FA PRE

POCKET ANNUAL 1995-96

Bruce Smith

3rd Year of Publication

FA Carling Premiership Annual 1995-96

Copyright © Bruce Smith – Author 1995

ISBN: 1-898351-29-5

The right of Bruce Smith to be identified as the Author of the Work has been asserted by him in accordance with the *Copyright, Designs and Patents Act 1988*.

First published August 1995 by
Words on Sport Ltd

Typeset by Bruce Smith Books Ltd

All photographs:
Empics Photo Agency

Words on Sport Ltd
PO Box 382, St. Albans,
Herts, AL2 3JD

Phone: 01923-894355
Fax: 01923-894366

Registered Office:
Worplesdon Chase, Worplesdon,
Guildford, Surrey, GU3 3LA
Reg. No.: 2917013

Printed and bound in Great Britain by
Bell & Bain Ltd, Glasgow

Disclaimer

In a book of this type it is inevitable that some errors will creep in. While every effort has been made to ensure that the details given in this annual are correct at the time of going to press, neither the editor nor the publishers can accept any responsibility for errors within.

CONTENTS

Introduction...

This is the third year of publication for the *FA Carling Premiership Pocket Annual* and for those of you who have seen a copy of the first two editions you will be aware that this latest issue has had some major improvements. Not least the addition of some 80 extra pages to allow the Club Directory section to be expanded to include full results for the 1994-95 season along with further enhancements to the statistics section. All-in-all we've ensured that the *FA Carling Premiership PA* remains the most comprehensive publication covering the top echelon of football in England.

Last season's extraordinary sales of the annual has allowed us to do this and we will be looking to refine and further improve the content for forthcoming editions of the annual. Suggestions and comments are always appreciated so if you have any ideas please feel free to write into us.

This year's cut off date for production purposes was the 31st July so I hope we have managed to get all confirmed/registered moves etc into place for publication. It has been particularly hairy in this area as clubs have been spending heavily pre-season and it's good to see that the vast sums of money injected into the game by TV are allowing the Premiership access to the top European stars. This is a trend that benefited Germany two seasons ago but I think will have an even greater effect in England. Significantly, I feel Nottingham Forest's signing of Andrea Silenzi is the most interesting. I anticipate a lot of Italians, no doubt aware of a move to the rigours our football, will be watching his progress with interest. If he does well I think we will see more travelling north but with less success than the English who have travelled south.

The 1995-96 season promises to be the most exciting season since 1993-94 which I regard as the best to date as a football spectacle and with the fillip of the European Championships to follow it could finish on the perfect note.

Bruce Smith

List of Acknowledgments
Many thanks to everyone who has contributed to this year's Annual – not least the following: Phil Heady, Mark Eames, Mark Webb, Jacqui Meechan, Dave Tavener and Dan Cristea. Thanks also to Carling – the sight of the annual's front cover on some 5 million beer mats last year was nearly too much to bear!

Blackburn Rovers FC 1994-95 – FA Carling Premiership Winners

Everton FC 1994-95 – FA Cup Winners

Liverpool FC 1994-95 – Coca-Cola League Cup Winners

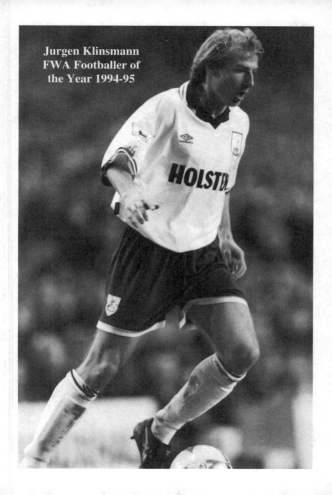

Jurgen Klinsmann
FWA Footballer of
the Year 1994-95

Stan
"The Man"
Collymore
£8,500,000

'94-95 Diary

August

By the start of August 1994 no less than 20 summer transfers in excess of £1 million had been completed. One quarter of the total was spent on one player when Chris Sutton's move from Norwich City cost Blackburn Rovers a British record fee of £5m, and which resulted in a pairing with Premiership hotshot Alan Shearer – a partnership that was to become known as the SAS. Foreign signings had also created many of the headlines with Tottenham Hotspur leading the way signing players who, only a month earlier had been on show at the World Cup Finals. Tottenham's coups brought Romanian Ilie Dumitrescu and German Jurgen Klinsmann to White Hart Lane, while North London rivals Arsenal signed Swede Stefan Schwartz from Benfica. Nottingham Forest, back in the top flight after a year's absence, had Dutchman Bryan Roy to bolster their midfield, while Nil Lamptey had swapped Belgium for Birmingham when he joined Aston Villa from Anderlecht.

The FA Charity Shield was played on a Sunday for the first time with FA Cup winners and Premiership Champions Manchester United facing league runners-up Blackburn Rovers, who were without both Shearer and Sutton. United won the game with a goal in each half – Eric Cantona scoring from the spot in the first period with Paul Ince adding a spectacular second nine minutes from time.

The big money signings were to continue up to the first Saturday of the new season. Phillipe Albert was another departure from Anderlecht, joining Newcastle United for £2.5m, while Dan Petrescu arrived at Hillsborough from Genoa in another £1m deal. Meanwhile at Upton Park, West Ham manager Billy Bonds left after a 27-year association with the East London club, claiming that the club wanted him to quit as manager and take up a directors post.

When the season finally got under way, the first sending-off in the Premiership came at Old Trafford with Clive Wilson of Queens Park Rangers being the first Premiership player to fall foul of the new FIFA directives after just seven minutes of play. Manchester United's Paul Parker followed four minutes after coming on as a second half substitute, but the Champions opened their bid for a hat-trick of titles with a comfortable 2-0 win. Bryan Roy, Jurgen Klinsmann and Dan Petrescu all made scoring debuts for their new clubs, as did Paul Furlong for Chelsea following his £2m move from Watford. One result stood out on the opening day though – Liverpool's 6-1 win at Crystal Palace. Leicester City's Premiership arrival was delayed for television until Sunday, but was spoilt by Newcastle's 3-1 win, while in midweek, the Shearer And Sutton (SAS) partnership bagged a goal apiece as the Foxes went down 3-0. Tottenham's six point penalty imposed on them by the Football Association was effectively whiped out by their second win as Klinsmann moved to the top of the goal charts with a brace in Spurs win over Vinnie Samway's new club Everton. Across Stanley Park, Liverpool bad-boy Don Hutchinson joined West Ham for £1.5m pounds after leaving in acrimonious circumstances.

The last league action of the month saw Leicester City win their first Premiership point with Phil Gee's last minute goal giving them a 1-1 draw at home to QPR. Manchester United remained unbeaten with a 3-0 win at home to Wimbledon. Also unbeaten were Blackburn, Newcastle and Liverpool, who put two past former 'keeper Bruce Grobbelaar at The Dell. In a bid to improve fortunes at Goodison Park, Mike Walker splashed out £3m on Nigerian World Cup star Daniel Amokachi.

September

September didn't see any let-up in clubs' spending power with two more £3m deals completed at the start of the month. Liverpool signed Phil Babb from Coventry and John Scales from Wimbledon to show the rest of the Premiership that, despite the lack of trophies, there was still plenty of money to be thrown around on Merseyside.

While action in the Premiership took a break in preparation for the international against the United States, the football world mourned the death of one of the true stars to have graced the game – Billy Wright CBE. He was the first Englishman to reach a century of caps, appearing 105 times in total, and captaining his country a record equalling 90 times. Wright won three league championship medals and the FA Cup, and was honoured by his fellow professionals with the accolade of Footballer of the Year in 1952.

Merseyside continued to be the focus of attention with David Burrows returning from West Ham to Everton, and Liverpool's John Barnes regaining a place in the starting line-up for England. The game against the USA at Wembley was settled by two Alan Shearer goals just before half-time,

Tottenham added to their international set with the capture of George Popescu from Dutch side PSV for £2.9m, while French captain Eric Cantona was reprimanded by the French Football Federation for threatening to punch a reporter. Another man in trouble was Manchester City's youth coach Neil McNab who was slapped with a five week ban for abusing a referee.

Two of only three teams with 100% records met at St.James' Park and Newcastle maintained their record with a 4-2 win over Chelsea. The third,

Liverpool, drew 0-0 with West Ham United at Anfield – John Scales making his debut for the home side. Blackburn and Nottingham Forest were both still unbeaten after victories against Everton and Sheffield Wednesday respectively. Champions Manchester United went down 2-1 to Leeds United, while Tottenham lost by the same score at home to Southampton. Arsenal striker Ian Wright was once again in trouble with the FA after he reportedly described referee Robbie Hart as a 'muppet' following the Gunners' goal-less draw with Norwich City.

The first round of European club matches got under way. In the UEFA Cup, Newcastle marked their return to Europe with a 5-0 thrashing of Royal Antwerp. Blackburn Rovers, in their Euro debut, sensationally crashed 1-0 at home to Swedish part-timers Trelleborgs, while a Dennis Bergkamp penalty in the San Siro sent Aston Villa to defeat against Internazionale. In their first UEFA Champions' League Group A game, Manchester United went a goal down to IFK Gothenburg but prevailed 4-2 to take the points. The Cup Winners' Cup also starts well for the two Premiership representatives – holders Arsenal won 3-1 in Cyprus against Omonia Nicosia, and Chelsea defeated Victoria Zizkov 4-2 at Stamford Bridge.

Back in Premiership action Manchester United ended Liverpool's unbeaten start to the season while Leicester City recorded their first win since promotion with a 3-1 victory over Tottenham. Elsewhere Dion Dublin scored on his £2m debut following his £2m transfer from Manchester United. Newcastle and Blackburn both visited London, Arsenal and Chelsea respectively, and both come away with their unbeaten records intact. Ipswich Town lost the East Anglian derby 2-1 at home to Norwich City.

Sheffield Wednesday manager Trevor Francis stated that he was disgusted by reports of a campaign by an anonymous player at Hillsborough to remove him from his post. Senior players including Des Walker and Chris Waddle said that the players supported Francis, and that there had been no dressing room bust-ups. Chelsea chairman Ken Bates ruled out any approach for manager Glenn Hoddle by his former club Monaco. Tottenham announced that they would challenge the FA over their six point penalty and FA Cup ban. Spurs chairman Alan Sugar caused concern at the FA when he publically announced that Terry Venables, the England coach, and former Spurs manager, would not be welcome at White Hart Lane until he stopped legal proceedings against the club for wrongful dismissal.

Ipswich Town recorded their first win at home since the previous February – an even bigger surprise was that it was achieved at the expense of champions Manchester United. Sky Blues' Dion Dublin maintained his goal a game record despite Coventry's defeat at home to Southampton. Newcastle and Liverpool took a point each from a 1-1 draw at St.James' Park, while the Sutton/Shearer partnership yielded another three goals with Aston Villa on the receiving end. Arsenal won 2-0 against a disappointing West Ham side at

Upton Park, and Sheffield Wednesday took a point from a 1-1 draw at home to Leeds despite having Gordon Watson sent off as early as the sixth minute.

In the second leg of the First Round European matches Newcastle wrapped up their tie with another five goals against Royal Antwerp for a 10-2 aggregate win, but goals from Alan Shearer and Chris Sutton failed to save Blackburn Rovers as they lost 3-2 to Trelleborgs over the two games. Manchester United stayed in Turkey just long enough to come away with a point from their UEFA Champions' League game against Galatasary in front of a hostile crowd of 34,000. Both Cup Winners' Cup sides safely progressed through to the Second Round – Arsenal rested players and still recorded a 2-0 win over Nicosia at Highbury, while Dmitri Kharine was Chelsea's hero, saving a penalty in a goalless draw against Zizkov. The drama was at Villa Park. Ray Houghton's goal had made it 1-1 against Internazionale, and after extra-time and nine penalties, Phil King converted the deciding spot kick to dump the holders unceremoniously out of the competition. Alan Parry's TV exclamation "You Beauty!" as the ball went in summed up the evening for most.

England captain David Platt announced that he would be out of action for four weeks, thereby missing out on his country's friendly against Romania at Wembley in October, after injuring his knee in Sampdoria's Cup Winners' Cup victory over Norwegians Bodo/Glimt.

October

Norwich City ended Blackburn Rovers' unbeaten start to the season. After former Canaries striker Chris Sutton had given Rovers the lead, goals from Mark Bowen and John Newsome gave Norwich the points. Two goals from John Salako for Crystal Palace gave the South Londoners a surprise win over Arsenal at Highbury. At Anfield, Liverpool trailed 1-0 to Sheffield Wednesday at half-time but Steve McManaman scored a second half hat-trick as the home side came through 4-1. Noel Whelan enhanced his growing reputation with both goals in Leeds United's 2-0 home win against Manchester City, Everton continued to struggle following defeat at Old Trafford by the same score. Nottingham Forest edged out Queen's Park Rangers in a game of five goals at the City Ground, while West Ham put one over London rivals Chelsea at Stamford Bridge. Leicester City and Coventry ended their 2-2 draw at Filbert Street with ten men each after Gary Gillespie and Jimmy Willis were dismissed by referee Philip Don.

Newcastle's Robert Lee won his first cap in place of the injured David Platt in the friendly against Romania at Wembley scoring in the 1-1 draw. The World Cup Quarter-Finalists had taken the lead through Tottenham's Ilie Dumitrescu. Arsenal skipper Tony Adams took over as captain of the international side in Platt's absence.

Everton manager Mike Walker continued in his quest to strengthen the Merseysiders with the double loan signing of Ian Durrant and Duncan Ferguson from Rangers. League leaders Newcastle United left it late at Selhurst Park – Peter Beardsley scoring the only goal of the game in the last minute against Crystal Palace. Blackburn Rovers maintained their challenge by defeating Liverpool 3-2 at Ewood Park.

Manchester City goalkeeper Andy Dibble and defender Richard Edgehill were sent-off in their 2-1 win at Queens Park Rangers while David Hirst scored a last minute winner for Sheffield Wednesday against Ipswich just six minutes after Bulgarian striker Bontcho Guentchev had missed a penalty for the home side. Nottingham Forest maintained their own good start in a 3-1 win over Wimbledon at the City Ground.

The European action resumed at Old Trafford as United hosted Barcelona in the UEFA Champions' League and preserved their unbeaten home record in Europe with a Lee Sharpe goal ten minutes from time giving them a 2-2 draw. Better luck – just – for Newcastle United over Spanish opposition, taking a 3-0 lead against Athletic Bilbao at St.James Park in the First Leg of their Second Round UEFA Cup tie, only to finish the match 3-2. Aston Villa went down 1-0 away to the Turkish side Trabzonspor. In the Cup Winners' Cup, holders Arsenal scraped a 2-1 lead in the home leg of their tie against Brondby of Denmark, while Chelsea only managed a goalless draw with FK Austria at Stamford Bridge.

Rumours were rife that Everton were said to be paying Duncan Ferguson £35,000 a week – a total of £420,000 for the three months of his loan. Tottenham defender Kevin Scott had his sending-off against Queens Park Rangers overturned by the Football Association. Referee Peter Jones reconsidered his verdict, and Scott's dismissal was reduced to a caution. Good news on the European front as the UEFA Fair Play Rankings list revealed that England, along with Norway and Luxembourg, were to be awarded an extra place in the 1995-96 UEFA Cup. Manchester United were told that they wouldn't be fined for not fielding a number of their first team players in the Coca Cola Cup games against Port Vale.

Tottenham's dream attack scored twice but the defence leaked five at Maine Road against Manchester City, while Newcastle and Liverpool both won at home to Sheffield Wednesday and Wimbledon respectively. Leading 1-0 at Ewood Park, Henning Berg is controversially sent-off after conceding a penalty in Blackburn Rovers home game against Manchester United. It proved to be the turning point as United went on to win 4-2. After their exploits in the Cup Winners' Cup, Arsenal and Chelsea beat Coventry City and Ipswich Town respectively. Pressure continued to mount on Tottenham manager Ossie Ardiles after his side lost 3-0 to Notts County in the Coca-Cola Cup while Manchester United, fielding another under strength side, bowed out of the same competition 2-0 to Newcastle at St.James' Park. David

Platt declared himself fit to play again in England's friendly against Nigeria at Wembley. As if on-cue Norwich City sold their Nigerian striker Efan Ekoku to Wimbledon for £800,000.

After the under-strength side had lost in the Cup, the full strength Manchester United side proved too strong for Newcastle in the Premiership, winning 2-0 at Old Trafford. More bad news for Magpies manager Kevin Keegan when he learned that shin splints would sideline leading scorer Andy Cole for at least a month. Blackburn Rovers beat Nottingham Forest by the same score at the City Ground, leaving Chelsea, who drew 1-1 at Hillsborough, as the only side to have scored in every Premiership game to date in the season. Tottenham created some breathing space for manager Ossie Ardiles with a 3-1 home win over West Ham United, while Liverpool went down 2-1 against Queen's Park Rangers at Loftus Road.

November

The speculation finally became reality as Ossie Ardiles was sacked as manager of Tottenham after just sixteen months in the hot-seat. The Football Association gave their backing to England coach Terry Venables after the BBC Panorama programme alleged irregularities concerning his business affairs. Queen's Park Rangers manager Gerry Francis tendered his resignation after Rodney Marsh was offered the position of Chief Executive without the knowledge of the Rangers' boss. Inevitably Francis was linked to the job vacancy at White Hart Lane along with Luton Town manager David Pleat.

Newcastle and Aston Villa ended their European campaigns as both were eliminated from the UEFA Cup on the away goals rule. Villa beat Trabzonspor 2-1 on the night to be level on aggregate at 2-2, while Newcastle were left to regret losing the 3-0 lead they held at St.James' Park after losing 1-0 in Bilbao to Athletic. In the UEFA Champions League Manchester United were handed a 4-0 hiding in the Nou Camp as Barcelona went top of Group A of the Champions League, while Arsenal and Chelsea both drew in the Cup Winners' Cup but went through to the Third Round.

In the Premiership an Alan Shearer goal secured Blackburn victory at Sheffield Wednesday, while Crystal Palace recorded their third successive win with a 4-1 victory over Coventry City at Highfield Road. There was some respite for Everton when they recorded their first win of the season with a Gary Ablett goal giving them three points at home to West Ham. A Robbie Fowler strike was enough to give Liverpool victory over Nottingham Forest at Anfield while Palace made it four wins in a row with a 3-0 win at home to Ipswich Town. Manchester United, Blackburn and Newcastle continued on their winning ways, but Forest and Newcastle ended scoreless at the City Ground.

After a win and two draws in their previous three games, Mike Walker found himself on the wrong side of the manager's door at Goodison Park, being sacked after ten months in the job. His last game in charge ironically turned out to be against his former side Norwich City! Former Everton favourite Joe Royle took over after a long association with Oldham Athletic.

Sensational accusations started to fly as allegations were published in a national newspaper that the Southampton goalkeeper Bruce Grobbelaar had been involved in match-fixing. The game at the centre of the allegation was Liverpool's 3-0 defeat by Newcastle United at St.James' Park during the 1993-94 season. Liverpool shrugged off the controversy surrounding their former 'keeper by beating Chelsea 3-1, while Aston Villa threw away a two goal lead and lost 4-3 at Wimbledon. Andrei Kanchelskis blasted a hat-trick as United thrashed City 5-0 in the Manchester derby.

Queens Park Rangers manager Gerry Francis finally had his resignation accepted by the board at Loftus Road, leaving him clear to take the reigns at White Hart Lane as Ray Wilkins replaced him after moving back from Crystal Palace following his free transfer in the summer. In a surprise move Aston Villa manager Ron Atkinson was sacked as the Midlands side's position at the foot of the Premiership failed to ease with Leicester City boss Brian Little favourite to take over.

Terry Venables' inclusion of Chelsea midfielder Dennis Wise proved a success as England beat World Cup Quarter-Finalists Nigeria in their friendly at Wembley. Captain David Platt scored the only goal of the game from a Wise free-kick. The England squad included Newcastle's uncapped defender Steve Howey, called into the England squad to replace Arsenal's Tony Adams, and Wimbledon defender Warren Barton called-up for the first time.

Manchester United maintained top spot in the Premiership with a 3-0 win over Crystal Palace with Blackburn moving second after Newcastle slipped up at Wimbledon. Joe Royle's first game in charge of Everton saw them record a 2-0 win over Liverpool in the Merseyside derby.

Newspaper headlines about activities off the field continued to dominate the game as Brian Little resigned as manager of Leicester City citing 'personal reasons' for his departure. Just days later he was in charge at Aston Villa.

Manchester United's dismal European campaign continued in the UEFA Champions League with Paul Ince sent-off as they lost 3-1 away to IFK Gothenburg. Their chances of progress into the Quarter Finals remained alive as Galatasaray surprisingly came from behind to beat Barcelona 2-1 in Turkey.

Tottenham's new manager Gerry Francis watched his side keep their first clean sheet of the season as they drew with Chelsea at White Hart Lane – the first time Glenn Hoddle's side had failed to score in the league this season.

Leicester City carried on after Brian Little's departure by recording a 2-1 win over Arsenal at Filbert Street.

The Football Association were told by an independent arbiter's investigation that they should review the deduction of six Premiership points and the FA Cup ban imposed on Tottenham Hotspur following financial irregularities at White Hart Lane. Manchester City midfielder Steve McMahon took over as player-manager at First Division Swindon Town.

The word 'sleeze' began to dominate the back pages as the Premier League started an investigation following allegations that a top official at Highbury received payment as part of the transfer that took Danish international John Jensen to Arsenal. The transfer of Pal Lydersen to the Gunners as well as Torben Piechnik's move to Liverpool were also being examined. The Southampton goalkeeper Bruce Grobbelaar was given more time to answer charges of misconduct.

There was more drama at Highbury as Mark Hughes was sent-off as Manchester United drew 0-0 with Arsenal. Newcastle United were held to a draw at home to lowly Ipswich Town, while Blackburn Rovers thrash Queens Park Rangers 4-0 at Ewood Park. Arsenal's season got no better when England striker Paul Merson revealed in a Sunday newspaper that he wass addicted to cocaine. Merson started to undergo months of rehabilitation, as the Football Association discussed the player's future with the Gunners.

Leicester City's attempt to gain an injunction against former manager Brian Little to prevent him from taking charge of Aston Villa's Coca-Cola Cup tie at Crystal Palace ended in failure – Palace thrashed Villa 4-1, while an Ian Rush hat-trick on his 600th appearance for Liverpool put the Reds through at Ewood Park against Blackburn Rovers. Arsenal put out Sheffield Wednesday, while Bolton and Millwall caused upsets by beating West Ham and Nottingham Forest respectively. Swindon and Norwich also went through, while Manchester City and Newcastle needed a replay. Wimbledon midfielder Vinnie Jones was the surprise name in the Welsh squad to face Bulgaria in a European Championship qualifier. Jones' grandfather, who was born in Wales, died over 15 years before!

December

Brian Little was given a hostile welcome at Filbert Street as he took his Aston Villa side to face his old team Leicester City for a draw 1-1. A single strike from Eric Cantona gave Manchester United victory over Norwich City at Old Trafford where they were still to concede a goal in the league during the season. Nottingham Forest ended their goal drought by drawing 2-2 with Arsenal at the City Ground. Blackburn won 3-0 at Wimbledon, while Tottenham beat Newcastle United 4-2 at White Hart Lane with Teddy

Sheringham scoring a hat-trick. John Lyall resigned as manager of Ipswich Town the day after a 2-1 home defeat by Manchester City.

Despite thrashing Turkish side Galatasary 4-0 at Old Trafford Manchester United bowed out of the Champions League. Barcelona drew 1-1 with IFK Gothenburg in Spain to finish level on points with United, but qualified with a superior goal difference.

The Football Association reinstated Tottenham Hotspur in the FA Cup and lifted the six point penalty imposed on them in the Premiership – the £1.5m fine remained though. Two weeks previously, the arbitrators on the Queen's Council had ruled that the punishment imposed on the north London club was too severe. Tottenham's gain was also Non-League Altrincham's who were their provisional opponents in the Third Round of the FA Cup.

After their midweek European exit, Manchester United won 3-2 at Queen's Park Rangers, while Blackburn won by the same scoreline in their game at home to Southampton. Newcastle and Nottingham Forest also secured three point each, but Liverpool were held to a 0-0 draw by Crystal Palace at Anfield. Mark McGee continued the managerial merry-go-round by leaving First Division Reading in favour of Leicester City.

The month's news hit new heights when the Arsenal manager George Graham was alleged to have received, but paid back, £285,000 as part of the transfer fee involved in bringing midfeidler John Jenson to Highbury from Danish club Brondby. It was reported that Graham had offered his resignation when Arsenal officials first became aware of the situation. An inquiry was set up, and the Premier League's commission was widened to investigate 23 transfers of Scandinavian players involving the Norwegian agent Rene Hauge.

Stan Collymore made the headlines on the field of play when he became the first visiting Premiership player to score at Old Trafford this season as Manchester United suffered a 2-1 home defeat by Nottingham Forest. Blackburn Rovers failed to take full advantage though with a goal-less draw at Filbert Street. Tottenham and Everton also failed to find the net at Goodison, while Chelsea and Liverpool had the same problem at Stamford Bridge. Leeds United increased the Highbury woe with a 3-1 win in north London as the Gunners board gave their backing to George Graham over the 'bung' allegations. Matthew Le Tissier scored a last minute winner for Southampton at home to Aston Villa.

Stuart Pearce publically apologised to England team-mate Paul Ince over alleged racist remarks which the Nottingham Forest skipper made to Ince during their weekend win at Old Trafford. Maurizio Gaudino joined Manchester City on loan from Eintracht Frankfurt until the end of the season, while Ian Taylor swapped Hillsborough for Villa Park as Guy Whittingham made the journey in the opposite direction.

With Christmas in full swing Manchester United started their holiday programme with a 3-2 win at Chelsea while Blackburn Rovers won 3-1 at Maine Road. Newcastle United and Leeds United though were score-less at Elland Road while Liverpool won 2-1 at Leicester City. A goal direct from a corner from Lars Bohinen gave Forest the points over Norwich at the City Ground, and Tottenham took a point from their clean sheet at home to Crystal Palace.

Ipswich Town started to take steps to try and get themselves out of the relegation zone by appointing former player George Burley as manager. No instant magic though as troubled Arsenal had a lift with a 2-0 win at Portman Road. Manchester United dropped two vital points in a 1-1 draw at home to bottom-placed Leicester City while Liverpool beat Manchester City 2-0 at Anfield. Sheffield Wednesday thrashed Coventry City 5-1 at Hillsborough with new signing Guy Whittingham scoring a brace. Unsettled Romanian striker Illie Dumitrescu moved to Spanish club Saville for the rest of the season from Tottenham. Manchester United's festive cheer to other teams continued as they were held to a 2-2 draw at The Dell, allowing Blackburn Rovers to extend their lead at the top with a 1-0 win at Crystal Palace. Liverpool defeated Leeds 2-0 at Elland Road as Nottingham Forest lost more ground 3-1 at Wimbledon. Tottenham thrashed Coventry City 4-0 at Highfield Road while Arsenal dropped nearer the relegation zone through a 3-1 home defeat by Queen's Park Rangers.

January

The New Year started more brightly in Suffolk as Ipswich Town won the battle of the bottom two at Portman Road as they ran out 4-1 victors over Leicester City. Liverpool put four past Norwich without reply at Anfield and Blackburn put the same number past West Ham at Ewood Park with the Hammers managing two in response. A goal from Dan Popescu gave Tottenham all three points from the derby clash with Arsenal at White Hart Lane. Aston Villa's Brian Little shelled out £2.9m to Derby County for striker Tommy Johnson and defender Gary Charles in an effort to halt their slide. Southampton's Alan Ball also had the cheque book open paying Chelsea a club record £1.2m for striker Neil Shipperley. The Southampton manager was also in the news when he was charged with misconduct by the Football Association for abusing a linesman at the end of December.

FA Cup Third Round action saw top sides Newcastle United and Blackburn Rovers drew 1-1 at St.James Park. Tottenham won 3-0 at home to Altrincham, while the remaining non-league interest ended with Aylesbury United, Marlow and Enfield losing at Queen's Park Rangers, Swindon and Cardiff respectively. Leeds United equalised in the last minute to force a replay at Walsall, Liverpool scraped a replay in a goal-less draw at resurgent

Birmingham City. Manchester United started their defence with a 2-0 win at Sheffield United – the third season in succession they had met in the Cup.

Leeds United's Howard Wilkinson continued his gradual rebuilding programme with the £3.4m capture of Ghanaian striker Anthony Yeboah from German side Eintracht Frankfurt – the fee set a new club record but was nothing compared to the £7m Manchester United paid in the audacious and sensational signing of Andy Cole from championship rivals Newcastle United. As part of the deal the highly rated winger Keith Gillespie moved to Tyneside.

Crystal Palace continued to put their sorry league form behind them finding four goals at Selhurst Park to reach the semi finals of the Coca Cola League Cup at the expense of Manchester City. Not such good news for fellow strugglers Norwich City though as a goal from David Lee put Bolton through, and Ian Rush secured Liverpool's place in the last four against Arsenal.

Arsenal manager George Graham – whose future at the Gunners' helm was coming under increasing speculation – announced two new signings – Welsh Under-21 international John Hartson from Luton Town and Chris Kiwomya of Ipswich Town for £2.5m and £1.25m respectively.

The Premiership resumed with top of the table clashes. Newcastle United and Manchester United drew 1-1 but the Reds' Mark Hughes was carried off with a serious knee injury following an accidental clash with Magpies' 'keeper Pavel Srnicek. Blackburn pressed home a further two point advantage with a 3-0 win at home to Nottingham Forest, Tottenham won 2-1 at West Ham, but Liverpool lost 1-0 at Anfield to strugglers Ipswich Town.

In FA Cup replays, South African Phil Masinga scored a hat-trick as Leeds United beat Walsall 5-2 at Elland Road, while Millwall dumped Arsenal out of the competition with a 2-0 win at Highbury. Liverpool continued to struggle against Birmingham City, being held 1-1 at Anfield but squeezed through over the Second Division side in a penalty shoot-out. Newcastle United won 2-1 at Ewood Park in their second game with Blackburn Rovers.

Manchester United won their six-pointer with Blackburn Rovers at Old Trafford thanks to a goal ten minutes from time from Eric Cantona. John Hartsen scored his first goal for Arsenal as the Gunners won 1-0 at Coventry City. Nottingham Forest, with manager Frank Clark, having signed a new three and a half year contract, lost 2-1 at home to Aston Villa and Newcastle were held 0-0 at Hillsborough. Leeds rattled four without reply at home to Queen's Park Rangers but goals were not in sight in the Merseyside derby at Anfield.

The season's growing *sleeze factor* reached new heights during the Crystal Palace v Manchester United encounter. Having been sent off, Eric Cantona attacked a Crystal Palace fan with a kung-fu style kick as he made his way to the changing rooms. In an incident that was televised around the world (I speak from experience watching it as a lead news item in Perth, Australia at the time!) the Football Association wasted no time in charging him with 'Bringing the game into disrepute'; Manchester United fined him two weeks wages (around £10,000) and banned him until the end of the season; the French Football Federation stripped him of the captaincy of the national team; and the police indicated that charges were likely to be brought against him and Paul Ince, who also allegedly struck a fan in the resulting post-kick incident.

In the Fourth Round of the FA Cup, Manchester United continued on in defence of their title but suffered a scare, going behind to Second Division Wrexham but recovering to win 5-2. Crystal Palace's Cup form continued on its winning ways with a 2-1 victory at Nottingham Forest, and Tottenham's cup reprieve continued with a 4-1 win at Sunderland. Aston Villa exited by the only goal of the tie at Manchester City and both Sheffield Wednesday and Liverpool were held to goal-less draws by First Division sides Wolves and Burnley.

February

Arsenal forward Paul Merson took the first step back into football action following his drug related problems when he came on as substitute for the first team in the 0-0 draw with Milan in the First Leg of the European Super Cup at Highbury. In the Premiership Blackburn and Leeds drew 1-1 at Ewood Park while Newcastle beat Everton 2-0 at St.James Park. The former chairman of Liverpool and the Sports Council, Sir John Smith, died of cancer at the age of 74. The bad news wouldn't go away as Wimbledon manager Joe Kinnear was charged by the FA of bringing the game into disrepute for accusing referee Mike Reed of cheating in their game at Newcastle.

Manchester United won 1-0 at home to Aston Villa and closed the gap at the top even further as Tottenham beat Blackburn 3-1 at White Hart Lane. Liverpool scored a late equaliser through Robbie Fowler to take a point from a 1-1 draw at Nottingham Forest, while Leeds United were held to a score-less draw at Wimbledon.

Terry Venables surprised many by calling up the Tottenham pair Nick Barmby and Sol Campbell into the England squad for the forthcoming international against the Republic of Ireland in Dublin, but Chelsea's Dennis Wise was dropped the day after the squad was announced when he was found guilty of assault and criminal damage but let out on bail.

In the Second Leg of the European Super Cup, Milan defeated Arsenal 2-0 in the San Siro and UEFA announced that England will be allocated an extra UEFA Cup place for the 95-96 season as a result of their fair play record.

No change at the very top as Blackburn Rovers and Manchester United both won. Blackburn recorded a 3-1 victory at home to Sheffield Wednesday while United triumphed in the Manchester derby with a 3-0 win at Maine Road. Tommy Johnson scored a hat-trick for Aston Villa as they thrashed Wimbledon 7-1 at Villa Park while Newcastle defeated Nottingham Forest 2-1 at St.James Park.

Wimbledon's Warren Barton made his expected international debut for England against the Republic of Ireland, but the match in Dublin was abandoned after serious crowd trouble with the Republic leading by a goal. Crystal Palace looked to be continuing their good cup form in the first leg of their Coca Cola League Cup semi final at Anfield. But, an injury time goal from Robbie Fowler gave Liverpool a 1-0 lead. Ron Atkinson returns to Premier Division management as a replacement for Phil Neal who left Coventry City by mutual consent. Vinnie Jones made their back pages when he was reported to the Football Association after allegedly biting the nose of a newspaper reporter!

In FA Cup replays, a single goal from John Barnes gave Liverpool a place in the next round at home to Burnley, Southampton hit Luton Town for six at The Dell while First Division sides Wolves and Millwall knocked out Premier Division Sheffield Wednesday and Chelsea on penalties after both games had finished level at 1-1 after extra time.

Arsenal signed the Dutch international Glenn Helder for £2.3m pounds from Vitesse Arnhem and just days later the Gunners sacked manager George Graham and placed assistant Stuart Houston in charge until the end of the season. Graham's dismissal came the day before the Football Association announced that the findings of their investigation suggested that Graham took around £425,000 in illegal payments for the transfer of two Scandinavian players.

Houston's first game in charge saw Arsenal beat Nottingham Forest 1-0 at Highbury. Blackburn beat Wimbledon 2-1 at Ewood Park with Manchester United winning 2-0 at Norwich. Aston Villa and Leicester City shared eight goals at Villa Park.

Off the pitch the FA held a press conference and announced that they had fined Eric Cantona a further £10,000 and extended his ban until 30th September for his attack on a Crystal Palace fan. FIFA confirmed it was a worldwide ban.

In the Fifth Round of the FA Cup, Manchester United beat Leeds 3-1 at Old Trafford with Newcastle United victorious over Manchester City by the same scoreline. Everton smashed five past a shell-shocked Norwich at Goodison, Queen's Park Rangers won 1-0 over Millwall, but Leicester bowed out to a David Kelly goal at Wolves. Liverpool were held at home 1-1 with Wimbledon, while Watford held Crystal Palace 0-0 at Vicarage Road.

Tottenham and Southampton caused a replay with a 1-1 draw at White Hart Lane. A Duncan Ferguson goal secured Everton a 1-0 win over Manchester United at Goodison Park as the Royle effect continued to take place, but leaders Blackburn Rovers failed to take advantage as they were held to a 0-0 draw at home to Norwich City. Newcastle beat Aston Villa 3-1 while Liverpool were 2-1 victors at Sheffield Wednesday.

Chelsea lost 1-0 in the First Leg of their Cup-Winners' Cup Quarter-Final tie away to FC Bruges in Belgium as trouble broke out in the streets around the ground after the game. Ian Rush equalled Denis Law's record of 41 post-war FA Cup goals in Liverpool's 2-0 Fifth Round Replay win at Wimbledon. Newcastle strengthened their third place in the league with a 2-0 win at Ipswich Town.

March

Almost forgotten Ronnie Rosenthal scored a sensational hat-trick as Tottenham beat Southampton 6-2 in an exciting game at the The Dell in their Fifth Round FA Cup Replay. A goal two minutes from the end of extra-time from George Ndah secured Crystal Palace a 1-0 win over First Division Watford. Arsenal though were held to a disappointing 1-1 draw by Auxerre in the First Leg of their Cup Winners' Cup Semi-Final at Highbury.

Drugs hit the headlines again as Crystal Palace striker Chris Armstrong was suspended by the Football Association after traces of cannabis were found in a random drugs test carried out at the end of January. It was later revealed that Armstrong had already undergone counselling and regular testing, and he was now temporarily suspended by the FA.

Manchester United recorded the biggest victory since the formation of the FA Premier League with a 9-0 thumping of strugglers Ipswich Town at Old Trafford – £7m man Andy Cole bagging five. Despite United's win, Blackburn stayed clear at the top after their 1-0 win at Aston Villa while Liverpool beat Newcastle 2-0 at Anfield. However, United's win gave them a better goal difference than Rovers.

Goals were harder to come by for the Reds at Wimbledon in their next match and it needed a Steve Bruce goal five minutes from the end to give them all three points in a 1-0 win. Blackburn, Newcastle and Tottenham all won to maintain their positions in the top six and Robbie Fowler repeated his feat of scoring the only goal of the game as Liverpool beat Crystal Palace 1-0 at Selhurst Park to record a 2-0 aggregate win and a place in the Coca Cola Cup Final.

Wimbledon manager Joe Kinnear took the extraordinary step of banning himself from the touchline after being ordered from the dug-out by referee Robbie Hart.

In the Quarter-Finals of the FA Cup, a late Jurgen Klinsmann goal gave Tottenham a 2-1 win against Liverpool at Anfield while Manchester United defeated Queen's Park Rangers 2-0 at Old Trafford. Dave Watson scored the only goal as Everton beat Newcastle United 1-0 at Goodison Park, but Wolves and Crystal Palace drew 1-1 at Selhurst Park. In the Premiership, Blackburn Rovers' jitters came back as they dropped two points at Highfield Road with a 1-1 draw with Coventry City, while Nottingham Forest won 4-2 at Leicester City.

Southampton's Bruce Grobbelaar, along with fellow goalkeeper Hans Segers from Wimbledon and Aston Villa striker John Fashanu, were all arrested by Hampshire police investigating match fixing allegations in a secret dawn raid that the press knew about. All three were held for 36 hours before being released on police bail. Chelsea midfielder Dennis Wise was sentenced to three months in prison for assault and criminal damage but was released on bail as he appealed against the sentence.

Better news as Chelsea progressed through to the Semi-Finals of the Cup Winners' Cup after goals from Mark Stein and Paul Furlong gave them a 2-0 win on the night against FC Bruges and a 2-1 win on aggregate. Arsenal also went through thanks to a first half goal from Ian Wright giving them a 1-0 win in Auxerre and a 2-1 aggregate victory. In the Semi-Final draw, Chelsea were drawn against Real Zaragoza with the First Leg to be played in Spain, while Arsenal would play Sampdoria with the First Leg at Highbury.

In the Premiership, Coventry City striker Peter Ndlovu became the first visiting player to score a hat-trick at Anfield since 1962 as the Sky Blues won 3-2 against Liverpool. Manchester United missed their chance to close the gap on Blackburn at the top when they failed to score at Old Trafford for the first time this season as Tottenham took a point. Blackburn though strengthened their squad as boss Kenny Dalglish signed Jeff Kenna from Southampton for £1.5m.

With a six figure fee laid out, Blackburn Rovers extended their lead at the top of the Premiership to six points with their 2-1 defeat of Chelsea at Ewood Park as Manchester United crashed 2-0 to Liverpool at Anfield. The race for the UEFA Cup places continued to add excitement at the top of the table – as well as Liverpool's win over United, there were also victories for Newcastle, Nottingham Forest, Tottenham and Leeds.

Terry Venables made changes to his squad for the forthcoming international match against Uruguay. Paul Ince was dropped, with the Manchester United midfielder facing assault changes, and Southampton's Matthew Le Tissier was left out. Tottenham 'keeper Ian Walker and Liverpool's Jamie Redknapp were included for the first time. Liverpool paid Millwall an initial fee of £1.5m for winger Mark Kennedy.

Manchester United returned to winning ways with a 3-0 win over Arsenal at Old Trafford, while neighbours City slipped closer to the relegation zone losing 2-0 at Wimbledon. Nottingham Forest won 3-0 at the City Ground in an important match at the top with Leeds United, while Newcastle conceded three goals in the last five minutes as they saw a 1-0 lead turn into a 3-1 defeat.

Crystal Palace secured their place in the Semi-Final of the FA Cup with a resounding 4-1 replay victory over Wolves at Molineux. Leeds United midfielder Gordon Strachan joined up again with former boss Ron Atkinson as he became coach at Coventry City. There were no major signings on transfer deadline day but Ray Houghton moved from Villa Park to join Crystal Palace. Andy Cole made his long awaited international debut, coming on as a late substitute in England's goal-less draw with Uruguay at Wembley. Steve McManaman and Nick Barmby also made their first appearances for the full national side.

April

Liverpool won the Coca-Cola League Cup for a record fifth time with a brace from Steve McManaman giving them a 2-1 victory over First Division Bolton Wanderers at Wembley. In the Premiership, Chris Sutton scored the fastest goal of the season after just 13 seconds to help leaders Blackburn on the road to a 2-1 victory at Everton while second placed Manchester United were held to a goalless draw by Leeds at Old Trafford. Arsenal returned to form with a 5-1 demolition of Norwich at Highbury, while Tottenham and Leicester City found themselves on the wrong end of a 4-3 scoreline against Southampton and Wimbledon respectively. Newcastle were held at Chelsea, while Nottingham Forest won 7-1 against Sheffield Wednesday at Hillsborough.

Blackburn's lead at the top of the table was increased to eight points with Chris Sutton's goal giving them a 1-0 win at Queens Park Rangers, while at the bottom Tony Yeboah's first half hat-trick for Leeds put Ipswich in deeper relegation trouble. Norwich were slipping alarmingly down the table and lost 1-0 at Leicester, while Liverpool beat Southampton 3-1 at Anfield.

There were mixed fortunes for Arsenal and Chelsea in the First Leg ties of their respective Cup Winner' Cup Semi-Final games. Two goals from Steve Bould and one from Ian Wright gave the Gunners a 3-2 advantage to take to Genoa for the Second Leg with Sampdoria. Trouble flared in Spain where Chelsea lost 3-0 to Real Zaragoza.

Daniel Amokachi scored twice as Everton overwhelmed Tottenham 4-1 in their FA Cup Semi-Final at Elland Road. The Merseysiders had to wait to see who they would face in the Final with Manchester United twice coming from behind to draw 2-2 with Crystal Palace at Villa Park after extra time. The game in Birmingham was overshadowed though by the death of a Palace fan prior to the match. In the Premiership, Newcastle beat troubled Norwich 3-0 at St.James' Park, while Nottingham Forest were held to a 1-1 draw by West Ham at the City Ground. Liverpool lost 1-0 to Leeds at Anfield with Brian Deane scoring the only goal of the game.

John Deehan resigned as the manager of Norwich City having only recorded 12 wins in the 56 matches since he replaced Mike Walker. Gary Megson took over as caretaker manager until the end of the season. Manchester United secured their place in the FA Cup Final with a 2-0 win over Crystal Palace thanks to goals from centre backs Steve Bruce and Gary Pallister, but the replay at Villa Park marked by the sending off of United's Roy Keane and Darren Patterson of Palace. Les Ferdinand scored the only goal as Queens Park Rangers beat Ipswich 1-0 at Portman Road, Southampton eased their relegation fears with a 2-0 win at Chelsea, while Norwich's slide continued with a late defeat at home to Nottingham Forest. Robbie Fowler scored the only goal of the game in injury time as Liverpool won at Arsenal.

The start of the Easter programme saw Everton repeat their FA Cup Quarter-Final win over Newcastle – a result that relegated Leicester after just one season in the top flight. A late Jurgen Klinsmann goal salvaged a point for Tottenham at Crystal Palace, while Liverpool went down 2-1 to Manchester City at Maine Road.

Manchester sprang two surprises on the Bank Holiday Monday, firstly United were held goalless at Old Trafford by Chelsea and City, with a stirring performance, overwhelmed Blackburn 3-2 at Ewood Park. A last minute goal by Jeroen Boere lifted West Ham out of the relegation places and denied Ipswich a rare win. Norwich slipped deeper into trouble with defeat at Tottenham while Cup finalists Everton picked up a point at Sheffield Wednesday. Leeds' first win at St James Park for 19 years took them to within four points of Newcastle and a place in Europe. Arsenal crushed Aston Villa 4-0 at Villa Park three days ahead of their return Cup-Winners' Cup tie with Sampdoria.

The Gunners then moved closer to being the first club to retain the Cup with an absorbing penalty shoot-out victory in Italy. Two goals in the last ten minutes put the Italians ahead on aggregate only for Stefan Schwarz to bring the scores level over the two games at 5-5. England 'keeper David Seaman was the hero with three penalty saves to put Arsenal through to the final for the second successive year. Chelsea fought gallantly to beat Real Zaragoza 3-1 at Stamford Bridge but the Spaniards' 3-0 lead from the 1st Leg proved decisive. On the same night, Blackburn closed in on their first championship for 81 years and nudged Crystal Palace closer to Division One with a 2-1 victory at Ewood Park.

The month ended with Blackburn slipping up again, this time going down to a 2-0 defeat at West Ham who were now seven games unbeaten. Leeds continued their good run with a last minute Carlton Palmer goal seeing off

Aston Villa. At the bottom end of the table, Chelsea beat Queens Park Rangers while Leicester beat Ipswich 2-0 in the battle to avoid being wooden spoonists. Norwich survival hopes slumped again with defeat at Liverpool.

May

Manchester United went into the final fourteen days of the Premiership season eight points adrift of a Blackburn side which was clearly struggling with the pressure of their lofty perch. Andy Cole scored twice as United increased the pressure with a 3-2 victory over Coventry, and on the seventh United moved to within two points of Dalglish's side when a David May goal saw off Sheffield Wednesday at Old Trafford. Sandwiched between those results, Nottingham Forest ensured a return to Europe with victory over Manchester City. Crystal Palace and Ipswich recorded their last wins in the Premiership, Southampton ensured survival with a draw at Everton but Norwich completed an East Anglian double when defeat at Leeds sent them down with Ipswich. Jurgen Klinsmann scored his last goal in the Premiership during a thrilling 3-3 draw at Newcastle, Peter Beardsley also scored his final goal of the season.

Newcastle's hopes of European football dipped when an Alan Shearer goal put Blackburn just three points away from the championship. Everton, Coventry and West Ham all moved clear of relegation with a game to spare, West Ham achieved it in the most impressive fashion with a 3-0 victory over Liverpool, former Red Don Hutchison scoring twice. Leeds made almost certain of qualifying for Europe with a 3-1 win over Crystal Palace at Elland Road that edged the south London club to within a whisker of relegation. Manchester United ensured that the battle for the championship went to the last day of the season with a 2-1 home win over Southampton, United's third successive win which came courtesy of a late, controversial, Denis Irwin penalty. Arsenal's amazing season had one more twist in the tail when the former Spurs midfielder Nayim scored an astonishing goal from close on the halfway line with almost the last kick of the Gunners Cup Winners' Cup Final with Real Zaragoza in Paris.

There was mixed news for Tottenham fans as Jurgen Klinsmann announced that he was off to join Bayern Munich but Gerry Francis confirmed that he would be manager for the following season. The final day of the league season saw Blackburn Rovers lose 2-1 to a last minute Jamie Redknapp goal at Anfield, after leading through Alan Shearer, but with Manchester United missing a host of chances at Upton Park during a 1-1 draw with West Ham, the title moved from Old Trafford to Ewood Park. At the opposite end of the table, Crystal Palace fought back from three down at Newcastle but still lost 3-2 and were relegated. Leeds picked up a point at White Hart Lane to deny Newcastle the last UEFA Cup place. Glenn Hoddle played his final game during Chelsea's 2-1 win over Arsenal.

Just twenty four hours after the end of the Premiership season, Alan Smith became the first managerial casualty when he left Crystal Palace by mutual consent. The following day saw Brian Horton dismissed at Manchester City. Arsenal's problems followed them abroad as 'keeper David Seaman suffered a broken ankle in Beijing and Stefan Schwarz was sent off during the friendly. Just six days after losing one half of their 'double,' Manchester United lost the other half as a Paul Rideout goal completed Everton's revival under Joe Royle as the FA Cup moved to Goodison Park. Transfer fever stepped up a gear at the end of the season with managers moving almost as freely as the players. One manager looking unlikely to move was Alan Ball who agreed a new contract at Southampton, but five weeks later he joined Manchester City.

June

Chelsea got the first full month of the close season off to a sensational start with the signing of Dutch superstar and former European Footballer of the Year Ruud Gullit from Sampdoria. It was just one of several big money moves. Les Ferdinand joined Newcastle from Queens Park Rangers in exchange for £6m, Isthmian League side Hayes benefitted by £600,000 from that move. Manchester United surprised many by agreeing to sell Mark Hughes to Chelsea for £1.5m, the deal making Chelsea a fashionable club following the earlier signing of Gullit.

More managerial changes came with Arsenal ending Stuart Houston's caretaker role at Highbury by appointing Bolton boss Bruce Rioch as the Gunners new manager. One of Rioch's first duties was to complete the £7m signing of renowned Dutch striker Dennis Bergkamp from Internazionale. The Italian club retaliated by taking Paul Ince from Manchester United for £8m. Liverpool joined in with the summer madness when spending £8.5m on persuading Nottingham Forest to let Stan Collymore move to Anfield.

Sheffield Wednesday found a replacement for Trevor Francis in the Luton Town manager David Pleat whose departure from Kenilworth Road almost resulted in High Court action. Comings and goings at Crystal Palace saw former manager Steve Coppell return to the club as technical director; striker Chris Armstrong departed for Tottenham in a £4.5m deal. ■

29

FINAL TABLES 1994-95

FA Carling Premiership

	P	HOME					AWAY					Pts
		W	D	L	F	A	W	D	L	F	A	
Blackburn Rovers	42	17	2	2	54	21	10	6	5	26	18	89
Manchester United	42	16	4	1	42	4	10	6	5	35	24	88
Nottingham Forest	42	12	6	3	36	18	10	5	6	36	25	77
Liverpool	42	13	5	3	38	13	8	6	7	27	24	74
Leeds United	42	13	5	3	35	15	7	8	6	24	23	73
Newcastle United	42	14	6	1	46	20	6	6	9	21	27	72
Tottenham Hotspur	42	10	5	6	32	25	6	9	6	34	33	62
Queens Park Rangers	42	11	3	7	36	26	6	9	6	25	33	60
Wimbledon	42	9	5	7	26	26	6	6	9	22	39	56
Southampton	42	8	9	4	33	27	4	9	8	28	36	54
Chelsea	42	7	7	7	25	22	6	8	7	25	33	54
Arsenal	42	6	9	6	27	21	7	3	11	25	28	51
Sheffield Wednesday	42	7	7	7	26	26	6	5	10	23	31	51
West Ham United	42	9	6	6	28	19	4	5	12	16	29	50
Everton	42	8	9	4	31	23	3	8	10	13	28	50
Coventry City	42	7	7	7	23	25	5	7	9	21	37	50
Manchester City	42	8	7	6	37	28	4	6	11	16	36	49
Aston Villa	42	6	9	6	27	24	5	6	10	24	32	48
Crystal Palace	42	6	6	9	16	23	5	6	10	18	26	45
Norwich City	42	8	8	5	27	21	2	5	14	10	33	43
Leicester City	42	5	6	10	28	37	1	5	15	17	43	29
Ipswich Town	42	5	3	13	24	34	2	3	16	12	59	27

Composite Table with Prize Money

	P	W	D	L	F	A	Pts	Prize Money	Psn
Blackburn Rovers	42	27	8	7	80	39	89	£897,820	1
Manchester United	42	26	10	6	77	28	88	£857,010	2
Nottingham Forest	42	22	11	9	72	43	77	£816,200	3
Liverpool	42	21	11	10	65	37	74	£775,390	4
Leeds United	42	20	13	9	59	38	73	£734,580	5
Newcastle United	42	20	12	10	67	47	72	£693,770	6
Tottenham Hotspur	42	16	14	12	66	58	62	£652,960	7
Queens Park Rangers	42	17	9	16	61	59	60	£612,150	8
Wimbledon	42	15	11	16	48	65	56	£571,340	9
Southampton	42	12	18	12	61	63	54	£530,530	10
Chelsea	42	13	15	14	50	55	54	£489,720	11
Arsenal	42	13	12	17	52	49	51	£448,720	12

	P	W	D	L	F	A	Pts		
Sheffield Wednesday	42	13	12	17	49	57	51	£408,100	13
West Ham United	42	13	11	18	44	48	50	£367,290	14
Everton	42	11	17	14	44	51	50	£326,480	15
Coventry City	42	12	14	16	44	62	50	£285,670	16
Manchester City	42	12	13	17	53	64	49	£244,860	17
Aston Villa	42	11	15	16	51	56	48	£204,050	18
Crystal Palace	42	11	12	19	34	49	45	£163,240	19
Norwich City	42	10	13	19	37	54	43	£122,430	20
Leicester City	42	6	11	25	45	80	29	£81,620	21
Ipswich Town	42	7	6	29	36	93	27	£40,810	22

Endsleigh League Division 1

	P	W	D	L	F	A	Pts		Pos
Middlesbrough	46	23	13	10	67	40	82	Promoted	1
Reading	46	23	10	13	58	44	79		2
Bolton Wanderers	46	21	14	11	67	45	77	Promoted	3
Wolverhampton Wanderers	46	21	13	12	77	61	76		4
Tranmere Rovers	46	22	10	14	67	58	76		5
Barnsley	46	20	12	14	63	52	72		6
Watford	46	19	13	14	52	46	70		7
Sheffield United	46	17	17	12	74	55	68		8
Derby County	46	18	12	16	66	51	66		9
Grimsby Town	46	17	14	15	62	56	65		10
Stoke City	46	16	15	15	50	53	63		11
Millwall	46	16	14	16	60	60	62		12
Southend United	46	18	8	20	54	73	62		13
Oldham Athletic	46	16	13	17	60	60	61		14
Charlton Athletic	46	16	11	19	58	66	59		15
Luton Town	46	15	13	18	61	64	58		16
Port Vale	46	15	13	18	58	64	58		17
Portsmouth	46	15	13	18	53	63	58		18
West Bromwich Albion	46	16	10	20	51	57	58		19
Sunderland	46	12	18	16	41	45	54		20
Swindon Town	46	12	12	22	54	73	48	Relegated	21
Burnley	46	11	13	22	49	74	46	Relegated	22
Bristol City	46	11	12	23	42	63	45	Relegated	23
Notts County	46	9	13	24	45	66	40	Relegated	24

Endsleigh League Division 2

	P	W	D	L	F	A	Pts		Pos
Birmingham City	46	25	14	7	84	37	89	Promoted	1
Brentford	46	25	10	11	81	39	85		2
Crewe Alexandra	46	25	8	13	80	68	83		3
Bristol Rovers	46	22	16	8	70	40	82		4
Huddersfield Town	46	22	15	9	79	49	81	Promoted	5

	P	W	D	L	F	A	Pts		Pos
Wycombe Wanderers	46	21	15	10	60	46	78		6
Oxford United	46	21	12	13	66	52	75		7
Hull City	46	21	11	14	70	57	74		8
York City	46	21	9	16	67	51	72		9
Swansea City	46	19	14	13	57	45	71		10
Stockport County	46	19	8	19	63	60	65		11
Blackpool	46	18	10	18	64	70	64		12
Wrexham	46	16	15	15	65	64	63		13
Bradford City	46	16	12	18	57	64	60		14
Peterborough United	46	14	18	14	54	69	60		15
Brighton & Hove Albion	46	14	17	15	54	53	59		16
Rotherham United	46	14	14	18	57	61	56		17
Shrewsbury Town	46	13	14	19	54	62	53		18
AFC Bournemouth	46	13	11	22	49	69	50		19
Cambridge United	46	11	15	20	52	69	48	Relegated	20
Plymouth Argyle	46	12	10	24	45	83	46	Relegated	21
Cardiff City	46	9	11	26	46	74	38	Relegated	22
Chester City	46	6	11	29	37	84	29	Relegated	23
Leyton Orient	46	6	8	32	30	75	26	Relegated	24

Endsleigh League Division 3

	P	W	D	L	F	A	Pts		Pos
Carlisle United	42	27	10	5	67	31	91	Promoted	1
Walsall	42	24	11	7	75	40	83	Promoted	2
Chesterfield Town	42	23	12	7	62	37	81	Promoted	3
Bury	42	23	11	8	73	36	80		4
Preston North End	42	19	10	13	58	41	67		5
Mansfield Town	42	18	11	13	84	59	65		6
Scunthorpe United	42	18	8	16	68	63	62		7
Fulham	42	16	14	12	60	54	62		8
Doncaster Rovers	42	17	10	15	58	43	61		9
Colchester United	42	16	10	16	56	64	58		10
Barnet	42	15	11	16	56	63	56		11
Lincoln City	42	15	11	16	54	55	56		12
Torquay United	42	14	13	15	54	57	55		13
Wigan Athletic	42	14	10	18	53	60	52		14
Rochdale	42	12	14	16	44	67	50		15
Hereford United	42	12	13	17	45	62	49		16
Northampton Town	42	10	14	18	45	67	44		17
Hartlepool United	42	11	10	21	43	69	43		18
Gillingham	42	10	11	21	46	64	41		19
Darlington	42	11	8	23	43	57	41		20
Scarborough	42	8	10	24	49	70	34		21
Exeter City	42	8	10	24	36	70	34		22

ALL-TIME TABLES
1992/93-94/95

Positions Based on Points

Psn		P	W	D	L	F	A	Pts	Yrs
1	Manchester United	126	77	33	16	224	97	264	3
2	Blackburn Rovers	126	72	28	26	211	121	244	3
3	Leeds United	126	50	44	32	181	139	194	3
4	Liverpool	126	54	31	41	186	147	193	3
5	QPR	126	50	33	43	186	175	183	3
6	Aston Villa	126	47	38	41	154	146	179	3
7	Arsenal	126	46	40	40	145	115	178	3
8	Wimbledon	126	47	34	45	160	173	175	3
9	Sheffield Wednesday ...	126	44	42	40	180	162	174	3
10	Norwich City	126	43	39	44	163	180	168	3
11	Tottenham Hotspur	126	43	37	46	180	183	166	3
12	Chelsea	126	40	41	45	150	162	161	3
13	Coventry City	126	39	41	46	139	164	158	3
14	Manchester City	126	36	43	47	147	164	151	3
15	Newcastle United	84	43	20	21	149	88	149	2
16	Everton	126	38	33	55	139	169	147	3
17	Southampton	126	37	36	53	164	190	147	3
18	Ipswich Town	126	28	38	60	121	206	122	3
19	Nottingham Forest	84	32	21	31	113	105	117	2
20	West Ham United	84	26	24	34	91	106	102	2
21	Crystal Palace	84	22	28	34	82	110	94	2
22	Sheffield United	84	22	28	34	96	113	94	2
23	Oldham Athletic	84	22	23	39	105	142	89	2
24	Middlesbrough	42	11	11	20	54	75	44	1
25	Swindon Town	42	5	15	22	47	100	30	1
26	Leicester City	42	6	11	25	45	80	29	1

Positions Based on Points-Games Average

Psn		P	W	D	L	F	A	Pts	%
1	Manchester United	126	77	33	16	224	97	264	69.84
2	Blackburn Rovers	126	72	28	26	211	121	244	64.55
3	Newcastle United	84	43	20	21	149	88	149	59.13
4	Leeds United	126	50	44	32	181	139	194	51.32
5	Liverpool	126	54	31	41	186	147	193	51.06
6	QPR	126	50	33	43	186	175	183	48.41

7	Aston Villa	126	47	38	41	154	146	179	47.35
8	Arsenal	126	46	40	40	145	115	178	47.09
9	Nottingham Forest	84	32	21	31	113	105	117	46.43
10	Wimbledon	126	47	34	45	160	173	175	46.30
11	Sheffield Wednesday	126	44	42	40	180	162	174	46.03
12	Norwich City	126	43	39	44	163	180	168	44.44
13	Tottenham Hotspur	126	43	37	46	180	183	166	43.92
14	Chelsea	126	40	41	45	150	162	161	42.59
15	Coventry City	126	39	41	46	139	164	158	41.80
16	West Ham United	84	26	24	34	91	106	102	40.48
17	Manchester City	126	36	43	47	147	164	151	39.95
18	Everton	126	38	33	55	139	169	147	38.89
19	Southampton	126	37	36	53	164	190	147	38.89
20	Crystal Palace	84	22	28	34	82	110	94	37.30
21	Sheffield United	84	22	28	34	96	113	94	37.30
22	Oldham Athletic	84	22	23	39	105	142	89	35.32
23	Middlesbrough	42	11	11	20	54	75	44	34.92
24	Ipswich Town	126	28	38	60	121	206	122	32.28
25	Swindon Town	42	5	15	22	47	100	30	23.81
26	Leicester City	42	6	11	25	45	80	29	23.02

PROMOTIONS and RELEGATIONS

1994-95*	Promoted	Middlesbrough	Champions
		Bolton Wanderers	Play-Off winners (3rd)
	Relegated	Crystal Palace	19th
		Norwich City	20th
		Leicester City	21st
		Ipswich Town	22nd
1993-94	Promoted	Crystal Palace	Champions
		Nottingham Forest	Runners-up
		Leicester City	Play-off winners (4th)
	Relegated	Sheffield United	20th
		Oldham Athletic	21st
		Swindon Town	22nd
1992-93	Promoted	Newcastle United	Champions
		West Ham United	Runners-up
		Swindon Town	Play-off winners (5th)
	Relegated	Crystal Palace	20th
		Middlesbrough	21st
		Nottingham Forest	22nd
1991-92†	Promoted	Ipswich Town	Champions
		Middlesbrough	Runners-up
		Blackburn Rovers	Play-off winners (6th)

FA Premier League reduced to 20 clubs

†*Promoted from Division 2 to newly formed FA Premier League*

FA PREMIER LEAGUE

	Arsenal	Aston Villa	Blackburn R	Chelsea	Coventry City	Crystal Palace	Everton	Ipswich Town	Leeds United	Leicester City	Liverpool
Arsenal	•	0-0	0-0	3-1	2-1	1-2	1-1	4-1	1-3	1-1	0-1
Aston Villa	0-4	•	0-1	3-0	0-0	1-1	0-0	2-0	0-0	4-4	2-0
Blackburn Rovers	3-1	3-1	•	2-1	4-0	2-1	3-0	4-1	1-1	3-0	3-2
Chelsea	2-1	1-0	1-2	•	2-2	0-0	0-1	2-0	0-3	4-0	0-0
Coventry City	0-1	0-1	1-1	2-2	•	1-4	0-0	2-0	2-1	4-2	1-1
Crystal Palace	0-3	0-0	0-1	0-1	0-2	•	1-0	3-0	1-2	2-0	1-6
Everton	1-1	2-2	1-2	3-3	2-0	0-2	•	4-1	3-0	1-1	2-0
Ipswich Town	0-2	0-1	1-3	2-2	2-0	3-1	1-0	•	2-0	4-1	1-3
Leeds United	1-0	1-0	1-1	2-3	3-0	0-1	2-2	4-0	•	2-1	0-2
Leicester City	2-1	1-1	0-0		2-2	0-1	0-0	2-0	1-3	•	1-2
Liverpool	3-0	3-2	2-1	3-1	2-3	1-1	4-0	0-1	0-1	2-0	•
Manchester City	1-2	2-2	1-3	1-2	0-0	3-0	2-0	2-0	0-0	0-1	2-1
Manchester United	3-0	1-0	1-0	0-0	2-0	3-2	2-0	9-0	1-2	1-1	2-0
Newcastle United	1-0	3-1	1-1	4-2	4-0	0-0	0-0	1-1	2-1	3-1	1-1
Norwich City	0-0	1-1	1-1	3-0	2-2	1-0	2-1	1-3	3-0	1-0	1-2
Nottingham Forest	2-2	1-2	0-2	0-1	2-0	1-0	2-3	4-1	3-2	1-0	1-1
QPR	3-1	2-0	0-1	1-0	2-2	0-1	0-0	1-2	1-1	2-2	2-1
Sheffield Wednesday	3-1	1-2	0-1	1-1	5-1	3-1	0-1	4-1	1-3	1-0	1-2
Southampton	1-0	2-1	1-1	0-1	0-0	0-0	2-1	3-1	1-1	1-0	0-2
Tottenham Hotspur	1-0	3-4	3-1	0-0	1-3	0-0	2-1	3-0	0-0	1-0	0-0
West Ham United	0-2	1-0	2-0	1-2	0-1	1-0	2-2	1-1	0-0	1-0	0-0
Wimbledon	1-3	4-3	0-3	1-1	2-0	2-0	2-1	1-1	0-0	2-1	0-0

	Manchester City	Manchester United	Newcastle Utd	Norwich City	Nottingham Forest	QPR	Sheffield Wed	Southampton	Tottenham Hot	West Ham Utd	Wimbledon
Arsenal	3-0	0-0	2-3	5-1	1-0	1-3	0-0	1-1	1-1	0-1	0-0
Aston Villa	1-1	1-2	0-2	1-1	0-2	2-1	1-1	1-1	1-0	0-2	7-1
Blackburn Rovers	2-3	2-4	1-1	0-0	3-0	4-0	3-1	3-2	2-0	4-2	2-1
Chelsea	3-0	2-3	1-1	1-0	0-2	1-0	1-1	0-2	1-1	1-2	1-1
Coventry City	1-0	2-3	0-0	1-0	0-0	0-1	2-0	1-3	0-4	2-0	1-1
Crystal Palace	2-1	1-1	0-1	0-1	1-2	0-0	2-1	0-0	1-1	1-0	0-0
Everton	1-1	1-0	2-0	2-1	0-1	2-1	1-4	2-1	0-3	1-0	2-2
Ipswich Town	1-1	3-2	0-0	1-2	0-1	0-1	1-2	0-1	1-3	1-1	3-1
Leeds United	1-2	2-1	0-0	2-1	1-0	4-0	0-1	0-0	1-1	2-2	3-4
Leicester City	2-0	0-4	1-3	1-0	2-4	1-1	0-1	4-3	3-1	1-0	3-0
Liverpool	0-1	2-0	2-0	4-0	1-0	2-3	4-1	3-1	5-2	0-0	2-0
Manchester City	•	5-0	0-0	2-0	3-3	2-0	3-2	3-3	0-0	1-0	3-0
Manchester United	0-3	•	2-0	1-0	1-2	2-1	1-0	2-1	0-2	2-0	2-1
Newcastle United	0-0	2-0	•	3-0	2-1	2-1	2-1	5-1	3-3	1-1	1-2
Norwich City	1-1	1-0	1-0	•	0-1	4-2	0-0	2-2	2-1	2-1	3-1
Nottingham Forest	1-1	1-1	0-0	1-0	•	3-2	4-1	3-0	2-1	1-0	0-1
QPR	1-2	1-1	3-0	2-0	1-1	•	3-2	2-2	3-4	2-1	2-3
Sheffield Wednesday	1-1	2-3	3-1	0-0	1-7	0-2	•	1-1	4-3	1-0	1-2
Southampton	2-2	2-2	4-2	0-1	1-1	2-1	0-0	•	3-4	1-1	3-0
Tottenham Hotspur	2-1	0-1	1-3	1-0	1-4	1-1	3-1	4-3	•	3-1	1-2
West Ham United	3-0	1-1	3-2	2-2	3-1	0-0	0-2	2-0	1-2	•	1-0
Wimbledon	2-0	0-1	1-2	1-0	2-2	1-3	0-1	0-2	1-2	1-0	•

FA PREMIER LEAGUE

	Arsenal	Aston Villa	Blackburn Rvr	Chelsea	Coventry City	Crystal Palace	Everton	Ipswich Town	Leeds United	Leicester City	Liverpool
Arsenal	•	34,452	37,629	38,234	31,725	34,136	34,473	36,818	38,098	31,373	38,036
Aston Villa	32,005	•	40,114	32,901	26,186	23,305	29,678	22,241	35,038	30,825	40,154
Blackburn Rovers	23,452	22,694	•	25,490	21,657	28,005	26,538	21,325	28,561	21,050	30,263
Chelsea	29,542	17,051	17,513	•	17,090	14,130	28,115	15,608	20,174	18,397	27,050
Coventry City	14,468	12,218	18,547	13,429	•	10,732	21,814	9,526	15,389	20,663	21,029
Crystal Palace	17,092	12,606	14,232	16,030	11,891	•	15,026	13,450	14,453	12,707	18,084
Everton	32,003	35,544	37,905	33,180	28,233	23,733	•	25,659	25,897	28,003	39,866
Ipswich Town	22,054	15,710	17,329	17,296	12,893	15,570	14,951	•	15,956	15,803	22,519
Leeds United	34,218	32,955	39,426	32,212	29,179	30,942	30,793	28,600	•	28,547	38,563
Leicester City	20,774	20,896	20,559	18,140	19,372	20,022	20,447	15,248	20,068	•	21,393
Liverpool	30,117	32,158	40,014	32,855	27,183	30,972	39,505	32,733	37,454	36,012	•
Manchester City	20,500	22,513	23,387	21,880	20,632	19,971	19,867	21,430	22,892	21,007	27,055
Manchester United	43,623	43,795	43,742	43,728	43,130	43,788	43,803	43,804	43,712	43,789	43,740
Newcastle United	35,611	34,637	34,344	34,435	34,163	35,626	34,465	34,459	35,626	34,400	34,435
Norwich City	17,768	19,374	18,146	18,246	14,024	19,015	18,377	17,510	17,390	20,567	21,843
Nottingham Forest	21,662	24,598	22,131	22,092	26,253	21,326	24,526	21,340	26,299	21,601	25,418
QPR	16,341	16,037	16,508	15,103	11,398	14,227	14,488	12,456	17,416	10,189	18,295
Sheffield Wednesday	23,468	24,063	24,207	25,450	26,056	21,930	27,880	30,213	23,227	22,551	31,964
Southampton	15,201	13,874	14,209	14,404	14,505	15,151	15,163	13,246	15,202	15,101	15,190
Tottenham Hotspur	28,747	26,899	28,124	27,037	24,134	27,730	24,553	24,930	33,040	30,851	31,988
West Ham United	18,498	18,326	24,202	21,500	17,251	16,959	21,081	20,959	18,610	18,780	22,446
Wimbledon	10,842	6,221	12,341	7,022	7,349	8,835	9,506	6,341	10,211	7,683	12,041

ATTENDANCES 1994-95

	Manchester City	Manchester Utd	Newcastle Utd	Norwich City	Nottingham Fst	QPR	Sheffield Wed	Southampton	Tottenham Hot	West Ham Utd	Wimbledon
Arsenal	38,368	38,301	36,819	36,942	35,441	32,393	33,705	27,213	38,377	36,295	32,822
Aston Villa	30,133	32,136	29,960	22,468	29,217	26,578	25,082	24,179	40,017	28,682	23,982
Blackburn Rovers	27,857	30,260	30,545	25,579	27,510	21,302	22,223	23,372	26,933	25,503	20,586
Chelsea	21,740	31,161	22,987	23,098	17,890	21,704	17,285	16,738	30,812	18,696	16,105
Coventry City	15,804	21,885	17,233	11,885	19,224	15,740	17,015	11,784	19,951	17,556	10,962
Crystal Palace	13,312	18,224	17,739	12,252	15,886	16,372	10,422	14,186	18,149	18,224	12,366
Everton	28,485	40,011	34,811	23,293	26,686	27,285	37,080	36,840	32,809	28,388	33,063
Ipswich Town	13,504	22,559	18,639	17,447	18,882	11,767	13,073	16,067	22,559	19,099	11,367
Leeds United	30,938	39,396	39,337	31,982	38,191	28,780	33,750	28,953	39,224	28,987	27,284
Leicester City	19,006	21,281	20,048	15,992	20,423	18,695	20,624	20,020	21,300	20,375	15,489
Liverpool	38,122	38,906	39,300	34,709	33,329	35,996	31,493	29,881	31,507	30,907	31,139
Manchester City	•	26,368	27,389	21,031	23,150	21,172	24,530	21,589	25,473	19,150	21,131
Manchester United	43,738	•	43,795	43,789	43,744	43,214	43,868	43,479	43,802	43,795	43,440
Newcastle United	34,437	34,471	•	35,518	34,471	34,278	34,408	34,181	35,603	34,595	34,374
Norwich City	16,266	21,824	22,102	•	19,005	19,431	13,530	18,361	21,814	19,110	13,530
Nottingham Forest	28,882	22,072	22,102	20,010	•	21,449	22,022	24,146	28,711	28,361	18,261
QPR	13,631	18,948	16,576	10,519	13,363	•	12,788	16,078	18,367	12,780	11,061
Sheffield Wednesday	26,776	33,441	31,215	25,072	30,060	22,766	•	28,424	34,051	25,350	20,395
Southampton	14,902	15,204	15,189	12,976	14,185	15,201	15,189	•	15,105	15,178	14,603
Tottenham Hotspur	27,410	24,502	28,002	32,304	24,558	25,799	25,912	22,387	•	26,271	27,258
West Ham United	17,286	24,783	18,580	21,464	20,544	22,932	14,554	18,853	24,573	•	21,804
Wimbledon	5,268	18,224	14,203	8,242	15,341	9,176	7,453	10,521	16,802	11,212	•

FA PREMIER LEAGUE
RECORDS 1994-95
SCORERS

Top Scorers – All Competitions

Player	Club	L	F	C	E	Total
Alan SHEARER	Blackburn Rovers	34	0	2	1	37
Robbie FOWLER	Liverpool	25	2	4	0	31
Matt LE TISSIER	Southampton	20	5	5	0	30
Ian WRIGHT	Arsenal	18	0	3	9	30
Jurgen KLINSMANN	Tottenham Hotspur	22	5	0	0	27
Andy COLE	Manchester United†	21	0	2	4	27
Les FERDINAND	QPR	24	1	1	0	26
Stan COLLYMORE	Nottingham Forest	23	1	2	0	26
Teddy SHERINGHAM	Tottenham Hotspur	17	4	0	0	21

† including Newcastle United
L=League, F=FA Cup, C=Coca-Cola Cup, E=Europe

FA Carling Premiership Top Scorers

Player	Club	Goals	All-time Total
Alan SHEARER	Blackburn Rovers	34	81
Robbie FOWLER	Liverpool	25	37
Stan COLLYMORE	Nottingham Forest	23	23
Les FERDINAND	QPR	23	60
Jurgen KLINSMANN	Tottenham Hotspur	22	22
Andy COLE	Newcastle United & Manchester United	21	55
Matt LE TISSIER	Southampton	20	60
Ian WRIGHT	Arsenal	18	56
Teddy SHERINGHAM	Tottenham Hotspur	17	85
Uwe ROSLER	Manchester City	15	15
Dean SAUNDERS	Aston Villa	15	39
Chris SUTTON	Blackburn Rovers	15	48
Andrei KANCHELSKIS	Manchester United	14	23
Peter BEARDSLEY	Newcastle United	13	44
Tony COTTEE	West Ham United	13	41
Dion DUBLIN	Coventry City	13	15

Bryan ROY	Nottingham Forest	13	13
Paul RIDEOUT	Everton	13	23
Eric CANTONA	Manchester United	12	45
Ian RUSH	Liverpool	12	40
Paul WALSH	Manchester City	12	16
Mark BRIGHT	Sheffield Wednesday	11	41
Peter NDLOVU	Coventry City	11	29
John SPENCER	Chelsea	11	14
Anthony YEBOAH	Leeds United	11	11
Ruel FOX	Newcastle United	10	24
Paul FURLONG	Chelsea	10	10
Kevin GALLEN	QPR	10	10

FA Carling Premiership Club Top Scorers

Club	*Scorers*
Arsenal	Wright 18, Hartson 7, Campbell 4
Aston Villa	Saunders 15, Staunton 5, Johnson 4
Blackburn Rovers	Shearer 34, Sutton 15, Atkins 6, Sherwood 6
Chelsea	Spencer 11, Furlong 10, Stein 8
Coventry City	Dublin 13, Ndlovu 11, Flynn 4
Crystal Palace	Armstrong 8, Salako 4, Preece 4, Dowie 4
Everton	Rideout 13, Ferguson 7, Amokachi 4
Ipswich Town	Thomsen 5, Wark 4, Sedgley 4
Leeds United	Yeboah 11, Whelan 7, Dean 7, McAllister 6
Leicester City	Roberts 9, Lowe 8, Robins 5
Liverpool	Fowler 25, Rush 12, McManaman 7, Barnes 7
Manchester City	Rosler 15, Walsh 12, Quinn 8
Manchester United	Kanchelskis 14, Cantona 12, Cole 12, Hughes 7
Newcastle United	Beardsley 13, Fox 10, Cole 9, Lee 9
Norwich City	Ward 8, Robins 4, Cureton 4, Newsome 3, Adams 3
Nottingham Forest	Collymore 23, Roy 13, Pearce 8
QPR	Ferdinand 23, Gallen 10, Sinclair 4, Barker 4
Sheffield Wednesday	Bright 11, Whittingham 9, Hyde 5
Southampton	Le Tissier 20, Magilton 6, Dowie 5, Ekelund 5
Tottenham Hotspur	Klinsmann 22, Sheringham 17, Barmby 9
West Ham United	Cottee 13, Hutchinson 8, Boere 6
Wimbledon	Ekoku 9, Holdsworth 7, Harford 6

FA Carling Premiership Hat-tricks

Player	*Goals*	*Match*	*Date*
Chris SUTTON	3	BLACKBURN v Coventry City (4-0)	27/8/94
Robbie FOWLER	3	LIVERPOOL v Arsenal (3-0)	28/8/94
A.KANCHELSKIS	3	MAN. UNITED v Man. City (5-0)	10/11/94
T. SHERINGHAM	3	TOTTENHAM v Newcastle Utd (4-2)	3/12/94

Tony COTTEE	3	WEST HAM UTD v Man.City (3-0)	17/12/94
Alan SHEARER	3	BLACKBURN v QPR (4-0)	2/1/95
Alan SHEARER	3	BLACKBURN v Ipswich Town (4-1)	28/1/95
Any COLE	5*	MAN. UNITED v Ipswich Town (9-0)	4/3/95
Peter NDLOVU	3	Liverpool v COVENTRY CITY (2-3)	4/3/95
JOHNSON	3	ASTON VILLA v Wimbledon (7-1)	11/2/95
Anthony YEBOAH	3	LEEDS UNITED v Ipswich Town (4-0)	5/4/95
Ian WRIGHT	3	ARSENAL v Ipswich Town (4-1)	15/4/95

5 goals, Premiership record

ATTENDANCES

Attendance Summaries by Club

Club	Total	Ave
Arsenal	741,650	35,317
Aston Villa	602,640	28,697
Blackburn Rovers	530,705	25,272
Chelsea	427,278	20,347
Coventry City	311,939	14,854
Crystal Palace	312,703	14,891
Everton	605,833	28,849
Ipswich Town	355,044	16,907
Leeds United	652,861	31,089
Leicester City	388,872	18,518
Liverpool	717,792	34,181
Manchester City	477,620	22,744
Manchester United	873,578	41,599
Newcastle United	728,537	34,692
Norwich City	391,034	18,621
Nottingham Forest	495,188	23,580
QPR	306,569	14,599
Sheffield Wednesday	531,783	25,323
Southampton	294,280	14,013
Tottenham Hotspur	550,049	26,193
West Ham United	405,659	19,317
Wimbledon	214,834	10,230
Total	**10,916,448**	**23,629**

Club	Posn	Total	Ave
Manchester United	2	873,578	41,599
Arsenal	12	741,650	35,317
Newcastle United	6	728,537	34,692
Liverpool	4	717,792	34,181
Leeds United	5	652,861	31,089
Everton	15	605,833	28,849
Aston Villa	18	602,640	28,697
Tottenham Hotspur	7	550,049	26,193
Sheffield Wednesday	13	531,783	25,323
Blackburn Rovers	1	530,705	25,272
Nottingham Forest	3	495,188	23,580
Manchester City	17	477,620	22,744
Chelsea	11	427,278	20,347
West Ham United	14	405,659	19,317
Norwich City	20	391,034	18,621
Leicester City	21	388,872	18,518
Ipswich Town	22	355,044	16,907
Crystal Palace	19	312,703	14,891
Coventry City	16	311,939	14,854
QPR	8	306,569	14,599
Southampton	10	294,280	14,013
Wimbledon	9	214,834	10,230

SCORES

Highest Aggregate Scorers

9-0	Manchester United v Ipswich Town	04/03/95
4-4	Aston Villa v Leicester City	22/02/95

Biggest Home Wins

9-0	Manchester United v Ipswich Town	04/03/95
7-1	Aston Villa v Wimbledon	11/02/95

Biggest Away Wins

1-7	Sheffield Wednesday v Nottingham Forest	01/04/95
1-6	Crystal Palace v Liverpool	20/08/94

Highest Score Draw

4-4   Aston Villa v Leicester City   22/02/95

Score Frequencies

	Home Win		Away Win		Draws	
Score	Total No.	Score	Total No.	Score	Total No.	
1-0	42	0-1	33	0-0	53	
2-0	39	0-2	19	1-1	55	
3-0	24	0-3	4	2-2	22	
4-0	8	0-4	2	3-3	4	
5-0	1	1-2	29	4-4	1	
2-1	36	1-3	14			
3-1	22	1-4	3			
4-1	8	1-6	1			
5-1	3	1-7	1			
7-1	1	2-3	10			
9-0	1	2-4	2			
3-2	10	3-4	3			
4-2	5					
4-3	3					
5-2	1					
Total	**204**	**Total**	**121**	**Total**	**135**	

BOOKINGS & DISMISSALS

Players Sent Off

	Player	Match	Date	Official
1	WILSON	Man.United v QPR	20/8/94	T.Gallagher
2	ROSLER	Arsenal v MAN. CITY	20/8/94	P.Durkin
3	PARKER	MAN.UNITED v QPR	20/8/94	T.Gallagher
4	SRNICEK	Leics.City v NEWCASTLE UTD	21/8/94	M.Reed
5	QUINN	Blackburn Rvrs v COVENTRY C.	27/8/94	G.Poll
6	MOHAN	N. Forest v LEICESTER CITY	27/8/94	G.Willard
7	CHETTLE	Everton v N.FOREST	30/8/94	G. Ashby
8	LEWIS	LEICS. CITY v N. Forest	31/8/94	P.Don
9	SINCLAIR	Leicester City v QPR	31/8/94	S.Lodge
10	WILCOX	Arsenal v BLACKBURN RVRS	31/8/94	K.Morton
11	JONES	WIMBLEDON v Leicester City	10/9/94	G.Poll

12	LOWE	Wimbledon v LEICESTER CITY	10/9/94	G.Poll
13	CAREY	Wimbledon v LEICESTER CITY	10/9/94	G.Poll
14	COTTEE	Liverpool v WEST HAM UTD	10/9/94	P.Danson
15	WISE	Newcastle v CHELSEA	10/9/94	P.Jones
16	CAMPBELL	TOTTENHAM H. v Southampton	12/9/94	A.Wilkie
17	ALBERT	NEWCASTLE UTD v Liverpool	24/9/94	P.Don
18	WATSON	SHEFF WEDS v Leeds United	26/9/94	A.Wilkie
19	CLARKE	CHELSEA v West Ham United	2/10/94	P.Don
20	GILLESPIE	Leicsr City v COVENTRY CITY	3/10/94	K.Cooper
21	WILLIS	LEICS. CITY v Coventry City	3/10/94	K.Cooper
22	ADAMS	Sheffield Weds v ARSENAL	6/10/94	K.Burge
23	HARTSON	Sheffield Wednesday v ARSENAL	6/10/94	K.Burge
24	DIBBLE	QPR v MAN. CITY	15/10/94	G.Willard
25	EDGHILL	QPR v MAN. CITY	15/10/94	G.Willard
26	WALKER	Ipswich Town v SHEFF WEDS	16/10/94	M.Reed
27	BERG	BLACKBURN RVRS v Man.Utd	23/10/94	G. Ashby
28	WILCOX	N.Forest v BLACKBURN RVRS	29/10/94	P.Danson
29	HUTCHISON	WEST HAM UTD v Leics.City	5/11/94	R.Dilkes
30	TOWNSEND	Wimbledon v ASTON VILLA	9/11/94	D.Elleray
31	JOHNSEN	Liverpool v CHELSEA	9/11/94	G.Poll
32	JONES	WIMBLEDON v Newcastle Utd	19/11/94	P.Don
33	SMITH	LEICS.CITY v Manchester City	20/11/94	K.Morton
34	REEVES	Manchester City v WIMBLEDON	26/11/94	A.Wilkie
35	HUGHES	Arsenal v MAN.UNITED	26/11/94	K.Morton
36	THORN	Southampton v WIMBLEDON	26/12/94	G.Poll
37	GRAYSON	LEICESTER CITY v Liverpool	26/12/94	G. Ashby
38	WHELAN	IPSWICH TOWN v Arsenal	28/12/94	P.Danson
39	KEOWN	Ipswich Town v ARSENAL	28/12/94	P.Danson
40	SCHWARZ	Tottenham Hotspur v ARSENAL	2/1/95	M.Reed
41	PRESSLEY	Man. United v COVENTRY C.	14/1/95	G.Willard
42	FERGUSON	Arsenal v EVERTON	14/1/95	R.Hart
43	BREACKER	WEST HAM UTD v Sheff. Weds	23/1/95	P.Danson
44	CANTONA	Crystal Palace v MAN.UNITED	25/1/95	A.Wilkie
45	FLOWERS	BLACKBURN RVRS v Leeds Utd	1/2/95	R.Gifford
46	BARRETT	Newcastle United v EVERTON	1/2/95	D.Elleray
47	HORNE	Newcastle United v EVERTON	1/2/95	D.Elleray
48	BABB	Nottingham Forest v LIVERPOOL	4/2/95	G.Willard
49	HUMPHREY	Ipswich Town v C. PALACE	4/2/95	S.Lodge
50	PRESSMAN	Blackburn Rovers v SHEFF WEDS	12/2/95	P.Jones
51	SAMWAYS	Leicester City v EVERTON	4/3/95	P.Durkin
52	FERGUSON	Leicester City v EVERTON	4/3/95	P.Durkin
53	JOHNSON	West Ham Utd v NORWICH CITY	11/3/95	A.Wilkie
54	PHELAN	Everton v MAN. CITY	15/3/95	G.Willard
55	HOLLOWAY	Coventry City v QPR	1/4/95	P.Danson
56	LEE	Everton v NEWCASTLE UTD	14/4/95	R.Gifford
57	TOWNSEND	Arsenal v ASTON VILLA	17/4/95	K.Morton

58	WHITLOW	Liverpool v LEICESTER CITY	17/4/95	G.Poll
59	WARK	Norwich City v IPSWICH TOWN	20/4/95	P.Durkin
60	BOSNICH	Leeds United v ASTON VILLA	29/4/95	D.Elleray
61	SRNICEK	NEWCASTLE UTD v Tottenham H.	3/5/95	T.Gallagher
62	CALDERWOOD	Newcastle Utd v TOTTENHAM H.	3/5/95	T.Gallagher
63	FERDINAND	QPR v Tottenham Hotspur	6/5/95	P.Jones
64	BARLOW	Ipswich Town v EVERTON	9/5/95	R.Hart
65	KIMBLE	WIMBLEDON v Man. United	7/3/95	R.Hart

Referees – Who They Sent Off

Referee	No.	Players
Ashby	3	Berg, Chettle, Grayson
Burge	2	Adams, Hartson
Cooper	3	Gillespie, Willis, Hughes
Danson	6	Brecker, Cottee, Holloway, Keown, Whelan, Wilcox
Dilkes	1	Hutchison
Don	4	Albert, Clarke, Jones, Lewis
Durkin	4	Ferguson, Rosler, Samways, Wark
Elleray	4	Barrett, Bosnich, Horne, Townsend
Gallagher	4	Calderwood, Parker, Srnicek, Wilson
Gifford	2	Flowers, Lee
Hart	3	Barlow, Ferguson, Kimble
Jones	3	Ferdinand, Pressman, Wise
Lodge	2	Humphrey, Sinclair
Morton	3	Smith, Townsend, Wilcox
Poll	7	Carey, Johnsen, Jones, Lowe, Quinn, Thorn, Whitlow
Reed	3	Schwarz, Srnicek, Walker
Wilkie	5	Campbell, Cantona, Johnson, Reeves, Watson
Willard	6	Babb, Dibble, Edghill, Mohan, Phelan, Pressley

Referees by Number of Bookings Issued

Twenty-two referees officiated in the 94-95 Premiership season. The following table demonstrates how many matches they have each officiated and gives a count of the number of yellow and red cards that have been shown. In all 1294 yellow cards were displayed (not including second yellow cards which are counted as reds for the purpose of the stats in this book) at an average rate of 1.4 per match.

The Bookings/Match column gives a rough illustration of which referees are more likely to reach for the paperwork. Equally it gives an indication of which referees have officiated at the toughest games. How much it reflects either situation is a matter for debate. In either case it can only be a rough estimation. The average is calculated on yellow cards alone.

Whistle Stop Tour
–
Graham Poll

	Referee	Matches	Yellow	Red	Average
1	WORRALL, Joe 44		26	0	0.59
2	HOLBROOK, Terry 41		29	0	0.71
3	HILL, Brian 42		37	0	0.88
4	GIFFORD, Roger 40		40	2	1.00
5	DILKES, Roger 24		26	1	1.08
6	GALLAGHER, Terry 47		55	4	1.17
7	BODENHAM, Martin 36		44	0	1.22
8	BURGE, Keith 42		53	2	1.26
9	ASHBY, Gerald 44		59	3	1.34
10	COOPER, Keith 44		60	3	1.36
11	HART, Robert 48		67	3	1.40
12	WILKIE, Alan 50		72	5	1.44
13	WILLARD, Gary 42		61	6	1.45
14	LODGE, Stephen 40		61	2	1.53
15	JONES, Peter 38		60	3	1.58
16	DURKIN, Paul 42		72	4	1.71
17	DON, Philip 46		79	4	1.72
18	POLL, Graham 45		81	7	1.80
19	MORTON, Keith 50		91	3	1.82
20	REED, Mike 50		91	3	1.82
21	DANSON, Paul 39		71	6	1.82
22	ELLERAY, David 30		59	4	1.97

Joe Worral heads our Fair Play chart at a rate of slightly more than one yellow card every two games, what's more he didn't feel the need to show the red plastic at all during the Premiership season. Intrestingly, the three referees who averaged under a booking per game all kept the red cards in their pockets. David Elleray takes the plastic spoon with a dish-out rate of nearly two yellows a game despite only officiating in 30 clashes.

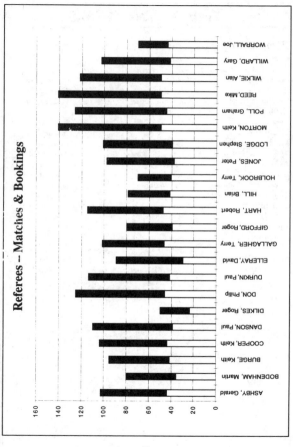

Referees – Matches & Bookings

49

THE MANAGERS

Premiership Managers by Length of Tenure

Club	Manager	Arrived
Manchester United	Alex Ferguson	November '86
Leeds United	Howard Wilkinson	October '88
Wimbledon	Joe Kinnear	January '91
Newcastle United	Kevin Keegan	February '92
Nottingham Forest	Frank Clark	June '93
Chelsea	Glenn Hoddle	June '93
Liverpool	Roy Evans	January '94
Middlesbrough	Bryan Robson	May '94
West Ham United	Harry Redknapp	August '94
Aston Villa	Brian Little	November '94
Everton	Joe Royle	November '94
Queens Park Rangers	Ray Wilkins	November '94
Tottenham Hotspur	Gerry Francis	November '94
Coventry City	Ron Atkinson	February '95
Arsenal	Bruce Rioch	May '95
Blackburn Rovers	Ray Harford	May '95
Bolton Wanderers	Roy McFarland	June '95
Manchester City	Alan Ball	July '95
Sheffield Wednesday	David Pleat	July '95
Southampton	Dave Merrington	July '95

FA PREMIER LEAGUE ALL-TIME RECORDS

† New record set in 1994-95 season.

Record Attendances by Club

Club	Att	Opponents	Date	
Arsenal	38,377	Tottenham Hotspur	29/04/95	†
Aston Villa	45,347	Liverpool	07/05/94	
Blackburn Rovers	30,545	Newcastle United	08/05/95	†
Chelsea	37,064	Manchester United	11/09/93	
Coventry City	24,410	Manchester United	12/04/94	
Crystal Palace	30,115	Manchester United	21/04/93	
Everton	40,011	Manchester United	25/02/95	†
Ipswich Town	22,559	Manchester United	01/05/94	
Leeds United	41,125	Manchester United	27/04/94	
Leicester City	21,393	Liverpool	26/12/94	†
Liverpool	44,619	Everton	20/03/93	
Manchester City	37,136	Manchester United	20/03/93	
Manchester Utd	44,751	Liverpool	04/01/94	
Middlesbrough	24,172	Manchester United	03/10/92	
Newcastle United	36,388	Leeds United	22/12/93	
Norwich City	21,843	Liverpool	29/04/95	†
Nottingham Forest	28,882	Manchester City	05/05/95	†
Queens Park Rangers	21,267	Manchester United	05/02/94	
Sheffield United	30,044	Sheffield Wednesday	23/10/93	
Sheffield Wednesday	38,668	Sheffield United	13/03/93	
Southampton	19,654	Tottenham Hotspur	15/08/92	
Tottenham Hotspur	33,709	Arsenal	12/12/92	
West Ham United	28,832	Manchester United	25/02/94	
Wimbledon	30,115	Manchester United	08/05/93	

Top 10 Attendances

Psn	Att	Match	Date
1	45,347	Aston Villa v Liverpool	07/05/94
2	44,751	Manchester United v Liverpool	30/03/94
3	44,750	Manchester United v Everton	22/01/94
4	44,748	Manchester United v Wimbledon	20/11/93
5	44,745	Manchester United v Chelsea	05/02/94
6	44,724	Manchester United v Leeds United	01/01/94

7	44,717	Manchester United v Coventry City	08/05/94
8	44,705	Manchester United v Southampton	04/05/94
9	44,694	Manchester United v Norwich City	04/12/93
10	44,686	Manchester United v Oldham Athletic	04/04/94

Lowest Attendances by Club

Club	Att	Opponents	Date
Arsenal	18,253	Wimbledon	10/02/92
Aston Villa	16,180	Southampton	24/11/93
Blackburn Rovers	13,505	Sheffield Utd	18/10/93
Chelsea	8,923	Coventry City	04/05/94
Coventry City	9,526	Ipswich Town	10/10/94†
Crystal Palace	10,422	Sheffield Wednesday	14/03/95†
Everton	13,660	Southampton	04/12/93
Ipswich Town	10,747	Sheffield United	21/08/93
Leeds United	25,774	Wimbledon	15/08/92
Leicester City	15,489	Wimbledon	01/04/95†
Liverpool	24,561	QPR	08/12/93
Manchester City	19,150	West Ham United	24/08/85†
Manchester United	29,736	Crystal Palace	02/09/92
Middlesbrough	12,290	Oldham Athletic	22/03/93
Newcastle United	32,067	Southampton	22/01/94
Norwich City	12,452	Southampton	05/09/92
Nottingham Forest	17,553	Arsenal	17/10/92
Oldham Athletic	9,633	Wimbledon	28/08/93
Queens Park Rangers	9,875	Swindon Town	30/04/94
Sheffield United	13,646	West Ham Utd	28/03/94
Sheffield Wednesday	18,509	Oldham Athletic	24/11/93
Southampton	9,028	Ipswich Town	08/12/93
Tottenham Hotspur	17,452	Aston Villa	02/03/94
Wimbledon	3,039	Everton	26/01/93

Bottom 10 Attendances

Psn	Att	Match	Date
1	3,039	Wimbledon v Everton	26/01/93
2	3,386	Wimbledon v Oldham Athletic	12/12/92
3	3,759	Wimbledon v Coventry City	22/08/92
4	3,979	Wimbledon v Sheffield United	20/02/93
5	4,534	Wimbledon v Southampton	06/03/93
6	4,714	Wimbledon v Manchester City	01/09/92
7	4,739	Wimbledon v Coventry City	26/12/93
8	4,954	Wimbledon v Ipswich Town	18/08/92
9	5,268	Wimbledon v Manchester City	21/03/95†
10	5,536	Wimbledon v Sheffield Wednesday	15/01/94

All-Time Biggest Home Wins

9-0	Manchester United v Ipswich Town	04/03/95	†
7-1	Aston Villa v Wimbledon	11/02/93	†
7-1	Blackburn Rovers v Norwich City	02/10/92	
7-1	Newcastle United v Swindon Town	12/03/94	
6-0	Sheffield United v Tottenham Hotspur	02/03/93	

All-Time Biggest Away Wins

1-7	Sheffield Wednesday v Nottingham Forest	01/04/95	†
1-6	Crystal Palace v Liverpool	20/08/94	†
0-5	Swindon Town v Liverpool	22/08/93	
0-5	Swindon Town v Leeds United	07/05/94	

All-Time Highest Score Draws

4-4	Aston Villa v Leicester City	22/02/95	†
3-3	Crystal Palace v Blackburn Rovers	15/08/92	
	Sheffield Wednesday v Manchester United	26/12/92	
	West Ham United v Norwich City	24/01/93	
	Swindon Town v Norwich City	19/02/93	
	West Ham United v Southampton	07/05/93	
	Coventry City v Leeds United	08/05/93	
	Middlesbrough v Norwich City	08/05/93	
	Oldham Athletic v Coventry City	24/08/93	
	Sheffield Wednesday v Norwich City	01/09/93	
	Southampton v Sheffield United	02/10/93	
	Leeds United v Blackburn Rovers	23/10/93	
	Sheffield Wednesday v Leeds United	30/10/93	
	Tottenham v Liverpool	18/12/93	
	Sheffield Wednesday v Swindon Town	29/12/93	
	Liverpool v Manchester United	04/01/94	
	Everton v Chelsea	03/05/95	†
	Manchester City v Nottingham Forest	08/10/94	†
	Manchester City v Southampton	05/11/94	†
	Newcastle United v Tottenham Hotspur	03/05/95	†

Crime Count – Year-by-Year

Season	Red Cards	Yellow Cards
1992-93	34	760
1993-94	25	599
1994-95	65	1294
Total	*124*	*2653*

Most Goals Scored in a Season	Newcastle United	84	1993-94	*
Fewest Goals Scored in a Season	Crystal Palace	34	1994-95	*
Most Goals Conceded in a Season	Swindon Town	100	1993-94	*
Fewest Goals Conceded in a Season	Arsenal	28	1993-94	*
	Manchester United	28	1994-95	*
Most Points in a Season	Manchester United	92	1993-94	*
Fewest Points in a Season	Ipswich Town	27	1994-95	*
Most Wins in a Season	Manchester United	27	1993-94	*
	Blackburn Rovers	27	1994-95	*
Fewest Wins in a Season	Swindon Town	5	1993-94	*
Fewest Defeats in a Season	Manchester United	4	1993-94	*
Most Defeats in a Season	Ipswich Town	29	1994-95	*
Most Draws in a Season	Manchester City	18	1993-94	*
	Sheffield United	18	1993-94	*
	Southampton	18	1994-95	*

* 42 games

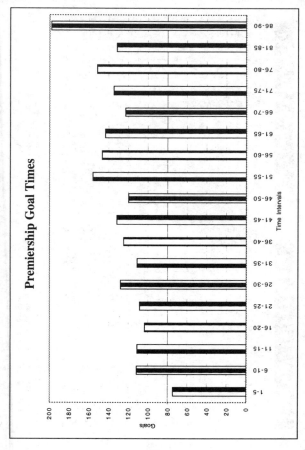

Premiership Goal Times

Final Table 1992-93 Season

		P	W	D	L	F	A	Pts	
1	Manchester United	42	24	12	6	67	31	84	
2	Aston Villa	42	21	11	10	57	40	74	
3	Norwich City	42	21	9	12	61	65	72	
4	Blackburn Rovers	42	20	11	11	68	46	71	
5	QPR	42	17	12	13	63	55	63	
6	Liverpool	42	16	11	15	62	55	59	
7	Sheffield Wednesday	42	15	14	13	55	51	59	
8	Tottenham Hotspur	42	16	11	15	60	66	59	
9	Manchester City	42	15	12	15	56	51	57	
10	Arsenal	42	15	11	16	40	38	56	
11	Chelsea	42	14	14	14	51	54	56	
12	Wimbledon	42	14	12	16	56	55	54	
13	Everton	42	15	8	19	53	55	53	
14	Sheffield United	42	14	10	18	54	53	52	
15	Coventry City	42	13	13	16	52	57	52	
16	Ipswich Town	42	12	12	18	50	55	52	
17	Leeds United	42	12	15	15	57	62	51	
18	Southampton	42	13	11	18	54	61	50	
19	Oldham Athletic	42	13	10	19	63	74	49	R
20	Crystal Palace	42	11	16	15	48	61	49	R
21	Middlesbrough	42	11	11	20	54	75	44	R
22	Nottingham Forest	42	10	10	22	41	62	40	R

Promoted:

Newcastle United – Champions
West Ham United – Runners-up
Swindon Town – Play-off Winners

Final Table 1993-94 Season

		P	W	D	L	F	A	Pts	
1	Manchester United	42	27	11	4	80	38	92	
2	Blackburn Rovers	42	25	9	8	63	36	84	
3	Newcastle United	42	23	8	11	82	41	77	
4	Arsenal	42	18	17	7	53	28	71	
5	Leeds United	42	18	16	8	65	39	70	
6	Wimbledon	42	18	11	13	56	53	65	
7	Sheffield Wednesday	42	16	16	10	76	54	64	
8	Liverpool	42	17	9	16	59	55	60	
9	QPR	42	16	12	14	62	61	60	
10	Aston Villa	42	15	12	15	46	50	57	
11	Coventry City	42	14	14	14	43	45	56	
12	Norwich City	42	12	17	13	65	61	53	
13	West Ham United	42	13	13	16	47	58	52	
14	Chelsea	42	13	12	17	49	53	51	
15	Tottenham Hotspur	42	11	12	19	54	59	45	
16	Manchester City	42	9	18	15	38	49	45	
17	Everton	42	12	8	22	42	63	44	
18	Southampton	42	12	7	23	49	66	43	
19	Ipswich Town	42	9	16	17	35	58	43	
20	Sheffield United	42	8	18	16	42	60	42	R
21	Oldham Athletic	42	9	13	20	42	68	40	R
22	Swindon Town	42	5	15	22	47	100	30	R

Promoted:

Crystal Palace – Champions
Nottingham Forest – Runners-up
Leicester City – Play-off Winners

Top Appearances by Player

Player	Total	Start	Sub	Goals
PALLISTER, Gary	125	125	0	4
BARRETT, Earl	123	122	1	1
SOUTHALL, Neville	123	123	0	0
FLOWERS, Tim	122	122	0	0
IRWIN, Dennis	122	122	0	9
ATHERTON, Peter	120	119	1	1
BOWEN, Mark	119	117	2	8
LE TISSIER, Matthew	119	119	0	60
SUTTON, Chris	119	113	6	48
WILSON, Clive	119	119	0	6
BRUCE, Steve	118	118	0	10
SAUNDERS, Dean	118	117	1	39
DEANE, Brian	117	115	2	35
RIPLEY, Stuart	117	114	3	11
INCE, Paul	116	116	0	19
SHERWOOD, Tim	116	115	1	11
McALLISTER, Gary	115	115	0	20
RICHARDSON, Kevin	115	114	1	8
RUDDOCK, Neil	114	114	0	8
SCHMEICHEL, Peter	114	114	0	0
SEGERS, Hans	114	113	1	0
SPEED, Gary	114	113	1	20
FOX, Ruel	113	111	2	23
IMPEY, Andy	113	110	3	8
MADDISON, Neil	113	109	4	14
BRIGHT, Mark	112	102	10	41
LINIGHAN, David	112	111	1	4
McGRATH, Paul	112	108	4	4
PEACOCK, Darren	112	109	3	6
BABB, Phil	111	103	8	3
HUGHES, Mark	111	110	1	35
FERDINAND, Les	110	109	1	60
PALMER, Carlton	110	109	1	9
RUSH, Ian	110	108	2	40
BART-WILLIAMS, Chris	109	83	26	17
SEAMAN, David	109	109	0	0
WILLIAMS, Geraint	109	109	0	1
ANDERTON, Darren	108	104	4	17
BEARDSLEY, Peter	108	108	0	44
GIGGS, Ryan	108	101	7	23
McCLAIR, Brian	108	88	20	15
DOWIE, Iain	107	105	2	25
KENNA, Jeff	107	104	3	5
MILLIGAN, Mike	107	106	1	5

57

PEACOCK, Gavin	107	104	3	24
SCALES, John	107	107	0	3
CROOK, Ian	106	103	3	3
HOLDSWORTH, Dean	106	103	3	43
WATSON, Dave	106	105	1	4
BENALI, Francis	105	97	8	0
HOUGHTON, Ray	105	93	12	8
TEALE, Shaun	105	104	1	2
TOWNSEND, Andy	105	105	0	8
GUNN, Bryan	104	104	0	0
KIWOMYA, Chris	104	90	14	21
REDKNAPP, Jamie	104	92	12	9
LE SAUX, Graeme	103	98	5	5
SHEARER, Alan	103	97	6	81
BARDSLEY, David	102	102	0	3
BORROWS, Brian	102	98	4	2
HENDRY, Colin	102	101	1	28
KEANE, Roy	102	97	5	13
NDLOVU, Peter	102	95	7	29
SHERINGHAM, Teddy	102	99	3	85
SINCLAIR, Frank	102	102	0	3
WINTERBURN, Nigel	102	102	0	1
BARTON, Warren	101	99	2	6
DIXON, Lee	101	100	1	1
LUKIC, John	101	101	0	0
McMANAMAN, Steve	101	96	5	13
NEWSOME, Jon	101	90	11	4
STAUNTON, Steve	101	100	1	10
WALLACE, Rod	101	95	6	28
WARK, John	101	100	1	13
WRIGHT, Ian	101	99	2	56
JONES, Vinny	100	100	0	7
NEWTON, Eddie	100	87	13	6

Top Substitute Appearances by Player

	Appearances			
Player	Sub	Total	Start	Goals
CLARKE, Andy	41	81	40	8
BARLOW, Stuart	38	59	21	10
WATSON, Gordon	33	69	36	18
CORK, Alan	28	46	18	5
WALTERS, Mark	28	68	40	11
BANGER, Nicky	26	34	8	8
BART-WILLIAMS, Chris	26	109	83	17
ADAMS, Neil	25	92	67	12
RADOSAVIJEVIC, Pedray	24	46	22	4

ROSENTHAL, Ronny	24	65	41	8
GUENTCHEV, Bontcho	22	61	39	6
KANCHELSKIS, Andrei	21	88	67	23
MATHIE, Alex	21	37	16	6
LIMPAR, Anders	20	69	49	13
McCLAIR, Brian	20	108	88	15
STUART, Graham	20	97	77	15

Top Goalscorers by Player

		Appearances		
Player	Goals	Total	Start	Sub
SHERINGHAM, Teddy	85	102	99	3
SHEARER, Alan	81	103	97	6
FERDINAND, Les	60	110	109	1
LE TISSIER, Matthew	60	119	119	0
WRIGHT, Ian	56	101	99	2
COLE, Andy	55	76	75	1
SUTTON, Chris	48	119	113	6
CANTONA, Eric	45	90	88	2
BEARDSLEY, Peter	44	108	108	0
HOLDSWORTH, Dean	43	106	103	3
BRIGHT, Mark	41	112	102	10
COTTEE, Tony	41	99	95	4
RUSH, Ian	40	110	108	2
SAUNDERS, Dean	39	118	117	1
FOWLER, Robbie	37	70	69	1
DEANE, Brian	35	117	115	2
HUGHES, Mark	35	111	110	1
NDLOVU, Peter	29	102	95	7
WALLACE, Rod	28	101	95	6
DOWIE, Iain	25	107	105	2
OLNEY, Ian	25	44	42	2
QUINN, Mick	25	64	57	7
ROBINS, Mark	25	84	73	11
WHITE, David	25	96	85	11
EKOKU, Efan	24	61	50	11
PEACOCK, Gavin	24	107	104	3
ARMSTRONG, Chris	23	75	75	0
CHAPMAN, Lee	23	96	78	18
COLLYMORE, Stan	23	39	37	2
FOX, Ruel	23	113	111	2
GIGGS, Ryan	23	108	101	7
KANCHELSKIS, Andrei	23	88	67	21
RIDEOUT, Paul	23	77	63	14
ATKINSON, Dalian	22	73	68	5
CAMPBELL, Kevin	22	97	79	18

KLINSMANN, Jurgen	22	41	41	0
QUINN, Niall	22	89	77	12
KIWOMYA, Chris	21	104	90	14
STEIN, Mark	21	42	39	3
BARMBY, Nicky	20	87	81	6
FASHANU, John	20	78	73	5
McALLISTER, Gary	20	115	115	0
SPEED, Gary	20	114	113	1

Top Goalscorers by Strike Percentage

NB: To qualify players must have played a minimum of 30 FAPL games and have a strike rate of 40% or more. A strike rate of 100% indicates a goal a game, 50% indicates a goal every two games.

Player	%	Goals	Total	Start	Sub
SHERINGHAM, Teddy	83.33	85	102	99	3
SHEARER, Alan	78.64	81	103	97	6
COLE, Andy	72.37	55	76	75	1
COLLYMORE, Stan	58.97	23	39	37	2
OLNEY, Ian	56.82	25	44	42	2
WRIGHT, Ian	55.45	56	101	99	2
FERDINAND, Les	54.55	60	110	109	1
KLINSMANN, Jurgen	53.66	22	41	41	0
FOWLER, Robbie	52.86	37	70	69	1
LE TISSIER, Matthew	50.42	60	119	119	0
CANTONA, Eric	50.00	45	90	88	2
STEIN, Mark	50.00	21	42	39	3
ROSLER, Uwe	48.39	15	31	29	2
COTTEE, Tony	41.41	41	99	95	4
BEARDSLEY, Peter	40.74	44	108	108	0
HOLDSWORTH, Dean	40.57	43	106	103	3
SUTTON, Chris	40.34	48	119	113	6

All-Time Player Most Goals in One Game

Gls	Player	Match	Date	Res
5	Andy COLE	MAN UNITED v Ipswich Town	04/03/95	9-0
4	Efan EKOKU	Everton v NORWICH CITY	25/09/93	1-5

FA CHALLENGE CUP 1994-95

Third Round – 7 January 1995

Aylesbury United *(played at QPR)*	v	Queen's Park Rangers	0-4	15,417
Barnsley	v	Aston Villa	0-2	11,469
Birmingham City	v	Liverpool	1-1	25,326
Bristol City	v	Stoke City	0-0	9,683
Bury	v	Tranmere Rovers	2-2	5,755
Cambridge United	v	Burnley	2-4	6,275
Chelsea	v	Charlton Athletic	3-0	24,485
Coventry City	v	West Bromwich Albion	1-1	16,555
Crystal Palace	v	Lincoln City	5-1	6,541
Everton	v	Derby County	1-0	10,425
Gillingham	v	Sheffield Wednesday	1-2	10,425
Grimsby Town	v	Norwich City	0-1	11,198
Leicester City	v	Enfield	2-0	17,351
Luton Town	v	Bristol Rovers	1-1	7,571
Mansfield Town	v	Wolves	2-3	6,701
Millwall	v	Arsenal	0-0	17,715
Newcastle United	v	Blackburn Rovers	1-1	31,721
Nottingham Forest	v	Plymouth Argyle	2-0	19,821
Notts County	v	Manchester City	2-2	12,376
Portsmouth	v	Bolton Wanderers	1-3	9,721
Reading	v	Oldham Athletic	1-3	8,886
Scarborough	v	Watford	0-0	3,544
Sheffield United	v	Manchester United	0-2	22,322
Southampton	v	Southend United	2-0	13,003
Sunderland	v	Carlisle United	1-1	15,523
Swansea City	v	Middlesbrough	1-1	8,407
Swindon Town	v	Marlow	2-0	7,007
Tottenham Hotspur	v	Altrincham	3-0	25,057
Walsall	v	Leeds United	1-1	8,619
Wimbledon	v	Colchester United	1-0	6,903
Wrexham	v	Ipswich Town	2-1	8,324
Wycombe	v	West Ham United	0-2	9,007

Third Round Replays

Arsenal	v	Millwall	0-2	32,319
Blackburn Rovers	v	Newcastle United	1-2	22,658
Bristol Rovers	v	Luton Town	0-1	8,218
Carlisle United	v	Sunderland	1-3	12,201
Leeds United	v	Walsall	5-2§	17,881
Liverpool	v	Birmingham City	1-1§	36,275
Manchester City	v	Notts County	5-2	14,261
Middlesbrough	v	Swansea City	1-2	13,940
Stoke City	v	Bristol City	1-3§	11,579
Tranmere Rovers	v	Bury	3-0	7,921
Watford	v	Scarborough	2-0	7,047
West Brom	v	Coventry City	1-2	23,230

Fourth Round – 28 January 1995

Bristol City	v	Everton	0-1	19,816
Burnley	v	Liverpool	0-0	20,551
Coventry City	v	Norwich City	0-0	15,101
Leeds United	v	Oldham Athletic	3-2	25,010
Luton Town	v	Southampton	1-1	9,938
Manchester City	v	Aston Villa	1-0	21,177
Manchester United	v	Wrexham	5-2	43,222
Millwall	v	Chelsea	0-0	18,573
Newcastle United	v	Swansea City	3-0	34,372
Nottingham Forest	v	Crystal Palace	1-2	16,970
Portsmouth	v	Leicester City	0-1	14,928
Queen's Park Rangers	v	West Ham United	1-0	17,694
Sheffield Wednesday	v	Wolves	0-0	21,757
Sunderland	v	Tottenham Hotspur	1-4	21,135
Tranmere Rovers	v	Wimbledon	0-2	11,637
Watford	v	Swindon Town	1-0	11,207

Fourth Round Replays

Chelsea	v	Millwall	1-1	†	25,515

(Millwall in 5-4 on penalties)

Liverpool	v	Burnley	1-0		32,109
Norwich City	v	Coventry City	3-1	†	14,673
Southampton	v	Luton Town	6-0		15,075
Wolves	v	Sheffield Wednesday	1-1	†	28,136

(Wolves win 3-2 on penalties)

Fifth Round – 18 February 1995

Everton	v	Norwich City	5-0	31,616
Liverpool	v	Wimbledon	0-0	25,124
Manchester United	v	Leeds United	3-1	42,744
Newcastle United	v	Manchester City	3-1	33,214
Queen's Park Rangers	v	Millwall	1-0	16,457
Tottenham Hotspur	v	Southampton	1-1	28,091
Watford	v	Crystal Palace	0-1	13,814
Wolves	v	Leicester City	1-0	28,544

Fifth Round Replays

Crystal Palace	v	Watford	1-0		10,321
Southampton	v	Tottenham Hotspur	2-6	†	15,172
Wimbledon	v	Liverpool	0-2		12,553

Sixth Round – 11 March 1995

Crystal Palace	v	Wolves	1-1	14,604
Everton	v	Newcastle United	1-0	35,213
Liverpool	v	Tottenham Hotspur	1-2	39,952
Manchester United	v	Queen's Park Rangers	2-0	42,830

Sixth Round Replay

Wolves	v	Crystal Palace	1-4	27,548

Semi Finals

Everton	v	Tottenham Hotspur	4-1	38,226
(Elland Road, Leeds, 9 April 94)				
Crystal Palace	v	Manchester United	2-2	38,256
(Villa Park, 9 April 94)		*after extra time*		

Semi Final Replay

Crystal Palace	v	Manchester United	0-2	17,987
(Villa Park, April 94)				

Final – 20 May 1994 at Wembley Stadium

Everton	v	Manchester United	1-0	79,592
Rideout (30)				

Everton: Southall; Jackson, Watson, Unsworth, Ablett; Limpar (Amokachi 69), Horne, Parkinson, Hinchcliffe; Stuart, Rideout (Ferguson 50). Sub not used: Kearton.

Manchester United: Schmeichel; G.Neville, Bruce (Giggs 45), Pallister, Irwin; Butt, Keane, Ince, Sharpe (Scholes 72); McClair, Hughes. Sub not used: Walsh.

Referee: Mr Gerald Ashby

† after extra time

FA CHALLENGE CUP FINALS 1872-1994

Year	Winners	Runners-up	Score
1872	The Wanderers	Royal Engineers	1-0
1873	The Wanderers	Oxford University	2-0
1874	Oxford University	Royal Engineers	2-0
1875	Royal Engineers	Old Etonians	1-1
	Royal Engineers	Old Etonians	2-0
1876	The Wanderers	Old Etonians	1-1 †
	The Wanderers	Old Etonians	3-0
1877	The Wanderers	Oxford University	2-1 †
1878	The Wanderers*	Royal Engineers	3-1
1879	Old Etonians	Clapham Rovers	1-0
1880	Clapham Rovers	Oxford University	1-0
1881	Old Carthusians	Old Etonians	3-0
1882	Old Etonians	Blackburn Rovers	1-0
1883	Blackburn Olympic	Old Etonians	2-1 †
1884	Blackburn Rovers	Queen's Park, Glasgow	2-1
1885	Blackburn Rovers	Queen's Park, Glasgow	2-0
1886	Blackburn Rovers**	West Bromwich Albion	0-0
	Blackburn Rovers**	West Bromwich Albion	2-0
1887	Aston Villa	West Bromwich Albion	2-0
1888	West Bromwich Albion	Preston North End	2-1
1889	Preston North End	Wolverhampton Wanderers	3-0
1890	Blackburn Rovers	Sheffield Wednesday	6-1
1891	Blackburn Rovers	Notts County	3-1
1892	West Bromwich Albion	Aston Villa	3-0
1893	Wolverhampton Wanderers	Everton	1-0
1894	Notts County	Bolton Wanderers	4-1
1895	Aston Villa	West Bromwich Albion	1-0
1896	Sheffield Wednesday	Wolverhampton Wanderers	2-1
1897	Aston Villa	Everton	3-2
1898	Nottingham Forest	Derby County	3-1
1899	Sheffield United	Derby County	4-1
1900	Bury	Southampton	4-0
1901	Tottenham Hotspur	Sheffield United	2-2
	Tottenham Hotspur	Sheffield United	3-1
1902	Sheffield United	Southampton	1-1
	Sheffield United	Southampton	2-1
1903	Bury	Derby County	6-0
1904	Manchester City	Bolton Wanderers	1-0

Year	Winners	Runners-up	Score
1905	Aston Villa	Newcastle United	2-0
1906	Everton	Newcastle United	1-0
1907	Sheffield Wednesday	Everton	2-1
1908	Wolverhampton Wanderers	Newcastle United	3-1
1909	Manchester United	Bristol City	1-0
1910	Newcastle United	Barnsley	1-1
	Newcastle United	Barnsley	2-0
1911	Bradford City	Newcastle United	0-0
	Bradford City	Newcastle United	1-0
1912	Barnsley	West Bromwich Albion	0-0 †
	Barnsley	West Bromwich Albion	1-0
1913	Aston Villa	Sunderland	1-0
1914	Burnley	Liverpool	1- 0
1915	Sheffield United	Chelsea	3-0
1920	Aston Villa	Huddersfield Town	1-0 †
1921	Tottenham Hotspur	Wolverhampton Wanderers	1-0
1922	Huddersfield Town	Preston North End	1-0
1923	Bolton Wanderers	West Ham United	2-0
1924	Newcastle United	Aston Villa	2-0
1925	Sheffield United	Cardiff City	1-0
1926	Bolton Wanderers	Manchester City	1-0
1927	Cardiff City	Arsenal	1-0
1928	Blackburn Rovers	Huddersfield Town	3-1
1929	Bolton Wanderers	Portsmouth	2-0
1930	Arsenal	Huddersfield Town	2-0
1931	West Bromwich Albion	Birmingham	2- 1
1932	Newcastle United	Arsenal	2-1
1933	Everton	Manchester City	3-0
1934	Manchester City	Portsmouth	2-1
1935	Sheffield Wednesday	West Bromwich Albion	4-2
1936	Arsenal	Sheffield United	1-0
1937	Sunderland	Preston North End	3-1
1938	Preston North End	Huddersfield Town	1-0 †
1939	Portsmouth	Wolverhampton Wanderers	4-1
1946	Derby County	Charlton Athletic	4-1 †
1947	Charlton Athletic	Burnley	1-0 †
1948	Manchester United	Blackpool	4-2
1949	Wolverhampton Wanderers	Leicester City	3-1
1950	Arsenal	Liverpool	2-0
1951	Newcastle United	Blackpool	2-0
1952	Newcastle United	Arsenal	1-0
1953	Blackpool	Bolton Wanderers	4-3
1954	West Bromwich Albion	Preston North End	3-2
1955	Newcastle United	Manchester City	3-1

Year	Winners	Runners-up	Score
1956	Manchester City	Birmingham City	3-1
1957	Aston Villa	Manchester United	2-1
1958	Bolton Wanderers	Manchester United	2-0
1959	Nottingham Forest	Luton Town	2-1
1960	Wolverhampton Wanderers	Blackburn Rovers	3-0
1961	Tottenham Hotspur	Leicester City	2-0
1962	Tottenham Hotspur	Burnley	3-1
1963	Manchester United	Leicester City	3-1
1964	West Ham United	Preston North End	3-2
1965	Liverpool	Leeds United	2-1 †
1966	Everton	Sheffield Wednesday	3-2
1967	Tottenham Hotspur	Chelsea	2-1
1968	West Bromwich Albion	Everton	1-0 †
1969	Manchester City	Leicester City	1-0
1970	Chelsea	Leeds United	2-2 †
	Chelsea	Leeds United	2-1 †
1971	Arsenal	Liverpool	2-1 †
1972	Leeds United	Arsenal	1-0
1973	Sunderland	Leeds United	1-0
1974	Liverpool	Newcastle United	3-0
1975	West Ham United	Fulham	2-0
1976	Southampton	Manchester United	1-0
1977	Manchester United	Liverpool	2-1
1978	Ipswich Town	Arsenal	1-0
1979	Arsenal	Manchester United	3-2
1980	West Ham United	Arsenal	1-0
1981	Tottenham Hotspur	Manchester City	1-1 †
	Tottenham Hotspur	Manchester City	3-2
1982	Tottenham Hotspur	Queens Park Rangers	1-1 †
	Tottenham Hotspur	Queens Park Rangers	1-0
1983	Manchester United	Brighton & Hove Albion	2-2
	Manchester United	Brighton & Hove Albion	4-0
1984	Everton	Watford	2-0
1985	Manchester United	Everton	1-0 †
1986	Liverpool	Everton	3-1 †
1987	Coventry City	Tottenham Hotspur	3-2 †
1988	Wimbledon	Liverpool	1-0
1989	Liverpool	Everton	3-2 †
1990	Manchester United	Crystal Palace	3-3 †
	Manchester United	Crystal Palace	1-0
1991	Tottenham Hotspur	Nottingham Forest	2-1 †
1992	Liverpool	Sunderland	2-0
1993	Arsenal	Sheffield Wednesday	1-1 †
	Arsenal	Sheffield Wednesday	2-1 †

Year	Winners	Runners-up	Score
1994	Manchester United	Chelsea	4-0
1995	Everton	Manchester United	1-0

Final Venues

1872	Kennington Oval
1873	Lillie Bridge
1874-92	Kennington Oval
1893	Fallowfield, Manchester
1894	Everton
1895-1914	Crystal Palace
1915	Old Trafford
1920-22	Stamford Bridge
1923 –1995	Wembley

Replay Venues

1886	Derby
1901	Bolton
1910	Everton
1911	Old Trafford
1912	Bramall Lane
1970	Old Trafford
1981	Wembley
1982	Wembley
1983	Wembley
1990	Wembley
1993	Wembley

* Trophy won outright by The Wanderers, but restored to the FA.

** Special trophy awarded for a third consecutive win.

† after extra time.

FA CHALLENGE CUP WINS BY CLUB

Manchester United	1909, 1948, 1963, 1977, 1983, 1985, 1990, 1994
Tottenham Hotspur	1901, 1921, 1961, 1962, 1967, 1981, 1982, 1991
Aston Villa	1887, 1895, 1897, 1905, 1913, 1920, 1957
Arsenal	1930, 1936, 1950, 1971, 1979, 1993
Blackburn Rovers	1884, 1885, 1886, 1890, 1891, 1928
Newcastle United	1910, 1924, 1932, 1951, 1952, 1955
Everton	1894, 1906, 1933, 1966, 1995
Liverpool	1965, 1974, 1986, 1989, 1992
The Wanderers	1872, 1873, 1876, 1877, 1878
West Bromwich Albion	1888, 1892, 1931, 1954, 1968
Bolton Wanderers	1923, 1926, 1929, 1958
Manchester City	1904, 1934, 1956, 1969
Sheffield United	1899, 1902, 1915, 1925
Wolverhampton Wdrers	1893, 1908, 1949, 1960
Sheffield Wednesday	1896, 1907, 1935
West Ham United	1964, 1975, 1980
Bury	1900, 1903
Nottingham Forest	1898, 1959
Old Etonians	1879, 1882
Preston North End	1889, 1938
Sunderland	1937, 1973

Club	Year	Club	Year
Barnsley	1912	Ipswich Town	1978
Blackburn Olympic	1883	Leeds United	1972
Blackpool	1953	Notts County	1894
Bradford City	1911	Old Carthusians	1881
Burnley	1914	Oxford University	1874
Cardiff City	1927	Portsmouth	1939
Charlton Athletic	1947	Royal Engineers	1875
Chelsea	1970	Southampton	1976
Clapham Rovers	1880	Wimbledon	1988
Coventry City	1987		
Derby County	1946		
Huddersfield Town	1922		

FA CHARITY SHIELD WINNERS 1908-94

1908	Manchester United v Queens Park Rangers	4-0
	after 1-1 draw	
1909	Newcastle United v Northampton Town	2-0
1910	Brighton & Hove Albion v Aston Villa	1-0
1911	Manchester United v Swindon Town	8-4
1912	Blackburn Rovers v Queens Park Rangers	2-1
1913	Professionals v Amateurs	7-2
1919	West Bromwich Albion v Tottenham Hotspur	2-0
1920	Tottenham Hotspur v Burnley	2-0
1921	Huddersfield Town v Liverpool	1-0
1922	Not Played	
1923	Professionals v Amateurs	2-0
1924	Professionals v Amateurs	3-1
1925	Amateurs v Professionals	6-1
1926	Amateurs v Professionals	6-3
1927	Cardiff City v Corinthians	2-1
1928	Everton v Blackburn Rovers	2-1
1929	Professionals v Amateurs	3-0
1930	Arsenal v Sheffield Wednesday	2-1
1931	Arsenal v West Bromwich Albion	1-0
1932	Everton v Newcastle United	5-3
1933	Arsenal v Everton	3-0
1934	Arsenal v Manchester City	4-0
1935	Sheffield Wednesday v Arsenal	1-0
1936	Sunderland v Arsenal	2-1
1937	Manchester City v Sunderland	2-0
1938	Arsenal v Preston North End	2-1
1948	Arsenal v Manchester United	4-3
1949	Portsmouth v Wolverhampton Wanderers	* 1-1
1950	World Cup Team v Canadian Touring Team	4-2
1951	Tottenham Hotspur v Newcastle United	2-1
1952	Manchester United v Newcastle United	4-2
1953	Arsenal v Blackpool	* 3-1
1954	Wolverhampton Wanderers v West Bromwich Albion	* 4-4
1955	Chelsea v Newcastle United	3-0
1956	Manchester United v Manchester City	1-0

1957	Manchester United v Aston Villa	4-0
1958	Bolton Wanderers v Wolverhampton Wanderers	4-1
1959	Wolverhampton Wanderers v Nottingham Forest	3-1
1960	Burnley v Wolverhampton Wanderers	* 2-2
1961	Tottenham Hotspur v FA XI	3-2
1962	Tottenham Hotspur v Ipswich Town	5-1
1963	Everton v Manchester United	4-0
1964	Liverpool v West Ham United	* 2-2
1965	Manchester United v Liverpool	* 2-2
1966	Liverpool v Everton	1-0
1967	Manchester United v Tottenham Hotspur	* 3-3
1968	Manchester City v West Bromwich Albion	6-1
1969	Leeds United v Manchester City	2-1
1970	Everton v Chelsea	2-1
1971	Leicester City v Liverpool	1-0
1972	Manchester City v Aston Villa	1-0
1973	Burnley v Manchester City	1-0
1974	Liverpool v Leeds United	1-1
	Liverpool won on penalties	
1975	Derby County v West Ham United	2-0
1976	Liverpool v Southampton	1-0
1977	Liverpool v Manchester United	* 0-0
1978	Nottingham Forest v Ipswich Town	5-0
1979	Liverpool v Arsenal	3-1
1980	Liverpool v West Ham United	1-0
1981	Aston Villa v Tottenham Hotspur	* 2-2
1982	Liverpool v Tottenham Hotspur	1-0
1983	Manchester United v Liverpool	2-0
1984	Everton v Liverpool	1-0
1985	Everton v Manchester United	2-0
1986	Everton v Liverpool	* 1-1
1987	Everton v Coventry City	1-0
1988	Liverpool v Wimbledon	2-1
1989	Liverpool v Arsenal	1-0
1990	Liverpool v Manchester United	* 1-1
1991	Arsenal v Tottenham Hotspur	* 0-0
1992	Leeds United v Liverpool	4-3
1993	Manchester United v Arsenal	1-1
	Manchester United won on penalties	
1994	Manchester United v Blackburn Rovers	2-0

* Each club retained Shield for six months

FOOTBALL LEAGUE
COCA-COLA CUP 94-95

First Round – two legs

			1st Leg	2nd Leg	Agg
Barnet	v	Leyton Orient	4-0	1-1	5-1
Blackpool	v	Chesterfield	1-2	2-4	3-6
Bournemouth	v	Northampton Town	2-0	1-0	3-0
Bradford City	v	Grimsby Town	2-1	2-1	4-2
Brighton & Hove Albion	v	Wycombe Wanderers	2-1	3-1	5-2
Bristol Rovers	v	Port Vale	1-3	1-1	2-4
Burnley	v	York City	1-0	2-2	3-2
Bury	v	Hartlepool United	2-0	1-5	3-5
Cardiff City	v	Torquay United	1-0	2-4	3-4
Colchester United	v	Brentford	0-2	0-2	0-4
Crewe Alexandra	v	Wigan Athletic	2-1	0-3	2-4
Darlington	v	Barnsley	2-2	0-0 †	2-2
(Barnsley win on away goals)					
Doncaster Rovers	v	Wrexham	2-4	1-1	3-5
Exeter City	v	Swansea City	2-2	0-2	2-4
Gillingham	v	Reading	0-1	0-3	0-4
Hereford United	v	West Bromwich Albion	0-0	1-0	1-0
Hull City	v	Scarborough	2-1	0-2	2-3
Lincoln City	v	Chester City	2-0	3-2	5-2
Luton Town	v	Fulham	1-1	1-1 †	2-2
(Fulham win 4-3 on penalties)					
Oxford United	v	Peterborough United	3-1	1-0	4-1
Portsmouth	v	Cambridge United	2-0	3-2	5-2
Preston North End	v	Stockport County	1-1	1-4	2-5
Rochdale	v	Mansfield Town	1-2	0-1	1-3
Rotherham United	v	Carlisle United	1-0	1-3	2-3
Scunthorpe United	v	Huddersfield Town	2-1	0-3	2-4
Shrewsbury Town	v	Birmingham City	2-1	0-2	2-3
Southend United	v	Watford	0-0	0-1	0-1
Walsall	v	Plymouth Argyle	4-0	2-2	6-2

Second Round

			1st	2nd	Agg
Aston Villa	v	Wigan Athletic	5-0	3-0	8-0
Barnet	v	Manchester City	1-0	1-4	2-4
Blackburn Rovers	v	Birmingham City	2-0	1-1	3-1
Brighton & Hove Albion	v	Leicester City	1-0	2-0	3-0
Bristol City	v	Notts County	0-1	0-3	0-4
Carlisle United	v	Queen's Park Rangers	0-1	0-2	0-3
Chelsea	v	Bournemouth	1-0	1-0	2-0

Chesterfield	v	Wolves	1-3	1-1	2-4
Everton	v	Portsmouth	2-3	1-1	3-4
Fulham	v	Stoke City	3-2	0-1 †	3-3
(Stoke City win on away goals)					
Hartlepool United	v	Arsenal	0-5	0-2	0-7
Huddersfield Town	v	Southampton	0-1	0-4	0-5
Ipswich Town	v	Bolton Wanderers	0-3	0-1	0-4
Leeds United	v	Mansfield Town	0-1	0-0	0-1
Lincoln City	v	Crystal Palace	1-0	0-3 †	1-3
Liverpool	v	Burnley	2-0	4-1	6-1
Millwall	v	Sunderland	2-1	1-1	3-2
Newcastle United	v	Barnsley	2-1	1-0	3-1
Norwich City	v	Swansea City	3-0	0-1	3-1
Nottingham Forest	v	Hereford United	2-1	0-0	2-1
Oxford United	v	Oldham Athletic	1-1	0-1	1-2
Port Vale	v	Manchester United	1-2	0-2	1-4
Reading	v	Derby County	3-1	0-2 †	3-3
(Derby County win on away goals)					
Scarborough	v	Middlesbrough	1-4	1-4	2-8
Sheffield Wednesday	v	Bradford City	2-1	1-1	3-2
Stockport County	v	Sheffield United	1-5	0-1	1-6
Swindon Town	v	Charlton Athletic	1-3	4-1	5-4
Tranmere Rovers	v	Brentford	1-0	0-0	1-0
Walsall	v	West Ham United	2-1	0-2	2-3
Watford	v	Tottenham Hotspur	3-6	3-2	6-8
Wimbledon	v	Torquay United	2-0	1-0	3-0
Wrexham	v	Coventry City	1-2	2-3	3-5

Third Round

Aston Villa	v	Middlesbrough	1-0	19,254
Blackburn Rovers	v	Coventry City	2-0	14,538
Brighton & Hove Alb.	v	Swindon Town	1-1	11,382
Liverpool	v	Stoke City	2-1	32,060
Mansfield Town	v	Millwall	0-2	5,359
Newcastle United	v	Manchester United	2-0	34,178
Notts County	v	Tottenham Hotspur	3-0	16,952
Oldham Athletic	v	Arsenal	0-0	9,303
Portsmouth	v	Derby County	0-1	8,568
Queen's Park Rangers	v	Manchester City	3-4	11,701
Sheffield United	v	Bolton Wanderers	1-2	6,939
Sheffield Wednesday	v	Southampton	1-0	16,715
Tranmere Rovers	v	Norwich City	1-1	10,232
West Ham United	v	Chelsea	1-0	18,815
Wimbledon	v	Crystal Palace	0-1	9,394
Wolves	v	Nottingham Forest	2-3	23,369

Third Round Replays

Arsenal	v	Oldham Athletic	2-0	22,746
Norwich City	v	Tranmere Rovers	4-2	13,311
Swindon Town	v	Brighton & Hove Alb.	4-1	6,482

Fourth Round

Arsenal	v	Sheffield Wednesday	2-0	27,390
Blackburn Rovers	v	Liverpool	1-3	30,115
Crystal Palace	v	Aston Villa	4-0	12,653
Manchester City	v	Newcastle United	1-1	25,162
Norwich City	v	Notts County	1-0	14,030
Nottingham Forest	v	Millwall	0-2	12,393
Swindon Town	v	Derby County	2-1	8,920
West Ham United	v	Bolton Wanderers	1-3	18,190

Fourth Round Replay

Newcastle United	v	Manchester City	0-2	30,156

Fifth Round

Bolton Wanderers	v	Norwich City	1-0	17,029
Crystal Palace	v	Manchester City	4-0	16,668
Liverpool	v	Arsenal	1-0	35,026
Swindon Town	v	Millwall	3-1	11,772

Semi-Finals First Leg

Swindon Town	v	Bolton Wanderers	2-1	15,341
Liverpool	v	Crystal Palace	1-0	25,480

Semi-Finals Second Leg

Bolton Wanderers	v	Swindon Town	3-1	19,851

(Bolton Wanderers win 4-3 on aggregate)

Crystal Palace	v	Liverpool	0-1	18,224

(Liverpool win 2-0 on aggregate)

Final – 2 April 1995 at Wembley Stadium

Bolton Wanderers	v	Liverpool	1-2	75,595

Thompson 68   McManaman 37,67

Bolton Wanderers: Branagan, Green (Bergsson 70), Phillips, McAteer, Seagraves, Stubbs, Lee, Sneekes, Paatelainen, McGinlay, Thompson. Subs not used: Patterson Davison.

Liverpool; James, Bjornebye, Ruddock, Scales, Babb, Jones, McManaman, Redknapp, Barnes, Rush, Fowler. Subs not used: Thomas, Walters, Chamberlain.
Ref: Philip Don.

† *after extra time*

73

FOOTBALL LEAGUE CUP
FINALS 1961-1994

Year	Winners	Runners-up	1st	2nd	Agg
1961	Aston Villa	Rotherham United	0-2†	3-0	3-2
1962	Norwich City	Rochdale	3-0	1-0	4-0
1963	Birmingham City	Aston Villa	3-1	0-0	3-1
1964	Leicester City	Stoke City	1-1	3-2	4-3
1965	Chelsea	Leicester City	3-2	0-0	3-2
1966	West Bromwich Albion	West Ham United	1-2	4-1	5-3
1967	Queens Park Rangers	West Bromwich Albion	3-2		
1968	Leeds United	Arsenal	1-0		
1969	Swindon Town	Arsenal	† 3-1		
1970	Manchester City	West Bromwich Albion	2-1		
1971	Tottenham Hotspur	Aston Villa	† 2-0		
1972	Stoke City	Chelsea	2-1		
1973	Tottenham Hotspur	Norwich City	1-0		
1974	Wolverhampton W	Manchester City	2-1		
1975	Aston Villa	Norwich City	1-0		
1976	Manchester City	Newcastle United	2-1		
1977	Aston Villa	Everton	† 3-2		
	after 0-0 draw and 1-1 draw aet				
1978	Nottingham Forest	Liverpool	1-0		
	after 0-0 draw aet				
1979	Nottingham Forest	Southampton	3-2		
1980	Wolverhampton W	Nottingham Forest	1-0		
1981	Liverpool	West Ham United	2-1		
	after 1-1 draw aet				

Milk Cup

Year	Winners	Runners-up	1st	2nd	Agg
1982	Liverpool	Tottenham Hotspur	† 3-1		
1983	Liverpool	Manchester United	† 2-1		
1984	Liverpool	Everton	1-0		
	after 0-0 draw aet				
1985	Norwich City	Sunderland	1-0		
1986	Oxford United	Queens Park Rangers	3-0		

Littlewoods Cup

1987	Arsenal	Liverpool	2-1
1988	Luton Town	Arsenal	3-2
1989	Nottingham Forest	Luton Town	3-1
1990	Nottingham Forest	Oldham Athletic	1-0

Rumbelows League Cup

| 1991 | Sheffield Wednesday | Manchester United | 1-0 |
| 1992 | Manchester United | Nottingham Forest | 1-0 |

Coca–Cola Cup

1993	Arsenal	Sheffield Wednesday	2-1
1994	Aston Villa	Manchester United	3-1
1995	Liverpool	Bolton Wanderers	2-1

FOOTBALL LEAGUE CUP WINS BY CLUB

Liverpool	1981, 1982, 1983, 1984, 1995
Nottingham Forest	1978, 1979, 1989, 1990
Aston Villa	1961, 1975, 1977, 1994
Arsenal	1987, 1993
Manchester City	1970, 1976
Tottenham Hotspur	1971, 1973
Norwich City (2)	1962, 1985
Wolverhampton Wders	1974, 1980
Birmingham City	1963
Leicester City	1964
Chelsea	1965
WBA	1966
QPR	1967
Leeds United	1968
Swindon Town	1969
Stoke City	1972
Oxford United	1986
Luton Town	1988
Sheffield Wednesday	1991
Manchester United	1992

CLUBS IN EUROPE 94-95

UEFA Champions' League – Manchester United

Group A Matches

Manchester United
Giggs (34,66), Kanchelskis (47)
Sharpe (71)
IFK Gothenburg
Pettersson (27), Rehn (50)
4-2 33,625

Galatasary
Manchester United
0-0 34,000

Manchester United
Hughes (20), Sharpe (80)
Barcelona
Romario (34), Bakero (49)
2-2 40,064

Barcelona
Stoichkov (9,52), Romario (45), Ferrer (88)
Manchester United
4-0 120,000

IFK Gothenburg
Blomqvist (10), Erlingmark (64),
Kamark (70 pen)
Manchester United
Hughes (63)
3-1 36,350

Manchester United
Davies (2), Beckham (37), Keane (48)
Bulent own goal (87)
Galatasaray
4-0 39,220

Final Group Table	P	W	D	L	F	A	Pts
IFK Gothenburg	6	4	1	1	10	7	9
Barcelona	6	2	2	2	11	8	6
Manchester United	6	2	2	2	11	11	6
Galatasaray	6	1	1	4	3	9	3

Cup-Winners' Cup – Arsenal, Chelsea

1st Round

Omonia Nicosia
Malekkas (72)
Arsenal
Merson (37,80), Wright (50)
1-3 20,000

Arsenal
Wright (9,70), Schwarz (31)
Omonia Nicosia
3-0 24,265

Arsenal win 6-1 on aggregate

Chelsea
Furlong (2), Sinclair (4)
Rocastle (54), Wise (69)
Victoria Zizkov
Majoros (35,41)
4-2 22,036

Victoria Zizkov
Chelsea
0-0

Chelsea win 4-2 on aggregate

2nd Round

Brondby
Arsenal
1-2 13,406

Strudal (53)	Wright (16), Smith (18)		
Arsenal Wright (25), Selley (46)	**Brondby** Hansen (2), Egen (69)	2-2	32,290

Arsenal win 4-3 on aggregate

Chelsea	**FK Austria**	0-0	22,560
FK Austria Narbekovas (73)	**Chelsea** Spencer (40)	1-1	25,000

1-1 on aggregate, Chelsea win on away goals rule

Quarter-Finals

Arsenal Wright (59 pen)	**Auxerre** Verlatt (68)	1-1	35,508
Auxerre	**Arsenal** Wright (15)	1-0	23,000

Arsenal win 2-1 on aggregate

FC Bruges Verhayen (83)	**Chelsea**	1-0	18,000
Chelsea Stein (16), Furlong (38)	**FC Bruges**	2-0	28,661

Chelsea win 2-1 on aggregate

Semi-Finals

Arsenal Bould (34,36), Wright (69)	**Sampdoria** Jugovic (51,78)	3-2	38,089
Sampdoria Mancini (13), Bellucci (82,84)	**Arsenal** Wright (60), Schwarz (87)	3-2	35,000

5-5 on aggregate aet – Arsenal win 3-2 on penalties

Real Zaragoza Pardeza (7), Esnaider (26,56)	**Chelsea**	3-0	35,000
Chelsea Furlong (30), Sinclair (62), Stein (86)	**Real Zaragoza** Aragon (54)	3-1	26,456

Real Zaragoza win 4-3 on aggregate

Final – 10 May 1994, Paris

Arsenal Hartson (76)	**Real Zaragoza** Esnaider (68), Nyaim (120)	1-2	42,424

Arsenal: Seaman, Dixon, Winterburn (Morrow 47), Schwarz, Linigan, Adams, Keown (Hillier 46), Wright, Hartson, Merson, Parlour: Subs not used: Bartram, McGoldrick, Kiwomya.
Real Zaragoza: Cedrun, Belsue, Cacares, Aguado, Solana, Poyet, Aragon, Nayim, Higuera (Sanjuan 68 (Geli 114)), Pardeza, Esnaider. Subs not used: Belman, Loreto, Oscar.
Referee: P. Ceccarini (Italy).

UEFA Cup – Aston Villa, Blackburn Rovers, Newcastle United

1st Round

Blackburn Rovers Sandell (71)	**Trelleborg**	0-1	**13,775**
Trelleborg Karlsson, J. (50,85)	**Blackburn Rovers** Sutton (18), Shearer (84)	2-2	**10,000**

Trelleborg win 3-2 on aggregate

Internazionale Bergkamp (75 pen)	**Aston Villa**	1-0	**22,639**
Aston Villa Houghton (41)	**Internazionale**	1-0	**30,533**

1-1 on aggregate aet, Aston Villa win 5-4 on penalties

Royal Antwerp	**Newcastle United** Lee (1,8,51), Sellars (39), Watson (78)	0-5	**19,700**
Newcastle United Lee (11), Cole (26,39,88) Beardsley (36 pen)	**Royal Antwerp** Kiekens (75), Severeyns (77)	5-2	**29,737**

Newcastle United win 10-2 on aggregate

2nd Round

Newcastle United Fox (9), Beardsley (34 pen) Cole (56)	**Athletico Bilbao** Ciganda (71), Suances (79)	3-2	**32,140**
Athletico Bilbao Ciganda (66)	**Newcastle United**	1-0	**47,000**

3-3 on aggregate. Athletico Bilbao win on away goals

Trabzonspor Orhan (78)	**Aston Villa**	1-0	**27,500**
Aston Villa Ehiogu (77,90)	**Trabzonspor** Orhan (89)	2-1	**23,858**

Aggregate 2-2. Trabzonspor win on away goals

Scorers by Club

Manchester United: 2: Giggs, Sharpe, Hughes; 1: Kanchelskis, Davies, Beckham, Keane, OG

Arsenal: 9: Wright; 2: Merson, Bould, Schwarz; 1: Smith, Selley, Hartson

Chelsea: 3: Furlong. 2: Sinclair,Stein; 1 Rocastle, Wise, Spencer

Aston Villa: 2 Ehiogu; 1: Houghton

Blackburn Rovers: 1: Sutton, Shearer

Newcastle United: 4: Lee, Cole; 2: Beardsley; 1: Watson, Sellars, Fox

FWA FOOTBALLER OF THE YEAR WINNERS

Season	Winner	Club
1947-48	Stanley Matthews	Blackpool & England
1948-49	Johnny Carey	Manchester United & Rep of Ireland
1949-50	Joe Mercer	Arsenal & England
1950-51	Harry Johnston	Blackpool & England
1951-52	Billy Wright	Wolverhampton Wanderers & England
1952-53	Nat Lofthouse	Bolton Wanderers & England
1953-54	Tom Finney	Preston North End & England
1954-55	Don Revie	Manchester City & England
1955-56	Bert Trautmann	Manchester City
1956-57	Tom Finney	Preston North End & England
1957-58	Danny Blanchflower	Tottenham Hotspur & Northern Ireland
1958-59	Syd Owen	Luton Town & England
1959-60	Bill Slater	Wolverhampton Wanderers & England
1960-61	Danny Blanchflower	Tottenham Hotspur & Northern Ireland
1961-62	Jimmy Adamson	Burnley
1962-63	Stanley Matthews	Stoke City & England
1963-64	Bobby Moore	West Ham United & England
1964-65	Bobby Collins	Leeds United & Scotland
1965-66	Bobby Charlton	Manchester United & England
1966-67	Jack Charlton	Leeds United & England
1967-68	George Best	Manchester United & Northern Ireland
1968-69	Dave Mackay	Derby County & Scotland
	Tony Book	Manchester City
1969-70	Billy Bremner	Leeds United & Scotland
1970-71	Frank McLintock	Arsenal & Scotland
1971-72	Gordon Banks	Stoke City & England
1972-73	Pat Jennings	Tottenham Hotspur & Northern Ireland
1973-74	Ian Callaghan	Liverpool & England
1974-75	Alan Mullery	Fulham & England
1975-76	Kevin Keegan	Liverpool & England
1976-77	Emlyn Hughes	Liverpool & England
1977-78	Kenny Burns	Nottingham Forest & Scotland
1978-79	Kenny Dalglish	Liverpool & Scotland
1979-80	Terry McDermott	Liverpool & England
1980-81	Frans Thijssen	Ipswich Town & Holland
1981-82	Steve Perryman	Tottenham Hotspur & England
1982-83	Kenny Dalglish	Liverpool & Scotland
1983-84	Ian Rush	Liverpool & Wales
1984-85	Neville Southall	Everton & Wales
1985-86	Gary Lineker	Everton & England
1986-87	Clive Allen	Tottenham Hotspur & England

1987-88	John Barnes	Liverpool & England
1988-89	Steve Nicol	Liverpool & England
1989-90	John Barnes	Liverpool & England
1990-91	Gordon Strachan	Leeds United & Scotland
1991-92	Gary Lineker	Tottenham Hotspur & England
1992-93	Chris Waddle	Sheffield Wednesday & England
1993-94	Alan Shearer	Blackburn Rovers & England
1994-95	Jurgen Klinsmann	Tottenham Hotspur & Germany

PFA AWARDS 1994-95

Player of the Year
1st	Alan Shearer	Blackburn Rovers
2nd	Matt Le Tissier	Southampton
3rd	Jurgen Klinsmann	Tottenham Hotspur

Young Player of the Year
1st	Robbie Fowler	Liverpool
2nd	Nick Barmby	Tottenham Hotspur
3rd	Chris Sutton	Blackburn Rovers

Merit Award
Gordon Strachan   Coventry City

Premiership Team
Goalkeeper	Tim Flowers	Blackburn Rovers
Defenders	Robbie Jones	Liverpool
	Graham Le Saux	Blackburn Rovers
	Gary Pallister	Manchester United
	Colin Hendry	Blackburn Rovers
Midfield	Paul Ince	Manchester United
	Matthew Le Tissier	Southampton
	Tim Sherwood	Blackburn Rovers
Forwards	Alan Shearer	Blackburn Rovers
	Jurgen Klinsmann	Tottenham Hotspur
	Chris Sutton	Blackburn Rovers

ENGLAND 1994-95

ENGLAND	UNITED STATES	2-0	38,629

Shearer (33, 40)

England: Seaman, Jones, Le Saux, Venison, Adams, Pallister, Anderton, Platt, Barnes, Shearer (Ferdinand 81), Sheringham (Wright 81).

ENGLAND	ROMANIA	1-1	48,754

Lee (43)   Dumitrescu (36)

England: Seaman, Jones (Pearce 59), Adams, Pallister, Le Saux, Lee (Wise 71), Ince, Le Tissier, Barnes, Shearer, Sheringham (Wright 71).

ENGLAND	NIGERIA	1-0	37,196

Platt (41)

England: Flowers, Jones, Le Saux, Lee (McManaman 26), Howey, Ruddock, Platt, Beardsley (Le Tissier 71), Shearer (Sheringham 78), Barnes, Wise.

REPUBLIC of IRELAND	ENGLAND	1-0

Kelly (22)

England: Seaman, Barton, Le Saux, Ince, Adams, Pallister, Platt, Beardsley, Shearer, Le Tissier, Anderton.

* Match abandoned after 27 minutes due to crowd trouble – caps awarded

ENGLAND	URUGUAY	0-0	34,849

England: Flowers, Jones, Adams, Pallister, Le Saux (McManaman 46), Venison, Platt, Barnes, Beardsley (Barmby 64), Sheringham (Cole 71), Anderton.

Umbro Cup

Wembley, June 3 1995

ENGLAND   **JAPAN**   **2-1**   **21,142**
Anderton (48), Platt (88 pen)   Ihara (62)

England: Flowers; Neville, Scales, Unsworth, Pearce; Anderton, Platt, Batty (Gascoigne 68), Beardsley (McManaman 68); Collymore (Sheringham 76), Shearer.

Leeds United FC, June 8 1995

ENGLAND   **SWEDEN**   **3-3**   **32,008**
Sheringham (44), Platt (89)   Mild (11, 37), Andersson (46)
Anderton (90)

England: Flowers; Barton, Pallister (Scales 81), Cooper, Le Saux; Barnes (Gascoigne 64), Platt, Anderton, Beardsley (Barmby 64), Shearer, Sheringham.

Wembley, June 11 1995

ENGLAND   **BRAZIL**   **1-3**   **67,318**
Le Saux (38)   Juninho (54), Ronaldo (61), Edmundo (76)

England: Flowers; G. Neville, Scales (Barton 90), Cooper, Pearce; Anderton, Batty (Gascoigne 79), Platt, Le Saux; Sheringham (Collymore 79), Shearer.

Other Matches

Brazil	Sweden	1-0	20,131	Aston Villa FC, 4 June 1995
Brazil	Japan	3-0	29,327	Everton FC, 6 June 1995
Sweden	Japan	2-2	5,591	Nottingham Forest, 10 June 1995

Final Table

		P	W	D	L	F	A	Pts
1.	Brazil	3	3	0	0	7	1	9
2.	England	3	1	1	1	6	7	4
3.	Sweden	3	0	2	1	5	6	2
4.	Japan	3	0	1	2	3	7	1

England Record 1994-95

P	W	D	L	F	A
7	3	3	2	10	8

(record does not include abandoned match)

1994-95 APPEARANCE CHART

	United States	Romania	Nigeria	Rep. Ireland	Uruguay	Japan	Sweden	Brazil
ADAMS	*	*	–	*	*	*	*	–
ANDERTON	*	–	–	–	*	*	*	–
BARTON	–	–	–	*	–	–	*	90†
BATTY	–	–	–	–	–	*†	–	*+
BARNES	*	*	*	–	*	–	*+	–
BARMBY	–	–	–	–	64+d	–	64§	–
BEARDSLEY	–	–	*+	*	*+	*+	*§	–
COLE	–	–	–	–	71§d	–	–	–
COLLYMORE	–	–	–	–	–	*d§	–	79§
COOPER	–	–	–	–	–	–	*d	*
FERDINAND	81†	–	–	–	–	–	–	–
FLOWERS	–	–	*	–	*	*	*	*
GASCOIGNE	–	–	–	–	–	68†	61+	79+
HOWEY	–	–	*	–	–	–	–	–
INCE	–	*	–	*	–	–	–	–
JONES	*	*†	*	–	*	–	–	–
LEE	–	*+d	*†	–	–	–	–	–
LE SAUX	*	*	*	*	*†	–	*	*
LE TISSIER	–	*d	71+	*	*	–	–	–
McMANAMAN	–	–	26†	–	46†	68+	–	–
NEVILLE G.	–	–	–	–	–	*d	–	*
PALLISTER	*	*	–	*	*	–	*†	–
PEARCE	–	59†	–	–	–	*	–	*
PLATT	*	–	*	*	*	*	*	*
RUDDOCK	–	–	*	–	–	–	–	–
SCALES	–	–	–	–	–	*d	81†	*†
SEAMAN	*	*	*	*	–	–	–	–
SHEARER	*†	*	*§	–	*	*	*	*
SHERINGHAM	*+	*§	78§	–	*§	76§	–	*§
UNSWORTH	–	–	–	–	–	*d	–	–
VENISON	*	–	–	–	*	–	–	–
WRIGHT	81+	71§	–	–	–	–	–	–
WISE	–	71+	*	–	–	–	–	–

• Started match. – No appearance. d International debut. A number indicates an appearance as substitute, the number relating the minute the player entered the match.

Player Summary 1994-95

Player	Club	Apps	Sub	Goals
Tony ADAMS	Arsenal	4	–	–
Darren ANDERTON	Tottenham Hotspur	6	–	2
Nick BARMBY	Tottenham Hotspur	–	2	–
David BATTY	Blackburn Rovers	2	–	–
John BARNES	Liverpool	5	–	–
Warren BARTON	Wimbledon	2	1	–
Peter BEARDSLEY	Newcastle United	5	–	–
Andy COLE	Newcastle United	–	1	–
Stan COLLYMORE	Nottingham Forest	1	1	–
Colin COOPER	Nottingham Forest	2	–	–
Les FERDINAND	Queen's Park Rangers	–	1	–
Tim FLOWERS	Blackburn Rovers	5	–	–
Paul GASCOIGNE	Lazio/Rangers	–	3	–
Steve HOWEY	Newcastle United	1	–	–
Paul INCE	Manchester United	2	–	–
Rob JONES	Liverpool	4	–	–
Robert LEE	Newcastle United	2	–	1
Graeme LE SAUX	Blackburn Rovers	7	–	1
Matthew LE TISSIER	Southampton	2	1	–
Steve McMANAMAN	Liverpool	–	3	–
Gary NEVILLE	Manchester United	2	–	–
Gary PALLISTER	Manchester United	5	–	–
Stuart PEARCE	Nottingham Forest	2	1	–
David PLATT	Sampdoria	7	–	3
Neil RUDDOCK	Liverpool	1	–	–
John SCALES	Liverpool	2	1	–
David SEAMAN	Arsenal	3	–	–
Alan SHEARER	Blackburn Rovers	7	–	2
Teddy SHERINGHAM	Tottenham Hotspur	4	2	1
David UNSWORTH	Everton	1	–	–
Barry VENISON	Newcastle United	2	–	–
Dennis WISE	Chelsea	1	1	–
Ian WRIGHT	Arsenal	–	2	–

CLUB DIRECTORY
1995-96

Arsenal

Formed as Dial Square, a workshop in Woolwich Arsenal with a sundial over the entrance, in October 1886, becoming Royal Arsenal, the 'Royal' possibly from a local public house, later the same year. Turned professional and became Woolwich Arsenal in 1891. Selected for an expanded Football League Division Two in 1893, the first southern team to join.

Moved from the Manor Ground, Plumstead south-east London, to Highbury, north London, in 1913 changing name again at the same time. Elected from fifth in Division Two to the expanded First Division for the 1919-20 season and never relegated. Premier League founder members 1992.

Ground: Arsenal Stadium, Highbury, London N5 1BU
Phone Club: 0171-226 0304
Box Office: 0171-354-5404   **Match Info:** 0171-359-0131
Capacity: 39,497   **News:**   0891 20 20 20
Colours: Red/White sleeves, White, Red   **Pitch size:** 110 yds x 71 yds
     Nickname: Gunners
Directions: *From North:* M1, J2 follow sign for City. After Holloway Rd station (c 6 miles) take third left into Drayton Park. Then right into Aubert Park after ¾ mile and 2nd left into Avenell Rd. *From South:* Signs for Bank of England then Angel from London Bridge. Right at traffic lights towards Highbury roundabout. Follow Holloway Rd then third right into Drayton Pk, thereafter as above. *From West:* A40(M) to A501 ring road. Left at Angel to Highbury roundabout, then as above.
Rail: Drayton Park/Finsbury Park   Highbury & Islington (North London)
Tube (Piccadilly line): Arsenal   Highbury & Islington (Victoria line)

Chairman: P.D. Hill-Wood   **Vice-Chairman:** David Dein
Managing Director and Secretary: Ken Friar
Manager: Bruce Rioch   **Assistant/Coach:** Stuart Houston
Physio: Gary Lewin MCSP SRP

League History: 1893 Elected to Division 2; 1904-13 Division 1; 1913-19 Division 2; 1919-92 Division 1; 1992-93 – FA Premier League.

Honours: *Football League: Division 1 – Champions:* 1930-31, 1932-33, 1933-34, 1934-35, 1937-38, 1947-48, 1952-53, 1970-71, 1988-89, 1990-91; *Runners-up:* 1925-26, 1931-32, 1972-73; *Division 2 – Runners-up:* 1903-04. *FA Cup: Winners:* 1929-30, 1935-36, 1949-50, 1970-71, 1978-79, 1992-93; *Runners-up:* 1926-27, 1931-32, 1951-52, 1971-72, 1977-78, 1979-80. *Football League Cup: Winners:* 1986-87, 1992-93; *Runners-up:* 1967-68, 1968-69, 1987-88. *League-Cup Double Performed:* 1970-71. *Cup-Cup*

Double Performed: 1992-93; *Cup-Winners' Cup Winners:* 1993-94 (winners), *Runners-up:* 1979-80, 1994-95; *Fairs Cup Winners:* 1969-70. *European Super Cup Runners-up:* 1994-95.

European Record: Champions' Cup (2): 71-72 (QF), 91-92 (2); Cup-Winners' Cup (3): 79-80 (F), 93-94 (W), 94-95 (F); UEFA Cup (6): 63-64 (2), 69-70 (W), 71-70 (Q), 78-79 (3), 81-82 (2), 82-83 (1)

Managers: Sam Hollis 1894-97; Tom Mitchell 1897-98; George Elcoat 1898-99; Harry Bradshaw 1899-1904; Phil Kelso 1904-08; George Morrell 1908-15; Leslie Knighton 1919-25; Herbert Chapman 1925-34; George Allison 1934-47; Tom Whittaker 1947-56; Jack Crayston 1956-58; George Swindin 1958-62; Billy Wright 1962-66; Bertie Mee 1966-76; Terry Neill 1976-83; Don Howe 1984-86; *(FAPL)* George Graham May 1986-Feb 1995; Stewart Houston (caretaker) Feb-1995-May 1995; Bruce Rioch May 1995–

Season 1994-95

Biggest Home Win: 5-1 v Norwich City, 1/4/95
Biggest Home Defeat: 1-3 v Leeds United, 17/12/94; QPR, 31/12/94
Biggest Away Win: 4-0 v Aston Villa, 17/4/95
Biggest Away Defeat: 0-3 v Liverpool 28/8/94; Manchester Utd 22/3/95
Biggest Home Att: 38,377 v Tottenham Hotspur 29/4/95
Smallest Home Att: 27,213 v Southampton 24/1/95
Average Attendance: 35,317
Leading Scorer: Ian Wright – 18
Last Season: *FAPL:* 12th *FA Cup:* 3rd Round *Coca-Cola Cup:* 5th Round, *Cup-Winners' Cup:* Runners-up

All-Time Records

Record FAPL Win: 5-1 v Ipswich Town 5/02/94 & Norwich City 1/4/95
Record FAPL Defeat: 0-3 v Leeds United, 21/11/92; Coventry City 14/8/93; Liverpool 28/8/94; Manchester United 22/3/95
Record FL Win: 12-0 v Loughborough Town, Division 2, 12/3/1900
Record FL Defeat: 0-8 v Loughborough Town, Division 2, 12/12/1896
Record Cup Win: 11-1 v Darwen, FA Cup R3, 9/1/32
Record Fee Received: £2m David Rocastle, Leeds United, 7/92
Record Fee Paid: £7.5m Dennis Bergkamp, Internazionale, 6/95
Most FL Apps: 547 – David O'Leary, 1975-92
Record Attendance (all-time): 73,295 v Sunderland, Division 1, 9/3/35
Record Attendance (FAPL):   38,377 v Tottenham Hotspur 29/4/95
Highest Scorer in FAPL Season: Ian Wright, 30, 1992-93
Most FAPL Goals in Season: 53, 1993-94
Most FAPL Points in Season: 71, 1993-94

5-Year League Record

	Div.	P	W	D	L	F	A	Pts	Pos	FAC	FLC
90-91	1	38	24	13	1	74	18	83*	1	SF	4
91-92	1	42	19	15	8	81	46	72	4	3	3
92-93	PL	42	15	11	16	40	38	56	10	W	W
93-94	PL	42	18	17	7	53	28	71	4	4	4
94-95	PL	42	13	12	17	52	49	51	12	3	5

*2 points deducted

Summary of FAPL Appearances and Goals 1994-95

Player	Tot	Start	Sub	SNU	PS	Goals	Yel	Red
ADAMS	27	27	0	0	4	3	4	1
BARTRAM	11	11	0	30	0	0	0	0
BOULD	31	30	1	0	1	0	4	0
CAMPBELL	23	19	4	1	0	4	1	0
CARTER	3	2	1	0	1	0	1	0
CLARKE	1	0	1	0	0	0	0	0
DAVIS	4	3	1	1	1	1	1	0
DICKOV	9	4	5	1	0	0	2	0
DIXON	39	39	0	0	0	1	0	0
FLATTS	3	1	2	1	1	0	0	0
HARPER	0	0	0	12	0	0	0	0
HARTSON	15	14	1	0	5	7	5	1
HELDER	13	12	1	0	5	0	0	0
HILLIER	9	5	4	0	1	0	0	0
HUGHES	1	1	0	0	1	0	0	0
JENSEN	24	24	0	0	8	1	2	0
KEOWN	31	24	7	2	3	1	6	1
KIWOMYA	14	5	9	0	0	3	1	0
LINIGHAN	20	13	7	7	2	2	1	0
MARSHALL	0	0	0	1	0	0	0	0
McGOLDRICK	11	9	2	1	2	0	3	0
McGOWAN	1	1	0	0	1	0	0	0
MERSON	24	24	0	0	5	4	3	0
MORROW	15	11	4	4	2	1	0	0
PARLOUR	30	22	8	0	5	0	0	0
SCHWARZ	34	34	0	0	1	2	8	1
SEAMAN	31	31	0	0	0	0	0	0
SELLEY	13	10	3	0	4	0	3	0
SHAW	1	0	1	0	0	0	0	0
SMITH	19	17	2	0	4	2	0	0
WINTERBURN	39	39	0	0	3	0	8	0
WRIGHT	31	30	1	0	5	18	8	0
						OGs 2		

Freak Show!

Rarely can a club have attracted such adverse publicity during a season as Arsenal during 1994/95. Manager George Graham had to contend with England international Paul Merson admitting to being a drug addict, but that was not the biggest cloud hanging over The Gunners' boss. In November he was accused of receiving an illegal payment totalling £286,000 following the transfer of John Jensen two years earlier. In February, Arsenal sacked Graham when the FA found him guilty of the charge; assistant manager Stuart Houston was installed as caretaker until the end of the season.

Europe again looked to be the outlet for Arsenal's trophy hunt as their defence of the Cup-Winners' Cup kept the season alive. Ian Wright revelled in the Euro action by scoring in every match to the final as Omonia Nicosia, Brondby, Auxerre and, most dramatically in the semi final, Sampdoria were removed from the competition. Against the Italians, David Seaman saved three penalties to put Arsenal on the verge of being the first team to successfully defend the cup. Wright needed just one more goal to become the first player to score in every game of a European competition but it wasn't to be. Defender Steve Bould was another hero with two goals in the 1st Leg against Sampdoria but a second yellow card put him out of the Final.

With one more penalty shoot-out less than ten seconds away at the end of extra time in the Final, Seaman's semi final heroics were forgotten as the former Spurs midfielder Nayim scored what was either the finest or flukiest cup winning goal of all time for Spanish side Real Zaragoza as he looped the ball over the 'keeper from fully forty five yards.

But at the start of the season things had seemed rosier as the league campaign got off to an excellent start with a 3-0 victory over Manchester City – but with just two points and two goals from the next five games things started to look bleak. However, the momentum was restablished with four wins from the next five outings. It was a brief respite though as the Gunners then ploughed through another six winless games. Such inconsistency typified Arsenal's season. A run of four successive defeats in March put Arsenal's unbroken run in the top flight since 1919 under threat until big wins over strugglers Norwich, Ipswich and Villa dispelled the threat of relegation.

Arsenal's European form carried some way into the domestic cups with wins over Hartlepool, Oldham and Wednesday in the Coca-Cola Cup. But at the height of the accusations surrounding Graham, Liverpool put the Gunners out of that competition. Worse was to come one week later when, Graham's old club Millwall won an FA Cup replay 2-0 at Highbury.

Building for the 95-96 season, Bolton Wanderers boss Bruce Rioch was appointed Arsenal manager and he immediately smashed the club record transfer fee and much maligned wage structure when signing Dennis Bergkamp from Internazionale in a transfer and pay package worth £8.5m to signal the start of what could be an even greater period of success for Arsenal, but with the style their faithful have been clamouring for. ∎

Results 1994-95

FA Carling Premiership

Date	Opponents	Ven	Res	Pos	Atten	Scorers
20-Aug	Man. City	H	3-0	2	38,368	Campbell (2); OG (36); Wright (76)
23-Aug	Leeds Utd	A	0-1	12	34,218	
28-Aug	Liverpool	H	0-3	13	30,117	
31-Aug	Blackburn R	H	0-0	13	37,629	
10-Sep	Norwich City	A	0-0	12	17,768	
18-Sep	Newcastle	H	2-3	15	36,819	Adams (9); Wright (88)
25-Sep	West Ham	A	2-0	14	18,498	Adams (17); Wright (53)
1-Oct	C. Palace	H	1-2	14	34,136	Wright (72)
8-Oct	Wimbledon	A	3-1	11	10,842	Wright (11); Smith (57); Campbell (65)
15-Oct	Chelsea	H	3-1	11	38,234	Wright (40,63); Campbell (54)
23-Oct	Coventry C	H	2-1	10	31,725	Wright (13,34)
29-Oct	Everton	A	1-1	10	32,003	Schwarz (24)
6-Nov	Sheffield W	H	0-0	10	33,705	
19-Nov	Southampton	A	0-0	11	15,201	
23-Nov	Leicester C	A	1-2	11	20,774	Wright (19 pen)
26-Nov	Man. United	H	0-0	12	38,301	
3-Dec	N. Forest	A	0-1	12	21,662	Keown (59); Davis (76)
12-Dec	Man City	A	2-1	11	20,580	Smith (31); Schwarz (34)
17-Dec	Leeds United	H	1-3	12	38,098	Linighan (86)
26-Dec	Aston Villa	H	0-0	12	34,452	
28-Dec	Ipswich Tn	A	2-0	9	22,054	Wright (16); Campbell (79)
31-Dec	QPR	H	1-3	13	32,393	Jensen (64)
2-Jan	Tottenham	A	0-1	13	28,747	
14-Jan	Everton	H	1-1	13	34,473	Wright (4)
21-Jan	Coventry C	A	1-0	11	14,468	Hartson (78)
24-Jan	Southampton	H	1-1	11	27,213	Hartson (21)
4-Feb	Sheffield W	A	1-3	11	23,468	Linighan (3)
11-Feb	Leicester C	H	1-1	12	31,373	Merson (52)
21-Feb	N. Forest	H	1-0	10	35,441	Kiwomya (81)
25-Feb	C. Palace	A	3-0	8	17,092	Merson (24); Kiwomya (39,78)
5-Mar	West Ham	H	0-1	11	36,295	
8-Mar	Blackburn R	A	1-3	12	23,452	Morrow (49)
19-Mar	Newcastle	A	0-1	13	35,611	
22-Mar	Man. United	A	0-3	14	43,623	
1-Apr	Norwich C	H	5-1	10	36,942	Hartsen (4,13); Dixon (6); Merson (75); OG (90)
8-Apr	QPR	A	1-3	12	16,341	Adams (90)
12-Apr	Liverpool	H	0-1	12	38,036	

Date	Opponents	Vn	Rnd	Res	Atten	Scorers
15-Apr	Ipswich Tn	H		4-1	13	36,818	Merson (33); Wright (47,50,56)
17-Apr	Aston Villa	A		4-0	10	32,005	Hartson (31,87); Wright (32,72 pen)
29-Apr	Tottenham	H		1-1	10	38,377	Wright (61 pen)
4-May	Wimbledon	H		0-0	12		
12-May	Chelsea	A		1-2	12	29,542	Hartson (23)

Cup-Winners' Cup

Date	Opponents	Vn	Rnd	Res	Atten	Scorers
15-Sep	Omonia	A	1R1L	3-1	20,000	Merson (37,80); Wright (50)
29-Sep		H	1R2L	3-0	24,265	Wright (9,70); Schwarz (31)
	Arsenal win 6-1 on aggregate					
20-Oc	Brondby	A	2R1L	2-1	13,406	Wright (16); Smith (18)
3-Nov		H	2R2L	2-2	32,290	Wright (25 pen); Selley (46)
	Arsenal win 4-3 on aggregate					
2-Mar	Auxerre	H	QF1L	1-1	35,508	Wright (59 pen)
16-Ma		A	QF2L	1-0	22,000	Wright (15)
	Arsenal win 2-1 on aggregate					
6-Apr	Sampdoria	H	SF1L	3-2	38,089	Bould (34,36); Wright (69)
20-Apr		A	SF2L	2-3	34,353	Wright (60); Schwarz (87)
	After extra time, 5-5 on aggregate. Arsenal win 3-2 on penalties					
10-May	Real Zaragoza	Final		1-2	42,424	Hartson (76)

FA Challenge Cup

Date	Opponents	Vn	Rnd	Res	Atten	Scorers
7-Jan	Millwall	A	3R	0-0	17,715	0-0
18-Jan	Millwall	H	3RR	0-2	32,319	0-2

Coca-Cola League Cup

Date	Opponents	Vn	Rnd	Res	Atten	Scorers
21-Sep	Hartlepool U	A	2R1L	5-0	4,421	Adams (32); Smith (37); Wright (54,85); Merson (75)
5-Oct	Hartlepool U	H	2R2L	2-0	20,520	Campbell (79); Dickov (89)
	Arsenal win 7-0 on aggregate					
26-Oct	Oldham Ath	A	3R	0-0	9,303	
9-Nov	Oldham Ath	H	3RR	2-0	22,746	Dickov (15,40)
30-Nov	Sheffield W	A	4R	2-0	27,390	Morrow (29); Wright (34)
11-Jan	Liverpool	A	QF	0-1	35,026	

European Super Cup

1 Feb	Milan	H	1L	0-0	38,041	
8 Feb		A	2L	0-2	23,953	*0-2 on aggregate*

Aston Villa

Founded in 1874 by cricketers from the Aston Wesleyan Chapel, Lozells, who played on Aston Park, moving to a field in Wellington Road, Perry Barr in 1876. Prominent nationally, the club was a founder member of the Football League in 1888.

The landlord at Perry Barr made such demands that the club sought its own ground and eventually moved back to Aston occupying the Aston Lower Grounds, which had already been used for some big games. Not known as Villa Park until some time later, the ground first saw League football in 1897. Premier League founder members 1992.

Ground: Villa Park, Trinity Rd, Birmingham, B6 6HE
Phone Club: 0121-327 2299   **News:** 0891 12 11 48
Box Office: 0121-327 5353   **Ticket:** 0891 12 18 48
Capacity: 40,530   **Pitch:** 115 yds x 75 yds
Colours: Claret/Blue, White, Blue/Claret   **Nickname:** The Villains
Directions: M6 J6, follow signs for Birmingham NE. 3rd exit at roundabout, then right into Ashton Hall Rd after $^1/_2$ mile.   **Rail:** Witton

President: Harold Musgrove   **Chairman:** Doug Ellis
Secretary: Steven Stride
Manager: Brian Little   **Assistant:** Allan Evans
First Team Coach: John Gregory   **Physio:** Jim Walker

League History: 1888 Founder Member of the League; 1936-38 Division 2; 1938-59 Division 1; 1959-60 Division 2; 1960-67 Division 1; 1967-70 Division 2; 1970-72 Division 3; 1972-75 Division 2; 1975-87 Division 1; 1987-88 Division 2; 1988-92 Division 1; 1992- FA Premier League.

Honours: *FA Premier League – Runners-up 1992-93; Football League: Division 1 – Champions* 1893-94, 1895-96, 1896-97, 1898-99, 1899-1900, 1909-10, 1980-81; *Runners-up* 1888-89, 1902-03, 1907-08, 1910-11, 1912-13, 1913-14, 1930-31, 1932-33, 1989-90; *Division 2 – Champions* 1937-38, 1959-60; *Runners-up* 1974-75, 1987-88; *Division 3 – Champions* 1971-72. *FA Cup: Winners* 1887, 1895, 1897, 1905, 1913, 1920, 1957; *Runners-up* 1892, 1924. *League-Cup Double Performed:* 1896-97. *Football League Cup: Winners* 1961, 1975, 1977, 1994; *Runners-up* 1963, 1971. *Champions' Cup Winners –* 1981-82; *European Super Cup Winners:* 1982-83; *World Club Championship Runners-up:* 1982-83.

European Record: CC (2): 81-82 (W), 82-83 (QF); CWC (0); UEFA (6): 75-76 (1), 77-78 (Q), 83-84 (2), 90-91 (2), 93-94 (2), 94-95 (2).

Managers: George Ramsay 1884-1926; W.J. Smith 1926-34; Jimmy McMullan 1934-35; Jimmy Hogan 1936-44; Alex Massie 1945-50; George Martin 1950-53; Eric Houghton 1953-58; Joe Mercer 1958-64; Dick Taylor 1965-67; Tommy Cummings 1967-68; Tommy Docherty 1968-70; Vic Crowe 1970-74; Ron Saunders 1974-82; Tony Barton 1982-84; Graham Turner 1984-86; Billy McNeill 1986-87; Graham Taylor 1987-91; Dr Jozef Venglos 1990-91; (FAPL) Ron Atkinson June 1991- Nov 1994, Brian Little Nov 1994-

Season 1994-95
Biggest Home Win: 7-1 v Wimbledon, 11/2/95
Biggest Home Defeat: 0-4 v Arsenal, 17/4/95
Biggest Away Win: 4-3 v Tottenham Hotspur, 19/11/94
Biggest Away Defeat: 1-3 v Blackburn Rvrs 24/9/94; Newcastle Utd 25/2/95
Biggest Home Attendance: 40,154 v Liverpool, 6/5/95
Smallest Home Attendance: 22,241 v Ipswich Town , 10/9/94
Average Attendance: 28,697
Last Season: *FAPL :* 18th *FA Cup:* 4th round *Coca-Cola Cup:* 4th Round *UEFA Cup:* 2nd round
Leading Scorer: Dean Saunders – 15

All-Time Records
Record FAPL Win: 7-1 v Wimbledon, 11/2/95
Record FAPL Defeat: 1-5 v Newcastle United, 27/4/94
Record FL Win: 12-2 v Accrington S, Division 1, 12/3/1892
Record FL Defeat: 1-8 v Blackburn R, FA Cup R3, 16/2/1889
Record Cup Win: 13-0 v Wednesbury Old Ath, FA Cup R1, 30/10/1886
Record Fee Received: £5.5m from Bari for David Platt, 8/1991
Record Fee Paid: £3.5m to Partizan Belgrade for Savo Milsosevic
Most FL Appearances: Charlie Aitken, 561, 1961-76
Record Attendance (all-time): 76,588 v Derby Co, FA Cup R6, 2/2/1946
Record Attendance (FAPL): 45,347 v Liverpool, 7/5/94
Highest Scorer in FAPL season: Dean Saunders, 17, 1992-93
Most FAPL Goals in Season: 57, 1992-93
Most FAPL Points in Season: 74, 1992-93

5-Year League Record

	Div.	P	W	D	L	F	A	Pts	Pos	FAC	FLC
90-91	1	38	9	14	15	46	58	41	17	3	5
91-92	1	42	17	9	16	48	44	60	7	2	6
92-93	PL	42	21	11	10	57	40	74	2	4	4
93-94	PL	42	15	12	15	46	50	57	10	5	W
94-95	PL	42	11	15	16	51	56	48	18	4	4

Summary of FAPL Appearances and Goals 1994-95

Player	Tot	Start	Sub	SNU	PS	Goals	Yel	Red
ATKINSON	16	11	5	2	5	3	1	0
BARRETT	25	24	1	0	1	0	3	0
BODEN	1	0	1	2	0	0	1	0
BOSNICH	30	30	0	6	0	0	4	1
CARR	2	0	2	2	0	0	0	0
CHARLES	16	14	2	2	0	0	1	0
EHIOGU	39	38	1	0	0	3	7	0
FASHANU	13	11	2	0	4	3	2	0
FENTON	17	7	10	7	4	2	4	0
HOUGHTON	26	19	7	1	7	1	1	0
JOHNSON	14	11	3	3	6	4	2	0
KING	16	13	3	2	4	0	1	0
LAMPTEY	6	1	5	1	1	0	2	0
McGRATH	40	36	4	1	0	0	5	0
OAKES	0	0	0	8	0	0	0	0
PARKER	14	12	2	3	1	1	1	0
RICHARDSON	19	18	1	1	1	0	5	0
SAUNDERS	39	39	0	0	5	15	2	0
SMALL	5	5	0	0	0	0	0	0
SPINK	13	12	1	27	0	0	0	0
STAUNTON	35	34	1	0	5	5	7	0
TAYLOR	22	22	0	0	1	1	2	0
TEALE	28	28	0	0	2	0	3	0
TOWNSEND	32	32	0	0	4	1	7	2
WHITTINGHAM	7	4	3	0	0	0	0	0
WRIGHT	8	8	0	0	1	0	0	0
YORKE	37	33	4	0	6	6	3	0

OGs 4

Little Change at End

A controversial season for Villa which saw the club only guarantee its place in the Premiership with a point at already doomed Norwich City on the last day of the campaign. The threat of relegation was hardly high on the agenda back in September when Ron Atkinson's side opened the season with a spell of five undefeated games and, an emphatic win over Wigan Athletic in the Coca-Cola Cup, before removing Internazionale from the UEFA Cup on a dramatic penalty shoot-out in front of a packed house.

But in October, Villa's season began to fall apart as his side embarked on a run of eight defeats and draw with Norwich in nine Premiership matches. A single goal defeat by Turks Trabzonspor precipitated an away goals ruling defeat in the 2nd Round of the UEFA Cup and the combination of those two events led to the dismissal of Atkinson just weeks after he had agreed an extension on his contract. Victory over Middlesbrough in the Coca-Cola Cup didn't help Atkinson's cause and at the end of November their interest in that competition ended with a heavy reversal at Crystal Palace.

A dramatic 4-3 win at Tottenham proved to be the only respite in a run of 16 games which heralded the arrival of new manager Brian Little. The former Villa player spent £4m on Ian Taylor, Gary Charles and Tommy Johnson, and picked up the Manager of the Month award for January as the club rose to 12th place on the strength of an eight match unbeaten run. But in the space of eight days Villa's fortunes turned again as two trips to Manchester brought about two significant defeats. City ended their short FA Cup run in the 4th Round and United terminated the unbeaten league run. A 7-1 thrashing of Wimbledon and a victory over Sheffield Wednesday took Little's side into the top ten but with just two more victories from the remaining thirteen league games the club came perilously close to ending their seven year stay in the top flight. Little was not afraid to make changes as he attempted to halt the slide. Earl Barrett, Garry Parker, and the experienced Ray Houghton all departed while Alan Wright joined from Blackburn and Franz Carr signed from nearby Leicester City.

Villa were involved in some remarkable games during the season, the 4-3 win at Tottenham was secured with a last minute goal by Dean Saunders after a 3-0 lead had been wiped out, and a three goal lead was also lost during a 4-4 draw at home to Little's old club, Leicester City. The thrashing of Wimbledon was Villa's biggest win for 33 years and saw Johnson score their only hat-trick of the season. Top scorer was Saunders who took his total of league goals to 145. Despite finishing eight places lower than the previous season, attendances at Villa Park rose by an average of 789 per game.

Villa fans may wonder how much the draining effects of USA94 had on their Irish contingent in that early part of the season. Little though has signalled his intent at Villa Park by making several expensive signings for the start of the 1995-96 season. ∎

Results 1994-95

FA Carling Premiership

Date	Opponents	Ven	Res	Pos	Atten	Scorers
20-Aug	Everton	A	2-2	7	35,544	Fashanu (68); Saunders (74)
24-Aug	Southampton	H	1-1	12	24,179	Saunders (32)
27-Aug	C Palace	H	1-1	12	23,305	Staunton (46)
29-Aug	Coventry	A	1-0	9	12,218	Yorke (3)
10-Sep	Ipswich Tn	H	2-0	9	22,241	Staunton (15); Saunders (85)
17-Sep	West Ham	A	0-1	8	18,326	
24-Sep	Blackburn R	A	1-3	9	22,694	Ehigou (90)
1-Oct	Newcastle U	H	0-2	12	29,960	
8-Oct	Liverpool	A	2-3	14	32,158	Whittingham (37); Staunton (90)
15-Oct	Norwich C	H	1-1	15	22,468	Saunders (62)
22-Oct	N Forest	H	0-2	16	29,217	
29-Oct	QPR	A	0-2	18	16,073	
6-Nov	Man United	H	1-2	19	32,136	Atkinson (29)
9-Nov	Wimbledon	A	3-4	19	6,221	Parker (19); Saunders (38,50)
19-Nov	Tottenham H	A	4-3	19	26,899	Atkinson (8); Fenton (20,26); Saunders (90)
27-Nov	Sheffield W	H	1-1	19	25,082	Atkinson (15)
3-Dec	Leicester C	A	1-1	19	20,896	Whittingham (61)
10-Dec	Everton	H	0-0	20	29,678	
19-Dec	Southampton	A	1-2	20	13,874	Houghton (80)
26-Dec	Arsenal	A	0-0	20	34,452	
28-Dec	Chelsea	H	3-0	19	32,901	OG (9); Yorke (32); Taylor (82)
31-Dec	Man City	A	2-2	20	22,513	OG (54); Staunton (59)
2-Jan	Leeds United	H	0-0	19	35,038	
14-Jan	QPR	H	2-1	18	26,578	Fashanu (7); Ehigu (76)
21-Jan	N. Forest	A	2-1	14	24,598	Fashanu (32); Saunders (68)
25-Jan	Tottenham	H	1-0	12	40,017	Saunders (18)
4-Feb	Man United	A	0-1	14	43,795	
11-Feb	Wimbledon	H	7-1	11	23,982	OG (12); Johnson (22,26,38); Saunders (48, 66 pen); Yorke (83)
18-Feb	Sheffield W	A	2-1	9	24,063	Saunders (26,44)
22-Feb	Leicester C	H	4-4	9	30,825	Saunders (8), Staunton (37); Yorke (60); Johnson (65)
25-Feb	Newcastle	A	1-3	11	34,674	Townsend (40)
4-Mar	Blackburn R	H	0-1	11	40,114	
6-Mar	Coventry C	H	0-0	10	26,186	
18-Mar	West Ham	H	0-2	15	28,682	
1-Apr	Ipswich Tn	A	1-0	13	16,710	Swales (OG 90)

4-Apr	C Palace	A		0-0	11	12,606	
15-Apr	Chelsea	A		0-1	16	17,015	
17-Apr	Arsenal	H		0-4	16	32,005	
29-Apr	Leeds United	A		0-1	17	32,955	
3-May	Man City	H		1-1	18	30,133	Eghiogu (9)
6-May	Liverpool	H		2-0	15	40,154	Yorke (25,36)
14-May	Norwich	A		1-1	18	19,374	Staunton (7)

UEFA Cup

Date	Opponents	Vn	Rnd	Res	Atten	Scorers
15-Sep	Inter	A	1R1L	0-1	22,630	
29-Sep	Inter	H	1R2L	1-0	30,533	Houghton (41)
	1-1 on aggregate aet. Aston Villa win 4-3 on penalties					
18-Oct	Trabzonspor	A	2R1L	0-1	27,500	
1-Nov		H	2R2L	2-1	23,858	Atkinson (77); Ehiogu (90)
	2-2 on aggregate. Trabzonspor win on away goals					

FA Challenge Cup

Date	Opponents	Vn	Rnd	Res	Atten	Scorers
7-Jan	Barnsley	A	3R	2-0	11,469	Yorke (48); Saunders (85)
28-Jan	Man City	A	4R	0-1	21,177	

Coca-Cola League Cup

Date	Opponents	Vn	Rnd	Res	Atten	Scorers
21-Sep	Wigan Ath	H	2R1L	5-0	12,433	Yorke (4); Atkinson (26,84); Saunders (69); Lamptey (73)
5-Oct	Wigan Ath	A	2R2L	3-0	2,633	Lamptey (43,85); Whittingham (60)
	Aston Villa win 8-0 on aggregate					
26-Oct	Middlesbro'	H	3R	1-0	19,254	Townsend (30)
30-Nov	C Palace	A	4R	1-4	12,653	Atkinson (32)

Villa – Premiership Fact File

- John Fashanu scored on his opening day debut for Villa as they drew 2-2 at Everton.
- Villa ended a run of ten Premiership games without a win when they win a seven goal thriller at White Hart Lane on 19 November. They had previously lost eight out of nine.
- Ian Taylor marked his debut with a goal in the 3-0 home win over Chelsea on 28 December.
- Villa's 7-1 win over Wimbledon on 11 February was their biggest for 33 years.

Blackburn Rovers

Founded in 1875 by local school-leavers. Used several pitches, including Alexander Meadows, the East Lancashire Cricket Club ground, and became known nationally for their FA Cup exploits, eclipsing the record of Blackburn Olympic, the first club to take the trophy away from London. Three consecutive wins in the 1880s, when in the finals Queen's Park (twice) and West Bromwich Albion were beaten, brought recognition by way of a special shield awarded by the FA to commemorate the achievement.

Founder member of the Football League in 1888, the club settled at Ewood Park in 1890, purchasing the ground outright in 1893-94. Premier League founder member 1992.

Ground: Ewood Park, Blackburn, BB2 4JF
Phone: 01254-698888 **Info:** 0891-12 11 79
Ticket: 0891-12 10 14
Capacity: 30,591 **Pitch:** 115yds x 76yds
Colours: Blue/White, White, Blue **Nickname:** Blue and Whites
Directions: *From North, South & West:* M6 J31 follow signs for Blackburn then Bolton Rd. Turn left after 1½ miles into Kidder St. *From East:* A677 or A679 following signs for Bolton Rd, then as above.
Rail: Blackburn Central

President: J. Walker **Chairman:** R.D. Coar BSC
Vice-Chairman: R.L. Matthewman **Secretary:** John W. Howarth FAAI
Director of Football: Kenny Dalglish MBE
Manager: Ray Harford **Assistant:**
Physio: M. Pettigrew

League History: 1888 Founder member of the League; 1936-39 Division 2; 1946-48 Division 1; 1948-58 Division 2; 1958-66 Division 1; 1966-71 Division 2; 1971-75 Division 3; 1975-79 Division 2; 1979-80 Division 3; 1980-92 Division 2; 1992 – FA Premier League.

Honours: *FA Premier League: Champions 1994-95; Runners up 1993-94; Football League: Division 1 – Champions 1911-12, 1913-14; Division 2 – Champions 1938-39; Runners-up 1957-58; Division 3 – Champions 1974-75;* Runners-up 1979-1980. *FA Cup: Winners* 1884, 1885, 1886, 1890, 1891, 1928; *Runners-up* 1882, 1960. *Full Members' Cup: Winners* 1986-87.

European Record: CC (1): 95-96; CWC (0): UEFA (1) : 94-95 (1).

Managers: Thomas Mitchell 1884-96; J. Walmsley 1896-1903; R.B. Middleton 1903-25; Jack Carr 1922-26 (TM under Middleton to 1925); Bob Crompton 1926-31 (Hon. TM); Arthur Barritt 1931-36 (had been Secretary from 1927); Reg Taylor 1936-38; Bob Crompton 1938-41; Eddie Hapgood 1944-47; Will Scott 1947; Jack Burton 1947-49; Jackie Bestall 1949-53; Johnny Carey 1953-58; Dally Duncan 1958-60; Jack Marshall 1960-67; Eddie Quigley 1967-70; Johnny Carey 1970-71; Ken Furphy 1971-73; Gordon Lee 1974-75; Jim Smith 1975-78; Jim Iley 1978; John Pickering 1978-79; Howard Kendall 1979-81; Bobby Saxton 1981-86; Don Mackay 1987-91; (FAPL) Kenny Dalglish October 1991-May 1995; Ray Harford May 1995-

Season 1994-95

Biggest Home Win: 4-0 v Coventry City 27/8/94; QPR 26/11//95
Biggest Home Defeat: 2-4 v Manchester United, 23/10/95
Biggest Away Win: 3-0 v Wimbledon, 3/12/94
Biggest Away Defeat: 1-3 v Tottenham Hotspur, 5/2/95
Biggest Home Attendance: 30,545 v Newcastle United, 8/6/95
Smallest Home Attendance: 20,586 v Wimbledon, 22/2/95
Average Attendance: 25,272
Last Season: *FAPL:* Champions *FA Cup:* 3rd round
            Coca-Cola Cup: 4th round. *UEFA Cup:* 1st Round
Leading Scorer: Alan Shearer – 34

All-Time Records

Record FAPL Win: 7-1 v Norwich City, 3/10/92
Record FAPL Defeat: 2-5 v Coventry City, 26/1/93;
            2-5 v Leeds United, 10/4/93
Record FL Win: 9-0 v Middlesbrough, Division 2, 6/11/1954
Record FL Defeat: 0-8 v Arsenal, Division 1, 25/2/1933
Record Cup Win: 11-0 v Rossendale, FA Cup R1, 13/10/1884
Record Fee Received: £1.4m from Manchester United for David May, 7/94
Record Fee Paid: £5m to Norwich City for Chris Sutton, 7/94
Most FL Appearances: Derek Fazackerley, 596, 1970-86
Record Attendance (all-time): 61,783 v Bolton W, FA Cup R6, 2/3/1929
Record Attendance (FAPL): 30,545 v Newcastle United, 8/6/95
Highest Scorer in FAPL Season: Alan Shearer, 34, 1994-95
Most FAPL Goals in Season: 80, 1994-95
Most FAPL Points in Season: 89, 1994-95

5-Year League Record

	Div.	P	W	D	L	F	A	Pts	Pos	FAC	FLC
90-91	2	46	14	10	22	51	66	52	19	3	3
91-92	2	46	21	11	14	70	53	74	6	4	1
92-93	PL	42	20	11	11	68	46	71	4	6	SF
93-94	PL	42	25	9	8	63	36	84	2	4	4
94-95	PL	42	27	8	7	80	39	89	1	3	4

Summary of FAPL Appearances and Goals 1994-95

Player	Tot	Start	Sub	SNU	PS	Goals	Yel	Red
ATKINS … … … …	34	30	4	4	7	6	1	0
BATTY… … … … …	5	4	1	1	0	0	2	0
BERG … … … … …	40	40	0	0	0	1	2	1
FLOWERS … … …	39	39	0	0	0	0	1	1
GALE … … … … …	15	15	0	3	2	0	1	0
GALLACHER … …	1	1	0	2	1	1	0	0
GIVEN … … … …	0	0	0	3	0	0	0	0
HENDRY … … …	38	38	0	0	1	4	3	0
KENNA … … … …	9	9	0	0	0	1	1	0
LE SAUX … … …	39	39	0	0	0	3	6	0
MARKER … … … …	0	0	0	1	0	0	0	0
MIMMS … … … …	4	3	1	38	0	0	0	0
NEWELL… … … …	12	2	10	16	0	0	1	0
PEARCE … … … …	28	22	6	7	0	0	1	0
RIPLEY … … … …	37	36	1	0	8	0	0	0
SHEARER … … …	42	42	0	0	2	34	4	0
SHERWOOD … …	38	38	0	0	1	6	8	0
SLATER … … … …	18	12	6	5	3	0	3	0
SUTTON … … … …	40	40	0	0	7	15	7	0
WARHURST … …	27	20	7	3	1	2	5	0
WILCOX… … … …	27	27	0	0	4	5	4	2
WITSCHGE … … …	1	1	0	2	0	0	0	0
WRIGHT … … … …	5	4	1	4	0	0	1	0
						OGs 2		

Rovers – Premiership Fact File

- Alan Shearer missed a penalty on the opening day of the season against his old club Southampton. Chris Sutton made his debut in the game which ended 1-1.
- Sutton scored his first Rovers goal in his home debut in a 3-0 win over Leicester City. Sutton went even better in his second home game scoring a second half hat-trick in a 4-0 win over Coventry City.

Title Money Talk

Much has been made of Jack Walker's open cheque book supposedly making life easy for manager Kenny Dalglish, but as was seen at Tottenham, without the right person at the helm it can all go to waste so easily. Dalglish broke the British transfer record to get Alan Shearer at Ewood Park and did so again to pair him up with Chris Sutton. But only one other major signing was made during the 94-95 season – Jeff Kenna moving from Southampton for £1.5m. But money was also being spent around the players as building was finally completed at Ewood Park to provide a fitting venue for the Champions.

The title race was always expected to be between Rovers and Manchester United and it was the reigning champions who fired the first shot with a 2-0 victory in the Charity Shield. In the league, when United maintained the upper hand with a 4-2 win at Ewood Park, Rovers responded by putting together a devastating seven match winning run. Indeed, with just two defeats from the opening 23 games, Dalglish's side were top by the end of November. They were never to lose their grip in pole position and with a ten match unbeaten run during late winter it appeared a formality that Rovers would win the title for the first time in 81 years. Even so, United stayed in contention and when Blackburn faltered with three defeats in their final five games the Reds came within one point of retaining the title. Just three weeks earlier Blackburn had held an eight point advantage.

As if anyone needed reminding Shearer emphasised his position as the leading English striker, claiming 34 goals including three hat tricks. Despite the goals Rovers failed to record any significant wins, their best result being a 4-0 drubbing of Coventry City and QPR. For all their success, Blackburn's season was not without its disappointments. Sutton scored on his return to Norwich and Shearer did likewise at Southampton, but the two games yielded just one point. Jason Wilcox was dismissed twice and Tim Flowers' outstanding season was marred by his departure after just 72 seconds at home to Leeds United.

Newcastle United put Rovers out of the FA Cup at the first hurdle but it was a home victory over the Magpies in May which put the club in touching distance of the title. Blackburn did better in the Coca-Cola Cup with wins over Birmingham City and Coventry City before the run was cut short by Liverpool in the 4th Round. But most disappointment was felt in the UEFA Cup where the part timers of Trelleborgs gained a sensational win at Blackburn in the 1st Leg and settled the issue with a late equaliser in the return match to ruin Rovers' European debut. They will hope to do a lot better in the UEFA Champions' League where they are guaranteed to earn several million from their six European games.

Six weeks after guiding Blackburn to the championship, the unpredictable Dalglish was appointed director of football at Ewood Park with Ray Harford taking charge of team affairs. During the summer Shearer signed a three year extension to his existing contract to put an end to speculation that he might move to Italy. ∎

Results 1994-95

FA Carling Premiership

Date	Opponents	Ven	Res	Pos	Atten	Scorers
20-Aug	Southampton	A	1-1	9	14,209	Shearer (60)
23-Aug	Leicester C	H	3-0		21,050	Sutton (18); Berg (59); Shearer (73)
27-Aug	Coventry C	H	4-0	2	21,657	Sutton (67,74,88); Wilcox (77)
31-Aug	Arsenal	A	0-0	7	37,629	
10-Sep	Everton	H	3-0	3	26,538	Shearer (17,60 pen); Wilcox (43)
18-Sep	Chelsea	A	2-1	2	17,513	OG (27); Sutton (66)
24-Sep	Aston Villa	H	3-1	2	22,694	Shearer (17 pen,72); Sutton (56)
1-Oct	Norwich C	A	1-2	3	18,146	Sutton (4)
9-Oct	Newcastle U	A	1-1	3	34,344	Shearer (58 pen)
15-Oct	Liverpool	H	3-2	2	30,263	Atkins (52); Sutton (57,72)
23-Oct	Man United	H	2-4	4	30,260	Warhurst (13), Hendry (31)
29-Oct	N Forest	A	2-0	4	22,131	Sutton (6,68)
2-Nov	Sheffield W	A	1-0	2	24,207	Shearer (9)
5-Nov	Tottenham H	H	2-0	2	26,933	Wilcox (8); Shearer (49 pen)
19-Nov	Ipswich Tn	A	3-1	2	17,329	Sutton (8); Sherwood (41); Shearer (70)
26-Nov	QPR	H	4-0	1	21,302	Sutton (9); Shearer (56,66 pen,85)
3-Dec	Wimbledon	A	3-0	1	12,341	Atkins (51); Wilcox (72); Shearer (74)
10-Dec	Southampton	H	3-2	1	23,372	Atkins (6); Shearer (13,74)
17-Dec	Leicester C	A	0-0	1	20,559	
26-Dec	Man City	A	3-1	1	23,387	Shearer (9); Atkins (16); Le Saux (67)
31-Dec	C Palace	A	1-0	1	14,232	Sherwood (66)
2-Jan	West Ham	H	4-2	1	25,503	Shearer (14 pen,75,79 pen); Le Saux (61)
14-Jan	N Forest	H	3-0	1	27,510	Warhurst (54); Wilcox (78); OG (88)
22-Jan	Man United	A	0-1	1	43,742	
28-Jan	Ipswich Tn	H	4-1	1	21,325	Shearer (3,29,90 pen); Sherwood (49)
1-Feb	Leeds Utd	H	1-1	1	28,561	Shearer (6 pen)
5-Feb	Tottenham H	A	1-3	1	28,124	Sherwood (46)
12-Feb	Sheffield W	H	3-1	1	22,223	Sherwood (26); Atkins (35); Shearer (66)
22-Feb	Wimbledon	H	2-1	1	20,586	Shearer 3), Atkins (25)

102

25-Feb	Norwich C	H	0-0	1	25,579	
4-Mar	Aston Villa	A	1-0	1	40,114	Hendry (12)
8-Mar	Arsenal	H	3-1	1	23,452	Shearer (4,48 pen);
						Le Saux (18)
11-Mar	Coventry C	A	1-1	1	18,547	Shearer (87)
18-Mar	Chelsea	H	2-1	1	25,490	Shearer (16); Sherwood (37)
1-Apr	Everton	A	2-1	1	37,905	Sutton (13 secs); Shearer (6)
4-Apr	QPR	A	1-0	1	16,508	Sutton (67)
15-Apr	Leeds Utd	A	1-1	1	39,426	Hendry (44)
17-Apr	Man City	A	2-3	1	27,857	Shearer (7); Hendry (39)
20-Apr	C Palace	H	2-1	1	28,005	Kenna (47); Gallacher (51)
30-Apr	West Ham	H	0-2	1	24,202	
8-May	Newcastle	H	1-0	1	30,545	Shearer (29)
14-May	Liverpool	A	1-2	1	40,014	Shearer (20)

UEFA Cup

Date	Opponents	Vn	Rnd	Res	Atten	Scorers
13-Sep	Trelleborg	H	1R1L	0-1	13,775	
27-Sep		A	1R2L	2-2	6,730	Sutton (18); Shearer (84)
	Trelleborg win 3-2 on aggregate					

FA Challenge Cup

Date	Opponents	Vn	Rnd	Res	Atten	Scorers
8-Jan	Newcastle	A	3R	1-1	31,721	Sutton (30)
18-Jan	Newcastle	H	3RR	1-2	22,658	Sutton (75)

Coca-Cola League Cup

Date	Opponents	Vn	Rnd	Res	Atten	Scorers
20-Sep	Bir'ham City	H	2R1L	2-0	14,517	Wilcox (55); Sutton (68)
4-Oct		A	2R2L	1-1	16,275	Sutton (71)
	Blackburn Rovers win 3-1 on aggregate					
26-Oct	Coventry C	H	3R	2-0	14,538	Shearer (54,63)
30-Nov	Liverpool	H	4R	1-3	30,115	Sutton (89)

Rovers – Premiership Fact File

- It was no April fool as a goal after just 13 seconds of play gave Sutton the distinction of scoring the fastest Premiership goal in a 2-1 win over Everton on 1st April 1994.
- Disaster for Kevin Gallacher though who was injured in his first game of the season – having missed the start of it through injury. It was bitter sweet for Gallacher who scored in the 2-1 win over Crystal Palace on 20 April.

Bolton Wanderers

Formed in 1874 as a Sunday School side, Christ Church. This connection ended in 1877 when they adopted their present name. Turned professional in 1895 and were Football League founder members. Moved from Pikes Lane to present ground in 1895. Members of the reorgainsed Division One on formation of the Premier League, they were last in the top flight in season 1979-80.

Ground: Burnden Park, Bolton.
Phone: 01204-389200   **Box Office:** 01204-521101
Info: 0891-12 11 64
Capacity: 22,500   **Pitch:** 113 x 76 yards
Colours: White, Navy Blue,Navy Blue   **Nickname:** The Trotters
Directions: *From North:* M61, J5. Follow signs towards Farnworth B653 into Manchester Road. After half mile turn left into Croft Lane for ground. *From South, West, East:* M62, J14 onto M61. At end of motorway (2 miles) take 1st exit on roundabout B6536. After 2 miles turn right into Croft Lane for ground. **Rail:** Bolton.

President: Nat Lofthouse   **Chairman:** G. Hargreaves
Secretary: Des McBain
Manager: Roy McFarland   **Chief Coach:** Colin Todd
Physio: E. Simpson

League History: 1892 Founder members of League; 1899-00 Division 2; 1900-03 Division 1; 1903-05 Division 2; 1905-08 Division 1; 1900-09 Division 2; 1909-10 Division 1; 1910-11 Division 2; 1911-33 Division 1; 1933-35 Division 2; 1935-64 Division 1; 1964-71 Division 2; 1971-73 Division 3; 1973-78 Division 2; 1978-80 Division 1; Division 2; 1983-87 Division 3; 1987-88 Division 4; 1988-92 Division 3; 1992-93 Division 2; 1993-94 Division 1; FAPL 1994-

Honours: *FA Cup Winners:* 1922-23, 1925-26. 1928-29, 1957-58; *Runners-up:* 1883-84, 1903-04, 1952-53; *League Cup Runners-up:* 1994-95; *Division Two Champions:* 1908-09, 1977-78; *Division Three Champions:* 1972-73; *FA Charity Shield Winners:* 1958; *Sherpa Van Trophy Winners:* 1988-89; *Freight Rover Trophy Runners-up:* 1985-86.

European Record: Never qualified

Managers: Tom Rawthorne 1874-85; JJ Bentley 1885-86; WG Struthers 1886-87; Fitzroy Norris 1887; JJ Bentley 1887-95; Harry Downs 1895-96;

Frank Brettell 1896-98; John Somerville 1889-1910; Will Settle 1910-15; Tom Mather 1915-19; Charles Foweraker 1991-44; Walter Rowley 1944-50; Bill Ridding 1951-68; Nat Lofthouse 1968-70; Jimmy McIlroy 1971; Jimmy Meadows 1971; Nat Lofthouse 1971; Jimmy Armfield 1971-74; Ian Greaves 1974-80; Stan Anderson 1980-81; George Mulhall 1981-82; John McGovern 1982-85; Charlie Wright 1985; Phil Neal 1985-92; Bruce Rioch 1992-1995; *(FAPL)* Roy McFarland June 1995-

Season 1994-95

Biggest Home Win: 5-1 v Charlton Athletic 21/1/95; Wolves 4/2/95
Biggest Home Defeat: 0-2 v Bristol City, 20/8/95
Biggest Away Win: 3-0 v Luton Town, 13/9/95
Biggest Away Defeat: 1-3 v Sheffield Utd 10/9/94; Wolves 23/11/94
Biggest Home Attendance: 18,370 v Middlesbrough 11/3/95
Smallest Home Attendance: 9,519 v Millwall 30/8/95
Average Attendance:
Last Season: *Division 1:* 3rd; *Play-off* Winners; *FA Cup* 3rd Round;
                           Coca-Cola Cup: Finalists
Leading Scorer: John McGinlay – 16

All Time Records

Record FAPL Win: –
Record FAPL Defeat: –
Record FL Win: 8-0 v Barnsley, Division 2 6/10/34
Record FL Defeat:
Record Cup Win: 13-0 v Sheffield Utd, FAC 2Rd, 1/2/1890
Record Fee Received: £340,000 from Birmingham City for
                                    Neil Whatmore 8/81
Record Fee Paid: £350,000 to WBA for Len Cantello, 5/79;
                                and to Sheffield Wednesday for Simon Coleman 10/94
Most FL Appearances: Eddie Hopkinson, 519, 1956-70
Record Attendance (all-time): 69,912 v Man City FAC 5Rd, 18/2/33
Record Attendance (FAPL): –
Highest Scorer in FAPL Season: –
Most FAPL Goals in Season: –
Most FAPL Points in Season: –

5-Year League Record

	Div.	P	W	D	L	F	A	Pts	Pos	FAC	FLC
90-91	3	46	24	11	11	64	50	83	4	4	2
91-92	3	46	14	17	15	57	56	59	13	5	2
92-93	2	46	27	9	10	80	41	90	2	5	2
93-94	1	46	15	14	11	63	64	59	14	6	2
94-95	1	42	21	14	11	67	45	77	3	3	F

Summary of Endsleigh League Apps and Goals 1994-95

Player	Tot	Start	Sub	SNU	PS	Goals	Yel	Red
BERGSSON	8	8	0	2	0	0	1	0
BRANAGAN	43	43	0	0	0	0	1	1
COLEMAN	22	22	0	0	1	4	1	0
COYLE	19	8	11	7	1	5	2	0
DAVISON...	4	3	1	41	0	0	0	0
De FREITAS	13	7	6	5	6	2	1	0
DREYER	2	1	1	4	0	0	0	0
FISHER	11	10	1	0	1	0	2	0
GREEN	31	26	5	1	0	1	2	0
KELLY...	4	4	0	0	1	0	1	0
KERNAGHAN	11	9	2	0	0	0	2	0
LEE	39	35	4	3	7	4	1	0
LYDIATE	19	18	1	8	1	0	2	0
McATEER	42	40	2	1	1	6	4	0
McDONALD	4	4	0	3	2	0	0	0
McGINLAY	37	34	3	1	10	16	3	0
PAATELAINEN ...	44	43	1	1	2	11	2	0
PATTERSON	27	24	3	3	1	3	5	1
PHILLIPS	46	46	0	0	1	0	3	0
RHODES	0	0	0	1	0	0	0	0
SEAGRAVES	13	13	0	1	1	0	0	0
SHILTON	1	0	1	1	0	0	0	0
SNEEKES	38	37	1	2	6	6	4	0
SPOONER...	1	1	0	1	0	0	0	0
STUBBS	38	36	2	0	1	1	5	0
THOMPSON	37	34	3	2	4	7	6	0
WESTHEAD	0	0	0	1	0	0	0	0
WHITTAKER	1	0	1	0	0	0	0	0

OGs 0

Cup Form Comes Good in League

In recent seasons Bolton have built a fine reputation as a cup side but what should not be overlooked is the excellent progress made in the league since Bruce Rioch's appointment as manager. Following promotion in 1993, Wanderers had a steady season in Division One and made a slow start to the 1994/95 campaign with just one point being picked up from the first three games. A late winner, against Millwall, got Bolton on their way at the end of August and a 4-0 thrashing of Stoke seemingly set the bandwagon rolling only for more hiccups to follow as two wins in eight games ensued. A draw at Burnley proved costly with Nicky Spooner breaking a leg and Jason Lydiate sent off. The tide turned at the end of October when Watford were beaten 3-0 and Bolton went third with a four match winning run.

Promotion rivals Wolves ended the run, a second successive defeat followed at Barnsley but two goals by Mark Patterson in the next two games accounted for Port Vale and Bristol City and set Bolton on a scintillating run of just one defeat in twenty one games. Nine different players were on the scoresheet as Charlton and Wolves were crushed 5-1 at Burnden Park in consecutive games as Bolton topped the table. Defeat at Derby then cost them top place. However, five wins, including victory over Middlesbrough, and three draws brought promotion closer and a win over Sunderland left Bolton just a couple of points behind the leaders. Bolton's hopes of grabbing the one automatic promotion place was lost when only two points were collected from the final three games.

Wanderers' cup fighting spirit came to the fore in the play-offs as a 2-1 reverse at Wolves was overturned into a 3-2 aggregate victory in the 2nd leg. The Wembley play-off final with Reading was equally dramatic as The Royals stormed into a two goal lead only for Bolton to dominate the second half and book their place in the Premiership with a 4-2 success in extra time.

Bolton made a swift exit from the FA Cup as Portsmouth shot them down 3-1 at Fratton Park. But they did not let the possibility of a cup run upset their league fortunes as they claimed three Premiership scalps on the way to Wembley for the Final of the Coca-Cola Cup. Ipswich were easily beaten in the 2nd Round and a last minute own goal put paid to Sheffield United. John McGinlay, a national hero after previous cup exploits, scored twice as West Ham were hammered at Upton Park before David Lee's spectacular goal edged Bolton past Norwich in the quarter final. Swindon Town put up stubborn resistance in the semi final, taking a 2-1 lead into the 2nd leg they held out until two goals in the last twenty minutes put Bolton through 4-3. In the final, Bolton fought boldly to come from two down against Liverpool and managed a consolation goal through Thompson.

The club suffered a big blow in the close season with Rioch taking the vacant manager's position at Arsenal. But Roy McFarland was soon appointed manager with his former Derby County teammate, Colin Todd, remaining in the assistant's post. ∎

Results 1994-95

Endsleigh First Division

Date	Opponents	Ven	Res	Pos	Atten	Scorers
13-Aug	Grimsby Tn	A	9	3-3	8,393	Paatelainan (10,28); McGinlay (63 pen)
20-Aug	Bristol City	H	16	0-2	12,127	
27-Aug	Middlesbro	A	16	0-1	19,570	
30-Aug	Millwall	H	10	1-0	9,519	Patterson (88)
3-Sep	Stoke City	H	9	4-0	11,515	McGinlay (41pen); McAteer (47,74); Paatelainen (50)
10-Sep	Sheffield U	A	15	1-3	14,116	McGinlay (70)
13-Sep	Luton Tn	A	5	3-0	5,764	McGinlay (51,71); Sneekes (69)
17-Sep	Portsmouth	H	10	1-1	11,284	McGinlay (21)
24-Sep	Southend	A	12	1-2	4,507	Sneekes (25)
1-Oct	Derby Co	H	7	1-0	12,015	McGinlay (81)
8-Oct	Burnley	A	9	2-2	16,687	McGinlay (5); Coleman (83)
16-Oct	Oldham Ath	H	11	2-2	11,106	Paatelainen (7); Lee (27)
22-Oct	Port Vale	A	12	1-1	10,003	Green (70)
29-Oct	Watford	H	7	3-0	10,483	Paatelainen (28); McGinlay (51,57)
1-Nov	Swindon Tn	H	5	3-0	10,046	Coleman (42); Thompson (77); De Freitas (89)
5-Nov	Charlton Ath	A	5	2-1	9,793	Sneekes (23,48)
19-Nov	Notts Co	H	3	2-0	11,698	De Freitas (30); Paatelainen (87)
23-Nov	Wolves	A	3	1-3	25,903	Paatelainen (15)
26-Nov	Barnsley	A	4	0-3	8,507	
6-Dec	Port Vale	H	4	1-0	10,324	Patterson (73)
10-Dec	Bristol City	A	4	1-0	6,144	Patterson (29 secs)
17-Dec	Grimsby Tn	H	3	3-3	10,522	Coyle (14,58); Lee (88)
26-Dec	Sunderland	A	5	1-1	19,758	Paatelainen (51)
27-Dec	Tranmere R	H	2	1-0	16,782	Thompson (41)
31-Dec	WBA	A	6	0-1	18,134	
2-Jan	Reading	H	4	1-0	14,705	Coleman (9)
14-Jan	Watford	A	3	0-0	9,113	
21-Jan	Charlton Ath	H	3	5-1	10,516	McGinlay (15,45); McAteer (57); Coyle (61); Paatelainen (74)
4-Feb	Wolves	H	1	5-1	16,964	Sneekes (9); Coleman (37); Phillips (60); Coyle (78); Thompson (83)

7-Feb	Notts Co	A	1	1-1	7,553	Coyle (71)
18-Feb	Barnsley	H	1	2-1	12,463	Thompson (17); Sneekes (26)
26-Feb	Derby Co	A	3	1-2	11,003	McAteer (1)
4-Mar	Southend U	H	3	3-0	10,786	Thompson (32); Lee (55); McAteer (71)
11-Mar	Middlesbro	H	3	1-0	18,370	Paatelainen (14)
19-Mar	Millwall	A	2	1-0	6,103	McGinlay (83)
22-Mar	Sheffield U	H	2	1-1	16,756	Stubbs (42)
25-Mar	Portsmouth	A	2	1-1	7,765	Paatelainen (12)
5-Apr	Swindon Tn	A	3	1-0	8,110	Thompson (88)
8-Apr	WBA	H	3	1-0	16,207	Thompson (85 pen)
11-Apr	Luton Town	H	2	0-0	13,619	
14-Apr	Tranmere R	A	3	0-1	15,595	
17-Apr	Sunderland	H	2	1-0	15,030	McGinlay (86)
21-Apr	Reading	A	2	1-2	13,223	Lee (48)
29-Apr	Oldham Ath	A	3	1-3	11,901	McGinlay (38)
3-May	Stoke City	A	2	1-0	15,557	McGinlay (32)
7-May	Burnley	H	3	1-1	16,853	Paatelainen (90)
14-May	Wolves	A	3	1-2	26,153	McAteer (46)

League Play-Offs

Date	Opponents	Vn	Rnd	Res	Atten	Scorers
14-May	Wolves	A	1L	1-2	26,153	McAteer (46)
17-May		H	2L	2-0†	20,041	McGinlay (44,109)
29-May	Reading	W	F	4-3†	64,107	Coyle (75); De Freitas (86,118); Paatelainen (105)

† after extra time

FA Challenge Cup

Date	Opponents	Vn	Rnd	Res	Atten	Scorers
7-Jan	Portsmouth	A	3R	1-3	9,721	Sneekes (42)

Coca-Cola League Cup

Date	Opponents	Vn	Rnd	Res	Atten	Scorers
21-Sep	Ipswich Tn	A	2R1L	3-0	7,787	McAteer (6); McGinlay (84); Thompson (88)
5-Oct	Ipswich Tn	H	2R2L	1-0	8,212	Sneekes (77)
25-Oct	Sheffield U	A	3R	2-1	6,989	Paatelainen (6); OG (89)
30-Nov	West Ham	A	4R	3-1	18,190	McGinlay (16,77); Lee (54)
11-Jan	Norwich C	H	QF	1-0	17,029	Lee (66)
12-Feb	Swindon Tn	A	SF1L	1-2	15,341	Stubbs (10)
9-Mar	Swindon Tn	H	SF2L	3-1	19,851	McAteer (64); Paatelainen (71); McGinlay (88)
2-Apr	Liverpool	A	F	1-2	75,595	Thompson (68)

Chelsea

Founded in 1905. The Mears brothers developed Stamford Bridge Athletic Ground, which they owned, into a football stadium for use for prestigious matches and, prospectively, nearby Fulham FC. But Fulham did not take up the chance so the Mears brothers established their own club, rejecting possible names such as 'London' and 'Kensington' in favour, eventually, of Chelsea.

Judging that the club would not be accepted into the Southern League, it sought membership of the Football League. This was gained at the first attempt and it started the 1906-07 season in Division Two. Premier League founder members 1992.

Ground: Stamford Bridge, London SW6 1HS
Phone: 0171-385 5545   **News:** 0891 12 11 59
Ticket News: 0891-12 10 11   **Booking:** 0171-386 7799
Capacity: 41,050   **Pitch:** 110 yds x 72 yds
Colours: Royal Blue, Royal Blue, White   **Nickname:** The Blues
Directions: *From North & East:* A1 or M1 to central London and Hyde Park corner. Follow signs for Guildford (A3) and then Knightsbridge (A4). After a mile turn left into Fulham Rd. *From South:* A219 Putney Bridge then follow signs for West End joining A308 and then into Fulham Rd. *From West:* M4 then A4 to central London. Follow A3220 to Westminster, after ¼ miles right at crossroads into Fulham Rd.   **Rail/Tube** (District line): Fulham Broadway

President: G.M. Thomson   **Chairman:** Ken W. Bates
Managing Director: Colin Hutchinson
Match Secretary: Keith Lacy   **Company Secretary:** Alan Shaw
Manager: Glenn Hoddle   **Assistant:** Peter Shreeves
Physio: Bob Ward

League History: 1905 Elected to Division 2; 1907-10 Division 1; 1910-12 Division 2; 1912-24 Division 1; 1924-30 Division 2; 1930-62 Division 1; 1962-63 Division 2; 1963-75 Division 1; 1975-77 Division 2; 1977-79 Division 1; 1979-84 Division 2; 1984-88 Division 1; 1988-89 Division 2; 1989-92 Division 1; 1992- FA Premier League.

Honours: *Football League: Division 1 Champions:* 1954-55; *Division 2 Champions:* 1983-84, 1988-89; *Runners-up:* 1906-7, 1911-12, 1929-30,1962-63, 1976-77. *FA Cup: Winners:* 1970; *Runners-up:* 1914-15, 1966-67, 1993-94. *Football League Cup: Winners:* 1964-65; *Runners-up:* 1971-72; *Full*

Members' Cup Winners: 1985-86. *Zenith Data Systems Cup Winners:* 1989-90.

European Record: CC (0) – ; CWC (3): 70-71 (W), 71-72 (2), 94-95 (SF); UEFA (2): 65-66 (SF), 68-69 (2).

Managers: John Tait Robertson 1905-07; David Calderhead 1907-33; A. Leslie Knighton 1933-39; Billy Birrell 1939-52; Ted Drake 1952-61; Tommy Docherty 1962-67; Dave Sexton 1967-74; Ron Stuart 1974-75; Eddie McCreadie 1975-77; Ken Shellito 1977-78; Danny Blanchflower 1978-79; Geoff Hurst 1979-81; John Neal 1981-85 (Director to 1986); John Hollins 1985-88; Bobby Campbell 1988-91; *(FAPL)* Ian Porterfield June 1991-1993; Dave Webb 1993; Glenn Hoddle July 1993-.

Season 1994-95
Biggest Home Win: 4-0 v Leicester City, 8/10/94
Biggest Home Defeat: 0-3 v Leeds United, 11/3/95
Biggest Away Win: 3-2 v Leeds United, 27/8/94
Biggest Away Defeat: 0-3 v Norwich City 10/12/94, Aston Villa 28/12/94
Biggest Home Attendance: 31,161 v Manchester United, 26/12/94
Smallest Home Attendance: 14,130 v Crystal Palace, 5/3/95
Average Attendance: 20,347
Last Season: *FAPL:* 11th *FA Cup:* 4th Round
　　　　　　　　Coca-Cola Cup: 3rd round. *Cup-Winners' Cup:* Semi Final
Leading Scorer: John Spencer – 11

All time Records
Record FAPL Win: 4-0 v Middlesbrough, 3/4/93; Leicester City, 8/10/94
Record FAPL Defeat: 1-4 v Leeds United, 6/11/93
Record FL Win: 9-2 v Glossop N E, Division 2, 1/9/1906
Record FL Defeat: 1-8 v Wolverhampton W, Division 1, 26/9/1953
Record Cup Win: 13-0 v Jeunesse Hautcharage, CWC, 1R2L, 29/9/1971
Record Fee Received: £2.2m from Tottenham H for Gordon Durie, 7/1991
Record Fee Paid: £2.3m to Watford for Paul Furlong, 6/94
Most FL Appearances: Ron Harris, 655, 1962-80
Record Attendance (all-time): 82,905 v Arsenal, Div 1, 12/10/1935
Record Attendance (FAPL): 37,064 v Manchester United, 11/9/93
Highest Scorer in FAPL Season: Mark Stein, 13, 1993-94
Most FAPL Goals in Season: 51, 1992-93
Most FAPL Points in Season: 56, 1992-93

5-Year League Record

	Div.	P	W	D	L	F	A	Pts	Pos	FAC	FLC
90-91	1	38	13	10	15	58	69	49	11	3	SF
91-92	1	42	13	14	15	50	60	53	14	6	2
92-93	PL	42	14	14	14	51	54	56	11	3	4
93-94	PL	42	13	12	17	49	53	51	14	F	3
94-95	PL	42	13	15	14	50	55	54	11	4	3

Summary of FAPL Appearances and Goals 1994-95

Player	Tot	Start	Sub	SNU	PS	Goals	Yel	Red
BARNESS	12	10	2	1	3	0	4	0
BURLEY	25	16	9	0	7	2	9	0
CLARKE	29	29	0	0	1	0	5	0
COLGAN	0	0	0	11	0	0	2	0
FLECK	0	0	0	1	0	0	1	0
FURLONG	36	30	6	0	3	10	7	1
HALL	6	4	2	3	0	0	0	0
HITCHCOCK	12	11	1	25	0	0	2	0
HODDLE	12	3	9	3	3	0	0	0
HOPKIN	15	7	8	1	1	1	3	0
JOHNSEN	33	33	0	0	1	0	0	0
JUDGE	0	0	0	2	0	0	1	0
KHARINE	31	31	0	3	1	0	1	0
KJELDBJERG	23	23	0	1	2	1	3	1
LEE	14	9	5	6	0	0	0	0
MINTO	19	19	0	0	0	0	2	0
MYERS	10	9	1	1	1	0	0	0
NEWTON	30	22	8	0	2	1	0	0
PEACOCK	38	38	0	0	2	4	0	0
RIX	1	0	1	0	0	0	4	1
ROCASTLE	28	26	2	1	17	0	5	0
SHIPPERLEY	10	6	4	1	3	2	0	0
SINCLAIR	35	35	0	0	1	3	0	0
SPACKMAN	36	36	0	1	6	0	1	0
SPENCER	29	26	3	0	6	11	1	0
STEIN	24	21	3	0	4	8	2	0
WISE	19	18	1	0	1	6	0	0

OGs 1

Chelsea – Premiership Fact File

- John Spencer scored what was to be the second fastest goal in a league game during the season, finding the net after just 17 seconds in the 4-0 home win over Leicester City.

Signing Coups Plan for Future

Chelsea went into their second season under Glenn Hoddle looking to build upon the previous campaign and a place in the Cup-Winners' Cup for the first time in over two decades. Transfer activity was modest with just David Rocastle moving to Stamford Bridge but expectations were high, especially when the opening three games brought wins over Norwich, Leeds United – after being two down – and Manchester City. Two defeats followed but a victory over Crystal Palace saw Chelsea finish September in fifth place.

But from then in it was all downhill in the league with the Blues failing to win two consecutive games during the rest of the season. In an amazingly tight battle at the foot of the table, which sucked in almost half of the Premiership during the final weeks of the season, Chelsea looked to be one of the sides in deepest trouble as just two wins were recorded in 19 outings. Chelsea drew 15 Premiership matches during the season and it was a run of three draws and three victories which finally secured their future. Top scorer was John Spencer with 11, supported by Paul Furlong on ten.

At a time when their league form began to lose its early momentum, Chelsea made progress in the Coca-Cola Cup with two 1-0 wins over Bournemouth, only for London rivals West Ham to terminate the run in the 3rd Round. It was another 'derby' clash which put paid to Chelsea's hopes of matching the previous season's run in the FA Cup as Millwall won a penalty shoot-out at the Bridge in the 4th Round which ended with a pitch invasion.

Disappointments in the domestic cup competitions were offset by an extended, if perhaps unexpected, run in the Cup-Winners' Cup. Hoddle's side successfully progressed through three rounds to the semi final despite winning just two games out of six. Viktoria Zizkov were seen off in the 1st Round before an away goals victory accounted for FK Austria. Chelsea recorded an excellent 2-0 win over Bruges in the 2nd Leg of their quarter final clash having lost to a solitary goal in Belgium. Spaniards Real Zaragoza were highly impressive when defeating Chelsea by three goals in the 1st Leg of their clash in the semis, but the Blues put up a brave fight in the return match before going down 4-3 on aggregate.

In common with many clubs, Chelsea's season was not without controversy. England international, and at the time club captain, Dennis Wise was sent off during their first defeat of the season – 4-2 at home to Newcastle – and later in the season he was charged but acquitted on appeal, of attacking a taxi driver. Neil Shipperley signed a new contract in November and was subsequently sold to Southampton for £1.3m just two months later.

It was during the close season that Chelsea really grabbed the headlines with the signing of *libero* Ruud Gullit from Sampdoria and then, perhaps an even greater coup, Mark Hughes from Manchester United at a bargain £1.5m, and which could prove to be one of the buys of the new season. ∎

Results 1994-95

FA Carling Premiership

Date	Opponents	Ven	Res	Pos	Atten	Scorers
20-Aug	Norwich C	H	2-0	3	23,098	Sinclair (44); Furlong (75)
27-Aug	Leeds Utd	A	3-2	6	32,212	Wise (37 pen); Spencer (61,88)
31-Aug	Man City	H	3-0	5	21,740	Peacock (4); Wise (73); OG (83)
10-Sep	Newcastle	A	2-4	6	34,435	Peacock (15); Furlong (27)
18-Sep	Blackburn R	H	1-2	7	17,513	Spencer (55)
24-Sep	C Palace	A	1-0	5	16,030	Furlong (50)
2-Oct	West Ham	H	1-2		18,696	Furlong (62)
8-Oct	Leicester C	H	4-0	6	18,397	Spencer (1,49); Peacock (4); Shipperley (77)
15-Oct	Arsenal	A	1-3	7	38,234	Wise (34)
23-Oct	Ipswich Tn	H	2-0	7	15,068	Wise (74), Shipperley (83)
29-Oct	Sheffield W	A	1-1	7	25,450	Wise (30)
6-Nov	Coventry	H	2-2	8	17,090	Spencer (46); Kjeldbjerg (69)
9-Nov	Liverpool	A	1-3	8	32,855	Spencer (3)
19-Nov	N Forest	H	1-0	7	22,092	Spencer (28)
23-Nov	Tottenham	A	0-0		27,037	
26-Nov	Everton	H	0-1	8	28,115	
3-Dec	Southampton	A	1-0	7	14,404	Furlong (89)
10-Dec	Norwich	A	0-3	8	18,246	
18-Dec	Liverpool	H	0-0	8	27,050	
26-Dec	Man United	H	2-3	9	31,161	Spencer (58pen); Newton (77)
28-Dec	Aston Villa	A	0-3	10	32,901	
31-Dec	Wimbledon	H	1-1	10	16,105	Furlong (65)
14-Jan	Sheffield W	H	1-1	12	17,285	Spencer (34)
21-Jan	Ipswich Tn	A	2-2	12	17,296	Stein (67); Burley (88)
25-Jan	N Forest	H	0-2	13	17,890	
4-Feb	Coventry C	A	2-2	12	13,429	Stein (14); Spencer (33 pen)
11-Feb	Tottenham	H	1-1	13	30,812	Wise (79)
25-Feb	West Ham	H	2-1	13	21,500	Burley (67); Stein (75)
5-Mar	C Palace	H	0-0	13	14,130	
8-Mar	Man City	A	2-1		21,880	Stein (5, 81)
11-Mar	Leeds Utd	H	0-3	11	20,174	
18-Mar	Blackburn R	A	1-2	14	25,490	Stein (3)
22-Mar	QPR	A	0-1	10	15,103	
1-Apr	Newcastle	H	1-1	15	22,987	Peacock (38)
10-Apr	Wimbledon	A	1-1	14	7,022	Sinclair (35)
12-Apr	Southampton	H	0-2	15	16,738	
15-Apr	Aston Villa	H	1-0	14	17,051	Stein (30)
17-Apr	Man United	A	0-0	14	43,728	

29-Apr	QPR	H	1-0	12	21,704	Sinclair (64)
3-May	Everton	H	3-3	12	33,180	Furlong (29, 77); Hopkin (52)
6-May	Leicester	A	1-1	12	18,140	Furlong (15)
14-May	Arsenal	H	2-1	11	29,542	Furlong (21); Stein (53)

Cup-Winners' Cup

Date	Opponents	Vn	Rnd	Res	Atten	Scorers
15-Sep	Vik Zizkov	H	1R1L	4-2	22,036	Furlong (2); Sinclair (4); Rocastle (54); Wise (69)
29-Sep		A	1R2L	0-0	6,000	
	Chelsea win 4-2 on aggregate					
20-Oct	FK Austria	H	2R1L	0-0	22,560	
3-Nov		A	2R2L	1-1	25,000	Spencer (40)
	Chelsea win on away goals					
28-Feb	FC Bruges	A	QF1L	0-1	18,000	
14-Mar		H	QF2L	2-0	28,661	Stein (16); Furlong (38)
	Chelsea win 2-1 on aggregate					
6-Apr	Real	A	SF1L	0-3	35,000	
20-Apr	Zaragoza	H	SF2L	3-1	26,456	Furlong (31); Sinclair (62); Stein (86)

Real Zaragoza win 4-3 on aggregate

FA Challenge Cup

Date	Opponents	Vn	Rnd	Res	Atten	Scorers
7-Jan	Charlton Ath	H	3R	3-0	24,485	Peacock (10); Sinclair (42); Spencer (90)
28-Jan	Millwall	A	4R	0-0	18,753	
8-Feb	Millwall	H	4RR	1-1	25,516	Stein (71)
	After Extra Time – Millwall win 5-4 on penalties					

Coca-Cola League Cup

Date	Opponents	Vn	Rnd	Res	Atten	Scorers
21-Sep	Bournemouth	A	2R1L	1-0	8,974	Rocastle (26)
4-Oct	Bournemouth	H	2R2L	1-0	9,784	Peacock (63)
	Chelsea win 2-0 on aggregate					
26-Oct	West Ham	A	3R	0-1	18,815	

Chelsea – Premiership Fact File

- Chelsea's 0-0 draw at Tottenham on 23rd November meant that they became the final Premiership club not to score in a match since the start of the season. Prior to that they had scored 25 and conceded 19 goals.
- Chelsea's 2-1 win over Arsenal on the final day of the season ensured they finished above their London rivals.

Coventry City

Founded as Singer's FC, cycle manufacturers, in 1883. Joined the Birmingham and District League in 1894; in 1898 changed name to Coventry City; and in 1905 moved to the Athletic Ground, Highfield Road. Elected to Division One of the Southern League in 1908, but relegated to the Second in 1914.

Joined the Wartime Midland Section of the Football League in 1918 and elected to an expanded Second Division of the Football League for 1919-20. Founder members of the Fourth Division in 1958. Promoted to Division One for the first time in 1967 and never relegated. Premier League founder members 1992.

Ground: Highfield Road Stadium, King Richard St, Coventry, CV2 4FW
Phone: 01203-223535   News: 0891 12 11 66
Capacity: 24,021   **Pitch:** 110 yds x 75 yds
Colours: All Sky Blue   **Nickname:** Sky Blues
Directions: *From North & West:* M6 J3, after 3½ miles turn left into Eagle St and straight on to Swan Lane. *From South & East:* M1 to M45 then A45 to Ryton-on-Dunsmore where 3rd exit at roundabout is A423. After 1 mile turn right into B4110. Left at T-junction then right into Swan Lane.
Rail: Coventry

Life President: Derrick H. Robbins   **Chairman:** Bryan Richardson
Deputy-Chairman: Mike McGinnity   **Secretary:** Graham Hover
Manager: Ron Atkinson
Assistants: Mick Brown & Gordon Strachan   **Physio:** George Dalton

League History: 1919 Elected to Division 2; 1925-26 Division 3 (N); 1926-36 Division 3 (S); 1936-52 Division 2; 1952-58 Division 3 (S); 1958-59 Division 4; 1959-64 Division 3; 1964-67 Division 2; 1967-92 Division 1; 1992 – FA Premier League.

Honours: *Football League Division 2 Champions:* 1966-67; *Division 3 Champions:* 1963-64; *Division 3 (S) Champions:* 1935-36; *Runners-up:* 1933-34; *Division 4 Runners-up:* 1958-59; *FA Cup Winners:* 1986-87.

European Record: CC (0): – ; CWC (0) – ; UEFA (1): 70-71 (2)

Managers: H.R. Buckle 1909-10; Robert Wallace 1910-13; Frank Scott-Walford 1913-15; William Clayton 1917-19; H. Pollitt 1919-20; Albert Evans 1920-24; Jimmy Ker 1924-28; James McIntyre 1928-31; Harry Storer 1931-45; Dick Bayliss 1945-47; Billy Frith 1947-48; Harry Storer 1948-53; Jack

Fairbrother 1953-54; Charlie Elliott 1954-55; Jesse Carver 1955-56; Harry Warren 1956-57; Billy Firth 1957-61; Jimmy Hill 1961-67; Noel Cantwell 1967-72; Bob Dennison 1972; Joe Mercer 1972-75; Gordon Milne 1972-81; Dave Sexton 1981-83; Bobby Gould 1983-84; Don Mackay 1985-86; George Curtis 1986-87 (became MD); John Sillett 1987-90; Terry Butcher 1990-92; Don Howe 1992; *(FAPL)* Bobby Gould July 1992-93; Phil Neal Nov 1993–Feb 1995; Ron Atkinson Feb 1995-

Season 1994-95

Biggest Home Win: 4-2 v Leicester City, 25/2/95
Biggest Home Defeat: 0-4 v Tottenham Hotspur, 31/12/94
Biggest Away Win: 3-1 v Tottenham Hotspur, 9/5/95
Biggest Away Defeat: 1-5 v Sheffield Wednesday, 28/12/94
Biggest Home Attendance: 21,885 v Manchester United, 1/5/95
Smallest Home Attendance: 9,526 v Ipswich Town, 10/10/94
Average Attendance: 14,854
Last Season: *FAPL:* 16th *FA Cup:* 4th round *Coca-Cola Cup:* 5th round
Leading Scorer: Dion Dublin – 13

All Time Records

Record FAPL Win: 5-1 v Liverpool, 19/12/92
Record FAPL Defeat: 0-5 v Manchester United, 28/12/92
Record FL Win: 9-0 v Bristol C, Division 3 (S), 28/4/1934
Record FL Defeat: 2-10 v Norwich C, Division 3 (S), 15/3/1930
Record Cup Win: 7-0 v Scunthorpe U, FA Cup R1, 24/11/1934
Record Fee Received: £3.6m from Liverpool for Phil Babb, 9/94
Record Fee Paid: £2m to Manchester United for Dion Dublin, 9/94
Most FL Appearances: George Curtis, 486, 1956-70
Record Attendance (all-time): 51,455 v Wolves, Division 2. 29/4/1967
Record Attendance (FAPL): 24,410 v Manchester United 12/04/93
Highest Scorer in FAPL Season: Mick Quinn, 17, 1992-93
Most FAPL Goals in Season: 62, 1992-93

5-Year League Record

	Div.	P	W	D	L	F	A	Pts	Pos	FAC	FLC
90-91	1	38	11	11	16	42	49	44	16	4	5
91-92	1	42	11	11	20	35	44	44	19	3	4
92-93	PL	42	13	13	16	52	57	52	15	3	2
93-94	PL	42	14	14	14	43	45	56	11	3	3
94-95	PL	42	12	14	16	44	62	50	16	4	3

Summary of FAPL Appearances and Goals 1994-95

Player	Tot	Start	Sub	SNU	PS	Goals	Yel	Red
BABB … … … … 3	3	0	0	0	0	0	1	0
BOLAND … … … 12	9	3	1	3	0	1	0	
BORROWS … … 35	33	2	2	1	0	8	0	
BURROWS … … 11	11	0	0	1	0	4	0	
BUSST … … … 20	20	0	0	2	2	2	0	
COOK… … … … 34	33	1	0	3	3	4	0	
DARBY … … … 29	27	2	1	2	0	5	0	
DAVIES … … … 0	0	0	1	0	0	0	0	
DUBLIN … … … 31	31	0	0	0	13	3	0	
FILAN … … … … 2	2	0	5	0	0	0	0	
FLYNN … … … 32	32	0	3	6	4	1	0	
GILLESPIE … … … 3	2	1	1	0	0	0	1	
GOULD … … … 7	7	0	34	0	0	0	0	
HALL … … … … 5	2	3	1	0	0	1	0	
JENKINSON … … 10	9	1	3	4	1	0	0	
JONES … … … 21	16	5	5	2	2	0	0	
MARSH … … … 15	15	0	2	2	2	2	0	
MORGAN … … … 28	26	2	2	1	0	6	0	
NDLOVU … … … 30	28	2	0	2	11	0	0	
OGRIZOVIC … … 33	33	0	2	0	0	1	0	
PICKERING… … … 31	27	4	7	1	0	2	0	
PRESSLEY … … … 19	18	1	3	1	1	6	1	
QUINN … … … … 6	3	3	3	0	0	0	1	
RENNIE … … … 28	28	0	1	2	0	2	0	
RICHARDSON… … 14	14	0	0	0	0	2	0	
ROBERTSON … … 1	0	1	0	0	0	0	0	
SHERIDAN … … … 0	0	0	1	0	0	0	0	
STRACHAN … … 5	5	0	0	1	0	1	0	
WEGERLE … … … 27	22	5	2	8	3	0	0	
WILLIAMS Paul … … 5	5	0	3	0	0	0	0	
WILLIAMS John … 7	1	6	1	0	0	1	0	

OGs 2

Foundations Being Laid

The Sky Blues went into the season with a flurry of activity in the transfer market. Paul Cook moved to Highfield Road from Wolves and veteran striker Mick Harford headed south to Wimbledon. To strengthen City's attacking prowess, Dion Dublin was signed for £2m from Manchester United and the USA international Cobi Jones joined at a cost of £300,000. In October, Phil Neal bolstered the defence with the signing of Steve Pressley from Rangers.

The season began with a home draw with the Dons but four goal thrashings at Newcastle and Blackburn, followed by a home defeat against Aston Villa, paved the way for central defender Phil Babb's £3.75m transfer to Liverpool. Coventry then put together a run of five wins and two draws from nine games which took Neal's side into the top ten. Amongst those nine games was a win at Everton and a draw at home to Liverpool.

But any hopes of spending winter in the higher echelons were dashed by a potentially disastrous run of eleven winless matches. A failure to beat fellow strugglers Sheffield Wednesday, Norwich City or Chelsea added to the tension at Highfield Road which, in February, led to the departure by mutual consent of Neal. City began a recovery with a 2-0 win at Crystal Palace and, now under new manager Ron Atkinson, continued the climb to safety with victories over West Ham United and Leicester City. March proved to be a big month for the club as draws with Southampton and Aston Villa were followed by taking a point off Blackburn Rovers and an outstanding 3-2 victory at Liverpool which saw Peter Ndlovu score a memorable hat trick.

Off the pitch Atkinson, who won the March Manager of the Month award, signed David Burrows from West Ham for £1m, Gordon Strachan from Leeds United and goalkeeper John Filan on loan from Cambridge United – the following month saw the long serving Steve Ogrizovic break an ankle during a friendly. Strachan retired at the end of the season to become coach.

City were unable to sustain their form of March for the remainder of the season although the season ended with a fine 3-1 win over Tottenham at White Hart Lane, a result which ensured survival, and a goalless draw with Everton. Whilst Ndlovu continued to entertain the spectators, it was Dublin who proved to be the success story as he demonstrated his recovery from almost two years of injury problems by scoring 13 times in the Premiership.

Coventry have struggled to live up to their FA Cup win of 1987 and last season was no different as Norwich, after extra time, put them out of the FA Cup in a 4th Round replay. Two late goals accounted for West Bromwich Albion in Round Three. The Coca-Cola Cup was also well beyond their grasp as Blackburn defeated them 2-0 in the 3rd Round after Coventry had disposed of Wrexham in the previous round.

It is the appointment of Gordon Strachan though as Atkinson's assistant with a view to taking over the managerial role in the future that could have the most significant impact at a club where chnages of manager have been frequent. ∎

Results 1994-95

FA Carling Premiership

Date	Opponents	Ven	Res	Pos	Atten	Scorers
20-Aug	Wimbledon	H	1-1	10	10,962	Busst (70)
24-Aug	Newcastle	A	0-4	19	34,163	
27-Aug	Blackburn R	A	0-4	21	21,657	
29-Aug	Aston Villa	H	0-1	21	12,218	
10-Sep	QPR	A	2-2	20	11,398	Cook (22); Dublin (86)
17-Sep	Leeds Utd	H	2-1	17	15,389	Dublin (50); Cook (83)
24-Sep	Southampton	H	1-3	20	11,784	Dublin (2)
3-Oct	Leicester	A	2-2	21	19,372	Wegerle (11); Dublin (73)
10-Oct	Ipswich Tn	H	2-0	17	9,526	OG (45); Cook (76 pen)
15-Oct	Everton	A	2-0	13	28,233	Dublin (6); Wegerle (17)
23-Oct	Arsenal	A	1-2	15	31,725	Wegerle (81 pen)
29-Oct	Man City	H	1-0	13	15,804	Dublin (85)
2-Nov	C Palace	A	1-4	15	10,732	Dublin (23)
6-Nov	Chelsea	A	2-2	15	17,090	Dublin (45); Ndlovu (77)
19-Nov	Norwich C	H	1-0	13	11,885	Jones (62)
26-Nov	West Ham	H	1-0	10	17,251	Busst (58)
3-Dec	Liverpool	H	1-1	10	21,029	Flynn (57)
10-Dec	Wimbledon	A	0-2	12	7,349	
17-Dec	Newcastle	H	0-0	13	17,233	
26-Dec	N Forest	H	0-0	12	19,224	
28-Dec	Sheffield W	A	1-5	15	26,056	Ndlovu (17 pen)
31-Dec	Tottenham	H	0-4	17	19,951	
2-Jan	Man United	A	0-2	17	43,130	
14-Jan	Man City	A	0-0	17	20,632	
21-Jan	Arsenal	H	0-1	19	14,468	
25-Jan	Norwich C	A	2-2	19	14,024	Dublin (22); Jenkinson (76)
4-Feb	Chelsea	H	2-2	20	13,429	Flyn (26); OG (36)
11-Feb	C Palace	H	2-0	17	11,871	Jones (74); Dublin (86)
18-Feb	West Ham	A	2-0	13	17,556	Ndlovu (25,67)
25-Feb	Leicester Cy	H	4-2	13	20,663	Flynn (18,76); Marsh (27); Ndlovu (87)
4-Mar	Southampton	A	0-0	12	14,505	
8-Mar	Aston Villa	A	0-0	11	26,186	
11-Mar	Blackburn R	H	1-1	12	18,547	Dublin (30)
14-Mar	Liverpool	A	3-2	9	27,183	Ndlovu (21,36 pen,87)
18-Mar	Leeds Utd	A	0-3	11	29,179	
1-Apr	QPR	H	0-1	12	15,740	
15-Apr	Sheffield W	H	2-0	12	17,015	Dublin (3); Ndlovu (88)
17-Apr	N Forest	A	0-2	15	26,253	
1-May	Man United	H	2-3	16	21,885	Ndlovu (39); Pressley (72)
6-May	Ipswich Tn	A	0-2	18	12,893	

Date	Opponents	Vn		Res	Atten	Scorers
9-May	Tottenham	A	3-1	15	24,134	Ndlovu (33, 64 pen); Dublin (68)
14-May	Everton	H	0-0	16	21,814	

FA Challenge Cup

Date	Opponents	Vn	Rnd	Res	Atten	Scorers
7-Jan	WBA	H	3R	1-1	16,555	Wegerle (52 pen)
18-Jan		A	3RR	2-1	23,230	Dublin (82); Ndlovu (84)
28-Jan	Norwich C	H	4R	0-0	15,101	
8-Feb		A	4RR	1-3	14,674	Ndlovu (32)
			after extra time			

Coca-Cola League Cup

Date	Opponents	Vn	Rnd	Res	Atten	Scorers
20-Sep	Wrexham	A	2R1L	2-1	5,286	Darby (37); Flynn (77)
5-Oct		H	2R2L	3-2	8,561	Dublin (17,60); Wegerle (64)
	Coventry City win 5-3 on aggregate					
26-Oct	Blackburn R	A	3R	0-2	14,538	

Coventry – Premiership Fact File

- Dion Dublin scored an equalisng goal for Coventry just four minutes from the end of his debut against QPR on 10th September at Loftus Road.
- Another Dublin goal helped City record their first win of the season on 17th September over Leeds United.
- Dublin scored eight goals in his first 10 games for the Sky Blues.
- Ron Atkinson won his first game in charge as manager on 18th February, beating West Ham 2-0 at Highfield Road.

Everton

The cricket team of St. Domingo's Church turned to football around 1878. Playing in Stanley Park, in late 1879 changed name to Everton FC, the name of the district to the west of the park.

Moved to a field at Priory Road in 1882 and then, in 1884, moved to a site in Anfield Road. As one of the country's leading teams, became founder members of the Football League in 1888. Moved to Goodison Park, a field on the north side of Stanley Park, in 1892 following a dispute with the ground's landlord. Premier League founder members 1992.

Ground: Goodison Park, Liverpool, L4 4EL
Phone: 0151 521 2020   **Box Office:** 0151 523 6666
Dial-a-Seat: 0151 525 1231   **Info:** 0891 12 11 99
Colours: Royal Blue, White, Blue   **Nickname:** The Toffees
Capacity: 40,160   **Pitch:** 112 yds x 78 yds
Radio Everton: 1602AM
Directions: *From North:* M6 J8 take A58 to A580 and follow into Walton Hall Ave. *From South & East:* M6 J21A to M62, turn right into Queen's Drive then, after 4 miles, left into Walton Hall Ave. *From West:* M53 through Wallasey Tunnel, follow signs for Preston on A580. Walton Hall Ave is signposted.   **Rail:** Liverpool Lime Street

Chairman: Peter Johnson   **Secretary:** Michael Dunford
Manager: Joe Royle
Physio: Les Helm

League History: 1888 Founder Member of the Football League; 1930-31 Division 2; 1931-51 Division 1; 1951-54 Division 2; 1954-92 Division 1; 1992-FA Premier League.

Honours: *Football League Division 1 Champions:* 1890-91, 1914-15, 1927-28, 1931-32, 1938-39, 1962-63, 1969-70, 1984-85, 1986-87; *Runners-up:* 1889-90, 1894-95, 1901-02, 1904-05, 1908-09, 1911-12, 1985-86; *Division 2 Champions:* 1930-31; *Runners-up:* 1953-54. *FA Cup Winners:* 1906, 1933, 1966, 1984, 1995; *Runners-up:* 1893, 1897, 1907, 1968, 1985, 1986, 1989. *Football League Cup Runners-up:* 1976-77, 1983-84. *League Super Cup Runners-up:* 1986. *Cup-Winners' Cup Winners:* 1984-85; *Simod Cup Runners-up:* 1989. *Zenith Data Systems Cup Runners-up:* 1991.

European Record: CC (2): 63-64(1), 70-71(QF); CWC (3): 66-67(2), 84-85(W), 95-96 (–). UEFA (6): 62-63(1), 64-65(3), 65-66(2), 75-76(1), 78-79(2), 79-80(1).

Managers: W.E. Barclay 1888-89; Dick Molyneux 1889-1901; William C. Cuff 1901-18; W.J. Sawyer 1918-19; Thomas H. McIntosh 1919-35; Theo Kelly 1936-48; Cliff Britton 1948-56; Ian Buchan 1956-58; Johnny Carey 1958-61; Harry Catterick 1961-73; Billy Bingham 1973-77; Gordon Lee 1977-81; Howard Kendall 1981-87; Colin Harvey 1987-90; (FAPL) Howard Kendall Nov 1990-93; Mike Walker Jan 1993-Nov 1994; Joe Royle Nov 1994-.

Season 1994-95

Biggest Home Win: 4-1 v Ipswich Town, 31/12/94
Biggest Home Defeat: 1-4 v Sheffield Wednesday, 26/12/94
Biggest Away Win: 3-2 v QPR, 18/3/95
Biggest Away Defeat: 0-4 v Manchester City, 27/8/95
Biggest Home Attendance: 40,011 v Manchester United, 25/2/95
Smallest Home Attendance: 23,293 v Norwich City, 4/2/95
Average Attendance: 28,849
Last Season: *PL:* 15th *FA Cup:* Winners *Coca-Cola Cup:* 2nd round
Leading Scorer: Paul Rideout – 14

All-time Records

Record FAPL Win: 6-2 v Swindon Town, 15/1/94
Record FAPL Defeat: 1-5 v Norwich City 25/9/93; Sheffield Wnd 2/4/94
Record FL Win: 9-1 v Manchester City, Division 1, 3/9/1906;
Plymouth Argyle, Division 2, 27/12/1930
Record FL Defeat: 4-10 v Tottenham H, Division 1, 11/10/1958
Record Cup Win: 11-2 v Derby County, FA Cup R1, 18/1/1890
Record Fee Received: £2.75m from Barcelona for Gary Lineker, 7/86
Record Fee Paid: £5m to Manchester United for Andrei Kanchelskis 7/95
Most FL Appearances: Ted Sagar, 465, 1929-53
Record Attendance (all-time): 78,299 v Liverpool, Division 1, 18/9/1948
Record Attendance (FAPL): 40,011 v Manchester United, 25/2/95
Highest Scorer in FAPL season: Tony Cottee, 16, 1993-94
Most FAPL Goals in Season: 53, 1992-93
Most FAPL Points in Season: 53, 1992-93

5-Year League Record

	Div.	P	W	D	L	F	A	Pts	Pos	FAC	FLC
90-91	1	38	13	12	13	50	46	51	9	6	3
91-92	1	42	13	14	15	52	51	53	12	4	4
92-93	PL	42	15	8	19	53	55	53	13	3	4
93-94	PL	42	12	8	22	42	63	44	17	3	4
94-95	PL	42	11	17	14	44	51	50	15	W	2

Summary of FAPL Appearances and Goals 1994-95

Player	Tot	Start	Sub	SNU	PS	Goals	Yel	Red
ABLETT	26	26	0	0	3	4	3	0
AMOKACHI ...	18	17	1	2	4	4	2	0
ANGELL	4	3	1	4	1	0	2	0
BARLOW ...	11	7	4	11	1	2	3	1
BARRETT ...	17	17	0	0	0	0	1	1
BURROWS	19	19	0	0	3	0	7	0
COTTEE ...	3	3	0	0	1	0	0	0
DURRANT ...	5	4	1	0	1	0	0	0
EBBRELL	26	26	0	0	2	0	10	0
FERGUSON... ...	23	22	1	0	1	7	2	2
GRANT ...	5	1	4	0	1	0	0	0
HINCHCLIFFE...	29	28	1	2	2	2	2	0
HOLMES	1	1	0	1	0	0	0	0
HORNE	31	31	0	0	0	0	5	1
JACKSON ...	29	26	3	6	2	0	3	0
KEARTON ...	1	1	0	32	0	0	1	0
LIMPAR ...	27	19	8	5	5	2	6	0
PARKINSON ...	34	32	2	2	6	0	6	0
REEVES	0	0	0	9	0	0	0	0
RIDEOUT ...	29	25	4	1	2	14	1	0
ROWETT ...	2	2	0	1	0	0	1	0
SAMWAYS	19	14	5	1	2	1	1	1
SNODIN	3	2	1	0	0	0	1	0
SOUTHALL... ...	41	41	0	0	0	0	3	0
SPEAR	0	0	0	1	0	0	0	0
STUART ...	28	20	8	3	3	3	0	0
UNSWORTH ...	38	37	1	0	3	3	7	0
WATSON	38	38	0	0	2	2	5	0

OGs 1

Royle Flush in Cup

The Blue corner of Stanley Park was staring relegation squarely in the eyes at the end of October with Mike Walker's side rooted to the foot of the table after a dozen Premiership games without a win and just four points in the bag. Despite investing £3m in Nigerian international Daniel Amokachi, Everton endured a run of four games without a goal and suffered heavy defeats at Manchester City and Blackburn Rovers. The Coca-Cola Cup provided no solace for Walker as The Toffees fell at the first hurdle to Division One side Portsmouth. The manager sought to arrest the slide by swapping David Burrows for Tony Cottee and signing Iain Durrant and Duncan Ferguson on loan from Rangers. Ferguson, despite his tarnished disciplinary record, was an instant hit with the supporters and in December completed a £4m move.

November proved to be the turning point in Everton's season. The month opened with a 1-0 win over Burrows' former club West Ham and just when it seemed as though the corner may have been turned Walker was sacked after less than ten months at Goodison Park. Walker's exit paved the way for the return of the prodigal son Joe Royle. A 2-0 home win over Liverpool in Royle's first home match lifted the club off the foot of the table and, with an eight match unbeaten run, Everton edged their way out of the bottom four. A new club record of seven successive clean sheets was set before Sheffield Wednesday devastated that statistic with a 4-1 win at Goodison on Boxing Day. The year ended with a 2-1 win over relegation bound Ipswich Town but a failure to win two consecutive matches from the turn of the year onwards kept the club perilously close to the relegation places. Even so, good wins were recorded over Manchester United and Newcastle United before a 1-0 win at Ipswich in the final week of the season secured Everton's presence in the Premiership.

Upon taking charge at Goodison, Royle's main task was to ensure Premiership survival, the prospect of honours was at least a full season away. With the Coca-Cola Cup long since gone Everton turned their attentions to the FA Cup in January and saw off Derby County with an Andy Hinchcliffe goal. Hinchcliffe earned a reputation for supplying the deadliest corner kicks in the country. Matt Jackson's first goal in nearly two years accounted for Bristol City at Ashton Gate before the second half of East Anglia's relegated duo, Norwich City, were thrashed 5-0 at Goodison in Round Five – five different scorers getting in on the demolition act. Veteran defender Dave Watson put Everton through to a record breaking 23rd semi final when his second half goal defeated Newcastle. With a powerful performance, and two late goals from substitute Amokachi, Everton hammered Tottenham 4-1 in the semi final at Elland Road. The Final itself against Manchester United may not have been the most memorable ever but Royle's side defied the bookies and ended a remarkable season with the FA Cup in their boardroom thanks to a first half goal from Paul Rideout. ■

Results 1994-95

FA Carling Premiership

Date	Opponents	Ven	Res	Pos	Atten	Scorers
20-Aug	Aston Villa	H	2-2	8	35,544	Stuart (22); Rideout (70)
24-Aug	Tottenham	A	1-2	15	24,553	Rideout (46)
27-Aug	Man City	A	0-4	19	19,867	
30-Aug	N Forest	H	1-2	20	26,689	Rideout (68)
10-Sep	Blackburn R	A	0-3	22	26,538	
17-Sep	QPR	H	2-2	22	27,285	Amokachi (10); Rideout (24)
24-Sep	Leicester C	H	1-1	22	28,003	Ablett (50)
1-Oct	Man United	A	0-2	22	43,803	
8-Oct	Southampton	A	0-2	22	15,163	
15-Oct	Coventry C	H	0-2	22	28,233	
22-Oct	C Palace	A	0-1	22	14,505	
29-Oct	Arsenal	H	1-1	22	32,003	Unsworth (14)
1-Nov	West Ham	H	1-0	22	28,338	Ablett (54)
5-Nov	Norwich C	A	0-0	22	18,377	
21-Nov	Liverpool	H	2-0	20	39,866	Ferguson (56); Rideout (89)
26-Nov	Chelsea	A	1-0	19	28,115	Rideout (39)
5-Dec	Leeds Utd	H	3-0	18	25,897	Rideout (7); Ferguson (58); Unsworth (66 pen)
10-Dec	Aston Villa	A	0-0	18	29,678	
17-Dec	Tottenham	H	0-0	19	32,809	
26-Dec	Sheffield W	H	1-4	19	37,080	Ferguson (36)
31-Dec	Ipswich Tn	H	4-1	19	25,659	Ferguson (27); Rideout (70,73); Watson (89)
2-Jan	Wimbledon	A	1-2	20	9,506	Rideout (16)
14-Jan	Arsenal	A	1-1	20	34,743	Watson (13)
21-Jan	C Palace	H	3-1	18	23,733	Ferguson (2,87); Rideout (53)
24-Jan	Liverpool	A	0-0	16	39,505	
1-Feb	Newcastle	A	0-2	18	34,465	
4-Feb	Norwich C	H	2-1	18	23,293	Stuart (42); Rideout (65)
13-Feb	West Ham	A	2-2	17	21,081	Rideout (44); Limpar (79)
22-Feb	Leeds Utd	A	0-1	18	30,793	
25-Feb	Man United	H	1-0	16	40,011	Ferguson (58)
4-Mar	Leicester City	A	2-2	17	20,447	Limpar (5); Samways (45)
8-Mar	N Forest	A	1-2	17	24,526	Barlow (45)
15-Mar	Man City	H	1-1	17	28,485	Unsworth (80 pen)
18-Mar	QPR	H	3-2	17	14,488	Barlow (58); OG (69); Hinchcliffe (90)
1-Apr	Blackburn R	H	1-2	17	37,905	Stuart (23)
14-Apr	Newcastle	H	2-0	17	34,811	Amokachi (23,49)
17-Apr	Sheffield W	A	0-0	17	27,880	
29-Apr	Wimbledon	H	0-0	16	33,063	

Date	Opponents	Vn	Res		Atten	Scorers
3-May	Chelsea	H	3-3	17	33,180	Hinchcliffe (39); Ablett(50); Amokachi (70)
6-May	Southampton	H	0-0	17	36,840	
9-May	Ipswich	A	1-0	15	14,951	Rideout (49)
14-May	Coventry C	A	0-0	15	21,814	

FA Challenge Cup

Date	Opponents	Vn	Rnd	Res	Atten	Scorers
7-Jan	Derby County	H	3R	1-0	29,406	Hinchcliffe (76)
29-Jan	Bristol City	A	4R	1-0	19,816	Jackson (78)
18-Feb	Norwich C	H	5R	5-0	31,616	Limpar (6); Parkinson (23); Rideout (56); Ferguson (63); Stuart (88)
12-Mar	Newcastle	H	QF	1-0	35,203	Watson (65)
9-Apr	Tottenham *(at Elland Road)*		SF	4-1	38,226	Jackson (35); Stuart (55); Amokachi (82,90)
20-May	Man United *(at Wembley)*		F	1-0	79,592	Rideout (30)

Coca-Cola League Cup

Date	Opponents	Vn	Rnd	Res	Atten	Scorers
20-Sep	Portsmouth	H	2R1L	2-3	14,043	Samways (57); Stuart (72 pen)
5-Oct	Portsmouth *Portsmouth win 4-3 on aggregate*	A	2R2L	1-1	13,605	Watson (17)

Everton – Premiership Fact File

- Daniel Amokachi scored on his home debut against QPR on 17th September.
- Everton had to wait until 1st November to record their first win of the season. It came in their 13th game with a 1-0 win over West Ham United. It meant they were the last club in England to record a league win for the season.
- Joe Royle took over the club when they were bottom of the Premiership and immediately secured a 2-0 win over Liverpool in the 151st Merseyside encounter.
- Everton set a new club record with seven successive clean sheets starting with the win over West Ham and ending with a 1-2 defeat by Sheffield Wednesday on Boxing Day.

Leeds United

Leeds City, founded in 1904, took over the Elland Road ground of the defunct Holbeck Club and in 1905 gained a Football League Division Two place. The club was, however, expelled in 1919 for disciplinary reasons associated with payments to players during the War. The club closed down.

Leeds United FC, a new professional club, emerged the same year and competed in the Midland League. The club was elected to Football League Division Two for season 1920-21. The club has subsequently never been out of the top two divisions. Premier League founder member 1992.

Ground: Elland Road, Leeds, LS11 0ES
Phone: 0113 271 6037 **Nickname:** United
Colours: All White
Capacity: 39,704 **Pitch:** 117 yds x 76 yds
Directions: *From North & East:* A58, A61, A63 or A64 into city centre and then onto M621. Leave Motorway after 1½ miles onto A643 and Elland Rd. *From West:* take M62 to M621 then as above. *From South:* M1 then M621 then as above. **Rail:** Leeds City

President: The Right Hon. The Earl of Harewood LLD
Chairman: Leslie Silver OBE **Vice-Chairman:** Peter Gilman
Managing Director: Bill Fotherby **Secretary:** Nigel Pleasants
Manager: Howard Wilkinson
First Team Coaches: Peter Gunby, Paul Hart, Mike Hennigan
Physios: Alan Sutton, Geoff Ladley

League History: 1920 Elected to Division 2; 1924-27 Division 1; 1927-28 Division 2; 1928-31 Division 1; 1931-32 Division 2; 1932-47 Division 1; 1947-56 Division 2; 1956-60 Division 1; 1960-64 Division 2; 1964-82 Division 1; 1982-90 Division 2; 1990-92 Division 1; 1992- FA Premier League.

Honours: *Football League Division 1 Champions:* 1968-69, 1973-74, 1991-92; *Runners-up:* 1964-65, 1965-66, 1969-70, 1970-71, 1971-72; *Division 2 Champions:* 1923-24, 1963-64, 1989-90; *Runners-up:* 1927-28, 1931-32, 1955-56. *FA Cup Winners:* 1971-72; *Runners-up:* 1964-65, 1969-70, 1972-73. *Football League Cup Winners:* 1967-68. *Champions' Cup Runners-up:* 1974-75; *Cup-Winners' Cup Runners-up:* 1972-73; *UEFA Cup Winners:* 1967-68, 1970-71; *Runners-up:* 1966-67.

European Record: CC (3): 69-70(SF), 74-75(F), 92-93(2). CWC (1): 72-73 (F); UEFA (7): 65-66(SF), 66-67(F), 67-68(W), 68-69(QF), 70-71(W), 71-72(1), 73-74(3), 79-80(2).

Managers: Dick Ray 1919-20; Arthur Fairclough 1920-27; Dick Ray 1927-35; Bill Hampson 1935-47; Willis Edwards 1947-48; Major Frank Buckley 1948-53; Raich Carter 1953-58; Bill Lambton 1958-59; Jack Taylor 1959-61; Don Revie 1961-74; Brian Clough 1974; Jimmy Armfield 1974-78; Jock Stein 1978; Jimmy Adamson 1978-80; Allan Clarke 1980-82; Eddie Gray 1982-85; Billy Bremner 1985-88; (FAPL) Howard Wilkinson October 1988 -

Season 1994-95
Biggest Home Win: 4-0 v QPR 23/1/95; Ipswich Town 5/4/95
Biggest Home Defeat: 0-2 v Liverpool, 31/12/94
Biggest Away Win: 3-0 v Chelsea, 11/3/95
Biggest Away Defeat: 0-3 v Everton 5/12/95; Nottingham Forest 22/3/95
Biggest Home Attendance: 39,396 v Manchester United, 11/9/94
Smallest Home Attendance: 27,284 v Wimbledon, 5/11/94
Average Attendance: 31,089
Last Season: *PL:* 5th *FA Cup:* 5th round *Coca-Cola Cup:* 2nd round
Leading Scorer: Tony Yeboah – 12

All-time Record
Record FAPL Win: 5-0 v Tottenham H, 25/8/92; Swindon Town, 7/5/94
Record FAPL Defeat: 0-4 v Manchester C, 7/11/92; Tottenham H, 20/2/93; Norwich City, 21/8/93
Record FL Win: 8-0 v Leicester City, Division 1, 7/4/1934
Record FL Defeat: 1-8 v Stoke City, Division 1, 27/8/1934
Record Cup Win: 10-0 v Lyn (Oslo), European Cup, R1 1st leg, 17/9/1969
Record Fee Received: £2.75 from Blackburn R. for David Batty, 10/1993
Record Fee Paid: £3.4m to Eintracht Frankfurt for Tony Yeboah, 1/1995
Most FL Appearances: Jack Charlton, 629, 1953-73
Record Attendance (all-time): 57,892 v Sunderland, FA Cup 5R replay, 15/3/1967
Record Attendance (FAPL): 41,125 v Manchester United, 27/4/94
Highest Scorer in FAPL Season: Rod Wallace, 17, 1993-94
Most FAPL Goals in Season: 65, 1993-94
Most FAPL Points in Season: 73, 1994-95

5-Year League Record

	Div.	P	W	D	L	F	A	Pts	Pos	FAC	FLC
90-91	1	38	19	7	12	65	47	64	4	4	SF
91-92	1	42	21	16	4	74	37	82	1	3	5
92-93	PL	42	12	15	15	57	62	51	17	4	3
93-94	PL	42	18	16	8	65	39	70	5	4	2
94-95	PL	42	20	13	9	59	38	73	5	5	2

Summary of FAPL Appearances and Goals 1994-95

Player	Tot	Start	Sub	SNU	PS	Goals	Yel	Red
BEENEY	0	0	0	42	0	0	0	0
COUZENS	4	2	2	1	0	0	1	0
DEANE	35	33	2	0	2	9	9	0
DORIGO	28	28	0	0	2	0	1	0
FAIRCLOUGH	5	1	4	2	0	0	0	0
KELLY	42	42	0	0	3	0	6	0
LUKIC	42	42	0	0	0	0	0	0
MASINGA	22	15	7	3	8	5	1	0
McALLISTER	41	41	0	0	1	6	1	0
PALMER	39	39	0	0	0	3	7	0
PEMBERTON	27	22	5	4	0	0	7	0
RADEBE	12	9	3	8	5	0	2	0
SHARP	2	0	2	1	0	0	0	0
SPEED	39	39	0	0	1	3	5	0
STRACHAN	6	5	1	1	2	0	0	0
TINKLER	3	3	0	5	1	0	0	0
WALLACE	32	30	2	0	7	4	5	0
WETHERALL	38	38	0	0	2	3	6	0
WHELAN	23	18	5	5	3	7	3	0
WHITE	23	18	5	2	4	3	3	0
WORTHINGTON	27	21	6	5	2	1	3	0
YEBOAH	18	16	2	1	3	12	0	0

OGs 3

Fifth Again as Leeds Threaten Better

Howard Wilkinson, at the start of his sixth season at Elland Road, was aware he needed to strengthen United's attacking options and was linked with various big names before landing Tony Yeboah in January for £3.4m. The Ghanian responded well with 12 Premiership goals but, with a total of 59 goals, the club were the lowest scorers of the sides to finish in the top eight.

The season began with four games against London sides. Two wins, a draw and a home defeat by Chelsea after leading 2-0 set the tone for a season that was at first steady and highly promising from the turn of the year.

In September, good home wins over the two Manchester clubs came either side of disappointing results at Coventry and Sheffield Wednesday. Defeats at the likes of Norwich and Ipswich deflected from good wins over Nottingham Forest, Arsenal and QPR, the latter by 4-0. Leeds went into the New Year in eighth position following a 2-0 home defeat by Liverpool, but of the next 21 league games just two ended in defeat. The run began with four draws in five games but a run of nine wins in twelve games paved the way for a draw at Tottenham on the last day of the season to clinch a place in Europe. Along the way struggling sides Chelsea, Leicester, Coventry and Ipswich were all convincingly beaten and an injury time goal at home to Norwich condemned the visitors to relegation. Leeds' form during April is what offers most hope that a serious title challenge can be launched. A Brian Deane goal ensured their first win at Anfield for 23 years, Newcastle were beaten at St. James Park and both Manchester United and Blackburn Rovers were held to draws.

Yeboah justified his large fee with 12 goals in just 18 games which included Leeds' only league hat-trick of the season, but Deane again struggled to live up to the form of earlier in his career and ended the season with nine league goals to his credit.

During the season, Wilkinson dispensed with the services of Steve Hodge, Frank Stradli and Gordon Strachan but extended the contract of skipper Gary McAllister to the end of the century. Leeds finished the season as the only side not to have a player sent–off in the Premiership.

Leeds have not won the Coca-cola Cup since 1968 and that poor record was easily maintained this time round as United suffered an embarrassing defeat at Elland Road against Division Three Mansfield Town, a draw in the return leg could not prevent a major cup upset. The FA Cup saw another Third Division side pose problems with Leeds requiring an extra time hat–trick from Phil Masinga to see off Walsall 5-2. Leeds were just three minutes from defeat at Walsall before David Wetherall popped up with a late face–saving equaliser. Masinga was again on target in the next round as Oldham Athletic were despatched 3-2 at Elland Road. Leeds found themselves two down in just four minutes at Old Trafford in Round Five before eventually bowing out of the competition 3-1. ■

Results 1994-95

FA Carling Premiership

Date	Opponents	Ven	Res	Pos	Atten	Scorers
20-Aug	West Ham	A	0-0	13	18,610	
23-Aug	Arsenal	H	1-0	9	34,218	Whelan (89)
27-Aug	Chelsea	H	2-3	10	32,212	Masinga (3); Whelan (18)
30-Aug	C Palace	A	2-1	6	13,654	White (17); Whelan (63)
11-Sep	Man United	H	2-1	6	39,396	Wetherall (12); Deane (48)
17-Sep	Coventry C	A	1-2	6	15,389	Speed (85)
26-Sep	Sheffield W	A	1-1	8	23,227	McAllister (13)
1-Oct	Man City	H	2-0	6	30,938	Whelan (27,90)
8-Oct	Norwich	A	1-2	9	17,390	Wallace (89)
15-Oct	Tottenham	H	1-1	9	39,224	Deane (62)
24-Oct	Leicester	H	2-1	9	28,547	McAllister (35), Whelan (67)
29-Oct	Southampton	A	3-1	6	15,202	OG (54); Wallace (84,90)
1-Nov	Ipswich Tn	A	0-2	6	15,956	
5-Nov	Wimbledon	H	3-1	6	27,284	Wetherall (13); Speed (38); White (45)
19-Nov	QPR	A	2-3	6	17,416	OG (55); Deane (72)
26-Nov	N Forest	H	1-0	6	38,191	Whelan (60)
5-Dec	Everton	A	0-3	8	25,897	
10-Dec	West Ham	H	2-2	7	28,987	Worthington (2); Deane (24)
17-Dec	Arsenal	A	1-3	6	38,098	Masinga (24,85); Deane (88)
26-Dec	Newcastle	H	0-0	6	39,337	
31-Dec	Liverpool	A	0-2	8	38,563	
2-Jan	Aston Villa	A	0-0	7	35,038	
14-Jan	Southampton	H	0-0	8	28,953	
23-Jan	QPR	H	4-0	7	28,780	Masinga (30,64); White (33); Deane (83)
1-Feb	Blackburn R	A	1-1	7	28,561	McAllister (85 pen)
4-Feb	Wimbledon	A	0-0	7	10,211	
22-Feb	Everton	H	1-0	7	30,793	Yeboah (81)
25-Feb	Man City	A	0-0	6	22,892	
4-Mar	Sheffield W	H	0-1	7	33,750	
11-Mar	Chelsea	A	3-0	7	20,174	Yeboah (23,61); McAllister (25)
15-Mar	Leicester C	A	3-1	6	20,068	Yeboah (32,59); Palmer (78)
18-Mar	Coventry C	H	3-0	6	29,179	Yeboah (39); OG (50); Wallace (60)
22-Mar	N Forest	A	0-3	6	26,299	
2-Apr	Man United	A	0-0	6	43,712	
5-Apr	Ipswich Tn	H	4-0	6	28,600	Yeboah (3,34,45); Speed (31)
9-Apr	Liverpool	A	1-0	6	37,454	Deane (29)
15-Apr	Blackburn R	H	1-1	6	39,426	Deane (90)

17-Apr	Newcastle	A	1-2	6	35,626	McAllister (25 pen);
						Yeboah (31)
29-Apr	Aston Villa	H	1-0	6	32,955	Palmer (89)
6-May	Norwich C	H	2-1	6	31,982	McAllister (79pen);
						Palmer (90)
9-May	C Palace	H	3-1	5	30,942	Yeboah (6,59);
						Wetherall (41)
14-May	Tottenham	A	1-1	5	33,040	Deane (67)

FA Challenge Cup

Date	Opponents	Vn	Rnd	Res	Atten	Scorers
7-Jan	Walsall	A	3R	1-1	8,619	Wetherall (87)
17-Mar	Walsall	H	3RR	5-2	17,881	Deane (8); Wetherall (37);
	after extra time					Masinga (105,107,114)
28-Jan	Oldham Ath	H	4R	3-2	25,010	White (81); Palmer (43);
						Masinga (66)
19-Feb	Man United	A	5R	1-3	42,744	Yeboah (52)

Coca-Cola League Cup

Date	Opponents	Vn	Rnd	Res	Atten	Scorers
21-Sep	Mansfield Tn	H	2R1L	0-1	7,844	
4-Oct		A	2R2L	0-0	7,227	
	Mansfield Town win 1-0 on aggregate					

Leeds – Premiership Fact File

- Leeds' draw with West Ham United on the opening day of the 1994-95 season was the only goalless draw in the Premiership on that day.
- Despite the new stricter rules, Leeds United didn't have a player sent off in a Premiership match during the season.
- Carlton Palmer's goal in the last seconds of their match with Norwich City at Elland Road, related the Canaries to the First Division.
- Spare a thought for substitute goalkeeper Mark Beeney. He was cover for John Lukic in every Premiership game but failed to make a single appearance!

Liverpool

Following a dispute between Everton and its Anfield landlord a new club, Liverpool AFC, was formed in 1892 by the landlord, former Everton committee-man John Houlding, with its headquarters at Anfield. An application for Football League membership was rejected without being put to the vote. Instead the team joined the Lancashire League and immediately won the championship.

After that one campaign, when the Liverpool Cup was won but there was early FA Cup elimination, Liverpool was selected to fill one of two vacancies in an expanded Football League Second Division in 1893. Premier League founder members 1992.

Ground: Anfield Road, Liverpool L4 0TH
Phone: 0151-263 2361　　　　**Match Info:** 0151-260 9999 (24 hrs)
News: 8091- 12 11 84　　　　**Box Office:** 0151-263 5727
Capacity: 44,243　　　　**Pitch:** 110 yds x 75 yds
Colours: All Red/White Trim　　　　**Nickname:** Reds or Pool
Directions: *From North:* M6 J8, follow A58 to Walton Hall Ave and pass Stanley Park then turn left into Anfield Rd. *From South & East:* to end of M62 and right into Queens Drive (A5058). Left after 3 miles into Utting Ave and right after another mile into Anfield Rd. *From West:* M53 through Wallasey Tunnel, follow signs for Preston then turn into Walton Hall Ave and right into Anfield Rd before Stanley Park.　　**Rail:** Liverpool Lime Street

Chairman: D.R. Moores
Chief Executive/General Secretary: Peter Robinson
Manager: Roy Evans　　　　**Coach:** Ronny Moran

League History: 1893 Elected to Division 2; 1894-95 Division 1; 1895-96 Division 2; 1896-1904 Division 1; 1904-05 Division 2; 1905-54 Division 1; 1954-62 Division 2; 1962-92 Division 1; 1992- FA Premier League.

Honours: *Football League Division 1 Champions:* 1900-01, 1905-06, 1921-22, 1922-23, 1946-47, 1963-64, 1965-66, 1972-73, 1975-76, 1976-77, 1978-79, 1979-80, 1981-82, 1982-83, 1983-84, 1985-86, 1987-88, 1989-90; *Runners-up:* 1898-99, 1909-10, 1968-69, 1973-74, 1974-75, 1977-78, 1984-85, 1986-87, 1988-89, 1990-91; *Division 2 Champions:* 1893-94, 1895-96, 1904-05, 1961-62. *FA Cup Winners:* 1965, 1974, 1986, 1989, 1992; *Runners-up:* 1914, 1950, 1971, 1977, 1988; *Football League Cup Winners:* 1981, 1982, 1983, 1984, 1995; *Runners-up:* 1977-78, 1986-87; *League Super Cup Winners:* 1985-86; *Champions' Cup Winners:* 1976-77; 1977-78, 1980-81;

1983-84; *Runners-up:* 1984-85; *Cup-Winners' Cup Runners-up:* 1965-66;
UEFA Cup Winners: 1972-73, 1975-76; *European Super Cup Winners:* 1977;
Runners-up: 1984; *World Club Championship Runners-up:* 1981, 1984.

European Record: CC (12): 64-65(SF), 66-67(2), 73-74(2), 76-77(W), 77-
78 (W), 78-79(1), 79-80(1), 80-81 (W), 81-82(QF), 82-83(QF), 83-84(W),
84-85 (F); CWC (4): 65-66 (F), 71-72(2), 74-75(2), 92-93(2); UEFA (8) 67-
68(3), 68-69(1), 69-70(2), 70-71(SF), 72-73 (W), 75-76 (W), 91-92(QF), 94-
95 (–).

Managers: W.E. Barclay 1892-96; Tom Watson 1896-1915; David
Ashworth 1920-22; Matt McQueen 1923-28; George Patterson 1928-36
(continued as secretary); George Kay 1936-51; Don Welsh 1951-56; Phil
Taylor 1956-59; Bill Shankly 1959-74; Bob Paisley 1974-83; Joe Fagan
1983-85; Kenny Dalglish 1985-91; Graeme Souness 1991-94; Roy Evans
January 1994-

Season 1994-95
Biggest Home Win: 4-0 v Norwich City, 2/1/95
Biggest Home Defeat: 2-3 v Coventry City, 14/3/95
Biggest Away Win: 6-1 v Crystal Palace, 20/8/94
Biggest Away Defeat: 0-3 v West Ham United, 10/5/95
Biggest Home Attendance: 40,014 v Blackburn Rovers, 14/5/95
Smallest Home Attendance: 27,183 v Coventry City, 14/3/95
Average Attendance: 34,181
Last Season: *FAPL:* 4th *FA Cup:* Quarter Final *Coca-Cola Cup:* Winners
Leading Scorer: Robbie Fowler – 25

All-time Record
Record FAPL Win: 6-1 v Crystal Palace, away, 20/8/94
Record FAPL Defeat: 1-5 v Coventry City, away, 19/12/92
Record FL Win: 10-1 v Rotherham Town, Division 2, 18/2/1896 *and*
         9-0 v Crystal Palace, Division 1, 12/9/89
Record FL Defeat: 1-9 v Birmingham C, Division 2, 11/12/1954
Record Cup Win: 11-0 v Stromsgodset Drammen, CWC 1R1L, 17/9/1974
Record Fee Received: £3.2m from Juventus for Ian Rush, 6/1986
Record Fee Paid: £8.5m to Nottingham Forest for Stan Collymore, 6/95
Most FL Appearances: Ian Callaghan, 640, 1960-78
Record Attendance (all-time): 61,905 v Wolves, FA Cup R4, 2/2/1952
Record Attendance (FAPL): 44,619 v Everton, 20/3/93
Highest Scorer in FAPL Season: Robbie Fowler, 25 1994/95
Most FAPL Goals in Season: 65, 1994-95
Most FAPL Points in Season: 74, 1994-95

5-Year League Record

	Div.	P	W	D	L	F	A	Pts	Pos	FAC	FLC
90-91	1	38	23	7	8	77	40	76	2	5	3
91-92	1	42	16	16	10	47	40	64	6	W	4
92-93	PL	42	16	11	15	62	55	59	6	3	4
93-94	PL	42	17	9	16	59	55	60	8	3	4
94-95	PL	42	21	11	10	65	37	74	4	QF	W

Summary of FAPL Appearances and Goals 1994-95

Player	Tot	Start	Sub	SNU	PS	Goals	Yel	Red
BABB … … … … …	34	33	1	1	1	0	3	1
BARNES … … … …	38	38	0	0	3	0	0	0
BJORNEBYE … …	31	31	0	0	7	0	5	0
CHAMBERLAIN …	0	0	0	5	0	0	0	0
CLOUGH … … …	10	3	7	15	0	0	0	0
FOWLER… … … …	42	42	0	0	4	25	4	0
HARKNESS … … …	8	8	0	3	0	1	2	0
JAMES … … … …	42	42	0	0	0	0	0	0
JONES Rob … …	31	31	0	0	2	0	5	0
JONES Lee … … …	1	0	1	2	0	0	0	0
KENNEDY … … …	6	4	2	0	1	0	1	0
MATTEO … … …	7	2	5	2	2	0	0	0
McMANAMAN …	40	40	0	0	1	7	5	0
MOLBY … … …	14	12	2	2	3	2	0	0
NICOL … … … …	4	4	0	1	0	0	0	0
PRUDHOE … … …	0	0	0	7	0	0	0	0
REDKNAPP… … …	40	36	4	2	1	3	5	0
RUDDOCK … … …	37	37	0	0	1	2	5	0
RUSH … … … … …	36	36	0	0	5	12	1	0
SCALES … … … …	35	35	0	0	3	2	3	0
STENSGAARD … …	0	0	0	20	0	0	0	0
STEWART … … …	0	0	0	1	0	0	0	0
THOMAS … … …	23	16	7	6	1	0	2	0
WALTERS … … …	17	7	10	7	5	0	1	0
WARNER … … … …	0	0	0	10	0	0	0	0
WRIGHT … … … …	6	5	1	2	0	0	1	0

OGs 4

Kop Back on Course

Are Liverpool on the way back? By most clubs' standards they have never been away but with the Coca-Cola Cup stashed away in the trophy cabinet, and their highest league position for four years behind them, it does seem that Roy Evans is moving the Reds towards a new era of greatness.

Liverpool started the campaign in irresistible fashion as Crystal Palace were crushed 6-1 at Selhurst Park, Arsenal went down 3-0 at Anfield to a five minute Robbie Fowler hat trick and Southampton were beaten 2-0 at The Dell. After three games Fowler had five goals in the bank. West Ham dented the winning start with a draw at Anfield and Manchester United ended the unbroken start with a 2-0 win at Old Trafford. Three bursts of two successive wins, interspersed with defeats at Blackburn – one of the great matches of the season – and at QPR, lifted the side into third position. The momentum was lost during December when a 2-0 reversal at Everton was followed with four straight draws, three of which were against lowly opposition. The winless run came to an abrupt halt with wins during the Christmas period over Leicester, Manchester City, Leeds and Norwich being sufficient to reclaim third place, Fowler scored in all four games. The eight match unbeaten run ended with Ipswich notching their last away win in the Premiership and their first ever win at Anfield. Whether the fact that the club had won the Coca-Cola Cup early in March played a part in Liverpool's performances thereafter or not, the facts show that five of the last 13 league games were lost compared with five of the previous 29. The Reds still managed to damage United's title aspirations during this period with a 2-0 home victory, and the season was rounded off with an almost last kick of the game victory over Blackburn.

Having crashed out of the FA Cup in the 3rd Round for each of the previous two seasons, Liverpool began nervously to record a 2-0 penalty shoot-out replay win over Birmingham City at Anfield. Two games were also needed to overcome Burnley in the 4th. After a draw on Merseyside, Wimbledon were defeated 2-0 at Selhurst thanks to first half goals by Barnes and the evergreen Ian Rush to set up a fascinating quarter final tie with Tottenham. Despite being ahead the Reds eventually succumbed to a late goal from Klinsmann.

Liverpool experienced no such problems in the Coca-Cola Cup as Burnley were seen off 6-1 on aggregate in Round One before Stoke City bowed out to two more goals from Rush. The Welshman went one better in the 4th Round with his hat trick destroying Blackburn at Ewood Park, and it was Rush who struck the decisive blow to add to Arsenal's problems in the quarter final. Another London club, Crystal Palace, stood before them in the semi final, but goals in both legs by Fowler clinched a 2-0 victory. Steve McManaman capped a quite magnificent personal season at the Wembley Final with his brace of goals being too much for Premiership bound Bolton Wanderers.

Building for the future continued during the close season as Liverpool secured the services of Stan Collymore from Forest for a cool £8.5m. ■

Results 1994-95

Date	Opponents	Ven	Res	Pos	Atten	Scorers
20-Aug	C Palace	A	6-1	1	18,084	Molby (11 pen); McManaman (14,69); Fowler (44); Rush (60,72)
28-Aug	Arsenal	H	3-0	5	30,117	Fowler (26,29,31)
31-Aug	Southampton	A	2-0	4	15,190	Fowler (21); Barnes (77)
10-Sep	West Ham	H	0-0	4	30,907	
17-Sep	Man United	A	0-2	5	43,740	
24-Sep	Newcastle	A	1-1	6	34,435	Rush (70)
1-Oct	Sheffield W	H	4-1	5	31,493	Rush (51); OG(66), McManaman (54,86),
8-Oct	Aston Villa	H	3-2	4	32,158	Ruddock (20); Fowler (26,57)
15-Oct	Blackburn R	A	2-3	5	30,263	Fowler (29); Barnes (59)
22-Oct	Wimbledon	H	3-0	5	31,139	McManaman (20), Fowler (35), Barnes (63)
29-Oct	Ipswich Tn	A	3-1	5	22,513	Barnes (39); Fowler (56,60)
31-Oct	QPR	A	1-2	5	18,295	Barnes (65)
5-Nov	N Forest	H	1-0	4	33,329	Fowler (14)
9-Nov	Chelsea	H	3-1	3	32,855	Fowler (8,9); Ruddock (24)
21-Nov	Everton	A	0-2	4	39,866	
26-Nov	Tottenham	H	1-1	4	35,007	Fowler (39 pen)
3-Dec	Coventry C	A	1-1	4	21,029	Rush (2)
11-Dec	C Palace	H	0-0	4	30,972	
18-Dec	Chelsea	A	0-0	5	27,050	
26-Dec	Leicester C	H	2-1	4	21,393	Fowler (67 pen); Rush (77)
28-Dec	Man City	A	2-0	3	38,122	OG (Phelan 55); Fowler (82)
31-Dec	Leeds Utd	H	2-0	3	38,563	Redknapp (17); Fowler (75)
2-Jan	Norwich C	H	4-0	3	34,709	Scales (14); Fowler (38,47); Rush (83)
14-Jan	Ipswich Tn	H	0-1	3	32,733	
24-Jan	Everton	H	0-0	3	39,505	
4-Feb	N Forest	A	1-1	4	25,418	Fowler (90)
11-Feb	QPR	H	1-1	4	35,996	Scales (71)
25-Feb	Sheffield W	A	2-1	4	31,964	Barnes (42); McManaman (59)
4-Mar	Newcastle U	H	2-0	4	39,300	Fowler (57); Rush (63)
14-Mar	Coventry C	A	2-3	5	27,183	Molby (72pen); OG (90)
19-Mar	Man United	H	2-0	4	38,906	Redknapp (24); OG (86)
22-Mar	Tottenham	A	0-0	5	31,988	
5-Apr	Southampton	H	3-1	5	29,881	Rush (28,50); Fowler (71 pen)
9-Apr	Leeds Utd	H	0-1	5	37,454	

12-Apr	Arsenal	A	1-0	5	38,036	Fowler (90)
14-Apr	Man City	A	1-2	5	27,055	McManaman (21)
17-Apr	Leicester C	H	2-0	4	36,012	Fowler (74); Rush (80)
29-Apr	Norwich C	A	2-1	4	21,843	Harkness (7); Rush (84)
2-May	Wimbledon	A	0-0	4	12,041	
6-May	Aston Villa	A	0-2	4	40,154	
10-May	West Ham	A	0-3	4	22,446	
14-May	Blackburn R	H	2-1	4	40,014	Barnes (65); Redknapp (90)

FA Challenge Cup

Date	Opponents	Vn	Rnd	Res	Atten	Scorers
7-Jan	Birmingham	A	3R	0-0	25,326	
18-Jan	Birmingham	H	3RR	1-1	36,275	OG (21)
	Liverpool win 2-0 on penalties					
28-Jan	Burnley	A	4R	0-0	20,551	
7-Feb	Burnley	H	4RR	1-0	32,109	Barnes (44)
19-Feb	Wimbledon	H	5R	1-1	25,124	Fowler (33)
28-Feb	Wimbledon	H	5RR	2-0	12,553	Barnes (10); Rush (38)
11-Mar	Tottenham	H	QF	1-2	39,592	Fowler (38)

Coca-Cola League Cup

Date	Opponents	Vn	Rnd	Res	Atten	Scorers
21-Sep	Burnley	H	2R1L	2-0	23,359	Scales (42); Fowler (84)
5-Oct		A	2R2L	4-1	19,032	Redknapp (15,68); Fowler (50); Clough (75)
	Liverpool win 6-1 on aggregate					
25-Oct	Stoke City	H	3R	2-1	32,060	Rush (4,55)
30-Nov	Blackburn R	A	4R	3-1	30,115	Rush (19,57,73)
11-Jan	Arsenal	H	QF	1-0	36,004	Rush (59)
15-Feb	C Palace	A	SF1L	1-0	25,480	Fowler (90)
8-Mar		H	SF2L	1-0	18,224	Fowler (27)
	Liverpool win 2-0 on aggregate					
2-Apr	Bolton Wders	N	F	2-1	75,595	McManaman (37,67)
	(at Wembley)					

Liverpool – Premiership Fact File

- Robbie Fowler's hat-trick against Arsenal on 28th August was scored in the shortest period ever recorded in the Premiership – the three goals coming within a 4minute 33 second period.
- Liverpool completed the 1994 part of the season undefeated at home. They soon lost that record in 1995 when strugglers Ipswich won 1-0 at Anfield on 14th January while Liverpool were in third position in the table.

Manchester City

Founded in 1880 as West Gorton AFC. Following ground difficulties, having lost the use of the Kirkmanshulme Cricket Ground, was relaunched as Gorton AFC in 1884. There were more ground problems before, in 1889, the club moved to Hyde Road, adopted the title of Ardwick, and employed its first professional.

Ardwick joined the Football Alliance in 1891, finishing seventh, and was founder member of Football League Division Two in 1892. Ardwick too encountered difficulties and the club was restarted as Manchester City in 1894, retaining the Football League place. In 1923 the club moved to Maine Road. Premier League founder member 1992.

Ground: Maine Road, Moss Side, Manchester, M14 7WN
Phone: 0161-226 1191/2   **Info:** 0891-12 11 91
Box Office: 0161-226 2224   **Dial-a-Seat:** 0161-227 9229
Capacity: 45,053   **Pitch:** 118 yds x 76 yds
Colours: Sky Blue, White, Sky Blue   **Nickname:** Blues or The Citizens
Directions: *From North & West:* M61 to M63 J9. Follow signs into Manchester (A5103). Turn right after 3 miles into Claremont Rd. Turn right after 400 yards into Maine Rd. *From South:* M6 J19 to A556 joining M56. Leave at junction 3 following A5103 as above. *From East:* M62 J17 and follow signs for Manchester Airport (A56 and A57(M)). Then follow Birmingham signs to A5103. Left into Claremont Rd after 1 mile then right into Maine Rd.   **Rail:** Manchester Piccadilly

Chairman: Francis Lee   **Vice-Chairman:** Freddie Pye
Managing Director: Colin Barlow   **General Secretary:** Bernard Halford
Manager: Alan Ball   **Assistant:** Asa Hartford
First Team Coach: Tony Book   **Physio:** Eamonn Salmon

League History: 1892 Ardwick elected founder member of Division 2; 1894 Newly-formed Manchester C elected to Division 2; Division 1 1899-1902, 1903-09, 1910-26, 1928-38, 1947-50, 1951-63, 1966-83, 1985-87, 1989-92; Division 2 1902-03, 1909-10, 1926-28, 1938-47, 1950-51, 1963-66, 1983-85, 1987-89; 1992 – FA Premier League.

Honours: *Football League: Division 1 Champions:* 1936-37, 1967-68; *Runners-up:* 1903-04, 1920-21, 1976-77; *Division 2 Champions:* 1898-99, 1902-03, 1909-10, 1927-28, 1946-47, 1965-66; *Runners-up:* 1895-96, 1950-51, 1987-88. *FA Cup Winners:* 1969-70; *Runners-up:* 1973-74, 1980-81. *Cup-Winners' Cup Winners:* 1969-70.

European Competitions: CC (1): 68-69. CWC (2): 69-70 (W), 70-71. UEFA (4): 72-73, 76-77, 77-78, 78-79.

Managers: Joshua Parlby 1893-95; Sam Omerod 1895-1902; Tom Maley 1902-06; Harry Newbould 1906-12; Ernest Magnall 1912-24; David Ashworth 1924-25; Peter Hodge 1926-32; Wilf Wild 1932-46 (continued as secretary to 1950); Sam Cowan 1946-47; John 'Jock' Thomson 1947-50; Leslie McDowall 1950-63; George Poyser 1963-65; Joe Mercer 1965-71 (continued as GM to 1972); Malcolm Allison 1972-73; Johnny Hart 1973; Ron Saunders 1973-74; Tony Book 1974-79; Malcolm Allison 1979-80; John Bond 1980-83; John Benson 1983; Billy McNeill 1983-86; Jimmy Frizzell 1986-87 (continued as GM); Mel Machin 1987-89; Howard Kendall 1990; (FAPL) Peter Reid 1990-93; Brian Horton Sept 1993-May 1995. Alan Ball July 1995–

Season 1994-95

Biggest Home Win: 4-0 v Everton, 27/8/94
Biggest Home Defeat: 0-3 v Manchester United, 11/2/95
Biggest Away Win: 3-2 v Blackburn Rovers, 17/4/95
Biggest Away Defeat: 0-5 v Manchester United, 10/11/94
Biggest Home Attendance: 27,850 v Queens Park Rangers, 14/5/95
Smallest Home Attendance: 19,150 v West Ham United, 24/8/94
Average Attendance: 22,744
Last Season: *PL:* 17th *FA Cup:* 5th round *Coca-Cola Cup:* 5th round
Leading Scorer: Uwe Rosler – 15

All-time Record

Record FAPL Win: 4-0 v Leeds United, 7/11/92 & Everton, 27/8/94
Record FAPL Defeat: 0-5 v Manchester United, 10/11/94
Record FL Win: 10-1 v Huddersfield Town, Division 2, 7/11/1987
Record FL Defeat: 1-9 v Everton, Division 1, 3/9/1906
Record Cup Win: 10-1 v Swindon Town, FA Cup R4, 29/1/1930
Record Fee Received: £1.7m from Tottenham H for Paul Stewart, 6/1988
Record Fee Paid: £2.5m to Wimbledon for Keith Curle, 8/1991
Most FL Appearances: Alan Oakes, 565, 1959-76
Record Attendance (all-time): 84,569 v Stoke C, FA Cup R6, 3/3/1934
British record for any game outside London or Glasgow
Record Attendance (FAPL): 37,136 v Manchester United, 7/11/1993
Highest Scorer in FAPL season: David White, 16, 1992-93
Most FAPL Goals in Season: 56, 1992-93
Most FAPL Points in Season: 57, 1992-93

5-Year League Record

	Div.	P	W	D	L	F	A	Pts	Pos	FAC	FLC
90-91	1	38	17	11	10	64	53	62	5	5	3
91-92	1	42	20	10	12	61	48	70	5	3	4
92-93	PL	42	15	12	15	56	51	57	9	6	3
93-94	PL	42	9	18	15	38	49	45	16	4	4
94-95	PL	42	12	13	17	53	64	49	17	5	5

Summary of FAPL Appearances and Goals 1994-95

Player	Tot	Start	Sub	SNU	PS	Goals	Yel	Red
BEAGRIE	37	33	4	0	3	2	3	0
BRIGHTWELL Ian	29	28	1	0	2	0	6	0
BRIGHTWELL D. ...	9	9	0	6	2	0	3	0
BURRIDGE	4	3	1	10	0	0	1	0
COTON	22	21	1	1	2	0	0	0
CURLE	31	31	0	0	1	2	4	0
DIBBLE	16	15	1	15	0	0	1	1
EDGHILL	14	14	0	1	0	0	2	1
FLITCROFT.........	37	37	0	0	2	5	6	0
FOSTER	11	9	2	3	1	0	1	0
GAUDINO	20	17	3	1	6	3	0	0
GRIFFITHS	2	0	2	1	0	0	0	0
HILL	13	10	3	4	3	0	1	0
KERNAGHAN	22	18	4	2	0	1	4	0
KERR	2	2	0	0	2	0	0	0
LOMAS	20	18	2	1	0	2	3	0
MARGETSON	0	0	0	11	0	0	0	0
McMAHON	7	6	1	1	1	0	1	0
MIKE	2	1	1	7	1	0	0	0
PHELAN	27	26	1	0	3	0	7	1
QUINN	35	24	11	3	2	8	4	0
ROSLER	31	29	2	0	5	15	7	1
SIMPSON	16	10	6	2	2	2	2	0
SUMMERBEE	41	39	2	1	2	1	4	0
THOMAS	2	0	2	0	0	0	0	0
TRACEY	3	3	0	2	0	0	0	0
VONK	21	19	2	2	4	0	2	0
WALSH	40	40	0	0	8	12	0	0

OGs 0

A Different Ball Game Now?

Having finished a lowly 16th in the Premiership the previous season, and seen rivals United complete the League and Cup Double, City manager Brian Horton was always likely to be one of the favourites for an early exit if results did not match up to expectations. The signs looked ominous from the off with German striker Uwe Rosler dismissed during a 3-0 defeat at Arsenal on the opening day of the season. However, emphatic 3-0 and 4-0 wins over West Ham and Everton at Maine Road quelled early discontent but just one point was extracted from the next three away games before QPR were beaten at Loftus Road, this despite having two players sent off. Fortunately, City's home form was very impressive, good wins over Norwich and Tottenham were supplemented by 3-3 draws with Nottingham Forest and Southampton. City's world appeared to be shattered on 10 November as they crashed 5-0 at Old Trafford but an instant response was made with three straight wins which took Horton's side up to a season's high of sixth. Powerful German Maurizio Gaudino was signed on loan as confidence grew.

Just when City seemed to be on the right track everything fell apart in spectacular fashion. The unbeaten home run was ended by Arsenal in mid December and the club embarked on a ten match run without a win, and a run of just two wins in 19 games. In the middle of that lot came a 3-0 reversal at home to United. The depression was lifted with a mini revival at Easter which saw the Blues record significant victories over both Liverpool and Blackburn Rovers. City avoided defeat against Newcastle United for the fourth time in five meetings during the season at the end of April but with just one point from the last three games they slipped down to 17th place and Horton's name was added to the lengthy list of former City managers. Rosler's form provided one of the high points of the season with 15 league goals, whilst Steve McMahon was released to join Swindon as manager.

Twenty five years have passed since Manchester City last won a piece of silverware and that statistic seemed to hang around the necks of the City players as the cup season kicked off with a 1-0 Coca-Cola Cup defeat at Barnet. Being a goal down in 27 seconds did not help City's cause. Two goals from Niall Quinn brilliantly helped turn things round at Maine Road to the tune of 4-1 and then City pulled off two excellent results. QPR were beaten 4-3 at Loftus Road – this time City were one down in 15 seconds – and Newcastle, following a draw, lost their unbeaten home record to goals from Rosler and Walsh. Crystal Palace, though, chalked up a very surprising 4-0 win at Selhurst Park in the quarter final as City's new year form dipped.

The FA Cup saw Rosler score four goals during a 5-2 replay victory over Notts County. In Round Four an early goal from Walsh accounted for Aston Villa but in the 5th Round Newcastle took full revenge and effectively ended City's season with a 3-1 win.

In the end City's 17th position in the Premiership lead to the departure of Brian Horton and the arrival of Alan Ball as manager. ∎

Results 1994-95

FA Carling Premiership

Date	Opponents	Ven	Res	Pos	Atten	Scorers
20-Aug	Arsenal	A	0-3	21	38,368	
24-Aug	West Ham	H	3-0	10	19,150	Walsh (14); Beagrie (42); Rosler (56)
27-Aug	Everton	H	4-0	5	19,867	Rosler (56,80); Walsh (61,63)
31-Aug	Chelsea	A	0-3	9	21,740	
10-Sep	C Palace	H	1-1	9	19,971	Walsh (18)
17-Sep	Sheffield W	A	1-1	10	26,776	Walsh (44)
24-Sep	Norwich C	H	2-0	7	21,031	Quinn (53); Rosler (62)
1-Oct	Leeds Utd	A	0-2	11	30,938	
8-Oct	N Forest	H	3-3	11	23,150	Quinn (41,54); Lomas (59)
15-Oct	QPR	A	2-1	8	13,361	Flitcroft (56); Walsh (58)
22-Oct	Tottenham	H	5-2	7	25,473	Walsh (15,45); Quinn (41), Lomas (52); Flitcroft (79)
29-Oct	Coventry C	A	0-1	9	15,804	
5-Nov	Southampton	H	3-3	9	21,589	Walsh (50,61); Beagrie (79)
10-Nov	Man United	A	0-5	9	47,738	
20-Nov	Leicester C	A	1-0	8	19,006	Quinn (16)
26-Nov	Wimbledon	H	2-0	7	21,131	Flitcroft (7); Rosler (88)
3-Dec	Ipswich Tn	A	2-1	6	13,504	Flitcroft (20); Rosler (42)
12-Dec	Arsenal	H	1-2	6	20,500	Simpson (80)
17-Dec	West Ham	A	0-3	8	17,286	
26-Dec	Blackburn R	H	1-3	10	23,387	Quinn (21)
28-Dec	Liverpool	A	0-2	11	38,122	
31-Dec	Aston Villa	H	2-2	11	22,513	Rosler (14,52)
2-Jan	Newcastle	A	0-0	11	34,437	
14-Jan	Coventry C	H	0-0	11	20,632	
25-Jan	Leicester C	H	0-1	14	21,007	
4-Feb	Southampton	A	2-2	13	14,902	Kernaghan (29); Flitcroft (88)
11-Feb	Man United	H	0-3	14	26,368	
22-Feb	Ipswich T	A	2-0	13	21,430	Quinn(68); Rosler (71)
25-Feb	Leeds Utd	H	0-0	15	22,892	
4-Mar	Norwich C	A	1-1	15	16,266	Simpson (86)
8-Mar	Chelsea	H	1-2	16	21,880	Gaudino (4)
15-Mar	Everton	A	1-1	16	28,405	Gaudino (25)
18-Mar	Sheffield	H	3-2	12	23,355	Rosler (37,83); Walsh (52)
21-Mar	Wimbledon	A	0-2	13	5,268	
1-Apr	C Palace	A	1-2	16	13,312	Rosler (58)
11-Apr	Tottenham	A	1-2	16	27,410	Rosler (49)
14-Apr	Liverpool	H	2-1	15	27,055	Summerbee (17); Gaudino (73)

17-Apr	Blackburn R	A	3-2	12	27,851	Curle (32 pen); Rosler (57); Walsh (71)
29-Apr	Newcastle	H	0-0	13	27,389	
3-May	Aston Villa	A	1-1	13	30,133	Rosler (63)
6-May	N Forest	A	0-1	13	28,882	
14-May	QPR	H	2-3	17	27,850	Quinn (26); Curle (80 pen)

FA Challenge Cup

Date	Opponents	Vn	Rnd	Res	Atten	Scorers
8-Jan	Notts County	A	3R	2-2	12,376	Beagrie (27); Brightwell, D (68)
18-Jan		H	3RR	5-2	14,261	Rosler (7,37,57,81); Gaudino (44)
28-Jan	Aston VIlla	H	4R	1-0	21,177	Walsh (7)
19-Feb	Newcastle	A	5R	1-3	33,219	Rosler (29)

Coca-Cola League Cup

Date	Opponents	Vn	Rnd	Res	Atten	Scorers
20-Sep	Barnet	A	2R1L	0-1	3,120	
5-Oct		H	2R2L	4-1	11,545	Quinn (56,88); Walsh (67); Summerbee (77)
	Manchester City win 4-1 on aggregate					
25-Oct	QPR	A	3R	4-3	11,701	Summerbee (36); Curle (46); Beagrie (53); Lomas (59)
30-Nov	Newcastle	H	4R	1-1	25,162	Rosler (69)
21-Dec	Newcastle	A	4RR	2-0	30,156	Rosler (11); Walsh (80)
11-Jan	C Palace	A	QF	0-4	16,668	

City – Premiership Fact File

- John Burridge made his senior debut for City at the end of April at the age of 43. It came against Newcastle United – the club where he was serving as goalkeeper/coach. The game ended goalless!
- Paul Walsh started 40 games for City – the most starts for any player – but he was also subbed the most – eight times. However, he still managed to finish City's second highest scorer in the Premiership.

Manchester United

Came into being in 1902 upon the bankruptcy of Newton Heath. Predecessors appear to have been formed in 1878 as Newton Heath (LYR) when workers at the Carriage and Wagon Department at the Lancashire and Yorkshire Railway formed a club. This soon outgrew railway competition.

Turned professional in 1885 and founder member of Football Alliance in 1889. In 1892 Alliance runners-up Newton Heath was elected to an enlarged Division One of the Football League. In 1902 the club became Manchester United and, in February 1910, moved from Bank Street, Clayton, to Old Trafford. Premier League founder member 1992.

Ground: Old Trafford, Manchester, M16 0RA
Phone: 0161-872 1661   **Info:** 0891 12 11 61
Manchester United Radio: 1413AM
Capacity: 44,622   **Pitch:** 116yds x 76yds
Colours: Red, White, Black   **Nickname:** Red Devils
Directions: *From North:* M63 J4 follow signs for Manchester (A5081). Right after 2½ miles into Warwick Rd. *From South:* M6 J19 follow A556 then A56 (Altrincham). From Altrincham follow signs for Manchester turning left into Warwick Rd after 6 miles. *From East:* M62 J17 then A56 to Manchester. Follow signs for South and then Chester. Turn right into Warwick Rd after two miles.

Chairman/Chief Executive: Martin Edwards
Secretary: Kenneth Merrett
Manager: Alex Ferguson   **Assistant:** Brian Kidd

League History: 1892 Newton Heath elected to Division 1; 1894-1906 Division 2; 1906-22 Division 1; 1922-25 Division 2; 1925-31 Division 1; 1931-36 Division 2; 1936-37 Division 1; 1937-38 Division 2; 1938-74 Division 1; 1974-75 Division 2; 1975-92 Division 1; 1992 – FA Premier League.

Honours: *FA Premier League Champions:* 1992-93, 1993-94; *Runners-up:* 1994-95; *Football League: Division 1 Champions:* 1907-8, 1910-11, 1951-52, 1955-56, 1956-57, 1964-65, 1966-67; *Runners-up:* 1946-47, 1947-48, 1948-49, 1950-51, 1958-59, 1963-64, 1967-68, 1979-80, 1987-88, 1991-92. *Division 2 Champions:* 1935-36, 1974-75; *Runners-up:* 1896-97, 1905-06, 1924-25, 1937-38. *FA Cup Winners:* 1909, 1948, 1963, 1977, 1983, 1985, 1990, 1994; *Runners-up:* 1957, 1958, 1976, 1979, 1995; *Football League*

Cup Winners: 1991-92; *Runners-up:* 1982-83, 1990-91, 1993-94.
Champions' Cup Winners: 1967-68; *Cup-Winners' Cup Winners:* 1990-91.

European Record: CC (7): 56-57(SF), 57-58(SF), 65-66(SF), 67-68(W), 68-69(SF), 93-94(SF), 94-95(CL): CWC (5): 63-64(QF), 77-78(2), 83-84(SF), 90-91(W) , 91-92 (2). UEFA (6): 64-65(SF), 76-77(2), 80-81(1), 82-83(1), 84-85(QF), 92-93(1).

Managers: Ernest Magnall 1900-12; John Robson 1914-21; John Chapman 1921-26; Clarence Hildrith 1926-27; Herbert Bamlett 1927-31; Walter Crickmer 1931-32; Scott Duncan 1932-37; Jimmy Porter 1938-44; Walter Crickmer 1944-45; Matt Busby 1945-69 (continued as GM then Director); Wilf McGuinness 1969-70; Frank O'Farrell 1971-72; Tommy Docherty 1972-77; Dave Sexton 1977-81; Ron Atkinson 1981-86; (FAPL) Alex Ferguson Nov 1986-

Season 1994-95

Biggest Home Win: 9-0 v Ipswich Town, 4/3/95
Biggest Home Defeat: 1-2 v Nottingham Forest, 17/12/94
Biggest Away Win: 4-0 v Leicester City, 15/4/95
Biggest Away Defeat: 0-2 v Liverpool, 19/3/95
Biggest Home Attendance: 43,868 v Sheffield Wednesday, 7/5/95
Smallest Home Attendance: 43,130 v Coventry City, 3/1/95
Average Attendance: 41,599
Last Season: *FAPL:* 2nd *FA Cup:* Runners-up *Coca-Cola Cup:* 3rd round.
       UEFA Champions League: 3rd Group A
Leading Scorer: Andrei Kanchelskis – 14

All-time Records

Record FAPL Win: 9-0 v Ipswich Town, 4/3/95
Record FAPL Defeat: 0-3 v Everton, 19/8/92
Record FL Win: 10-1 v Wolverhampton W, Division 2, 15/10/1892
Record FL Defeat: 0-7 v Blackburn R, Division 1, 10/4/1926;
                Aston Villa, Division 1, 27/12/1930;
                Wolves, Division 2, 26/12/1931
Record Cup Win: 10-0 v RSC Anderlecht, European Cup, PR L2, 26/9/1956
Record Fee Received: £7m from Internazionale (Italy) for Paul Ince 6/95
Record Fee Paid: £7m to Newcastle United for Andy Cole 1/95
                (inc. part exchange of Keith Gillespie – £1m).
Most FL Appearances: Bobby Charlton, 606, 1956-73
Record Attendance (all-time): 70,504 v Aston Villa, Division 1, 27/12/1920
Record Attendance (FAPL): 44,751 v Liverpool, 30/3/94
Highest Scorer in FAPL Season: Cantona, 18, 1993-94
Most FAPL Goals in Season: 80, 1993-94
Most FAPL Points in Season: 92, 1993-94

5-Year League Record

	Div.	P	W	D	L	F	A	Pts	Pos	FAC	FLC
90-91	1	38	16	12	10	58	45	59	6	5	F
91-92	1	42	21	15	6	63	33	78	2	4	W
92-93	PL	42	24	12	6	67	31	84	1	5	3
93-94	PL	42	27	11	4	80	38	92	1	W	F
94-95	PL	42	26	10	6	77	28	88	2	F	3

Summary of FAPL Appearances and Goals 1994-95

Player	Tot	Start	Sub	SNU	PS	Goals	Yel	Red
BECKHAM	4	2	2	1	1	0	0	0
BRUCE	35	35	0	0	1	2	12	0
BUTT	22	11	11	8	5	1	4	0
CANTONA...	21	21	0	0	0	12	4	1
CASPER	0	0	0	1	0	0	0	0
COLE	18	17	1	0	0	12	1	0
DAVIES	5	3	2	1	4	0	0	0
DUBLIN	0	0	0	2	0	0	0	0
GIGGS	29	29	0	0	6	1	3	0
GILLESPIE	9	3	6	1	2	1	2	0
HUGHES	34	33	1	0	6	8	7	1
INCE...	36	36	0	0	2	5	5	0
IRWIN	40	40	0	1	0	2	1	0
KANCHELSKIS ...	30	25	5	0	3	14	0	0
KEANE	25	23	2	0	4	2	7	0
MAY	19	15	4	3	3	2	2	0
McCLAIR	40	35	5	2	6	5	1	0
McGIBBON	0	0	0	1	0	0	0	0
NEVILLE Gary ...	18	16	2	2	2	0	5	0
NEVILLE Phil ...	2	1	1	0	1	0	0	0
PALLISTER	42	42	0	0	0	2	0	0
PARKER	2	1	1	1	1	0	0	1
PILKINGTON	1	0	1	17	0	0	0	0
SCHMEICHEL ...	32	32	0	0	1	0	0	0
SCHOLES	17	6	11	4	3	5	0	0
SHARPE	28	26	2	0	6	3	7	0
WALSH...	10	10	0	24	0	0	0	0
						OGs 1		

United – Premiership Fact File

- United scored in their first eight Premiership games.
- United did not concede a goal at Old Trafford in the Premiership for their first nine home games. Stan Collymore finally broke through for Forest after 1,135 minutes.
- United recorded the biggest ever win in the Premiership – 9-0 over Ipswich – on 4th March. It was United's biggest win of the century. Andy Cole set a new Premiership scoring record by scoring five goals in the game.

Second Double is Double Second

Having won the championship the previous two seasons and performed the double in 1993-94, United's major target was the Champions' Cup. The Reds started their campaign well with a 4-2 win over Gothenburg, but after draws with Galatasaray, away, and Barcelona, home, United were crushed 4-0 in the Nou Camp. A 3-1 defeat in Gothenburg made elimination almost certain and despite preserving their unbeaten home European record with a 4-0 win over Galatasaray, United went out of Europe.

On the home front, United began their title defence with three wins and a draw from the opening four league matches. Defeats were then suffered at each of the next three away games at Leeds, Ipswich and Sheffield Wednesday as they slipped to fifth place. The slide was arrested in stunning fashion as six consecutive wins and 17 goals took Alex Ferguson's side to the top of the table. Amongst those beaten were title challengers Blackburn and Newcastle while top scorer Andrei Kanchelskis scored a hat-trick during the 5-0 thrashing of Manchester City. United were top for only a week as a draw with Arsenal returned Blackburn to pole position. After ten successive home wins, and without a goal conceded in 1,135 minutes, United lost to Nottingham Forest at Old Trafford. United lost just two of the remaining 23 league games and returned to the summit on 11 February when completing an 8-0 aggregate double over rivals City. An inferior goal difference to Blackburn was wiped out during a 9-0 annihilation of Ipswich, £7m striker Andy Cole, from Newcastle, scored five. Despite their consistency, United could not hold back Blackburn although three successive wins early in May almost closed the gap – a winning goal on the final day at West Ham would have taken the title to Old Trafford again.

United's grip on the FA Cup looked to be invincible in the early rounds. Two late goals eased the Red Devils past Sheffield United at Bramall Lane (the third year running the two sides had met), while Wrexham were dispatched 5-2. Leeds hardly knew what had hit them as United went two up in four minutes in the 5th Round and Premiership side QPR bowed out 2-0. A year after United had problems in dealing with struggling Oldham, they encountered equally stubborn resistance in Crystal Palace who took the tie to a replay before defenders Steve Bruce and Gary Pallister clinched a place in the Final. United though, capped a disappointing end to their season with a 1-0 defeat by Everton at Wembley.

Whatever United did or did not achieve on the pitch, their good name was dented by mercurial Frenchman Eric Cantona. Dismissed four times, he was sent for 120 days community service after landing a kick on an aggressive supporter in January. Cantona was also fined £20,000 and suspended from all football until October. The headlines were hit off the pitch at the end of the season when Paul Ince signed for Internazionale in an £8m deal that was followed by Mark Hughes joining Chelsea for £1.5m and Andrei Kanchelskis going to Everton for £5m. ∎

Results 1994-95

FA Carling Premiership

Date	Opponents	Ven	Res	Pos	Atten	Scorers
20-Aug	QPR	H	2-0	4	43,214	Hughes (47); McClair (68)
22-Aug	N Forest	A	1-1	3	22,072	Kanchelskis (22)
27-Aug	Tottenham	A	1-0	3	24,502	Bruce (48)
31-Aug	Wimbledon	H	3-0	2	43,440	Cantona (40); McClair (81); Giggs (85)
11-Sep	Leeds Utd	A	1-2	5	39,396	Cantona (73 pen)
17-Sep	Liverpool	H	2-0	3	43,740	Kanchelskis (72); McClair (73)
24-Sep	Ipswich Tn	A	2-3	4	22,559	Cantona (70); Scholes (73)
1-Oct	Everton	H	2-0	4	43,803	Kanchelskis (41); Sharpe (88)
8-Oct	Sheffield W	A	0-1	5	33,441	
15-Oct	West Ham	H	1-0	4	43,795	Cantona (45)
23-Oct	Blackburn R	A	4-2	3	30,260	Cantona (45pen); Hughes (67); Kanchelskis (52,82)
29-Oct	Newcastle	H	2-0	4	43,795	Pallister (12); Gillespie (76)
6-Nov	Aston Villa	A	2-1	3	32,136	Ince (44); Kanchelskis (50)
10-Nov	Man City	H	5-0	2	43,738	Cantona (24); Hughes (70) Kanchelskis (43,47,89);
19-Nov	C Palace	H	3-0	1	43,788	Irwin (8); Cantona (33); Kanchelskis (50)
26-Nov	Arsenal	A	0-0	2	38,301	
3-Dec	Norwich C	H	1-0	2	43,789	Cantona (36)
10-Dec	QPR	A	3-2	2	18,948	Scholes (32,47); Keane (38)
17-Dec	N Forest	H	1-2	2	43,744	Cantona (68)
26-Dec	Chelsea	A	3-2	2	31,161	Hughes (21); Cantona (45pen); McClair (78)
28-Dec	Leicester C	H	1-1	2	43,789	Kanchelskis (61)
31-Dec	Southampton	A	2-2	2	15,204	Butt (50); Pallister (79)
3-Jan	Coventry C	H	2-0	2	43,130	Scholes (29); Cantona (50pen)
15-Jan	Newcastle	A	1-1	2	34,471	Hughes (12)
22-Jan	Blackburn R	H	1-0	2	43,742	Cantona (80)
25-Jan	C Palace	A	1-1	2	18,224	May (56)
4-Feb	Aston Villa	H	1-0	2	43,795	Cole (17)
11-Feb	Man City	A	3-0	1	26,368	Ince (58); Kanchelskis (74); Cole (77)
22-Feb	Norwich C	A	2-0	2	21,824	Ince (2); Kanchelskis (16)
25-Feb	Everton	A	0-1	2	40,011	
4-Mar	Ipswich Tn	H	9-0	2	43,804	Keane (15); Cole (23,36,52,64,88); Hughes (54,58); Ince (72)

150

7-Mar	Wimbledon	A	1-0	2	18,224	Bruce (84)
15-Mar	Tottenham	H	0-0	2	43,802	
19-Mar	Liverpool	A	0-2	2	38,906	
22-Mar	Arsenal	H	3-0	2	43,623	Hughes (27); Sharpe (32); Kanchelskis (79)
2-Apr	Leeds Utd	H	0-0	2	43,712	
15-Apr	Leicester C	A	4-0	2	21,281	Sharpe (33); Cole (45,52); Ince (90)
17-Apr	Chelsea	H	0-0	2	43,728	
1-May	Coventry C	A	3-2	2	21,885	Scholes (32); Cole (55,79)
7-May	Sheffield W	H	1-0	2	43,868	May (5)
10-May	Southampton	H	2-1	2	43,479	Cole (21); Irwin (82 pen)
14-May	West Ham	A	1-1	2	24,785	McClair (52)

UEFA Champions' League

Date	Opponents	Vn	Rnd	Res	Atten	Scorers
14-Sep	IFK	H	Gp A	4-2	33,625	Giggs (34,66); Kanchelskis (47); Sharpe (71)
28-Sep	Galatasaray	A	Gp A	0-0	28,605	
19-Oct	Barcelona	H	Gp A	2-2	40,064	Hughes (20), Sharpe (80)
2-Nov	Barcelona	A	Gp A	0-4	114,273	
23-Nov	IFK	A	Gp A	1-3	36,350	Hughes (64)
7-Dec	Galatasaray	H	Gp A	4-0	39,220	Davies (2); Beckham (37); Keane (48); OG (87)

FA Challenge Cup

Date	Opponents	Vn	Rnd	Res	Atten	Scorers
9-Jan	Sheffield U	A	3R	2-0	22,322	Hughes (80); Cantona (82)
28-Jan	Wrexham	H	4R	5-2	43,222	Irwin (16,73 pen); Giggs (26); McClair (66); OG (89)
19-Feb	Leeds Utd	H	5R	3-1	42,744	Bruce (1); McClair (4); Hughes (71)
12-Mar	QPR	H	QF	2-0	42,830	Sharpe (22); Irwin (53)
9-Apr	C Palace	N	SF	2-2	38,256	Irwin (70); Pallister (96)
12-Apr	C Palace	N	SFR	2-0	17,987	Bruce (30); Pallister (40)
	(both semi final matches played at Villa Park)					
20-May	Everton	N	F	0-1	79,592	*(at Wembley)*

Coca-Cola League Cup

Date	Opponents	Vn	Rnd	Res	Atten	Scorers
21-Sep	Port Vale	A	2R1L	2-1	18,605	Scholes (36,53)
5-Oct		H	2R2L	2-0	31,615	McClair (34); May (61)
	Manchester United win 4-1 on aggregate					
26-Oct	Newcastle	A	3R	0-2	34,178	

Middlesbrough

Formed in 1876 and played first game in 1877. Turned professional in 1889, but reverted to amateur status shortly afterwards, being early winners of the FA Amateur Cup. League football was first played in Middlesbrough by the Ironpolis side for one season, 1893-94. Middlesbrough turned professional again, were elected to Division Two in 1899, and moved to Ayresome Park in 1903. They were founder members of the Premier League in 1993 but were relegated in their first season. Moved to purpose built stadium in 1995 coinciding with return to Premiership.

Ground: The Cellnet Riverside Stadium, South Bank, Middlesbrough
Phone: 01642 227227   **Nickname:** The Boro
Colours: Red with Black, White with Black, Red with Black.
Capacity: 31,000
Directions: *From North:* A19 towards Middlesbrough. Cross Tees Bridge and join A66 towards South Bank/Harbour. Ground signposted at site of harbour. *From South:* A19 towards Middlesbrough. Join A66 towards South Bank/Harbour. Ground signposted at site of harbour. *From West:* Join A66 and ground signposted at site of harbour.

Chairman: Steve Gibson   **CEO/Secretary:** Keith Lamb
Manager: Bryan Robson   **Assistant:** Viv Anderson
First Team Coach: John Pickering   **Physio:** Bob Ward, Tommy Johnson

League History: 1899 Elected to Division 2; 1902-24 Division 1; 1924-27 Division 2; 1927-28 Division 1; 1928-29 Division 2; 1929-54 Division 1; 1954-66 Divsion 2; 1966-67 Division 1; 1967-74 Division 2; 1974-82 Division 2; 1982-86 Division 2; 1986-87 Division 3; 1988-89 Division 1; 1989-92 Division 2; 1992-93 FAPL; 1993-95 Division 1; 1995- FAPL.

Honours: *Division 1 (new) Champions:*1994-95; *Division 2 Champions* 1926-27, 1928-29, 1973-74; *Runners-up:* 1901-02, 1991-92; *Division 3 Runners up:* 1966-67, 1986-87; *FA Amateur Cup Winners:* 1895, 1898; *Anglo-Scottish Cup Winners:* 1975-76.

European Record: Never qualified

Managers: John Robson 1899-05; Alex Massie 1905-06; Andy Atkin 1906-09; J.Gunter 1908-10; Andy Walker 1910-11; Tom McIntosh 1911-19; James Howie 1920-23; Herbert Bamlett 1923-26; Peter McWilliam 1927-34; Wilf Gillow 1933-44; David Jack 1944-52; Walter Rowley 1952-54; Bob Dennison 1954-63; Raich Carter 1963-66; Stan Anderson 1966-73; Jack

Charlton 1973-77; John Neal 1977-81; Bobby Murdoch 1981-82; Malcolm Allison 1982-84; Willie Maddren 1984-86; Bruce Rioch 1986-90; Colin Todd 1990-91; Lennie Lawrence 1991-94; *(FAPL)*: Bryan Robson May 1994-

Season 1994-95

Biggest Home Win: 4-0 v Portsmouth, 3/12/94
Biggest Home Defeat: 2-4 v Derby County, 16/3/95
Biggest Away Win: 3-0 v Burnley, 18/12/94
Biggest Away Defeat: 1-5 v Luton Town, 15/10/94
Biggest Home Attendance: 23,903 v Luton Town, 30/4/95
Smallest Home Attendance: 14, 878 v WBA, 14/9/94
Average Attendance: 18,641
Last Season: *D1:* Champions *FA Cup* 3rd round
           Coca-Cola Cup 3rd round
Leading Scorer: John Hendrie – 15

All-time Record

Record FAPL Win: 4-1 v Leeds United, 22/8/92
Record FAPL Defeat: 1-5 v Aston Villa, 17/1/93
Record FL Win: 9-0 v Brighton &HA, D2 23/8/58
Record FL Defeat: 0-9 v Blackburn Rovers, D2 6/11/54
Record Cup Win: 9-3 v Goole Town, FAC1, 9/1/15
Record Fee Received: £2.3m, Gary Pallister to Manchester Utd, Aug 89
Record Fee Paid: £1.3m to Swindon for Jan Aage Fjortoft, 3/95
Record Attendance (all-time): 53,596 v Newcastle Utd, D1 27/12/49
Record Attendance (FAPL): 24,172 v Manchester United, 3/10/92
        Both at Ayresome Park
Highest Scorer in FAPL Season: Paul Wilkinson 15, 1992-93
Most FAPL Goals in Season: 54, 1992-93
Most FAPL Points in Season: 44, 1992-93

5-Year League Record

	Div.	P	W	D	L	F	A	Pts	Pos	FAC	FLC
90-91	2	46	20	9	17	66	47	69	7	4	4
91-92	2	46	23	11	12	58	41	80	2	5	SF
92-93	PL	42	11	11	20	54	75	44	21	4	2
93-94	1	46	18	13	15	66	54	67	9	3	3
94-95	1	46	23	13	10	67	40	82	1	3	3

Summary of League Appearances and Goals 1994-95

Player	Tot	Start	Sub	SNU	PS	Goals	Yel	Red
ANDERSON	2	2	0	2	0	0	0	0
BLACKMORE	30	26	4	5	5	2	7	0
COX	40	39	1	0	2	1	4	0
FJORTOFT	8	8	0	0	0	3	0	0
FLEMING	21	21	0	1	0	0	6	0
FREESTONE	1	0	1	0	0	0	0	0
FUCHS	15	13	2	2	2	9	3	0
HENDRIE	39	37	2	1	3	15	3	0
HIGNETT	26	19	7	8	5	8	2	0
KAVANAGH	7	5	2	6	0	0	1	0
LIDDLE	1	1	0	0	0	0	0	0
MILLER	41	41	0	1	0	0	0	1
MOORE	37	35	2	1	5	4	3	0
MORENO	14	6	8	10	2	1	1	0
MORRIS	15	14	1	3	0	0	2	0
MUSTOE	27	24	3	3	0	3	5	1
O'HALLORAN	1	1	0	0	1	0	0	0
PEARS	5	5	0	16	0	0	0	0
PEARSON	33	33	0	0	2	3	7	0
POLLOCK	41	41	0	0	3	5	8	0
ROBERTS	0	0	0	28	0	0	0	0
ROBSON	22	21	1	0	4	1	1	0
STAMP	3	1	2	0	0	0	0	0
TODD	5	5	0	1	1	0	0	0
VICKERS	44	44	0	0	1	3	3	0
WHYTE	36	36	0	2	0	1	5	0
WILKINSON	30	27	3	4	1	6	2	0
WRIGHT	1	1	0	4	1	0	0	0
						OGs 2		

Boro' Bow Out of Ayresome in Style

Middlesbrough made a bold step in handing former England captain Bryan Robson his first managerial position in May 1994. Bold it may have been, but that Robson successfully combined managing the club with playing came as a surprise to few people. Boro' kicked off the campaign in front of 23,343 spectators against Burnley and with a brace of goals from top scorer John Hendrie they made the perfect start. Another Hendrie double saw off Southend and goals from Paul Wilkinson and Clayton Blackmore maintained the 100% record. The Teessiders retained top place at the start of September despite dropping their first points and conceding their first goal in a 1-1 draw at Watford. North east rivals Sunderland were the first visiting side to take a point from Ayresome Park as Boro' came back from two down to preserve the unbeaten record. Port Vale ended that record in mid September and with it went top position. A swift recovery was made with victories over Bristol City and Millwall but the unbeaten home record went as Tranmere recorded their first away win of the season, a 5-1 defeat at Luton saw Boro' slip to fourth. A drawn game at Swindon was followed by five wins in six games as Robson's side moved back to the top of the table. December kicked off with a 4-0 victory over Portsmouth but despite winning just three of seven matches during the month – including a Hendrie hat-trick at Burnley – Boro ended the year five points clear of second placed Wolves.

The New Year saw Boro' in unconvincing form as a run of four winless games cost them top place. Robson steadied the ship with the on-loan signing of Uwe Fuchs from Kaiserlautern and it was his goal that got Boro' going again with a 1-0 win over Charlton. Fuchs scored again during a 2-0 win over Wolves in front of 26,611 at Molineux and followed up with a hat trick against Bristol City. Boro's fourth win in five games, against Watford, closed the gap on the top but they dropped to third after three games without a win, a run which ended with a Jamie Pollock goal at Sunderland which took Boro back to the top. Boro strengthened their position with the signing of Jan Fjortoft from Swindon and Robson scored his first goal during a 3-0 win over Port Vale. Boro closed in on the championship with wins over WBA and Stoke coming either side of defeat at Oldham, but their end of season form was less impressive as just one of the final five games was won. Fortunately all of the challengers also slipped up and when Hendrie scored twice in a 2-1 win against Luton in the last ever match at Ayresome Park, and chasing sides Wolves and Bolton failed to win in midweek, Boro were crowned champions.

Boro's determination to win promotion meant that cup football took second place. In the FA Cup, Swansea City won a 3rd Round replay at Ayresome Park and after seeing off Scarborough in the Coca-Cola Cup, Boro went down 1-0 away to Aston Villa.

The 1995-96 campaign sees Middlesbrough installed in a brand new 31,000 all-seater stadium – the Cellnet Riverside Stadium. Situated in the harbourside redevelopment area it should provide a fitting backdrop for Robson's team. ■

155

Results 1994-95

Date	Opponents	Ven	Res	Pos	Atten	Scorers
13-Aug	Burnley	H	2-0	4	23,343	Hendrie (26,34)
20-Aug	Southend U	A	2-0	1	6,722	Hendrie (30,49)
27-Aug	Bolton Wds	H	1-0	1	19,570	Wilkinson (9)
31-Aug	Derby Co	A	1-0	1	14,659	Blackmore (19)
3-Sep	Watford	A	1-1	1	9,478	Blackmore (34)
11-Sep	Sunderland	H	2-2	1	19,578	Moore (79); Pearson (82)
14-Sep	WBA	H	2-1	1	14,878	Mustoe (42); Hignett (89pen)
17-Sep	Port Vale	A	1-2	2	10,313	Pollock (38)
24-Sep	Bristol City	A	1-0	2	8,642	Hendrie (70)
1-Oct	Millwall	H	3-0	2	17,229	Hendrie (46); Wilkinson (52); OG(74)
8-Oct	Tranmere R	H	0-1	2	18,497	
15-Oct	Luton Town	A	1-5	4	8,412	Whyte (83)
23-Oct	Portsmouth	A	0-0	3	7,281	
29-Oct	Swindon Tn	H	3-1	2	17,328	Cox (2); Hendrie (63); Wilkinson (65 pen)
1-Nov	Oldham Ath	H	2-1	2	15,929	Moore (53); Hignett (74)
5-Nov	Grimsby Tn	A	1-2	2	8,488	Hignett (73)
20-Nov	Wolves	H	1-0	1	19,953	Hendrie (67)
26-Nov	Charlton Ath	A	2-0	1	10,019	Hendrie (4); Pollock (55)
3-Dec	Portsmouth	H	4-0	1	17,185	Wilkinson (26,75); Hignett (28,59)
6-Dec	Reading	A	1-1	1	10,301	Wilkinson (70pen)
10-Dec	Southend U	A	1-2	1	16,843	Hendrie (79)
18-Dec	Burnley	A	3-0	1	12,049	Hendrie (15,64,90)
26-Dec	Sheffield U	H	1-1	1	20,693	Hignett (73)
28-Dec	Notts Co	H	2-1	1	21,558	Hignett (30); Pearson (36)
31-Dec	Stoke City	A	1-1		15,914	Vickers (9)
15-Jan	Swindon Tn	A	1-2	1	8,888	Hignett (14)
21-Jan	Grimsby Tn	H	1-1	1	15,360	Mustoe (85)
4-Feb	Reading	H	0-1	3	17,982	
18-Feb	Charlton Ath	H	1-0	3	16,301	Fuchs (16)
21-Feb	Wolves	A	2-0	2	26,611	Vickers (51); Fuchs (81)
26-Feb	Millwall	A	0-0	2	7,427	
4-Mar	Bristol City	H	3-0	2	17,371	Fuchs (9,48,65)
7-Mar	Watford	H	2-0	2	16,630	Mustoe (31); Fuchs (51)
11-Mar	Bolton Ws	A	0-1	2	18,370	
14-Mar	Barnsley	H	1-1	2	19,655	Moreno (37)
16-Mar	Derby Co	H	2-4	3	18,163	Fuchs (51); Pollock (54)
21-Mar	Sunderland	A	1-0	1	16,501	Pollock (65)

26-Mar	Port Vale	H	3-0	1	17,041	Robson (13); Vickers (18); Fuchs (77)
1-Apr	WBA	A	3-1	1	20,256	Pollock (57); OG(62); Moore (67)
5-Apr	Oldham Ath	A	0-1	1	11,024	
8-Apr	Stoke City	H	2-1	1	20,867	Pearson (13); Moore (70)
15-Apr	Notts Co	A	1-1	1	9,377	Fuchs (83)
17-Apr	Sheffield U	H	1-1	1	23,225	Fjortoft (7)
22-Apr	Barnsley	A	1-1	1	11,711	Fjortoft (40)
30-Apr	Luton Town	H	2-1	1	23,903	Hendrie (45,71)
7-May	Tranmere R	A	1-1	1	16,377	Fjortoft (51)

Anglo-Italian Cup

Date	Opponents	Vn	Rnd	Res	Atten	Scorers
24-Aug	Piacenza	H	GpB	0-0	5,348	
5-Oct	Cesena	H	GpB	1-0	3,273	Moreno (56)
18-Oct	Udinese	A	GpB	0-0	300	
15-Nov	Ancona	A	GpB	1-3	1,500	

FA Challenge Cup

Date	Opponents	Vn	Rnd	Res	Atten	Scorers
8-Jan	Swansea City	A	1-1	3R	8,407	Moore (61)
17-Jan	Swansea City	H	1-2	3RR	13,940	Hendrie (78)

Coca-Cola League Cup

Date	Opponents	Vn	Rnd	Res	Atten	Scorers
20-Sep	Scarborough	A	4-1	2R1L	4,751	Hendrie (7); Pollock (23); Moore (33); Mustoe (40)
27-Sep	Scarborough	H	4-1	2R2L	7,739	Wilkinson (40,61,65); Hignett (68)
	Middlesbrough win 8-2 on aggregate					
26-Oct	Aston Villa	A	0-1	3R	19,254	

Boro – Premiership Fact File

- Middlesbrough took part in the first Premiership season but were one of the teams to be relegated at the end of the 1992-93 season.
- Boro have moved to a 31,000 all purpose stadium that has cost £13m and is part of a £120m redevelopment of the Middlesbrough Harbour area that includes winter storage for tall ships!
- At the start of the 1995-96 season Paul Wilkinson was Boro's top player with 41 Premiership appearances and 15 goals.

Newcastle United

Formed 1882 as Newcastle East End on the amalgamation of Stanley and Rosewood. Founder members, as a professional club, of the Northern League in 1889. Moved from Chillington Road, Heaton in 1892 to take over the home of the defunct Newcastle West End, with several of those associated with the West End side joining the newcomers.

Applied for Football League Division One membership in 1892, failed and decided against a place in the new Second Division, staying in the Northern League. Later in 1892 changed name to Newcastle United. Elected to an expanded Football League Division Two in 1893.

Ground: St James' Park, Newcastle-upon-Tyne, NE1 4ST
Phone: 0191-232 8361   **Info:** 0891 12 11 90
Colours: Black/White, Black, Black   **Nickname:** Magpies
Capacity: 36,401   **Pitch:** 115 yds x 75 yds.
Directions: *From South:* Follow A1, A68 then A6127 to cross the Tyne. At roundabout, first exit into Moseley St. Left into Neville St, right at end for Clayton St. and then Newgate St. Left for Leazes Park Rd. *From West:* A69 towards city centre. Left into Clayton Street for Newgate St, left again for Leazes Park Rd. *From North:* A1 then follow signs for Hexham until Percy St. Right into Leazes Park Rd. *Rail:* Newcastle Central ($^1/_2$ mile).

President: Trevor Bennett   **Chairman:** Sir John Hall
General Manager/Secretary: Russell Cushing
Manager: Kevin Keegan   **Assistant:** Terry McDermott
Coaches: Chris McMenemy, Arthur Cox   **Physio:** Derek Wright

League History: 1893 Elected to Division 2; 1898-1934 Division 1; 1934-48 Division 2; 1948-61 Division 1; 1961-65 Division 2; 1965-78 Division 1; 1978-84 Division 2; 1984-89 Division 1; 1989-92 Division 2; 1992-1993 Division 1; 1993- FA Premier League.

Honours: *Football League: Division 1 Champions:* 1904-05, 1906-07, 1908-09, 1926-27, 1992-93; *Division 2 Champions:* 1964-65; *Runners-up:* 1897-98, 1947-48. *FA Cup Winners:* 1910, 1924, 1932, 1951, 1952, 1955; *Runners-up:* 1905, 1906, 1908, 1911, 1974; *Football League Cup Runners-up:* 1975-76; *Texaco Cup Winners:* 1973-74, 1974-75. *UEFA Cup Winners:* 1968-69.

European Record: CC (0): –; CWC (0): – ; UEFA (5): 68-69(W), 69-70(QF), 70-71(2), 77-78 (2), 94-95 (2).

Managers: Frank Watt 1895-1932 (secretary until 1932); Andy Cunningham 1930-35; Tom Mather 1935-39; Stan Seymour 1939-47 (hon manager); George Martin 1947-50; Stan Seymour 1950-54 (hon manager); Duggie Livingstone; 1954-56, Stan Seymour (Non manager) 1956-58; Charlie Mitten 1958-61; Norman Smith 1961-62; Joe Harvey 1962-75; Gordon Lee 1975-77; Richard Dinnis 1977; Bill McGarry 1977-80; Arthur Cox 1980-84; Jack Charlton 1984; Willie McFaul 1985-88; Jim Smith 1988-91; Ossie Ardiles 1991-92; *(FAPL)* Kevin Keegan Feb. 1992-

Season 1994-95

Biggest Home Win: 5-1 v Southampton, 27/8/94
Biggest Home Defeat: 1-2 v Leeds United, 17/4/95
Biggest Away Win: 3-1 v Leicester City 21/8/94, West Ham United 31/8/94
Biggest Away Defeat: 0-3 v Queens Park Rangers, 4/2/95
Biggest Home Attendance: 35,626 v Leeds United 17/4/95;
Crystal Palace 14/5/95
Smallest Home Attendance: 34,163 v Coventry City, 24/8/94
Average Attendance: 34,692
Last Season: *FAPL:* 6th *FA Cup:* Quarter Final
Coca-Cola Cup: 4th round *UEFA Cup:* 2nd round
Leading Scorer: Peter Beardsley – 13

All-time Record

Record FAPL Win: 7-1 v Swindon Town, 12/3/94
Record FAPL Defeat: 0-3 v Queens Park Rangers, 4/2/95
Record FL Win: 13-0 v Newport County, Division 2, 5/10/1946
Record FL Defeat: 0-9 v Burton Wanderers, Division 2, 15/4/1895
Record Cup Win: 9-0 v Southport (at Hillsborough), FA Cup R4, 1/2/1932
Record Fee Received: £7m from Manchester United for Andy Cole, 1/1995
(inc part exchange)
Record Fee Paid: £6m to QPR for Les Ferdinand, 6/95
Most FL Appearances: Jim Lawrence, 432, 1904-22
Record Attendance (all-time): 68,386 v Chelsea, Division 1, 3/9/1930
Record Attendance (FAPL): 36,388 v Manchester United, 11/12/93
Highest Scorer in FAPL Season: Andy Cole, 34, 1993-94
Most FAPL Goals in Season: 82, 1993-94
Most FAPL Points in Season: 77, 1993-94

5-Year League Record

	Div.	P	W	D	L	F	A	Pts	Pos	FAC	FLC
90-91	2	46	14	17	15	49	56	59	11	4	2
91-92	2	46	13	13	20	66	84	52	20	3	3
92-93	1	46	29	4	8	85	37	93	1	5	3
93-94	PL	42	23	8	11	82	41	77	3	4	3
94-95	PL	42	20	12	10	67	47	72	6	QF	4

Summary of FAPL Appearances and Goals 1994-95

Player	Tot	Start	Sub	SNU	PS	Goals	Yel	Red
ALBERT	17	17	0	0	1	2	4	1
ALLEN	1	0	1	3	0	0	0	0
BEARDSLEY	34	34	0	0	4	13	3	0
BERESFORD	33	33	0	0	0	0	7	0
BRACEWELL	16	13	3	5	1	0	1	0
BURRIDGE	0	0	0	1	0	0	0	0
CLARK	19	9	10	9	0	1	0	0
COLE	18	18	0	0	0	9	2	0
DRYSDALE	0	0	0	3	0	0	0	0
ELLIOTT	14	10	4	0	2	2	4	0
FOX	40	40	0	0	6	10	0	0
GILLESPIE	17	15	2	0	1	2	2	0
HARPER	0	0	0	3	0	0	0	0
HOOPER	6	4	2	36	0	0	0	0
HOTTIGER	38	38	0	2	2	1	4	0
HOWEY	30	29	1	2	1	1	5	0
JEFFREY	0	0	0	1	0	0	0	0
KITSON	26	24	2	0	5	8	0	0
LEE	35	35	0	0	6	9	5	1
MATHIE	9	3	6	6	1	1	0	0
NEILSON	6	5	1	6	0	0	0	0
PEACOCK	35	35	0	1	1	1	6	0
SELLARS	12	12	0	0	4	0	2	0
SRNICEK	38	38	0	0	0	0	1	2
VENISON	28	28	0	0	1	1	3	0
WATSON	27	22	5	11	1	4	2	0

OGs 2

Newcastle – Premiership Fact File

- Newcastle win their first six Premiership games, scoring 22 goals in the process and conceding just seven.
- After 11 games undefeated (including nine wins) Manchester United inflict Newcastle's first defeat of the season at Old Trafford.
- Andy Cole scored eight goals in the first 11 games of the season.

Flying Start Before Magpies Falter

With an opening burst of six consecutive victories, Geordies were dreaming of their first top flight championship since 1927. Twenty two goals were scored in that explosive start – including six in five games for Andy Cole – the dreaming looked to have a very real foundation. The unspoilt record went when Liverpool picked up a point at St James' Park but the unbeaten run was stretched to eleven games before Manchester United cast the first serious doubts over Newcastle's seat at the top of the table. Keegan, often hailed as the Messiah on Tyneside, knew that he stood to become an outcast in supporters' eyes in January when he sold goalscoring hero Cole to Manchester United in a deal valued at £7m with Keith Gillespie moving to Newcastle.

That points were dropped against top sides during those ten weeks as league leaders suggested that the Magpies might not quite go the distance. Pole position was surrendered when losing 3-2 to Wimbledon.

A run of one win in eleven games from early November saw the club slip to fourth in the table and 13 points behind the leaders. Keegan, often hailed as the Messiah on Tyneside, knew that he stood to become an outcast in supporters' eyes in January when he sold goalscoring hero Cole to Manchester United in a deal valued at £7m with Keith Gillespie moving to Newcastle.

The loss of Cole was offset by an excellent run of seven wins in nine games, the goals were evenly spread between Paul Kitson (a £2.25m signing from Derby), Ruel Fox and the influential Peter Beardsley – the club's top scorer. United failed to maintain that form and having resurfaced in third place fell away again to finish sixth. During this spell United lost at home to Leeds, a result that ended their 28 match unbeaten home league run and, ultimately, earned Leeds a place in Europe ahead of Newcastle.

In addition to their bright start in the league, United made good progress in three cup competitions. In the UEFA Cup both Robert Lee and Cole hit hat tricks as Royal Antwerp were crushed 10-2. In the 2nd Round, United threw away a three goal lead against Athletic Bilbao to take a slender 3-2 advantage into the return and paid the price when going out on the away goals ruling.

The domestic cups saw Keegan's side handed tough draws. Blackburn were dismissed from the FA Cup in a replay thanks to Lee Clark's 85th minute strike, while a treble from Kitson removed Swansea in the 4th Round. Gillespie, proving to be more than a make-weight in the Cole deal, scored twice as Manchester City were defeated in Round Five but eventual winners Everton stopped the run in the Quarter Final.

United won both legs of their 2nd Round Coca-Cola Cup tie with Barnsley and looked well on course for success when seeing off Manchester United 2-0 at St James' Park in the 3rd Round with late goals from Phillipe Albert and Kitson. In the 4th Round Manchester City were held at Maine Road but City became the first Premier side to win at St James' since the previous January when recording a surprise 2-0 replay victory.

Keegan finally replaced Cole in the close season with the £6m signing of Les Ferdinand from QPR and continued to strengthen his side by acquiring England defender Warren Barton from Wimbledon and the 1994 French Footballer of the Year, David Ginola, from Paris St Germain. ∎

Results 1994-95

Date	Opponents	Ven	Res	Pos	Atten	Scorers
21-Aug	Leicester C	A	3-1	1	20,048	Cole (51); Beardsley (58); Elliott (74)
24-Aug	Coventry C	H	4-0	1	34,163	Lee (21,34); Watson (26); Cole (73)
27-Aug	Southampton	H	5-1	1	34,181	Watson (30, 37); Cole (40,73); Lee (85)
31-Aug	West Ham	A	3-1	1	18,580	OG (31); Lee (35); Mathie (89)
10-Sep	Chelsea	H	4-2	1	34,435	Cole (7,66); Fox (21); Lee (55)
18-Sep	Arsenal	A	3-2	1	36,819	OG (6); Beardsley (45 pen); Fox (74)
24-Sep	Liverpool	H	1-1	1	34,435	Lee (50)
1-Oct	Aston Villa	A	2-0	1	29,960	Lee (66); Cole (83)
9-Oct	Blackburn R	H	1-1	1	34,344	OG (88)
15-Oct	C Palace	A	1-0	1	17,760	Beardsley (89)
22-Oct	Sheffield W	H	2-1	1	34,408	Watson (35), Cole (37)
29-Oct	Man United	A	0-2	1	33,795	
5-Nov	QPR	H	2-1	1	34,278	Kitson (20); Beardsley (42)
7-Nov	N Forest	A	0-0	1	22,102	
19-Nov	Wimbledon	A	2-3	3	14,203	Beardsley (29); Kitson (32)
26-Nov	Ipswich Tn	H	1-1	3	34,459	Cole (86)
3-Dec	Tottenham	A	2-4	3	28,002	Fox (29,41)
10-Dec	Leicester C	H	3-1	3	34,400	Albert (32,70); Howey (50)
17-Dec	Coventry C	A	0-0	3	17,233	
26-Dec	Leeds Utd	A	0-0	3	39,337	
31-Dec	Norwich C	A	1-2	4	21,172	Fox (39 pen)
2-Jan	Man City	H	0-0	5	34,437	
15-Jan	Man United	H	1-1	5	34,471	Kitson (67)
21-Jan	Sheffield W	A	0-0	3	31,215	
25-Jan	Wimbledon	H	2-1	4	34,374	Fox (34); Kitson (51)
1-Feb	Everton	H	2-0	3	34,465	Fox (74); Beardsley (80 pen)
4-Feb	QPR	A	0-3	3	16,576	
11-Feb	N Forest	H	2-1	3	34,471	Fox (47); Lee (73)
25-Feb	Aston Villa	H	3-1	3	34,674	Venison (31); Beardsley (55,66)
28-Feb	Ipswich Tn	A	2-0	3	18,632	Fox (12); Kitson (38)
4-Mar	Liverpool	A	0-2	3	39,300	
8-Mar	West Ham	H	2-0	3	34,595	Clark (17); Kitson (52)
19-Mar	Arsenal	H	1-0	3	35,611	Beardsley (89)
22-Mar	Southampton	A	1-3	3	14,676	Kitson (18)

1-Apr	Chelsea	A	1-1	3	22,987	Hottiger (88)
8-Apr	Norwich C	H	3-0	3	35,518	Beardsley (8 pen, 42); Kitson (74)
14-Apr	Everton	A	0-2	4	34,811	
17-Apr	Leeds Utd	A	1-2	5	35,626	Elliott (30)
29-Apr	Man City	H	0-0	5	27,389	
3-May	Tottenham	H	3-3	5	35,603	Gillespie (7); Peacock (10); Beardsley (70)
8-May	Blackburn R	A	0-1	5	30,545	
14-May	C Palace	H	3-2	6	35,626	Fox (6); Lee (26); Gillespie (28)

UEFA Cup

Date	Opponents	Vn	Rnd	Res	Atten	Scorers
13-Sep	R Antwerp	A	1R1L	5-0	19,700	Lee (1,8,51); Sellars (39); Watson (78)
27-Sep		H	1R2L	5-2	31,383	Lee (11), Cole (26,39,88); Beardsley (36 pen)

Newcastle United win 10-2 on aggregate

| 18-Sep | A Bilbao | H | 2R1L | 3-2 | 32,440 | Fox (9); Beardsley (34 pen); Cole (56) |
| 1-Nov | | A | 2R2L | 0-1 | 47,000 | |

Athletic Bilbao win on away goals – 3-3 on aggregate

FA Challenge Cup

Date	Opponents	Vn	Rnd	Res	Atten	Scorers
8-Jan	Blackburn R	H	3R	1-1	31,721	Lee (56)
18-Jan		A	3RR	2-1	22,658	Hottiger (58); Clark (85)
28-Jan	Swansea City	H	4R	3-0	34,372	Kitson (41,46,72)
19-Feb	Man City	H	5R	3-1	33,219	Gillespie (18,64); Beresford (34)
12-Mar	Everton	A	QF	0-1	35,203	

Coca-Cola League Cup

Date	Opponents	Vn	Rnd	Res	Atten	Scorers
21-Sep	Barnsley	H	2R1L	2-1	27,208	Cole (25); Fox (85)
5-Oct		A	2R2L	1-0	10,992	Cole (39)

Newcastle win 3-1 on aggregate

26-Oct	Man United	H	3R	2-0	34,178	Albert (82); Kitson (87)
30-Nov	Man City	A	4R	1-1	25,162	Jeffrey (11)
21-Dec		H	4RR	0-2	31,056	

Nottingham Forest

Founded in 1865 by players of a hockey-like game, shinney, who played at the Forest Recreation Ground. They played their first game in 1866. Had several early homes, including a former Notts County ground, The Meadows, and Trent Bridge Cricket Ground.

Founder members of the Football Alliance in 1889 and champions in 1892 when elected to an extended Football League top division. In 1898 moved from the Town Ground to the City Ground at West Bridgford. Run by a Committee until 1982, the last League club to become a limited company. Premier League founder members 1992. Relegated after one season, but promoted back at the first attempt.

Ground: City Ground, Nottingham NG2 5FJ
Phone: 0115-952 6000   **News:** 0891 12 11 74
Box Office: 0115-952-6002   **Info:** 0115-952 6016 (24 hrs)
Capacity: 24,000   **Pitch:** 115x78 yd.
Colours: Red, White, Red   **Nickname:** Reds
Directions: *From North:* Leave M1 at Junction 26 for A610 And A606, left into Radcliffe Road for the ground. *From South:* Leave M1 at Junction 24 to Trent Bridge right into Radcliffe Road. *From East:* A52 to West Bridgford and right to the ground. *From West:* A52 To A606 and then as for the North.
Rail: Nottingham

Chairman: Fred Reacher   **Vice-Chairman:** I.I. Korn
Secretary: Paul White
Manager: Frank Clark   **Assistant Manager:** Alan Hill
First Team Coach: Liam O'Kane   **Physio:** John Haselden

League History: 1892 elected to Division 1; 1906-07 Divison 2; 1907-11 Division 1; 1911-22 Division 2; 1922-25 Division 1; 1925-49 Division 2; 1949-51 Division 3(S); 1951-57 Division 2; 1957-72 Division 1; 1972-77 Division 2; 1977-92 Division 1; 1992-93 FA Premier League; 1993-94 Division 1; 1994- FA Premier League.

Honours: *Football League Division 1 Champions:* 1977-78; *Runners-up:* 1966-67, 1978-79; *Division 2 Champions:* 1906-07, 1921-22; *Runners-up:* 1956-57; *Division 3(S) Champions:* 1950-51. *FA Cup Winners:* 1898, 1959; *Runners-up:* 1991. *Anglo-Scottish Cup Winners:* 1976-77. *Football League Cup Winners:* 1977-78, 1978-79, 1988-89, 1989-90; *Runners-up:* 1979-80, 1991-92; *Simod Cup Winners:* 1989; *Zenith Data Systems Cup Winners:*

1991-92; *Champions' Cup Winners:* 1978-79, 1979-80; *European Super Cup Winners:* 1979-80; *Runners-up:* 1980-81. *World Club Championship Runners-up:* 1980-81.

European Record: CC (3): 78-79(W), 79-80(W), 80-81(1); CWC(0): –; UEFA (4): 61-62(1), 67-68(2), 83-84(3), 84-85(1).

Managers: Harry Radford 1889-97; Harry Haslam 1897-09; Fred Earp 1909-12; Bob Masters 1912-25; Jack Baynes 1925-29; Stan Hardy 1930-31; Noel Watson 1931-36; Harold Wightman 1936-39; Billy Walker 1939-60; Andy Beattie 1960-63; John Carey 1963-68; Matt Gillies 1969-72; Dave Mackay 1972-73; Allan Brown 1973-75; (FAPL) Brian Clough 1975-93; Frank Clark June 1993-

Season 1994-95
Biggest Home Win: 4-1 v Sheffield Wed. 10/9/94; Ipswich Town 10/12/94
Biggest Home Defeat: 0-2 v Blackburn Rovers, 29/10/94
Biggest Away Win: 7-1 v Sheffield Wednesday, 1/4/95
Biggest Away Defeat: 0-3 v Blackburn Rovers, 14/1/95
Biggest Home Attendance: 28,882 v Manchester City, 6/5/95
Smallest Home Attendance: 20,010 v Norwich City, 27/12/94
Average Attendance: 23,580
Last Season: *FAPL:* 3rd, *FA Cup:* 4th round, *Coca-Cola Cup:* 4th round
Leading Scorer: Stan Collymore – 23

All-time Record
Record FAPL Win: 7-1 v Sheffield Wednesday, 1/4/95
Record FAPL Defeat: 1-4 v Blackburn, 0-3 v Everton *and* Norwich
Record FL Win: 12-0 v Leicester Fosse, Division 1, 12/4/1909
Record FL Defeat: 1-9 v Blackburn R, Division 2, 10/4/1937
Record Cup Win: 14-0 v Clapton (away), FA Cup R1, 17/1/1891
Record Fee Received: £8.5m from Liverpool for Stan Collymore, 6/1995
Record Fee Paid: £2.2m to Foggia for Bryan Roy, 7/1994
        (Tribunal fees for Bart-Williams/Campbell pending)
Most FL Appearances: Bob McKinlay, 614, 1951-70
Record Attendance (all-time): 49,945 v Manchester Utd., Div 1 28/10/1967
Record Attendance (FAPL): 28,882 v Manchester City, 6/5/95
Highest Scorer in FAPL Season: Stan Collymore, 23, 1994/95
Most FAPL Goals in Season: 72, 1994-95
Most FAPL Points in Season: 77, 1994-95

5-Year League Record

	Div.	P	W	D	L	F	A	Pts	Pos	FAC	FLC
90-91	1	38	14	12	12	65	50	54	8	F	4
91-92	1	42	16	11	15	60	58	59	8	6	F
92-93	PL	42	10	10	22	41	62	40	22	5	5
93/94	1	46	23	14	9	74	49	83	2	3	5
94-95	PL	42	22	11	9	72	43	77	3	4	4

Summary of FAPL Appearances and Goals 1994-95

Player	Tot	Start	Sub	SNU	PS	Goals	Yel	Red
BLACK	10	5	5	4	1	2	1	0
BOHINEN	34	30	4	1	6	6	8	0
BULL	1	1	0	2	0	1	0	0
CHETTLE	41	41	0	0	0	0	4	1
COLLYMORE	37	37	0	0	1	23	4	0
COOPER	35	35	0	0	1	1	7	0
CROSSLEY	42	42	0	0	0	0	1	0
FILAN	0	0	0	9	0	0	0	0
GEMMILL	19	19	0	4	6	1	1	0
HAALAND	20	18	2	4	1	1	1	0
LEE	22	5	17	11	0	3	3	0
LYTTLE	38	38	0	0	1	0	7	0
McGREGOR	10	0	10	9	0	1	1	0
MERCER	0	0	0	7	0	0	0	0
PEARCE	36	36	0	0	0	8	7	0
PHILLIPS	38	38	0	0	1	1	2	0
RIGBY	0	0	0	17	0	0	0	0
ROSARIO	1	0	1	1	0	0	0	0
ROY	37	37	0	0	16	13	4	0
STONE	41	41	0	0	1	5	4	0
TILER	3	3	0	0	0	0	1	0
WARNER	1	1	0	1	0	0	0	0
WEBB	0	0	0	4	0	0	0	0
WOAN	37	35	2	2	6	5	5	0
WRIGHT	0	0	0	9	0	0	0	0

OGs 1

Roy Sparks Collymore

Having regained their place in the Premiership at the first attempt under Frank Clark, Forest strengthened their squad with the £2.2m signing of Dutch international Bryan Roy from Foggia. A flying start to the season was made with an eleven match unbeaten run which took Clark's side to second in the table. The campaign opened with Roy scoring the winner at Ipswich. Stan Collymore then got in on the act with a goal in a 1-1 draw with Manchester United and he went on to score seven times in the next nine games. During the unbeaten run both Sheffield Wednesday and Tottenham were hammered 4-1, England defender Stuart Pearce scored the first of his eight goals for the season during the match with Wednesday. The winning streak, however, came to an abrupt end as Clark's side went five games without a goal.

Blackburn Rovers and Liverpool both took maximum points before Forest salvaged a point at home to Newcastle only for Chelsea and Leeds to extend the winless run. A draw with Arsenal signalled the end of Forest's worst run under Clark. After completing the double over Ipswich, Forest became the first visiting side (1,135 minutes) to score at Old Trafford as United were beaten 2-1 thanks to Collymore and Pearce. The year ended in inconsistent form with just one win against three lowly sides and Forest struggled to regain their touch during the floods of January and February. Wins over Crystal Palace and Chelsea were the high points during a disappointing eight match run, Forest then hit a rich vein of form that no side in the Premiership could hope to match. A draw with QPR was followed by another draw with Spurs before twelve goals were scored during four successive victories but that record almost paled into insignificance on 1st April when Roy and Collymore scored two apiece during a 7-1 destruction of Sheffield Wednesday at Hillsborough. West Ham halted the winning run but four more sides from the wrong end of the table Norwich, Coventry, Palace and Manchester City were all disposed of as Forest won nine games in ten outings; that last win clinched third place for Clark's side. The season closed with a 2-2 draw with Wimbledon.

Forest may have re-established themselves as a force in the Premiership but in the cup competitions the club experienced a disappointing campaign. Early goals from Collymore and Scott Gemmill eased Plymouth out of the FA Cup only for Forest to suffer a surprise home defeat in the 4th Round against Palace just three weeks after beating them in the league. Better progress was made in the Coca-Cola Cup as a brace from Collymore clinched a 2-1 aggregate victory over Hereford United. In the 3rd Round two goals from Pearce helped to see off Wolves 3-2 at Molineux before Millwall claimed their scalp with a two goal victory at the City ground in Round Four.

During the close season another Roy made an impression on Collymore. Roy Evans the Liverpool manager secured his signature for Liverpool for £8.5m. Clark invested around £4m of that on Kevin Campbell (Arsenal) and Chris Bart-Williams (Sheffield Wednesday). ■

Results 1994-95

Date	Opponents	Ven	Res	Pos	Atten	Scorers
20-Aug	Ipswich Tn	A	1-0	6	18,882	Roy (40)
22-Aug	Man United	H	1-1	4	22,072	Collymore (26)
27-Aug	Leicester C	H	1-0	4	21,601	Collymore (38)
30-Aug	Everton	A	2-1	3	26,689	OG (24); Cooper (60)
10-Sep	Sheffield W	H	4-1	2	22,022	Black (34); Bohinen (52); Pearce (63 pen); Roy (82)
17-Sep	Southampton	A	1-1	2	14,185	Collymore (43)
24-Sep	Tottenham	A	4-1	3	24,558	Stone (9); Roy (52,69); Bohinen (79)
2-Oct	QPR	H	3-2	2	21,449	Black (51); Roy (63); Collymore (88)
8-Oct	Man City	A	3-3	2	23,150	Collymore (22,51); Woan (90)
17-Oct	Wimbledon	H	3-1	2	20,187	Bohinen (40); Collymore (66); Woan (74)
22-Oct	Aston Villa	A	2-0	2	29,217	Pearce (1 pen), Stone (70)
29-Oct	Blackburn R	H	0-2	2	22,131	
5-Nov	Liverpool	A	0-1	5	33,329	
7-Nov	Newcastle	H	0-0	5	22,102	
19-Nov	Cheslea	H	0-1	5	22,092	
26-Nov	Leeds Utd	A	0-1	5	38,191	
3-Dec	Arsenal	H	2-2	5	21,662	Pearce (36pen); Roy (60)
10-Dec	Ipswich Tn	H	4-1	4	21,340	Collymore (4); Gemmill (11); Haarland (26); Pearce (42)
17-Dec	Man United	A	2-1	4	43,744	Collymore (35); Pearce (62)
26-Dec	Coventry C	A	0-0		19,224	
27-Dec	Norwich C	H	1-0		20,010	Bohinen (51)
31-Dec	West Ham	H	1-3		20,644	McGregor (89)
2-Jan	C Palace	H	1-0	4	21,326	Bull (76)
14-Jan	Blackburn R	A	0-3	4	27,510	
21-Jan	Aston Villa	H	1-2	5	24,598	Collymore (53pen)
25-Jan	Chelsea	A	2-0	5	17,890	Collymore (33,54)
4-Feb	Liverpool	H	1-1	5	25,418	Collymore (10)
11-Feb	Newcastle	A	1-2	5	34,471	Lee (74)
21-Feb	Arsenal	A	0-1	5	35,441	
26-Feb	QPR	A	1-1	5	13,363	Stone (57)
4-Mar	Tottenham	H	2-2	5	28,711	Bohinen (84); Lee (85)
8-Mar	Everton	H	2-1	5	24,526	Collymore (19); Pearce (54)
11-Mar	Leicester C	A	4-2	5	20,423	Pearce (8 pen); Collymore (64); Woan (68); Lee (90)
18-Mar	Southampton	H	3-0	4	24,146	Roy (38,81); Collymore (63)

Date	Opponents	Vn	Res		Atten	Scorers
22-Mar	Leeds Utd	H	3-0	4	26,299	Roy (9,35); Collymore (44)
1-Apr	Sheffield W	A	7-1	4	30,060	Pearce (17); Woan (20); Roy (48,64); Collymore (78,80); Bohinen (85)
8-Apr	West Ham	H	1-1	4	28,361	Collymore (78)
12-Apr	Norwich C	A	1-0	3	19,005	Stone (85)
17-Apr	Coventry C	H	2-0	3	26,253	Woan (9); Collymore (42)
29-Apr	C Palace	A	2-1	3	15,886	Roy (14); Collymore (67)
6-May	Man City	H	1-0	3	28,882	Collymore (18)
13-May	Wimbledon	A	2-2	3	15,341	Phillips (13); Stone (75)

FA Challenge Cup

Date	Opponents	Vn	Rnd	Res	Atten	Scorers
7-Jan	Plymouth Ar	H	3R	2-0	19,821	Collymore (7); Gemmill (16)
28-Jan	C Palace	H	4R	1-2	16,790	Bohinen (32)

Coca-Cola League Cup

Date	Opponents	Vn	Rnd	Res	Atten	Scorers
21-Sep	Hereford U	H	2R1L	2-1	10,076	Collymore (48,53)
4-Oct		A	2R2L	0-0	8,965	
	Nottingham Forest win 2-1 on aggregate					
26-Oct	Wolves	A	3R	3-2	28,369	Pearce (5,87); Roy (21)
30-Nov	Millwall	H	4R	0-2	12,393	

Forest – Premiership Fact File

- Brian Roy scored on his debut for Forest with the only goal of the game against Ipswich on the opening day of the season.
- Forest were unbeaten in their first 11 Premiership games and scored in every one. The duck was broken by their 2-0 home defeat by Blackburn Rovers on 29 October.
- The Blackburn defeat marked the start of a five match run in which four games were lost and Forest failed to score.
- McGregor scored his first Premiership goal for Forest and it proved to be a last minute winner at West Ham United on the last day of 1994.

Queens Park Rangers

Founded in 1885 as St. Jude's Institute. Changed name to Queens Park Rangers in 1887; joined the London League in 1896; and turned professional in 1898. Moved to the Southern League, 1899, and were twice champions.

Led a nomadic existence in West London but in 1917 took over the home of the amateurs Shepherds Bush, Loftus Road, where, apart from a couple of seasons at White City, it has stayed. Founder members of Football League Division Three in 1920 (this becoming Division Three (South) the following season); of Division Three at the end of regionalisation in 1958; and of the Premier League, 1992.

Ground: Loftus Road, South Africa Road, W12 7PA
Phone: 0181-743 0262   **News:** 0891 12 11 62
Box Office: 0181-749 5744   **Info:** 0181-749 7798 (24Hrs)
Capacity: 19,300   **Pitch:** 112 yds x 72 yds
Colours: Blue/White Hoops, White, White   **Nickname:** Rangers or Rs
Directions: *From North:* M1 to north circular A406 towards Neasden. Turn left onto A404 follow signs for Hammersmith past White City Stadium then right into South Africa Rd. *From South:* A3 across Putney Bridge and signs for Hammersmith. Follow A219 to Shepherds Bush and join A4020 towards Acton. Turn right after ¼ mile into Loftus Rd. *From East:* From A40(M) towards M41 roundabout. Take 3rd exit at roundabout to A4020 then as above. *From West:* M4 to Chiswick then A315 and A402 to Shepherd's Bush joining A4020 (then as above).
Rail: Shepherd's Bush   **Tube** (Central Line): White City

Chairman/Chief Executive: Richard Thompson
Secretary: Sheila Marson
Manager: Ray Wilkins MBE   **Coach:** Frank Sibley
Physio: Brian Morris

League History: 1920 Original Member of Divison 3; 1921 Division 3 (S); 1948-52 Division 2; 1952-58 Division 3 (S); 1958-67 Division 3; 1967-68 Division 2; 1968-69 Division 1; 1969-73 Division 2; 1973-79 Division 1; 1979-83 Division 2; 1983-92 Division 1; 1992 – FA Premier League.

Honours: *Football League: Division 1 Runners-up:* 1975-76; *Division 2 Champions:* 1982-83; *Runners-up:* 1967-68, 1972-73; *Division 3 (S) Champions:* 1947-48; *Runners-up:* 1946-47; *Division 3 Champions:* 1966-67; *FA Cup Runners-up:* 1982; *Football League Cup Winners:* 1966-67;

Runners-up: 1985-86. (In 1966-67 won Division 3 and Football League Cup.)

European Record: CC (0): –; CWC (0): –; UEFA (2): 76-77(QF), 84-85(2).

Managers: James Cowan 1906-13; James Howie 1913-20; Ted Liddell 1920-24; Will Wood 1924-25 (had been secretary since 1903); Bob Hewison 1925-30; John Bowman 1930-31; Archie Mitchell 1931-33; Mick O'Brien 1933-35; Billy Birrell 1935-39; Ted Vizard 1939-44; Dave Mangnall 1944-52; Jack Taylor 1952-59; Alec Stock 1959-65 (GM to 1968); Jimmy Andrews 1965; Bill Dodgin Jnr 1968; Tommy Docherty 1968; Les Allen 1969-70; Gordon Jago 1971-74; Dave Sexton 1974-77; Frank Sibley 1977-78; Steve Burtenshaw 1978-79; Tommy Docherty 1979-80; Terry Venables 1980-84; Gordon Jago 1984; Alan Mullery 1984; Frank Sibley 1984-85; Jim Smith 1985-88; Trevor Francis 1988-90; Don Howe 1990-91; *(FAPL)* Gerry Francis June 1991-Nov 1994; Ray Wilkins Nov 1994-.

Season 1994-95
Biggest Home Win: 3-0 v Newcastle United, 4/2/95
Biggest Home Defeat: 2-3 v Manchester United 10/12/94; Everton 18/3/95
Biggest Away Win: 3-1 v Arsenal 31/12/94; Wimbledon 4/3/95
Biggest Away Defeat: 0-4 v Leeds United, 24/1/95
Biggest Home Attendance: 18,948 v Manchester United, 10/12/94
Smallest Home Attendance: 10,189 v Leicester City, 8/3/95
Average Attendance: 14,499
Last Season: *PL:* 9th *FA Cup:* 3rd round *Coca-Cola Cup:* 4th round
Leading Scorer: Les Ferdinand – 24

All-time Record
Record FAPL Win: 5-1 v Coventry City 23/10/93
Record FAPL Defeat: 0-4 v Leeds Utd 4/4/94, Backburn Rovers 26/11/94
Record FL Win: 9-2 v Tranmere R, Division 3, 3/12/1960
Record FL Defeat: 1-8 v Mansfield Town, Division 3, 15/3/1965;
  Manchester United, Division 1, 19/3/1969
Record Cup Win: 8-1 v Bristol Rovers (away), FA Cup R1, 27/11/1937;
  Crewe Alexandra, Milk Cup R1, 3/10/1983
Record Fee Received: £6m from Newcastle for Les Ferdinand, 5/94
Record Fee Paid: £1m to Luton Town for Roy Wegerle, 12/1989
Most FL Appearances: Tony Ingham, 519, 1950-63
Record Attendance (all-time): 35,353 v Leeds U, Division 1, 27/4/1974
Record Attendance (FAPL): 21,267 v Manchester United, 5/2/94
Highest Scorer in FAPL Season: 24, Les Ferdinand, 1994-95
Most FAPL Goals in Season: 63, 1992-93
Most FAPL Points in Season: 63, 1992-93

5-Year League Record

	Div.	P	W	D	L	F	A	Pts	Pos	FAC	FLC
90-91	1	38	12	10	16	44	53	46	12	3	4
91-92	1	42	12	18	12	48	47	54	11	3	3
92-93	PL	42	17	12	13	63	55	63	5	4	4
93-94	PL	42	16	12	14	62	61	60	9	3	4
94-95	PL	42	17	9	16	61	59	60	8	QF	3

Summary of FAPL Appearances and Goals 1994-95

Player	Tot	Start	Sub	SNU	PS	Goals	Yel	Red
ALLEN	5	2	3	4	0	2	0	0
BARDSLEY	30	30	0	0	0	0	8	0
BARKER	37	37	0	0	4	4	9	0
BREVETT	19	17	2	3	1	0	6	0
CALDWELL	0	0	0	2	0	0	0	0
DICHIO	9	4	5	1	0	3	0	0
DYKSTRA	11	11	0	30	0	0	2	0
FERDINAND	37	37	0	0	5	24	6	1
GALLEN	37	31	6	3	10	10	2	0
HODGE	15	15	0	0	3	0	4	0
HOLLOWAY	31	28	3	2	1	1	6	1
IMPEY	40	40	0	0	3	3	3	0
MADDIX	27	21	6	6	0	1	7	0
McCARTHY	2	0	2	1	0	0	0	0
McDONALD	39	39	0	0	1	1	6	0
MEAKER	8	7	1	0	2	1	0	0
PENRICE	19	9	10	6	3	3	1	0
REEDY	13	11	2	6	1	1	0	0
ROBERTS	31	31	0	10	0	0	1	0
SINCLAIR	33	32	1	2	3	4	4	1
WHITE	1	1	0	0	0	0	0	0
WILKINS	2	1	1	2	1	0	0	0
WILSON	36	36	0	0	3	2	4	1
YATES	23	22	1	5	2	1	1	0
						OGs 1		

Wilkins Leads Rangers Recovery

After two seasons inside the top ten, Rangers fans could be excused for thinking that another decent campaign lay ahead. Eleven games into the season and just one win recorded, those same fans were wondering what else could go wrong. The resignation of manager Gerry Francis answered that question and with top scorer Les Ferdinand departing for Newcastle in June in exchange for £6m a remarkable season was complete. On the plus side, one of the success stories was the form of young Kevin Gallen.

Rangers hardly made the most encouraging of starts with Clive Wilson sent off after just seven minutes of an opening day defeat at Old Trafford. A 3-2 win over Sheffield Wednesday eased the first day blues only for nine games without a victory to send the club to 20th in the table. That run was terminated by four successive home wins which included excellent victories over Liverpool and Leeds, and Danny Dichio's first goals for the club. November, however, ended in near turmoil for Rangers as Francis quit on a point of principle and the team went down to a 4-0 defeat at Blackburn – their third successive away defeat. A replacement was swiftly appointed in Ray Wilkins, who did a fine job in turning around their fortunes.

Manchester United, on 10th December, boosted their title hopes with a 3-2 win at Loftus Road but Rangers hit back with their first away win of the season, 2-0 at Hillsborough. Ferdinand, with seven goals in seven Premiership matches, was in superb form. The year ended with an excellent 3-1 win at Arsenal which took Rangers to their highest position, 14th, for over three months. The new year began disappointingly with just one win in five outings, though that was a comprehensive 3-0 victory over Newcastle. Two good draws with Liverpool and Forest saw Rangers in 17th place before seven wins in nine games – and just six goals conceded – took the club into the top ten for the first time since the previous season. A goal drought was suffered during the latter part of April with just two goals being scored in five games. Ferdinand, though, increased his value by scoring six of Rangers last seven goals of the season. A potentially traumatic campaign ended on a high with a 2-1 victory over Francis' new club, Spurs, being followed by a first ever win over Manchester City at Maine Road.

The city of Manchester had a lot to do with QPR failing to have lengthy runs in the two major cups. After seeing off Aylesbury United 4-0 in the 3rd Round of the FA Cup (complete with their Duck Walk), Rangers faced two successive London derbies. Just four days after losing 4-0 at Leeds, Wilkins' side recovered to put West Ham out of the cup with a Neil Impey goal. In Round Five a replay with Millwall was beckoning before Wilson put Rangers through to the quarter final for the first time since 1989-90 with a last minute penalty. The party ended there as Manchester United saw them off for the third time in the season. ∎

Results 1994-95

Date	Opponents	Ven	Res	Pos	Atten	Scorers
20-Aug	Man United	A	0-2	20	43,214	
24-Aug	Sheffield W	H	3-2	15	12,788	Ferdinand (22); Sinclair (57); Gallen (78)
27-Aug	Ipswich Tn	H	1-2	15	12,456	Ferdinand (90)
31-Aug	Leicester C	A	1-1	14	18,695	OG (41)
10-Sep	Coventry C	H	2-2	20	11,398	Penrice (35,37)
17-Sep	Everton	A	2-2	12	27,285	Ferdinand (4,47)
24-Sep	Wimbledon	H	0-1	15	11,061	
2-Oct	N Forest	A	2-3	13	21,449	Ferdinand (54); Allen (84)
8-Oct	Tottenham	A	1-1	17	25,799	Impey (45)
15-Oct	Man City	H	1-2	19	13,361	Wilson (62)
22-Oct	Norwich C	A	2-4	20	19,431	Barker (24), Gallen (61)
29-Oct	Aston Villa	H	2-0	18	16,037	Dichio (36); Penrice (90)
31-Oct	Liverpool	H	2-1	16	18,295	Sinclair (28); Ferdinand (85)
5-Nov	Newcastle	A	1-2	16	34,278	Dichio (60)
19-Nov	Leeds Utd	H	3-2	18	17,416	Ferdinand (30,39); Gallen (68)
26-Nov	Blackburn R	A	0-4	18	21,302	
4-Dec	West Ham	H	2-1	16	12,780	Ferdinand (2); Sinclair (37)
10-Dec	Man United	A	2-3	17	18,948	Ferdinand (24,64)
17-Dec	Sheffield W	A	2-0	13	22,766	Maddix (60); Ferdinand (84)
26-Dec	C Palace	A	0-0	16	16,372	
28-Dec	Southampton	H	2-2	16	16,078	Barker (7); Gallen (49)
31-Dec	Arsenal	A	3-1	14	32,393	Gallen (3); Allen (76); Impey (77)
14-Jan	Aston Villa	A	1-2	15	26,578	Yates (88)
24-Jan	Leeds Utd	A	0-4	16	28,780	
4-Feb	Newcastle	H	3-0	17	16,576	Ferdinand (4,7); Barker (19)
11-Feb	Liverpool	A	1-1	16	35,996	Gallen (6)
26-Feb	N Forest	H	1-1	17	13,363	Barker (87)
4-Mar	Wimbledon	A	3-1	16	9,176	Ferdinand (24,60); Holloway (49)
8-Mar	Leicester C	H	2-0	14	10,189	McDonald (71); Wilson (73)
15-Mar	Norwich C	H	2-0	11	10,519	Ferdinand (66); Gallen (86)
18-Mar	Everton	H	2-3	11	14,488	Ferdinand (36); Gallen (59)
22-Mar	Chelsea	H	1-0	9	15,103	Gallen (62)
1-Apr	Coventry C	A	1-0	9	15,740	Sinclair (85)
4-Apr	Blackburn R	H	0-1	7	16,508	
8-Apr	Arsenal	H	3-1	9	16,341	Impey (27); Gallen (59); Reddy (82)
11-Apr	Ipswich Tn	A	1-0	8	11,767	Ferdinand (68)

15-Apr	Southampton	A	1-2	8	15,210	Ferdinand (63)
17-Apr	C Palace	H	0-1	8	14,227	
29-Apr	Chelsea	A	0-1	8	21,704	
3-May	West Ham	A	0-0	8	22,923	
6-May	Tottenham	H	2-1	8	18,367	Ferdinand (64,, 75)
14-May	Man City	A	3-2	8	27,850	Ferdinand (13,89); Dichio (77)

FA Challenge Cup

Date	Opponents	Vn	Rnd	Res	Atten	Scorers
7-Jan	Aylesbury U	A	3R	4-0	15,417	Maddix (10); Ferdinand (26); Gallen (40); Meaker (74)
	(at Loftus Road)					
28-Jan	West Ham	H	4R	1-0	17,694	Impey (20)
18-Feb	Millwall	H	5R	1-0	16,457	Wilson (90 pen)
12-Mar	Man United	A	QF	0-2	42,830	

Coca-Cola League Cup

Date	Opponents	Vn	Rnd	Res	Atten	Scorers
20-Sep	Carlisle Utd	A	2R1L	1-0	9,570	Ferdinand (16)
5-Oct		H	2R2L	2-0	6,561	Allen (8); Wilson (pen 38)
	Queens Park Rangers win 3-0 on aggregate					
25-Oct	Man City	H	3R	3-4	11,701	Gallen (15 secs); Sinclair (37); Penrice (87)

QPR – Premiership Fact File

- Kevin Wilson became the first player of the 1994-95 season to be sent off in the Premiership when he was dismissed after eight minutes of the game against Manchester United at Old Trafford.
- Kevin Gallen scored his first Premiership goal against Sheffield Wednesday in QPR's second game of the season while Daniele Dichio made it a scoring debut against Aston Villa in October.
- Ray Wilkins made it a winning start in his first match in charge as manager with a 3-2 defeat of Leeds United.
- QPR had to wait until 17 December to record their first away win of the season. It came at Hillsborough as Sheffield Wednesday were beaten 2-0.

Sheffield Wednesday

Founded in 1867 by members of the Wednesday Cricket Club and played at Highfield before moving to Myrtle Road. Were first holders of the Sheffield FACup. The club played at Sheaf House then Endcliff and became professionals in 1886. In 1887 moved to Olive Grove.

Refused admission to the Football League, the club was founder member, and first champions, of the Football Alliance in 1889. In 1892 most Alliance clubs became founder members of Football League Division Two, but Wednesday were elected to an enlarged top division. The club moved to Hillsborough in 1899. Founder member of the Premier League 1992.

Ground: Hillsborough, Sheffield, S6 1SW
Phone: 0114-234 3122 **News:** 0891 12 11 86
Box Office: 0114-234 7233
Capacity: 40,000 **Pitch:** 115 yds x 77 yds
Colours: Blue/White, Blue, Blue **Nickname:** The Owls
Directions: *From North:* M1 J34 then A6109 to Sheffield. At roundabout after 1½ miles take 3rd exit then turn left after 3 miles into Herries Rd. *From South & East:* M1 J31 or J33 to A57. At roundabout take Prince of Wales Rd exit. A further 6 miles then turn left into Herries Rd South. *From West:* A57 to A6101 then turn left after 4 miles at T junction into Penistone Road.
Rail: Sheffield Midland

Chairman: D.G. Richards **Vice-Chairman:** K.T. Addy
Secretary: G.H. Mackrell FCCA
Manager: David Pleat **Assistant:** Danny Bergara
Physio: D.Galley

League History: 1892 Elected to Division 1; 1899-1900 Division 2; 1900-20 Division 1; 1920-26 Division 2; 1926-37 Division 1; 1937-50 Division 2; 1950-51 Division 1; 1951-52 Division 2; 1952-55 Division 1; 1955-56 Division 2; 1956-58 Division 1; 1958-59 Division 2; 1959-70 Division 1; 1970-75 Division 2; 1975-80 Division 3; 1980-84 Division 2; 1984-90 Division 1; 1990-91 Division 2; 1991-92 Division 1; 1992- FA Premier League.

Honours: *Football League: Division 1 Champions:* 1902-03, 1903-04, 1928-29, 1929-30; *Runners-up:* 1960-61; *Division 2 Champions:* 1899-1900, 1925-26, 1951-52, 1955-56, 1958-59; *Runners-up:* 1949-50, 1983-84. *FA Cup Winners:* 1895-96, 1906-07, 1934-35; *Runners-up:* 1889-90, 1965-66, 1992-93; *Football League Cup Winners:* 1990-91; *Runners-up:* 1992-93.

European Record: CC (0): –; CWC (0): – ; UEFA (3): 61-62(QF), 63-64(2), 92-93(2).

Managers: Arthur Dickinson 1891-1920; Robert Brown 1920-33; Billy Walker 1933-37; Jimmy McMullan 1937-42; Eric Taylor 1942-58 (continued as GM to 1974); Harry Catterick 1958-61; Vic Buckingham 1961-64; Alan Brown 1964-68; Jack Marshall 1968-69; Danny Williams 1969-71; Derek Dooley 1971-73; Steve Burtenshaw 1974-75; Len Ashurst 1975-77; Jackie Charlton 1977-83; Howard Wilkinson 1983-88; Peter Eustace 1988-89; Ron Atkinson 1989-91; *(FAPL)* Trevor Francis June 1991-May 1995; David Pleat July 1995–

Season 1994-95
Biggest Home Win: 5-1 v Coventry City, 28/12/94
Biggest Home Defeat: 1-7 v Nottingham Forest, 1/4/95
Biggest Away Win: 4-1 v Everton, 26/12/94
Biggest Away Defeat: 1-4 v Nottingham Forest 10/9/94, Liverpool 1/10/94
Biggest Home Attendance: 34,051 v Tottenham Hotspur, 20/8/91
Smallest Home Attendance: 20,395 v Wimbledon, 11/3/95
Average Attendance: 25.323
Last Season: *FAPL:* 13th *FA Cup:* 4th round *Coca-Cola Cup:* 4th round
Leading Scorer: Mark Bright – 11

All-time Record
Record FAPL Win: 5-0 v Ipswich Town, 23/4/94; West Ham, 18/12/93
Record FAPL Defeat: 1-7 v Nottingham Forest, 1/4/95
Record FL Win: 9-1 v Birmingham, Division 1, 13/12/1930
Record FL Defeat: 0-10 v Aston Villa, Division 1, 5/10/1912
Record Cup Win: 12-0 v Halliwell, FA Cup R1, 17/1/1891
Record Fee Received: £2.7m from Blackburn R. for Paul Warhurst, 9/1993
Record Fee Paid: £2.7m to Sampdoria for Des Walker, 7/1993 *and* £2.7m to QPR for Andy Sinton, 8/1993
Most FL Appearances: Andy Wilson, 502, 1900-20
Record Attendance (all-time): 72,841 v Man City, FA Cup R5, 17/2/1934
Record Attendance (FAPL): 37,708 v Manchester United, 26/12/92
Highest Scorer in FAPL Season: Bright, 19, 1993-94
Most FAPL Goals in Season: 76, 1993-94
Most FAPL Points in Season: 64, 1993-94

5-Year League Record

	Div.	P	W	D	L	F	A	Pts	Pos	FAC	FLC
90-91	2	46	22	16	8	80	51	82	3	5	W
91-92	1	42	21	12	9	62	49	75	3	4	3
92-93	PL	42	15	14	13	55	51	59	7	F	F
93-94	PL	42	16	16	10	76	54	64	7	4	SF
94-95	PL	42	13	12	17	49	57	51	13	4	4

Summary of FAPL Appearances and Goals 1994-95

Player	Tot	Start	Sub	SNU	PS	Goals	Yel	Red
ATHERTON	41	41	0	0	2	1	5	0
BART-WILLIAMS	38	32	6	0	7	2	6	0
BRIGHT	37	33	4	0	8	11	3	0
BRISCOE	6	6	0	0	3	0	0	0
COLEMAN	1	1	0	1	0	0	1	0
DONALDSON	1	0	1	0	0	0	0	0
HIRST	15	13	2	0	4	3	2	0
HYDE	35	33	2	0	5	5	7	0
INGESSON	13	9	4	0	3	2	2	0
JONES	5	3	2	0	1	0	0	0
KEARN	0	0	0	1	0	0	0	0
KEY	0	0	0	27	0	0	0	0
NOLAN	42	42	0	0	1	3	4	0
PEARCE	34	34	0	1	0	0	12	0
PETRESCU	29	20	9	0	8	3	3	0
PORIC	4	1	3	1	1	0	0	0
PRESSMAN	34	34	0	5	0	0	1	1
SHERIDAN	36	34	2	0	6	1	3	0
SINTON	25	22	3	1	7	0	1	0
TAYLOR	14	9	5	1	2	1	1	0
WADDLE	25	20	5	1	6	4	1	0
WALKER	38	38	0	0	3	0	2	1
WATSON	23	5	18	1	3	2	0	1
WATTS	0	0	0	3	0	0	0	0
WHITTINGHAM	21	16	5	0	4	9	0	0
WILLIAMS	10	8	2	1	0	1	0	0
WOODS	9	8	1	8	0	0	0	0

OGs 1

Francis Out as Owls Play the Fool

Since his appointment as manager of Sheffield Wednesday in 1991, Trevor Francis had enjoyed reasonable success although it was often a case of so near. Having finished seventh in the Premiership for the past two seasons, and having been finalists in both the FA and Coca-Cola Cups, and semi finalists again in the Coca-Cola the following year, Francis was busy in the transfer market during the close season in an effort to finally secure some silverware. Klas Ingesson, Dan Petrescu, Ian Nolan, Ian Taylor and Peter Atherton were purchased at a cost of £6.6m although Taylor departed in December for £1m. Other departures were Carlton Palmer, Nigel Worthington and Phil King for a total of £3.1m. The squad was strengthened in December when Chris Waddle's long lay-off though injury ended.

Owls supporters witnessed an entertaining start to the season although the first two games were lost, 4-3 to Tottenham (Petrescu scored his first goal) and 5-1 at QPR. Two successive clean sheets suggested better things defensively before the illusion was shattered with a 4-1 defeat at Francis' former club Nottingham Forest. Two draws preceded another 4-1 thrashing, this time at Anfield, as October began with the Owls down in 18th position. Successive wins over Manchester United, surprisingly, and Ipswich, not such a surprise, lifted Wednesday five places. But just two wins from the next nine games put Wednesday back in 18th place, only for Christmas presents to come in the form of 4-1 and 5-1 victories over Everton and Coventry, a win over Leicester took Francis' side up to ninth. Just when it seemed that Wednesday were on the right path, supported by wins over West Ham and Arsenal, The Owls embarked on a dismal run of only three wins in fifteen outings – two of the wins were against relegation bound sides. Solace was found in the form of a Yorkshire derby victory over Leeds but that became almost meaningless once the side went down to a humiliating 7-1 defeat to Nottingham Forest at Hillsborough on April Fools Day.

Wednesday's inconsistent and frustrating season was never better illustrated than during their brief FA Cup run. Following a 2-1 win at Gillingham, in which 'keeper Kevin Pressman was dismissed, they drew at home to Wolves having tossed away the chance of victory through a missed penalty. The replay at Molineux ended level after extra time. Wednesday went three up in the penalty shoot-out but completely lost their nerve as Wolves came back to gain surely the most outrageous victory of the season.

Having reached at least the semi-final of the Coca-Cola Cup in three of the previous four seasons, Wednesday were none too convincing when overcoming county rivals Bradford City over two legs but went through 2-1 and progressed through to the 4th Round with a Chris Bart-Williams goal seeing off Southampton. But hopes of matching previous runs were ended by Arsenal in Round Four.

In the close season Trevor Francis was dismissed with the Luton Town manager David Pleat taking over, as Bart-Williams moved for £2m. ∎

Results 1994-95

Date	Opponents	Ven	Res	Pos	Atten	Scorers
20-Aug	Tottenham	H	3-4	17	34,051	Petrescu (54); OG (66); Hirst (83)
24-Aug	QPR	A	2-3	14	12,788	Sheridan (38); Hyde (74)
27-Aug	Wimbledon	A	1-0	14	7,453	Watson (79)
31-Aug	Norwich C	H	0-0	12	25,072	
10-Sep	N Forest	A	1-4	15	22,022	Hyde (56)
17-Sep	Man City	H	1-1	16	26,776	Watson (76)
26-Sep	Leeds Utd	H	1-1	17	23,227	Bright (15)
1-Oct	Liverpool	A	1-4	18	31,493	Nolan (33)
8-Oct	Man United	H	1-0	16	33,441	Hirst (44)
16-Oct	Ipswich Tn	A	2-1	13	13,073	Bright (8); Hirst (89)
22-Oct	Newcastle	A	1-2	14	34,408	Taylor (55)
29-Oct	Chelsea	H	1-1	15	25,450	Bright (67)
2-Nov	Blackburn R	H	0-1	17	24,207	
6-Nov	Arsenal	A	0-0	16	33,705	
19-Nov	West Ham	H	1-0	16	25,350	Petrescu (28)
27-Nov	Aston Villa	A	1-1	15	25,082	Atherton (58)
3-Dec	C Palace	H	1-0	14	21,930	Bart-Williams (19)
10-Dec	Tottenham	A	1-3	14	25,912	Nolan (37)
17-Dec	QPR	H	0-2	18	22,766	
26-Dec	Everton	A	4-1	15	37,080	Bright (39); Whittingham (42,79); Ingesson (47)
28-Dec	Coventry C	H	5-1	13	26,056	Bright (14,45); Waddle (38); Whittingham (57,64)
31-Dec	Leicester C	A	1-0	9	20,624	Hyde (40)
2-Jan	Southampton	A	1-1	10	28,424	Hyde (19)
14-Jan	Chelsea	A	1-1	10	17,285	Nolan (90)
21-Jan	Newcastle	H	0-0	9	31,215	
23-Jan	West Ham	A	2-0	7	14,554	Waddle (32); Bright (82)
4-Feb	Arsenal	H	3-1	8	23,468	Petrescu (8); Ingesson (25); Bright (90)
12-Feb	Blackburn R	A	1-3	8	22,223	Waddle (32)
18-Feb	Aston Villa	H	1-2	8	24,063	Bright (71)
25-Feb	Liverpool	H	1-2	9	31,932	Bart-Williams (14)
4-Mar	Leeds Utd	A	1-0	8	33,750	Waddle (11)
8-Mar	Norwich C	A	0-0	8	13,530	
11-Mar	Wimbledon	H	0-1	8	20,395	
14-Mar	C Palace	A	1-2	8	10,422	Whittingham (31)
18-Mar	Man City	A	2-3	9	23,255	Whittingham (13); Hyde (21)

1-Apr	N Forest	H	1-7	11	30,060	Bright (52pen)
8-Apr	Leicester C	H	1-0	10	22,551	Whittingham (38)
15-Apr	Coventry C	A	0-2	11	15,710	
17-Apr	Everton	A	0-0	12	27,880	
29-Apr	Southampton	A	0-0	14	15,189	
7-May	Man United	A	0-1	14	43,868	
14-May	Ipswich Tn	H	4-1	13	30,213	Whittingham (7,58); Williams (55); Bright (89)

FA Challenge Cup

Date	Opponents	Vn	Rnd	Res	Atten	Scorers
7-Jan	Gillingham	A	3R	2-1	10,452	Waddle (31); Bright (32)
29-Jan	Wolves	H	4R	0-0	21,757	
8-Feb	Wolves	A	4RR	1-1	28,136	Bright (56)

after extra time – Wolves won 4-3 on penalties

Coca-Cola League Cup

Date	Opponents	Vn	Rnd	Res	Atten	Scorers
21-Sep	Bradford C	H	2R1L	2-1	15,705	Taylor (71); Hyde (81)
4-Oct	Bradford City	A	2R2L	1-1	13,092	Bart-Williams (29)

Sheffield Wednesday win 3-2 on aggregate

| 26-Oct | Southampton | H | 3R | 1-0 | 16,715 | Bart-Williams (50) |
| 30-Nov | Arsenal | A | 4R | 0-2 | 27,390 | |

Wednesday – Premiership Fact File

- Dan Petrescu scored a debut goal on the opening day of the season against Tottenham, while Ian Noland's first Premiership goal came against Liverpool at the start of October.
- Gordon Watson was shown the Red Card against Leeds United in September. Yet despite making a total of 23 appearances for Wednesday that was his only indiscretion of the season – no yellow cards!
- Wednesday's 7-1 home defeat by Nottingham Forest on April Fools Day was their biggest ever defeat in the Premiership.

Southampton

Formed 1885 by members of the St Mary's Young Men's Association, St Mary's FC. The church link was dropped, though the name retained, in 1893. In 1895 applied for a Southern League place, but was refused only to be invited to fill a subsequent vacancy. 'St. Mary's' was dropped after two seasons. Moved from the County Cricket Ground to the Dell in 1898.

Six times Southern League champions, Southampton were founder members of Football League Division Three in 1920 (this becoming Division Three (South) the following season); of Division Three at the end of regionalisation in 1958; and of the Premier League, 1992.

Ground: The Dell, Milton Road, Southampton, SO9 4XX
Phone: 01703-220505   **News:** 0891 12 15 93
Box Office: 01703-228575
Capacity: 15,288   **Pitch:** 110 yds x 72 yds
Colours: Red/White, Black, Black   **Nickname:** The Saints
Directions: *From North:* A33 into The Avenue then right into Northlands Rd. Right at the end into Archer's Rd. *From East:* M27 then A334 and signs for Southampton along A3024. Follow signs for the West into Commercial Rd, right into Hill Lane then first right into Milton Rd. *From West:* Take A35 then A3024 towards city centre. Left into Hill Lane and first right into Milton Rd.
Rail: Southampton Central

President: J. Corbett   **Chairman:** F.G. Askham FCA
Vice-Chairman: K. St. J. Wiseman   **Secretary:** Brian Truscott
Director of Football: Lawrie Mcmenemy
Manager: Dave Merrington   **Assistant:** Lew Chatterley
Physio: Don Taylor

League History: 1920 Original Member of Division 3; 1921 Division 3 (S); 1922-53 Division 2; 1953-58 Division 3 (S); 1958-60 Division 3; 1960-66 Division 2; 1966-74 Division 1; 1974-78 Division 2; 1978-92 Division 1; 1992 – FA Premier League.

Honours: *Football League: Division 1 Runners-up:* 1983-84; *Division 2 Runners-up:* 1965-66, 1977-78; *Division 3 (S) Champions:* 1921-22; *Runners-up:* 1920-21; *Division 3 Champions:* 1959-60. *FA Cup Winners:* 1975-76; *Runners-up:* 1900, 1902. *Football League Cup Runners-up:* 1978-79. *Zenith Data Systems Cup Runners-up:* 1991-92.

European Record: CWC (1): 76-77(QF). UEFA (5): 69-70(3), 71-72(1), 81-82(2), 82-83(1), 84-85(1).

Managers: Cecil Knight 1894-95; Charles Robson 1895-97; E. Arnfield 1897-1911 (continued as secretary); George Swift 1911-12; E. Arnfield 1912-19; Jimmy McIntyre 1919-24; Arthur Chadwick 1925-31; George Kay 1931-36; George Cross 1936-37; Tom Parker 1937-43; J.R. Sarjantson stepped down from the board to act as secretary-manager 1943-47 with the next two listed being team managers during this period); Arthur Dominy 1943-46; Bill Dodgin Snr 1946-49; Sid Cann 1949-51; George Roughton 1952-55; Ted Bates 1955-73; Lawrie McMenemy 1973-85; Chris Nicholl 1985-91; *(FAPL)* Ian Branfoot 1991-94; Alan Ball Jan 1994-July 1995.

Season 1994-95
Biggest Home Win: 3-1 v Ipswich Town 1/10/94; Newcastle United 22/3/95; Crystal Palace 3/5/95
Biggest Home Defeat: 1-3 v Leeds United, 29/10/94
Biggest Away Win: 3-1 v Coventry City, 24/9/94
Biggest Away Defeat: 1-5 v Newcastle United, 27/8/94
Biggest Home Attendance: 15,204 v Manchester United, 31/12/94
Smallest Home Attendance: 12,976 v Norwich City, 2/11/94
Average Attendance: 14,013
Last Season: *PL:* 10th *FA Cup:* 5th round *Coca-Cola Cup:* 3rd round
Leading Scorer: Matt Le Tissier – 20

All-time Record
Record FAPL Win: 5-1 v Swindon Town, 25/8/93
Record FAPL Defeat: 1-5 v Newcastle United, 27/8/94
Record FL Win: 9-3 v Wolverhampton Wanderers, Division 2, 18/9/1965
Record FL Defeat: 0-8 v Tottenham Hotspur, Division 2, 28/3/1936; Everton, Division 1, 20/11/1971
Record Cup Win: 7-1 v Ipswich Town, FA Cup R3, 7/1/1961
Record Fee Received: £3.3m from Blackburn R. for Alan Shearer, 7/1992
Record Fee Paid: £1.2m to Chelsea for Neil Shipperley, 1/1995
Most FL Appearances: Terry Payne, 713, 1956-74
Record Attendance (all-time): 31,044 v Man United, Division 1, 8/10/1969
Record Attendance (FAPL): 19,654 v Tottenham Hotspur, 15/8/92
Highest Scorer in FAPL Season: 25, Matthew Le Tissier, 1993-94
Most FAPL Goals in Season: 61, 1994-95
Most FAPL Points in Season: 54, 1994-95

5-Year League Record

	Div.	P	W	D	L	F	A	Pts	Pos	FAC	FLC
90-91	1	38	12	9	17	58	69	45	14	5	5
91-92	1	42	14	10	18	39	55	52	16	6	4
92-93	PL	42	13	11	18	54	61	50	18	3	3
93-94	PL	42	12	7	23	49	66	43	18	3	2
94-95	PL	42	12	18	12	61	63	54	10	5	3

Summary of FAPL Appearances and Goals 1994-95

Player	Tot	Start	Sub	SNU	PS	Goals	Yel	Red
ALLAN	0	0	0	1	0	0	0	0
ALLEN	11	11	0	1	1	0	2	0
BANGER	4	4	0	3	0	2	0	0
BEASANT	13	12	1	29	0	0	0	0
BENALI	35	32	3	1	3	0	11	0
CHARLTON	25	25	0	1	5	1	1	0
DODD	26	24	2	1	0	2	4	0
DOWIE	17	17	0	0	0	5	2	0
EKELUND	17	15	2	0	4	5	1	0
GROBBELAAR	30	30	0	9	1	0	1	0
HALL	37	36	1	0	3	4	4	0
HEANEY	34	21	13	1	7	2	4	0
HOPPER	0	0	0	3	0	0	0	0
HUGHES	12	2	10	3	1	2	2	0
KENNA	28	28	0	0	1	0	1	0
LE TISSIER	41	41	0	0	3	20	5	0
MADDISON	35	35	0	0	7	3	2	0
MAGILTON	42	42	0	0	2	6	3	0
MASKELL	6	2	4	4	1	0	1	0
McDONALD	2	0	2	0	0	0	0	0
MONKOU	31	31	0	0	3	1	11	0
OAKLEY	1	0	1	0	0	0	0	0
ROBINSON	1	0	1	0	0	0	0	0
SHIPPERLEY	19	19	0	0	2	4	3	0
TISDALE	6	0	6	5	0	0	0	0
WATSON	12	12	0	0	2	3	2	0
WHISTON	1	0	1	4	0	0	0	0
WIDDRINGTON	28	23	5	8	6	0	6	0

OGs 1

Le Tizz Still the Bizz

With crowd favourite Alan Ball at the helm for his first full season at the Dell, Saints supporters looked forward to better days after three successive battles against relegation and poor cup results. Ball made minor changes to his squad which included the signing of Bruce Grobbelaar. The Zimbabwe international saved an Alan Shearer penalty on his debut but Saints made a sorry start with just one win in six games and were thrashed 5-1 at Newcastle. Matt Le Tissier, who again proved himself to be the most gifted Englishman in the Premiership but who was consistently overlooked at international level, opened his account with a cracking effort at Aston Villa. Defender Ken Monkou was not so fortunate as he suffered a collapsed lung when colliding with David James during a home defeat against Liverpool.

The corner was turned on 12th September with a 2-1 win at Tottenham; three wins and a draw from the next four games took Southampton to seventh. The winning streak came to an unlikely end at bottom dogs Leicester although Saints battled back from four down to almost rescue a point. Defeats followed against West Ham and Leeds but a mid-table position was maintained during two successive draws and a win over Arsenal. The cry of *Le Tissier for England* was never heard louder than on 10th December when he scored twice during a 3-2 defeat at Blackburn which included a stupendous effort past Tim Flowers from all of 35 yards. The Channel Islander scored a last minute winner as Saints defeated Villa nine days later in what turned out to be their last league success for three months. During that period Neil Shipperley joined from Chelsea for £1.2m while Jeff Kenna signed for Blackburn for £1.5 and Iain Dowie moved to Crystal Palace. A remarkable sequence of seven consecutive draws, followed by two defeats and two draws, edged Ball's side down to 18th before excellent wins over Newcastle and Spurs eased the threat of relegation. A trio of wins over Chelsea, QPR and Wimbledon, made them almost certain of safety which was finally secured on the final day of the season with a point at home to Leicester.

Southampton put their slow start to the league behind them in the Coca Cola Cup with a 5-0 aggregate victory over Huddersfield in the 1st Round, Le Tissier scored all five goals. Sheffield Wednesday maintained Saints poor recent cup form in the 3rd Round with a 1-0 win at Hillsborough. Southampton kicked off the new year with a Neil Heaney goal in just 16 seconds as Southend were put out of the FA Cup 2-0 at the Dell. A backs to the wall draw was salvaged at Luton in the 4th Round before the Saints went on a goal spree with a 6-0 replay victory. Southampton recorded an impressive draw away to Spurs in the 5th Round and led 2-0 at half time in the replay only for Ronny Rosenthal to turn the tide and send the Saints sliding to an astonishing 6-2 extra time defeat. Midway through the close season Ball departed The Dell to join Manchester City as manager. ■

Results 1994-95

FA Carling Premiership

Date	Opponents	Ven	Res	Pos	Atten	Scorers
20-Aug	Blackburn R	H	1-1	11	14,209	Banger (15)
24-Aug	Aston Villa	A	1-1	17	24,179	Le Tissier (89)
27-Aug	Newcastle	A	1-5	17	34,181	Banger (53)
31-Aug	Liverpool	H	0-2	18	15,190	
12-Sep	Tottenham	A	2-1	15	22,387	Le Tissier (75,89)
17-Sep	N Forest	H	1-1	14	14,185	Le Tissier (54 pen)
24-Sep	Coventry	A	3-1	13	11784	Dowie (34,55); Ekelund (81)
1-Oct	Ipswich Tn	H	3-1	8	13,246	Maddison (53); Ekelund (65); Dowie (90)
8-Oct	Everton	H	2-0	7	15,163	Ekelund (19); Le Tissier (72)
15-Oct	Leicester C	A	3-4	10	20,020	Dowie (78,90); Le Tissier (90)
22-Oct	West Ham	A	0-2	10	18,853	
29-Oct	Leeds Utd	H	1-3	12	15,202	Maddison (44)
2-Nov	Norwich C	H	1-1	13	12,876	Le Tissier (89 pen)
5-Nov	Man City	A	3-3	12	21,589	Hall (26); Ekelund (62,66)
19-Nov	Arsenal	H	1-0	9	15,201	Magilton (60)
26-Nov	C Palace	A	0-0	11	14,007	
3-Dec	Chelsea	H	0-1	13	14,404	
10-Dec	Blackburn R	A	2-3	13	23,372	Le Tissier (65,78)
19-Dec	Aston Villa	H	2-1	12	13,874	Hall (8); Le Tissier (90)
26-Dec	Wimbledon	H	2-3	14	14,603	Dodd (10); Le Tissier (43)
28-Dec	QPR	A	2-2	14	16,078	Dodd (14); Hughes (71)
31-Dec	Man United	H	2-2	15	15,204	Magilton (45); Hughes (73)
2-Jan	Sheffield W	A	1-1	15	28,424	Le Tissier (70 pen)
14-Jan	Leeds Utd	A	0-0	14	28,953	
24-Jan	Arsenal	A	1-1	14	27,213	Magilton (74)
4-Feb	Man City	H	2-2	15	14,902	OG (24); Le Tissier (60)
11-Feb	Norwich C	H	2-2	15	18,361	Hall (33); Magilton (36)
25-Feb	Ipswich Tn	A	1-2	18	16,076	Maddison (38)
4-Mar	Coventry C	A	0-0	18	14,505	
15-Mar	West Ham	H	1-1	20	15,178	Shipperley (48)
18-Mar	N Forest	A	0-3	20	24,146	
22-Mar	Newcastle	H	3-1	19	14,676	Heaney (86); Watson (89); Shipperley (90)
2-Apr	Tottenham	H	4-3	17	15,105	Heaney (13); Le Tissier (44,58); Magilton (62)
5-Apr	Liverpool	A	1-3	17	29,881	Hall (13)
12-Apr	Chelsea	A	2-0	14	16,738	Shipperley (10); Le Tissier (32)

15-Apr	QPR	H	2-1	13	15,201	Shipperley (50); Watson (67)
17-Apr	Wimbledon	A	2-0	11	10,521	Le Tissier (9); Magilton (30)
29-Apr	Sheffield W	H	0-0	11	15,189	
3-May	C Palace	H	3-1	10	15,151	Le Tissier (1); Watson (9); Le Tissier (86)
6-May	Everton	A	0-0	10	36,840	
10-May	Man United	A	1-2	10	43,479	Charlton (6)
14-May	Leicester C	H	2-2		15,101	Monkou (21); Le Tissier (55)

FA Challenge Cup

Date	Opponents	Vn	Rnd	Res	Atten	Scorers
7-Jan	Southend Utd	H	3R	2-0	13,003	Heaney (16 secs); Le Tissier (42)
28-Jan	Luton Town	A	4R	1-1	9,938	Shipperley (54)
8-Feb		H	4RR	6-0	15,075	Le Tissier (6,36 pen); Magilton (32); Heaney (40); Monkou (50); Hughes (67)
18-Feb	Tottenham	A	5R	1-1	28,091	Le Tissier (21 pen)
1-Mar		H	5RR	2-6	15,172	Shipperley (5); Le Tissier (39 pen)

Coca-Cola League Cup

Date	Opponents	Vn	Rnd	Res	Atten	Scorers
20-Sep	Huddersfield	A	2R1L	1-0	13,814	Le Tissier (90)
5-Oct	Huddersfield	H	2R2L	4-0	12,042	Le Tissier (40,66,69,83)
	Southampton win 5-0 on aggregate					
26-Oct	Sheffield W	A	3R	0-1	16,715	

Saints – Premiership Fact File

- Bruce Grobbelaar saved an Alan Shearer penalty on his home debut in the first game of the season to earn Saints a point.
- Jim Magilton scored his first Premiership goal in the 1-0 win over Arsenal in November.
- Matt Le Tissier scored no less than five goals in the last minute of play, three of which earned the Saints a win and the other two draws!
- Southampton failed to score in just nine of their Premiership games.

Tottenham Hotspur

Formed in 1882 by members of the schoolboys' Hotspur Cricket Club and Hotspur FC and had early Church connections. Added 'Tottenham' to distinguish club from others with similar names in 1885. Turned professional in 1895 and elected to the Southern League in 1896 having been rebuffed by the Football League.

Played at several places before moving to the site which became known as White Hart Lane in 1899. Joined the Football League Second Division 1908. Having failed to gain a place in the re-election voting, it secured a vacancy caused by a late resignation. Premier League founder members 1992.

Ground: 748 High Road, Tottenham, London, N17 0AP
Phone: 0181-365 5000   **News:** 0891-100 500
Box Office: 0181-365 5050
Capacity: 30,246   **Pitch:** 110yds x 73 yds
Colours: White, Navy Blue, White   **Nickname:** Spurs
Directions: A406 North Circular to Edmonton. At traffic lights follow sign for Tottenham along A1010 then Fore St for ground.
Rail: White Hart Lane (adjacent)
Tube: Seven Sisters (Victoria Line) or Manor House (Piccadilly Line)

Chairman: Alan Sugar   **President:** W.E. Nicholson OBE
Chief Executive: C. Littner   **Secretary:** Peter Barnes
Manager: Gerry Francis   **Physio:** Tony Lenaghan

League History: 1908 Elected to Division 2; 1909-15 Division 1; 1919-20 Division 2; 1920-28 Division 1; 1928-33 Division 2; 1933-35 Division 1; 1935-50 Division 2; 1950-77 Division 1; 1977-78 Division 2; 1978-92 Division 1; 1992- FA Premier League.

Honours: *Football League: Division 1 Champions:* 1950-51, 1960-61; *Runners-up:* 1921-22, 1951-52, 1956-57, 1962-63; *Division 2 Champions:* 1919-20, 1949-50; *Runners-up:* 1908-09, 1932-33; *FA Cup Winners:* 1900-01, 1920-21, 1960-61, 1961-62, 1966-67, 1980-81, 1981-82, 1990-91; *Runners-up:* 1986-87; *Football League Cup Winners:* 1970-71, 1972-73; *Runners-up:* 1981-82; *Cup-Winners' Cup Winners:* 1962-63; *Runners-up:* 1981-82; *UEFA Cup Winners:* 1971-72, 1983-84; *Runners-up:* 1973-74.

European Record: CC (1): 61-62(SF); CWC (6): 62-63 (W), 63-64(2), 67-68(2), 81-82 (F), 82-83(2), 91-92(QF). UEFA (5): 71-72 (W), 72-73(SF), 73-74 (F), 83-84 (W), 84-85(QF).

Managers: Frank Brettell 1898-99; John Cameron 1899-1906; Fred Kirkham 1907-08; Peter McWilliam 1912-27; Billy Minter 1927-29; Percy Smith 1930-35; Jack Tresadern 1935-38; Peter McWilliam 1938-42; Arthur Turner 1942-46; Joe Hulme 1946-49; Arthur Rowe 1949-55; Jimmy Anderson 1955-58; Bill Nicholson 1958-74; Terry Neill 1974-76; Keith Burkinshaw 1976-84; Peter Shreeves 1984-86; David Pleat 1986-87; Terry Venables 1987-91; Peter Shreeves 1991-92; Ossie Ardiles June 1993-Nov 1994; Gerry Francis Nov 1994-.

Season 1994-95

Biggest Home Win: 3-0 v Ipswich Town, 8/3/95
Biggest Home Defeat: 1-4 v Nottingham Forest, 24/9/94
Biggest Away Win: 4-0 v Coventry City, 31/12/94
Biggest Away Defeat: 2-5 v Manchester City, 22/10/94
Biggest Home Attendance: 33,040 v Leeds United, 14/5/95
Smallest Home Attendance: 22,387 v Southampton, 12/9/94
Average Attendance: 26,193
Last Season: *FAPL:* 7th *FA Cup:* Semi Final *Coca-Cola Cup:* 3rd round
Leading Scorer: Jurgen Kinsmann – 24

All-time Record

Record FAPL Win: 5-0 v Oldham Athletic, 18/9/93
Record FAPL Defeat: 0-6 v Sheffield United, 2/3/93
Record FL Win: 9-0 v Bristol Rovers, Division 2, 22/10/1977
Record FL Defeat: 0-7 v Liverpool, Division 1, 2/9/1978
Record Cup Win: 13-2 v Crewe Alex, FA Cup, R4 replay, 3/2/1960
Record Fee Received: £5.5m from Lazio for Paul Gascoigne, 5/1992
Record Fee Paid: £4.5m to Crystal Palace for Chris Armstrong, 6/1995
Most FL Appearances: Steve Perryman, 655, 1969-86
Record Attendance (all-time): 75,038 v Sunderland, FA Cup R6, 5/3/1938
Record Attendance (FAPL): 33,709 v Arsenal, 12/12/92
Highest Scorer in FAPL Season: Jurgen Klinsmann, 24, 1994-95
Most FAPL Goals in Season: 66, 1994-95
Most FAPL Points in Season: 62, 1994-95

5-Year League Record

	Div.	P	W	D	L	F	A	Pts	Pos	FAC	FLC
90-91	1	38	11	16	11	51	50	49	10	W	5
91-92	1	42	15	7	20	58	63	52	15	3	SF
92-93	PL	42	16	11	15	60	66	59	8	SF	4
93-94	PL	42	11	12	19	54	59	45	15	4	5
94-95	Pl	42	16	14	12	66	58	62	7	SF	3

Summary of FAPL Appearances and Goals 1994-95

Player	Tot	Start	Sub	SNU	PS	Goals	Yel	Red
ANDERTON	37	37	0	0	2	5	3	0
AUSTIN	24	23	1	1	0	0	5	0
BARMBY	38	37	1	1	9	9	0	0
CALDERWOOD	36	35	1	2	3	2	4	1
CAMPBELL	30	29	1	0	5	0	0	1
CASKEY	4	1	3	8	1	0	0	0
CUNDY	0	0	0	0	0	0	0	0
DAY	0	0	0	20	0	0	0	0
DOZZELL	7	6	1	0	3	0	1	0
DUMITRESCU	13	11	2	1	3	4	1	0
EDINBURGH	31	29	2	3	1	0	6	0
HAZARD	11	2	9	2	2	0	2	0
HILL	3	1	2	0	0	0	0	0
HOWELLS	26	26	0	0	5	1	2	0
KERSLAKE	18	16	2	0	1	0	2	0
KLINSMANN	41	41	0	0	1	22	6	0
MABBUTT	36	33	3	3	1	0	1	0
McMAHON	2	2	0	0	1	0	0	0
NETHERCOTT	17	8	9	15	3	0	0	0
POPESCU	23	23	0	1	2	3	3	0
ROSENTHAL	20	14	6	1	1	0	4	0
SCOTT	4	4	0	1	0	0	0	0
SHERINGHAM	42	41	1	0	0	17	3	0
THORSTVEDT	1	1	0	21	0	0	0	0
TURNER	1	1	0	1	0	0	0	0
WALKER	41	41	0	1	0	0	1	0
						OGs 3		

Spurs – Premiership Fact File

- Jurgen Klinsmann scored on his debut at Sheffield Wednesday as Spurs won 4-3 but was then carried off injured.
- Teddy Sheringham – the Premiership's all-time top scorer – missed three successive penalties at the start of the season v Manchester United, Southampton and Nottingham Forest.
- Gerry Francis' first game in charge as manager was against Aston Villa on 19th November – Spurs lost 3-4.

Jurgen is King but Cup Hopes Dive

During the close season, chairman Alan Sugar and manager Ossie Ardiles produced a masterstroke in securing the signature of German international Jurgen Klinsmann, whose reputation for diving had won him few friends in England. At the end of a phenomenally successful campaign personally, Klinsmann moved to Bayern Munich and it seemed as though Tottenham had lost one of their favourite sons, such was his impact on English football that rightly earned him the FWA Footballer of the Year Award.

The signing of Klinsmann and Romanian internationals Gica Popescu and Ilie Dumitrescu deflected from Spurs' battle to win back twelve points which had been deducted by the FA for financial irregularities prior to Sugar taking control of the club. During a lengthy legal battle the Amstrad chairman not only retrieved the points but also got Spurs back in the FA Cup as they had also been banned from that competition. The fine of £1.5m, however, stood.

Klinsmann was an instant hit with six goals in his first six league games as Ardiles' entertaining side began stylishly but conceded goals at a far too regular rate. As entertaining as Spurs may have been, enough games were not being won and with a run of just two victories in twelve games during September and through November something had to give. By mid November Spurs had won just twice at White Hart Lane in the league. Ardiles, amid intense speculation, was dismissed and Gerry Francis was installed as the new Spurs boss. His first game saw Tottenham trail 3-0 to Aston Villa and, pull level, and only to lose to almost the last kick of the game. Four days later Spurs kept their first clean sheet of the season during a goalless draw with Chelsea. That draw sparked a run of 23 league games with just three defeats. Impressive home wins over Newcastle 4-2 and Blackburn 3-1 were recorded while Coventry were crushed 4-0 at Highfield Road. Spurs had got themselves in with a realistic chance of a place in Europe but with only two wins from the final ten games the chance was lost and with it, one suspects, Klinsmann. During this time Dumitrescu was sent on loan to Seville while Popescu's place was held by an impressive Howells.

Tottenham's Coca-Cola Cup form mirrored their early league form. Klinsmann scored a hat trick in a 6-3 win at Watford. The Hornets won the return match although Spurs still went through only to be humbled 3-0 at Notts County. The FA Cup was more to Spurs' liking as Altrincham and Sunderland were despatched. In the 5th Round, Spurs stuttered into a replay at Southampton and were two down when Ronny Rosenthal entered the fray and scored a scintillating hat trick in a 6-2 extra time victory. Goals from Sheringham and Klinsmann overturned a Liverpool lead to put Francis' side through to the semi final. The run floundered at Elland Road when a resurgent Everton side overpowered Spurs to cruise through to the Final as worthy 4-1 winners. At the end of the season, Klinsmann and Popescu were exported to Bayern Munich and Barcelona and question marks hung over the future of Dumitrescu. Money was spent though as Chris Armstrong arrived from Crystal Palace. ∎

Results 1994-95

FA Carling Premiership

Date	Opponents	Ven	Res	Pos	Atten	Scorers
20-Aug	Sheffield W	A	4-3	5	34,051	Sheringham (19); Anderton (30); Barmby (71); Klinsmann (82)
24-Sep	Everton	H	2-1	7	24,553	Klinsmann (21,35)
27-Sep	Man United	H	0-1	7	24,502	
30-Aug	Ipswich Tn	A	3-1	6	22,559	Klinsmann (15,38); Dumitrescu (28)
12-Sep	Southampton	H	1-2	7	22,387	Klinsmann (6)
17-Sep	Leicester C	A	1-3	9	21,300	Klinsmann (88)
24-Sep	N Forest	A	1-4	12	24,558	Dumitrescu (32)
1-Oct	Wimbledon	A	2-1	10	16,802	Sheringham (26); Popescu (61)
8-Oct	QPR	H	1-1	10	25,799	Barmby (79)
15-Oct	Leeds Utd	A	1-1	12	39,224	Sheringham (27)
22-Oct	Man City	A	2-5	13	25,473	Dumitrescu (29 pen,46)
29-Oct	West Ham	H	3-1	11	26,271	Klinsmann (18); Sheringham (48); Barmby (63)
5-Nov	Blackburn R	A	0-2	13	26,933	
19-Nov	Aston Villa	H	3-4	15	26,899	Sheringham (39); Klinsmann (52 pen,72)
23-Nov	Chelsea	H	0-0	14	27,037	
26-Nov	Liverpool	A	1-1	14	35,007	OG (Ruddock 77)
3-Dec	Newcastle	H	4-2	11	28,002	Sheringham (14,38,70); Popescu (79)
10-Dec	Sheffield W	H	3-1	10	25,912	Barmby (60); Klinsmann (70); Calderwood (79)
17-Dec	Everton	A	0-0	10	32,809	
26-Dec	Norwich C	A	2-0		21,814	Barmby (11); Sheringham (90)
27-Dec	C Palace	H	0-0		27,730	
31-Dec	Coventry C	A	4-0		19,951	OG(7); Barmby (67); Anderton (77); Sheringham (81)
2-Jan	Arsenal	H	1-0	6	28,747	Popescu (22)
14-Jan	West Ham	A	2-1	6	24,573	Sheringham (59); Klinsmann (79)
25-Jan	Aston Villa	A	0-1	6	40,017	
5-Feb	Blackburn R	H	3-1	6	28,124	Klinsmann (18); Anderton (29); Barmby (79)
11-Feb	Chelsea	A	1-1	6	30,812	Sheringham (8)

Date	Opponents	Vn	Res		Atten	Scorers
25-Feb	Wimbledon	H	1-2	7	27,258	Klinsmann (49)
4-Mar	N Forest	A	2-2	6	28,711	Sheringham (79); Calderwood (87)
8-Mar	Ipswich T	H	3-0	6	24,930	Klinsmann (2); Barmby (15); OG (83)
15-Mar	Man United	A	0-0	7	43,802	
18-Mar	Leicester C	H	1-0	7	30,851	Klinsmann (82)
22-Mar	Liverpool	H	0-0	7	31,988	
2-Apr	Southampton	A	3-4	7	15,105	Sheringham (17); Klinsmann (35,59)
11-Apr	Man City	H	2-1	7	27,410	Howells (53); Klinsmann (85)
14-Apr	C Palace	A	1-1	7	18,149	Klinsmann (87)
17-Apr	Norwich C	H	1-0	7	32,304	Sheringham (36)
29-Apr	Arsenal	A	1-1	7	38,377	Klinsmann (74)
3-May	Newcastle	A	3-3	7	35,603	Barmby (22); Klinsmann (24); Anderton (26)
6-May	QPR	A	1-2	7	18,367	Sheringham (45)
9-May	Coventry C	H	1-3	7	24,134	Anderton (83)
14-May	Leeds Utd	H	1-1	7	33,040	Sheringham (30)

FA Challenge Cup

Date	Opponents	Vn	Rnd	Res	Atten	Scorers
7-Jan	Altrincham	H	3R	3-0	25,057	Sheringham (9); Rosenthal (34); Nethercott (82)
29-Jan	Sunderland	A	4R	4-1	21,135	Klinsmann (51pen ,86); Sheringham (57); Mabbutt (64)
18-Feb	Southampton	H	5R	1-1	28,091	Klinsmann (20)
1-Mar	Southampton *after extra time*	A	5RR	6-2	15,172	Rosenthal (56,58,101); Sheringham (112); Barmby (115); Anderton (120)
11-Mar	Liverpool	A	QF	2-1	39,952	Sheringham (45); Klinsmann (88)
9-Apr	Everton *(at Elland Road)*	N	SF	1-4	38,226	Klinsmann (63 pen)

Coca-Cola League Cup

Date	Opponents	Vn	Rnd	Res	Atten	Scorers
21-Sep	Watford	A	2R1L	6-3	13,659	Anderton (4); Sheringham (75); Klinsmann (17,34,45); Dumitrescu (88)
4-Oct		H	2R2L	2-3	17,798	Barmby (30); Klinsmann (62)
	Tottenham Hotspur win 8-6 on aggregate					
26-Oct	Notts County	A	3R	0-3	16,952	

West Ham United

Thames Ironworks founded 1895, to give recreation for the shipyard workers. Several different grounds were used as the club entered the London League (1896) and won the championship (1898). In 1899, having become professional, won the Southern League Second Division (London) and moved into Division One.

On becoming a limited liability company the name was changed to West Ham United. Moved from the Memorial Ground to a pitch in the Upton Park area, known originally as 'The Castle', in 1904. Elected to an expanded Football League Division Two for the 1919-20 season and never subsequently out of the top two divisions.

Ground: Boleyn Ground, Green Street, Upton Park, London E13 9AZ
Phone: 0181-548-2748   **News:** 0891 12 11 65
Capacity: 24,500   **Pitch:** 112 yds x 72 yds
Colours: Claret, White, White   **Nickname:** The Hammers
Directions: *From North & West:* North Circular to East Ham then Barking Rd for 1½ miles until traffic lights. Turn right into Green St. *From South:* Blackwall Tunnel then A13 to Canning Town. Then A124 to East Ham, Green St on left after 2 miles. *From East:* A13 then A117 and A124. Green St on right after ¾ miles.   **Rail/Tube:** Upton Park (¼ mile)

Chairman: T Brown   **Vice-Chairman:** Martin Cearns
Managing Director: Peter Storrie   **Secretary:** Richard Skirrow
Manager: Harry Redknapp   **Assistant:** Frank Lampard
First Team Coach: Paul Hilton, Tony Carr
Physio: John Green

League History: 1919 Elected to Division 2; 1923-32 Division 1; 1932-58 Division 2; 1958-78 Division 1; 1978-81 Division 2; 1981-89 Divison 1; 1989-91 Division 2; 1991-1993 Division 1; 1993- FA Premier League.

Honours: *Football League: Division 1 Runners-up: 1992-93; Division 2 Champions: 1957-58, 1980-81; Runners-up: 1922-23, 1990-91. FA Cup Winners: 1964, 1975, 1980; Runners-up: 1922-23. Football League Cup Runners-up: 1966, 1981. Cup-Winners' Cup Winners: 1964-65; Runners-up: 1975-76.*

European Record: CC (0): –; CWC (4): 64-65(W), 65-66(SF), 75-76 (F), 80-81(QF); UEFA (0): –.

Managers: Syd King 1902-32; Charlie Paynter 1932-50; Ted Fenton 1950-61; Ron Greenwood 1961-74 (continued as GM to 1977); John Lyall 1974-89; Lou Macari 1989-90; *(FAPL)* Billy Bonds Feb 1990-Aug 1994; Harry Redknapp Aug 1994-.

Season 1994-95

Biggest Home Win: 3-0 v Manchester City 17/12/94; Wimbledon 13/4/95; Liverpool 10/5/95
Biggest Home Defeat: 1-3 v Newcastle United, 31/8/94
Biggest Away Win: 2-0 v Aston villa, 18/3/95
Biggest Away Defeat: 0-3 v Manchester City, 24/8/94
Biggest Home Attendance: 24,783 v Manchester United, 14/5/95
Smallest Home Attendance: 14,554 v Sheffield Wednesday, 23/1/95
Average Attendance: 19,317
Last Season: *FAPL:* 14th *FA Cup:* 4th round *Coca-Cola Cup:* 4th round
Leading Scorer: Tony Cottee – 13

All-time Record

Record FAPL Win: 4-1 v Tottenham Hotspur, 4/4/94
Record FAPL Defeat: 0-5 v Sheffield Wednesday, 18/12/93
Record FL Win: 8-0 v Rotherham United, Division 2, 8/3/1958; Sunderland, Division 1, 19/10/1968
Record FL Defeat: 2-8 v Blackburn Rovers, Division 1, 26/12/1963
Record Cup Win: 10-0 v Bury, League Cup, R2 2nd leg, 25/10/1983
Record Fee Received: £2m from Everton for Tony Cottee, 7/1988
Record Fee Paid: £1.5m to Liverpool for Don Hutchison, 8/1994
Most FL Appearances: Billy Bonds, 663, 1967-88
Record Attendance (all-time): 42,322 v Tottenham H, Div 1, 17/10/1970
Record Attendance (FAPL): 28,832 v Manchester United, 26/2/94
Highest Scorer in FAPL Season: 13 – Trevor Morley, 1993-94; Tony Cottee 1994-95
Most FAPL Goals in Season: 47, 1993-94
Most FAPL Points in Season: 52, 1993-94

5-Year League Record

	Div.	P	W	D	L	F	A	Pts	Pos	FAC	FLC
90-91	2	46	24	15	7	60	34	87	2	SF	3
91-92	1	42	9	11	22	37	59	38	22	5	4
92-93	1	46	26	10	10	81	41	88	2	4	2
93-94	PL	42	13	13	16	47	58	52	13	6	3
94-95	PL	42	13	11	18	44	48	50	14	4	4

Summary of FAPL Appearances and Goals 1994-95

Player	Tot	Start	Sub	SNU	PS	Goals	Yel	Red
ALLEN	29	26	3	1	5	2	8	0
BISHOP	31	31	0	2	2	1	1	0
BOERE	20	15	5	0	3	6	3	0
BREACKER... ...	33	33	0	0	0	0	8	1
BROWN	9	8	1	4	0	0	0	0
BURROWS	4	4	0	0	0	0	0	0
BUTLER	5	5	0	0	2	0	2	0
CHAPMAN	10	7	3	2	2	0	0	0
COTTEE	31	31	0	0	0	13	1	1
DICKS	29	29	0	0	1	5	9	0
FEUER	0	0	0	16	0	0	0	0
HOLMES...	24	24	0	1	8	0	4	0
HUGHES	17	15	2	0	4	2	0	0
HUTCHISON	23	22	1	1	6	9	6	1
JONES	2	1	1	0	0	0	2	0
MARSH	16	13	3	1	1	0	1	0
MARTIN	24	24	0	0	1	0	2	0
MIKLOSKO... ...	42	42	0	0	0	0	1	0
MONCUR	30	30	0	0	2	2	7	0
MORLEY	14	10	4	3	1	0	1	0
POTTS	42	42	0	0	2	0	4	0
RIEPER	21	17	4	3	1	1	0	0
ROWLAND	12	11	1	8	2	0	1	0
RUSH	23	15	8	1	3	2	5	0
SEALEY	0	0	0	26	0	0	0	0
WEBSTER	5	0	5	0	0	0	0	0
WHITBREAD	8	3	5	8	0	0	0	0
WILLIAMSON	4	4	0	3	0	0	1	0

OGs 0

Late Flurry Saves Hammers

No side had their pre-season rocked more than West Ham who lost the services of manager Billy Bonds as the long serving Hammer quit Upton Park. The club moved swiftly to appoint a replacement with former player Harry Redknapp moving into the hot seat.

It was a quiet summer on the transfer front for West Ham although £1.5m was spent on bringing Don Hutchison down from Liverpool. Having struggled the previous season, the last thing West Ham needed was to score just twice in the opening seven games, one of which was a Hutchison penalty. The second came from Tony Cottee who rejoined the club from Everton at the start of September with David Burrows moving in the opposite direction. Cottee's goal gave West Ham their first goal in open play and their first win of the season, at the sixth attempt, and was a distinct improvement on his first game since his return which saw him dismissed at Liverpool. Wins over Chelsea and Crystal Palace lifted the Hammers clear of any immediate danger but it was the only occasion when consecutive games were won. Redknapp moved shrewdly in the transfer market to bring hard man Julian Dicks back from Liverpool.

A run of three home wins on the trot went some way towards shoring up a poor away record which did not see West Ham win on their travels again until early February. The third of those games saw Cottee score a hat trick against Manchester City. The run floundered in mid January when Spurs won at Upton Park to push The Hammers into the relegation zone for the first time since August. Alvin Martin, during a 2-0 defeat by Sheffield Wednesday, was controversially dismissed but later had the offence reduced to just a caution. Cottee scored his 100th goal for the club during a home win over Leicester but two more defeats kept the club in the bottom four. A 1-0 win at Arsenal sparked a recovery despite the next match at Newcastle being lost. With two late goals Cottee rescued a point against ten man Norwich and with a six match unbeaten run behind them West Ham moved closer to safety with an inspired 2-0 win over leaders Blackburn. Just one point was taken from games with QPR and Palace before survival was secured with an excellent 3-0 win over Liverpool, former Red Hutchison scoring twice. The season ended with a titanic battle against Manchester United which saw The Hammers cling on for a draw and deny United the championship.

West Ham made little impact in the FA Cup. After seeing off Wycombe Wanderers at Adams Park, Redknapp's side bowed out of the competition with a 1-0 defeat at QPR. Their Coca-Cola Cup campaign was a touch more successful although extra time was required to dispose of Division Three side Walsall in the 2nd Round. A goal after just two minutes by Hutchison removed Chelsea only for promotion chasing Bolton to cause an upset with a 3-1 win at Upton Park in the 4th Round. ∎

Results 1994-95

FA Carling Premiership

Date	Opponents	Ven	Res	Pos	Atten	Scorers
20-Aug	Leeds Utd	H	0-0	14	18,610	
24-Aug	Man City	A	0-3	17	19,150	
27-Aug	Norwich C	A	0-1	18	19,110	
31-Aug	Newcastle	H	1-3	21	18,580	Hutchison (87 pen)
10-Sep	Liverpool	A	0-0	19	30,907	
17-Sep	Aston Villa	H	1-0	19	18,326	Cottee (86)
25-Sep	Arsenal	H	0-2	19	18,498	
2-Oct	Chelsea	A	2-1	15	18,696	Allen (53); Moncur (67)
8-Oct	C Palace	H	1-0	13	16,959	Hutchinson (71)
15-Oct	Man United	A	0-1	14	43,795	
22-Oct	Southampton	H	2-0	12	18,853	Allen (49), Rush (62)
29-Oct	Tottenham	A	1-3	14	26,271	Rush (41)
1-Nov	Everton	A	0-1	13	28,338	
5-Nov	Leicester C	H	1-0	14	18,780	Dicks (77 pen)
19-Nov	Sheffield W	A	0-1	17	35,300	
26-Nov	Coventry C	H	0-1	17	17,251	
4-Dec	QPR	A	1-2	18	12,780	Boere (90)
10-Dec	Leeds Utd	A	2-2	19	28,987	Boere (45,78)
17-Dec	Man City	H	3-0	17	17,286	Cottee (6,9,57)
26-Dec	Ipswich Tn	H	1-1	18	20,542	Cottee (16)
28-Dec	Wimbledon	A	0-1	18	11,212	
31-Dec	N Forest	H	3-1	16	20,544	Cottee (24); Bishop (26); Hughes (44)
2-Jan	Blackburn R	A	2-4	16	25,503	Cottee (33); Dicks (58)
14-Jan	Tottenham	H	1-2	19	24,573	Boere (10)
23-Jan	Sheffield W	H	0-2	19	14,554	
4-Feb	Leicester C	A	2-1	20	20,375	Cottee (28); Dicks (43 pen)
13-Feb	Everton	H	2-2	20	21,081	Cottee (22,60)
18-Feb	Coventry C	A	0-2	20	17,554	
25-Feb	Chelsea	H	1-2	20	21,500	Hutchison (11)
5-Mar	Arsenal	A	1-0	19	36,295	Hutchison (20)
8-Mar	Newcastle	A	0-2	19	34,595	
11-Mar	Norwich C	H	2-2	18	21,464	Cottee (82,88)
15-Mar	Southampton	A	1-1	19	15,178	Hutchinson (38)
18-Mar	Aston Villa	A	2-0	18	28,682	Moncur (11); Hutchison (49)
8-Apr	N Forest	A	1-1	19	28,361	Dicks (65)
13-Apr	Wimbledon	H	3-0	16	21,804	Dicks (41 pen); Boere (76); Cottee (78)
17-Apr	Ipswich Tn	A	1-1	18	19,099	Boere (90)
30-Apr	Blackburn R	H	2-0	16	24,202	Rieper (50); Hutchison (83)
3-May	QPR	H	0-0	15	23,932	

6-May	C Palace	A	0-1	16	18,224	
10-May	Liverpool	H	3-0	14	22,446	Holmes (28);
						Hutchison (60,62)
14-May	Man United	H	1-1	14	24,783	Hughes (30)

FA Challenge Cup

Date	Opponents	Vn	Rnd	Res	Atten	Scorers
7-Jan	Wycombe W	A	3R	2-0	9,007	Cottee (48); Brown (78)
28-Jan	QPR	A	4R	0-1	17,694	

Coca-Cola League Cup

Date	Opponents	Vn	Rnd	Res	Atten	Scorers
20-Sep	Walsall	A	2R1L	1-2	5,994	OG (42)
5-Oct		H	2R2L	2-0	14,076	Hutchison (62); Moncur (94)
	After extra time. West Ham United win 2-1 on aggregate					
26-Oct	Chelsea	H	3R	1-0	18,815	Hutchison (2)
30-Nov	Bolton Wdrs	H	4R	1-3	18,190	Cottee (80)

Hammers – Premiership Fact File

- United's 0-0 draw with Leeds on the opening day of the season was the only game in the Premiership on that day not to have a goal.
- West Ham fans had to wait 357 minutes into the season to see their side score a Premiership goal – a penalty three minutes from time by Don Hutchison. The Hammer's lost 1-3 at home to Newcastle.
- United scored just two goals in their first seven games.
- West Ham didn't score in the first half of a game until the 29th October against London rivals Spurs.

Wimbledon

Founded 1889 as Wimbledon Old Centrals, an old boys' side of the Central School playing on Wimbledon Common. Member of the Southern Suburban League, the name was changed to Wimbledon in 1905. Moved to Plough Lane in 1912. Athenian League member for two seasons before joining the Isthmian League in 1921.

FA Amateur Cup winners 1963 and seven times Isthmian League champions. Turned professional in 1965 joining the Southern League of which they were champions three times before being elected to Football League Division Four in 1977. Started ground sharing at Selhurst Park in 1991 and founder member of the Premier League 1992.

Ground: Selhurst Park, South Norwood, London SE25 6PY
Phone: 0181-771 2233   **News:** 0891 12 11 75
Box Office: 0181-771 8841
Colours: All Blue with Yellow trim   **Nickname:** The Dons
Capacity: 26,995   **Pitch:** 110 yds x 74 yds
Directions: *From North:* M1/A1 to North Circular A406 and Chiswick. Follow South Circular A205 to Wandsworth then A3 and A214 towards Streatham and A23. Then left onto B273 for 1 mile and turn left at end into High St and Whitehorse Lane. *From South:* On A23 follow signs for Crystal Palace along B266 going through Thornton Heath into Whitehorse Lane. *From East:* A232 Croydon Rd to Shirley joining A215, Norwood Rd. Turn left after 2½ miles into Whitehorse Lane. *From West:* M4 to Chiswick then as above. **Rail:** Selhurst, Norwood Junction or Thornton Heath.

Chairman: S.G.Reed   **Vice-Chairman:** J. Lelliott
Owner: Sam Hamman   **Chief Executive:** David Barnard
Secretary: Steve Rooke   **Manager:** Joe Kinnear
Assistant: Terry Burton   **Physio:** Steve Allen

League History: 1977 Elected to Division 4; 1979-80 Division 3; 1980-81 Division 4; 1981-82 Division 3; 1982-83 Division 4; 1983-84 Division 3; 1984-86 Division 2; 1986-92 Division 1; 1992- FA Premier League.

Honours: *Football League Division 3 Runners-up:* 1983-84; *Division 4 Champions:* 1982-83. *FA Cup Winners:* 1987-88. *FA Amateur Cup Winners:* 1963

European Record: Never qualified. InterToto Cup (1995)

Managers: Les Henley 1955-71; Mike Everitt 1971-73; Dick Graham 1973-74; Allen Batsford 1974-78; Dario Gradi 1978-81; Dave Bassett 1981-87; Bobby Gould 1987-90; Ray Harford 1990-91; Peter Withe 1991; (FAPL) Joe Kinnear January 1992-

Season 1994-95

Biggest Home Win: 2-0 v Crystal Palace 18/3/95; Manchester City 21/3/95
Biggest Home Defeat: 0-3 v Blackburn Rovers, 3/12/94
Biggest Away Win: 4-3 v Leicester City, 1/4/95
Biggest Away Defeat: 1-7 v Aston Villa, 11/2/95
Biggest Home Attendance: 18,224 v Manchester United, 7/3/95
Smallest Home Attendance: 5,268 v Manchester City, 21/3/95
Average Attendance: 10,230
Last Season: *FAPL:* 9th *FA Cup:* 5th round *Coca-Cola Cup:* 3rd round
Leading Scorer: Efan Ekoku – 9

All-time Record

Record FAPL Win: 4-0 v Crystal Palace, 9/4/1993
Record FAPL Defeat: 1-7 v Aston Villa, 11/2/1995
Record FL Win: 6-0 v Newport County, Division 3, 3/9/1983
Record FL Defeat: 0-8 v Everton, League Cup R2, 29/8/1978
Record Cup Win: 7-2 v Windsor & Eton, FA Cup R1, 22/11/1980
Record Fee Received: £4.5m from Newcastle for Warren Barton, 6/1995
Record Fee Paid: £1m to Norwich for Efan Ekoku, 10/1994
Most FL Appearances: Alan Cork, 430, 1977-92
Record Attendance (all-time): 30,115 v Manchester United, 8/5/93
Record Attendance (FAPL): 30,115 v Manchester United, 8/5/93
Record Scorer in FAPL Season: Holdsworth, 19, 1992-93
Most FAPL Goals in Season: 56, 1992-93 *and* 56, 1993-94
Most FAPL Points in Season: 65, 1993-94

5-Year League Record

	Div.	P	W	D	L	F	A	Pts	Pos	FAC	FLC
90-91	1	38	14	14	10	53	46	56	7	4	2
91-92	1	42	13	14	15	53	53	53	13	3	2
92-93	PL	42	14	12	16	56	55	54	12	5	3
93-94	PL	42	18	11	13	56	53	65	6	5	5
94-95	Pl	42	15	11	16	48	65	56	9	5	3

Summary of FAPL Appearances and Goals 1994-95

Player	Tot	Start	Sub	SNU	PS	Goals	Yel	Red
ARDLEY...	14	9	5	2	1	1	1	0
BARTON...	39	39	0	0	2	2	4	0
BLISSETT...	9	4	5	1	2	0	0	0
CASTLEDINE	6	5	1	0	1	1	1	0
CLARKE...	25	8	17	2	3	1	2	0
CUNNINGHAM ...	28	28	0	0	0	0	1	0
EARLE...	9	9	0	0	1	0	0	0
EKOKU	24	24	0	0	6	9	6	0
ELKINS	36	33	3	0	3	1	6	0
FEAR	14	8	6	2	3	1	2	0
FITZGERALD ...	17	14	3	2	0	0	2	0
GAYLE	23	22	1	0	12	2	0	0
GOODMAN...	19	13	6	0	5	4	0	0
HARFORD	27	17	10	4	5	6	7	0
HOLDSWORTH ...	28	27	1	1	10	7	5	0
JONES	33	33	0	0	2	3	9	2
JOSEPH	3	3	0	0	0	0	1	0
KIMBLE	26	26	0	0	2	0	4	1
LEONHARDSEN ...	20	18	2	0	3	4	2	0
MURPHY	0	0	0	1	0	0	0	0
PERRY	21	16	5	3	1	0	2	0
REEVES	32	32	0	0	1	3	5	1
SCALES	3	3	0	0	0	0	0	0
SEGERS	32	31	1	10	0	0	3	0
SULLIVAN	11	11	0	30	1	0	0	0
TALBOYS...	7	7	0	1	2	1	1	0
THORN	23	22	1	0	1	1	4	1
						OGs 1		

Dons Continue to Confound

Having finished sixth in the Premier the previous season, Wimbledon manager Joe Kinnear once again proved how to enjoy reasonable success on limited resources. As usual, the Dons' finances were hardly overflowing but the sale of John Fashanu to Aston Villa in August did give the manager some leeway, his replacement was veteran striker Mick Harford.

The season began badly for Wimbledon with just eight points collected from the first 33 available. By the start of November three wins had been recorded, two of which were against sides heading for relegation. The first full month of the season, September, saw the bank balance swelled by £3.5m with John Scales moving to Liverpool. Kinnear invested almost £2m of that during the following six weeks on Efan Ekoku, Alan Reeves and Kenny Cunningham. Ekoku justified the £1m spent on him by being the Dons' top scorer with nine, two of which were match winners against his former club Norwich. With Scales gone, Jones was appointed team captain and celebrated his new position with a dismissal against Leicester.

A single goal victory over Norwich, courtesy of Ekoku, lifted Wimbledon out of the relegation places at the end of October and with consecutive 4-3 and 3-2 wins over Aston Villa and Newcastle, the Dons continued to climb – Jones was again first in the dressing room during the Newcastle match. Some momentum was lost with reversals against Manchester City and Blackburn but four wins and a draw between Christmas and mid January revived hopes of the club pushing on to secure a place in Europe for the first time. Those hopes were seriously dashed on 11 February when they were annihilated 7-1 at Villa Park for their heaviest defeat since joining the league in 1977. Wimbledon's reputation for upsetting the 'big boys' was not so evident during the 1994/95 season although two goals by Ekoku clinched victory over Spurs at White Hart Lane to end a three match winless run.

Two more defeats followed before maximum points were taken from games with Sheffield Wednesday, Crystal Palace, Manchester City and Leicester City – the latter by 4-3 with two late goals. It proved to be Wimbledon's last win of the season as a draw with Chelsea was followed by five games without a goal, two of which were drawn, before the curtains came down on the season with a 2-2 home with Nottingham Forest.

In the Coca-Cola Cup Wimbledon completed the double over Torquay United before going down 1-0 to Crystal Palace in a 'home' tie at Selhurst Park. A longer run was achieved in the FA Cup with Colchester United and Tranmere Rovers being defeated before the side The Dons beat in the 1988 Final, Liverpool, won a 4th Round replay in south London.

The season, as with most Wimbledon seasons, was not without its talking points. Many were provided by Jones who, in addition to his two dismissals, was fined by the FA and warned his future conduct after, allegedly, swearing at the Newcastle boss Kevin Keegan and biting a journalist's nose in Dublin. Kinnear, too, was fined £15,500 and banned from the touchline. ∎

Results 1994-95

Date	Opponents	Ven	Res	Pos	Atten	Scorers
20-Aug	Coventry C	A	1-1	12	10,962	Castledine (55)
23-Aug	Ipswich Tn	H	1-1	16	6,341	Holdsworth (19)
27-Aug	Sheffield W	H	0-1	16	7,453	
31-Aug	Man United	A	0-3	16	43,440	
10-Sep	Leicester C	H	2-1	14	7,683	Harford (28); OG (44)
17-Sep	C Palace	A	0-0	13	12,100	
24-Sep	QPR	A	1-0	10	11,059	Reeves (48)
1-Oct	Tottenham	H	1-2	13	16,802	Talboys (28)
8-Oct	Arsenal	H	1-3	15	10,842	Jones (81)
17-Oct	N Forest	A	1-3	19	20,287	Gayle (82)
22-Oct	Liverpool	A	0-3	19	31,139	
30-Oct	Norwich C	H	1-0	18	8,242	Ekoku (62)
5-Nov	Leeds Utd	A	1-3	18	27,284	Ekoku (25)
9-Nov	Aston Villa	H	4-3	16	6,221	Barton (8 pen); Ardley (60); Jones (83); Leonhardson (90)
19-Nov	Newcastle	H	3-2	14	14,203	Clarke (1); Ekoku (27); Harford (46)
26-Nov	Man City	A	0-2	15	21,131	
3-Dec	Blackburn R	H	0-3	16	12,341	
10-Dec	Coventry C	H	2-0	15	7,349	Leonhardson (4); Harford (17)
16-Dec	Ipswich Tn	A	2-2	14	11,367	Holdsworth (2); Goodman (62)
26-Dec	Southampton	A	3-2		14,603	Holdsworth (20,72 pen); Harford (37)
28-Dec	West Ham	H	1-0	12	11,212	Fear (57)
31-Dec	Chelsea	A	1-1		16,105	Ekoku (74)
2-Jan	Everton	H	2-1	9	9,506	Harford (3,8)
14-Jan	Norwich C	A	2-1	7	18,261	Reeves (44); Ekoku (49)
25-Jan	Newcastle	A	1-2	9	34,374	Ekoku (78)
4-Feb	Leeds Utd	H	0-0	9	10,211	
11-Feb	Aston Villa	A	1-7	9	23,982	Barton (11)
21-Feb	Blackburn R	A	1-2	10	20,586	Ekoku (39)
25-Feb	Tottenham	A	2-1	10	27,258	Ekoku (38,64)
4-Mar	QPR	H	1-3	10	9,116	Holdsworth (12)
7-Mar	Man United	H	0-1	9	18,224	
11-Mar	Sheffield W	A	1-0	9	20,395	Reeves (63)
18-Mar	C Palace	H	2-0	8	8,835	Jones (37); Gayle (60)
21-Mar	Man City	H	2-0		5,268	Thorn (59); Elkins (76)
1-Apr	Leicester C	A	4-3	8	15,489	Goodman (63,90); Leonhardson (65,85)

10-Apr	Chelsea	H	1-1	9	7,022	Goodman (56)
13-Apr	West Ham	A	0-3	9	21,804	
17-Apr	Southampton	H	0-2	9	10,521	
29-Apr	Everton	A	0-0	9	33,063	
2-May	Liverpool	H	0-0	9	12,041	
4-May	Arsenal	A	0-0	9	32,822	
13-May	N Forest	H	2-2	9	15,341	Holdsworth (35,40 pen)

FA Challenge Cup

Date	Opponents	Vn	Rnd	Res	Atten	Scorers
7-Jan	Colchester U	H	3R	1-0	6,903	Harford (8)
29-Jan	Tranmere R	A	4R	2-0	11,637	Leonhardson (31); Earle (51)
19-Feb	Liverpool	A	5R	1-1	25,124	Clarke (2)
28-Feb		H	5RR	0-2	12,553	

Coca-Cola League Cup

Date	Opponents	Vn	Rnd	Res	Atten	Scorers
20-Sep	Torquay U	H	2R1L	2-0	2,451	Gayle (35); Harford (43)
5-Oct		A	2R2L	1-0	4,244	Holdsworth (38)
	Wimbledon win 3-0 on aggregate					
25-Oct	C Palace	H	3R	0-1	9,394	

Dons – Premiership Fact File

- Efan Ekoku scored his first goal for Wimbledon against the club he left to join them – Norwich City. It earned the Dons a 1-0 win at the end of October.
- Wimbledon breathed a sigh of relief when Dean Holdsworth netted two to earn the Dons a 2-2 draw with Nottingham Forest on the final day of the season. Prior to that they had gone five games without scoring!
- Wimbledon have set the ten lowest recorded attendance figures for Premiership games.

D1: Crystal Palace

Founded in 1905 to play at the Crystal Palace Ground where, earlier, a Crystal Palace staff team had successfully played. Joined the Southern League for 1905/06 when they were Champions of Division Two. Soon moved to Herne Hill, then to The Nest, Selhurst. Founder members and first champions of the Football League Third Division 1920/21. Moved to Selhurst Park in 1924.

Founder members of the old Fourth Division in 1958, they reached the First Division for the first time as Second Division runners-up in 1969. Premier League founder members 1992. Relegated after one season, but promoted back at the first attempt.

Ground: Selhurst Park, South Norwood, London SE25 6PU
Phone: 0181 653 1000 **News:** 0891-400 333
Box Office: 0181 771-8841 **Dial-a-Seat:** 0891-516 161
Capacity: 26,995 **Pitch:** 110 x 74 yd.
Colours: Red/Blue, Red, Red **Nickname:** The Eagles
Directions: *From North:* M1 or A1 to A406 for Chiswick, then A205 to Wandsworth. A3 and then A214 for Streatham, And then A23 to B273 for Whitehorse Lane. *From South:* A23 and then B266. Turn right onto High Street and left into Whitehorse Lane. *From East:* A232 and then A215 to B266 for High Street, and then as above. *From West:* M4 To Chiswick, and then as for North.
Rail: Thornton Heath, Northwood Junction or Selhurst.

Chairman: Ron G. Noades **Secretary:** Mike Hurst
Director of Football: Steve Coppell
First Team Coach: Steve Harrison **Physio:** Peter McClean

League History: 1920 Original Members of Division 3; 1921-25 Division 2; 1925-58 Division 3(S); 1958-61 Division 4; 1961-64 Division 3, 1964-69 Division 2; 1969-73 Division 1; 1973-74 Division 2; 1974-77 Division 3; 1977-79 Division 2; 1979-81 Division 1; 1981-89 Division 2; 1989-92 Division 1; 1992-93 FA Premier League; 1993-94 Division 1; 1994-95 FA Premier League; 1995- Division 1.

Honours: *Football League Division 1 (new) Champions:* 1993/94; *Division 2 Champions:* 1978-79; *Runners-up:* 1968-69; *Division 3 Runners-up:* 1963-64; *Division 3(S) Champions:* 1920-21; *Runners-up:* 1928-29, 1930-31, 198-39; *Division 4 Runners-up:* 1960-61; *FA Cup:Runners-up:* 1989-90; *Zenith Data System Cup Winners:* 1991.

European Record: Never qualified

Managers: John T. Robson 1905-07; Edmund Goodman 1907-25 (had been secretary since 1905 and afterwards continued in this position to 1933); Alec Maley 1925-27; Fred Maven 1927-30; Jack Tresadern 1930-35; Tom Bromilow 1935-36; R.S. Moyes 1936; Tom Bromilow 1936-39; George Irwin 1939-47; Jack Butler 1947-49; Ronnie Rooke 1949-50; Charlie Slade and Fred Dawes (joint managers) 1950-51; Laurie Scott 1951-54; Cyril Spiers 1954-58; George Smith 1958-60; Authur Rowe 1960-62; Dick Graham 1962-66; Bert Head 1966-72 (continued as GM until 1973); Malcolm Allison 1973-76; Terry Venables 1976-80; Ernie Walley 1980; Malcolm Allison 1980-81; Dario Gradi 1981; Steve Kember 1981-82; Alan Mullery 1982-84; (FAPL) Steve Coppell 1984-93; Alan Smith June 1993-May 1995.

Season 1994-95
Biggest Home Win: 3-0 v Ipswich Town, 5/11/94
Biggest Home Defeat: 1-6 v Liverpool, 20/8/94
Biggest Away Win: 4-1 v Coventry City, 2/11/94
Biggest Away Defeat: 0-3 v Manchester United, 19/11/94
Biggest Home Attendance: 18,224 v West Ham United, 6/5/95
Smallest Home Attendance: 10,442 v Sheffield Wednesday, 14/3/95
Average Attendance: 14,891
Last Season: *FAPL:* 19th *FA Cup:* Semi Final *Coca-Cola Cup:* Semi Final
Leading Scorer: Chris Armstong – 8

All-time Records
Record FAPL Win: 4-1 v Middlesbrough 12/4/93
Record FAPL Defeat: 0-5 v Liverpool 28/11/92
Record FL Win: 9-0 v Barrow, Division 4, 10/10/1959
Record FL Defeat: 0-9 v Burnley, FA Cup R2 replay, 10/2/1909; Liverpool, Division 1, 12/9/90
Record Cup Win: 8-0 v Southend U, League Cup, 2R2L, 25/9/90
Record Fee Received: £4.5m from Tottenham for Chris Armstrong, 6/95
Record Fee Paid: £1.8m to Sunderland for Marco Gabbiadini, 9/91
Most FL Appearances: Jim Cannon, 571, 1973-88
Record Attendance (all-time): 41,482 v Burnley, Division 2, 11/5/1979
Record Attendance (FAPL): 36,380 Away v. Liverpool 28/11/92
Highest Scorer in FAPL season: Chris Armstrong,15, 1992-93
Most FAPL Goals in Season: 48, 1992-93
Most FAPL Points in Season: 49, 1992-93

5-Year League Record

	Div.	P	W	D	L	F	A	Pts	Pos	FAC	FLC
90-91	1	38	20	9	9	50	41	69	3	3	4
91-92	1	42	14	15	13	53	61	57	10	3	5
92-93	PL	42	11	16	15	48	61	49	20	3	SF
93-94	1	46	27	9	10	73	46	90	1	3	3
94-95	PL	42	11	12	19	34	49	45	19r	SF	SF

Summary of FAPL Appearances and Goals 1994-95

Player	Tot	Start	Sub	SNU	PS	Goals	Yel	Red
ARMSTRONG	40	40	0	0	1	8	6	0
BOWRY	18	13	5	4	5	0	2	0
COLEMAN	35	35	0	0	2	1	4	0
COX	11	1	10	3	2	0	0	0
DOWIE	15	15	0	0	2	4	3	0
DYER	16	7	9	7	4	1	1	0
GLASS	0	0	0	5	0	0	0	0
GORDON	41	38	3	0	0	2	4	0
HOUGHTON	10	10	0	0	1	2	1	0
HUMPHREY	21	19	2	2	2	0	5	1
LAUNDERS	2	1	1	1	1	0	0	0
MARTYN	37	37	0	0	1	0	1	0
MATTHEW	4	2	2	2	1	0	0	0
NDAH	12	5	7	2	2	1	0	0
NEWMAN	35	32	3	0	4	3	4	0
PATTERSON	22	22	0	2	4	1	7	0
PITCHER	25	21	4	9	2	0	5	0
PREECE	20	17	3	1	5	4	0	0
RODGER	4	4	0	0	2	0	0	0
SALAKO	39	39	0	0	6	4	2	0
SHAW	41	41	0	0	1	0	4	0
SOUTHGATE	42	42	0	0	0	3	5	0
WILKINS	1	1	0	0	1	0	1	0
WILLIAMS	4	2	2	0	0	0	0	0
WILMOT	6	5	1	36	0	0	0	0
YOUNG	13	13	0	0	3	0	2	0

OGs 0

Cup Runs Out

Few sides can match the topsy-turvy existence of Crystal Palace in recent seasons and just three months after winning promotion there was little doubt that Palace would face a tough campaign as Liverpool romped to a 6-1 opening day victory at Selhurst Park. Scoring was always likely to be a problem for Alan Smith's side and in the first dozen games only once did they score more than one goal, John Salako's double at Highbury at the start of October secured Palace's first win of the campaign. Four draws had been achieved during the early weeks of the season but the lack of wins left Palace short of points. The onset of winter coincided with a fine run as four wins in succession were chalked up. Seven goals in two games suggested that the attacking problems were over, but the goals against Ipswich, on Bonfire Night, were the last for three months. Having climbed to tenth in the table, the nine goalless games saw Palace slump to 18th. On the plus side, some pride was recouped with draws at Liverpool and Tottenham.

The New Year got off to a lively start with a defeat at Nottingham Forest being followed by the first goals in 836 minutes as the double was completed over Leicester. Smith boosted his attacking options by signing Iain Dowie from Southampton. The month ended with Palace in the headlines following the infamous Cantona incident at Selhurst Park. Hopes of avoiding the drop were boosted with a second win over Ipswich but consecutive defeats at home to Arsenal and Chelsea put them firmly in the mire. A season full of controversy saw Palace suffer with Armstrong banned having proved positive in a drugs test, but when he returned he was in rich scoring form. But with three more defeats Palace were in deep trouble and when a win over West Ham was followed by losses at Leeds and Newcastle their one year stay in the top flight was over.

Cup football proved to be more to the Eagles liking. In the FA Cup, Lincoln City were thrashed at Selhurst before Palace sprung a surprise with an excellent win at Nottingham Forest. Watford provided stubborn resistance before succumbing to a George Ndah goal two minutes from the end of extra time; a replay was also required before Wolves were hammered 4-1. In the semi final, Armstrong and Dowie took their total of cup goals to nine but it was not enough to stop Manchester United from getting to Wembley after a replay.

The Coca-Cola Cup run was equally lengthy as Lincoln, again, and 'lodgers' Wimbledon were beaten in the early rounds. Top form was hit in the next two rounds as 4-1 and 4-0 victories over Aston Villa and Manchester City put The Eagles through to the semi finals. Winning the cup may have helped to secure Smith's future but Liverpool comfortably won the two legged semi and at the end of the season Smith resigned, Armstrong joined Spurs for £4.5m and former manager Steve Coppell returned to the club in a directorial role with a brief to secure the long-term future of the Eagles. ∎

Results 1994-95

FA Carling Premiership

Date	Opponents	Ven	Res	Pos	Atten	Scorers
20-Aug	Liverpool	H	1-6	22	18,084	Armstrong (49)
24-Aug	Norwich C	A	0-0	20	19,015	
27-Aug	Aston Villa	A	1-1	18	23,305	Southgate (86)
30-Aug	Leeds Utd	H	1-2	17	14,453	Gordon (55)
10-Sep	Man City	A	1-1	17	19,971	Dyer (31)
17-Sep	Wimbledon	H	0-0	21	12,366	
24-Sep	Chelsea	A	0-1	21	16,064	
1-Oct	Arsenal	A	2-1	16	34,136	Salako (19,41)
8-Oct	West Ham	A	0-1	18	16,595	
15-Oct	Newcaslte	H	0-1	21	17,739	
22-Oct	Everton	H	1-0	19	15,026	Preece (53)
29-Oct	Leicester C	A	1-0	16	20,022	Preece (36)
2-Nov	Coventry C	A	4-1	12	10,732	Preece (18,49); Salako (20); Newman (80)
5-Nov	Ipswich Tn	H	3-0	10	13,450	Newman (18); Armstrong (83); Salako (87)
19-Nov	Man United	A	0-3	12	43,788	
26-Nov	Southampton	H	0-0	13	14,186	
3-Dec	Sheffield W	A	0-1	15	21,930	
11-Dec	Liverpool	A	0-0	13	30,972	
17-Dec	Norwich C	H	0-1	16	12,252	
26-Dec	QPR	H	0-0	17	16,372	
27-Dec	Tottenham	A	0-0	16	27,730	
31-Dec	Blackburn R	H	0-1	18	14,232	
2-Jan	N Forest	A	0-1	18	21,326	
14-Jan	Leicester C	H	2-0	16	12,707	Newman (23); Ndah (44)
21-Jan	Everton	A	1-3	17	23,733	Coleman (79)
25-Jan	Man United	H	1-1	16	18,224	Southgate (80)
4-Feb	Ipswich Tn	A	2-0	16	15,570	Dowie (55); Gordon (86 pen)
11-Feb	Coventry C	H	0-2	18	11,891	
25-Feb	Arsenal	H	0-3	19	17,092	
5-Mar	Chelsea	A	0-0	20	14,130	
14-Mar	Sheffield W	H	2-1	21	10,422	Armstrong (55); Dowie (65)
18-Mar	Wimbledon	A	0-2	19	8,835	
1-Apr	Man City	H	2-1	19	13,312	Armstrong (34); Patterson (65)
4-Apr	Aston Villa	H	0-0	19	12,606	
14-Apr	Tottenham	H	1-1	20	18,149	Armstrong (41)
17-Apr	QPR	A	1-0	19	14,227	Dowie (56)
20-Apr	Blackburn R	A	1-2	19	28,005	Houghton (71)
29-Apr	N Forest	H	1-2	19	15,886	Dowie (79)

Date		Vn	Res		Atten	Scorers
3-May	Southampton	A	1-3	19	15,151	Southgate (26)
6-May	West Ham	H	1-0	19	18,224	Armstrong (51)
9-May	Leeds Utd	A	1-3	19	30,942	Armstrong (67)
14-May	Newcastle	A	2-3	19	35,626	Armstrong (51);
						Houghton (81)

FA Challenge Cup

Date	Opponents	Vn	Rnd	Res	Atten	Scorers
7-Jan	Lincoln City	H	3R	5-1	6,541	Coleman (7); Armstrong (24); Gordon (33 pen); Salako (62,87)
28-Jan	N Forest	A	4R	2-1	16,790	Armstrong (5); Dowie (53)
18-Feb	Watford	A	5R	0-0	13,814	
1-Mar		H	5RR	1-0	10,321	Ndah (118)
11-Mar	Wolves	H	QF	1-1	14,604	Dowie (53)
22-Mar		A	QFR	4-1	27,548	Armstrong (33,67); Dowie (38); Pitcher (44)
9-Apr	Man United	N	SF	2-2	38,256	Dowie (33); Armstrong (92)
	(at Villa Park – after extra time)					
12-Apr	Man United	N	SFR	0-2	17,987	
	(at Villa Park)					

Coca-Cola League Cup

Date	Opponents	Vn	Rnd	Res	Atten	Scorers
20-Sep	Lincoln City	A	2R1L	0-1	4,310	
4-Oct		H	2R2L	3-0	7,041	Gordon (90); Armstrong (101); Dyer (110)
	Crystal Palace win 3-1 on aggregate					
25-Oct	Wimbledon	A	3R	1-0	9,394	Armstrong (72)
30-Nov	Aston Villa	H	4R	4-1	12,807	Armstrong (48,88); Southgate (59,75)
11-Jan	Man City	H	QF	4-0	16,668	Pitcher (60); Salako (87); Armstrong (84); Preece (87)
15-Feb	Liverpool	A	SF1L	0-1	25,480	
8-Mar	Liverpool	H	SF2L	0-1	18,224	
	Liverpool win 2-0 on aggregate					

Palace – Premiership Fact File

- Palace went through a period of over nine Premiership games – 837 minutes – without scoring a goal from early November to January.
- Palace have now been relegated twice from the Premiership.
- Gareth Southgate was the only Palace player to feature in all of their Premiership games.

D1: Ipswich Town

Originally founded in the 1880s, a strictly amateur set up and founder member of the AFA's Southern Amateur League in 1907. Four times League champions and seven times County Cup winners. In 1936 under the leadership of the Cobbold family a professional Ipswich Town was formed.

The new club used Portman Road, only recently occupied by the amateur side and the site of several sporting activities. After two Southern League campaigns and one championship, elected to Football League Division Three (South) in 1938. Football League Champions in 1963, the club's debut season in the top section. Premier League founder member 1992.

Ground: Portman Road, Ipswich, Suffolk, IP1 2DA
Phone: 01473-219211   **News:** 0839-66 44 88
Ticket News: 0839-66 44 99
Capacity: 22,823   **Pitch:** 112 yds x 70 yds
Colours: Blue/White, White, Blue   **Nickname:** Blues or Town
Directions: Follow A45 and signs for Ipswich West. Through Post House traffic lights and turn right at second roundabout into West End Rd. Ground on left.   **Rail:** Ipswich

Chairman: John Kerr MBE   **Secretary:** David Rose
Manager: George Burley   **Assistant:** Dale Roberts
Coach: John Wark   **Physio:** David Bingham

League History: 1938 Elected to Division 3 (S); 1954-55 Division 2; 1955-57 Division 3 (S); 1957-61 Division 2; 1961-64 Division 1; 1964-68 Division 2; 1968-86 Division 1; 1986-92 Division 2; 1992-95 FA Premier League: 1995- Division 1.

Honours: *Football League Division 1 Champions:* 1961-62; *Runners-up:* 1980-81. 1981-82; *Division 2 Champions:* 1960-61, 1967-68, 1991-92; *Division 3 (S) Champions:* 1953-54,, 1956-57; *FA Cup Winners:* 1977-78; *UEFA Cup Winners:* 1980-81.

European Record: CC (1): 62-63(2); CWC (1): 78-79(QF). UEFA (8): 73-74(QF), 74-75(1), 75-76(2), 77-78(3), 79-80(2), 80-81(W), 81-82(1), 82-83(1).

Managers: Mick O'Brien 1936-37; Scott Duncan 1937-55 (continued as secretary); Alf Ramsey 1955-63; Jackie Milburn 1963-64; Bill McGarry

1964-68; Bobby Robson 1969-82; Bobby Ferguson 1982-87; Johnny Duncan 1987-90; John Lyall,1990-July 1992; *(FAPL)* Mick McGiven 1992-93; John Lyall May 1993-Dec 1994; George Burley Dec 1994–

Season 1994-95
Biggest Home Win: 4-1 v Leicester City, 2/1/95
Biggest Home Defeat: 1-3 v Tottenham H, 30/8/94; Liverpool, 29/10/94; Blackburn Rovers, 19/11/94
Biggest Away Win: 3-0 v Crystal Palace, 5/11/94
Biggest Away Defeat: 0-9 v Manchester United, 4/3/95
Biggest Home Attendance: 22,559 v Tottenham H, 30/8/94
Smallest Home Attendance: 11,367 v Wimbledon, 16/12/94
Average Attendance: 16,907
Last Season: *FAPL:* 22nd. *FA Cup:* 3rd round. *Coca-Cola Cup:* 2nd round
Leading Scorer: Claus Tomsen – 5

All-time Record
Record FAPL Win: 4-1 v Leicester City, 2/1/95
Record FAPL Defeat: 0-9 v Manchester United, 4/3/95
Record FL Win: 7-0 v Portsmouth, Div 2, 7/11/64; WBA, Div 1, 11/64
Record FL Defeat: 1-10 v Fulham, Division 1, 26/12/63
Record Cup Win: 10-0 v Floriana, European Cup, PrRd 25/9/62
Record Fee Received: £1.75m from Tottenham H for Jason Dozzell
Record Fee Paid: £1m to Tottenham H for Steve Sedgley, 7/94
Most FL Appearances: Mick Mills, 591, 1966-82
Record Attendance (all-time): 38.010 v Leeds Utd, FA Cup R6, 8/3/75
Record Attendance (FAPL): 22.559 v Manchester United, 1/5/94 and Tottenham H, 30/8/94
Highest Scorer in FAPL Season: Chris Kiwomya, 10, 1992-93 *and* Ian Marshall, 10, 1993-94
Most FAPL Goals in Season: 50, 1992-93
Most FAPL Points in Season: 52. 1992-93

5-Year League Record

	Div.	P	W	D	L	F	A	Pts	Pos	FAC	FLC
90-91	2	46	13	18	15	60	68	57	14	3	3
91-92	2	46	24	12	10	70	50	84	1	5	2
92-93	PL	42	12	16	14	50	55	52	16	6	5
93-94	PL	42	9	16	17	35	58	43	19	5	3
94-95	PL	42	7	6	29	36	93	27	22r	3	2

Summary of FAPL Appearances and Goals 1994-95

Player	Tot	Start	Sub	SNU	PS	Goals	Yel	Red
BAKER	2	2	0	23	0	0	0	0
CHAPMAN	16	9	7	2	2	1	1	0
COTERELL	2	0	2	0	0	0	0	0
ELLIS	1	1	0	0	1	0	0	0
FORREST	36	36	0	0	0	0	1	0
GREGORY Neil	1	0	1	2	0	0	0	0
GREGORY David	3	1	2	1	1	0	0	0
GUENTCHEV	16	11	5	1	2	1	1	0
JOHNSON	17	14	3	4	1	0	1	0
KIWOMYA	15	13	2	0	2	3	0	0
LINIGHAN	32	31	1	0	5	0	7	0
MARSHALL	18	14	4	2	4	3	0	0
MASON	21	19	2	4	4	3	1	0
MATHIE	13	13	0	0	3	2	0	0
MILTON	25	19	6	1	2	2	3	0
MORGAN	1	1	0	18	0	0	0	0
NORFOLK	3	1	2	0	0	0	0	0
PALMER	12	10	2	6	1	0	2	0
PAZ	17	13	4	1	5	1	1	0
SEDGLEY	26	26	0	0	1	4	2	0
SLATER	27	22	5	0	4	1	1	0
STOCKWELL	15	14	1	0	0	0	0	0
SWAILES	4	4	0	0	0	0	0	0
TANNER	10	9	1	0	2	2	1	0
TARICCO	0	0	0	1	0	0	0	0
THOMPSON	10	9	1	0	0	0	0	0
THOMSEN	33	31	2	0	3	5	3	0
VAUGHAN	10	10	0	0	1	0	4	0
WARK	26	26	0	0	4	4	3	1
WHELAN	13	12	1	0	2	0	4	1
WILLIAMS	38	38	0	0	4	1	4	0
WRIGHT	3	3	0	1	0	0	0	0
YALLOP	41	41	0	1	1	1	4	0
YOUDS	10	9	1	3	0	0	4	0

OGs 2

Burley Approach Fails to Keep Status

In a bid to arrest two years of struggle near to the foot of the Premiership, Ipswich turned to former manager John Lyall at the end of the previous season. Attention was focused on Ipswich's lack of attacking prowess with just 35 goals scored during 1993-94. Lyall attempted to improve a squad short on genuine quality with the £1m transfer of Steve Sedgley from Tottenham and £250,000 signing of Claus Thomsen from Aarhus.

The first week brought a mixed bag for Ipswich with an opening day home defeat being followed by a draw at Wimbledon and a promising victory over QPR at Loftus Road. Sadly for Ipswich fans, though, that is pretty much where their season finished as the month ended with a comprehensive reversal against Tottenham at Portman Road. Lyall took further steps to bolster the squad early in September with the imaginative swoop for the South American pair of Adrian Paz for £1m and Mauricio Taricho from Argentinos Juniors.

The side was, however, already on a downward spiral and defeats against Aston Villa and East Anglian rivals Norwich had the doom merchants in full voice. Ipswich pulled off a major surprise on 24 September when beating Manchester United 3-2, a result which brought to an end their run of eleven matches without victory at Portman Road. Town failed to build on that result and in 15 more league games before the turn of the year just one more win, against Leeds, was achieved and just six points collected – such form could only have one outcome.

Lyall resigned during December to be replaced by former Blues defender George Burley who, at the time, was in charge of Division Three neighbours Colchester. Going into the New Year rooted to the foot of the table was hardly uplifting but Ipswich showed true grit to firstly hammer Leicester 4-1 and then astound the Premiership with their first victory at Anfield courtesy of Adam Tanner's second goal in consecutive games. Only one other player, Thomsen, found the net two games in succession during the season. Those wins lifted Ipswich above Leicester but with just one point from the next three games, relegation was a matter of when rather than if. Burley turned to experience by signing Lee Chapman but his return of one goal in 16 games highlighted Town's problems. Chapman's only goal helped Town to victory over Southampton but their fate was then sealed by seven consecutive reversals which included the highest ever score in the Premiership when Manchester United turned them over 9-0 at Old Trafford. Ian Marshall ended Ipswich's seven match run without scoring with a consolation goal at Highbury in mid April but the 4-1 defeat confirmed their relegation.

Ipswich could find no escape from their misery in the cup competitions with lower league opposition adding to their woes. In the FA Cup, Wrexham added to their list of giant cup killings with a 2-1 at the Racecourse Ground, and in the Coca-Cola Cup Bolton waltzed to a 3-0 win at Portman Road and completed the double at Burden Park. ∎

Results 1994-95

FA Carling Premiership

Date	Opponents	Ven	Res	Pos	Atten	Scorers
20-Aug	N Forest	H	0-1	18	18,882	
23-Aug	Wimbledon	A	1-1	8	5,853	Milton (61)
27-Aug	QPR	A	2-1	8	12,456	OG (19); Guentchev (50)
30-Aug	Tottenham	H	1-3	15	22,559	Kiwomya (86)
10-Sep	Aston Villa	A	0-2	16	22,241	
19-Sep	Norwich C	H	1-2	14	17,447	Wark (45 pen)
24-Sep	Man United	H	3-2	14	22,559	Mason (15,43); Sedgley (80)
1-Oct	Southampton	A	1-3	16	13,246	Marshall (77)
10-Oct	Coventry C	A	0-2	20	9,526	
16-Oct	Sheffield W	H	1-2	21	13,073	Wark (50)
23-Oct	Chelsea	A	0-2	21	15,068	
29-Oct	Liverpool	H	1-3	21	22,519	Paz (64)
1-Nov	Leeds Utd	H	2-0	20	15,956	Sedgley (7); Williams (64)
5-Nov	C Palace	A	3-0	20	13,349	
19-Nov	Blackburn R	H	1-3	20	17,329	Thomsen (28)
26-Nov	Newcastle	A	1-1	22	34,459	Thomsen (89)
3-Dec	Man City	H	1-2	22	13,504	Mason (73)
10-Dec	N Forest	A	1-4	22	21,340	Thomsen (45)
16-Dec	Wimbledon	H	2-2	22	11,367	Milton (7); Sedgley (83)
26-Dec	West Ham	H	1-1	22	20,562	Thomsen (70)
28-Dec	Arsenal	H	0-2	22	22,054	
31-Dec	Everton	A	1-4	22	25,659	Sedgley (14)
2-Jan	Leicester C	H	4-1	21	15,803	Kiwomya (34,62); Tanner (54); Yallop (73)
14-Jan	Liverpool	A	1-0	21	32,733	Tanner (30)
21-Jan	Chelsea	H	2-2	21	17,296	Slater (74); Wark (80 pen)
28-Jan	Blackburn R	A	1-4	21	21,325	Wark (76 pen)
4-Feb	C Palace	H	0-2	21	15,570	
22-Feb	Man City	A	0-2	21	21,430	
25-Feb	Southampton	H	2-1	21	16,067	Mathie (70); Chapman (77)
28-Feb	Newcastle	H	0-2	21	18,639	
4-Mar	Man United	A	0-9	21	43,804	
8-Mar	Tottenham	A	0-3	21	24,930	
20-Mar	Norwich C	A	0-3	21	17,510	
1-Apr	Aston Villa	H	0-1	21	15,710	
5-Apr	Leeds Utd	A	0-4	22	28,600	
11-Apr	QPR	H	0-1	22	11,767	
15-Apr	Arsenal	A	1-4	22	36,818	Marshall (71)
17-Apr	West Ham	H	1-1	22	19,099	Thomsen (11)
29-Apr	Leicester C	A	0-2	22	15,248	

6-May	Coventry C	H	2-0	22	12,893	Marshall (52); OG (62)
9-May	Everton	H	0-1	22	14.951	
14-May	Sheffield W	A	1-4	22	30.213	Mathie (50)

FA Challenge Cup

| Date | Opponents | Vn | Rnd | Res | Atten | Scorers |
| 7-Jan | Wrexham | A | 3R | 1-2 | 8,324 | Linighan (84) |

Coca-Cola League Cup

Date	Opponents	Vn	Rnd	Res	Atten	Scorers
21-Sep	Bolton Wdrs	H	2R1L	0-3	7,787	
5-Oct		A	2R2L	0-1	8,212	

Bolton Wanderers win 4-0 on aggregate

Ipswich – Premiership Fact File

- Town's 3-2 win over Manchester United on 24th September was their first home win since February 1994.
- Ipswich were not involved in a goalless draw all season!
- During February, March and April Ipswich went through a period of seven games without a goal.
- Ipswich suffered a 9-0 humiliation at Old Trafford as Manchester United recorded the highest ever Premiership score.
- Ipswich's total of 29 defeats set a new Premiership record as did their tally of 27 points – the lowest ever in a season.

D1: Leicester City

Founded in 1884 as Leicester Fosse by former pupils of the Wyggeston School from the western part of the city near the old Roman Fosse. Moved to their present ground in 1891 and, from the Midland League joined Division Two of the Football League in 1894. Promoted for the first time in 1908, they have been relegated seven times from the top flight. FA Cup runners-up four times, they gained European Cup-Winners' Cup experience in 1961/62. Members of the new Division One in its first season, 1992/93, and promoted to the Premier League following play-off success in 1994.

Ground: City Stadium, Filbert Street, Leicester LE2 7FL
Phone: 0116-255 55000   **News:** 0891 12 11 85
Box Office: 0116-291 5232
Colours: All Blue   **Club Nickname:** Filberts or Foxes
Capacity: 24,000   **Pitch:** 112x75 yd.
Directions: *From North:* Leave M1 at junction 22, or take A46, A607 to town centre. Towards Rugby via Almond Road, Aylestone Road, and then left into Walnut Street and Filbert Street for the ground. *From South:* M1 or M69 and then A46 to Upperton Road and Filbert Street. *From East:* A47 into town centre, then right along Oxford Street to Aylestone Road and as North. *From West:* M69 and A50 to Aylestone Road, and then as North.
Rail: Leicester

President: K.R. Brigstock   **Chairman:** Martin George
Chief Executive: Barry Pierpoint
Secretary: Ian Silvester   **Company Secretary:** Steve Kind
Manager: Mark McGee   **Assistant:** Colin Lee
Coach: Mike Hickman   **Physio:** Alan Smith

League History: 1894 Elected to Division 2; 1908-09 Division 1; 1009-25 Division 2; 1925-35 Division 1; 1935-37 Division 2; 1937-39 Division 1; 1946-54 Division 2; 1954-55 Division 1; 1955-57 Divsion 2; 1957-69 Division 1; 1969-71 Division 2; 1971-78 Division 1; 1978-80 Division 2; 1980-81 Division 1; 1981-83 Division 2; 1983-87 Division 1; 1987-92 Division 2; 1992-94 Division 1; 1994-95 FA Premier League; 1995 - Division 1.

Honours: *Football League Division 1 Runners-up:* 1928-29; *Division 2 Champions:* 1924-25, 1936-37, 1953-54, 1956-57, 1970-71, 1979-80; *Runners-up:* 1907-08. *FA Cup Runners-up:* 1949, 1961, 1963, 1969. *Football League Cup Winners:* 1963-64; *Runners-up:* 1964-65.

218

European Record: CC (0): –; CWC (1): 61-62 (2); UEFA (0): –.

Managers: William Clarke 1896-97; George Johnson 1898-1907; James Blessington 1907-09; Andy Aitkin 1909-11; J.W. Bartlett 1912-14; Peter Hodge 1919-26; William Orr 1926-32; Peter Hodge 1932-34; Andy Lochead 1934-36; Frank Womack 1936-39; Tom Bromilow 1939-45; Tom Mather 1945-46; Johnnny Duncan 1946-49; Norman Bullock 1949-55; David Halliday 1955-58; Matt Gillies 1959-68; Frank O'Farrell 1968-71; Jimmy Bloomfield 1971-77; Frank McLintock 1977-78; Jock Wallace 1978-82; Gordon Milne 1982-86; Bryan Hamilton 1986-87; David Pleat 1987-91; *(FAPL)* Brian Little May 1991-Nov 1994; Mark McGee Dec 1994-

Season 1994-95

Biggest Home Win: 4-3 v Southampton, 15/10/94
Biggest Home Defeat: 0-4 v Manchester United, 15/4/95
Biggest Away Win: 1-0 v Manchester City, 25/1/95
Biggest Away Defeat: 0-4 v Chelsea, 8/10/94
Biggest Home Attendance: 21,393 v Liverpool, 26/12/94
Smallest Home Attendance: 15,248 v Ipswich Town, 29/4/95
Average Attendance: 18,518
Last Season: *FAPL:* 21st *FA Cup 5th round. Coca-Cola Cup:* 2nd round
Leading Scorer: Iwan Roberts – 9

All-time Record

Record FAPL Win: 4-3 v Southampton, 15/10/94
Record FAPL Defeat: – 0-4 v Manchester United, 15/4/95
Record FL Win: 10-0 v Portsmouth, Division 1, 20/10/1928
Record FL Defeat: 0-12 v Nottingham Forest, Division 1, 21/4/1909
Record Cup Win: 8-1 v. Coventry City (away), League Cup R5, 1/12/64
Record Fee Received: £3.5m from Aston Villa for Mark Draper, 7/95
Record Fee Paid: £1.25m to Notts County for Mark Draper, 8/94
Most FL Appearances: Adam Black, 528, 1920-35
Record Attendance (all-time): 47,298 v. Tottenham H, FAC Rd5, 18/2/1928
Record Attendance (FAPL): 21,393 v Liverpool, 26/12/94
Highest Scorer in FAPL season: Iwan Roberts (9)
Most FAPL Goals in Season: 49, 1994-95
Most FAPL Points in Season: 29, 1994-95

5-Year League Record

	Div.	P	W	D	L	F	A	Pts	Pos	FAC	FLC
90-91	2	46	14	8	24	60	83	50	22	3	2
91-92	2	46	23	8	15	62	55	77	4	4	2
92-93	1	46	22	10	14	71	64	76	6	3	3
93-94	1	46	19	16	11	72	59	73	4	3	3
94-95	PL	42	6	11	25	45	80	29	21r	5	2

Summary of FAPL Appearances and Goals 1994-95

Player	Tot	Start	Sub	SNU	PS	Goals	Yel	Red
AGNEW 11	7	4	2	1	0	1	0
BLAKE 30	26	4	2	5	3	8	0
CAREY 12	11	1	0	2	0	2	1
CARR 13	12	1	0	5	1	0	0
DRAPER 39	39	0	0	3	5	5	0
GALLOWAY 5	4	1	0	0	0	3	0
GEE 7	3	4	2	3	2	1	0
GRAYSON 34	34	0	0	6	0	7	1
HESKEY 1	1	0	1	1	0	0	0
HILL 24	24	0	0	3	0	2	0
HOULT 0	0	0	2	0	0	0	0
JOACHIM 15	11	4	0	2	3	0	0
LAWRENCE 17	9	8	1	1	1	0	0
LEWIS 16	13	3	0	3	0	1	1
LOWE 29	19	10	2	5	8	3	1
McMAHON 1	0	1	3	0	0	0	0
MILLS 1	1	0	0	0	0	0	0
MOHAN 23	23	0	1	1	0	5	1
MUGGLETON 0	0	0	1	0	0	0	0
OLDFIELD 14	8	6	1	2	1	1	0
ORMONDROYD ... 6	6	0	1	3	1	0	0
PARKER 14	14	0	0	0	2	0	0
PHILPOTT 23	19	4	1	5	0	2	0
POOLE 36	36	0	6	0	0	0	0
ROBERTS 37	32	5	2	2	9	2	0
ROBINS 17	16	1	0	1	5	0	0
SMITH 12	10	2	2	3	0	4	1
THOMPSON 19	16	3	0	3	0	0	0
WALSH 5	5	0	0	0	0	0	0
WARD 6	6	0	33	0	0	0	0
WHITLOW 28	28	0	0	2	2	7	1
WILLIS 29	29	0	1	0	2	8	1

OGs 0

Little Change for Foxes

Having shown no small amount of persistence in making their way into the Premiership – three successive appearances in the play offs – Leicester manager Brian Little strengthened his squad preseason with the signing of Mark Draper from Notts County for £1.25m. Despite this, Leicester were the bookies' favourites for the drop and at the end of the first week, when the Foxes were the only side in the Premiership without a point from three games, the bookies' doubts seemed fully justified. Leicester stopped the rot when taking a point off ten man QPR but the first victory did not arrive until the middle of September when Ardiles' leaky Spurs side were beaten 3-1 at Filbert Street. A draw at Everton the following week took Leicester out of the relegation places but a 4-0 thumping at Chelsea brought them down to earth.

Little's response was to buy Franz Carr from Sheffield United. Leicester moved out of the bottom four for the last time in mid October with a 4-3 win over Southampton, three goals for the visitors in the last twelve minutes almost denied Leicester that rare victory. The Foxes were five points clear of bottom side Everton at the end of October but a run of four successive defeats, three by just 1-0, set the trend for the rest of the campaign. Following the third of those defeats, at West Ham, Little quit the club and shortly after joined Aston Villa amid much outrage at Filbert Street. The players put the turmoil behind them to beat Arsenal but again any possible recovery was thwarted by nine more winless matches.

December got off to a hostile start with Little receiving an extremely volatile reception when he took his new Villa side to Filbert Street when the match ended in an honourable draw. After a 3-1 defeat at Newcastle, Reading manager Mark McGhee was handed the same position at Leicester. His first match saw Leicester keep their first clean sheet of the season in a draw with Blackburn, eleven days later another unlikely point was gathered at Old Trafford. A return trip to Manchester saw Mark Robins' first goal for his new club secure Leicester's only away win of the season as City were beaten 1-0.

Far from heralding a new beginning, the New Year began with a crushing 4-1 defeat at Ipswich, a result which took Leicester to the bottom of the pile. By the end of March, Leicester were 16 points adrift of safety and resigned to their fate. Ipswich's abysmal form offered hope for Leicester to avoid finishing in last place and with wins over fellow relegated sides Norwich and Ipswich, Leicester did finish above the Suffolk club.

Leicester could have been humiliated in the FA Cup when presented with a home tie against non-leaguers Enfield, but the Premier side cruised through to the 4th Round where McGhee's men overcame nine man Portsmouth. The Foxes' run ended in the 5th Round with Wolves winning 1-0 at Molineux. In the Coca-Cola Cup, Leicester were humbled by Brighton who won both legs of the 2nd Round clash.

The close season saw Mark Draper reunited with his former manager at Aston Villa as Leicester looked to build to a return. ■

Results 1994-95

FA Carling Premiership

Date	Opponents	Ven	Res	Pos	Atten	Scorers
21-Aug	Newcastle	H	1-3	22	20,048	Joachim (90)
23-Aug	Blackburn R	A	0-3	22	21,050	
27-Aug	N Forest	A	0-1	22	21,601	
31-Aug	QPR	H	1-1	20	18,695	Gee (89)
10-Sep	Wimbledon	A	1-2	21	7,683	Lowe (23)
17-Sep	Tottenham	H	3-1	20	21,300	Joachim (45,90); Lowe (87)
24-Sep	Everton	A	1-1	18	28,003	Draper (81)
3-Oct	Coventry C	H	2-2	19	19,372	Roberts (45,85)
8-Oct	Chelsea	A	0-4	20	18,397	
15-Oct	Southampton	H	4-3	18	20,020	Blake (3,54); Roberts (21); Carr (81)
24-Oct	Leeds Utd	A	1-2	18	28,547	Blake (53)
29-Oct	C Palace	H	0-1	19	20,022	
5-Nov	West Ham	A	0-1	21	18,780	
20-Nov	Man City	H	0-1	21	19,006	
23-Nov	Arsenal	H	2-1	21	20,774	Ormondroyd (16); Lowe (28)
26-Nov	Norwich C	A	1-2	21	20,657	Draper (22)
3-Dec	Aston Villa	H	1-1	21	20,896	Gee (5)
10-Dec	Newcastle	A	1-3	21	34,400	Oldfield (48)
17-Dec	Blackburn R	H	0-0	21	20,559	
26-Dec	Liverpool	H	1-2	21	21,393	Roberts (87)
28-Dec	Man United	A	1-1	21	43,789	Whitlow (65)
31-Dec	Sheffield W	H	0-1	21	20,624	
2-Jan	Ipswich Tn	A	1-4	22	15,803	Roberts (53)
14-Jan	C Palace	A	0-2	22	12,707	
25-Jan	Man City	A	1-0	22	21,007	Robins (69)
4-Feb	West Ham	H	1-2	22	20,375	Robins (44)
11-Feb	Arsenal	A	1-1	22	31,373	Draper (78)
22-Feb	Aston Villa	A	4-4	22	30,825	Robins (61); Roberts (67); Lowe (80,90)
25-Feb	Coventry C	A	2-4	22	20,663	Lowe (64); Roberts (74)
4-Mar	Everton	H	2-2	22	20,447	Draper (59); Roberts (83)
8-Mar	QPR	A	0-2	22	10,189	
11-Mar	N Forest	H	2-4	22	20,423	Lowe (16); Draper (71)
15-Mar	Leeds United	H	1-3	22	20,068	Roberts (21)
18-Mar	Tottenham	A	0-1	22	30,851	
1-Apr	Wimbledon	H	3-4	22	15,489	Robins (13); Willis (79); Lawrence (84)
5-Apr	Norwich C	H	1-0	21	15,992	Parker (48)
8-Apr	Sheffield W	A	0-1	21	22,551	
15-Apr	Man United	H	0-4	21	21,281	

17-Apr	Liverpool	A	0-2	21	36,012	
29-Apr	Ipswich Tn	H	2-0	21	15,248	Whitlow (67); Lowe (90)
6-May	Chelsea	H	1-1	21	18,140	Willis (24)
14-May	Southampton	A	2-2	21	15,101	Parker (58); Robins (87)

FA Challenge Cup

Date	Opponents	Vn	Rnd	Res	Atten	Scorers
7-Jan	Enfield	H	3R	2-0	17,351	Oldfield (9); Roberts (67)
28-Jan	Portsmouth	A	4R	1-0	14,928	Roberts (44)
18-Feb	Wolves	A	5R	0-1	28,544	

Coca-Cola League Cup

Date	Opponents	Vn	Rnd	Res	Atten	Scorers
21-Sep	Brighton & H	A	2R1L	0-1	11,041	
5-Oct		H	2R2L	0-2	14,258	

Brighton & Hove Albion win 3-0 on aggregate

Foxes – Premiership Fact File

- A last minute goal by Phil Gee earned Leicester their first Premiership point in a 1-1 draw with QPR on the last day of August.
- Mark McGee's first game in charge came against Blackburn Rovers on 17th December. Leicester secured a draw and their first clean sheet of the season.
- Foxes 4-4 draw at Aston Villa on 22 February set a new record high for a score draw in the Premiership.

D1: Norwich City

Formed following a June 1902 public meeting organised by two loc[al]
schoolteachers which agreed the desirability of a Norwich City Football Clu[b]
Started in the Norwich & Suffolk League. Turned professional and elected [to]
the Southern League in 1905. Moved from Newmarket Road to The Nes[t]
Rosary Road in 1908.

Founder members of Football League Divison Three with other Souther[n]
Leaguers in 1920, this becoming Divison Three (South) in 1921. Moved [to]
Carrow Road, the home of Boulton & Paul Sports Club in 1935. Found[er]
members of Division Three on the end of regionalisation in 1958. Premi[er]
League founder members 1992.

Ground: Carrow Road, Norwich, NR1 1JE
Phone: 01603-612131   **News:** 0891-42 42 12
Capacity: 25,000   **Pitch:** 114yds x 74 yds
Colours: Yellow, Green, Yellow   **Nickname:** The Canaries
Directions: *From North:* A140 to ring road and follow signs for Yarmou[th]
A47. Turn right at T junction after 3½ miles then left after ½ mile [onto]
Carrow Rd. *From South & West:* A11/A140 onto ring road. Follow signs f[or]
Yarmouth A47 etc. *From East:* A47 into Norwich then left onto ring road.

President: Geoffrey Watling   **Chairman:** Robert Chase JP
Vice-Chairman: J.A. Jones   **Secretary:** Andrew Neville
Manager: Martin O'Neill
Physio: Tim Sheppard MCSP, SRP

League History: 1920 Original Member of Division 3; 1921 Division 3 (S)
1934-39 Division 2; 1946-58 Division 3 (S); 1958-60 Division 3; 1960-7[2]
Division 2; 1972-74 Division 1; 1974-75 Division 2; 1975-81 Division [1]
1981-82 Division 2; 1982-85 Division 1; 1985-86 Division 1; 1986-9[5]
Division 1; 1992-95 – FA Premier League; 1995- Division 1.

Honours: *Football League Division 2 Champions:* 1971-72, 1985-8[6]
Division 3 (S) Champions: 1933-34; *Division 3 Runners-up:* 1959-6[0]
Football League Cup Winners: 1962, 1985; *Runners-up:* 1973, 1975.

European Record: CC (0): –; CWC (0):–; UEFA (1): 93-94(2).

Managers: John Bowman 1905-07; James McEwen 1907-08; Arthur Turne[r]
1909-10; Bert Stansfield 1910-15; Major Frank Buckley 1919-20; Charle[s]
O'Hagan 1920-21; Albert Gosnell 1921-26; Bert Stansfield 1926; Cecil Potte[r]
1926-29; James Kerr 1929-33; Tom Parker 1933-37; Bob Young 1937-39[...]

Jimmy Jewell 1939; Bob Young 1939-45; Cyril Spiers 1946-47; Duggie Lochhead 1945-50; Norman Low 1950-55; Tom Parker 1955-57; Archie Macaulay 1957-61; Willie Reid 1961-62; George Swindin 1962; Ron Ashman 1962-66; Lol Morgan 1966-69; Ron Saunders 1969-73; John Bond 1973-80; Ken Brown 1980-87; Dave Stringer December 1987-92; (FAPL) Mike Walker 1992-93; John Deehan Jan 1994-Apr 1995; Gary Megson April 1995-June 1995; Martin O'Neill June 1995–

Season 1994-95
Biggest Home Win: 4-2 v QPR, 22/10/94
Biggest Home Defeat: 0-2 v Tottenham H 26/12/94; Man United 22/2/95
Biggest Away Win: 2-1 v Ipswich Town, 19/9/94
Biggest Away Defeat: 1-5 v Arsenal, 1/4/95
Biggest Home Attendance: 21,843 v Liverpool, 29/4/95
Smallest Home Attendance: 13,350 v Sheffield Wednesday, 8/3/95
Average Attendance: 18,621
Last Season: *FAPL:* 20th *FA Cup:* 5th round *Coca-Cola Cup:* 5th round
Leading Scorer: Mark Robbins & Cureton – 4

All-time Record
Record FAPL Win: 5-1 v Everton 25/9/93
Record FAPL Defeat: 1-7 v Blackburn Rovers, 3/10/92
Record FL Win: 10-2 v Coventry City, Division 3 (S), 15/3/1930
Record FL Defeat: 2-10 v Swindon Town, Southern League, 5/9/1908
Record Cup Win: 8-0 v Sutton United, FA Cup R4, 28/1/1989
Record Fee Received: £5m from Blackburn Rovers for Chris Sutton, 7/94
Record Fee Paid: £925,000 to Port Vale for Darren Beckford, 6/1991
Most FL Appearances: Ron Ashman, 592, 1947-64
Record Attendance (all-time): 43,984 v Leicester C, FA Cup R6, 30/3/1963
Record Attendance (FAPL): 21,181 v Tottenham Hotspur, 2/4/94
Highest Scorer in FAPL Season: Chris Sutton, 25, 1993-94
Most FAPL Goals in Season: 65, 1993-94
Most FAPL Points in Season: 72, 1992-93

5-Year League Record

	Div.	P	W	D	L	F	A	Pts	Pos	FAC	FLC
90-91	1	38	13	6	19	41	64	45	15	6	3
91-92	1	42	11	12	19	47	63	45	18	SF	5
92-93	PL	42	21	9	12	61	65	72	3	4	3
93-94	PL	42	12	17	13	65	61	53	12	4	3
94-95	Pl	42	10	13	19	37	54	43	20r	5	5

Summary of FAPL Appearances and Goals 1994-95

Player	Tot	Start	Sub	SNU	PS	Goals	Yel	Red
ADAMS	33	23	10	1	8	3	2	0
AKINBIYI	13	6	7	0	5	0	1	0
BOWEN	36	34	2	0	2	1	5	0
BRADSHAW	26	25	1	0	4	1	6	0
BROWNRIGG	0	0	0	1	0	0	0	0
CROOK	34	33	1	0	7	0	5	0
CROWFOOT	0	0	0	6	0	0	0	0
CURETON	17	9	8	1	5	4	0	0
EADIE	26	22	4	0	2	2	0	0
EKOKU	6	5	1	0	4	0	1	0
GOSS	25	19	6	0	1	2	6	0
GUNN	21	21	0	0	1	0	0	0
HOWIE...	0	0	0	6	0	0	0	0
JOHNSON...	7	6	1	0	1	0	2	1
MARSHALL	21	20	1	14	0	0	0	0
MEGSON	1	1	0	0	1	0	1	0
MILLIGAN	26	25	1	1	5	2	7	0
MILLS	0	0	0	1	0	0	0	0
NEWMAN	32	23	9	2	5	1	6	0
NEWSOME	35	35	0	0	0	3	4	0
O'NEIL...	1	0	1	0	0	0	0	0
POLSTON	38	38	0	0	1	0	7	0
PRIOR	17	12	5	1	1	0	2	0
RHODES	0	0	0	10	0	0	0	0
ROBINS	17	14	3	0	7	4	0	0
SHERON...	21	17	4	0	5	1	0	0
SUTCH	30	20	10	1	3	1	2	0
TRACEY	1	1	0	5	0	0	0	0
ULLATHORNE ...	27	27	0	0	7	2	5	0
WARD	25	25	0	0	0	8	5	0
WRIGHT	2	1	1	0	1	0	1	0
						OGs 1		

Player Sales Take Toll

Following on from a disastrous second half to the 1993-94 season, Norwich made several changes to the playing staff, all of which were funded by the £5m sale of Chris Sutton to Blackburn. Manager John Deehan brought in Jon Newsome from Leeds and Mike Sheron from Manchester City both for £1m, Mike Milligan from Oldham for £800,000 and Carl Bradshaw from Sheffield United for £500,000.

The new look Norwich made a disappointing start with a 2-0 defeat at Chelsea but then put together their best form of the season with a run of one defeat in ten games. Norwich's first away win came in the East Anglian derby at Ipswich as Bradshaw's first goal for the club clinched a 2-1 success. Clean sheets were maintained in the opening three home games before, ironically, Sutton scored for Blackburn only for Norwich to hit back to claim a memorable victory. The following week a Bryan Gunn penalty save and a last minute Neil Adams goal accounted for Leeds at Carrow Road and lifted Norwich into sixth place. A draw at Villa Park and a resounding 4-2 home win over QPR strengthened their position.

October ended with Norwich losing to Wimbledon and failing to win any of the next three games, all against struggling sides. A last minute goal by Daryl Sutch earned Norwich their only league win during November, 2-1 against Leicester, and after a defeat at Old Trafford, The Canaries edged back into the top seven with wins over Chelsea and Crystal Palace.

Christmas was hardly a time for celebration at Carrow Road as their season turned with defeats by Tottenham and Forest, and an ankle injury to goalkeeper Gunn which proved costly for the club. The next home match, against Newcastle, was won but it was one of just two victories in the final 23 league games. The slide was unstoppable, other than for a second win over Ipswich, as a succession of draws and then seven successive defeats culminated in relegation.

Norwich's good first half of the season form was reflected in the Coca-Cola Cup where Swansea City were comfortably beaten and four second half goals put paid to Tranmere. In the 4th Round Darren Eadie's first minute goal disposed of Notts County only for Wembley bound Bolton to curtail the run in the quarter final. The FA Cup also saw good progress made with wins over Grimsby Town and Coventry, after a replay, setting up a 5th Round tie at Goodison which, in keeping with their league form at that time, saw Norwich hammered 5-0.

During the season the club signed Ashley Ward from Crewe, who proved to be an excellent signing, but the £1m sale of Efan Ekoku was counter productive as he twice scored the winner against Norwich for his new club Wimbledon. Mark Robins also left, joining Leicester for £1m. Deehan quit during the slump with Gary Megson taking over in a caretaker capacity. In the close season Megson was subsequently replaced by crowd favourite Martin O'Neill. ■

Results 1994-95

FA Carling Premiership

Date	Opponents	Ven	Res	Pos	Atten	Scorers
20-Aug	Chelsea	A	0-2	19	23,098	
24-Aug	C Palace	H	0-0	10	19,015	
27-Aug	West Ham	H	1-0	10	19,110	Robins (64)
31-Aug	Sheffield W	A	0-0	11	25,072	
10-Sep	Arsenal	H	0-0	11	17,768	
19-Sep	Ipswich Tn	A	2-1	11	17,447	Newman (11); Bradshaw (52 pen)
24-Sep	Man City	A	0-2	11	21,031	
1-Oct	Blackburn R	H	2-1	9	18,146	Bowen (30); Newsome (55)
8-Oct	Leeds Utd	H	2-1	8	17,390	Robins (61); Adams (90)
15-Oct	Aston Villa	A	1-1	6	22,468	Milligan (49)
22-Oct	QPR	H	4-2	6	19,431	Robins (44); Bowen (54), Sheron (57); OG (62)
30-Oct	Wimbledon	A	0-1	7	8,242	
2-Nov	Southampton	A	1-1	7	12,976	Robins (48)
5-Nov	Everton	H	0-0	7	18,377	
19-Nov	Coventry C	A	0-1	8	11,885	
26-Nov	Leicester C	H	2-1	9	20,567	Newsome (56); Sutch (90)
3-Dec	Man United	A	0-1	9	43,789	
10-Dec	Chelsea	H	3-0	9	18,246	Ward (23,45); Cureton (88)
17-Dec	C Palace	A	1-0	7	12,252	Ward (48)
26-Dec	Tottenham	A	0-2		21,814	
27-Dec	N Forest	A	0-1		20,010	
31-Dec	Newcastle	H	2-1		21,172	Adams (1); Ward (10)
2-Jan	Liverpool	A	0-4	8	34,709	
14-Jan	Wimbledon	H	1-2	9	18,261	Goss (22)
25-Jan	Coventry C	H	2-2	10	14,024	Adams (32pen); Ward (58)
4-Feb	Everton	A	1-2	10	23,293	Milligan (80)
11-Feb	Southampton	H	2-2	10	18,361	Newsome (37); Ward (90)
22-Feb	Man United	H	0-2	14	21,824	
25-Feb	Blackburn R	A	0-0	14	25,579	
4-Mar	Man City	H	1-1	13	16,266	Cureton (82)
8-Mar	Sheffield W	H	0-0	14	13,530	
11-Mar	West Ham	A	2-2	14	21,464	Eadie (22); Ullathorne (55)
15-Mar	QPR	A	0-2	16	10,519	
20-Mar	Ipswich Tn	H	3-0		17,510	Cureton (53); Ward (58); Eadie (77)
1-Apr	Arsenal	A	1-5	14	36,942	Cureton (32)
5-Apr	Leicester C	A	0-1		15,992	
8-Apr	Newcastle	A	0-3	14	35,518	
12-Apr	N Forest	H	0-1	18	19,005	

228

17-Apr	Tottenham	A	0-1	20	32,304	
29-Apr	Liverpool	H	1-2	20	21,843	Ullathorne (16)
6-May	Leeds Utd	A	1-2	20	31,982	Ward (36)
14-May	Aston Villa	H	1-1	20	19,374	Goss (56)

FA Challenge Cup

Date	Opponents	Vn	Rnd	Res	Atten	Scorers
7-Jan	Grimsby Tn	A	3R	1-0	11,198	Crook (56)
28-Jan	Coventry C	A	4R	0-0	15,101	
8-Feb		H	4RR	3-1	14,673	Sheron (8,108); Eadie (103);
			after extra time			
18-Feb	Everton	A	5R	0-5	31,616	

Coca-Cola League Cup

Date	Opponents	Vn	Rnd	Res	Atten	Scorers
21-Sep	Swansea City	H	2R1L	3-0	8,053	Sheron (36); Bradshaw (48pen); Adams (63)
4-Oct		A	2R2L	0-1	3,568	
	Norwich City win 3-1 on aggregate					
26-Oct	Tranmere R	A	3R	1-1	10,232	Polston (45)
9-Nov		H	3RR	4-2	13,311	Prior (56); McGreal (61); Polston (65); Newman (85)
30-Nov	Notts County	H	4R	1-0	14,040	Eadie (1)
11-Jan	Bolton Wdrs	A	5R	0-1	17,029	

Canaries – Premiership Fact File

- Norwich scored just one in their first five games of the season but still managed to gain six points.
- Ashley Ward scored two goals for Norwich on his debut in the 3-0 win over Chelsea in December.
- Carlton Palmer's last minute goal for Leeds United in the penultimate match of the season, resigned City to relegation.

FA PREMIER LEAGUE CLUB TRANSFERS 1994-95

Player	From	To	Fee
Chris Sutton	Norwich City	Blackburn Rovers	£5,000,000
Carlton Palmer	Sheffield Wednesday	Leeds United	£2,800,000
Paul Furlong	Watford	Chelsea	£2,300,000
Vinnie Samways	Tottenham Hotspur	Everton	£2,000,000
Stefan Schwarz	Benfica	Arsenal	£1,750,000
Nicky Summerbee	Swindon Town	Manchester City	£1,500,000
David May	Blackburn Rovers	Manchester United	£1,400,000
Tony Daley	Aston Villa	Wolves	£1,300,000
Steve Froggatt	Aston Villa	Wolves	*£1,000,000
Jon Newsome	Leeds United	Norwich City	£1,000,000
Steve Sedgley	Tottenham Hotspur	Ipswich Town	£1,000,000
Ian Taylor	Port Vale	Sheffield Wednesday	**£1,000,000
Joey Beauchamp	Oxford United	West Ham United	***£850,000
Neil Cox	Aston Villa	Middlesbrough	†£850,000
John Moncur	Swindon Town	West Ham United	††£850,000
Scott Minto	Charlton Athletic	Chelsea	£775,000
Nigel Pearson	Sheffield Wednesday	Middlesbrough	£750,000
Mark Robinson	Newcastle United	Swindon Town	£600,000
Carl Bradshaw	Sheffield United	Norwich City	£500,000
Alan Miller	Arsenal	Middlebrough	£500,000
Nicky Mohan	Middlesbrough	Leicester City	£300,000
Lee Glover	Nottingham Forest	Port Vale	£200,000
Dariusz Kubicki	Aston Villa	Sunderland	£100,000
Simon Osborn	Crystal Palace	Reading	£90,000
Rhys Wilmot	Grimsby Town	Crystal Palace	£80,000
Malcolm Rigby	Notts County	Nottingham Forest	£50,000
Clayton Blackmore	Manchester United	Middlesbrough	Free
Bryan Robson	Manchester United	Middlesbrough	Free
David Foot	Tottenham Hotspur	Southend United	Free
Mike Phelan	Manchester United	West Bromwich Albion	Free

*Plus £500,000 after appearances. ** Plus £25,000 for every 10 goals up to 50.*
****** – Plus £150,000 after appearances.*

Player	From	To	Fee
Daniel Amokachi	FC Bruges	Everton	£3,000,000
Philippe Albert	Anderlecht	Newcastle United	£2,650,000
Ilie Dumitrescu	Steaua Bucharest	Tottenham Hotspur	£2,600,000
Brian Roy	Foggia	Nottingham Forest	£2,500,000
Jurgen Klinsmann	Monaco	Tottenham Hotspur	£2,000,000
Don Hutchinson	Liverpool	West Ham United	£1,500,000
Ian Nolan	Tranmere Rovers	Sheffield Wednesday	£1,500,000
John Fashanu	Wimbledon	Aston Villa	£1,350,000
Dan Petrescu	Genoa	Sheffield Wednesday	£1,300,000
Mark Draper	Notts County	Leicester City	£1,250,000
David Rocastle	Manchester City	Chelsea	£1,250,000
Nil Lamptey	Anderlecht	Aston Villa	£1,000,000
Mike Sheron	Manchester City	Norwich City	£1,000,000
John Moncur	Swindon Town	West Ham United	£1,000,000
Mike Milligan	Oldham Athletic	Norwich City	£850,000
Paul Cook	Wolves	Coventry City	£600,000
Marc Hottiger	Sion	Newcastle United	£600,000
Mark Robinson	Newcastle United	Swindon Town	£600,000
Joey Beauchamp	West Ham United	Swindon Town	*£500,000
Carl Bradshaw	Sheffield United	Norwich City	£500,000
Alan Miller	Arsenal	Middlesbrough	£500,000
Jason Drysdale	Watford	Newcastle United	£425,000
Vince Bartram	Bournemouth	Arsenal	£400,000
Nicky Mohan	Middlesbrough	Leicester City	£330,000
Robbie Slater	Lens	Blackburn Rovers	£300,000
Mixu Paatelainen	Aberdeen	Bolton Wanderers	£300,000
Philomen Masinga	Mamolodi Sundowns	Leeds United	£275,000
Phil King	Sheffield Wednesday	Aston Villa	£250,000
Bruce Grobbelaar	Liverpool	Southampton	£250,000
Lucas Radebe	Kaizer Chiefs	Leeds United	£250,000
Lee Glover	Nottingham Forest	Port Vale	£200,000
Mark Ward	Everton	Birmingham City	£200,000
Steve Guppy	Wycombe Wanderers	Newcastle United	£150,000
Richard Sneekes	Fortuna Sitard	Bolton Wanderers	£150,000
Alphonse Groenendijk	Manchester City	Spartak Rotterdam	£100,000
Paul Miller	Wimbledon	Bristol Rovers	£100,000
Simon Osborn	Crystal Palace	Reading	£90,000
Rhys Wilmot	Grimsby Town	Crystal Palace	£80,000
Mick Harford	Coventry City	Wimbledon	£70,000
Simon Ireland	Blackburn Rovers	Mansfield Town	£60,000
Darren Pitcher	Charlton Athletic	Crystal Palace	**£40,000
Ray Kelly	Athlone Town	Manchester City	£30,000
Peter Whiston	Exeter City	Southampton	£30,000

Player	From	To	Fee
Shay Given	Celtic	Blackburn Rovers	Undisclosed
Paul Mortimer	Crystal Palace	Charlton Athletic	**Swap
David Whyte	Crystal Palace	Charlton Athletic	**Swap
Adrian Whitbread	Swindon Town	West Ham United	*Swap
Alan Judge	Hereford United	Chelsea	***Non-Contract
Andy Scott	Blackburn Rovers	Cardiff City	Free
Tony Gale	West Ham United	Blackburn Rovers	Free
Glynn Hurst	Tottenham Hotspur	Barnsley	Free
Rod McAree	Liverpool	Bristol City	Free
Scott Paterson	Liverpool	Bristol City	Free
Chris Adams	Oldham Athletic	Norwich City	Free
Viv Anderson	Barnsley	Middlesbrough	Free
Ray Byrne	Nottingham Forest	Northampton Town	Free
Richard Crisp	Aston Villa	Telford United	Free
Martin Davies	Coventry City	Stafford Rangers	Free
Danny Foot	Tottenham Hotspur	Southend United	Free
Colin Gibson	Leicester City	Blackpool	Free
Billy Kenny	Everton	Oldham Athletic	Free
Ian Kilford	Nottingham Forest	Wigan Athletic	Free
Criag Lawton	Manchester United	Port Vale	Free
Jeff Minton	Tottenham Hotspur	Brighton & Hove Albion	Free
Bryan Robson	Manchester United	Middlesbrough	Free
Paul Tait	Everton	Wigan Athletic	Free
Nicky Tanner	Liverpool	Bath	Free
Ray Wallace	Leeds United	Stoke City	Free
Kevin Brock	Newcastle United	Colchester United	Trial
Jan Eriksson	Kaiserslautern	Everton	Trial
Peter Lassen	Hvidovre	Southampton	Trial
Brian Law	Queen's Park Rangers	Millwall	Trial

*Swap with Beauchamp plus £500,000. ** Swap with Pitcher plus £40,000*
*** Now with Bromsgrove Rovers but available for Chelsea on non-contract basis*

September 1994

Player	From	To	Fee
Phil Babb	Coventry City	Liverpool	£3,600,000
John Scales	Wimbledon	Liverpool	*£3,000,000
Gheorghe Popescu	PSV Eindhoven	Tottenham Hotspur	£2,900,000
Paul Kitson	Derby County	Newcastle United	£2,250,000
Dion Dublin	Manchester United	Coventry City	£2,000,000
Klas Ingesson	PSV Eindhoven	Sheffield Wednesday	£2,000,000
Adrian Paz	Penarol	Ipswich Town	£900,000
Ronnie Ekelund	Barcelona	Southampton	£500,000
Nigel Jemson	Sheffield Wednesday	Notts County	£350,000
Cobi Jones	USSF	Coventry City	£300,000
Alan Reeves	Rochdale	Wimbledon	£300,000

232

Colin McKee	Manchester United	Kilmarnock	£265,000
Neil Whitworth	Manchester United	Kilmarnock	£265,000
Mauricio Taricco	Argentina Juniors	Ipswich Town	£175,000
Keith Jones	Southend United	Charlton Athletic	£150,000
John Gayle	Coventry City	Burnley	£70,000
Colin Cramb	Southampton	Falkirk	£70,000
Peter Beadle	Tottenham Hotspur	Watford	Undisclosed
John Gayle	Coventry City	Burnley	Undisclosed
Gary Mills	Leicester City	Notts County	Undisclosed
Tony Cottee	Everton	West Ham United	**Swap
David Burrows	West Ham United	Everton	**Swap
Colin Gibson	Leicester City	Walsall	Non-Contract
Gary Crosby	Nottingham Forest	Huddersfield Town	Free
David Culverhouse	Tottenham Hotspur	Dagenham & Redbridge	Free
Andy Gray	Tottenham Hotspur	Marbella	Free
Shaun Brooks	Bournemouth	West Ham United	Trial
Gary Gillespie	Celtic	Coventry City	Trial
Elijah Litana	Zambia	Everton	Trial
Glen Thomas	Fulham	Crystal Palace	Trial
Guilano Majorana	Manchester United	Watford	Trial

*Plus £500,000 on first England cap. ** Plus £300,000 to Everton.*

October 1994

Player	From	To	Fee
Efan Ekoku	Norwich City	Wimbledon	£800,000
Steve Pressley	Rangers	Coventry City	£600,000
Julian Dicks	Liverpool	West Ham United	*£500,000
Peter Butler	West Ham United	Notts County	£350,000
Simon Coleman	Sheffield Wednesday	Bolton Wanderers	£350,000
Steve Hodge	Leeds United	Queen's Park Rangers	£300,000
Scott Howie	Norwich City	Motherwell	£300,000
Matthew Bound	Southampton	Stockport County	£125,000
Franz Carr	Sheffield United	Leicester City	£100,000
Gary Mills	Leicester City	Notts County	£50,000
Mark Humphries	Leeds United	Bristol City	Undisclosed
Craig Lawton	Manchester United	Port Vale	Free
Steve Robinson	Tottenham Hotspur	Bournemouth	Free
Andy Thorn	Crystal Palace	Wimbledon	Free
Ronnie Whelan	Liverpool	Southend United	Free
Neil Young	Tottenham Hotspur	Bournemouth	Free
John Burridge	Newcastle United	Dumbarton	Non-Contract
Oyvind Leonhardsen	Rosenborg	Wimbledon	Trial
Peter Huistra	Rangers	Queen's Park Rangers	Trial
Bruno Pasquale	Torino	Crystal Palace	Trial

May rise to £1,000,000.

November 1994

Player	From	To	Fee
Jon Goodman	Millwall	Wimbledon	*£1,300,000
Kenny Cunningham	Millwall	Wimbledon	*See Above
Nicky Banger	Southampton	Oldham Athletic	£250,000
Steve Guppy	Newcastle United	Port Vale	£225,000
Steve Jones	West Ham United	Bournemouth	£150,000
Frank Strandli	Leeds United	Brann	£100,000
Steve McMahon	Manchester City	Swindon Town	**Free
Ray Wilkins	Crystal Palace	Queen's Park Rangers	**Free
Mark Powell	Everton	Bolton Wanderers	Free
Les Sealey	Blackpool	West Ham United	Free
Mike Small	West Ham United	Stevenage Borough	Free
John Burridge	Manchester City	Falkirk	Non-Contract
Christian Karlsson	Trelleborg	Crystal Palace	Trial
Joachim Karlsson	Trelleborg	Crystal Palace	Trial
Teddy Luvic	Vastra	Crystal Palace	Trial
Frankie Shonhaye	Cape Town	Southampton	Trial

*Combined fee. ** As player-manager*

December 1994

Player	From	To	Fee
Duncan Ferguson	Rangers	Everton	£4,000,000
Ian Taylor	Sheffield Wednesday	Aston Villa	£1,000,000
Guy Whittingham	Aston Villa	Sheffield Wednesday	£700,000
Mike Marsh	West Ham United	Coventry City	£500,000
Marc Rieper	Brondby	West Ham United	£500,000
Ashley Ward	Crewe Alexandra	Norwich Cty	* £350,000
Ian Culverhouse	Norwich City	Swindon Town	** £250,000
Brian Law	Queen's Park Rangers	Wolves	*** £100,000
Tony Witter	Queen's Park Rangers	Millwall	£100,000
Devon White	Queen's Park Rangers	Notts County	£100,000
Wilfred Mugeyi	Umtata	West Ham United	Trial
Peter Thorne	Blackburn Rovers	Southampton	Trial
Ian Culverhouse	Norwich City	Swindon Town	Tribunal

*Plus £150,000 after appearances. ** Figure set by transfer tribunal.*
*** Plus £34,000 to insurers*

January 1995

Player	From	To	Fee
Andy Cole	Newcastle United	Manchester United	*£7,000,000
Anthony Yeboah	Eintracht Frankfurt	Leeds United	£3,400,000
Tommy Johnson	Derby County	Aston Villa	**£2,900,000

Player	From	To	Fee
Gary Charles	Derby County	Aston Villa	**See Above
John Hartson	Luton Town	Arsenal	£2,500,000
Earl Barrett	Aston Villa	Everton	£1,700,000
Chris Kiwomya	Ipswich Town	Arsenal	***£1,550,000
Neil Shiperley	Chelsea	Southampton	£1,250,000
Keith Gillespie	Manchester United	Newcastle United	†£1,000,000
Mark Robins	Norwich City	Leicester City	£1,000,000
Oyvind Leonhardsen	Rosenborg	Wimbledon	£650,000
Iain Dowie	Southampton	Crystal Palace	£400,000
Steve Agnew	Leicester City	Sunderland	£250,000
Ian Culverhouse	Norwich City	Swindon Town	***£250,000
Peter Thorne	Blackburn Rovers	Swindon Town	£200,000
James Lawrence	Doncaster Rovers	Leicester City	£175,000
Lee Chapman	West Ham United	Ipswich Town	£70,000
Paul Smith	Hastings Town	Nottingham Forest	£50,000
Perry Groves	Southampton	Dagenham & Redbridge	Free
Steve Nicol	Liverpool	Notts County	Free
Chris Priest	Everton	Chester City	Free
Ian Snodin	Everton	Oldham Athletic	Free
Ryan Nicholls	Leeds United	Cardiff City	Non-Contract
Dieter Exkstein	Schalke 04	Crystal Palace	Trial
Sam Hyppia	MyPa	Newcastle United	Trial

*Includes valuation of Keith Gillespie. ** Combined fee.*
*** Figure set by transfer tribunal. † Included as part of the fee for Andy Cole*

February 1995

Player	From	To	Fee
Glenn Helder	Vitesse Arnhem	Arsenal	£2,300,000
Garry Parker	Aston Villa	Leicester City	*£550,000
Alex Mathie	Newcastle United	Ipswich Town	£500,000
Kevin Richardson	Aston Villa	Coventry City	£300,000
Franz Carr	Leicester City	Aston Villa	*£250,000
Steve Thompson	Leicester City	Burnley	£200,000
Bjorn Enqvist	Malmo	Crystal Palace	£70,000
Niall Thompson	Crystal Palace	Colchester United	Free
Peter Shilton	Plymouth Argyle	Wimbledon	Non-Contract
Trifon Ivanov	Neuchatel Zamax	Coventry City	Trial
Justin Le Tissier	Vale Recreation	Sothamton	Trial
Ian Richardson	Dagenham & Red.	Wimbledon	Trial
Tony Sheridan	Coventry City	Brighton & Hove Albion	Trial
Anthony Tohill	Park	Manchester United	Trial

Exchange deal – Villa receive Carr plus £300,000

March 1995

Player	From	To	Fee
Mark Kennedy	Millwall	Liverpool	*£1,500,000
Jeff Kenna	Southampton	Blackburn Rovers	£1,500,000
Gordon Watson	Sheffield Wednesday	Southampton	£1,200,000
David Burrows	Everton	Coventry City	£1,100,000
Alan Wright	Blackburn Rovers	Aston Villa	£1,000,000
Brett Angell	Everton	Sunderland	£600,000
Jason Drysdale	Newcastle United	Swindon Town	£340,000
John Filan	Cambridge United	Coventry City	£300,000
Ray Houghton	Aston Villa	Crystal Palace	£300,000
Phil Whelan	Ipswich Town	Middlesbrough	£300,000
Chris Boden	Aston Villa	Derby County	£150,000
Chris Swailes	Doncaster Rovers	Ipswich Town	**£150,000
Eddie Younds	Ipswich Town	Bradford City	£150,000
Andy Brownrigg	Hereford United	Norwich City	£100,000
James Crawford	Bohemians	Newcastle United	£75,000
Gudni Bergsson	Tottenham Hotspur	Bolton Wanderers	£65,000
Christer Warren	Cheltenham Town	Southampton	£40,000
Matt Dickens	Blackburn Rovers	Stockport County	Undisclosed
Lee Marshall	Nottingham Forest	Stockport County	Free
Carl Rookyard	Nottingham Forest	Walsall	Free
Richard Smith	Nottingham Forest	Walsall	Free
Gordon Strachan	Leeds United	Coventry City	Free
Sigurdt Rushfeldt	Tromso	Everton	Trial
Scott Mean	Bournemouth	Norwich City	Trial
Deigo Tur	FC Copenhagen	Newcastle United	Trial

*Rises to £2 million after appearances. ** Rises to £225,000 after appearances.*

May 1995

Player	From	To	Fee
Glca Popescu	Tottenham Hotspur	Barcelona	£3,500,000
Ruud Gullit	Sampdoria	Chelsea	£1,000,000
Carlos Batista	Farense (Portugal)	Coventry City	£125,000

June 1995

Player	From	To	Fee
Dennis Bergkamp	Internazional	Arsenal	£7,500,000
Paul Ince	Manchester United	Internazionale (Italy)	£7,000,000
Les Ferdinand	QPR	Newcastle United	£6,000,000
Chris Armstrong	Crystal Palace	Tottenham Hotspur	£4,500,000
Warren Barton	Wimbledon	Newcastle United	*£4,000,000

Savo Milosevic	Partizan Belgrade	Aston Villa	£3,500,000
Gareth Southgate	Crystal Palace	Aston Villa	£2,500,000
Mark Hughes	Manchester United	Chelsea	£1,500,000

*Plus further £1,000,000 after 50 appearances.

July 1995

Player	From	To	Fee
Stan Collymore	Liverpool	Nottingham Forest	£8,500,000
Andrei Kanchelskis	Manchester United	Everton	£5,000,000
David Platt	Sampdoria	Arsenal	£4,750,000
Mark Draper	Leicester City	Aston Villa	£3,250,000
Stefan Schwarz	Arsenal	Fiorentina (Italy)	£2,750,000
David Ginola	PSG (France)	Newcastle United	£2,500,000
Craig Short	Derby County	Everton	£2,500,000
Dean Saunders	Aston Villa	Galatasaray (Turkey)	£1,500,000
Mike Marsh	Coventry City	Galatasaray (Turkey)	£1,000,000
Barry Venison	Newcastle United	Galatasaray (Turkey)	£750,000
Marques Isaias	Benfica (Portugal)	Coventry City	£500,000
Paul Telfer	Luton Town	Coventry City	Tribunal
Peter Shilton	Bolton Wanderers	Coventry City	Free

FA PREMIER LEAGUE CLUBS PLAYER LOANS 1994-95

August 1994

Player	From	To
John Gayle	Coventry City	Burnley
Steve Hodge	Leeds United	Derby County
Russell Hoult	Leicester City	Lincoln City
Alan Kernaghan	Manchester City	Bolton Wanderers
David Lee	Chelsea	Portsmouth
Scott Marshall	Arsenal	Sheffield United
Stephen Robinson	Tottenham Hotspur	Leyton Orient
Justin Skinner	Wimbledon	Chester
Andy Turner	Tottenham Hotspur	Wycombe Wanderers

September 1994

Player	From	To
Richard Appleby	Newcastle United	Darlington
Jeroen Boare	West Ham Untied	WBA
Gary Bull	Nottingham Forest	Birmingham City
Franz Carr	Sheffield United	Leicester City
Darren Currie	West Ham United	Shrewsbury Town
Matt Dickens	Blackburn Rovers	Grimsby Town
Jamie Forrester	Leeds United	Southend United
Paul Harford	Blackburn Rovers	Wigan Athletic
Neil Moore	Everton	Blackpool
Chris Priest	Everton	Chester
Fitzroy Simpson	Manchester City	Bristol City
Bryan Small	Aston Villa	Birmingham City
Paul Stewart	Liverpool	Wolves
Mark Walters	Liverpool	Wolves

October 1994

Player	From	To
Nicky Banger	Southampton	Oldham Athletic
Nick Colgan	Chelsea	Grimsby Town
Martin Davies	Coventry City	Stafford Rangers
Matt Dickens	Blackburn Rovers	Rochdale
Andy Dow	Chelsea	Bradford City
Ian Durrant	Rangers	Everton
Duncan Ferguson	Rangers	Everton
John Hendry	Tottenham Hotspur	Swansea City
Steve Jones	West Ham United	Bournemouth
Gerard McMahon	Tottenham Hotspur	Barnet
Ian Snodin	Everton	Sunderland
Simon Tracey	Sheffield United	Manchester City
Andy Turner	Tottenham Hotspur	Doncaster Rovers
Neil Webb	Nottingham Forest	Swindon Town
John Williams	Coventry City	Notts County
Tony Witter	QPR	Millwall

November 1994

Player	From	To
Ade Akinbiwi	Norwich City	Brighton & Hove Alb
Darren Barnard	Chelsea	Reading
Scott Eustace	Leicester City	Shelbourne
Michael Hughes	Stratsbourg	West Ham United

Player	From	To
Mick Quinn	Coventry City	Plymouth Argyle
Mark Prudhoe	Stoke City	Liverpool
Carl Tiler	Nottingham Forest	Swindon Town
Jamie Vincent	Crystal Palace	Bournemouth
Paul Williams	Coventry City	Huddersfield Town

December 1994

Player	From	To
Paul Allen	Southampton	Luton Town
Craig Armstrong	Nottingham Forest	Burnley
Marvin Bryan	QPR	Doncaster Rovers
Jimmy Carter	Arsenal	Oxford United
Ilie Dumitrescu	Tottenham Hotspur	Sevilla*
Mario Gaudino	Eindhoven Frankfurt	Manchester City
John Filan	Cambridge United	Nottingham Forest
Bryan Griffiths	Blackpool	Scarborough
Steve Howe	Nottingham Forest	Kettering Town
Aidan	Wimbledon	Portsmouth
Paul Pettinger	Leeds United	Torquay United
Neil Shipperley	Chelsea	Watford

*Sevilla paying £275, 000

January 1995

Player	From	To
Paul Allen	Southampton	Stoke City
Dennis Bailey	QPR	Brentford
Lee Chapman	West Ham United	Southend United*
Robert Fleck	Chelsea	Bristol City
Uwe Fuchs	Kaiserslautern	Middlesbrough
Mike Galloway	Celtic	Leicester City
Phil Gee	Leicester City	Plymouth Argyle
Shay Given	Blackburn Rovers	Swindon Town
David Gregory	Ipswich Town	Hereford United
Matt Holand	West Ham United	Bournemouth
Jason Kearton	Everton	Notts County
Ian Ormondroyd	Leicester City	Hull City
Grant Payne	Wimbledon	Woking
Gary Rowett	Everton	Blackpool
Kevin Scott	Tottenham Hotspur	Port Vale
Richard Smith	Nottingham Forest	Nuneaton
Paul Williams	Crystal Palace	Sunderland
Eddie Youds	Ipswich Town	Bradford City

*Later joined Ipswich

February 1995

Player	From	To
David Beckham	Manchester United	Preston North End
Darren Currie	West Ham United	Shrewsbury Town
Matt Dickens	Blackburn Rovers	Stockport County
Tony Feuer	West Ham United	Peterborough United
James Glass	Crystal Palace	Portsmouth
Jon Hallworth	Oldham Athletic	Norwich City
Steve Harkness	Liverpool	Southend United
Paul Hayward	Nottingham Forest	Grantham
Russell Hoult	Leicester City	Derby County
Gareth Knott	Tottenham Hotspur	Gillingham
Jason Lillis	Cambridge United	Dover
Lee Marshall	Nottingham Forest	Grantham
Neil Moore	Everton	Oldham Athletic
David Oldfield	Leicester City	Millwall
Paul Pettinger	Leeds United	Halifax
Mick Quinn	Coventry City	Portsmouth
Terry Skiverton	Chelsea	Wycombe Wanderers
Paul Stewart	Liverpool	Burnley
Kevin Watson	Tottenham Hotspur	Barnet
John Williams	Coventry City	Swansea City

March 1995

Player	From	To
Kingsley Black	Nottingham Forest	Sheffield United
Alec Chamberlain	Sunderland	Liverpool
Owen Coll	Tottenham Hotspur	Yeovil Town
Dieter Eckstein	Schalke 04	West Ham United
Gareth Farrelly	Aston Villa	Rotherham United
Mark Flatts	Arsenal	Bristol City
Dale Gordon	West Ham United	Peterborough United
Neil Gregory	Ipswich Town	Scunthorpe United
Roger Joseph	Wimbledon	Millwall
Martyn Margetson	Manchester City	Luton Town
Billy Mercer	Sheffield United	Nottingham Forest
Paul Read	Arsenal	Leyton Orient
Paul Shaw	Arsenal	Burnley
Simon Webster	West Ham United	Oldham Athletic
Paul A Williams	Crystal Palace	Birmingham
Paul R C Williams	Coventry City	Huddersfield Town
Richard Witschge	Bordeaux	Blackburn Rovers

*£10, 000 for loan – £65,000 follows at end of season

FA PREMIER LEAGUE CLUBS £1m+ PLAYERS in 1994

The following players were transferred for a £1m or more during 1994.

Player	From	To	Fee
Chris Sutton	Norwich City	Blackburn Rovers	£5m
Duncan Ferguson	Rangers	Everton	£4m
Phil Babb	Coventry City	Liverpool	£3.6m
John Scales	Wimbledon	Liverpool	£3.5m
Daniel Amokachi	FC Bruges	Everton	£3m
Gica Popescu	Eindhoven	Tottenham Hotspur	£2.9m
Carlton Palmer	Sheffield Wednesday	Leeds United	£2.8m
Darren Peacock	QPR	Newcastle United	£2.7m
Philippe Albert	Anderlecht	Newcastle United	£2.65m
Ilie Dumitrescu	St Bucharest	Tottenham Hotspur	£2.6m
Bryan Roy	Foggia	Nottingham Forest	£2.5m
Paul Furlong	Watford	Chelsea	£2.3m
Ruel Fox	Norwich City	Newcastle United	£2.25m
Paul Kitson	Derby County	Newcastle United	£2.25m
Vinny Samways	Tottenham Hotspur	Everton	£2.2m
Dion Dublin	Manchester United	Coventry City	£2m
Jurgen Klinsmann	Monaco	Tottenham Hotspur	£2m
Stefan Schwarz	Benfica	Arsenal	£1.75m
Anders Limpar	Arsenal	Everton	£1.6m
Steve Froggatt	Aston Villa	Wolves	£1.5m
Don Hutchison	Liverpool	West Ham United	£1.5m
Ian Nolan	Tranmere Rovers	Sheffield Wednesday	£1.5m
Nicky Summerbee	Swindon Town	Manchester City	£1.5m
David May	Blackburn Rovers	Manchester United	£1.4m
John Fashanu	Wimbledon	Aston Villa	£1.35m
Tony Daley	Aston Villa	Wolves	£1.3m
Dan Petrescu	Genoa	Sheffield Wednesday	£1.3m
Mark Draper	Notts County	Leicester City	£1.25m
David Rocastle	Manchester City	Chelsea	£1.25m
Peter Beagrie	Everton	Manchester City	£1.1m
Bruce Dyer	Watford	Crystal Palace	£1.1m
Don Goodman	Sunderland	Wolves	£1.1m
Joey Beauchamp	Oxford United	West Ham United	£1m
Neil Cox	Aston Villa	Middlesbrough	£1m
Neil Emblen	Millwall	Wolves	£1m
Nii Lamptey	Anderlecht	Aston Villa	£1m
John Moncur	Swindon Town	West Ham United	£1m

Jon Newsome	Leeds United	Norwich City	£1m
Steve Sedgley	Tottenham Hotspur	Ipswich Town	£1m
Mike Sheron	Manchester City	Norwich City	£1m
Ian Taylor	Port Vale	Sheffield Wednesday	£1m
Ian Taylor	Sheffield Wednesday	Aston Villa	£1m

A-Z
FA Premier League Players
1995-96

Notes: The players are listed in alphabetical order and are those who are likely to feature in the Premiership action during the 1995-96 season. Fringe players who played at least one game in 1994-95 are included. Generally players who did not feature in 1994-95 are included in the Ex-Players list. There are exceptions though – for instance Mark Beeney the Leeds United 'keeper was sub for all 42 of their Premiership games in 1994-95 but never entered the fray! *Previous Club Details* includes all Premiership games played to date. Specific appearance details for 1994-95 can be found in the *Club Directory* section.

ABLETT Gary   Everton

Fullname: Gary Ian Ablett   DOB: 20-10-69 Liverpool
Debut: EVERTON v Sheffield Wednesday 15/8/92
Debut Goal: Southampton v EVERTON 14/8/93

Previous Clubs Details			Apps					Goals		
Club	Signed	Fee	Tot	Start	Sub	FA	FL	Lge	FA	FL
Liverpool	Nov-83		109	103	6	18	11	1	0	0
Derby County	Jan-85	Loan	6	3	3	0	0	0	0	0
Hull City	Sep-86	Loan	5	5	0	0	0	0	0	0
Everton	Jan-92	£750,000	115	115	0	9	11	5	0	0
FAPL Summary by Club										
Everton	92/3 to 94/5		98	98	0	8	11	4	0	0
Total			*98*	*98*	*0*	*8*	*11*	*4*	*0*	*0*

ADAMS Tony   Arsenal

Fullname: Anthony Alexander Adams   DOB: 11-10-70 Romford
Debut: ARSENAL v Norwich City 15/8/92
Debut Goal: ARSENAL v Newcastle United 18/9/94

Previous Clubs Details			Apps					Goals		
Club	Signed	Fee	Tot	Start	Sub	FA	FL	Lge	FA	FL
Arsenal	Jan-84		346	343	3	30	49	23	5	3
FAPL Summary by Club										
Arsenal	92/93 to 94/5		97	95	2	12	15	3	4	1
Total			*97*	*95*	*2*	*12*	*15*	*3*	*4*	*1*

ALBERT Philippe   Newcastle United

Fullname: Philippe Albert   DOB: 11-08-71 Belgium
Debut: Leicester City v NEWCASTLE UNITED 21/8/94
Debut Goal: NEWCASTLE UNITED v Leicester City 10/12/94

Previous Clubs Details			Apps					Goals		
Club	Signed	Fee	Tot	Start	Sub	FA	FL	Lge	FA	FL
Anderlecht										
Newcastle Utd	Aug-94	£2.65m	17	17	0	0	4	2	0	1
FAPL Summary by Club										
Newcastle Utd	94/5		17	17	0	0	4	2	0	1
Total			*17*	*17*	*0*	*0*	*4*	*2*	*0*	*1*

ALLEN Bradley QPR

Fullname: Bradley James Allen DOB: 14-09-75 Romford
Debut: Norwich City v QPR 17/10/92 as sub
Debut Goal: Norwich City v QPR 17/10/92

Previous Clubs Details

Club	Signed	Fee	Tot	Start	Sub	FA	FL	Lge	FA	FL
QPR	Sep-88		73	51	22	3	7	26	0	5

FAPL Summary by Club

QPR	92/3 to 94/5		51	37	14	2	6	19	0	4
Total			*51*	*37*	*14*	*2*	*6*	*19*	*0*	*4*

ALLEN Martin West Ham United

Fullname: Martin J Allen DOB: 15-08-69 Reading
Debut: WEST HAM UNITED v Wimbledon 14/8/93
Debut Goal: WEST HAM UNITED v Aston Villa 15/1/94

Previous Clubs Details

Club	Signed	Fee	Tot	Start	Sub	FA	FL	Lge	FA	FL
QPR	Jun-83		136	128	8	9	18	16	1	1
West Ham Utd	Aug-89	£675,000	187	160	27	14	18	25	4	5

FAPL Summary by Club

West Ham Utd	93/4 to 94/5		55	46	9	7	5	9	2	1
Total			*55*	*46*	*9*	*7*	*5*	*9*	*2*	*1*

ALLEN Malcolm Newcastle United

Fullname: Malcolm Allen DOB: 22-03-71 Caernarfon
Debut: NEWCASTLE UNITED v Tottenham Hotspur 14/8/93
Debut Goal: NEWCASTLE UNITED v Everton 25/8/93

Previous Clubs Details

Club	Signed	Fee	Tot	Start	Sub	FA	FL	Lge	FA	FL
Watford	Mar-85		39	27	12	14	5	5	6	2
Aston Villa	Sep-87	Loan	4	4	0	0	0	0	0	0
Norwich City	Aug-88	£175,000	35	24	11	5	3	8	7	0
Millwall	Mar-90	£400,000	81	64	17	1	7	24	0	2
Newcastle Utd	Aug-93	£300,000	10	9	1	0	3	5	0	2

FAPL Summary by Club

Newcastle Utd	93/4 to 94/5		10	9	1	0	3	5	0	0
Total			*10*	*9*	*1*	*0*	*3*	*5*	*0*	*0*

ALLEN Paul Southampton

Fullname: Paul Kevin Allen DOB: 29-08-66 Reading
Debut: Southampton v TOTTENHAM HOTSPUR 15/8/92
Debut Goal: TOTTENHAM HOTSPUR v Everton 5/9/92

Previous Clubs Details

Club	Signed	Fee	Tot	Start	Sub	FA	FL	Lge	FA	FL
West Ham Utd	Aug-79		152	149	3	18	24	6	3	2
Tottenham H	Jun-85	£400,000	292	276	16	27	44	23	1	4

Club	Signed	Fee	Tot	Start	Sub	FA	FL	Lge	FA	FL
Southampton	Sep-93	£550,000	43	40	3	2	4	1	0	0
Luton Town	Dec-94	Loan								
Stoke City	Jan-95	Loan								
FAPL Summary by Club										
Tottenham H	92/3 to 93/4		39	38	1	5	4	3	0	0
Southampton	93/4 to 94/5		43	40	3	2	4	1	0	0
Total			*82*	*78*	*4*	*7*	*8*	*4*	*0*	*0*

AMOKACHI Daniel   Everton

Fullname: Daniel Amokachi   DOB: 31-12-76 Nigeria
Debut: Blackburn Rovers v EVERTON 10/9/94
Debut Goal: EVERTON v QPR 17/10/94

Previous Clubs Details			Apps					Goals		
Club	Signed	Fee	Tot	Start	Sub	FA	FL	Lge	FA	FL
FC Bruge										
Everton	Aug-94	£3m	18	17	1	2	2	4	2	0
FAPL Summary by Club										
Everton	94/5 to 93/4		18	17	1	2	2	4	2	0
Total			*18*	*17*	*1*	*2*	*2*	*4*	*2*	*0*

ANDERSON Viv   Middlesbrough

Fullname: Vivian Anderson   DOB: 30-08-60 Nottingham
Debut: Nottingham Forest v SHEFFIELD WEDNESDAY 12/9/92
Debut Goal: SHEFFIELD WEDNESDAY v Tottenham Hotspur 27/9/92

Previous Clubs Details			Apps					Goals		
Club	Signed	Fee	Tot	Start	Sub	FA	FL	Lge	FA	FL
N Forest	Aug-74	Amateur	328	323	5	24	39	15	1	5
Arsenal	Aug-84	£250,000	120	120	0	12	18	9	3	3
Manchester U	Jul-87	£250,000	54	50	4	7	7	3	1	1
Sheffield W	Jan-91	Free	70	60	10	10	9	8	2	1
Barnsley	Jul-93	Free	20	20	0	0	2	3	0	0
Middlesbrough	Jul-93	Free	2	2	0	0	0	0	0	0
FAPL Summary by Club										
Sheffield W	92-93 to 93/4		25	23	2			3		
Total			*25*	*23*	*2*			*3*		

ANDERTON Darren   Tottenham Hotspur

Fullname: Darren Robert Anderton   DOB: 04-03-76 Southampton
Debut: Southampton v TOTTENHAM HOTSPUR 15/8/92
Debut Goal: TOTTENHAM HOTSPUR v Southampton 7/2/93

Previous Clubs Details			Apps					Goals		
Club	Signed	Fee	Tot	Start	Sub	FA	FL	Lge	FA	FL
Portsmouth	Feb-90		62	53	9	7	5	7	5	1
Tottenham H	Jun-92	£1.75m	108	104	4	14	9	17	2	1

| | | | 108 | 104 | 4 | 14 | 9 | 17 | 2 | 1 |
| | | | *108* | *104* | *4* | *14* | *9* | *17* | *2* | *1* |

ARDLEY Neal   **Wimbledon**

Fullname: Neal Christopher Ardley   DOB: 02-09-76 Epsom
Debut: WIMBLEDON v Arsenal 5/9/92 as sub
Debut Goal: WIMBLEDON v Blackburn Rovers 19/9/92

Previous Clubs Details

Club	Signed	Fee	Tot	Start	Sub	FA	FL	Lge	FA	FL
				Apps				*Goals*		
Wimbledon	Jul-91		65	55	10	8	10	6	0	2

FAPL Summary by Club

Club			Tot	Start	Sub	FA	FL	Lge	FA	FL
Wimbledon	92-93 to 94/5		56	47	9	8	10	6	0	2
Total			*56*	*47*	*9*	*8*	*10*	*6*	*0*	*2*

ARMSTRONG Chris   **Tottenham Hotspur**

Fullname: Christopher P Armstrong   DOB: 20-06-75 Newcastle
Debut: Manchester United v CRYSTAL PALACE 2/9/92
Debut Goal: CRYSTAL PALACE v Oldham Athletic 12/9/92

Previous Clubs Details

Club	Signed	Fee	Tot	Start	Sub	FA	FL	Lge	FA	FL
				Apps				*Goals*		
Wrexham	Mar-89		60	40	20	1	3	13	0	0
Millwall	Aug-91	£50,000	28	11	17	1	4	5	0	2
Crystal Palace	Sep-92	£1m	118	118	0	8	8	46	5	6
Tottenham H	Jul-94	£4.5m								

FAPL Summary by Club

Club			Tot	Start	Sub	FA	FL	Lge	FA	FL
C Palace	92-93 to 94/5		75	75	0	6	5	23	5	5
Total			*75*	*75*	*0*	*6*	*5*	*23*	*5*	*5*

ATHERTON Peter   **Sheffield Wednesday**

Fullname: Peter Atherton   DOB: 07-04-74 Orrell
Debut: COVENTRY CITY v Middlesbrough 15/8/92
Debut Goal: Aston Villa v SHEFFIELD WEDNESDAY 27/11/94

Previous Clubs Details

Club	Signed	Fee	Tot	Start	Sub	FA	FL	Lge	FA	FL
				Apps				*Goals*		
Wigan Athletic	Feb-88		149	145	4	7	8	1	0	0
Coventry City	Aug-91	£300,000	114	113	1	2	4	0	0	0
Sheffield W	Jun-94	£800,000	41	41	0	3	1	0	0	0

FAPL Summary by Club

Club			Tot	Start	Sub	FA	FL	Lge	FA	FL
Coventry City	92/3 to 93/4		79	78	1	2	4	0	0	0
Sheffield W	94/5		41	41	0	3	4	1	0	0
Total			*120*	*119*	*1*	*5*	*8*	*1*	*0*	*0*

ATKINS Mark   **Blackburn Rovers**

Fullname: Mark Nigel Atkins   DOB: 15-09-72 Doncaster
Debut: Crystal Palace v BLACKBURN ROVERS 15/8/92

Debut Goal: Coventry City v BLACKBURN ROVERS 29/8/92

Previous Clubs Details

Club	Signed	Fee	Apps Tot	Start	Sub	FA	FL	Goals Lge	FA	FL
Scunthorpe Utd	Jul-86		50	45	5	5	4	2	0	0
Blackburn R	Jun-88	£45,000	253	224	29	14	22	33	0	4
FAPL Summary by Club										
Blackburn R	92/3 to 94/5		80	62	18	7	13	12	0	1
Total			*80*	*62*	*18*	*7*	*13*	*12*	*0*	*1*

ATKINSON Dalian — Aston Villa

Fullname: Dalian Robert Atkinson   DOB: 22-03-72 Shrewsbury
Debut: Ipswich Town v ASTON VILLA 15/8/92
Debut Goal: Ipswich Town v ASTON VILLA 15/8/92

Previous Clubs Details

Club	Signed	Fee	Apps Tot	Start	Sub	FA	FL	Goals Lge	FA	FL
Ipswich Town	Jun-85		60	49	11	0	6	18	0	3
Sheffield W	Jul-87	£450,000	38	38	0	2	3	10	1	3
Real Sociedad	Aug-90	£1.7m	0	0	0	0	0	0	0	0
Aston Villa	Jul-91	£1.6m	87	79	8	4	15	23	0	11
FAPL Summary by Club										
Aston Villa	92/3 to 94/5		73	68	5	3	14	22	0	11
Total			*73*	*68*	*5*	*3*	*14*	*22*	*0*	*11*

AUSTIN Dean — Tottenham Hotspur

Fullname: Dean Barry Austin   DOB: 27-04-74 Hemel Hempstead
Debut: TOTTENHAM HOTSPUR v Crystal Palace 22/8/92
Debut Goal:

Previous Clubs Details

Club	Signed	Fee	Apps Tot	Start	Sub	FA	FL	Goals Lge	FA	FL
Southend Utd	Mar-90	£12,000	96	96	0	2	4	2	0	0
Tottenham H	Jun-92	£375,000	81	76	5	12	6	0	0	0
FAPL Summary by Club										
Tottenham H	92/3 to 94/5		81	76	5	12	6	0	0	0
Total			*81*	*76*	*5*	*12*	*6*	*0*	*0*	*0*

BABB Phil — Liverpool

Fullname: Phillip A Babb   DOB: 01-12-74 London
Debut: COVENTRY CITY v Middlesbrough 15/8/92
Debut Goal: Arsenal v COVENTRY CITY 14/8/93

Previous Clubs Details

Club	Signed	Fee	Apps Tot	Start	Sub	FA	FL	Goals Lge	FA	FL
Bradford City	Aug-90		80	73	7	3	6	14	0	0
Coventry City	Jul-92	£500,000	77	70	7	2	5	3	0	1
Liverpool	Sep-94	£3.6m	34	33	1	6	7	0	0	0

FAPL Summary by Club

Club	Season	Tot	Start	Sub	FA	FL	Lge	FA	FL
Coventry City	92/3 to 94/5	77	70	7	2	5	3	0	1
Liverpool	94/5	34	33	1	6	7	0	0	0
Total		111	103	8	8	12	3	0	1

BAILEY Dennis
QPR

Fullname: Dennis Lincoln Bailey   DOB: 14-12-69 Lambeth
Debut: Manchester City v QPR 17/8/92
Debut Goal: QPR v Sheffield United 22/8/92

Previous Clubs Details

Club	Signed	Fee	Tot	Start	Sub	FA	FL	Lge	FA	FL
C Palace	Dec-87	£10,000	5	0	5	0	0	1	0	0
Bristol R	Feb-89	Loan	17	17	0	0	0	9	0	0
Birmingham C	Aug-89	£80,000	75	65	10	6	6	23	0	2
Bristol R	Mar-91	Loan	6	6	0	0	0	1	0	0
QPR	Jun-91	£175,000	39	32	7	2	5	10	0	3
Charlton Athl	Oct-93	Loan	4	0	4	0	0	0	0	0
Watford	Mar-94	Loan	8	2	6	0	0	0	0	0
Brentford	Jan-95	Loan						4	0	0

FAPL Summary by Club

Club	Season	Tot	Start	Sub	FA	FL	Lge	FA	FL
QPR	92/3 to 94/5	15	13	2	1	2	1	0	1
Total		15	13	2	1	2	1	0	1

BARDSLEY David
QPR

Fullname: David John Bardsley   DOB: 12-09-68 Manchester
Debut: Manchester City v QPR 17/8/92
Debut Goal: QPR v Southampton 19/8/92

Previous Clubs Details

Club	Signed	Fee	Tot	Start	Sub	FA	FL	Lge	FA	FL
Blackpool	Nov-82		45	45	0	2	2	0	0	1
Watford	Nov-83	£150,000	100	97	3	14	6	7	1	1
Oxford Utd	Sep-87	£265,000	74	74	0	5	12	7	0	0
QPR	Sep-89	£500,000	212	212	0	18	18	4	0	1

FAPL Summary by Club

Club	Season	Tot	Start	Sub	FA	FL	Lge	FA	FL
QPR	92/3 to 94/5	102	102	0	7	10	3	0	0
Total		102	102	0	7	10	3	0	0

BARKER Simon
QPR

Fullname: Simon Barker   DOB: 05-11-68 Farnworth
Debut: QPR v Sheffield United 22/8/92
Debut Goal: QPR v Sheffield United 22/8/92

Previous Clubs Details

Club	Signed	Fee	Tot	Start	Sub	FA	FL	Lge	FA	FL
Blackburn R	Nov-82		182	180	2	12	11	35	0	4
QPR	Jul-88	£400,000	221	200	21	21	23	21	3	5

BARLOW Stuart   Everton
Fullname: Stuart Barlow   DOB: 17-07-72 Liverpool
Debut: Tottenham Hotspur v EVERTON 5/9/92 as sub
Debut Goal: Queens Park Rangers v EVERTON 28/12/92

Previous Clubs Details			*Apps*					*Goals*		
Club	Signed	Fee	Tot	Start	Sub	FA	FL	Lge	FA	FL
Everton	Jun-90		68	24	44	7	7	10	2	1
Rotherham Utd	Jan-92	Loan								
FAPL Summary by Club										
Everton	92/3 to 94/5		59	21	38	7	7	10	2	1
Total			*59*	*21*	*38*	*7*	*7*	*10*	*2*	*1*

BARMBY Nicky   Tottenham Hotspur
Fullname: Nicholas Jonathan Barmby   DOB: 12-(?-78 Hull
Debut: Sheffield Wednesday v TOTTENHAM H 7/9/92
Debut Goal: TOTTENHAM H v Middlesbrough 17/10/92

Previous Clubs Details			*Apps*					*Goals*		
Club	Signed	Fee	Tot	Start	Sub	FA	FL	Lge	FA	FL
Tottenham H	Apr-91		87	81	6	13	8	20	5	1
FAPL Summary by Club										
Tottenham H	92/3 to 94/5		87	81	6	13	8	20	5	1
Total			*87*	*81*	*6*	*13*	*8*	*20*	*5*	*1*

BARNARD Darren   Chelsea
Fullname: Darren Sean Barnard   DOB: 01-12-75 Germany
Debut: Coventry v CHELSEA 24/10/92
Debut Goal: CHELSEA v Middlesbrough 3/4/93

Previous Clubs Details			*Apps*					*Goals*		
Club	Signed	Fee	Tot	Start	Sub	FA	FL	Lge	FA	FL
Chelsea	Jul-90	£50,000	29	18	11	2	2	2	0	0
Reading	Nov-94	Loan								
FAPL Summary by Club										
Chelsea	92/3 to 93/4		25	17	8	2	2	2	0	0
Total			*25*	*17*	*8*	*2*	*2*	*2*	*0*	*0*

BARNES John   Liverpool
Fullname: John Charles Bryan Barnes   DOB: 08-11-67 Jamaica
Debut: QPR v LIVERPOOL 23/11/92 as sub
Debut Goal: LIVERPOOL v Aston Villa 9/1/92

Previous Clubs Details			*Apps*					*Goals*		
Club	Signed	Fee	Tot	Start	Sub	FA	FL	Lge	FA	FL
Watford	Jul-81		233	232	1	31	21	65	11	7

Liverpool	Jun-87	£900,000	242	240	2	42	20	77	14	3
FAPL Summary by Club										
Liverpool	92/3 to 94/5		91	88	3	10	10	15	0	0
Total			*91*	*88*	*3*	*10*	*10*	*15*	*0*	*0*

BARNESS Tony   Chelsea

Fullname: Anthony Barness   DOB: 26-03-77 Lewisham
Debut: CHELSEA v Norwich City 12/9/92
Debut Goal:

Previous Clubs Details

			Apps					Goals		
Club	Signed	Fee	Tot	Start	Sub	FA	FL	Lge	FA	FL
Charlton Ath	Mar-91		27	21	6	3	2	1	0	0
Chelsea	Sep-92	£350,000	14	12	2	0	1	0	0	0
Middlesbrough	Aug-93	Loan								
FAPL Summary by Club										
Chelsea	92/3 to 94/5		14	12	2	0	1	0	0	0
Total			*14*	*12*	*2*	*0*	*1*	*0*	*0*	*0*

BARRETT Earl   Everton

Fullname: Earl Delisser Barrett   DOB: 29-04-71 Rochdale
Debut: Ipswich Town v ASTON VILLA 15/8/92
Debut Goal: ASTON VILLA v Everton 20/2/93

Previous Clubs Details

			Apps					Goals		
Club	Signed	Fee	Tot	Start	Sub	FA	FL	Lge	FA	FL
Manchester C	Apr-85		3	2	1	0	1	0	0	0
Chester City	Mar-86	Loan	12	12	0	0	0	0	0	0
Oldham Ath	Nov-87	£35,000	183	181	2	14	20	7	1	1
Aston Villa	Feb-92	£1.7m	119	118	1	9	15	1	0	1
Everton	Jan-95	£1.7m	17	17	0	0	0	0	0	0
FAPL Summary by Club										
Aston Villa	92/3 to 94/5		106	105	1	9	15	1	0	0
Everton	94/5		17	17	0	0	0	0	0	0
Total			*123*	*122*	*1*	*9*	*15*	*1*	*0*	*0*

BARRON Michael   Middlesbrough

Fullname: Michael Barron   DOB: 23-12-78 Salford
Debut: Debut Goal:
Previous Clubs Details   Apps   Goals

| Club | Signed | Fee | Tot | Start | Sub | FA | FL | Lge | FA | FL |
| Middlesbrough | Feb-93 | Trainee | | | | | | | | |

BART-WILLIAMS Chris   Nottingham Forest

Fullname: Christopher Gerald Bart-Williams
                            DOB: 17-06-78 Sierra Leone
Debut: Everton v SHEFFIELD WEDNESDAY 15/8/92 as sub
Debut Goal: EVERTON v Coventry City 2/9/92

Previous Clubs Details			*Apps*					*Goals*		
Club	Signed	Fee	Tot	Start	Sub	FA	FL	Lge	FA	FL
Leyton Orient	Jul-91		36	34	2	0	4	2	0	0
Sheffield W	Nov-91	£275,000	124	95	29	12	16	16	2	4
Nottingham Forest	Jun-95	£2m								
FAPL Summary by Club										
Sheffield W	92/3 to 94/5		109	83	26	11	16	17	1	3
Total			*109*	*83*	*26*	*11*	*16*	*17*	*1*	*3*

BARTON Warren   Newcastle United

Fullname: Warren Dean Barton   DOB: 20-03-73 S. Newington
Debut: Leeds United v WIMBLEDON 15/8/92
Debut Goal: Leeds United v WIMBLEDON 15/8/92

Previous Clubs Details			*Apps*					*Goals*		
Club	Signed	Fee	Tot	Start	Sub	FA	FL	Lge	FA	FL
Maidstone Utd	Jul-87	£10,000	42	41	1	3	2	0	1	0
Wimbledon	Jun-90	£300,000	180	178	2	11	16	10	0	1
Newcastle Utd	Jun-95	£4m +								
PFAPL Summary by Club										
Wimbledon	92/3 to 94/5		101	99	2	6	12	6	0	1
Total			*101*	*99*	*2*	*6*	*12*	*6*	*0*	*1*

BARTRAM Vince   Arsenal

Fullname: Vincent L Bartram   DOB: 08-08-72 Birmingham
Debut: Nottingham Forest v ARSENAL 3/12/94
Debut Goal: (Goalkeeper)

Previous Clubs Details			*Apps*					*Goals*		
Club	Signed	Fee	Tot	Start	Sub	FA	FL	Lge	FA	FL
Wolves	Aug-85		5	5	0	3	2	0	0	0
Blackpool	Oct-89	Loan	9	9	0	0	0	0	0	0
Bournemouth	Jul-91	£65,000	132	132	0	14	10	0	0	0
Arsenal	Aug-94	£400,000	11	11	0	0	0	0	0	0
FAPL Summary by Club										
Arsenal	94/5		11	11	0	0	1	0	0	0
Total			*11*	*11*	*0*	*0*	*1*	*0*	*0*	*0*

BATISTA Carlos   Coventry City

Fullname: Carlos Batista   DOB:
Debut: Debut Goal:

Previous Clubs Details			*Apps*					*Goals*		
Club	Signed	Fee	Tot	Start	Sub	FA	FL	Lge	FA	FL
Farense (Portugal)										
Coventry City	May-95	£125,000								

BATTY David
Blackburn Rovers

Fullname: David Batty
DOB: 03-12-72 Leeds
Debut: LEEDS UNITED v Wimbledon 15/8/92
Debut Goal: LEEDS UNITED v Middlesbrough 31/1/93

Previous Clubs Details			*Apps*					*Goals*		
Club	Signed	Fee	Tot	Start	Sub	FA	FL	Lge	FA	FL
Leeds Utd	Jul-87		211	201	10	12	17	4	0	0
Blackburn R	Oct-93	£2.75m	31	30	1	4	2	0	0	0
FAPL Summary by Club										
Leeds Utd	92/3 to 93/4		39	38	1	3	2	1	0	0
Blackburn R	93/4 to 94/5		31	30	1	4	2	0	0	0
Total			*70*	*68*	*2*	*7*	*4*	*1*	*0*	*0*

BEAGRIE Peter
Manchester City

Fullname: Peter Sydney Beagrie
DOB: 30-11-69 Middlesbrough
Debut: EVERTON v Sheffield Wednesday 15/8/92
Debut Goal: EVERTON v Coventry City 17/10/92

Previous Clubs Details			*Apps*					*Goals*		
Club	Signed	Fee	Tot	Start	Sub	FA	FL	Lge	FA	FL
Middlesbrough	Sep-83		32	24	8	0	1	2	0	0
Sheffield W	Aug-86	£35,000	84	81	3	5	5	11	0	0
Stoke City	Jun-88	£210,000	54	54	0	3	4	7	1	0
Everton	Nov-89	£750,000	149	88	61	2	9	11	1	3
Sunderland	Sep-91	Loan	5	5	0	0	0	0	0	0
Manchester C	Mar-94	£1.1m	46	42	4	4	6	3	1	1
FAPL Summary by Club										
Everton	92/3 to 93/4		51	40	11	2	7	7	0	0
Manchester City	93/4 to 94/5		46	42	4	4	6	3	1	1
Total			*97*	*82*	*15*	*6*	*13*	*10*	*1*	*1*

BEARDSLEY Peter
Newcastle United

Fullname: Peter Andrew Beardsley
DOB: 19-01-65 Newcastle
Debut: EVERTON v Sheffield Wednesday 15/8/92
Debut Goal: Manchester United v EVERTON 19/8/92

Previous Clubs Details			*Apps*					*Goals*		
Club	Signed	Fee	Tot	Start	Sub	FA	FL	Lge	FA	FL
Carlisle Utd	Aug-79		104	93	11	15	7	22	7	0
Vancouver	Apr-81	£275,000								
Manchester Utd	Sep-82	£300,000	0	0	0	0	1	0	0	0
Vancouver	Sep-83									
Newcastle Utd	Sep-83	£150,000	147	146	1	6	10	61	0	0
Liverpool	Jul-87	£1.9m	131	120	11	25	14	46	11	1
Everton	Aug-91	£1m	81	81	0	4	8	25	1	5
Newcastle Utd	Jul-93	£1.4m	69	69	0	6	7	34	2	1

253

BEASANT Dave   Southampton

Fullname: David John Beasant   DOB: 21-03-63 Willesden
Debut: CHELSEA v Oldham Athletic 15/8/92
Debut Goal: (Goalkeeper)

Previous Clubs Details			*Apps*					*Goals*		
Club	Signed	Fee	Tot	Start	Sub	FA	FL	Lge	FA	FL
Wimbledon	Aug-79	£1,000	340	340	0	27	21	0	0	0
Newcastle Utd	Jun-88	£800,000	20	20	0	2	2	0	0	0
Chelsea	Jan-89	£725,000	116	116	0	5	11	0	0	0
Grimsby Town	Oct-92	Loan	6	6	0	0	0	0	0	0
Wolves	Jan-93	Loan	4	4	0	0	1	0	0	0
Southampton	Nov-93	£300,000	38	37	1	2	0	0	0	0
FAPL Summary by Club										
Chelsea	92/3 to 93/4		17	17	0	0	0	0	0	0
Southampton	93/4 to 94/5		38	37	1	2	0	0	0	0
Total			*55*	*54*	*1*	*2*	*0*	*0*	*0*	*0*

BECKHAM David   Manchester United

Fullname: David Beckham   DOB: 03-05-79 Leytonstone
Debut: MANCHESTER UNITED v Leeds United 2/4/95
Debut Goal:

Previous Clubs Details			*Apps*					*Goals*		
Club	Signed	Fee	Tot	Start	Sub	FA	FL	Lge	FA	FL
Manchester Utd	Jan-93	Trainee	4	2	2	2	3	0	0	0
Preston North End	Feb-95	Loan								
FAPL Summary by Club										
Manchester Utd	94/5 to 93/4		4	2	2	2	3	0	0	0
Total			*4*	*2*	*2*	*2*	*3*	*0*	*0*	*0*

BEENEY Mark   Leeds United

Fullname: Mark R Beeney   DOB: 31-12-71 Tunbridge Wells
Debut: Coventry City v LEEDS UNITED 8/5/93
Debut Goal: (Goalkeeper)

Previous Clubs Details			*Apps*					*Goals*		
Club	Signed	Fee	Tot	Start	Sub	FA	FL	Lge	FA	FL
Gillingham	Aug-86		2	2	0	0	1	0	0	0
Maidstone Utd	Feb-87		50	50	0	11	3	0	0	0
Aldershot	Mar-90	Loan	7	7	0	0	0	0	0	0
Brighton & H	Mar-91	£30,000	69	68	1	7	6	0	0	0
Leeds Utd	Apr-93	£350,000	23	23	0	3	2	0	0	0

Leeds Utd	92/3 to 93/4	23	23	0	3	2	0	0	0
Total		*23*	*23*	*0*	*3*	*2*	*0*	*0*	*0*

BENALI Francis   Southampton

Fullname: Francis Vincent Benali   DOB: 11-12-72 Southampton
Debut: SOUTHAMPTON v Tottenham Hotspur 15/8/92
Debut Goal:

Previous Clubs Details

Club	Signed	Fee	Apps					Goals		
			Tot	Start	Sub	FA	FL	Lge	FA	FL
Southampton	Dec-86		173	151	22	17	19	0	0	0

FAPL Summary by Club

Southampton	92/3 to 94/5	105	97	8	6	8	0	0	0
Total		*105*	*97*	*8*	*6*	*8*	*0*	*0*	*0*

BENNETT Frank   Southampton

Fullname: Frank Bennett   DOB: 04-01-73 Birmingham
Debut: SOUTHAMPTON v Everton 14/8/93
Debut Goal: SOUTHAMPTON v Chelsea 27/12/93

Previous Clubs Details

Club	Signed	Fee	Apps					Goals		
			Tot	Start	Sub	FA	FL	Lge	FA	FL
Southampton	Feb-93	£7,500	8	0	8	1	1	1	0	0

FAPL Summary by Club

Southampton	93/4 to 94/5	8	0	8	1	1	1	0	0
Total		*8*	*0*	*8*	*1*	*1*	*1*	*0*	*0*

BERESFORD John   Newcastle United

Fullname: John Beresford   DOB: 05-09-70 Sheffield
Debut: NEWCASTLE UTD v Tottenham Hotspur 14/8/93
Debut Goal:

Previous Clubs Details

Club	Signed	Fee	Apps					Goals		
			Tot	Start	Sub	FA	FL	Lge	FA	FL
Manchester C	Sep-83		0	0	0	0	0	0	0	0
Barnsley	Aug-86	Free	88	79	9	5	7	5	1	2
Portsmouth	Mar-89	£300,000	107	102	5	11	12	8	0	2
Newcastle Utd	Jul-92	£650,000	109	109	0	11	11	1	1	0

FAPL Summary by Club

Newcastle Utd	93/4 to 94/5	67	67	0	7	7	0	1	0
Total		*67*	*67*	*0*	*7*	*7*	*0*	*1*	*0*

BERG Henning   Blackburn Rovers

Fullname: Henning Berg   DOB: 02-09-73 Eidsvell
Debut: BLACKBURN ROVERS v Crystal Palace 2/2/93
Debut Goal: BLACKBURN ROVERS v Chelsea 14/8/93

| *Previous Clubs Details* | | | *Apps* | | | | | *Goals* | | |
Club	Signed	Fee	Tot	Start	Sub	FA	FL	Lge	FA	FL
KFMU Oslo										
Blackburn R	Dec-92	£400,000	85	80	5	6	9	2	0	0
FAPL Summary by Club										
Blackburn R	92/3 to 94/5		85	80	5	6	9	2	0	0
Total			*85*	*80*	*5*	*6*	*9*	*2*	*0*	*0*

BERGKAMP Dennis   Arsenal
Fullname: Dennis Nicolaas Bergkamp   DOB: 11-05-73 Amsterdam
Debut: Debut Goal:

| *Previous Clubs Details* | | | *Apps* | | | | | *Goals* | | |
Club	Signed	Fee	Tot	Start	Sub	FA	FL	Lge	FA	FL
Ajax	Jul-86		185	185	0	0	0	103	0	0
Internazionale	Jul-93	£12m								
Arsenal	Jun-95	£7.5m								

BERGSSON Gudni   Bolton Wanderers
Fullname: Gudni Bergsson   DOB: 22-07-69 Iceland
Debut: TOTTENHAM HOTSPUR v Nottm Forest 28/12/92
Debut Goal:

| *Previous Clubs Details* | | | *Apps* | | | | | *Goals* | | |
Club	Signed	Fee	Tot	Start	Sub	FA	FL	Lge	FA	FL
Tottenham H	Dec-88	£100,000	71	51	20	4	6	3	0	0
Bolton Wders	Mar-95	£65,000	8	8	0	0	1	0	0	0
FAPL Summary by Club										
Tottenham H	92/3 to 94/5		5	0	5	1	0	0	0	0
Total			*5*	*0*	*5*	*1*	*0*	*0*	*0*	*0*

BISHOP Ian   West Ham United
Fullname: Ian W Bishop   DOB: 30-05-69 Liverpool
Debut: WEST HAM UNITED v Swindon Town 11/9/93
Debut Goal: Sheffield United v WEST HAM UNITED 28/3/94

| *Previous Clubs Details* | | | *Apps* | | | | | *Goals* | | |
Club	Signed	Fee	Tot	Start	Sub	FA	FL	Lge	FA	FL
Everton	Jun-83		1	0	1	0	0	0	0	0
Crewe Alex	Mar-84	Loan	4	4	0	0	0	0	0	0
Carlisle Utd	Oct-84	£15,000	132	131	1	5	8	14	1	1
Bournemouth	Jul-88	£35,000	44	44	0	5	4	2	0	0
Manchester C	Aug-89	£465,000	19	18	1	0	4	2	0	1
West Ham Utd	Dec-89	Exchange	187	176	11	18	13	9	3	0
FAPL Summary by Club										
West Ham Utd	93/4 to 94/5		67	67	0	8	6	2	1	0
Total			*67*	*67*	*0*	*8*	*6*	*2*	*1*	*0*

BJORNEBYE Stig Inge Liverpool

Fullname: Stig Inge Bjornebye DOB: 12-12-73 Norway
Debut: Coventry City v LIVERPOOL 19/12/92
Debut Goal:

Previous Clubs Details			*Apps*					*Goals*		
Club	Signed	Fee	Tot	Start	Sub	FA	FL	Lge	FA	FL
Rosenborg (Norway)										
Liverpool	Dec-92	£600,000	51	48	3	9	7	0	0	0
FAPL Summary by Club										
Liverpool	92/3 to 94/5		51	48	3	8	8	0	0	0
Total			*51*	*48*	*3*	*8*	*8*	*0*	*0*	*0*

BLACK Kinglsey Nottingham Forest

Fullname: Kinglsey Black DOB: 23-06-72 Luton
Debut: NOTTINGHAM FOREST v Liverpool 16/8/93
Debut Goal: NOTTINGHAM FOREST v Middlesbrough 21/10/93

Previous Clubs Details			*Apps*					*Goals*		
Club	Signed	Fee	Tot	Start	Sub	FA	FL	Lge	FA	FL
Luton Town	Jul-86		127	123	4	6	18	25	2	1
N Forest	Sep-91	£1.5m	96	79	17	4	20	14	0	5
Sheffield Utd	Mar-95	Loan								
FAPL Summary by Club										
N Forest	92/3 to 94/5		34	24	10	0	6	7	0	1
Total			*34*	*24*	*10*	*0*	*6*	*7*	*0*	*1*

BLACKMORE Clayton Middlesbrough

Fullname: Clayton Graham Blackmore DOB: 24-09-68 Neath
Debut: MANCHESTER UNITED v Sheffield United 15/8/93
Debut Goal:

Previous Clubs Details			*Apps*					*Goals*		
Club	Signed	Fee	Tot	Start	Sub	FA	FL	Lge	FA	FL
Manchester Utd	Sep-82		186	150	36	21	25	19	1	3
Middlesbrough	Jul-94	Free	30	26	4	0	1	2	0	0
FAPL Summary by Club										
Manchester Utd	92/3 to 94/5		14	12	2	1	1	0	0	0
Total			*14*	*12*	*2*	*1*	*1*	*0*	*0*	*0*

BLACKWELL Dean Wimbledon

Fullname: Dean Robert Blackwell DOB: 16-12-73 Camden
Debut: Leeds United v WIMBLEDON 15/8/92
Debut Goal:

Previous Clubs Details			*Apps*					*Goals*		
Club	Signed	Fee	Tot	Start	Sub	FA	FL	Lge	FA	FL
Wimbledon	Jul-88		84	67	17	8	3	1	0	0
Plymouth Arg	Mar-90	Loan	7	5	2	0	0	0	0	0

Wimbledon	92/3 to 93/4	42	35	7	5	1		0	0	0
Total		*42*	*35*	*7*	*5*	*1*		*0*	*0*	*0*

BLISSETT Gary   Wimbledon

Fullname: Gary P Blissett   DOB: 30-06-68 Manchester
Debut: WIMBLEDON v QPR 27/09/93 as sub
Debut Goal: Sheffield Wednesday v WIMBLEDON 16/10/93

Previous Clubs Details			*Apps*					*Goals*		
Club	Signed	Fee	Tot	Start	Sub	FA	FL	Lge	FA	FL
Crewe Alex	Aug-83		221	112	109	4	0	39	0	3
Brentford	Mar-87	£60,000	233	220	13	14	19	79	7	9
Wimbledon	Aug-93	£350,000	27	10	17	2	2	3	0	0
FAPL Summary by Club										
Wimbledon	93/4 to 94/5		27	10	17	2	2	3	0	0
Total			*27*	*10*	*17*	*2*	*2*	*3*	*0*	*0*

BOERE Jeroem   West Ham United

Fullname: Jeroem Boere   DOB: 19-11-71 Arnhem, Belgium
Debut: Newcastle Utd v WEST HAM UNITED 25/9/93 as sub
Debut Goal:

Previous Clubs Details			*Apps*					*Goals*		
Club	Signed	Fee	Tot	Start	Sub	FA	FL	Lge	FA	FL
Go Ahead Eagles										
West Ham Utd	Sep-93		24	15	9	2	2	6	0	0
Portsmouth	Mar-94	Loan	5	4	1	0	0	0	0	0
WBA	Sep-94	Loan								
FAPL Summary by Club										
West Ham Utd	93/4 to 94/5		24	15	9	2	2	6	0	0
Total			*24*	*15*	*9*	*2*	*2*	*6*	*0*	*0*

BOHINEN Lars   Nottingham Forest

Fullname: Lars Bohinen   DOB: 09-09-73 Norway
Debut: Ipswich Town v NOTTM FOREST 20/8/94 as sub
Debut Goal: NOTTM FOREST v Sheffield Wednesday 10/9/94

Previous Clubs Details			*Apps*					*Goals*		
Club	Signed	Fee	Tot	Start	Sub	FA	FL	Lge	FA	FL
Langes, Lillestrom										
N Forest	Oct-93	£450,000	57	52	5	1	4	6	0	0
FAPL Summary by Club										
N Forest	94/5		34	30	4	1	4	6	0	0
Total			*34*	*30*	*4*	*1*	*4*	*6*	*0*	*0*

BOLAND Willie   Coventry City

Fullname: Willie Boland   DOB: 07-08-79 Republic of Ireland
Debut: Chelsea v COVENTRY CITY 1/5/93 as sub

Debut Goal:

Previous Clubs Details

Club	Signed	Fee	Apps					Goals		
			Tot	Start	Sub	FA	FL	Lge	FA	FL
Coventry City	Nov-92		40	33	7	1	4	0	0	0

FAPL Summary by Club

Coventry City	92/3 to 94/5		40	33	7	0	4	0	0	0
Total			*40*	*33*	*7*	*0*	*4*	*0*	*0*	*0*

BORROWS Brian

Coventry City

Fullname: Brian Borrows
Debut: Sheffield Wednesday v COVENTRY CITY 2/9/92   DOB: 21-12-64 Liverpool
Debut Goal: COVENTRY CITY v Liverpool 19/12/92

Previous Clubs Details

Club	Signed	Fee	Apps					Goals		
			Tot	Start	Sub	FA	FL	Lge	FA	FL
Everton	Apr-80									
Bolton Wdrs	Mar-83	£10,000	29	27	2	0	0	0	0	0
Coventry City	Jun-85	£80,000	95	95	0	4	7	0	0	0
Bristol City	Sep-93	Loan	365	359	6	22	35	11	0	1
			6	6	0	0	0	0	0	0

FAPL Summary by Club

Coventry City	92/3 to 94/5		102	98	4	6	4	2	0	1
Total			*102*	*98*	*4*	*6*	*4*	*2*	*0*	*1*

BOSNICH Mark

Aston Villa

Fullname: Mark John Bosnich
Debut: Sheffield Wednesday v ASTON VILLA 5/12/92   DOB: 14-01-76 Sydney
Debut Goal: (Goalkeeper)

Previous Clubs Details

Club	Signed	Fee	Apps					Goals		
			Tot	Start	Sub	FA	FL	Lge	FA	FL
Manchester Utd	Jun-89		3	3	0	0	0	0	0	0
Croatia Sydney	Aug-91									
Aston Villa	Feb-92	Free	75	75	0	5	11	0	0	0

FAPL Summary by Club

Aston Villa	92/3 to 94/5		75	75	0	5	11	0	0	0
Total			*75*	*75*	*0*	*5*	*11*	*0*	*0*	*0*

BOULD Steve

Arsenal

Fullname: Stephen Andrew Bould
Debut: ARSENAL v Norwich City 15/8/92   DOB: 17-11-66 Stoke
Debut Goal: ARSENAL v Norwich City 15/8/92

Previous Clubs Details

Club	Signed	Fee	Apps					Goals		
			Tot	Start	Sub	FA	FL	Lge	FA	FL
Stoke City	Nov-80		183	179	4	10	13	6	0	1
Torquay Utd	Oct-82	Loan	9	9	0	2	0	0	0	0
Arsenal	Jun-89	£390,000	192	184	8	17	23	5	0	0

BRACEWELL Paul   Newcastle United

Fullname: Paul W Bracewell   DOB: 20-07-66 Heswall
Debut: NEWCASTLE UNITED v Tottenham Hotspur 14/8/93
Debut Goal: NEWCASTLE UNITED v Aston Villa 23/2/94

Previous Clubs Details			*Apps*					*Goals*	
Club	Signed	Fee	Tot	Start	Sub	FA	FL	Lge	FA	FL
Stoke City	Feb-80		129	123	6	6	6	5	0	1
Sunderland	Jul-83	£250,000	38	38	0	2	4	4	0	0
Everton	May-84	£425,000	95	95	0	21	11	7	0	2
Sunderland	Sep-89	£250,000	113	112	1	10	9	2	0	0
Newcastle Utd	Jun-92	£250,000	73	64	9	8	3	3	0	1

FAPL Summary by Club
Newcastle Utd	93/4 to 94/5	48	45	3	4	3	1	0	1
Total		*48*	*45*	*3*	*4*	*3*	*1*	*0*	*1*

BRANAGAN Keith   Bolton Wanderers

Fullname: Keith Branagan   DOB: 11-07-70 Fulham
Debut: Debut Goal:

Previous Clubs Details			*Apps*					*Goals*	
Club	Signed	Fee	Tot	Start	Sub	FA	FL	Lge	FA	FL
Cambridge Utd	Aug-83	Junior	110	110	0	6	12	0	0	0
Millwall	Mar-88	£100,000	46	46	0	5	1	0	0	0
Brentford	Nov-89	Loan	2	2	0	0	0	0	0	0
Gillingham	Oct-91	Loan	1	1	0	0	0	0	0	0
Bolton Wders	Jul-92	Free	99	99	0	8	16	0	0	0

BREACKER Tim   West Ham United

Fullname: Timothy S Breacker   DOB: 03-07-69 Bicester
Debut: WEST HAM UNITED v Wimbledon 14/8/93
Debut Goal: WEST HAM UNITED v Coventry City 11/12/93

Previous Clubs Details			*Apps*					*Goals*	
Club	Signed	Fee	Tot	Start	Sub	FA	FL	Lge	FA	FL
Luton Town	May-83		210	204	6	21	24	3	0	0
West Ham Utd	Oct-90	£600,000	170	168	2	22	11	8	0	0

FAPL Summary by Club
West Ham Utd	93/4 to 94/5	73	73	0	8	5	3	0	0
Total		*73*	*73*	*0*	*8*	*5*	*3*	*0*	*0*

BREVETT Rufus   QPR

Fullname: Rufus Emanuel Brevett   DOB: 25-09-73 Derby
Debut: Manchester United v QPR 26/9/92
Debut Goal:

Previous Clubs Details

Club	Signed	Fee	Apps					Goals		
			Tot	Start	Sub	FA	FL	Lge	FA	FL
Doncaster R	Jun-88		109	106	3	4	5	3	0	0
QPR	Feb-91	£250,000	58	50	8	2	3	0	0	0

FAPL Summary by Club

QPR	92/3 to 94/5		41	34	7	2	2	0	0	0
Total			*41*	*34*	*7*	*2*	*2*	*0*	*0*	*0*

BRIGHT Mark   Sheffield Wednesday

Fullname: Mark Abraham Bright   DOB: 07-06-66 Stoke
Debut: SHEFFIELD WED v Blackburn Rovers 15/8/92
Debut Goal: SHEFFIELD WED v Blackburn Rovers 15/8/92

Previous Clubs Details

Club	Signed	Fee	Apps					Goals		
			Tot	Start	Sub	FA	FL	Lge	FA	FL
Port Vale	Oct-81		29	18	11	1	2	10	1	0
Leicester City	Jul-84	£33,000	42	26	16	1	4	6	0	0
C Palace	Nov-86	£75,000	227	224	3	14	22	90	2	11
Sheffield W	Sep-92	£375,000	107	97	10	13	17	43	7	8

FAPL Summary by Club

C Palace	92/3 to 94/5		5	5	0	0	0	0	0	0
Sheffield W	92/3 to 94/5		107	97	10	13	17	41	7	8
Total			*112*	*102*	*10*	*13*	*17*	*41*	*7*	*8*

BRIGHTWELL Ian   Manchester City

Fullname: Ian Robert Brightwell   DOB: 10-04-72 Lutterworth
Debut: MANCHESTER CITY v QPR 17/8/92
Debut Goal: MANCHESTER CITY v Leeds United 7/11/92

Previous Clubs Details

Club	Signed	Fee	Apps					Goals		
			Tot	Start	Sub	FA	FL	Lge	FA	FL
Manchester C	May-85		233	203	30	17	26	16	1	0

FAPL Summary by Club

Manchester C	92/3 to 94/5		57	55	2	5	8	1	0	0
Total			*57*	*55*	*2*	*5*	*8*	*1*	*0*	*0*

BRIGHTWELL David   Manchester City

Fullname: David John Brightwell   DOB: 08-01-75 Lutterworth
Debut: Coventry City v MANCHESTER CITY 21/11/92
Debut Goal: MANCHESTER CITY v Newcastle United 9/4/94

Previous Clubs Details

Club	Signed	Fee	Apps					Goals		
			Tot	Start	Sub	FA	FL	Lge	FA	FL
Manchester C	Apr-88		43	35	8	7	3	1	1	0
Chester City	Mar-91	Loan	6	6	0	0	0	0	0	0

FAPL Summary by Club

Manchester C	92/3 to 94/5		39	32	7	7	4	1	1	0
Total			*39*	*32*	*7*	*7*	*4*	*1*	*1*	*0*

BRISCOE Lee — Sheffield Wednesday

Fullname: Lee Briscoe
DOB: 01-10-79 Pontefract
Debut: Tottenham Hotspur v SHEFFIELD WED 5/2/94 as sub
Debut Goal:

Previous Clubs Details			Apps					Goals		
Club	Signed	Fee	Tot	Start	Sub	FA	FL	Lge	FA	FL
Sheffield W	May-94		7	6	1	0	0		0	0	0

FAPL Summary by Club

Sheffield W	93/4 to 94/5		7	6	1	0	0	0	0	0
Total			*7*	*6*	*1*	*0*	*0*	*0*	*0*	*0*

BROWN Kenny — West Ham United

Fullname: Kenneth J Brown
DOB: 12-07-71 Barking
Debut: Newcastle United v WEST HAM UNITED 25/9/93
Debut Goal:

Previous Clubs Details			Apps					Goals		
Club	Signed	Fee	Tot	Start	Sub	FA	FL	Lge	FA	FL
Norwich City	Jul-85		25	24	1	0	0		0	0	0
Plymouth Arg	Aug-88		126	126	0	6	9	4	0	0
West Ham Utd	Aug-91	£175,000	60	52	8	9	2	5	1	0

FAPL Summary by Club

West Ham Utd	93/4 to 94/5		18	14	4	4	1	0	1	0
Total			*18*	*14*	*4*	*4*	*1*	*0*	*1*	*0*

BRUCE Steve — Manchester United

Fullname: Stephen Roger Bruce
DOB: 01-01-65 Corbridge
Debut: Sheffield United v MANCHESTER UNITED 15/8/93
Debut Goal: MANCHESTER UNITED v Leeds United 6/9/93

Previous Clubs Details			Apps					Goals		
Club	Signed	Fee	Tot	Start	Sub	FA	FL	Lge	FA	FL
Gillingham	Oct-78		205	203	2	14	15	29	1	6
Norwich City	Aug-84	£125,000	141	141	0	9	20	14	1	5
Manchester Utd	Dec-87	£800,000	279	279	0	36	32	2	3	6

FAPL Summary by Club

Manchester Utd	92/3 to 94/5		118	118	0	15	13	10	2	2
Total			*118*	*118*	*0*	*15*	*13*	*10*	*2*	*2*

BULL Gary — Nottingham Forest

Fullname: Gary W Bull
DOB: 13-06-70 Tipton
Debut: NOTTINGHAM FOREST v Crystal Palace 2/1/95
Debut Goal: NOTTINGHAM FOREST v Crystal Palace 2/1/95

Previous Clubs Details			Apps					Goals		
Club	Signed	Fee	Tot	Start	Sub	FA	FL	Lge	FA	FL
Cambridge Utd	Mar-88		19	13	6	0	1	4	0	0
Barnet	Mar-89	£2,000	83	83	0	11	4	37	3	4

| N Forest | Jul-93 | Free | 12 | 4 | 8 | 3 | 2 | | 1 | 0 | 0 |
| Birmingham City | Sep-94 | Loan | | | | | | | | | |

FAPL Summary by Club

| Nottingham Forest | 94/5 | | 1 | 1 | 0 | 1 | 0 | | 1 | 0 | 0 |
| *Total* | | | *1* | *1* | *0* | *1* | *0* | | *1* | *0* | *0* |

BURLEY Craig   Chelsea

Fullname: Craig William Burley   DOB: 25-09-75 Irvine
Debut: Tottenham Hotspur v CHELSEA 5/12/92
Debut Goal: CHELSEA v Everton 3/1/94

Previous Clubs Details			Apps						Goals		
Club	Signed	Fee	Tot	Start	Sub	FA	FL		Lge	FA	FL
Chelsea	Sep-89		60	43	17	11	3		5	3	0

FAPL Summary by Club

| Chelsea | 92/3 to 94/5 | | 51 | 37 | 14 | 11 | 0 | | 5 | 3 | 0 |
| *Total* | | | *51* | *37* | *14* | *11* | *0* | | *5* | *3* | *0* |

BURRIDGE John   Manchester City

Fullname: John Burridge   DOB: 3/12/51 Workington
Debut: MANCHESTER UTD v Newcastle Utd 29/4/95 as sub
Debut Goal: (Goalkeeper)

Previous Clubs Details			Apps						Goals		
Club	Signed	Fee	Tot	Start	Sub	FA	FL		Lge	FA	FL
Workington			27	27	0				0		
Blackpool	Apr-71		134	134	0				0		
Aston Villa	Sep-75		65	65	0				0		
Southend U	Jan-78	Loan	6	6	0				0		
C Palace	Mar-78		88	88	0				0		
QPR	Dec-80		39	39	0				0		
Wolves	Aug-88		74	74	0				0		
Derby Co	Sep-84	Loan	6	6	0				0		
Sheff.Utd	Oct-84		109	109	0				0		
Southampton	Aug-87		62	62	0				0		
Newcastle U	Oct-89		67	67	0				0		
Hibernian	1991		65	65	0				0		
Scarborough	1993		3	3	0				0		
Lincoln City	1994		4	4	0				0		
Aberdeen	1994		3	3	0				0		
Dumbarton	Oct-94	NC									
Manchester C	Apr-95		4	3	1	0	0		0	0	0

FAPL Summary by Club

| Manchester C | 94/5 | | 4 | 3 | 1 | 0 | 0 | | 0 | 0 | 0 |
| *Total* | | | *4* | *3* | *1* | *0* | *0* | | *0* | *0* | *0* |

BURROWS David   Coventry City

Fullname: David Burrows   DOB: 26-10-72 Dudley
Debut: Nottingham Forest v WEST HAM UNITED 16/8/92
Debut Goal: WEST HAM UNITED v Coventry City 11/12/93

Previous Clubs Details			*Apps*					*Goals*		
Club	Signed	Fee	Tot	Start	Sub	FA	FL	Lge	FA	FL
WBA	Oct-86		46	37	9	2	4	1	0	0
Liverpool	Oct-88	£550,000	146	135	11	17	16	3	0	0
West Ham Utd	Sep-93	Swap	29	29	0	3	3	1	0	1
Everton	Sep-94	Swap +	19	19	0	2	2	0	0	0
Coventry City	Mar-95	£1.1m	11	11	0	0	0	0	0	0
FAPL Summary by Club										
Liverpool	92/3 to 94/5		30	29	1	0	5	2	0	0
West Ham Utd	93/4 to 94/5		29	29	0	3	3	1	0	1
Everton	94/5		19	19	0	2	2	0	0	0
Coventry City	94/5		11	11	0	0	0	0	0	0
Total			*89*	*88*	*1*	*5*	*10*	*3*	*0*	*1*

BUSST David   Coventry City

Fullname: David John Busst   DOB: 01-07-71 Birmingham
Debut: Norwich City v COVENTRY CITY 16/1/93
Debut Goal: COVENTRY CITY v Everton 20/8/94

Previous Clubs Details			*Apps*					*Goals*		
Club	Signed	Fee	Tot	Start	Sub	FA	FL	Lge	FA	FL
Coventry City	Jan-92	Free	13	12	1	1	1	0	0	0
FAPL Summary by Club										
Coventry City	92/3 to 94/5		33	32	1	1	4	2	0	0
Total			*33*	*32*	*1*	*1*	*4*	*2*	*0*	*0*

BUTT Nicky   Manchester United

Fullname: Nicholas Butt   DOB: 22-01-79 Manchester
Debut: MANCHESTER UNITED v Oldham Athletic 21/11/92
Debut Goal: Southampton v MANCHESTER UNITED 31/12/94

Previous Clubs Details			*Apps*					*Goals*		
Club	Signed	Fee	Tot	Start	Sub	FA	FL	Lge	FA	FL
Manchester Utd	Jan-93		24	11	13	4	3	1	0	0
FAPL Summary by Club										
Manchester Utd	92/3 to 94/5		24	11	13	5	3	1	0	0
Total			*24*	*11*	*13*	*5*	*3*	*1*	*0*	*0*

CALDERWOOD Colin   Tottenham Hotspur

Fullname: Colin Calderwood   DOB: 21-01-69 Stranraer
Debut: Newcastle United v TOTTENHAM HOTSPUR 14/8/93
Debut Goal: TOTTENHAM HOTSPUR v Sheffield Wed 10/12/94

Previous Clubs Details			*Apps*					*Goals*		
Club	Signed	Fee	Tot	Start	Sub	FA	FL	Lge	FA	FL
Mansfield Tn	Mar-82		100	97	3	6	4	1	1	0
Swindon Town	Jul-85	£30,000	330	328	2	17	35	20	1	0
Tottenham H	Jul-93	£1.25m	62	61	1	9	6	2	0	0
FAPL Summary by Club										
Tottenham H	93/4 to 94/5		62	61	1	9	6	2	0	0
Total			62	61	1	9	6	2	0	0

CAMPBELL Kevin   Nottingham Forest

Fullname: Kevin Joseph Campbell   DOB: 05-02-74 Lambeth
Debut: ARSENAL v Norwich City 15/8/92
Debut Goal: ARSENAL v Norwich City 15/8/92

Previous Clubs Details			*Apps*					*Goals*		
Club	Signed	Fee	Tot	Start	Sub	FA	FL	Lge	FA	FL
Arsenal	Feb-88		166	124	42	19	14	46	2	6
Leyton Orient	Jan-89	Loan	16	16	0	0	0	9	0	0
Leicester City	Nov-89	Loan	11	11	0	0	0	5	0	0
N Forest	Jun-95	£2m								
FAPL Summary by Club										
Arsenal	92/3 to 94/5		97	79	18	12	18	22	1	6
Total			97	79	18	12	18	22	1	6

CAMPBELL Sol   Tottenham Hotspur

Fullname: Sulzeer Campbell   DOB: 19-09-78 Newham
Debut: TOTTENHAM HOTSPUR v Chelsea 5/12/92 as sub
Debut Goal: TOTTENHAM HOTSPUR v Chelsea 5/12/92

Previous Clubs Details			*Apps*					*Goals*		
Club	Signed	Fee	Tot	Start	Sub	FA	FL	Lge	FA	FL
Tottenham H	Sep-92		65	56	9	6	8	1	0	1
FAPL Summary by Club										
Tottenham H	92/3 to 94/5		65	56	9	6	8	1	0	1
Total			65	56	9	6	8	1	0	1

CANTONA Eric   Manchester United

Fullname: Eric Cantona   DOB: 25-05-70 Paris, France
Debut: MANCHESTER UNITED v Wimbledon 15/8/92
Debut Goal: Middlesbrough v MANCHESTER UNITED 22/8/92

Previous Clubs Details			*Apps*					*Goals*		
Club	Signed	Fee	Tot	Start	Sub	FA	FL	Lge	FA	FL
Auxerre			81					23		
Martiques		Loan								
Marseille	1988	£2.2m	55					13		
Bordeaux		Loan	11					6		
Montpellier		Loan	33					10		
Nimes	1991	£1m								

Club	Signed	Fee	Tot	Start	Sub	FA	FL	Lge	FA	FL
Leeds Utd	Feb-92	£900,000	28	18	10	0	1	9	0	0
Manchester Utd	Nov-92	£1.2m	77	76	1	7	5	39	5	1
FAPL Summary by Club										
Leeds Utd	92/3 to 94/5		13	12	1	0	1	6	0	0
Manchester Utd	92/3 to 94/5		77	76	1	7	5	39	5	1
Total			*90*	*88*	*2*	*7*	*6*	*48*	*5*	*1*

CARR Franz — Aston Villa

Fullname: Franz A Carr   DOB: 25-09-70 Preston
Debut: Coventry City v SHEFFIELD UNITED 24/3/93
Debut Goal: Manchester United v SHEFFIELD UNITED 6/2/93

Previous Clubs Details   *Apps*   *Goals*

Club	Signed	Fee	Tot	Start	Sub	FA	FL	Lge	FA	FL
Blackburn R	Jul-84		0	0	0	0	0	0	0	0
N Forest	Aug-84	£100,000	131	122	9	4	18	17	0	5
Sheffield W	Dec-89	Loan	12	9	3	2	0	0	0	0
West Ham Utd	Mar-91	Loan	3	1	2	0	0	0	0	0
Newcastle Utd	May-91	£250,000	24	20	4	0	4	3	0	0
Sheffield Utd	Jan-93	£120,000	18	18	0	4	0	4	0	0
Leicester City	Oct-94	£100,000	13	12	1	0	0	1	0	0
Aston Villa	Dec-95	£250,000	2	2	0	0	0	0	0	0
FAPL Summary by Club										
Sheffield Utd	92/3 to 93/4		18	18	0	4	0	4	0	0
Leicester City	94/5		13	12	1	0	0	1	0	0
Aston Villa	94/5		2	0	2	0	0	0	0	0
Total			*33*	*30*	*3*	*4*	*0*	*5*	*0*	*0*

CASKEY Darren — Tottenham Hotspur

Fullname: Darren Mark Caskey   DOB: 22-08-78 Basildon
Debut: TOTTENHAM HOTSPUR v Arsenal 16/8/93
Debut Goal: TOTTENHAM HOTSPUR v Everton 3/10/93

Previous Clubs Details   *Apps*   *Goals*

Club	Signed	Fee	Tot	Start	Sub	FA	FL	Lge	FA	FL
Tottenham H	Mar-92		29	17	12	4	4	4	0	1
FAPL Summary by Club										
Tottenham H	93/4 to 94/5		29	17	12	4	4	4	0	1
Total			*29*	*17*	*12*	*4*	*4*	*4*	*0*	*1*

CASTLEDINE Stewart — Wimbledon

Fullname: Stewart Mark Castledine   DOB: 23-01-77 Wandsworth
Debut: Coventry City v WIMBLEDON 2/4/94
Debut Goal: Coventry City v WIMBLEDON 2/4/94

Previous Clubs Details   *Apps*   *Goals*

Club	Signed	Fee	Tot	Start	Sub	FA	FL	Lge	FA	FL
Wimbledon	Jul-91		11	8	3	0	0	2	0	0

Wimbledon	93/4 to 94/5	9	8	1	0	0	2	0	0
Total		*9*	*8*	*1*	*0*	*0*	*2*	*0*	*0*

CHARLES Gary Aston Villa

Fullname: Gary Andrew Charles DOB: 14-04-74 Newham
Debut: Manchester United v ASTON VILLA 4/2/95
Debut Goal:

Previous Clubs Details			*Apps*					*Goals*		
Club	Signed	Fee	Tot	Start	Sub	FA	FL	Lge	FA	FL
N Forest	Nov-87		56	54	2	10	9	1	0	1
Leicester City	Mar-89	Loan	8	5	3	0	0	0	0	0
Derby County	Jul-93	£750,000	43	43	0	1	3	1	0	0
Aston Villa	Jan-95	£2.9m +	16	14	2	0	0	0	0	0

FAPL Summary by Club

Aston Villa	94/5	16	14	2	0	0	0	0	0
Total		*16*	*14*	*2*	*0*	*0*	*0*	*0*	*0*

CHARLTON Simon Southampton

Fullname: Simon T Charlton DOB: 26-10-75 Huddersfield
Debut: SOUTHAMPTON v Everton 14/8/93
Debut Goal: SOUTHAMPTON v Chelsea 27/12/93

Previous Clubs Details			*Apps*					*Goals*		
Club	Signed	Fee	Tot	Start	Sub	FA	FL	Lge	FA	FL
Huddersfield T	Jul-89		124	121	3	10	9	1	0	1
Southampton	Aug-93	£250,000	58	54	4	2	4	2	0	0

FAPL Summary by Club

Southampton	93/4 to 94/5	58	54	4	2	4	2	0	0
Total		*58*	*54*	*4*	*2*	*4*	*2*	*0*	*0*

CHETTLE Steve Nottingham Forest

Fullname: Stephen Chettle DOB: 28-09-72 Nottingham
Debut: NOTTINGHAM FOREST v Liverpool 16/8/92
Debut Goal:

Previous Clubs Details			*Apps*					*Goals*		
Club	Signed	Fee	Tot	Start	Sub	FA	FL	Lge	FA	FL
N Forest	Aug-86		256	243	13	25	39	7	0	1

FAPL Summary by Club

Nottingham Forest	92/3 to 94/5	71	71	0	6	8	0	0	0
Total		*71*	*71*	*0*	*6*	*8*	*0*	*0*	*0*

CLARK Lee Newcastle United

Fullname: Lee R Clark DOB: 28-10-76 Wallsend
Debut: NEWCASTLE UNITED v Tottenham United 14/8/93
Debut Goal: Swindon Town v NEWCASTLE UNITED 18/9/93

Previous Clubs Details			Apps					Goals		
Club	Signed	Fee	Tot	Start	Sub	FA	FL	Lge	FA	FL
Newcastle Utd	Nov-89		132	112	20	11	13	20	2	0
FAPL Summary by Club										
Newcastle Utd	93/4 to 94/5		48	38	10	5	5	3	1	0
Total			*48*	*38*	*10*	*5*	*5*	*3*	*1*	*0*

CLARKE Steve Chelsea

Fullname: Stephen Clarke   DOB: 30-08-67 Saltcoats
Debut: CHELSEA v Oldham Athletic 15/8/92
Debut Goal:

Previous Clubs Details			Apps					Goals		
Club	Signed	Fee	Tot	Start	Sub	FA	FL	Lge	FA	FL
St Mirren			151					6		
Chelsea	Jan-87	£422,000	251	247	4	20	16	6	1	1
FAPL Summary by Club										
Chelsea	92/3 to 94/5		88	86	2	12	6	0	0	0
Total			*88*	*86*	*2*	*12*	*6*	*0*	*0*	*0*

CLARKE Adrian Arsenal

Fullname: Adrian Clarke   DOB:
Debut: ARSENAL v QPR 31/12/94 as sub
Debut Goal:

Previous Clubs Details			Apps					Goals		
Club	Signed	Fee	Tot	Start	Sub	FA	FL	Lge	FA	FL
Arsenal			1	0	1	0	0	0	0	0
FAPL Summary by Club										
Arsenal	94/5		1	0	1	0	0	0	0	0
Total			*1*	*0*	*1*	*0*	*0*	*0*	*0*	*0*

CLARKE Andy Wimbledon

Fullname: Andrew Weston Clarke   DOB: 23-07-71 Islington
Debut: Leeds United v WIMBLEDON 15/8/92
Debut Goal: WIMBLEDON v Aston Villa 3/10/92

Previous Clubs Details			Apps					Goals		
Club	Signed	Fee	Tot	Start	Sub	FA	FL	Lge	FA	FL
Non-League										
Wimbledon	Feb-91	£250,000	127	60	67	8	14	14	1	2
FAPL Summary by Club										
Wimbledon	92/3 to 94/5		81	40	41	3	3	8	1	0
Total			*81*	*40*	*41*	*3*	*3*	*8*	*1*	*0*

CLOUGH Nigel Liverpool

Fullname: Nigel Howard Clough   DOB: 20-03-70 Sunderland
Debut: NOTTINGHAM FOREST v Liverpool 16/8/92
Debut Goal: Norwich City v NOTTINGHAM FOREST 31/8/92

Previous Clubs Details			*Apps*					*Goals*		
Club	Signed	Fee	Tot	Start	Sub	FA	FL	Lge	FA	FL
N Forest	Sep-84		311	307	4	28	46	101	22	6
Liverpool	Aug-93	£2.275m	37	28	9	2	3	7	0	2
FAPL Summary by Club										
N Forest	92/3 to 94/5		42	42	0	4	5	10	1	1
Liverpool	93/4 to 94/5		37	28	9	2	3	7	0	1
Total			*79*	*70*	*9*	*6*	*8*	*17*	*1*	*2*

COLE Andy   Manchester United

Fullname: Andrew Alexander Cole   DOB: 20-10-75 Nottingham
Debut: NEWCASTLE UNITED v Tottenham Hotspur 14/8/93
Debut Goal: Manchester United v NEWCASTLE UNITED 21/8/93

Previous Clubs Details			*Apps*					*Goals*		
Club	Signed	Fee	Tot	Start	Sub	FA	FL	Lge	FA	FL
Arsenal	Oct-89		1	0	1	0	0	0	0	0
Fulham	May-91	Loan	0	0	0	0	0	0	0	0
Bristol City	Mar-92	£500,000	41	41	0	0	0	20	0	0
Newcastle Utd	Mar-93	£1.75m	70	69	1	4	7	54	1	8
Manchester Utd	Jan-95	£7m +	18	17	1	0	0	12	0	0
FAPL Summary by Club										
Newcastle Utd	93/4 to 94/5		58	58	0	4	7	43	1	8
Manchester Utd	94/5		18	17	1	0	0	12	0	0
Total			*76*	*75*	*1*	*4*	*7*	*55*	*1*	*8*

COLEMAN Simon   Bolton Wanderers

Fullname: Simon Coleman   DOB: 14-03-72 Worksop
Debut: SHEFFIELD WEDNESDAY v Liverpool 4/12/93
Debut Goal: Tottenham Hotspur v SHEFFIELD WED 5/2/94

Previous Clubs Details			*Apps*					*Goals*		
Club	Signed	Fee	Tot	Start	Sub	FA	FL	Lge	FA	FL
Mansfield T	Jul-85		96	96	0	7	9	7	0	0
Middlesbrough	Sep-89	£400,000	55	51	4	5	0	2	0	0
Derby County	Aug-91	£300,000	70	62	8	5	6	2	0	0
Sheffield W	Jan-94	£250,000	16	11	5	2	3	1	0	0
Bolton Wders	Oct-94	£350,000	22	22	0	1	5	4	0	0
FAPL Summary by Club										
Sheffield W	93/4 to 94/5		16	11	5	2	3	1	0	0
Total			*16*	*11*	*5*	*2*	*3*	*1*	*0*	*0*

COLLYMORE Stan   Liverpool

Fullname: Stanley Victor Collymore   DOB: 23-01-75 Stone
Debut: CRYSTAL PALACE v Southampton 26/9/92 as sub
Debut Goal: NOTTINGHAM FOREST v Manchester United 22/8/94

Previous Clubs Details			Apps					Goals		
Club	Signed	Fee	Tot	Start	Sub	FA	FL	Lge	FA	FL
C Palace	Jan-91	£100,000	20	4	16	0	5	1	0	0
Southend Utd	Nov-92	£100,000	30	30	0	3	0	15	3	0
N Forest	Jul-93	£2.1m	65	64	1	2	9	41	1	7
Liverpool	Jul-95	£8.5m								
FAPL Summary by Club										
C Palace	92/3 to 94/5		2	0	2	0	2	0	0	0
N Forest	94/5		37	37	0	2	4	23	1	2
Total			*39*	*37*	*2*	*2*	*6*	*23*	*1*	*2*

COOK Paul   Coventry City

Fullname: Paul A Cook   DOB: 23-02-71 Liverpool
Debut: COVENTRY CITY v Wimbledon 20/8/94 as sub
Debut Goal: QPR v COVENTRY CITY 10/9/94

Previous Clubs Details			Apps					Goals		
Club	Signed	Fee	Tot	Start	Sub	FA	FL	Lge	FA	FL
Wigan Athletic	Jul-84		83	77	6	7	4	14	0	0
Norwich City	May-88	£73,000	6	3	3	0	0	0	0	0
Wolves	Nov-89	£250,000	193	191	2	7	7	19	1	0
Coventry City	Aug-94	£600,000	34	33	1	3	3	3	0	0
FAPL Summary by Club										
Coventry City	94/5		34	33	1	3	3	3	0	0
Total			*34*	*33*	*1*	*3*	*3*	*3*	*0*	*0*

COOPER Colin   Nottingham Forest

Fullname: Colin T Cooper   DOB: 01-03-71 Durham
Debut: Ipswich Town v NOTTINGHAM FOREST 20/8/94
Debut Goal: Everton v NOTTINGHAM FOREST 30/8/94

Previous Clubs Details			Apps					Goals		
Club	Signed	Fee	Tot	Start	Sub	FA	FL	Lge	FA	FL
Middlesbrough	Jul-84		189	183	6	13	18	6	0	0
Millwall	Jul-91	£300,000	77	77	0	2	6	6	0	0
N Forest	Jun-93	£1.5m	72	71	1	3	8	8	1	1
FAPL Summary by Club										
N Forest	94/5		35	35	0	1	4	1	0	0
Total			*35*	*35*	*0*	*1*	*4*	*1*	*0*	*0*

COTON Tony   Manchester City

Fullname: Anthony Philip Coton   DOB: 20-05-65 Tamworth
Debut: MANCHESTER CITY v QPR 17/8/92
Debut Goal:

Previous Clubs Details			Apps					Goals		
Club	Signed	Fee	Tot	Start	Sub	FA	FL	Lge	FA	FL
Birmingham C	Oct-78		94	94	0	10	10	0	0	0
Watford	Sep-84	£300,000	233	233	0	32	18	0	0	0

			163	162	1	11	16		0	0	0

Manchester C   Jul-90   £1m

FAPL Summary by Club

Manchester C	92/3 to 94/5		93	92	1	4	9		0	0	0
Total			*93*	*92*	*1*	*4*	*9*		*0*	*0*	*0*

COTTEE Tony   West Ham United

Fullname: Anthony Richard Cottee   DOB: 12-07-69 West Ham

Debut: Blackburn Rovers v EVERTON 15/9/92

Debut Goal: Blackburn Rovers v EVERTON 15/9/92

Previous Clubs Details

Club	Signed	Fee	Apps					Goals			
			Tot	Start	Sub	FA	FL	Lge	FA	FL	
West Ham Utd	Sep-82		212	203	9	24	19	92	11	14	
Everton	Aug-88	£2.3m	184	161	23	21	23	72	11	4	
West Ham Utd	Sep-94	Swap+									
		£300,000	31	31	0	2	3	13	1	1	

FAPL Summary by Club

Everton	92/3-94/5		64	61	4	2	8	16	3	0	
West Ham Utd	94/5		31	31	0	2	3	13	1	1	
Total											

COUZENS Andy   Leeds United

Fullname: Andrew Couzens   DOB: 05-06-79 Shipley

Debut: LEEDS UNITED v Coventry City 18/3/95 as sub

Debut Goal:

Previous Clubs Details

Club	Signed	Fee	Apps					Goals			
			Tot	Start	Sub	FA	FL	Lge	FA	FL	
Leeds Utd			4	2	2	0	0	0	0	0	

FAPL Summary by Club

Leeds Utd	94/5		4	2	2	0	0	0	0	0	
Total			*4*	*2*	*2*	*0*	*0*	*0*	*0*	*0*	

COX Neil   Middlesbrough

Fullname: Neil James Cox   DOB: 09-10-75 Scunthorpe

Debut: Sheffield Wednesday v ASTON VILLA 5/12/92

Debut Goal: ASTON VILLA v Everton 20/2/93

Previous Clubs Details

Club	Signed	Fee	Apps					Goals			
			Tot	Start	Sub	FA	FL	Lge	FA	FL	
Scunthorpe Utd	Mar-90		17	17	0	4	0	1	0	0	
Aston Villa	Feb-91	£400,000	7	4	3	0	0	0	0	0	
Middlesbrough	Jul-94	£850,000	40	39	1	0	3	1	0	0	

FAPL Summary by Club

Aston Villa	92/3 to 93/4		35	22	13	6	7	3	0	0	
Total			*35*	*22*	*13*	*6*	*7*	*3*	*0*	*0*	

COYLE Owen — Bolton Wanderers

Fullname: Owen Coyle
DOB: 15-07-70 Glasgow
Debut:
Debut Goal:

Previous Clubs Details

Club	Signed	Fee	Tot	Start	Sub	FA	FL	Lge	FA	FL
Dumbarton			103	85	18	2	4	36	0	0
Clydebank	Aug-88	£175,000	63	63	0	3	2	33	1	0
Airdrieonians	Feb-90	£175,000	123	116	7	10	6	50	1	2
Bolton Wders	Jun-93	£250,000	49	33	16	8	7	5	0	0

CROSSLEY Mark — Nottingham Forest

Fullname: Mark Geoffrey Crossley
DOB: 17-06-73 Barnsley
Debut: NOTTINGHAM FOREST v Liverpool 16/8/92
Debut Goal:

Previous Clubs Details

Club	Signed	Fee	Tot	Start	Sub	FA	FL	Lge	FA	FL
N Forest	Jul-87		200	199	1	22	29	0	0	0

FAPL Summary by Club

N Forest	92/3 to 94/5		79	79	0	2	4	0	0	0
Total			79	79	0	2	4	0	0	0

CUNDY Jason — Tottenham Hotspur

Fullname: Jason Victor Cundy
DOB: 13-11-73 Wandsworth
Debut: Southampton v TOTTENHAM HOTSPUR 15/8/92
Debut Goal: Ipswich Town v TOTTENHAM HOTSPUR 30/8/92

Previous Clubs Details

Club	Signed	Fee	Tot	Start	Sub	FA	FL	Lge	FA	FL
Chelsea	Aug-88		41	40	1	6	6	2	0	0
Tottenham H	Mar-92	£750,000	25	23	2	0	2	1	0	0

FAPL Summary by Club

Tottenham H	92/3 to 94/5		15	13	2	0	2	1	0	0
Total			15	13	2	0	2	1	0	0

CUNNINGHAM Kenny — Wimbledon

Fullname: Kenneth E Cunningham
DOB: 29-06-75 Dublin
Debut: WIMBLEDON v Newcastle United 19/11/94
Debut Goal:

Previous Clubs Details

Club	Signed	Fee	Tot	Start	Sub	FA	FL	Lge	FA	FL
Millwall	Sep-89		121	117	4	1	8	1	0	0
Wimbledon	Nov-94	£1.3m +	28	28	0	4	0	0	0	0

FAPL Summary by Club

Wimbledon	94/5		28	28	0	4	0	0	0	0
Total			28	28	0	4	0	0	0	0

CURLE Keith — Manchester City

Fullname: Keith Curle
Debut: MANCHESTER CITY v QPR 17/8/92   DOB: 15-11-67 Bristol
Debut Goal: Coventry City v MANCHESTER CITY 21/11/92

Previous Clubs Details

Club	Signed	Fee	Apps					Goals		
			Tot	Start	Sub	FA	FL	Lge	FA	FL
Bristol R	Nov-81		32	21	11	1	3	4	0	0
Torquay Utd	Nov-83	£5,000	16	16	0	1	0	5	1	0
Bristol City	Mar-84	£10,000	121	113	8	5	8	1	0	0
Reading	Oct-87	£150,000	40	40	0	0	8	0	0	0
Wimbledon	Oct-88	£500,000	93	91	2	5	7	3	0	0
Manchester C	Aug-91	£2.5m	139	139	0	9	15	11	0	1

FAPL Summary by Club

Manchester City	92/3 to 94/5		99	99	0	8	11	6	0	1
Total			*99*	*99*	*0*	*8*	*11*	*6*	*0*	*1*

DARBY Julian — Coventry City

Fullname: Julian T Darby
Debut: COVENTRY CITY v Everton 6/11/93   DOB: 04-10-71 Bolton
Debut Goal: West Ham v COVENTRY CITY 11/12/93

Previous Clubs Details

Club	Signed	Fee	Apps					Goals		
			Tot	Start	Sub	FA	FL	Lge	FA	FL
Bolton Wders	Jul-86		270	258	12	19	25	36	3	8
Coventry City	Oct-93	£150,000	55	52	3	4	30	5	0	1

FAPL Summary by Club

Coventry City	93/4 to 94/5		55	52	3	4	30	5	0	1
Total			*55*	*52*	*3*	*4*	*30*	*5*	*0*	*1*

DAVIES Simon — Manchester United

Fullname: Simon Davies
Debut: MANCHESTER UNITED v Crystal Palace 19/11/94   DOB: 24-12-78 Winsford
Debut Goal:

Previous Clubs Details

Club	Signed	Fee	Apps					Goals		
			Tot	Start	Sub	FA	FL	Lge	FA	FL
Manchester Utd	Jul-92	Trainee	5	3	2	0	0	0	0	0
Exeter City	Dec-93	Loan	6	5	1	1	0	1	0	0

FAPL Summary by Club

Manchester Utd	94/5		5	3	2	0	3	0	0	0
Total			*5*	*3*	*0*	*0*	*3*	*0*	*0*	*0*

DAVISON Aidan — Bolton Wanderers

Fullname: Aidan Davison
Debut: DOB: 12-05-72 Sedgefield
   Debut Goal:

Previous Clubs Details

Club	Signed	Fee	Apps					Goals		
			Tot	Start	Sub	FA	FL	Lge	FA	FL
Notts County	Mar-88		1	1	0	0	0	0	0	0

Bury	07-10-89	£6,000								
Millwall	Aug-91	Free	34	34	0	3	3	0	0	0
Bolton Wders	Jul-93	£25,000	35	33	2	8	0	0	0	0

De FREITAS Fabian   Bolton Wanderers

Fullname: Fabian De Freitas   DOB:
Debut: Debut Goal:

Previous Clubs Details			*Apps*					*Goals*		
Club	Signed	Fee	Tot	Start	Sub	FA	FL	Lge	FA	FL
Volendam										
Bolton Wders	Aug-94	£350,000	13	7	6	0	3	2	0	0

DEANE Brian   Leeds United

Fullname: Brian Christopher Deane   DOB: 08-02-72 Leeds
Debut: LEEDS UNITED v Manchester United 15/8/93
Debut Goal: LEEDS UNITED v Manchester United 15/8/93

Previous Clubs Details			*Apps*					*Goals*		
Club	Signed	Fee	Tot	Start	Sub	FA	FL	Lge	FA	FL
Doncaster R	Dec-85		66	59	7	3	3	12	1	0
Sheffield Utd	Jul-88	£30,000	197	197	0	24	16	93	11	11
Leeds Utd	Jul-93	£2.7m	76	74	2	5	5	20	2	0
FAPL Summary by Club										
Sheffield Utd	92/3 to 94/5		41	41	0	6	4	15	3	2
Leeds Utd	93/4 to 94/5		76	74	2	6	3	20	2	0
Total			*117*	*115*	*2*	*12*	*7*	*35*	*5*	*2*

DIBBLE Andy   Manchester City

Fullname: Andrew Gerald Dibble   DOB: 09-05-69 Cwmbran
Debut: QPR v MANCHESTER CITY 6/2/93
Debut Goal: (Goalkeeper)

Previous Clubs Details			*Apps*					*Goals*		
Club	Signed	Fee	Tot	Start	Sub	FA	FL	Lge	FA	FL
Cardiff City	Aug-82		62	62	0	4	4	0	0	0
Luton Town	Jul-84	£125,000	30	30	0	1	4	0	0	0
Sunderland	Feb-86	Loan	12	12	0	0	0	0	0	0
Huddersfield T	Feb-87	Loan	5	5	0	0	0	0	0	0
Manchester C	Jul-88	£240,000	103	101	2	9	12	0	0	0
Aberdeen	Oct-90	Loan	5	5	0			0	0	0
Middlesbrough	Feb-91	Loan	19	19	0			0	0	0
Bolton Wdrers	Sep-91	Loan	13	13	0			0	0	0
WBA	Feb-92	Loan	9	9	0			0	0	0
FAPL Summary by Club										
Manchester C	92/3 to 94/5		29	27	2	4	6	0	0	0
Total			*29*	*27*	*2*	*4*	*6*	*0*	*0*	*0*

DICHIO Danny   QPR
Fullname: Daniele Dichio   DOB: 20-10-78 Hammersmith
Debut: QPR v Aston Villa 29/10/94
Debut Goal: QPR v Aston Villa 29/10/94

Previous Clubs Details

Club	Signed	Fee	Tot	Start	Sub	FA	FL	Lge	FA	FL
QPR	May-93	Trainee	9	4	5	1	1	3	0	0
Barnet	Mar-94	Loan	9	9	0	0	0	2	0	0
FAPL Summary by Club										
QPR	94/5		9	4	5	1	1	3	0	0
Total			9	4	5	1	1	3	0	0

DICKOV Paul   Arsenal
Fullname: Paul Dickov   DOB: 02-11-76 Livingstone
Debut: ARSENAL v Southampton 20/3/93
Debut Goal: ARSENAL v Crystal Palace 8/5/93

Previous Clubs Details

Club	Signed	Fee	Tot	Start	Sub	FA	FL	Lge	FA	FL
Arsenal	Dec-90		13	5	8	0	4	2	0	0
Luton Town	Oct-93	Loan	15	8	7	0	0	1	0	0
Brighton & H	03-Oct	Loan	8	8	0	0	0	5	0	0
FAPL Summary by Club										
Arsenal	92/3 to 94/5		13	5	8	0	4	2	0	3
Total			13	5	8	0	4	2	0	3

DICKS Julian   West Ham United
Fullname: Julian A Dicks   DOB: 09-08-72 Bristol
Debut: WEST HAM UNITED v Wimbledon 14/8/93
Debut Goal: Everton v LIVERPOOL 14/8/93

Previous Clubs Details

Club	Signed	Fee	Tot	Start	Sub	FA	FL	Lge	FA	FL
Birmingham C	Apr-86		89	83	6	5	6	1	0	0
West Ham Utd	Mar-88	£300,000	159	159	0	14	19	29	2	5
Liverpool	Sep-93	£1.6m	24	24	0	1	3	3	0	0
West Ham Utd	Oct-94	£500,000+	29	29	0	2	2	5	0	0
FAPL Summary by Club										
West Ham Utd	93/4 to 94/5		7	7	0	0	0	1	0	0
Liverpool	93/4 to 93/4		24	24	0	1	3	3	0	0
West Ham Utd	94/5		29	29	0	2	2	5	0	0
Total			60	60	0	3	5	9	0	0

DIXON Lee   Arsenal
Fullname: Lee Michael Dixon   DOB: 18-03-68 Manchester
Debut: ARSENAL v Norwich City 15/8/92
Debut Goal: ARSENAL v Norwich City 1/4/95

Previous Clubs Details			Apps					Goals		
Club	Signed	Fee	Tot	Start	Sub	FA	FL	Lge	FA	FL
Burnley	Jul-82		4	4	0	0	1	0	0	0
Chester City	Feb-84	Free	57	56	1	1	2	1	0	0
Bury	Jul-85	Free	45	45	0	8	4	6	1	0
Stoke City	Jul-86	£40,000	71	71	0	7	6	5	0	0
Arsenal	Jan-88	£400,000	254	251	3	26	32	16	1	0
FAPL Summary by Club										
Arsenal	92/3 to 94/5		101	100	1	13	16	1	0	0
Total			*101*	*100*	*1*	*13*	*16*	*1*	*0*	*0*

DODD Jason   Southampton
Fullname: Jason Robert Dodd   DOB: 03-11-74 Bath
Debut: SOUTHAMPTON v Tottenham Hotspur 15/8/92
Debut Goal: Sheffield Wednesday v SOUTHAMPTON 13/4/93

Previous Clubs Details			Apps					Goals		
Club	Signed	Fee	Tot	Start	Sub	FA	FL	Lge	FA	FL
Southampton	Mar-89	£50,000	135	119	16	16	19	3	0	0
FAPL Summary by Club										
Southampton	92/3 to 94/5		66	56	10	6	4	3	0	0
Total			*66*	*56*	*10*	*6*	*4*	*3*	*0*	*0*

DONALDSON O'Neill   Sheffield Wednesday
Fullname: O'Neill Donaldson   DOB:
Debut: Manchester City v SHEFFIELD WED 18/3/95 as sub
Debut Goal:

Previous Clubs Details			Apps					Goals		
Club	Signed	Fee	Tot	Start	Sub	FA	FL	Lge	FA	FL
Sheffield W			1	1	0	0	0	0	0	0
FAPL Summary by Club										
Sheffield W	94/5		1	0	1	0	0	0	0	0
Total			*1*	*0*	*1*	*0*	*0*	*0*	*0*	*0*

DORIGO Tony   Leeds United
Fullname: Anthony Robert Dorigo   DOB: 01-02-69 Melbourne
Debut: LEEDS UNITED v Wimbledon 15/8/92
Debut Goal: LEEDS UNITED v Ipswich Town 27/2/93

Previous Clubs Details			Apps					Goals		
Club	Signed	Fee	Tot	Start	Sub	FA	FL	Lge	FA	FL
Aston Villa	Jul-83		111	106	5	7	15	1	0	0
Chelsea	May-87	£475,000	146	146	0	4	14	11	0	0
Leeds Utd	May-91	£1.3m	136	136	0	9	9	4	0	0
FAPL Summary by Club										
Leeds Utd	92/3 to 94/5		98	98	0	8	4	1	0	0
Total			*98*	*98*	*0*	*8*	*4*	*1*	*0*	*0*

DOW Andy   Chelsea

Fullname: Andrew Dow   DOB: 08-02-77 Dundee
Debut: CHELSEA v Blackburn Rovers 14/8/93 as sub
Debut Goal:

Previous Clubs Details			Apps					Goals		
Club	Signed	Fee	Tot	Start	Sub	FA	FL	Lge	FA	FL
Dundee	Nov-90		18					1		
Chelsea	Aug-93		14	13	1	1	2	0	0	0
Bradford City	Sep-94	Loan								
FAPL Summary by Club										
Chelsea	93/4 to 94/5		14	13	1	1	2	0	0	0
Total			*14*	*13*	*1*	*1*	*2*	*0*	*0*	*0*

DOZZELL Jason   Tottenham Hotspur

Fullname: Jason Alvin Winans Dozzell   DOB: 10-12-71 Ipswich
Debut: IPSWICH TOWN v Aston Villa 15/8/92
Debut Goal: IPSWICH TOWN v Liverpool 25/8/92

Previous Clubs Details			Apps					Goals		
Club	Signed	Fee	Tot	Start	Sub	FA	FL	Lge	FA	FL
Ipswich Town	Dec-84		291	271	20	18	23	45	10	3
Tottenham H	Aug-93	£1.9m	39	34	5	2	6	8	1	0
FAPL Summary by Club										
Ipswich Town	92/3 to 94/5		41	41	0	4	7	7	2	0
Tottenham H	93/4 to 94/5		39	34	5	2	6	8	1	0
Total			*80*	*75*	*5*	*6*	*13*	*15*	*3*	*0*

DRAPER Mark   Aston Villa

Fullname: Mark Draper   DOB: 12-11-74 Long Eaton
Debut: LEICESTER CITY v Newcastle United 21/8/94
Debut Goal: Everton v LEICESTER CITY 24/9/94

Previous Clubs Details			Apps					Goals		
Club	Signed	Fee	Tot	Start	Sub	FA	FL	Lge	FA	FL
Notts County	Dec-88		222	206	16	10	15	40	1	1
Leicester City	Jul-94	£1.25m	39	39	0	2	2	5	0	0
Aston Villa	Jul-95	£3.25m								
FAPL Summary by Club										
Leicester City	94/5		39	39	0	2	2	5	0	0
Total			*39*	*39*	*0*	*2*	*2*	*5*	*0*	*0*

DUBLIN Dion   Coventry City

Fullname: Dion Dublin   DOB: 23-04-73 Leicester
Debut: Sheffield United v MANCHESTER UTD 15/8/92 as sub
Debut Goal: Southampton v MANCHESTER UNITED 24/8/92

Previous Clubs Details			*Apps*					*Goals*		
Club	Signed	Fee	Tot	Start	Sub	FA	FL	Lge	FA	FL
Norwich City	Mar-88		0	0	0	0	0	0	0	0
Cambridge Utd	Aug-88		156	133	23	21	10	53	11	5
Manchester Utd	Jul-92	£1m	12	4	8	2	2	2	0	1
Coventry City	Sep-94	£2m	31	31	0	4	3	13	1	2
FAPL Summary by Club										
Manchester Utd	92/3 to 93/4		12	4	8	2	2	2	0	1
Coventry City	94/5		31	31	0	4	3	13	1	2
Total			*43*	*35*	*8*	*6*	*5*	*15*	*1*	*3*

DUMITRESCU Ilie — Tottenham Hotspur

Fullname: Ilie Dumitrescu DOB: 07-01-73 Romania
Debut: Sheffield Wed v TOTTENHAM HOTSPUR 20/8/94
Debut Goal: TOTTENHAM HOTSPUR v Ipswich Town 30/8/94

Previous Clubs Details			*Apps*					*Goals*		
Club	Signed	Fee	Tot	Start	Sub	FA	FL	Lge	FA	FL
CSA Steaua Bucharest	Jun-87		2	2	0	0	0	0	0	0
FC Olt Scornicesti	Jul-8732		32	0	1	0	1	0	0	
CSA Steaua Bucharest	Jul-88		164	164	0	16	0	71	4	0
Tottenham H	Aug-94	£2.6m	26	24	2	0	2	8	0	0
FC Seville	Dec-94	Loan								
FAPL Summary by Club										
Tottenham H	94/5 to 93/4		13	11	2	0	2	4	0	0
Total			*13*	*11*	*2*	*0*	*2*	*4*	*0*	*0*

DYKSTRA Sieb — QPR

Fullname: Sieb Dykstra DOB: 21-10-70 Kerkrade
Debut: Norwich City v QPR 22/10/94
Debut Goal:

Previous Clubs Details			*Apps*					*Goals*		
Club	Signed	Fee	Tot	Start	Sub	FA	FL	Lge	FA	FL
Roda JC			0	0	0	0	0	0	0	0
Motherwell			80	80	0	4	3	0	0	0
QPR	Jul-94	£250,000	11	11	0	0	1	0	0	0
FAPL Summary by Club										
QPR	94/5 to 93/4		11	11	0	0	1	0	0	0
Total			*11*	*11*	*0*	*0*	*1*	*0*	*0*	*0*

EARLE Robbie — Wimbledon

Fullname: Robert Gerald Earle DOB: 28-01-69 Newcastle-u-Lyme
Debut: Leeds United v WIMBLEDON 15/8/92
Debut Goal: WIMBLEDON v Arsenal 5/9/92

Previous Clubs Details			Apps					Goals		
Club	Signed	Fee	Tot	Start	Sub	FA	FL	Lge	FA	FL
Port Vale	Jul-82		294	284	10	21	23	77	4	4
Wimbledon	Jul-91	£775,000	133	133	0	14	12	30	2	3
FAPL Summary by Club										
Wimbledon	92/3 to 94/5		93	93	0	12	10	16	2	3
Total			*93*	*93*	*0*	*12*	*10*	*16*	*2*	*3*

EBBRELL John
Everton
Fullname: John Keith Ebbrell   DOB: 02-10-73 Bromborough
Debut: EVERTON v Sheffield Wednesday 15/8/92
Debut Goal: Blackburn Rovers v EVERTON 15/9/92

Previous Clubs Details			Apps					Goals		
Club	Signed	Fee	Tot	Start	Sub	FA	FL	Lge	FA	FL
Everton	Nov-86		185	176	9	16	16	9	2	1
FAPL Summary by Club										
Everton	92/3 to 94/5		89	89	0	6	7	5	0	0
Total			*89*	*89*	*0*	*6*	*7*	*5*	*0*	*0*

EDGEHILL Richard
Manchester City
Fullname: Richard Arlon Edgehill   DOB: 24-09-78 Oldham
Debut: Wimbledon v MANCHESTER CITY 20/9/93
Debut Goal:

Previous Clubs Details			Apps					Goals		
Club	Signed	Fee	Tot	Start	Sub	FA	FL	Lge	FA	FL
Manchester C	Jul-92		35	34	1	1	7	0	0	0
FAPL Summary by Club										
Manchester C	93/4 to 94/5		22	22	0	1	4	0	0	0
Manchester C	94/5		14	14	0	0	3	0	0	0
Total			*36*	*36*	*0*	*1*	*7*	*0*	*0*	*0*

EDINBURGH Justin
Tottenham Hotspur
Fullname: Justin Charles Edinburgh   DOB: 19-12-73 Brentwood
Debut: Southampton v TOTTENHAM HOTSPUR 15/8/92
Debut Goal:

Previous Clubs Details			Apps					Goals		
Club	Signed	Fee	Tot	Start	Sub	FA	FL	Lge	FA	FL
Southend Utd	Jul-88		62	60	2	5	6	0	0	0
Tottenham H	Jul-90	£150,000	127	120	7	17	17	1	0	0
FAPL Summary by Club										
Tottenham H	92/3 to 94/5		88	84	4	12	9	0	0	0
Total			*88*	*84*	*4*	*12*	*9*	*0*	*0*	*0*

EHIOGU Ugo
Aston Villa
Fullname: Ugochuku Ehiogu   DOB: 01-01-77 Hackney
Debut: ASTON VILLA v Southampton 22/8/92

Debut Goal:

Club	Signed	Fee	Tot	Start	Sub	FA	FL	Lge	FA	FL
					Apps				*Goals*	
WBA	Jul-89		2	0	2	0	0	0	0	0
Aston Villa	Jul-91	£40,000	67	56	11	4	5	0	0	0
FAPL Summary by Club										
Aston Villa	92/3 to 94/5		60	53	7	3	5	0	0	0
Total			*60*	*53*	*7*	*3*	*5*	*0*	*0*	*0*

EKELUND Ronnie   Southampton

Fullname: DOB: 22-08-76 Denmark
Debut: Nottingham Forest v SOUTHAMPTON 12/9/94 as sub
Debut Goal: Coventry City v SOUTHAMPTON 24/9/94

Club	Signed	Fee	Tot	Start	Sub	FA	FL	Lge	FA	FL
					Apps				*Goals*	
Barcelona										
Southampton	Sep-94	£500,000	17	15	2	0	3	5	0	0
FAPL Summary by Club										
Southampton	94/5		17	15	2	0	3	5	0	0
Total			*17*	*15*	*2*	*0*	*3*	*5*	*0*	*0*

EKOKU Efan   Wimbledon

Fullname: Efan Ekoku   DOB: 19-06-71 Manchester
Debut: NORWICH CITY v Manchester United 5/4/93 as sub
Debut Goal: Tottenham Hotspur v NORWICH CITY 9/4/93

Club	Signed	Fee	Tot	Start	Sub	FA	FL	Lge	FA	FL
					Apps				*Goals*	
Bournemouth	May-90		62	43	19	7	7	21	2	0
Norwich City	Mar-93	£500,000	37	26	11	2	3	15	0	1
Wimbledon	Oct-94	£800,000	24	24	0	3	0	9	0	0
FAPL Summary by Club										
Norwich City	92/3 to 94/5		37	26	11	1	3	15	0	2
Wimbledon	94/5		24	24	0	3	0	9	0	0
Total			*61*	*50*	*11*	*4*	*3*	*24*	*0*	*2*

ELKINS Gary   Wimbledon

Fullname: Gary Elkins   DOB: 05-05-70 Wallingford
Debut: Leeds United v WIMBLEDON 15/8/92
Debut Goal: WIMBLEDON v Liverpool 4/4/94

Club	Signed	Fee	Tot	Start	Sub	FA	FL	Lge	FA	FL
					Apps				*Goals*	
Fulham	Dec-83		104	100	4	4	6	2	0	0
Exeter City	Dec-89	Loan	5	5	0	0	0	0	0	0
Wimbledon	Aug-90	£20,000	100	93	7	7	7	3	1	0

Wimbledon	92/3 to 94/5	72	68	4	7	6	2	0	0
Total		*72*	*68*	*4*	*7*	*6*	*2*	*0*	*0*

ELLIOTT Robert   Newcastle United

Fullname: Robert J Elliott   DOB: 26-12-77 Newcastle
Debut: Oldham Athletic v NEWCASTLE UNITED 23/2/94
Debut Goal: Leicester City v NEWCASTLE UNITED 21/8/94 as sub

Previous Clubs Details			*Apps*				*Goals*		
Club	Signed	Fee	Tot	Start	Sub	FA	FL	Lge	FA FL
Newcastle Utd	Apr-91		44	37	7	5	1	2	0 0
FAPL Summary by Club									
Newcastle Utd	93/4 to 94/5		29	23	6	5	0	2	0 0
Total			*29*	*23*	*6*	*5*	*0*	*2*	*0 0*

FAIRCLOUGH Chris   Leeds United

Fullname: Courtney Huw Fairclough   DOB: 13-04-68 Nottingham
Debut: LEEDS UNITED v Wimbledon 15/8/92
Debut Goal: LEEDS UNITED v Coventry City 31/10/92

Previous Clubs Details			*Apps*					*Goals*		
Club	Signed	Fee	Tot	Start	Sub	FA	FL	Lge	FA	FL
N Forest	Oct-81		107	102	5	6	10	1	0	1
Tottenham H	Jun-87	£387,000	60	60	0	3	7	5	0	0
Leeds Utd	Mar-89	£500,000	193	187	6	15	19	23	0	2
FAPL Summary by Club										
Leeds Utd	92/3 to 94/5		75	70	5	7	6	8	0	0
Total			*75*	*70*	*5*	*7*	*6*	*8*	*0*	*0*

FARRELL Dave   Aston Villa

Fullname: David William Farrell   DOB: 12-11-75 Birmingham
Debut: Oldham Athletic v ASTON VILLA 24/10/92 as sub
Debut Goal:

Previous Clubs Details			*Apps*					*Goals*		
Club	Signed	Fee	Tot	Start	Sub	FA	FL	Lge	FA	FL
Aston Villa	Jan-92	£45,000	6	5	1	0	2	0	0	0
Scunthorpe Utd	Jan-93	Loan	5	4	1	0	0	1	0	0
FAPL Summary by Club										
Aston Villa	92/3 to 94/5		6	5	1	0	2	0	0	0
Total			*6*	*5*	*1*	*0*	*2*	*0*	*0*	*0*

FASHANU John   Aston Villa

Fullname: John Fashanu   DOB: 19-09-66 Kensington
Debut: WIMBLEDON v Manchester City 1/9/92
Debut Goal: WIMBLEDON v Arsenal 5/9/93

Previous Clubs Details

Club	Signed	Fee	Apps					Goals		
			Tot	Start	Sub	FA	FL	Lge	FA	FL
Norwich City	Oct-79		7	6	1	0	0	1	0	0
C Palace	Aug-83	Loan	1	1	0	0	1	0	0	0
Lincoln City	Sep-83		36	31	5	3	2	11	0	0
Millwall	Nov-84	£55,000	50	50	0	9	4	12	4	2
Wimbledon	Mar-86	£125,000	276	271	5	27	23	107	11	9
Aston Villa	Aug-94	£1.35m	13	11	2	0	3	3	0	0
FAPL Summary by Club										
Wimbledon	92/3 to 93/4		65	62	3	8	9	17	2	1
Aston Villa	94/5		13	11	2	2	0	3	0	0
Total			*78*	*73*	*5*	*10*	*9*	*20*	*2*	*1*

FEAR Peter   Wimbledon

Fullname: Peter Fear   DOB: 11-09-77 Sutton
Debut: Arsenal v WIMBLEDON 10/2/93
Debut Goal: WIMBLEDON v Leeds United 26/3/94

Previous Clubs Details

Club	Signed	Fee	Apps					Goals		
			Tot	Start	Sub	FA	FL	Lge	FA	FL
Wimbledon	Jul-92		41	33	8	2	5	2	0	0
FAPL Summary by Club										
Wimbledon	92/3 to 94/5		41	33	8	2	5	2	0	0
Total			*41*	*33*	*8*	*2*	*5*	*2*	*0*	*0*

FENTON Graham   Aston Villa

Fullname: Graham Anthony Fenton   DOB: 23-05-78 Wallsend
Debut: ASTON VILLA v Manchester City 22/2/94
Debut Goal: Sheffield United v ASTON VILLA 16/4/94

Previous Clubs Details

Club	Signed	Fee	Apps					Goals		
			Tot	Start	Sub	FA	FL	Lge	FA	FL
Aston Villa	Feb-92		29	16	13	0	5	3	0	0
WBA	Jan-94	Loan	7	7	0	0	0	3	0	0
FAPL Summary by Club										
Aston Villa	93/4 to 94/5		29	16	13	0	5	3	0	0
Total			*29*	*16*	*13*	*0*	*5*	*3*	*0*	*0*

FERDINAND Les   Newcastle United

Fullname: Leslie Ferdinand   DOB: 19-12-70 Acton
Debut: Manchester City v QPR 17/8/92
Debut Goal: QPR v Southampton 19/8/92

Previous Clubs Details

Club	Signed	Fee	Apps					Goals		
			Tot	Start	Sub	FA	FL	Lge	FA	FL
QPR	Apr-87	£15,000	163	152	11	8	13	80	3	7
Brentford	Mar-88	Loan	3	3	0	0	0	0	0	0
Besiktas (Turkey)	Jun-88	Loan								
Newcastle Utd	Jun-95	£6m								

FERGUSON Duncan   Everton

Fullname: Duncan Ferguson
Debut: EVERTON v Coventry City 15/10/94   DOB: 28-12-75 Carse Thistle
Debut Goal: EVERTON v Liverpool 21/11/94

Previous Clubs Details			*Apps*					*Goals*		
Club	Signed	Fee	Tot	Start	Sub	FA	FL	Lge	FA	FL
Dundee U			77					28		
Rangers			14					2		
Everton	Oct-94	Loan								
Everton	Dec-94	£4m +	23	22	1	4	1	7	1	0
FAPL Summary by Club										
Everton		94/5	23	22	1	4	1	7	1	0
Total			*23*	*22*	*1*	*4*	*1*	*7*	*1*	*0*

FILAN John   Coventry City

Fullname: John Filan
Debut: Tottenham Hotspur v COVENTRY CITY 9/5/95   DOB: 09-02-74 Sydney
Debut Goal:

Previous Clubs Details			*Apps*					*Goals*		
Club	Signed	Fee	Tot	Start	Sub	FA	FL	Lge	FA	FL
Sydney Budapest			0	0	0	0	0	0	0	0
Cambridge Utd	Mar-93	£40,000	52	52	0	3	4	0	0	0
N Forest	Dec-94	Loan								
Coventry City	Mar-95	£300,000	2	2	0	0	0	0	0	0
FAPL Summary by Club										
Coventry City		94/5	2	2	0	0	0	0	0	0
Total			*2*	*2*	*0*	*0*	*0*	*0*	*0*	*0*

FISHER Neil   Bolton Wanderers

Fullname: Neil Fisher
Debut: DOB: 08-11-74 St Helens
                                                          Debut Goal:

Previous Clubs Details			*Apps*					*Goals*		
Club	Signed	Fee	Tot	Start	Sub	FA	FL	Lge	FA	FL
Bolton Wders	Jul-89	Trainee	24	17	7	1	4	0	0	0

FITZGERALD Scott   Wimbledon

Fullname: Scott Brian Fitzgerald
Debut: Leeds United v WIMBLEDON 15/8/92   DOB: 14-08-73 Westminster
Debut Goal:

Previous Clubs Details			*Apps*					*Goals*		
Club	Signed	Fee	Tot	Start	Sub	FA	FL	Lge	FA	FL
Wimbledon	Jul-87		102	93	9	9	8	13	0	0

FJORTOFT Jan-Aage   Middlesbrough

Fullname: Jan-Aage Fjortoft   DOB: 11-01-71 Aalesund, Norway
Debut: Sheffield United v SWINDON TOWN 14/8/93
Debut Goal: SWINDON TOWN v Tottenham Hotspur 22/1/94

Previous Clubs Details			Apps					Goals		
Club	Signed	Fee	Tot	Start	Sub	FA	FL	Lge	FA	FL
Rapid Vienna										
Swindon Town	Aug-93	£500,000	36	26	10	2	1	12	1	0
Middlesbrough	Mar-95	£1.3m	8	8	0	0	0	3	0	0
FAPL Summary by Club										
Swindon Town	93/4 to 94/5		36	26	10	2	1	12	1	0
Total			*36*	*26*	*10*	*2*	*1*	*12*	*1*	*0*

FLATTS Mark   Arsenal

Fullname: Mark Michael Flatts   DOB: 15-10-76 Islington
Debut: Sheffield United v ARSENAL 19/9/92
Debut Goal:

Previous Clubs Details			Apps					Goals		
Club	Signed	Fee	Tot	Start	Sub	FA	FL	Lge	FA	FL
Arsenal	Dec-90		16	9	7	1	1	0	0	0
Cambridge Utd	Oct-93	Loan	5	5	0	0	0	1	0	0
Brighton & H	Dec-93	Loan	10	9	1	0	0	1	0	0
Bristol City	Mar-95	Loan								
FAPL Summary by Club										
Arsenal	92/3 to 94/5		16	9	7	1	1	0	0	0
Total			*16*	*9*	*7*	*1*	*1*	*0*	*0*	*0*

FLECK Robert   Chelsea

Fullname: Robert Fleck   DOB: 12-08-69 Glasgow
Debut: CHELSEA v Oldham Athletic 15/8/92
Debut Goal: Aston Villa v CHELSEA 2/9/92

Previous Clubs Details			Apps					Goals		
Club	Signed	Fee	Tot	Start	Sub	FA	FL	Lge	FA	FL
Rangers										
Norwich City	Dec-87	£580,000	143	130	13	18	13	40	11	11
Chelsea	Aug-92	£2.1m	40	35	5	1	7	3	0	1
Bolton Wders	Dec-93	Loan	7	6	1	0	0	1	0	0
Bristol City	Jan-95	Loan								
FAPL Summary by Club										
Chelsea	92/3 to 93/4		40	35	5	1	7	3	0	1
Total			*40*	*35*	*5*	*1*	*7*	*3*	*0*	*1*

FLEMING Curtis — Middlesbrough

Fullname: Curtis Fleming
Debut:
DOB: 09-10-72 Manchester
Debut Goal:

Previous Clubs Details			Apps					Goals		
Club	Signed	Fee	Tot	Start	Sub	FA	FL	Lge	FA	FL
Middlesbrough	Aug-91	£50,000	113	101	12	7	9	0	0	0

FLITCROFT Gary — Manchester City

Fullname: Gary William Flitcroft
Debut: MANCHESTER CITY v Oldham Athletic 29/8/92
Debut Goal: Ipswich Town v MANCHESTER CITY 12/12/92
DOB: 07-12-76 Bolton

Previous Clubs Details			Apps					Goals		
Club	Signed	Fee	Tot	Start	Sub	FA	FL	Lge	FA	FL
Manchester C	Jul-91		90	84	6	6	10	13	1	0
Bury	Mar-92	Loan	12	12	0	0	0	0	0	0
FAPL Summary by Club										
Manchester City	92/3 to 94/5		90	84	6	10	11	13	1	0
Total			90	84	6	10	11	13	1	0

FLOWERS Tim — Blackburn Rovers

Fullname: Timothy David Flowers
Debut: SOUTHAMPTON v Tottenham Hotspur 15/8/92
Debut Goal: (Goalkeeper)
DOB: 04-02-71 Kenilworth

Previous Clubs Details			Apps					Goals		
Club	Signed	Fee	Tot	Start	Sub	FA	FL	Lge	FA	FL
Wolves	Aug-84		63	63	0	2	5	0	0	0
Southampton	Jun-86	£70,000	192	192	0	16	26	0	0	0
Swindon Tn	Mar-87	Loan	2	2	0	0	0	0	0	0
Swindon Tn	Nov-87	Loan	5	5	0	0	0	0	0	0
Blackburn R	Nov-93	£2.4m	68	68	0	6	4	0	0	0
FAPL Summary by Club										
Southampton	92/3 to 93/4		54	54	0	1	5	0	0	0
Blackburn R	93/4 to 94/5		68	68	0	2	8	0	0	0
Total			122	122	0	3	13	0	0	0

FLYNN Sean — Coventry City

Fullname: Sean Michael Flynn
Debut: COVENTRY CITY v Middlesbrough 15/8/92
Debut Goal: Arsenal v COVENTRY CITY 14/8/93
DOB: 14-03-72 Birmingham

Previous Clubs Details			Apps					Goals		
Club	Signed	Fee	Tot	Start	Sub	FA	FL	Lge	FA	FL
Coventry City	Dec-91	£20,000	97	90	7	3	5	9	0	1
FAPL Summary by Club										
Coventry City	92/3 to 94/5		75	69	6	3	5	7	0	1
Total			75	69	6	3	5	7	0	1

FORRESTER Jamie — Leeds United

Fullname: Jamie Forrester DOB: 02-11-78 Bradford
Debut: Nottingham Forest v LEEDS UNITED 21/3/93
Debut Goal:

Previous Clubs Details			*Apps*					*Goals*		
Club	Signed	Fee	Tot	Start	Sub	FA	FL	Lge	FA	FL
Auxerre (France)										
Leeds Utd	Oct-92	£120,000	9	7	2	2	0	0	0	0
Southend Utd	Sep-94	Loan								
FAPL Summary by Club										
Leeds Utd	92/3 to 93/4		9	7	2	2	0	0	0	0
Total			*9*	*7*	*2*	*2*	*0*	*0*	*0*	*0*

FOSTER John — Manchester City

Fullname: John Colin Foster DOB: 20-09-77 Manchester
Debut: Newcastle United v MANCHESTER CITY 1/1/94
Debut Goal:

Previous Clubs Details			*Apps*					*Goals*		
Club	Signed	Fee	Tot	Start	Sub	FA	FL	Lge	FA	FL
Manchester C	Jul-92		12	10	2	3	2	0	0	0
FAPL Summary by Club										
Manchester C	93/4 to 94/5		12	10	2	3	2	0	0	0
Total			*12*	*10*	*2*	*3*	*2*	*0*	*0*	*0*

FOWLER Robbie — Liverpool

Fullname: Robert Bernard Fowler DOB: 10-04-78 Liverpool
Debut: Chelsea v LIVERPOOL 25/9/93
Debut Goal: LIVERPOOL v Oldham Athletic 16/10/93

Previous Clubs Details			*Apps*					*Goals*		
Club	Signed	Fee	Tot	Start	Sub	FA	FL	Lge	FA	FL
Liverpool	Apr-92		70	69	1	8	13	37	0	10
FAPL Summary by Club										
Liverpool	93/4 to 94/5		70	69	1	8	13	37	0	10
Total			*70*	*69*	*1*	*8*	*13*	*37*	*0*	*10*

FOX Ruel — Newcastle United

Fullname: Ruel Adrian Fox DOB: 15-01-72 Ipswich
Debut: Arsenal v NORWICH CITY 15/8/92
Debut Goal: Arsenal v NORWICH CITY 15/8/92

Previous Clubs Details			*Apps*					*Goals*		
Club	Signed	Fee	Tot	Start	Sub	FA	FL	Lge	FA	FL
Norwich City	Jan-86		172	148	24	13	16	22	0	3
Newcastle Utd	Feb-94	£2.25m	54	54	0	5	2	12	0	1

FREESTONE Chris   Middlesbrough

Fullname: Christopher Freestone   DOB:
Debut: Debut Goal:

Previous Clubs Details			*Apps*				*Goals*		
Club	Signed	Fee	Tot	Start	Sub	FA	FL	Lge	FA	FL
Arnold Town										
Middlesbrough	Nov-94	£10,000	1	0	1	0	0	0	0	0

FUCHS Uwe   Middlesbrough

Fullname: Uwe Fuchs   DOB:
Debut: Debut Goal:

Previous Clubs Details			*Apps*				*Goals*		
Club	Signed	Fee	Tot	Start	Sub	FA	FL	Lge	FA	FL
Kaiserslautern										
Middlesbrough	Jan-95	Loan	15	13	2	0	0	9	0	0

FURLONG Paul   Chelsea

Fullname: Paul Anthony Furlong   DOB: 02-10-72 Wood Green
Debut: CHELSEA v Norwich City 20/8/94
Debut Goal: CHELSEA v Norwich City 20/8/94

Previous Clubs Details			*Apps*				*Goals*		
Club	Signed	Fee	Tot	Start	Sub	FA	FL	Lge	FA	FL
Coventry City	Jul-91		37	27	10	2	4	4	0	1
Watford	Jul-92	£250,000	79	79	0	2	7	39	0	4
Chelsea	May-94	£2.3m	36	30	6	2	2	10	0	0

FAPL Summary by Club

Chelsea	94/5 to 93/4	36	30	6	2	2	10	0	0
Total		*36*	*30*	*6*	*2*	*2*	*10*	*0*	*0*

GALLACHER Kevin   Blackburn Rovers

Fullname: Kevin William Gallacher DOB: 24-11-70 Clydebank
Debut: COVENTRY CITY v Blackburn Rovers 29/8/92
Debut Goal: Oldham Athletic v COVENTRY CITY 5/9/92

Previous Clubs Details			*Apps*				*Goals*		
Club	Signed	Fee	Tot	Start	Sub	FA	FL	Lge	FA	FL
Coventry City	Jan-90		100	99	1	4	11	28	0	7
Blackburn R	Mar-93	£1.6m	40	37	3	4	4	13	1	0

FAPL Summary by Club

Coventry City	92/3 to 93/4	20	19	1	1	2	6	0	0
Blackburn R	92/3 to 94/5	40	37	3	4	4	13	1	0
Total		*60*	*56*	*4*	*5*	*6*	*19*	*1*	*0*

GALLEN Kevin   QPR

Fullname: Kevin Gallen   DOB: 22-09-79 Chiswick
Debut: Manchester United v QPR 20/8/94
Debut Goal: QPR v Sheffield Wednesday 24/8/94

Previous Clubs Details			*Apps*					*Goals*		
Club	Signed	Fee	Tot	Start	Sub	FA	FL	Lge	FA	FL
QPR	Sep-92	Trainee	37	31	6	4	2	10	1	1
FAPL Summary by Club										
QPR	94/5 to 93/4		37	31	6	4	2	10	1	1
Total			*37*	*31*	*6*	*4*	*2*	*10*	*1*	*1*

GAUDINO Maurizio   Manchester City

Fullname: Maurizio Gaudino   DOB:
Debut: MANCHESTER CITY v Blackburn Rovers 26/12/94
Debut Goal: MANCHESTER CITY v Chelsea 8/3/95

Previous Clubs Details			*Apps*					*Goals*		
Club	Signed	Fee	Tot	Start	Sub	FA	FL	Lge	FA	FL
Eintracht Frankfurt										
Manchester C	Dec-94	Loan	20	17	3	3	2	3	1	0
FAPL Summary by Club										
Manchester C	94/5		20	17	3	3	2	3	1	0
Total			*20*	*17*	*3*	*3*	*2*	*3*	*1*	*0*

GAYLE Marcus   Wimbledon

Fullname: Marcus A Gayle   DOB: 28-09-74 Hammersmith
Debut: WIMBLEDON v Leeds United 26/3/94
Debut Goal: Nottingham Forest v WIMBLEDON 17/10/94

Previous Clubs Details			*Apps*					*Goals*		
Club	Signed	Fee	Tot	Start	Sub	FA	FL	Lge	FA	FL
Brentford	Jul-89		156	118	38	8	9	22	2	0
Wimbledon	Mar-94	£250,000	33	32	1	0	2	2	0	1
FAPL Summary by Club										
Wimbledon	93/4 to 94/5		33	32	1	0	2	2	0	1
Total			*33*	*32*	*1*	*0*	*2*	*2*	*0*	*1*

GEMMILL Scot   Nottingham Forest

Fullname: Scot Gemmill   DOB: 03-01-75 Paisley
Debut: NOTTINGHAM FOREST v Liverpool 16/8/92
Debut Goal: Tottenham Hotspur v NOTTM FOREST 28/10/92

Previous Clubs Details			*Apps*					*Goals*		
Club	Signed	Fee	Tot	Start	Sub	FA	FL	Lge	FA	FL
N Forest	Jan-90		126	123	3	10	22	22	1	3
FAPL Summary by Club										
N Forest	92/3 to 94/5		52	52	0	6	6	2	1	0
Total			*52*	*52*	*0*	*6*	*6*	*2*	*1*	*0*

GIGGS Ryan   Manchester United

Fullname: Ryan Joseph Giggs   DOB: 30-11-77 Cardiff
Debut: Sheffield United v MANCHESTER UNITED 15/8/92
Debut Goal: Nottingham Forest v MANCHESTER UNITED 29/8/92

Previous Clubs Details			*Apps*				*Goals*		
Club	Signed	Fee	Tot	Start	Sub	FA	FL	Lge	FA	FL
Manchester Utd	Dec-90		144	134	10	19	25	26	4	7
FAPL Summary by Club										
Manchester Utd	92/3 to 94/5		108	101	7	16	10	23	4	3
Total			*108*	*101*	*7*	*16*	*10*	*23*	*4*	*3*

GILLESPIE Keith   Newcastle United

Fullname: Keith Gillespie   DOB: 19-02-79 Bangor
Debut: Sheffield Wednesday v MANCHESTER UTD 8/10/94
Debut Goal: MANCHESTER UTD v Newcastle Utd 29/10/94 as sub

Previous Clubs Details			*Apps*				*Goals*		
Club	Signed	Fee	Tot	Start	Sub	FA	FL	Lge	FA	FL
Manchester Utd	Feb-93	Trainee	0	0	0	2	3	0	1	0
Wigan Ath	Sep-93	Loan	8	8	0	0	0	4	0	0
Newcastle Utd	Jan-95	£1m +	17	15	2	3	0	2	2	0
FAPL Summary by Club										
Manchester Utd	94/5		9	3	6	0	3	1	0	0
Newcastle Utd	94/5		17	15	2	3	0	2	2	0
Total			*26*	*18*	*8*	*3*	*3*	*3*	*2*	*0*

GINOLA David   Newcastle United

Fullname: David Ginola   DOB:
Debut: Debut Goal:

Previous Clubs Details			*Apps*				*Goals*		
Club	Signed	Fee	Tot	Start	Sub	FA	FL	Lge	FA	FL
Paris St.Germain										
Newcastle Utd	Jul-95	£2.5m								

GOODMAN Jon   Wimbledon

Fullname: Jonathan Goodman   DOB: 03-06-75 Walthamstow
Debut: WIMBLEDON v Newcastle United 19/11/94
Debut Goal: Ipswich Town v WIMBLEDON 16/12/94

Previous Clubs Details			*Apps*				*Goals*		
Club	Signed	Fee	Tot	Start	Sub	FA	FL	Lge	FA	FL
Bromley										
Millwall	Aug-90	£50,000	94	82	12	6	6	27	0	0
Wimbledon	Nov-94	£1.3m +								
FAPL Summary by Club										
Wimbledon	94/5		19	13	6	1	0	4	0	0
Total			*19*	*13*	*6*	*1*	*0*	*4*	*0*	*0*

GOULD Jonathon — Coventry City

Fullname: Jonathon A Gould   DOB: 19-07-72 London
Debut: COVENTRY CITY v Liverpool 19/12/92
Debut Goal: (Goalkeeper)

Previous Clubs Details

Club	Signed	Fee	Tot	Start	Sub	FA	FL	Lge	FA	FL
Halifax Town	Jul-90	Free	32	32	0	5	2	0	0	0
Coventry City	Jul-92	Free	25	25	0	0	0	0	0	0
FAPL Summary by Club										
Coventry City	92/3 to 94/5		25	25	0	0	0	0	0	0
Total			*25*	*25*	*0*	*0*	*0*	*0*	*0*	*0*

GRANT Tony — Everton

Fullname: Anthony Grant   DOB: 15-11-78 Liverpool
Debut: Newcastle United v EVERTON 1/2/95 as sub
Debut Goal:

Previous Clubs Details

Club	Signed	Fee	Tot	Start	Sub	FA	FL	Lge	FA	FL
Everton			5	1	4	0	0	0	0	0
FAPL Summary by Club										
Everton	94/5		5	1	4	0	0	0	0	0
Total			*5*	*1*	*4*	*0*	*0*	*0*	*0*	*0*

GREEN Scott — Bolton Wanderers

Fullname: Scott Green   DOB: 16-01-74 Walsall
Debut: Debut Goal:

Previous Clubs Details

Club	Signed	Fee	Tot	Start	Sub	FA	FL	Lge	FA	FL
Derby County	Jul-88	Trainee								
Bolton Wders	Mar-90	£50,000	177	133	44	18	18	20	2	1

GRIFFITHS Carl — Manchester City

Fullname: Carl B Griffiths   DOB: 17-07-75 Welshpool
Debut: West Ham United v MANCHESTER CITY 1/11/93
Debut Goal: Leeds United v MANCHESTER CITY 4/12/93

Previous Clubs Details

Club	Signed	Fee	Tot	Start	Sub	FA	FL	Lge	FA	FL
Shrewsbury T	Sep-88		143	110	33	6	11	53	2	3
Manchester C	Oct-93	£500,000	7	18	5	2	1	4	0	0
FAPL Summary by Club										
Manchester C	93/4 to 94/5		18	11	7	2	1	0	0	0
Total			*18*	*11*	*7*	*2*	*1*	*0*	*0*	*0*

GROBBELAAR Bruce — Southampton

Fullname: Bruce David Grobbelaar   DOB: 17-10-61 Durban, SA
Debut: LIVERPOOL v Wimbledon 26/9/92

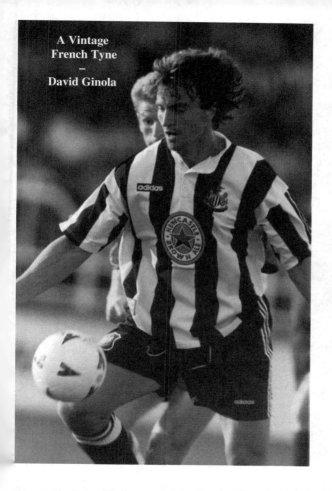

A Vintage
French Tyne
–
David Ginola

Debut Goal: (Goalkeeper)

Previous Clubs Details

Club	Signed	Fee	Apps					Goals		
			Tot	Start	Sub	FA	FL	Lge	FA	FL
Crewe Alex	Dec-79		24	24	0	0	0	0	0	0
Vancouver	May-80									
Liverpool	Mar-81	£250,000	440	440	0	62	70	0	0	0
Stoke City	Mar-93	Loan	4	4	0	0	0	0	0	0
Southampton	Aug-94	£250,000	30	30	0	5	3	0	0	0
Southampton	94/5		30	30	0	5	3	0	0	0

FAPL Summary by Club

Liverpool	92/3 to 93/4		34	34	0	2	7	0	0	0
Southampton	94/5		30	30	0	5	3	0	0	0
Total			*64*	*64*	*0*	*7*	*10*	*0*	*0*	*0*

GULLIT Ruud   Chelsea
Fullname: Dil Ruud Gullit   DOB: 02-09-66 Amsterdam
Debut: Debut Goal:

Previous Clubs Details

Club	Signed	Fee	Apps					Goals		
			Tot	Start	Sub	FA	FL	Lge	FA	FL
Haarlem	Jul-79		91	91				32		
Feyenoord	Jul-82		85	85				30		
PSV	Jul-85		68	68				46		
Milan	Jul-87		117	117				35		
Sampdoria	Jul-93									
Milan	Jul-94									
Sampdoria	Dec-94									
Chelsea	May-95	£1m								

HAALAND Alf-Inge   Nottingham Forest
Fullname: Alf-Inge Haaland   DOB: 24-11-76 Stavanger, Norway
Debut: Southampton v NOTTINGHAM FOREST 17/9/94
Debut Goal: NOTTINGHAM FOREST v Ipswich Town 10/12/94

Previous Clubs Details

Club	Signed	Fee	Apps					Goals		
			Tot	Start	Sub	FA	FL	Lge	FA	FL
N Forest			23	21	2	1	1	1	0	0

FAPL Summary by Club

N Forest	94/5 to 93/4		20	18	2	1	1	1	0	0
Total			*20*	*18*	*2*	*1*	*1*	*1*	*0*	*0*

HALL Marcus   Coventry City
Fullname: Marcus Hall   DOB:
Debut: COVENTRY CITY v Tottenham Hotspur 31/12/94 as sub
Debut Goal:

Previous Clubs Details

Club	Signed	Fee	Apps					Goals		
			Tot	Start	Sub	FA	FL	Lge	FA	FL
Coventry City			5	2	3	0	0	0	0	0

		Coventry City	94/5 to 93/4	5	2	3	0	0		0	0	0
		Total		*5*	*2*	*3*	*0*	*0*		*0*	*0*	*0*

HALL Gareth   Chelsea

Fullname: Gareth David Hall   DOB: 21-03-73 Croydon
Debut: CHELSEA v Oldham Athletic 15/8/92
Debut Goal: CHELSEA v Ipswich Town 17/10/92

Previous Clubs Details			*Apps*					*Goals*			
Club	Signed	Fee	Tot	Start	Sub	FA	FL	Lge	FA	FL	
Chelsea	May-86		133	115	18	6	13	3	0	0	
FAPL Summary by Club											
Chelsea	92/3 to 94/5		50	44	6	0	6	2	0	0	
Total			*50*	*44*	*6*	*0*	*6*	*2*	*0*	*0*	

HALL Richard   Southampton

Fullname: Richard Anthony Hall   DOB: 15-03-76 Ipswich
Debut: SOUTHAMPTON v Tottenham Hotspur 15/8/92
Debut Goal: Oldham Athletic v SOUTHAMPTON 31/10/92

Previous Clubs Details			*Apps*					*Goals*			
Club	Signed	Fee	Tot	Start	Sub	FA	FL	Lge	FA	FL	
Scunthorpe Utd	Mar-90		22	22	0	3	2	3	0	0	
Southampton	Feb-91	£200,000	96	89	7	7	10	10	2	0	
FAPL Summary by Club											
Southampton	92/3 to 94/5		69	68	1	5	3	8	0	0	
Total			*69*	*68*	*1*	*5*	*3*	*8*	*0*	*0*	

HARFORD Mick   Wimbledon

Fullname: Michael G Harford   DOB: 13-05-63 Sunderland
Debut: CHELSEA v Oldham Athletic 15/8/92
Debut Goal: CHELSEA v Oldham Athletic 15/8/92

Previous Clubs Details			*Apps*					*Goals*			
Club	Signed	Fee	Tot	Start	Sub	FA	FL	Lge	FA	FL	
Lincoln City	Jul-77		115	109	6	3	8	41	0	5	
Newcastle Utd	Dec-80	£180,000	19	18	1	0	0	4	0	0	
Bristol City	Aug-81	£160,000	30	30	0	5	5	11	2	1	
Birmingham C	Mar-82	£100,000	92	92	0	7	10	25	2	6	
Luton Town	Dec-84	£250,000	139	135	4	27	16	57	11	10	
Derby County	Jan-90	£450,000	58	58	0	1	7	15	0	3	
Luton Town	Sep-91	£325,000	29	29	0	0	1	12	0	0	
Chelsea	Aug-92	£300,000	28	27	1	5	1	9	2	0	
Sunderland	Mar-93	£250,000	11	10	1	0	0	2	0	0	
Coventry City	Jul-93	£200,000	0	0	1	0	0	1	0	0	
Wimbledon	Aug-94	£70,000	27	17	10	4	3	6	1	1	

FAPL Summary by Club

		Tot	Start	Sub	FA	FL	Lge	FA	FL
Chelsea	92/3 to 94/5	28	27	1	1	5	9	0	2
Coventry City	93/4 to 93/4	1	0	1	0	0	1	0	0
Wimbledon	94/5	27	17	10	4	3	6	1	1
Total		*56*	*44*	*12*	*5*	*8*	*16*	*1*	*3*

HARKNESS Steve   Liverpool

Fullname: Steven Harkness   DOB: 28-08-75 Carlisle
Debut: Ipswich Town v LIVERPOOL 25/8/92
Debut Goal: LIVERPOOL v Tottenham Hotspur 8/5/93

Previous Clubs Details

			Apps				Goals		
Club	Signed	Fee	Tot	Start	Sub	FA	FL	Lge	FA	FL
Carlisle Utd	Mar-89		13	12	1	0	0	0	0	0
Liverpool	Jul-89	£75,000	40	34	6	2	5	2	0	0
Huddersfield T	Sep-93	Loan	5	5	0	0	0	0	0	0
Southend Utd	Feb-95	Loan								

FAPL Summary by Club

		Tot	Start	Sub	FA	FL	Lge	FA	FL
Liverpool	92/3 to 94/5	29	27	2	0	3	2	0	0
Total		*29*	*27*	*2*	*0*	*3*	*2*	*0*	*0*

HARTSON John   Arsenal

Fullname: John Hartson   DOB: 06-04-79 Swansea
Debut: ARSENAL v Everton 14/1/95
Debut Goal: Coventry City v ARSENAL 21/1/95

Previous Clubs Details

			Apps				Goals		
Club	Signed	Fee	Tot	Start	Sub	FA	FL	Lge	FA	FL
Luton Town	Dec-92		54	32	22	6	1	11	1	1
Arsenal	Jan-95	£2.5m	15	14	1	0	0	7	0	0

FAPL Summary by Club

		Tot	Start	Sub	FA	FL	Lge	FA	FL
Arsenal	94/5	15	14	1	0	0	7	0	0
Total		*15*	*14*	*1*	*0*	*0*	*7*	*0*	*0*

HAZARD Micky   Tottenham Hotspur

Fullname: Michael Hazard   DOB: 06-02-64 Sunderland
Debut: SWINDON TOWN v Oldham Athletic 18/8/93
Debut Goal: TOTTENHAM HOTSPUR v Liverpool 18/12/93

Previous Clubs Details

			Apps				Goals		
Club	Signed	Fee	Tot	Start	Sub	FA	FL	Lge	FA	FL
Tottenham H	Feb-78		91	73	18	10	14	13	2	5
Chelsea	Sep-85	£310,000	81	78	3	6	10	9	1	1
Portsmouth	Jan-90	£100,000	8	8	0	0	0	1	0	0
Swindon Town	Sep-90	£130,000	119	112	7	7	12	17	0	1
Tottenham H	Nov-93	£50,000	28	15	13	5	2	2	2	1

Swindon Town	93/4 to 94/5	9	7	2	0	2	0	0	0
Tottenham H	93/4 to 94/5	28	15	13	2	2	2	0	0
Total		*37*	*22*	*15*	*2*	*4*	*2*	*0*	*0*

HEANEY Neil   Southampton

Fullname: Neil Andrew Heaney   DOB: 04-11-75 Middlesbrough
Debut: ARSENAL v Liverpool 31/1/93
Debut Goal: Newcastle United v SOUTHAMPTON 22/3/95 as sub

Previous Clubs Details			Apps				Goals		
Club	Signed	Fee	Tot	Start	Sub	FA	FL	Lge	FA	FL
Arsenal	Nov-89		7	4	3	0	1	0	0	0
Hartlepool Utd	Jan-91	Loan	3	2	1	0	0	0	0	0
Cambridge Utd	Jan-92	Loan	13	9	4	1	0	2	0	0
Southampton	Mar-94	£300,000	36	23	13	5	2	2	2	1

FAPL Summary by Club									
Arsenal	92/3 to 93/4	6	4	2	0	1	0	0	0
Southampton	93/4 to 94/5	42	25	17	5	2	2	2	1
Total		*48*	*29*	*19*	*5*	*3*	*2*	*2*	*1*

HELDER Glenn   Arsenal

Fullname: Glenn Helder   DOB:
Debut: ARSENAL v Nottingham Forest 21/2/95
Debut Goal:

Previous Clubs Details			Apps				Goals		
Club	Signed	Fee	Tot	Start	Sub	FA	FL	Lge	FA	FL
Vitesse Arnhem										
Arsenal	Feb-95	£2.3m	13	12	1	0	0	0	0	0

FAPL Summary by Club									
Arsenal	94/5 to 93/4	13	12	1	0	0	0	0	0
Total		*13*	*12*	*1*	*0*	*0*	*0*	*0*	*0*

HENDRIE John   Middlesbrough

Fullname: John Hendrie   DOB: 25-10-67 Lennoxtown
Debut: Coventry City v MIDDLESBROUGH 15/8/92
Debut Goal: MIDDLESBROUGH v Leeds United 22/8/92

Previous Clubs Details			Apps				Goals		
Club	Signed	Fee	Tot	Start	Sub	FA	FL	Lge	FA	FL
Coventry City	May-81	Amateur	21	15	6	0	2	2	0	0
Hereford Utd	Jan-84	Loan	0	6	0	0	0	0	0	0
Bradford City	Jul-84	Free	173	173	0	11	17	46	6	4
Newcastle Utd	Jun-88	£500,000	34	34	0	4	2	4	0	1
Leeds Utd	Jun-89	£600,000	27	22	5	1	1	5	0	0
Middlesbrough	Jul-90	£550,000	179	174	5	12	20	44	2	6

Middlesbrough	92/3	32	31	1		9
Total		*32*	*31*	*1*		*9*

HENDRY Colin — Blackburn Rovers

Fullname: Edward Colin James Hendry   DOB: 08-12-69 Keith
Debut: Crystal Palace v BLACKBURN ROVERS 15/8/92
Debut Goal: BLACKBURN ROVERS v Coventry City 26/1/93

Previous Clubs Details

			Apps				Goals		
Club	Signed	Fee	Tot	Start	Sub	FA	FL	Lge	FA	FL
Blackburn R	Mar-87	£30,000	102	99	3	3	4	22	0	0
Manchester C	Nov-89	£700,000	63	57	6	5	5	5	2	1
Blackburn R	Nov-91	£700,000	129	124	5	10	16	9	0	0

FAPL Summary by Club

Blackburn R	92/3 to 94/5	102	101	1	9	16	5	0	0
Total		*102*	*101*	*1*	*9*	*16*	*5*	*0*	*0*

HIGNETT Craig — Middlesbrough

Fullname: Craig Hignett   DOB: 13-01-74 Prescot
Debut: Oldham Athletic v MIDDLESBROUGH 28/11/92
Debut Goal: Aston Villa v MIDDLESBROUGH 17/1/93

Previous Clubs Details

			Apps				Goals		
Club	Signed	Fee	Tot	Start	Sub	FA	FL	Lge	FA	FL
Liverpool (T)										
Crewe Alex	May-88	Free	121	108	13	12	10	42	8	4
Middlesbrough	Nov-92	£500,000	76	62	14	3	7	17	0	6

FAPL Summary by Club

Middlesbrough	92/3	21	18	3		4
Total		*21*	*18*	*3*		*4*

HILL Danny — Tottenham Hotspur

Fullname: Daniel Hill   DOB: 02-10-77 Enfield
Debut: Chelsea v TOTTENHAM HOTSPUR 23/3/93 as sub
Debut Goal:

Previous Clubs Details

			Apps				Goals		
Club	Signed	Fee	Tot	Start	Sub	FA	FL	Lge	FA	FL
Tottenham H	Sep-92		10	4	6	0	2	0	0	0

FAPL Summary by Club

Tottenham H	92/3 to 94/5	10	4	6	0	2	0	0	0
Total		*10*	*4*	*6*	*0*	*2*	*0*	*0*	*0*

HILL Andy — Manchester City

Fullname: Andrew Rowland Hill   DOB: 21-01-69 Maltby
Debut: MANCHESTER CITY v QPR 17/8/92
Debut Goal: MANCHESTER CITY v Leeds United 7/11/92

Previous Clubs Details			*Apps*					*Goals*		
Club	Signed	Fee	Tot	Start	Sub	FA	FL	Lge	FA	FL
Manchester Utd	Jan-83		0	0	0	0	0	0	0	0
Bury	Jul-84		264	264	0	12	22	10	0	1
Manchester C	Dec-90	£200,000	98	91	7	3	11	6	0	0
FAPL Summary by Club										
Manchester C	92/3 to 94/5		54	48	6	3	6	1	0	0
Total			*54*	*48*	*6*	*3*	*6*	*1*	*0*	*0*

HILLIER David Arsenal

HILLIER David   **Arsenal**

Fullname: David Hillier   DOB: 20-12-73 Blackheath
Debut: ARSENAL v Norwich City 15/8/92
Debut Goal: ARSENAL v Sheffield United 9/1/93

Previous Clubs Details			*Apps*					*Goals*		
Club	Signed	Fee	Tot	Start	Sub	FA	FL	Lge	FA	FL
Arsenal	Feb-88		97	79	18	15	13	2	0	0
FAPL Summary by Club										
Arsenal	92/3 to 94/5		54	43	11	10	11	1	0	0
Total			*54*	*43*	*11*	*10*	*11*	*1*	*0*	*0*

HINCHCLIFFE Andy   **Everton**

Fullname: Andrew George Hinchcliffe   DOB: 06-02-73 Manchester
Debut: EVERTON v Sheffield Wednesday 15/8/92
Debut Goal: EVERTON v Nottingham Forest 13/3/93

Previous Clubs Details			*Apps*					*Goals*		
Club	Signed	Fee	Tot	Start	Sub	FA	FL	Lge	FA	FL
Manchester C	Jun-86		112	107	5	12	11	8	1	1
Everton	Jul-90	£800,000	247	224	23	17	21	86	7	10
FAPL Summary by Club										
Everton	92/3 to 94/5		80	78	2	6	11	3	1	0
Total			*80*	*78*	*2*	*6*	*11*	*3*	*1*	*0*

HIRST David   **Sheffield Wednesday**

Fullname: David Eric Hirst   DOB: 08-12-71 Cudworth
Debut: Everton v SHEFFIELD WEDNESDAY 15/8/92
Debut Goal: SHEFFIELD WED v Nottingham Forest 19/8/92

Previous Clubs Details			*Apps*					*Goals*		
Club	Signed	Fee	Tot	Start	Sub	FA	FL	Lge	FA	FL
Barnsley	Nov-85		28	26	2	0	1	9	0	0
Sheffield W	Aug-86	£200,000	233	209	24	16	31	87	6	10
FAPL Summary by Club										
Sheffield W	92/3 to 94/5		44	41	3	6	9	15	1	3
Total			*44*	*41*	*3*	*6*	*9*	*15*	*1*	*3*

HITCHCOCK Kevin
Chelsea

Fullname: Kevin Joseph Hitchcock DOB: 06-10-66 Canning Town
Debut: Manchester City v CHELSEA 20/9/92
Debut Goal:

Previous Clubs Details

Club	Signed	Fee	Apps					Goals		
			Tot	Start	Sub	FA	FL	Lge	FA	FL
N Forest	Aug-83	£15,000	0	0	0	0	0	0	0	0
Mansfield T	Feb-84	Loan	14	14	0	0	0	0	0	0
Mansfield T	Jun-84	£140,000	168	168	0	10	12	0	0	0
Chelsea	Mar-88	£250,000	69	68	1	5	8	0	0	0
Northampton T	Dec-90	Loan	17	17	0	0	0	0	0	0
West Ham Utd	Mar-93	Loan								
FAPL Summary by Club										
Chelsea	92/3 to 94/5		34	33	1	1	6	0	0	0
Total			*34*	*33*	*1*	*1*	*6*	*0*	*0*	*0*

HODGE Steve
QPR

Fullname: Stephen Brian Hodge DOB: 26-10-66 Nottingham
Debut: LEEDS UNITED v Wimbledon 15/8/92 as sub
Debut Goal: LEEDS UNITED v Aston Villa 13/9/93

Previous Clubs Details

Club	Signed	Fee	Apps					Goals		
			Tot	Start	Sub	FA	FL	Lge	FA	FL
N Forest	Oct-80		123	122	1	6	10	30	0	2
Aston Villa	Aug-85	£450,000	53	53	0	4	12	12	1	3
Tottenham H	Dec-86	£650,000	45	44	1	7	2	7	2	0
N Forest	Aug-88	£550,000	82	79	3	12	21	20	2	6
Leeds Utd	Jul-91	£900,000	54	28	26	3	7	10	0	0
Derby County	Aug-94	Loan								
QPR	Oct-94	£300,000	15	15	0	1	0	0	0	0
FAPL Summary by Club										
Leeds Utd	92/3 to 93/4		31	16	15	2	2	3	0	0
QPR	94/5		15	15	0	1	0	0	0	0
Total			*46*	*31*	*15*	*3*	*2*	*3*	*0*	*0*

HOLDSWORTH Dean
Wimbledon

Fullname: Dean C Holdsworth DOB: 09-11-72 London
Debut: Leeds United v WIMBLEDON 15/8/92
Debut Goal: WIMBLEDON v Coventry City 22/8/92

Previous Clubs Details

Club	Signed	Fee	Apps					Goals		
			Tot	Start	Sub	FA	FL	Lge	FA	FL
Watford	Nov-86		16	2	14	0	0	3	0	0
Carlisle Utd	Feb-88	Loan	4	4	0	0	0	1	0	0
Port Vale	Mar-88	Loan	6	6	0	0	0	2	0	0
Swansea City	Aug-88	Loan	5	4	1	0	0	1	0	0

Club	Signed	Fee	Tot	Start	Sub	FA	FL	Lge	FA	FL
Brentford	Oct-88	Loan	7	2	5	0	0	1	0	0
Brentford	Sep-89	£125,000	110	106	4	6	8	53	7	6
Wimbledon	Jul-92	£720,000	106	103	3	9	11	43	3	5
FAPL Summary by Club										
Wimbledon	92/3 to 94/5		106	103	3	9	11	43	3	5
Total			*106*	*103*	*3*	*9*	*11*	*43*	*3*	*5*

HOLLAND Chris   Newcastle United

Fullname: Christopher J Holland
Debut:
DOB: 12-09-83 Whalley
Debut Goal:

Previous Clubs Details			*Apps*					*Goals*		
Club	Signed	Fee	Tot	Start	Sub	FA	FL	Lge	FA	FL
Preston NE			2	0	2	0	0	0	0	0
Newcastle Utd	Jan-94	£100,000	0	0	0	0	0	0	0	0

HOLLOWAY Ian   QPR

Fullname: Ian Scott Holloway
Debut: Manchester City v QPR 17/8/92
DOB: 13-03-67 Kingswood
Debut Goal: QPR v Tottenham Hotspur 3/10/92

Previous Clubs Details			*Apps*					*Goals*		
Club	Signed	Fee	Tot	Start	Sub	FA	FL	Lge	FA	FL
Bristol R	Mar-81		111	104	7	8	10	14	2	1
Wimbledon	Jul-85	£35,000	19	19	0	1	3	2	0	0
Brentford	Mar-86	£25,000	30	27	3	3	2	2	0	0
Torquay Utd	Jan-87	Loan	5	5	0	0	0	0	0	0
Bristol R	Aug-87	£10,000	179	179	0	10	5	26	1	0
QPR	Aug-91	£230,000	117	101	16	7	11	3	1	0
FAPL Summary by Club										
QPR	92/3 to 94/5		80	70	10	6	8	3	1	0
Total			*80*	*70*	*10*	*6*	*8*	*3*	*1*	*0*

HOLMES Paul   Everton

Fullname: Paul Holmes
Debut: EVERTON v Ipswich Town 24/3/92
DOB: 19-02-72 Wortley
Debut Goal:

Previous Clubs Details			*Apps*					*Goals*		
Club	Signed	Fee	Tot	Start	Sub	FA	FL	Lge	FA	FL
Doncaster R	Feb-86		47	45	2	4	0	1	1	0
Torquay Utd	Aug-88	£6,000	138	127	11	11	9	4	0	0
Birmingham C	Jun-92		12	12	0	1	0	0	0	0
Everton	Mar-93	£100,000	19	19	0	1	4	0	0	0
FAPL Summary by Club										
Everton	92/3 to 94/5		20	20	0	1	5	0	0	0
Total			*20*	*20*	*0*	*1*	*5*	*0*	*0*	*0*

HOLMES Mattie
West Ham United

Fullname: Matthew J Holmes   DOB: 02-08-73 Luton
Debut: WEST HAM UNITED v Wimbledon 14/8/93
Debut Goal: WEST HAM UNITED v Manchester City 1/11/93

Previous Clubs Details

Club	Signed	Fee	Tot	Start	Sub	FA	FL	Lge	FA	FL
Bournemouth	Sep-88		114	105	9	10	7	8	0	0
Cardiff City	Mar-89	Loan	1	0	1	0	0	0	0	0
West Ham Utd	Aug-92	£40,000	76	63	13	6	4	5	0	0

FAPL Summary by Club

| West Ham Utd | 93/4 to 94/5 | | 58 | 57 | 1 | 5 | 4 | 4 | 0 | 0 |
| *Total* | | | *58* | *57* | *1* | *5* | *4* | *4* | *0* | *0* |

HOOPER Mike
Newcastle United

Fullname: Michael Dudley Hooper   DOB: 11-02-68 Bristol
Debut: LIVERPOOL v Middlesbrough 7/11/92
Debut Goal: (Goalkeeper)

Previous Clubs Details

Club	Signed	Fee	Tot	Start	Sub	FA	FL	Lge	FA	FL
Bristol City	Jan-84		1	1	0	1	0	0	0	0
Wrexham	Feb-85		34	34	0	0	4	0	0	0
Liverpool	Oct-85	£40,000	51	50	1	5	10	0	0	0
Leicester City	Sep-90	Loan	14	14	0	0	0	0	0	0
Newcastle Utd	Sep-93	£550,000	25	23	2	3	2	0	0	0

FAPL Summary by Club

Liverpool	92/3 to 94/5		9	8	1	2	3	0	0	0
Newcastle Utd	94/5		6	4	2	0	0	0	0	0
Total			*15*	*12*	*3*	*2*	*3*	*0*	*0*	*0*

HOPKIN David
Chelsea

Fullname: David Hopkin   DOB: 22-08-74 Greenock
Debut: Liverpool v CHELSEA 10/2/92
Debut Goal: Everton v CHELSEA 3/5/95

Previous Clubs Details

Club	Signed	Fee	Tot	Start	Sub	FA	FL	Lge	FA	FL
Morton			18					0		
Chelsea	Sep-92	£300,000	40	21	19	5	1	2	0	0

FAPL Summary by Club

| Chelsea | 92/3 to 94/5 | | 40 | 21 | 19 | 5 | 1 | 1 | 0 | 0 |
| *Total* | | | *40* | *21* | *19* | *5* | *1* | *1* | *0* | *0* |

HORNE Barry
Everton

Fullname: Barry Horne   DOB: 19-05-66 St Asaph
Debut: EVERTON v Sheffield Wednesday 15/8/92
Debut Goal: EVERTON v Sheffield Wednesday 15/8/92

Previous Clubs Details			Apps					Goals		
Club	Signed	Fee	Tot	Start	Sub	FA	FL	Lge	FA	FL
Wrexham	Jun-84		136	136	0	7	10	17	2	1
Portsmouth	Jul-87	£60,000	70	66	4	6	3	7	0	0
Southampton	Mar-89	£700,000	112	111	1	15	17	6	3	3
Everton	Aug-92	£695,000	97	93	4	8	11	2	0	0
FAPL Summary by Club										
Everton	92/3 to 94/5		97	93	4	8	10	2	0	0
Total			*97*	*93*	*4*	*8*	*10*	*2*	*0*	*0*

HOTTIGER Marc — Newcastle United

Fullname: Marc Hottiger

Debut: Leicester City v NEWCASTLE UNITED 21/8/94

DOB: 08-11-71 Lausanne

Debut Goal: Chelsea v NEWCASTLE UNITED 1/4/95

Previous Clubs Details			Apps					Goals		
Club	Signed	Fee	Tot	Start	Sub	FA	FL	Lge	FA	FL
Sion										
Newcastle Utd	Aug-94	£600,000	38	38	0	4	5	1	1	0
FAPL Summary by Club										
Newcastle Utd	94/5		38	38	0	4	5	1	1	0
Total			*38*	*38*	*0*	*4*	*5*	*1*	*1*	*0*

HOWE Stephen — Nottingham Forest

Fullname: Stephen Robert Howe

Debut:

DOB: 07-01-77 Annitsford

Debut Goal:

Previous Clubs Details			Apps					Goals		
Club	Signed	Fee	Tot	Start	Sub	FA	FL	Lge	FA	FL
N Forest			4	2	2	0	1	0	0	0
Kettering Tn	Dec-94	Loan								

HOWELLS David — Tottenham Hotspur

Fullname: David G Howells

Debut: Southampton v TOTTENHAM HOTSPUR 15/8/92

DOB: 16-12-71 Guildford

Debut Goal: Blackburn Rovers v TOTTENHAM HOTSPUR 7/11/92

Previous Clubs Details			Apps					Goals		
Club	Signed	Fee	Tot	Start	Sub	FA	FL	Lge	FA	FL
Tottenham H	Jan-85		196	163	33	18	24	17	1	3
FAPL Summary by Club										
Tottenham H	92/3 to 94/5		62	57	5	9	5	3	0	1
Total			*62*	*57*	*5*	*9*	*5*	*3*	*0*	*1*

HOWEY Steve — Newcastle United

Fullname: Stephen N Howey

Debut: NEWCASTLE UNITED v Tottenham Hotspur 14/8/93

DOB: 27-10-75 Sunderland

Debut Goal: NEWCASTLE UNITED v Leicester City 10/12/94

Previous Clubs Details			*Apps*					*Goals*		
Club	Signed	Fee	Tot	Start	Sub	FA	FL	Lge	FA	FL
Newcastle Utd	Dec-89		118	99	19	12	11	4	0	1
FAPL Summary by Club										
Newcastle Utd	93/4 to 94/5		44	42	2	4	6	1	0	0
Total			*44*	*42*	*2*	*4*	*6*	*1*	*0*	*0*

HUGHES Stephen   Arsenal

Fullname: Stephen Hughes   DOB:
Debut: ARSENAL v Aston Villa 26/12/94
Debut Goal:

Previous Clubs Details			*Apps*					*Goals*		
Club	Signed	Fee	Tot	Start	Sub	FA	FL	Lge	FA	FL
Arsenal			1	1	0	0	0	0	0	0
FAPL Summary by Club										
Arsenal		94/5	1	1	0	0	0	0	0	0
Total			*1*	*1*	*0*	*0*	*0*	*0*	*0*	*0*

HUGHES Michael   West Ham United

Fullname: Michael Hughes   DOB:
Debut: QPR v WEST HAM UNITED 4/12/94
Debut Goal: WEST HAM UNITED v Nottingham Forest 31/12/94

Previous Clubs Details			*Apps*					*Goals*		
Club	Signed	Fee	Tot	Start	Sub	FA	FL	Lge	FA	FL
Strasbourg										
West Ham Utd	Nov-94	Loan	17	15	2	2	0	2	0	0
FAPL Summary by Club										
West Ham Utd		94/5	17	15	2	2	0	2	0	0
Total			*17*	*15*	*2*	*2*	*0*	*2*	*0*	*0*

HUGHES Mark   Chelsea

Fullname: Leslie Mark Hughes   DOB: 02-11-67 Wrexham
Debut: Sheffield United v MANCHESTER UNITED 15/8/92
Debut Goal: Sheffield United v MANCHESTER UNITED 15/8/92

Previous Clubs Details			*Apps*					*Goals*		
Club	Signed	Fee	Tot	Start	Sub	FA	FL	Lge	FA	FL
Manchester Utd	Nov-80		89	85	4	10	6	37	4	4
Barcelona	Jul-86	£2.5m								
Bayern Munich	Oct-87	Loan								
Manchester Utd	Jul-88	£1.5m	256	251	5	36	32	83	9	7
Chelsea	Jun-95	£1.5m								
FAPL Summary by Club										
Manchester Utd	92/3 to 94/5		111	110	1	15	11	35	6	6
Total			*111*	*110*	*1*	*15*	*11*	*35*	*6*	*6*

HUGHES David — Southampton

Fullname: David R Hughes
DOB: 31-12-76 St Albans
Debut: Oldham Athletic v SOUTHAMPTON 5/12/94 as sub
Debut Goal: QPR v SOUTHAMPTON 28/12/94 as sub

Previous Clubs Details			*Apps*					*Goals*		
Club	Signed	Fee	Tot	Start	Sub	FA	FL	Lge	FA	FL
Southampton	Jul-91		14	2	12	4	0	2	1	0
FAPL Summary by Club										
Southampton	93/4 to 94/5		14	2	12	4	0	2	1	0
Total			*14*	*2*	*12*	*4*	*0*	*2*	*1*	*0*

HUTCHISON Don — West Ham United

Fullname: Donald Hutchison
DOB: 10-05-75 Gateshead
Debut: Aston Villa v LIVERPOOL 19/9/92
Debut Goal: LIVERPOOL v Sheffield Wednesday 3/10/92

Previous Clubs Details			*Apps*					*Goals*		
Club	Signed	Fee	Tot	Start	Sub	FA	FL	Lge	FA	FL
Hartlepool Utd	Mar-90		24	19	5	2	2	3	0	0
Liverpool	Nov-90	£175,000	45	33	12	3	8	7	0	2
West Ham Utd	Aug-94	£1.5m	23	22	1	1	3	9	0	2
FAPL Summary by Club										
Liverpool	92/3 to 93/4		42	33	9	3	8	7	0	2
West Ham Utd	94/5		23	22	1	1	3	9	0	2
Total			*65*	*55*	*10*	*4*	*11*	*16*	*0*	*4*

HYDE Graham — Sheffield Wednesday

Fullname: Graham Hyde
DOB: 11-11-74 Doncaster
Debut: Everton v SHEFFIELD WEDNESDAY 15/8/92
Debut Goal: Nottingham Forest v SHEFFIELD WED 3/10/92

Previous Clubs Details			*Apps*					*Goals*		
Club	Signed	Fee	Tot	Start	Sub	FA	FL	Lge	FA	FL
Sheffield W	May-88		104	83	21	13	16	7	1	2
FAPL Summary by Club										
Sheffield W	92/3 to 94/5		91	74	17	11	15	7	1	2
Total			*91*	*74*	*17*	*11*	*15*	*7*	*1*	*2*

IMPEY Andy — QPR

Fullname: Andrew Rodney Impey
DOB: 01-10-75 Hammersmith
Debut: Manchester City v QPR 17/8/92
Debut Goal: Coventry City v QPR 26/8/92

Previous Clubs Details			*Apps*					*Goals*		
Club	Signed	Fee	Tot	Start	Sub	FA	FL	Lge	FA	FL
QPR	Jun-90	£35,000	126	123	3	5	10	8	1	1
FAPL Summary by Club										
QPR	92/3 to 94/5		113	110	3	5	9	8	1	1
Total			*113*	*110*	*3*	*5*	*9*	*8*	*1*	*1*

INGESSON Klas — Sheffield Wednesday

Fullname: Klas Ingesson
DOB:
Debut: Nottingham Forest v SHEFFIELD WED 10/9/94
Debut Goal: Everton v SHEFFIELD WEDNESDAY 26/12/94

Previous Clubs Details

Club	Signed	Fee	Tot	Start	Sub	FA	FL	Lge	FA	FL
PSV Eindhoven										
Sheffield W	Sep-94	£2m	13	9	4	1	1	2	0	0

FAPL Summary by Club

Club	Signed	Fee	Tot	Start	Sub	FA	FL	Lge	FA	FL
Sheffield W	94/5		13	9	4	1	1	2	0	0
Total			*13*	*9*	*4*	*1*	*1*	*2*	*0*	*0*

IRWIN Dennis — Manchester United

Fullname: Dennis Joseph Irwin
DOB: 01-11-69 Cork
Debut: Sheffield United v MANCHESTER UNITED 15/8/92
Debut Goal: MANCHESTER UNITED v Ipswich Town 22/8/92

Previous Clubs Details

Club	Signed	Fee	Tot	Start	Sub	FA	FL	Lge	FA	FL
Leeds Utd	Oct-83		72	72	0	3	5	1	0	0
Oldham Ath	May-86		167	166	1	13	19	4	0	3
Manchester Utd	Jun-90	£625,000	194	192	2	23	29	13	4	0

FAPL Summary by Club

Club	Signed	Fee	Tot	Start	Sub	FA	FL	Lge	FA	FL
Manchester Utd	92/3 to 94/5		122	122	0	17	14	9	6	0
Total			*122*	*122*	*0*	*17*	*14*	*9*	*6*	*0*

ISAIAS Marques — Coventry City

Fullname: Marques Isaias
DOB:
Debut:
Debut Goal:

Previous Clubs Details

Club	Signed	Fee	Tot	Start	Sub	FA	FL	Lge	FA	FL
Benfica (Portugal)										
Coventry City	Jul-95	£500,000								

JACKSON Matthew — Everton

Fullname: Matthew Alan Jackson
DOB: 20-10-75 Leeds
Debut: Sheffield Wednesday v EVERTON 15/8/92
Debut Goal: Crystal Palace v EVERTON 9/1/93

Previous Clubs Details

Club	Signed	Fee	Tot	Start	Sub	FA	FL	Lge	FA	FL
Luton Town	Jul-90		9	7	2	0	2	0	0	0
Preston NE	Mar-91	Loan	4	3	1	0	0	0	0	0
Everton	Oct-91	£600,000	124	118	6	12	8	4	2	0

FAPL Summary by Club

Club	Signed	Fee	Tot	Start	Sub	FA	FL	Lge	FA	FL
Everton	92/3 to 94/5		94	88	6	10	8	3	2	0
Total			*94*	*88*	*6*	*10*	*8*	*3*	*2*	*0*

JAMES David   Liverpool
Fullname: David James   DOB: 02-08-74 Welwyn Garden City
Debut: Nottingham Forest v LIVERPOOL 16/892
Debut Goal: (Goalkeeper)

Previous Clubs Details

Club	Signed	Fee	Tot	Start	Sub	FA	FL	Lge	FA	FL
						Apps			*Goals*	
Watford	Jul-88		89	89	0	2	6	0	0	0
Liverpool	Jun-92	£1m	85	84	1	7	9	0	0	0
FAPL Summary by Club										
Liverpool	92/3 to 94/5		85	84	1	8	8	0	0	0
Total			*85*	*84*	*1*	*8*	*8*	*0*	*0*	*0*

JEFFREY Mike   Newcastle United
Fullname: Michael R Jeffrey   DOB: 12-08-75 Liverpool
Debut: Tottenham Hotspur v NEWCASTLE UNITED 4/12/93
Debut Goal:

Previous Clubs Details

Club	Signed	Fee	Tot	Start	Sub	FA	FL	Lge	FA	FL
						Apps			*Goals*	
Bolton Wders	Feb-89		15	9	6	42	0	1	0	0
Doncaster R	Mar-92	£20,000	41	40	1	0	2	18	0	0
Newcastle Utd	Oct-93	£60,000	2	2	0	0	1	0	0	1
FAPL Summary by Club										
Newcastle Utd	93/4 to 94/5		2	2	0	0	1	0	0	1
Total			*2*	*2*	*0*	*0*	*1*	*0*	*0*	*1*

JENKINSON Leigh   Coventry City
Fullname: Leigh Jenkinson   DOB: 10-07-73 Thorne
Debut: COVENTRY CITY v Arsenal 13/3/93
Debut Goal: Norwich City v COVENTRY CITY 25/1/95

Previous Clubs Details

Club	Signed	Fee	Tot	Start	Sub	FA	FL	Lge	FA	FL
						Apps			*Goals*	
Hull City	Jun-87		130	95	35	7	9	13	0	0
Rotherham Utd	Sep-90	Loan	7	5	2	0	0	0	0	0
Coventry City	Mar-93	£300,000	31	21	10	3	1	1	0	0
Birmingham C	Nov-93	Loan	3	2	1	0	0	0	0	0
FAPL Summary by Club										
Coventry City	92/3 to 94/5		31	21	10	5	2	1	0	0
Total			*31*	*21*	*10*	*5*	*2*	*1*	*0*	*0*

JENSEN John   Arsenal
Fullname: John Jensen   DOB: 04-05-69 Copenhagen
Debut: ARSENAL v Norwich City 15/8/92
Debut Goal: ARSENAL v QPR 31/12/94

Previous Clubs Details

Club	Signed	Fee	Tot	Start	Sub	FA	FL	Lge	FA	FL
						Apps			*Goals*	
Brondby (Denmark)										

Hamburg (Germany)
Brondby (Denmark)

Club	Signed	Fee	Tot	Start	Sub	FA	FL	Lge	FA	FL
Arsenal	Aug-92	£1.1m	83	80	3	7	10	1	0	0

FAPL Summary by Club

Club			Tot	Start	Sub	FA	FL	Lge	FA	FL
Arsenal	92/3 to 94/5		83	80	3	7	10	1	0	0
Total			*83*	*80*	*3*	*7*	*10*	*1*	*0*	*0*

JOHNSEN Erland   Chelsea

Fullname: Erland Johnsen   DOB: 06-04-71 Fredrikstad, Norway
Debut: Nottingham Forest v CHELSEA 16/1/93
Debut Goal: CHELSEA v Blackburn Rovers 14/8/93

Previous Clubs Details			*Apps*					*Goals*		
Club	Signed	Fee	Tot	Start	Sub	FA	FL	Lge	FA	FL
Chelsea	Nov-89	£306,000	105	103	2	14	4	1	0	0

FAPL Summary by Club

Club			Tot	Start	Sub	FA	FL	Lge	FA	FL
Chelsea	92/3 to 94/5		74	73	1	10	4	1	0	0
Total			*74*	*73*	*1*	*10*	*4*	*1*	*0*	*0*

JOHNSON Tommy   Aston Villa

Fullname: Thomas Johnson   DOB: 16-01-75 Newcastle
Debut: ASTON VILLA v QPR 14/1/95
Debut Goal: ASTON VILLA v Wimbledon 11/2/95

Previous Clubs Details			*Apps*					*Goals*		
Club	Signed	Fee	Tot	Start	Sub	FA	FL	Lge	FA	FL
Notts County	Jan-89		118	100	18	5	9	47	5	1
Derby County	Mar-92	£1.3m	84	77	7	5	6	23	2	1
Aston Villa	Jan-95	£2.9m +	14	11	3	1	0	4	0	0

FAPL Summary by Club

Club			Tot	Start	Sub	FA	FL	Lge	FA	FL
Aston Villa	94/5		14	11	3	1	0	4	0	0
Total			*14*	*11*	*3*	*1*	*0*	*4*	*0*	*0*

JONES Lee   Liverpool

Fullname: Philip Lee Jones   DOB: 30-05-77 Wrexham
Debut: LIVERPOOL v Wimbledon 22/10/94 as sub
Debut Goal:

Previous Clubs Details			*Apps*					*Goals*		
Club	Signed	Fee	Tot	Start	Sub	FA	FL	Lge	FA	FL
Wrexham	Jul-91		39	24	15	5	3	9	1	0
Liverpool	Mar-92	£300,000	1	0	1	0	1	0	0	0
Crewe Alex		Loan	8	4	4	0	0	0	0	0

FAPL Summary by Club

Club			Tot	Start	Sub	FA	FL	Lge	FA	FL
Liverpool	94/5		1	0	1	0	1	0	0	0
Total			*1*	*0*	*1*	*0*	*1*	*0*	*0*	*0*

JONES Rob — Liverpool

Fullname: Robert Marc Jones DOB: 06-11-75 Wrexham
Debut: LIVERPOOL v Sheffield United 19/8/92
Debut Goal:

Previous Clubs Details

Club	Signed	Fee	Tot	Start	Sub	FA	FL	Lge	FA	FL
					Apps				Goals	
Crewe Alex	Dec-88		75	59	16	3	9	2	0	0
Liverpool	Oct-91	£300,000	127	127	0	20	16	0	0	0

FAPL Summary by Club

Liverpool	92/3 to 94/5		99	99	0	11	16	0	0	0
Total			*99*	*99*	*0*	*11*	*16*	*0*	*0*	*0*

JONES Ryan — Sheffield Wednesday

Fullname: Ryan Anthony Jones DOB: 24-07-77 Sheffield
Debut: Coventry City v SHEFFIELD WEDNESDAY 3/3/93
Debut Goal: SHEFFIELD WEDNESDAY v Wimbledon 16/10/93

Previous Clubs Details

Club	Signed	Fee	Tot	Start	Sub	FA	FL	Lge	FA	FL
					Apps				Goals	
Sheffield W	Jun-91		41	36	5	3	5	6	1	0

FAPL Summary by Club

Sheffield W	92/3 to 94/5		41	36	5	3	5	6	1	0
Total			*41*	*36*	*5*	*3*	*5*	*6*	*1*	*0*

JONES Vinny — Wimbledon

Fullname: Vincent Peter Jones DOB: 06-01-69 Watford
Debut: CHELSEA v Oldham Athletic 15/8/92
Debut Goal: Sheffield Wednesday v CHELSEA 22/8/92

Previous Clubs Details

Club	Signed	Fee	Tot	Start	Sub	FA	FL	Lge	FA	FL
					Apps				Goals	
Non-League			0	0	0	0	0	0	0	0
Wimbledon	Nov-86	£10,000	77	77	0	13	8	9	1	0
Leeds Utd	Jun-89	£650,000	46	44	2	1	2	5	0	0
Sheffield Utd	Sep-90	£700,000	35	35	0	1	4	2	0	0
Chelsea	Aug-91	£575,000	42	42	0	4	1	4	1	0
Wimbledon	Sep-92	£700,000	93	93	0	8	11	6	0	2

FAPL Summary by Club

Chelsea	92/3		7	7	0	0	0	1	0	0
Wimbledon	92/3 to 94/5		93	93	0	8	11	6	0	2
Total			*100*	*100*	*0*	*8*	*11*	*7*	*0*	*2*

JOSEPH Roger — Wimbledon

Fullname: Roger Anthony Joseph DOB: 25-12-69 Paddington
Debut: Leeds United v WIMBLEDON 15/8/92
Debut Goal:

Previous Clubs Details			Apps					Goals		
Club	Signed	Fee	Tot	Start	Sub	FA	FL	Lge	FA	FL
Brentford	Oct-84		104	103	1	1	7	2	0	0
Wimbledon	Aug-88	£150,000	162	155	7	12	19	0	0	0
Millwall	Mar-95	Loan								
FAPL Summary by Club										
Wimbledon	92/3 to 94/5		48	47	1	6	7	0	0	0
Total			*48*	*47*	*1*	*6*	*7*	*0*	*0*	*0*

KANCHELSKIS Andrei   Everton

Fullname: Andrei Kanchelskis   DOB: 24-01-73 Kirovograd, USSR
Debut: Sheffield United v MANCHESTER UNITED 15/8/93
Debut Goal: MANCHESTER UNITED v Leeds United 6/9/93

Previous Clubs Details			Apps					Goals		
Club	Signed	Fee	Tot	Start	Sub	FA	FL	Lge	FA	FL
Shakhtyor Donezts										
Manchester Utd	Mar-91		123	96	27	12	16	27	4	3
Everton	Jul-95	£5m								
FAPL Summary by Club										
Manchester Utd	92/3 to 94/5		88	67	21	11	15	23	3	1
Total			*88*	*67*	*21*	*11*	*15*	*23*	*3*	*1*

KEANE Roy   Manchester United

Fullname: Roy Maurice Keane   DOB: 11-08-75 Cork
Debut: NOTTINGHAM FOREST v Liverpool 16/8/92
Debut Goal: Leeds United v NOTTINGHAM FOREST 5/12/92

Previous Clubs Details			Apps					Goals		
Club	Signed	Fee	Tot	Start	Sub	FA	FL	Lge	FA	FL
Cobh Ramblers										
N Forest	May-90	£10,000	114	114	0	18	17	22	3	6
Manchester Utd	Jul-93	£3.75m	61	57	4	13	8	7	1	0
FAPL Summary by Club										
N Forest	92/3 to 93/4		40	40	0	4	5	6	1	1
Manchester Utd	93/4 to 94/5		62	57	5	13	8	7	1	0
Total			*102*	*97*	*5*	*17*	*13*	*13*	*2*	*1*

KEARTON Jason   Everton

Fullname: Jason Brett Kearton   DOB: 10-07-73 Australia
Debut: QPR v EVERTON 28/12/92
Debut Goal:

Previous Clubs Details			Apps					Goals		
Club	Signed	Fee	Tot	Start	Sub	FA	FL	Lge	FA	FL
Everton	Oct-88		7	3	4	1	1	0	0	0
Stoke City	Aug-91	Loan	16	16	0	0	0	0	0	0

Blackpool	Jan-92	Loan	14	14	0	0	0		0	0	0
Notts County	Jan-95	Loan									

FAPL Summary by Club

Everton	92/3 to 94/5		6	3	3	1	1		0	0	0
Total			*6*	*3*	*3*	*1*	*1*		*0*	*0*	*0*

KELLY Ray   Manchester City
Fullname: Raymond Kelly   DOB:
Debut: Debut Goal:

Previous Clubs Details			*Apps*					*Goals*			
Club	Signed	Fee	Tot	Start	Sub	FA	FL	Lge	FA	FL	
Athlone Town											
Manchester C	Aug-94	£30,000									

KELLY Gary   Leeds United
Fullname: Gary Kelly   DOB: 10-07-78 Drogheda
Debut: Manchester City v LEEDS UNITED 14/8/93
Debut Goal:

Previous Clubs Details			*Apps*					*Goals*			
Club	Signed	Fee	Tot	Start	Sub	FA	FL	Lge	FA	FL	
Leeds Utd	Sep-91		84	84	0	7	4	0	0	0	

FAPL Summary by Club

Leeds Utd	93/4 to 94/5		84	84	0	7	4	0	0	0	
Total			*84*	*84*	*0*	*7*	*4*	*0*	*0*	*0*	

KENNA Jeff   Blackburn Rovers
Fullname: Jeffrey Jude Kenna   DOB: 28-08-74 Dublin
Debut: QPR v SOUTHAMPTON 19/8/92
Debut Goal: SOUTHAMPTON v Sheffield United 27/2/92

Previous Clubs Details			*Apps*					*Goals*			
Club	Signed	Fee	Tot	Start	Sub	FA	FL	Lge	FA	FL	
Southampton	Apr-89		114	110	4	11	4	4	0	0	
Blackburn R	Mar-95	£1.5m	9	9	0	0	0	1	0	0	

FAPL Summary by Club

Southampton	92/3 to 94/5		98	95	3	7	4	4	0	0	
Blackburn R	94/5		9	9	0	0	0	1	0	0	
Total			*107*	*104*	*3*	*7*	*4*	*5*	*0*	*0*	

KENNEDY Mark   Liverpool
Fullname: Mark Kennedy DOB: 16-05-80 Dublin, Republic of Ireland
Debut: LIVERPOOL v Leeds United 9/4/95 as sub
Debut Goal:

Previous Clubs Details			*Apps*					*Goals*			
Club	Signed	Fee	Tot	Start	Sub	FA	FL	Lge	FA	FL	
Millwall	May-92	Trainee									
Liverpool	Mar-95	£1.5m +	6	4	2	0	0	0	0	0	

FAPL Summary by Club

Liverpool	94/5	6	4	2	0	0	0	0	0
Total		*6*	*4*	*2*	*0*	*0*	*0*	*0*	*0*

KEOWN Martin   Arsenal

Fullname: Martin Raymond Keown   DOB: 25-07-70 Oxford
Debut: EVERTON v Coventry City 17/10/92
Debut Goal: Nottingham Forest v ARSENAL 3/12/94

Previous Clubs Details			*Apps*					*Goals*		
Club	Signed	Fee	Tot	Start	Sub	FA	FL	Lge	FA	FL
Arsenal	Jan-84		22	22	0	5	0	0	0	0
Brighton & HA	Feb-85	Loan	23	21	2	0	2	1	0	1
Aston Villa	Jun-86	£200,000	112	109	3	6	13	3	0	0
Everton	Jun-89	£750,000	96	92	4	12	11	0	0	0
Arsenal	Feb-93	£2m	80	62	18	5	8	1	0	0
FAPL Summary by Club										
Everton	92/3 to 94/5		13	13	0	2	4	0	0	0
Arsenal	92/3 to 94/5		80	62	18	5	8	1	0	0
Total			*93*	*75*	*18*	*7*	*12*	*1*	*0*	*0*

KERNAGHAN Alan   Manchester City

Fullname: Alan Nigel Kernaghan   DOB: 26-04-71 Otley
Debut: Coventry City v MIDDLESBROUGH 15/8/92
Debut Goal: MIDDLESBROUGH v Ipswich Town 1/9/92

Previous Clubs Details			*Apps*					*Goals*		
Club	Signed	Fee	Tot	Start	Sub	FA	FL	Lge	FA	FL
Middlesbrough	Mar-85		212	172	40	11	29	16	3	1
Charlton Ath	Jan-91	Loan	13	13	0	0	0	0	0	0
Manchester C	Sep-93	£1.6m	46	41	5	5	7	1	1	1
Bolton Wders	Aug-94	Loan	11	9	2	0	0	0	0	0
FAPL Summary by Club										
Middlesbrough	92/3 to 94/5		22	22	0	0	2	2	0	0
Manchester City	93/4 to 94/5		46	41	5	5	7	1	1	0
Total			*68*	*63*	*5*	*5*	*9*	*3*	*1*	*0*

KERR David   Manchester City

Fullname: David William Kerr   DOB: 07-09-78 Dumfries
Debut: MANCHESTER CITY v Crystal Palace 5/5/93 as sub
Debut Goal:

Previous Clubs Details			*Apps*					*Goals*		
Club	Signed	Fee	Tot	Start	Sub	FA	FL	Lge	FA	FL
Manchester C	Sep-91		5	4	1	0	0	0	0	0
FAPL Summary by Club										
Manchester C	92/3 to 94/5		5	4	1	0	0	0	0	0
Total			*5*	*4*	*1*	*0*	*0*	*0*	*0*	*0*

KERSLAKE David
Tottenham Hotspur

Fullname: David Kerslake
DOB: 20-06-70 Stepney
Debut: LEEDS UNITED v Manchester City 13/3/93
Debut Goal:

Previous Clubs Details

Club	Signed	Fee	Apps					Goals		
			Tot	Start	Sub	FA	FL	Lge	FA	FL
QPR	Jun-83		58	38	20	4	8	6	0	4
Swindon Town	Nov-89	£110,000	135	133	2	8	12	1	0	0
Leeds Utd	Mar-93	£500,000	8	8	0	0	0	0	0	0
Tottenham H	Sep-93	£450,000	35	32	3	2	5	0	0	0

FAPL Summary by Club

Leeds Utd	92/3 to 94/5		8	8	0	0	0	0	0	0
Tottenham H	93/4 to 94/5		35	32	3	2	5	0	0	0
Total			*43*	*40*	*3*	*2*	*5*	*0*	*0*	*0*

KEY Lance
Sheffield Wednesday

Fullname: Lance Key
DOB: 14-05-72 Kettering
Debut:
Debut Goal:

Previous Clubs Details

Club	Signed	Fee	Apps					Goals		
			Tot	Start	Sub	FA	FL	Lge	FA	FL
Histon										
Sheffield W	Apr-90	£10,000	0	0	0	1	0	0	0	0
Oldham Athl	Oct-93	Loan	2	2	0	0	0	0	0	

KHARINE Dimitri
Chelsea

Fullname: Dimitri Kharine
DOB: 17-08-72 Moscow
Debut: QPR v CHELSEA 27/1/93
Debut Goal:

Previous Clubs Details

Club	Signed	Fee	Apps					Goals		
			Tot	Start	Sub	FA	FL	Lge	FA	FL
CSKA Moscow										
Chelsea	Dec-92	£200,000	76	76	0	11	6	0	0	0

FAPL Summary by Club

Chelsea	92/3 to 94/5		76	76	0	11	6	0	0	0
Total			*76*	*76*	*0*	*11*	*6*	*0*	*0*	*0*

KIMBLE Alan
Wimbledon

Fullname: Alan F Kimble
DOB: 07-08-70 Dagenham
Debut: West Ham United v WIMBLEDON 14/8/93
Debut Goal:

Previous Clubs Details

Club	Signed	Fee	Apps					Goals		
			Tot	Start	Sub	FA	FL	Lge	FA	FL
Charlton Ath	Aug-84		6	6	0	0	0	0	0	0
Exeter City	Aug-85	Loan	1	1	0	0	1	0	0	0
Cambridge Utd	Aug-86	Free	299	295	4	29	24	24	1	0
Wimbledon	Jul-93	£175,000	40	40	0	3	5	0	0	0

| Wimbledon | 93/4 to 94/5 | 40 | 40 | 0 | 3 | 5 | 0 | 0 | 0 |
| *Total* | | *40* | *40* | *0* | *3* | *5* | *0* | *0* | *0* |

KING Phil   Aston Villa

Fullname: Philip Geoffrey King   DOB: 29-01-71 Bristol
Debut: Everton v SHEFFIELD WEDNESDAY 15/8/92
Debut Goal: SHEFFIELD WEDNESDAY v Southampton 12/4/93

Previous Clubs Details			*Apps*				*Goals*		
Club	Signed	Fee	Tot	Start	Sub	FA	FL	Lge	FA FL
Exeter City	Jan-85		27	24	3	0	1	0	0 0
Torquay Utd	Jul-86	£3,000	24	24	0	1	2	3	0 0
Swindon Town	Feb-87	£15,000	116	112	4	5	11	4	0 0
Sheffield Wed	Nov-89	£400,000	139	124	15	9	17	2	0 0
Notts County	Oct-93	Loan	6	6	0	0	0	0	0 0
Aston Villa	Aug-94	£250,000	16	13	3	0	3	0	0 0

FAPL Summary by Club									
Sheffield W	92/3 to 93/4	22	18	4	1	4	1	0	0
Aston Villa	94/5	16	13	3	0	3	0	0	0
Total		*38*	*31*	*7*	*1*	*7*	*1*	*0*	*0*

KITSON Paul   Newcastle United

Fullname: Paul Kitson   DOB: 10-01-75 Peterlee
Debut: Aston Villa v NEWCASTLE UNITED 1/10/94
Debut Goal: NEWCASTLE UNITED v QPR 5/11/94

Previous Clubs Details			*Apps*				*Goals*		
Club	Signed	Fee	Tot	Start	Sub	FA	FL	Lge	FA FL
Leicester City	Dec-88		50	39	11	2	5	6	3 1
Derby County	Mar-92	£1.3m	97	97	0	5	7	34	3 1
Newcastle Utd	Sep-94	£2.25m	26	24	2	5	3	8	3 1

FAPL Summary by Club									
Newcastle Utd	94/5	26	24	2	5	3	8	3	1
Total		*26*	*24*	*2*	*5*	*3*	*8*	*3*	*1*

KIWOMYA Chris   Arsenal

Fullname: Christopher Mark Kiwomya   DOB: 03-12-73 Huddersfield
Debut: IPSWICH TOWN v Aston Villa 15/8/92
Debut Goal: Manchester United v IPSWICH TOWN 223/8/92

Previous Clubs Details			*Apps*				*Goals*		
Club	Signed	Fee	Tot	Start	Sub	FA	FL	Lge	FA FL
Ipswich Town	Mar-87		226	197	29	14	14	50	2 8
Arsenal	Jan-95	£1.55m +	14	5	9	0	0	3	0 0

FAPL Summary by Club									
Ipswich Town	92/3 to 94/5	90	85	5	6	8	18	1	7
Arsenal	94/5	14	5	9	0	0	3	0	0
Total		*104*	*90*	*14*	*6*	*8*	*21*	*1*	*7*

KJELDBERG Jakob · Chelsea

Fullname: Jakob Kjeldberg DOB: 22-10-73 Denmark
Debut: Wimbledon v CHELSEA 17/8/93
Debut Goal: CHELSEA v Sheffield United 7/5/94

Previous Clubs Details			*Apps*					*Goals*		
Club	Signed	Fee	Tot	Start	Sub	FA	FL	Lge	FA	FL
Silkeborg (Denmark)										
Chelsea	Aug-93	£400,000	52	52	0	8	5	2	0	0
FAPL Summary by Club										
Chelsea	93/4 to 94/5		52	52	0	8	5	1	0	0
Total			*52*	*52*	*0*	*8*	*5*	*1*	*0*	*0*

LAMPTEY Nil · Aston Villa

Fullname: Nil Lamptey DOB: 11-12-78 Accra, Ghana
Debut: Blackburn Rovers v ASTON VILLA 24/9/94 as sub
Debut Goal:

Previous Clubs Details			*Apps*					*Goals*		
Club	Signed	Fee	Tot	Start	Sub	FA	FL	Lge	FA	FL
Anderlecht										
Aston Villa	Aug-94	£1m	6	1	5	0	3	0	0	3
FAPL Summary by Club										
Aston Villa	94/5		6	1	5	0	3	0	0	3
Total			*6*	*1*	*5*	*0*	*3*	*0*	*0*	*3*

LE SAUX Graeme · Blackburn Rovers

Fullname: Graeme Pierre Le Saux DOB: 18-10-72 Jersey
Debut: CHELSEA v Ipswich Town 17/10/92
Debut Goal: Chelsea v BLACKBURN ROVERS 14/8/93

Previous Clubs Details			*Apps*					*Goals*		
Club	Signed	Fee	Tot	Start	Sub	FA	FL	Lge	FA	FL
Chelsea	Dec-87		90	77	13	8	13	8	0	1
Blackburn R	Mar-93	Swap	89	88	1	6	8	5	0	0
FAPL Summary by Club										
Chelsea	92/3 to 94/5		14	10	4	1	4	0	0	0
Blackburn R	92/3 to 94/5		89	88	1	6	8	5	0	0
Total			*103*	*98*	*5*	*7*	*12*	*5*	*0*	*0*

LE TISSIER Matthew · Southampton

Fullname: Matthew Paul Le Tissier DOB: 15-10-72 Guernsey
Debut: SOUTHAMPTON v Tottenham Hotspur 15/8/92
Debut Goal: QPR v SOUTHAMPTON 189/8/92

Previous Clubs Details			*Apps*					*Goals*		
Club	Signed	Fee	Tot	Start	Sub	FA	FL	Lge	FA	FL
Southampton	Oct-86		292	262	30	24	32	120	11	18

Southampton	92/3 to 94/5	119	119	0	8	6	60	6	7
Total		*119*	*119*	*0*	*8*	*6*	*60*	*6*	*7*

LEE Robert   Newcastle United

Fullname: Robert M Lee   DOB: 02-02-70 West Ham
Debut: NEWCASTLE UNITED v Tottenham Hotspur 14/8/93
Debut Goal: NEWCASTLE UNITED v Swindon Town 12/3/94

Previous Clubs Details			*Apps*				*Goals*		
Club	Signed	Fee	Tot	Start	Sub	FA	FL	Lge	FA	FL
Charlton Ath	Jul-83		298	274	24	14	19	58	2	1
Newcastle Utd	Sep-92	£700,000	112	112	0	11	8	26	3	2

FAPL Summary by Club

Newcastle Utd	93/4 to 94/5	76	76	0	7	5	16	1	1
Total		*76*	*76*	*0*	*7*	*5*	*16*	*1*	*1*

LEE Dave   Bolton Wanderers

Fullname: David M Lee   DOB: 06-11-71 Blackburn
Debut: SOUTHAMPTON v Manchester United 24/8/92 as sub
Debut Goal:

Previous Clubs Details			*Apps*				*Goals*		
Club	Signed	Fee	Tot	Start	Sub	FA	FL	Lge	FA	FL
Bury	Aug-86		208	203	5	6	15	35	0	1
Southampton	Aug-91	£350,000	20	11	9	1	0	0	0	0
Bolton Wders	Nov-92	£300,000	112	102	10	12	12	14	0	2

FAPL Summary by Club

Southampton	92/3	1	0	1	0	0	0	0	0
Total		*1*	*0*	*1*	*0*	*0*	*0*	*0*	*0*

LEE David   Chelsea

Fullname: David John Lee   DOB: 27-11-73 Kingswood
Debut: Aston Villa v CHELSEA 2/9/92
Debut Goal: CHELSEA v Manchester United 19/12/92

Previous Clubs Details			*Apps*				*Goals*		
Club	Signed	Fee	Tot	Start	Sub	FA	FL	Lge	FA	FL
Chelsea	Jun-88		118	88	30	7	16	9	0	1
Reading	Jan-92	Loan	5	5	0	0	0	5	0	0
Plymouth Arg	Mar-92	Loan	9	9	0	0	0	1	0	0
Portsmouth	Aug-94	Loan								

FAPL Summary by Club

Chelsea	92/3 to 94/5	46	35	11	2	9	3	0	0
Total		*46*	*35*	*11*	*2*	*9*	*3*	*0*	*0*

LEE Jason   Nottingham Forest

Fullname: Jason B Lee   DOB: 10-05-75 Newham
Debut: Ipswich Town v NOTTINGHAM FOREST 20/8/94

Debut Goal: Newcastle United v NOTTM FOREST 11/2/95 as sub

Previous Clubs Details

Club	Signed	Fee	Apps					Goals		
			Tot	Start	Sub	FA	FL	Lge	FA	FL
Charlton Ath	Jun-89		1	0	1	0	0	0	0	0
Stockport Co	Feb-91	Loan	2	2	0	0	0	0	0	0
Lincoln City	Mar-91	£35,000	93	86	7	3	6	21	1	0
Southend Utd	Jul-93		24	18	6	1	1	3	0	0
N Forest	Mar-94	£200,000	35	15	20	0	1	3	0	0

FAPL Summary by Club

N Forest		94/5	22	5	17	0	1	3	0	0
Total			*22*	*5*	*17*	*0*	*1*	*3*	*0*	*0*

LEONHARDSEN Oyvind   Wimbledon

Fullname: Oyvind Leonhardsen   DOB:
Debut: WIMBLEDON v Aston Villa 9/11/94
Debut Goal: WIMBLEDON v Aston Villa 9/11/94

Previous Clubs Details

Club	Signed	Fee	Apps					Goals		
			Tot	Start	Sub	FA	FL	Lge	FA	FL
Rosenborg										
Wimbledon	Oct-94	Trial								
Wimbledon	Jan-95	£650,000	20	18	2	3	0	4	1	0

FAPL Summary by Club

Wimbledon		94/5	20	18	2	3	0	4	1	0
Total			*20*	*18*	*2*	*3*	*0*	*4*	*1*	*0*

LIMPAR Anders   Everton

Fullname: Anders Limpar   DOB: 25-09-69 Sweden
Debut: ARSENAL v Norwich City 15/8/92
Debut Goal: Liverpool v ARSENAL 23/8/92

Previous Clubs Details

Club	Signed	Fee	Apps					Goals		
			Tot	Start	Sub	FA	FL	Lge	FA	FL
Arsenal	Jul-90	£1m	96	76	20	7	9	18	2	0
Everton	Mar-94	£1.6m	35	27	8	6	0	2	1	0

FAPL Summary by Club

Arsenal		92/3 to 93/4	33	21	12	2	6	2	0	0
Everton		93/4 to 94/5	36	28	8	6	0	11	1	0
Total			*69*	*49*	*20*	*8*	*6*	*13*	*1*	*0*

LINIGHAN Andy   Arsenal

Fullname: Andrew Linighan   DOB: 19-06-66 Hartlepool
Debut: Sheffield United v ARSENAL 19/9/92
Debut Goal: Oldham Athletic v ARSENAL 20/2/93

Previous Clubs Details

Club	Signed	Fee	Apps					Goals		
			Tot	Start	Sub	FA	FL	Lge	FA	FL
Hartlepool Utd	Sep-80		110	110	0	8	8	4	0	1

			Tot	Start	Sub	FA	FL	Lge	FA	FL
Leeds Utd	May-84	£200,000	66	66	0	2	6	3	0	1
Oldham Ath	Jan-86	£65,000	87	87	0	3	8	6	0	2
Norwich City	Mar-88	£350,000	86	86	0	10	6	8	0	0
Arsenal	Jun-90	£1.25m	89	74	15	13	12	4	1	1

FAPL Summary by Club

Arsenal	92/3 to 94/5		62	52	10	9	10	4	1	1
Total			*62*	*52*	*10*	*9*	*10*	*4*	*1*	*1*

LOMAS Stephen — Manchester City

Fullname: Stephen Martin Lomas   DOB: 19-01-78 Hanover
Debut: Sheffield United v MANCHESTER CITY 25/9/93
Debut Goal: MANCHESTER CITY v Nottingham Forest 8/10/94

Previous Clubs Details				*Apps*					*Goals*	
Club	Signed	Fee	Tot	Start	Sub	FA	FL	Lge	FA	FL
Manchester C	Jan-91		43	35	8	3	10	2	0	2

FAPL Summary by Club

Manchester C	93/4 to 94/5		43	35	8	3	10	2	0	2
Total			*43*	*35*	*8*	*3*	*10*	*2*	*0*	*2*

LUKIC John — Leeds United

Fullname: Jovan Lukic   DOB: 12-12-64 Chesterfield
Debut: LEEDS UNITED v Wimbledon 15/8/92
Debut Goal: (Goalkeeper)

Previous Clubs Details				*Apps*					*Goals*	
Club	Signed	Fee	Tot	Start	Sub	FA	FL	Lge	FA	FL
Leeds Utd	Dec-78		146	146	0	9	7	0	0	0
Arsenal	Jul-83	£50,000	223	223	0	21	32	0	0	0
Leeds Utd	Jun-90	£1m	181	181	0	14	16	0	0	0

FAPL Summary by Club

Leeds Utd	92/3 to 94/5		101	101	0	7	5	0	0	0
Total			*101*	*101*	*0*	*7*	*5*	*0*	*0*	*0*

LYTTLE Des — Nottingham Forest

Fullname: Desmond Lyttle   DOB: 25-09-75 Wolverhampton
Debut: Ipswich Town v NOTTINGHAM FOREST 20/8/94
Debut Goal:

Previous Clubs Details				*Apps*					*Goals*	
Club	Signed	Fee	Tot	Start	Sub	FA	FL	Lge	FA	FL
Swansea City	Jul-92	£12,500	46	46	0	5	2	1	0	0
N Forest	Jul-93	£375,000	75	75	0	4	10	1	0	0

FAPL Summary by Club

N Forest	94/5		38	38	0	2	4	0	0	0
Total			*38*	*38*	*0*	*2*	*4*	*0*	*0*	*0*

MABBUTT Gary   Tottenham Hotspur

Fullname: Gary Vincent Mabbutt   DOB: 24-09-65 Bristol
Debut: Wimbledon v TOTTENHAM HOTSPUR 25/10/92
Debut Goal: TOTTENHAM HOTSPUR v Nottm Forest 18/12/92

Previous Clubs Details

Club	Signed	Fee	Tot	Start	Sub	FA	FL	Lge	FA	FL
Bristol Rovers	Jan-79		131	122	9	6	10	10	1	1
Tottenham H	Aug-82	£105,000	430	417	13	41	58	27	4	2

FAPL Summary by Club

Tottenham H	92/3 to 94/5		91	91	0	11	7	2	1	0
Total			*91*	*91*	*0*	*11*	*7*	*2*	*1*	*0*

MADDISON Neil   Southampton

Fullname: Neil Stanley Maddison   DOB: 03-10-73 Darlington
Debut: SOUTHAMPTON v Middlesbrough 29/8/92
Debut Goal: SOUTHAMPTON v Arsenal 5/12/92

Previous Clubs Details

Club	Signed	Fee	Tot	Start	Sub	FA	FL	Lge	FA	FL
Southampton	Apr-88		130	117	13	10	7	16	0	0

FAPL Summary by Club

Southampton	92/3 to 94/5		113	109	4	7	5	14	0	0
Total			*113*	*109*	*4*	*7*	*5*	*14*	*0*	*0*

MADDIX Danny   QPR

Fullname: Daniel Shawn Maddix   DOB: 12-10-71 Ashford, Kent
Debut: Southampton v QPR 12/9/92
Debut Goal: Sheffield Wednesday v QPR 17/12/94

Previous Clubs Details

Club	Signed	Fee	Tot	Start	Sub	FA	FL	Lge	FA	FL
Tottenham H	Jul-85		0	0	0	0	0	0	0	0
Southend U	Oct-86	Loan	2	2	0	0	0	0	0	0
QPR	Jul-87	Free	166	143	23	18	15	7	2	2

FAPL Summary by Club

QPR	92/3 to 94/5		41	30	11	5	1	1	1	0
Total			*41*	*30*	*11*	*5*	*1*	*1*	*1*	*0*

MAGILTON Jim   Southampton

Fullname: James Magilton   DOB: 07-05-73 Belfast, Nth Ireland
Debut: SOUTHAMPTON v Liverpool 14/2/94
Debut Goal: Arsenal v SOUTHAMPTON 19/11/94

Previous Clubs Details

Club	Signed	Fee	Tot	Start	Sub	FA	FL	Lge	FA	FL
Liverpool	May-86		0	0	0	0	0	0	0	0
Oxford Utd	Oct-90	£100,000	150	150	0	8	9	34	4	1
Southampton	Feb-94	£600,000	57	57	0	5	3	6	1	0

FAPL Summary by Club

		Tot	Start	Sub	FA	FL	Lge	FA	FL
Southampton	93/4 to 94/5	57	57	0	5	3	6	1	0
Total		*57*	*57*	*0*	*5*	*3*	*6*	*1*	*0*

MARTIN Alvin   West Ham United

Fullname: Alvin E Martin   DOB: 21-07-62 Liverpool
Debut: WEST HAM UNITED v Manchester City 1/11/93
Debut Goal: WEST HAM UNITED v Oldham Athletic 20/11/93

Previous Clubs Details			*Apps*				*Goals*		
Club	Signed	Fee	Tot	Start	Sub	FA	FL	Lge	FA	FL
West Ham Utd	Aug-74		455	452	3	39	69	27	0	6

FAPL Summary by Club

West Ham Utd	93/4 to 94/5	31	30	1	5	3	2	0	0
Total		*31*	*30*	*1*	*5*	*3*	*2*	*0*	*0*

MASINGA Philomen   Leeds United

Fullname: Philomen Masinga   DOB: 29-06-73 Johannesburg, SA
Debut: West Ham United v LEEDS UNITED 20/8/94 as sub
Debut Goal: LEEDS UNITED v Chelsea 27/8/94

Previous Clubs Details			*Apps*				*Goals*		
Club	Signed	Fee	Tot	Start	Sub	FA	FL	Lge	FA	FL
Mamolodi Sun										
Leeds Utd	Aug-94	£250,000	22	15	7	4	1	5	4	0

FAPL Summary by Club

Leeds Utd	94/5	22	15	7	4	1	5	4	0
Total		*22*	*15*	*7*	*4*	*1*	*5*	*4*	*0*

MASKELL Craig   Southampton

Fullname: Craig D Maskell   DOB: 11-04-72 Aldershot
Debut: Sheffield United v SWINDON TOWN 14/8/93
Debut Goal: Southampton v SWINDON TOWN 25/8/93

Previous Clubs Details			*Apps*				*Goals*		
Club	Signed	Fee	Tot	Start	Sub	FA	FL	Lge	FA	FL
Southampton	Apr-86		6	2	4	0	0	1	0	0
Huddersfield T	May-88	£20,000	87	86	1	8	6	43	3	4
Reading	Aug-90	£250,000	72	60	12	6	2	27	0	0
Swindon T	Jul-92	Exchange	47	40	7	3	4	21	0	1
Southampton	Feb-94	£250,000	16	8	8	1	0	1	0	0

FAPL Summary by Club

Swindon T	93/4 to 94/5	14	8	6	2	2	3	0	0
Southampton	93/4 to 94/5	16	8	8	1	0	1	0	0
Total		*30*	*16*	*14*	*3*	*2*	*4*	*0*	*0*

MATTEO Dominic   Liverpool

Fullname: Dominic Matteo   DOB: 29-04-78 Dumfries
Debut: Manchester City v LIVERPOOL 23/10/93

Debut Goal:

Previous Clubs Details			Apps					Goals		
Club	Signed	Fee	Tot	Start	Sub	FA	FL	Lge	FA	FL
Liverpool	May-92		18	13	5	1	2	0	0	0
FAPL Summary by Club										
Liverpool	93/4 to 94/5		18	2	16	1	2	0	0	0
Total			*18*	*2*	*16*	*1*	*2*	*0*	*0*	*0*

MAY David — Manchester United

Fullname: David May
Debut: Crystal Palace v BLACKBURN ROVERS 15/8/92   DOB: 25-06-74 Oldham
Debut Goal: Everton v BLACKBURN ROVERS 3/3/93

Previous Clubs Details			Apps					Goals		
Club	Signed	Fee	Tot	Start	Sub	FA	FL	Lge	FA	FL
Blackburn R	Jun-88		122	122	0	10	13	3	1	2
Manchester Utd	Jul-94	£1.4m	19	15	4	1	2	2	0	1
FAPL Summary by Club										
Blackburn Rovers	92/3 to 93/4		74	74	0	7	10	2	1	2
Manchester Utd	94/5		19	15	4	1	2	2	0	1
Total			*93*	*89*	*4*	*8*	*12*	*4*	*1*	*3*

McALLISTER Gary — Leeds United

Fullname: Gary McAllister
Debut: LEEDS UNITED v Wimbledon 15/8/92   DOB: 26-12-68 Motherwell
Debut Goal: LEEDS UNITED v Liverpool 29/8/92

Previous Clubs Details			Apps					Goals		
Club	Signed	Fee	Tot	Start	Sub	FA	FL	Lge	FA	FL
Leicester C	Aug-85	£125,000	201	199	2	5	15	46	2	3
Leeds Utd	Jun-90	£1m	195	194	1	18	18	27	3	3
FAPL Summary by Club										
Leeds Utd	92/3 to 94/5		115	115	0	11	7	20	2	1
Total			*115*	*115*	*0*	*11*	*7*	*20*	*2*	*1*

McALLISTER Brian — Wimbledon

Fullname: Brian McAllister
Debut: Sheffield United v WIMBLEDON 25/8/92   DOB: 01-12-74 Glasgow
Debut Goal:

Previous Clubs Details			Apps					Goals		
Club	Signed	Fee	Tot	Start	Sub	FA	FL	Lge	FA	FL
Wimbledon	Feb-89		53	49	4	3	5	0	0	0
Plymouth Arg	Dec-90	Loan	8	7	1	0	0	0	0	0
FAPL Summary by Club										
Wimbledon	92/3 to 93/4		40	39	1	3	5	0	0	0
Total			*40*	*39*	*1*	*3*	*5*	*0*	*0*	*0*

McATEER Jason — Bolton Wanderers

Fullname: Jason McAteer
Debut:

DOB: 19-06-75 Birkenhead
Debut Goal:

Previous Clubs Details			Apps					Goals		
Club	Signed	Fee	Tot	Start	Sub	FA	FL	Lge	FA	FL
Bolton Wdrs	Jan-92		109	104	5	11	11	9	3	2

McCARTHY Alan — QPR

Fullname: Alan James McCarthy
Debut: Ipswich Town v QPR 26/3/94
Debut Goal:

DOB: 12-01-76 Wandsworth

Previous Clubs Details			Apps					Goals		
Club	Signed	Fee	Tot	Start	Sub	FA	FL	Lge	FA	FL
QPR	Dec-89		11	8	3	1	0	0	0	0
Watford	Nov-93	Loan	9	8	1	0	0	0	0	0
Plymouth Arg	Feb-94	Loan	2	1	1	0	0	0	0	0
FAPL Summary by Club										
QPR	93/4 to 94/5		6	4	2	0	0	0	0	0
Total			*6*	*4*	*2*	*0*	*0*	*0*	*0*	*0*

McCLAIR Brian — Manchester United

Fullname: Brian John McClair
Debut: Sheffield United v MANCHESTER UNITED 15/8/92
Debut Goal: Everton v MANCHESTER UNITED 12/9/92

DOB: 09-12-67 Bellshill

Previous Clubs Details			Apps					Goals		
Club	Signed	Fee	Tot	Start	Sub	FA	FL	Lge	FA	FL
Aston Villa										
Motherwell			39					15		
Celtic	Jul-83		145					99		
Manchester Utd	Jul-87	£850,000	298	278	20	39	41	86	14	18
FAPL Summary by Club										
Manchester Utd	92/3 to 94/5		108	88	20	15	13	15	3	5
Total			*108*	*88*	*20*	*15*	*13*	*15*	*3*	*5*

McDONALD Alan — QPR

Fullname: Alan McDonald
Debut: Manchester City v QPR 17/8/92
Debut Goal: Wimbledon v QPR 27/9/93

DOB: 13-10-67 Belfast, N.Ireland

Previous Clubs Details			Apps					Goals		
Club	Signed	Fee	Tot	Start	Sub	FA	FL	Lge	FA	FL
QPR	Aug-81		337	332	5	28	38	10	1	2
Charlton Ath	Mar-83	Loan	9	9	0	0	0	0	0	0
FAPL Summary by Club										
QPR	92/3 to 94/5		90	90	0	6	10	2	0	0
Total			*90*	*90*	*0*	*6*	*10*	*2*	*0*	*0*

McDONALD Neil — Bolton Wanderers

Fullname: Neil McDonald
DOB: 03-11-69 Wallsend
Debut: OLDHAM ATHLETIC v Aston Villa 24/10/92 as sub
Debut Goal:

Previous Clubs Details

Club	Signed	Fee	Tot	Start	Sub	FA	FL	Lge	FA	FL
Newcastle Utd	Feb-83	Amateur	180	163	17	11	12	24	1	3
Everton	Aug-88	£535,000	90	76	14	17	7	4	0	3
Oldham Ath	Oct-91	£500,000	24	19	5	2	3	1	0	0
Bolton Wdrs		Free	28	23	5	2	3	1	0	0

FAPL Summary by Club

Club			Tot	Start	Sub	FA	FL	Lge	FA	FL
Oldham Ath	92/3 to 93/4		7	5	2	2	1	0	0	0
Total			7	5	2	2	1	0	0	0

McDONALD Paul — Southampton

Fullname: Paul McDonald
DOB: 21-04-72 Motherwell
Debut: Norwich City v SOUTHAMPTON 2/11/94 as sub
Debut Goal:

Previous Clubs Details

Club	Signed	Fee	Tot	Start	Sub	FA	FL	Lge	FA	FL
Hamilton Academicals										
Southampton	Jun-93	£75,000	2	0	2	0	0	0	0	0

FAPL Summary by Club

Club			Tot	Start	Sub	FA	FL	Lge	FA	FL
Southampton	94/5 to 93/4		2	0	2	0	0	0	0	0
Total			2	0	2	0	0	0	0	0

McGINLAY John — Bolton Wanderers

Fullname: John McGinlay
DOB: 09-04-68 Inverness
Debut:
Debut Goal:

Previous Clubs Details

Club	Signed	Fee	Tot	Start	Sub	FA	FL	Lge	FA	FL
Shrewsbury T	Feb-89		60	58	2	1	4	27	2	0
Bury	Jul-90	£175,000	25	16	9	1	1	9	0	0
Millwall	Jan-91	£80,000	34	27	7	2	3	10	0	0
Bolton Wdrs	Sep-92	£125,000	110	104	6	14	11	57	8	5

McGOLDRICK Eddie — Arsenal

Fullname: Edward John Paul McGoldrick
DOB: 01-05-69 Islington
Debut: CRYSTAL PALACE v Blackburn Rovers 15/8/92
Debut Goal: Oldham Athletic v CRYSTAL PALACE 19/8/92

Previous Clubs Details

Club	Signed	Fee	Tot	Start	Sub	FA	FL	Lge	FA	FL
Northampton T	Aug-86	£10,000	107	97	10	7	9	9	1	0
Crystal Palace	Jan-89	£200,000	147	139	8	5	22	11	0	2
Arsenal	Jul-93	£1m	37	32	5	2	9	0	0	0

McGOWAN Gavin   Arsenal

Fullname: Gavin McGowan   DOB: 17-01-80 Blackheath
Debut: Sheffield Wednesday v ARSENAL 6/5/93 as sub
Debut Goal:

Previous Clubs Details			*Apps*					*Goals*		
Club	Signed	Fee	Tot	Start	Sub	FA	FL	Lge	FA	FL
Arsenal			3	1	2	0	0	0	0	0

FAPL Summary by Club

Arsenal	92/3 to 94/5	3	1	2	0	0	0	0	0
Total		*3*	*1*	*2*	*0*	*0*	*0*	*0*	*0*

McGRATH Paul   Aston Villa

Fullname: Paul McGrath   DOB: 05-12-73 Ealing
Debut: ASTON VILLA v Ipswich Town 15/8/92
Debut Goal: ASTON VILLA v Nottingham Forest 12/12/92

Previous Clubs Details			*Apps*					*Goals*		
Club	Signed	Fee	Tot	Start	Sub	FA	FL	Lge	FA	FL
Manchester Utd	Apr-82	£30,000	163	159	4	17	13	12	2	2
Aston Villa	Jul-89	£400,000	222	218	14	20	24	6	1	0

FAPL Summary by Club

Aston Villa	92/3 to 94/5	112	108	4	8	15	4	0	1
Total		*112*	*108*	*4*	*8*	*15*	*4*	*0*	*1*

McGREGOR Paul   Nottingham Forest

Fullname: Paul A McGregor   DOB:
Debut: NOTTM FOREST v Ipswich Town 10/12/94 as sub
Debut Goal: West Ham United v NOTTM FOREST 31/12/94 as sub

Previous Clubs Details			*Apps*					*Goals*		
Club	Signed	Fee	Tot	Start	Sub	FA	FL	Lge	FA	FL
N Forest			10	0	10	0	0	1	0	0

FAPL Summary by Club

N Forest	94/5	10	0	10	0	0	1	0	0
Total		*10*	*0*	*10*	*0*	*0*	*1*	*0*	*0*

McMAHON Gerry   Tottenham Hotspur

Fullname: Gerard McMahon   DOB: 30-12-77 Belfast, Nth Ireland
Debut: TOTTENHAM HOTSPUR v Coventry City 9/5/95
Debut Goal:

Previous Clubs Details			*Apps*					*Goals*		
Club	Signed	Fee	Tot	Start	Sub	FA	FL	Lge	FA	FL
Glenavon										

			Tot	Start	Sub	FA	FL	Lge	FA	FL
Tottenham H	Jul-92	£100,000	2	2	0	0	0	0	0	0
Barnet	Oct-94	Loan								

FAPL Summary by Club

			Tot	Start	Sub	FA	FL	Lge	FA	FL
Tottenham H	94/5		2	2	0	0	0	0	0	0
Total			*2*	*2*	*0*	*0*	*0*	*0*	*0*	*0*

McMANAMAN Steve — Liverpool

Fullname: Steven McManaman   DOB: 12-02-76 Bootle
Debut: Nottingham Forest v LIVERPOOL 16/8/92
Debut Goal: LIVERPOOL v Wimbledon 26/9/92

Previous Clubs Details			Apps					Goals		
Club	Signed	Fee	Tot	Start	Sub	FA	FL	Lge	FA	FL
Liverpool	Feb-90		133	122	11	19	20	18	3	7

FAPL Summary by Club

			Tot	Start	Sub	FA	FL	Lge	FA	FL
Liverpool	92/3 to 94/5		101	96	5	10	15	13	0	4
Total			*101*	*96*	*5*	*10*	*15*	*13*	*0*	*4*

MEAKER Michael — QPR

Fullname: Michael John Meaker   DOB: 19-08-75 Greenford
Debut: QPR v Norwich City 6/3/93
Debut Goal: Leeds United v QPR 29/12/93

Previous Clubs Details			Apps					Goals		
Club	Signed	Fee	Tot	Start	Sub	FA	FL	Lge	FA	FL
QPR	Dec-89		33	21	12	3	2	1	1	1
Plymouth Arg	Nov-91	Loan	4	4	0	0	0	0	0	0

FAPL Summary by Club

			Tot	Start	Sub	FA	FL	Lge	FA	FL
QPR	92/3 to 94/5		25	21	4	3	2	1	1	1
Total			*25*	*21*	*4*	*3*	*2*	*1*	*1*	*1*

MERSON Paul — Arsenal

Fullname: Paul Charles Merson   DOB: 21-03-72 Harlesden
Debut: ARSENAL v Norwich City 15/8/92
Debut Goal: ARSENAL v Sheffield Wednesday 29/8/92

Previous Clubs Details			Apps					Goals		
Club	Signed	Fee	Tot	Start	Sub	FA	FL	Lge	FA	FL
Arsenal	Nov-85		257	219	38	26	30	66	4	9
Brentford	Jan-87	Loan	7	6	1	0	0	0	0	0

FAPL Summary by Club

			Tot	Start	Sub	FA	FL	Lge	FA	FL
Arsenal	92/3 to 94/5		90	80	10	11	15	17	1	3
Total			*90*	*80*	*10*	*11*	*15*	*17*	*1*	*3*

MIKE Adrian — Manchester City

Fullname: Adrian Roosevelt Mike   DOB: 17-11-77 Manchester
Debut: MANCHESTER CITY v Middlesbrough 12/9/92
Debut Goal: Swindon Town v MANCHESTER CITY 1/9/93

Previous Clubs Details			*Apps*					*Goals*		
Club	Signed	Fee	Tot	Start	Sub	FA	FL	Lge	FA	FL
Manchester C	Jun-92		16	5	11	1	2	2	0	0
Bury	Mar-93	Loan	7	5	2	0	0	1	0	0
FAPL Summary by Club										
Manchester C	92/3 to 94/5		14	3	11	1	2	1	0	0
Total			*14*	*3*	*11*	*1*	*2*	*1*	*0*	*0*

MIKLOSKO Ludek   West Ham United

Fullname: Ludek Miklosko   DOB: 10-12-65 Protesov, Czech'kia
Debut: WEST HAM UNITED v Wimbledon 14/8/93
Debut Goal: (Goalkeeper)

Previous Clubs Details			*Apps*					*Goals*		
Club	Signed	Fee	Tot	Start	Sub	FA	FL	Lge	FA	FL
Banik Ostrava										
West Ham Utd	Feb-90	£300,000	230	230	0	20	17	0	0	0
FAPL Summary by Club										
West Ham Utd	93/4 to 94/5		84	84	0	8	7	0	0	0
Total			*84*	*84*	*0*	*8*	*7*	*0*	*0*	*0*

MILLER Alan   Middlesbrough

Fullname: Alan John Miller   DOB: 30-03-74 Epping
Debut: Leeds United v ARSENAL 21/11/92
Debut Goal: (Goalkeeper)

Previous Clubs Details			*Apps*					*Goals*		
Club	Signed	Fee	Tot	Start	Sub	FA	FL	Lge	FA	FL
Arsenal	May-88		8	6	2	0	0	0	0	0
Plymouth Arg	Nov-88	Loan	13	13	0	2	0	0	0	0
WBA	Aug-91	Loan	3	3	0	0	0	0	0	0
Birmingham C	Dec-91	Loan	15	15	0	0	0	0	0	0
Middlesbrough	Aug-94	£500,000	41	41	0	2	1	0	0	0
FAPL Summary by Club										
Arsenal	92/3 to 93/4		8	6	2	0	0	0	0	0
Total			*8*	*6*	*2*	*0*	*0*	*0*	*0*	*0*

MILOSEVIC Savo   Aston Villa

Fullname: Savo Milosevic   DOB:
Debut: Debut Goal:

Previous Clubs Details			*Apps*					*Goals*		
Club	Signed	Fee	Tot	Start	Sub	FA	FL	Lge	FA	FL
Partizan Belgrade										
Aston Villa	Jun-95	£3.5m								

MIMMS Bobby   Blackburn Rovers

Fullname: Robert Andrew Mimms   DOB: 13-10-67 York
Debut: Crystal Palace v BLACKBURN ROVERS 15/8/93

Debut Goal: (Goalkeeper)

Previous Clubs Details

Club	Signed	Fee	Apps					Goals		
			Tot	Start	Sub	FA	FL	Lge	FA	FL
Halifax T	Aug-81		0	0	0	0	0	0	0	0
Rotherham Utd	Nov-81	£15,000	83	83	0	3	7	0	0	0
Everton	May-85	£150,000	29	29	0	2	2	0	0	0
Notts County	Mar-86	Loan	2	2	0	0	0	0	0	0
Sunderland	Dec-86	Loan	4	4	0	0	0	0	0	0
Blackburn R	Jan-87	Loan	6	6	0	0	0	0	0	0
Manchester C	Sep-87	Loan	3	3	0	0	0	0	0	0
Tottenham H	Feb-88	£325,000	37	37	0	2	5	0	0	0
Aberdeen	Feb-90	Loan	0	0	0	0	0	0	0	0
Blackburn R	Dec-90	£250,000	126	125	1	9	14	0	0	0

FAPL Summary by Club

Blackburn Rovers	92/3 to 94/5		59	58	1	5	12	0	0	0
Total			*59*	*58*	*1*	*5*	*12*	*0*	*0*	*0*

MINTO Scott — Chelsea

Fullname: Scott C Minto DOB: 07-08-75 Heswall
Debut: Nottingham Forest v CHELSEA 19/11/94
Debut Goal:

Previous Clubs Details

Club	Signed	Fee	Apps					Goals		
			Tot	Start	Sub	FA	FL	Lge	FA	FL
Charlton Ath	Feb-89		180	171	9	10	8	6	0	2
Chelsea	Jun-94	£775,000	19	19	0	2	0	0	0	0

FAPL Summary by Club

Chelsea	94/5		19	19	0	2	0	0	0	0
Total			*19*	*19*	*0*	*2*	*0*	*0*	*0*	*0*

MOLBY Jan — Liverpool

Fullname: Jan Molby DOB: 05-07-67 Jutland, Denmark
Debut: LIVERPOOL v Arsenal 23/8/92
Debut Goal: Ipswich Town v LIVERPOOL 25/8/92

Previous Clubs Details

Club	Signed	Fee	Apps					Goals		
			Tot	Start	Sub	FA	FL	Lge	FA	FL
Liverpool	Aug-84	£575,000	218	195	23	28	28	44	4	9

FAPL Summary by Club

Liverpool	92/3 to 94/5		35	31	4	0	5	7	0	1
Total			*35*	*31*	*4*	*0*	*5*	*7*	*0*	*1*

MONCUR John — West Ham United

Fullname: John F Moncur DOB: 23-09-70 Stepney
Debut: Sheffield United v SWINDON TOWN 14/8/93
Debut Goal: Sheffield United v SWINDON TOWN 14/8/93

Previous Clubs Details			Apps					Goals		
Club	Signed	Fee	Tot	Start	Sub	FA	FL	Lge	FA	FL
Tottenham H	Aug-84		21	10	11	0	3	1	0	0
Doncaster R	Sep-86	Loan	4	4	0	0	0	0	0	0
Cambridge Utd	Mar-87	Loan	4	3	1	0	0	0	0	0
Portsmouth	Mar-89	Loan	7	7	0	0	0	0	0	0
Brentford	Oct-89	Loan	5	5	0	0	0	0	0	0
Ipswich T	Oct-91	Loan	6	5	1	0	0	0	0	0
N Forest	Feb-92	Loan	0	0	0	0	0	0	0	0
Swindon T	Mar-92	£80,000	58	53	5	1	4	5	0	0
West Ham Utd	Aug-94	£1m	30	30	0	2	3	2	0	1
FAPL Summary by Club										
Swindon T	93/4 to 94/5		41	41	0	1	3	4	0	0
West Ham Utd	94/5		30	30	0	2	3	2	0	1
Total			71	71	0	3	6	6	0	1

MONKOU Ken   Southampton
Fullname: Kenneth John Monkou   DOB: 30-11-68 Necare, Surinam
Debut: SOUTHAMPTON v Manchester United 24/8/92
Debut Goal: SOUTHAMPTON v Sheffield Wednesday 28/12/92

Previous Clubs Details			Apps					Goals		
Club	Signed	Fee	Tot	Start	Sub	FA	FL	Lge	FA	FL
Chelsea	Mar-89	£100,000	94	92	2	3	12	2	0	0
Southampton	Aug-92	£750,000	99	99	0	7	6	6	0	0
FAPL Summary by Club										
Southampton	92/3 to 94/5		99	99	0	7	6	6	0	0
Total			99	99	0	7	6	6	0	0

MOORE Neil   Everton
Fullname: Neil Moore   DOB: 22-09-76 Liverpool
Debut: EVERTON v Sheffield United 4/5/93
Debut Goal:

Previous Clubs Details			Apps					Goals		
Club	Signed	Fee	Tot	Start	Sub	FA	FL	Lge	FA	FL
Everton	Jun-91		5	4	1	0	1	0	0	0
Blackpool	Sep-94	Loan								
Oldham Ath	Feb-95	Loan								
FAPL Summary by Club										
Everton	92/3 to 93/4		5	4	1	0	1	0	0	0
Total			5	4	1	0	1	0	0	0

MOORE Alan   Middlesbrough
Fullname: Alan Moore   DOB: 26-11-78 Dublin
Debut: MIDDLESBROUGH v Everton 10/4/92
Debut Goal:

Previous Clubs Details			Apps					Goals		
Club	Signed	Fee	Tot	Start	Sub	FA	FL	Lge	FA	FL
Middlesbrough	Dec-91	Trainee	81	77	4	3	6	15	2	0
FAPL Summary by Club										
Middlesbrough		92/3	2	0	2	0	0	0	0	0
Total			*2*	*0*	*2*	*0*	*0*	*0*	*0*	*0*

MORENO Jaime   Middlesbrough
Fullname: Jaime Moreno   DOB: 19-01-74 Bolivia
Debut: Debut Goal:

Previous Clubs Details			Apps					Goals		
Club	Signed	Fee	Tot	Start	Sub	FA	FL	Lge	FA	FL
Blooming (Bolivia)										
Middlesbrough		£250,000	14	6	8	0	1	1	0	0

MORGAN Steve   Coventry City
Fullname: Stephen A Morgan   DOB: 20-09-72 Oldham
Debut: Arsenal v COVENTRY CITY 14/8/93
Debut Goal: COVENTRY CITY v Chelsea 18/9/93

Previous Clubs Details			Apps					Goals		
Club	Signed	Fee	Tot	Start	Sub	FA	FL	Lge	FA	FL
Blackpool	Aug-86		144	135	9	16	13	10	1	2
Plymouth Arg	Jul-90	£115,000	121	120	1	6	7	6	0	0
Coventry C	Jul-93	£110,000	68	65	3	5	5	2	0	3
FAPL Summary by Club										
Coventry C	93/4 to 94/5		68	65	3	5	5	2	0	3
Total			*68*	*65*	*3*	*5*	*5*	*2*	*0*	*3*

MORLEY Trevor   West Ham United
Fullname: Trevor W Morley   DOB: 21-03-66 Nottingham
Debut: WEST HAM UNITED v Wimbledon 14/8/93
Debut Goal: Blackburn Rovers v WEST HAM UNITED 18/9/93

Previous Clubs Details			Apps					Goals		
Club	Signed	Fee	Tot	Start	Sub	FA	FL	Lge	FA	FL
Northampton T	Jun-85	£20,000	107	107	0	6	10	39	2	4
Manchester C	Jan-88	£175,000	72	69	3	1	7	18	0	3
West Ham Utd	Dec-89	£500,000	178	159	19	19	11	57	7	5
FAPL Summary by Club										
West Ham Utd	93/4 to 94/5		56	49	7	5	4	13	0	3
Total			*56*	*49*	*7*	*5*	*4*	*13*	*0*	*3*

MORROW Steve   Arsenal
Fullname: Stephen Joseph Morrow   DOB: 03-07-74 Bangor, N.Ireland
Debut: ARSENAL v Oldham Athletic 26/8/92
Debut Goal: Blackburn Rovers v ARSENAL 8/3/95

Previous Clubs Details			Apps					Goals		
Club	Signed	Fee	Tot	Start	Sub	FA	FL	Lge	FA	FL
Arsenal	May-88		44	31	13	5	8	1	0	2
Reading	Jan-91	Loan	10	10	0	0	0	0	0	0
Watford	Aug-91	Loan	8	7	1	0	0	0	0	0
Reading	Oct-91	Loan	3	3	0	0	0	0	0	0
Barnet	Mar-92	Loan	1	1	0	0	0	0	0	0
FAPL Summary by Club										
Arsenal	92/3 to 94/5		42	31	11	5	8	1	0	2
Total			42	31	11	5	8	1	0	2

MUSTOE Robbie   Middlesbrough
Fullname: DOB: 29-08-72 Witney
Debut: Coventry City v MIDDLESBROUGH 15/8/92
Debut Goal: Tottenham Hotspur v MIDDLESBROUGH 17/10/92

Previous Clubs Details			Apps					Goals		
Club	Signed	Fee	Tot	Start	Sub	FA	FL	Lge	FA	FL
Oxford Utd	Jul-86	Junior	91	78	13	2	2	10	0	0
Middlesbrough	Jul-90	£375,000	156	150	9	1	0	12	0	1
FAPL Summary by Club										
Middlesbrough	92/3 to 94/5		23	21	2			1		
Total			23	21	2	0	0	1	0	0

MYERS Andy   Chelsea
Fullname: Andrew John Myers   DOB: 04-11-77 Hounslow
Debut: Wimbledon v CHELSEA 28/12/92
Debut Goal:

Previous Clubs Details			Apps					Goals		
Club	Signed	Fee	Tot	Start	Sub	FA	FL	Lge	FA	FL
Chelsea	Jun-91		33	27	6	6	2	1	0	0
FAPL Summary by Club										
Chelsea	92/3 to 94/5		19	18	1	4	1	0	0	0
Total			19	18	1	4	1	0	0	0

NDLOVU Peter   Coventry City
Fullname: Peter Ndlovu   DOB: 26-02-77 Bulawayo, Zimbabwe
Debut: Tottenham Hotspur v COVENTRY CITY 19/8/92 as sub
Debut Goal: Sheffield Wednesday v COVENTRY CITY 2/9/92

Previous Clubs Details			Apps					Goals		
Club	Signed	Fee	Tot	Start	Sub	FA	FL	Lge	FA	FL
Coventry C	Jul-91	£10,000	125	104	21	5	7	31	1	1
FAPL Summary by Club										
Coventry C	92/3 to 94/5		102	95	7	5	4	29	1	1
Total			102	95	7	5	4	29	1	1

NEILSON Alan — Newcastle United

Fullname: Alan B Neilson DOB: 27-09-76 Wegburg, Germany
Debut: Ipswich Town v NEWCASTLE UNITED 31/8/93 as sub
Debut Goal:

Previous Clubs Details			*Apps*					*Goals*		
Club	Signed	Fee	Tot	Start	Sub	FA	FL	Lge	FA	FL
Newcastle Utd	Feb-91	Trainee	42	35	7	0	4	1	0	0
FAPL Summary by Club										
Newcastle Utd	93/4 to 94/5		20	15	5	0	1	0	0	0
Total			*20*	*15*	*5*	*0*	*1*	*0*	*0*	*0*

NETHERCOTT Stuart — Tottenham Hotspur

Fullname: Stuart D Nethercott DOB: 22-03-77 Ilford
Debut: TOTTENHAM HOTSPUR v Norwich City 9/4/93 as sub
Debut Goal:

Previous Clubs Details			*Apps*					*Goals*		
Club	Signed	Fee	Tot	Start	Sub	FA	FL	Lge	FA	FL
Tottenham H	Jul-91		32	20	12	5	0	0	1	0
Maidstone Utd	Sep-91	Loan	13	13	0	0	0	1	0	0
Barnet	Feb-92	Loan	3	3	0	0	0	0	0	0
FAPL Summary by Club										
Tottenham H	92/3 to 94/5		32	20	12	5	0	0	1	0
Total			*32*	*20*	*12*	*5*	*0*	*0*	*1*	*0*

NEVILLE Phil — Manchester United

Fullname: Phil Neville DOB:
Debut: Manchester City v MANCHESTER UNITED 11/2/95
Debut Goal:

Previous Clubs Details			*Apps*					*Goals*		
Club	Signed	Fee	Tot	Start	Sub	FA	FL	Lge	FA	FL
Manchester Utd			2	1	1	1	0	0	0	0
FAPL Summary by Club										
Manchester Utd	94/5		2	1	1	1	0	0	0	0
Total			*2*	*1*	*1*	*1*	*0*	*0*	*0*	*0*

NEVILLE Gary — Manchester United

Fullname: Gary Neville DOB: 19-02-79 Bury
Debut: MANCHESTER UNITED v Crystal Palace 19/11/94
Debut Goal:

Previous Clubs Details			*Apps*					*Goals*		
Club	Signed	Fee	Tot	Start	Sub	FA	FL	Lge	FA	FL
Manchester Utd	Jan-93	Trainee	18	16	2	4	3	0	0	0
FAPL Summary by Club										
Manchester Utd	94/5		18	16	2	4	3	0	0	0
Total			*18*	*16*	*2*	*4*	*3*	*0*	*0*	*0*

NEWELL Mike   Blackburn Rovers

Fullname: Michael Colin Newell   DOB: 28-01-69 Liverpool
Debut: Crystal Palace v BLACKBURN ROVERS 15/8/92
Debut Goal: BLACKBURN ROVERS v Manchester City 22/8/92

Previous Clubs Details			*Apps*					*Goals*		
Club	Signed	Fee	Tot	Start	Sub	FA	FL	Lge	FA	FL
Crewe Alex	Sep-83	Free	3	3	0	0	0	0	0	0
Wigan Ath	Oct-83	Free	72	64	8	8	6	25	6	1
Luton T	Jan-86	£100,000	63	62	1	5	0	18	1	0
Leicester C	Sep-87	£350,000	81	81	0	2	9	21	0	5
Everton	Jun-89	£1.1m	68	48	20	10	10	15	0	4
Blackburn R	Nov-91	£1.1m	98	85	13	9	12	26	6	7
FAPL Summary by Club										
Blackburn R	92/3 to 94/5		80	69	11	7	12	10	3	7
Total			*80*	*69*	*11*	*7*	*12*	*10*	*3*	*7*

NEWTON Eddie   Chelsea

Fullname: Edward John Ikem Newton   DOB: 14-12-75 Hammersmith
Debut: Norwich City v CHELSEA 19/8/92
Debut Goal: CHELSEA v Sheffield Wednesday 22/8/92

Previous Clubs Details			*Apps*					*Goals*		
Club	Signed	Fee	Tot	Start	Sub	FA	FL	Lge	FA	FL
Chelsea	May-90		101	87	14	9	12	7	0	1
Cardiff C	Jan-92	Loan	18	18	0	0	0	4	0	0
FAPL Summary by Club										
Chelsea	92/3 to 94/5		100	87	13	9	12	6	0	0
Total			*100*	*87*	*13*	*9*	*12*	*6*	*0*	*0*

NOLAN Ian   Sheffield Wednesday

Fullname: Ian R Nolan   DOB: 10-07-74 Liverpool
Debut: SHEFFIELD WED v Tottenham Hotspur 20/8/94
Debut Goal: Liverpool v SHEFFIELD WEDNESDAY 1/10/94

Previous Clubs Details			*Apps*					*Goals*		
Club	Signed	Fee	Tot	Start	Sub	FA	FL	Lge	FA	FL
Preston										
Tranmere R	Aug-91	£10,000	88	87	1	7	10	1	1	0
Sheffield W	Aug-94	£1.5m	42	42	0	3	4	3	0	0
FAPL Summary by Club										
Sheffield W	94/5		42	42	0	3	4	3	0	0
Total			*42*	*42*	*0*	*3*	*4*	*3*	*0*	*0*

O'HALLORAN Keith   Middlesbrough

Fullname: Keith O'Halloran   DOB:
Debut: Debut Goal:

Previous Clubs Details			Apps					Goals		
Club	Signed	Fee	Tot	Start	Sub	FA	FL	Lge	FA	FL
Cherry Orchard										
Middlesbrough	Sep-94		1	0	1	0	0	0	0	0

OAKLEY Matthew   Southampton

Fullname: Matthew Oakley   DOB:
Debut: Everton v TOTTENHAM HOTSPUR 6/5/95 as sub
Debut Goal:

Previous Clubs Details			Apps					Goals		
Club	Signed	Fee	Tot	Start	Sub	FA	FL	Lge	FA	FL
Southampton			1	0	1	0	0	0	0	0
FAPL Summary by Club										
Southampton		94/5	1	0	1	0	0	0	0	0
Total			*1*	*0*	*1*	*0*	*0*	*0*	*0*	*0*

OGRIZOVIC Steve   Coventry City

Fullname: Steven Ogrizovic   DOB: 13-09-61 Mansfield
Debut: COVENTRY CITY v Middlesbrough 15/8/92
Debut Goal:

Previous Clubs Details			Apps					Goals		
Club	Signed	Fee	Tot	Start	Sub	FA	FL	Lge	FA	FL
Chesterfield	Jul-77		16	16	0	0	2	0	0	0
Liverpool	Nov-77	£70,000	4	4	0	0	0	0	0	0
Shrewsbury T	Aug-82	£70,000	84	84	0	5	7	0	0	0
Coventry C	Jun-84	£72,000	415	415	0	25	40	1	0	0
FAPL Summary by Club										
Coventry C	92/3 to 94/5		99	99	0	6	8	0	0	0
Total			*99*	*99*	*0*	*6*	*8*	*0*	*0*	*0*

PAATELAINEN Mixu   Bolton Wanderers

Fullname: Mixu Paatelainen   DOB: 04-02-71 Helsinki
Debut: Debut Goal:

Previous Clubs Details			Apps					Goals		
Club	Signed	Fee	Tot	Start	Sub	FA	FL	Lge	FA	FL
Dundee Utd	1987		133					33		
Aberdeen	1991		75	53	22	8	6	23	1	3
Bolton Wdrs	Aug-94	£300,000	44	43	1	1	8	11	0	2

PALLISTER Gary   Manchester United

Fullname: Gary Andrew Pallister   DOB: 01-07-69 Ramsgate
Debut: Sheffield United v MANCHESTER UNITED 15/8/92
Debut Goal: MANCHESTER UNITED v Blackburn Rovers 3/5/93

Previous Clubs Details			Apps					Goals		
Club	Signed	Fee	Tot	Start	Sub	FA	FL	Lge	FA	FL
Middlesbrough	Nov-84		156	156	0	10	10	5	1	0

Club	Signed	Fee	Tot	Start	Sub	FA	FL	Lge	FA	FL
Darlington	Oct-85	Loan	7	7	0	0	0	0	0	0
Manchester Utd	Aug-89	£2.3m	236	233	3	31	34	8	2	0
FAPL Summary by Club										
Manchester Utd	92/3 to 94/5		125	125	0	17	14	4	2	0
Total			*125*	*125*	*0*	*17*	*14*	*4*	*2*	*0*

PALMER Carlton Leeds United

Fullname: Carlton Lloyd Palmer   DOB: 06-12-69 Rowley Regis
Debut: Everton v SHEFFIELD WEDNESDAY 15/8/92
Debut Goal: SHEFFIELD WEDNESDAY v Oldham Athletic 17/10/92

Previous Clubs Details			*Apps*					*Goals*		
Club	Signed	Fee	Tot	Start	Sub	FA	FL	Lge	FA	FL
WBA	Dec-84		121	114	7	4	8	4	0	1
Sheffield W	Feb-89	£750,000	205	204	1	18	31	14	2	1
Leeds Utd	Aug-94	£2.8m	39	39	0	3	2	3	1	0
FAPL Summary by Club										
Sheffield W	92/3 to 93/4		71	70	1	11	16	6	2	1
Leeds Utd	94/5		39	39	0	3	2	3	1	0
Total			*110*	*109*	*1*	*14*	*18*	*9*	*3*	*1*

PAPAVASSILLIOU Nicodenos Newcastle United

Fullname: Nicodenos Papavassilliou   DOB: 31-08-74 Limassol, Cyprus
Debut: NEWCASTLE UNITED v Tottenham Hotspur 14/8/93
Debut Goal:

Previous Clubs Details			*Apps*					*Goals*		
Club	Signed	Fee	Tot	Start	Sub	FA	FL	Lge	FA	FL
Newcastle Utd	Jul-93	£120,000	7	7	0	0	0	0	0	0
FAPL Summary by Club										
Newcastle Utd	93/4		7	7	0	0	0	0	0	0
Total			*7*	*7*	*0*	*0*	*0*	*0*	*0*	*0*

PARKER Paul Manchester United

Fullname: Paul Andrew Parker   DOB: 05-04-68 West Ham
Debut: MANCHESTER UNITED v Liverpool 18/10/92
Debut Goal: MANCHESTER UNITED v Tottenham Hotspur 9/1/93

Previous Clubs Details			*Apps*					*Goals*		
Club	Signed	Fee	Tot	Start	Sub	FA	FL	Lge	FA	FL
Fulham	Apr-82		153	140	13	11	16	2	0	1
QPR	Jun-87	£300,000	125	121	4	16	14	1	0	0
Manchester Utd	Aug-91	£2m	99	95	4	13	14	1	0	0
FAPL Summary by Club										
Manchester Utd	92/3 to 94/5		73	71	2	10	8	1	0	0
Total			*73*	*71*	*2*	*10*	*8*	*1*	*0*	*0*

PARKINSON Joe — Everton

Fullname: Joseph S Parkinson DOB: 12-06-75 Eccles
Debut: EVERTON v Aston Villa 20/8/94 as sub
Debut Goal:

Previous Clubs Details

Club	Signed	Fee	Tot	Start	Sub	FA	FL	Lge	FA	FL
Wigan Ath	Apr-89		119	115	4	9	11	6	0	1
Bournemouth	Jul-93	£35,000	30	30	0	4	4	1	0	1
Everton	Mar-94	£25,000	34	32	2	6	2	0	1	0

FAPL Summary by Club

Everton	94/5		34	32	2	6	2	0	1	0
Total			*34*	*32*	*2*	*6*	*2*	*0*	*1*	*0*

PARLOUR Ray — Arsenal

Fullname: Raymond Parlour DOB: 08-03-77 Romford
Debut: ARSENAL v Sheffield Wednesday 29/8/92
Debut Goal: ARSENAL v Sheffield Wednesday 29/8/92

Previous Clubs Details

Club	Signed	Fee	Tot	Start	Sub	FA	FL	Lge	FA	FL
Arsenal	Mar-91		84	64	20	9	11	4	1	0

FAPL Summary by Club

Arsenal	92/3 to 94/5		78	62	16	9	11	3	1	0
Total			*78*	*62*	*16*	*9*	*11*	*3*	*1*	*0*

PEACOCK Darren — Newcastle United

Fullname: Darren Peacock DOB: 04-02-72 Bristol
Debut: Manchester City v QPR 17/8/92
Debut Goal: QPR v Coventry City 20/2/93

Previous Clubs Details

Club	Signed	Fee	Tot	Start	Sub	FA	FL	Lge	FA	FL
Newport C	Feb-86		28	24	4	1	2	0	0	0
Hereford Utd	Mar-89		59	56	3	6	6	5	0	1
QPR	Dec-90	£200,000	126	123	3	3	12	6	0	1
Newcastle Utd	Mar-94	£2.7m	44	44	0	5	4	1	0	0

FAPL Summary by Club

QPR	92/3 to 93/4		68	65	3	2	8	5	0	1
Newcastle Utd	93/4 to 94/5		44	44	0	5	4	1	0	0
Total			*112*	*109*	*3*	*7*	*12*	*6*	*0*	*1*

PEACOCK Gavin — Chelsea

Fullname: Gavin K Peacock DOB: 19-11-71 Welling, Kent
Debut: CHELSEA v Blackburn Rovers 14/8/92
Debut Goal: CHELSEA v Blackburn Rovers 14/8/92

Previous Clubs Details

Club	Signed	Fee	Tot	Start	Sub	FA	FL	Lge	FA	FL
QPR	Nov-84		17	7	10	1	0	1	0	0

			Apps					Goals		
Gillingham	Oct-87	£40,000	70	69	1	2	4	11	0	0
Bournemouth	Aug-89	£250,000	56	56	0	2	6	8	0	0
Newcastle Utd	Nov-90	£150,000	106	102	4	6	6	35	2	5
Chelsea	Aug-93	£1.25m	75	75	0	11	5	12	7	1
FAPL Summary by Club										
Newcastle Utd	92/3 to 93/4		32	29	3	4	4	12	2	2
Chelsea	93/4 to 94/5		75	75	0	11	5	12	7	1
Total			*107*	*104*	*3*	*15*	*9*	*24*	*9*	*3*

PEARCE Ian   Blackburn Rovers
Fullname: Ian Anthony Pearce   DOB: 08-05-78 Bury St Edmunds
Debut: CHELSEA v Liverpool 5/9/92 as sub
Debut Goal: West Ham United v BLACKBURN ROVERS 27/4/94

Previous Clubs Details			Apps					Goals		
Club	Signed	Fee	Tot	Start	Sub	FA	FL	Lge	FA	FL
Chelsea	Aug-91		4	0	4	0	0	0	0	0
Blackburn R	Oct-93	£300,000	33	23	10	3	3	1	0	1
FAPL Summary by Club										
Chelsea	92/3 to 93/4		1	0	1	0	0	0	0	0
Blackburn Rovers	93/4 to 94/5		33	23	10	3	3	1	0	1
Total			*34*	*23*	*11*	*3*	*3*	*1*	*0*	*1*

PEARCE Stuart   Nottingham Forest
Fullname: Stuart Pearce   DOB: 25-04-66 Shepherds Bush
Debut: NOTTINGHAM FOREST v Liverpool 16/8/92
Debut Goal: Oldham Athletic v NOTTINGHAM FOREST 22/8/92

Previous Clubs Details			Apps					Goals		
Club	Signed	Fee	Tot	Start	Sub	FA	FL	Lge	FA	FL
Coventry C	Oct-83	£25,000	52	52	0	2	0	4	0	0
N Forest	Jun-85	£200,000	337	337	0	31	57	55	7	9
FAPL Summary by Club										
N Forest	92/3 to 94/5		59	59	0	4	8	10	0	2
Total			*59*	*59*	*0*	*4*	*8*	*10*	*0*	*2*

PEARCE Andy   Sheffield Wednesday
Fullname: Andrew John Pearce   DOB: 21-04-70 Bradford on Avon
Debut: COVENTRY CITY v Middlesbrough 15/8/92
Debut Goal: COVENTRY CITY v Crystal Palace 3/10/92

Previous Clubs Details			Apps					Goals		
Club	Signed	Fee	Tot	Start	Sub	FA	FL	Lge	FA	FL
Coventry C	May-90	£15,000	71	68	3	3	6	4	0	0
Sheffield W	Aug-93	£500,000	66	63	3	7	11	3	1	0
FAPL Summary by Club										
Coventry C	92/3 to 94/5		24	21	3	1	2	1	0	0
Sheffield W	93/4 to 94/5		66	63	3	7	11	3	0	1
Total			*90*	*84*	*6*	*8*	*13*	*4*	*0*	*1*

PEARS Stephen   Middlesbrough
Fullname: Stephen Pears   DOB: 23-01-66 Brandon
Debut: Coventry City v MIDDLESBROUGH 15/8/92
Debut Goal:

Previous Clubs Details

Club	Signed	Fee	Apps					Goals		
			Tot	Start	Sub	FA	FL	Lge	FA	FL
Manchester Utd	Jan-79	Apprentice	4	4	0	0	1	0	0	0
Middlesbrough	Nov-83	Loan	12	12	0	2	0	0	0	0
Middlesbrough	Jul-85	£80,000	327	327	0	23	32	0	0	0

FAPL Summary by Club

Middlesbrough	92/3		26	26	0			26		
Total			*26*	*26*	*0*	*0*	*0*	*26*	*0*	*0*

PEARSON Nigel   Middlesbrough
Fullname: Nigel Graham Pearson   DOB: 22-08-67 Nottingham
Debut: Everton v SHEFFIELD WEDNESDAY 15/8/92
Debut Goal: Everton v SHEFFIELD WEDNESDAY 15/8/92

Previous Clubs Details

Club	Signed	Fee	Apps					Goals		
			Tot	Start	Sub	FA	FL	Lge	FA	FL
Shrewsbury T	Nov-81	£5,000	153	153	0	6	19	5	0	0
Sheffield W	Oct-87	£250,000	180	176	4	15	19	14	1	5
Middlesbrough	Jul-94	£750,000	9	6	3	0	0	0	0	0

FAPL Summary by Club

Sheffield W	92/3 to 93/4		21	17	4	2	5	1	0	0
Total			*21*	*17*	*4*	*2*	*5*	*1*	*0*	*0*

PEMBERTON John   Leeds United
Fullname: John Matthew Pemberton   DOB: 19-11-68 Oldham
Debut: Norwich City v SHEFFIELD UNITED 21/11/92
Debut Goal:

Previous Clubs Details

Club	Signed	Fee	Apps					Goals		
			Tot	Start	Sub	FA	FL	Lge	FA	FL
Rochdale	Sep-84		1	1	0	0	0	0	0	0
Crewe Alex	Mar-85		121	116	5	3	7	1	0	1
Crystal Palace	Mar-88	£80,000	78	76	2	8	7	2	0	0
Sheffield Utd	Jul-90	£300,000	68	67	1	4	4	0	0	0
Leeds Utd	Nov-93	£250,000	36	28	8	4	1	0	0	0

FAPL Summary by Club

Sheffield Utd	92/3 to 93/4		19	19	0	4	0	0	0	0
Leeds Utd	93/4 to 94/5		36	28	8	4	1	0	0	0
Total			*55*	*47*	*8*	*8*	*1*	*0*	*0*	*0*

PENRICE Gary   QPR
Fullname: Gary Kenneth Penrice   DOB: 24-03-68 Bristol
Debut: Coventry City v QPR 26/8/92 as sub
Debut Goal: QPR v Middlesbrough 19/9/92

			Apps					Goals		
Previous Clubs Details										
Club	Signed	Fee	Tot	Start	Sub	FA	FL	Lge	FA	FL
Bristol Rovers	Nov-84		188	186	2	11	11	53	7	3
Watford	Nov-89	£500,000	43	41	2	4	0	17	1	0
Aston Villa	Mar-91	£1m	20	14	6	0	0	1	0	0
QPR	Oct-91	£625,000	79	55	24	4	7	17	0	2
FAPL Summary by Club										
QPR	92/3 to 94/5		59	42	17	3	6	17	1	1
Total			*59*	*42*	*17*	*3*	*6*	*17*	*1*	*1*

PERRY Chris   Wimbledon

Fullname: Christopher John Perry   DOB: 26-12-79 Surrey
Debut: WIMBLEDON v Liverpool 4/4/94 as sub
Debut Goal:

			Apps					Goals		
Previous Clubs Details										
Club	Signed	Fee	Tot	Start	Sub	FA	FL	Lge	FA	FL
Wimbledon	Jul-91		23	16	7	3	2	0	0	0
FAPL Summary by Club										
Wimbledon	93/4 to 94/5		23	16	7	3	2	0	0	0
Total			*23*	*16*	*7*	*3*	*2*	*0*	*0*	*0*

PETRESCU Dan   Sheffield Wednesday

Fullname: Dan Vasile Petrescu   DOB: 23-12-71 Bucharest
Debut: SHEFFIELD WED v Tottenham Hotspur 20/8/94
Debut Goal: SHEFFIELD WED v Tottenham Hotspur 20/8/94

			Apps					Goals		
Previous Clubs Details										
Club	Signed	Fee	Tot	Start	Sub	FA	FL	Lge	FA	FL
CSA Steaua Bucharest	Jun-86		2	2	0	0	0	0	0	0
FC Olt Scornicesti	Jul-86		24	24	0	1	0	0	0	0
CSA Steaua Bucharest	Jul-87		93	93	0	14	0	27	3	0
Foggia	Jul-91		55	55	0	6	–	7	0	–
Genoa	Jul-93		24	24	0	1	–	1	0	–
Sheffield W	Aug-94	£1.3m	29	20	9	2	2	3	0	0
FAPL Summary by Club										
Sheffield W	94/5		29	20	9	2	2	3	0	0
Total			*29*	*20*	*9*	*2*	*2*	*3*	*0*	*0*

PHELAN Terry   Manchester City

Fullname: Terence M Phelan   DOB: 17-03-71 Manchester
Debut: MANCHESTER CITY v Norwich City 26/8/92
Debut Goal: MANCHESTER CITY v Southampton 28/12/93

			Apps					Goals		
Previous Clubs Details										
Club	Signed	Fee	Tot	Start	Sub	FA	FL	Lge	FA	FL
Leeds Utd	Aug-84		14	12	2	0	3	0	0	0
Swansea C	Jul-86	Free	45	45	0	5	4	0	0	0

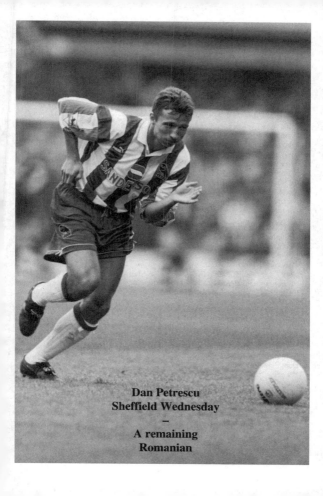

Dan Petrescu
Sheffield Wednesday
–
A remaining
Romanian

Wimbledon	Jul-87	£100,000	159	155	4	16	15	1	2	0
Manchester C	Aug-92	£2.5m	93	92	1	8	10	1	1	0

FAPL Summary by Club

Manchester C	92/3 to 94/5		94	93	1	8	10	1	1	0
Total			*94*	*93*	*1*	*8*	*10*	*1*	*1*	*0*

PHILLIPS David   Nottingham Forest
Fullname: David Owen Phillips   DOB: 30-07-67 Wegberg, Germany
Debut: Arsenal v NORWICH CITY 15/8/92
Debut Goal: Arsenal v NORWICH CITY 15/8/92

Previous Clubs Details

			Apps					Goals		
Club	Signed	Fee	Tot	Start	Sub	FA	FL	Lge	FA	FL
Plymouth Arg	Aug-81		73	65	8	13	3	15	0	0
Manchester C	Aug-84	£65,000	81	81	0	5	8	13	0	0
Coventry C	Jun-86	£150,000	100	93	7	9	8	8	1	0
Norwich C	Jun-89	£525,000	152	152	0	14	12	17	1	0
N Forest	Aug-93	£600,000	81	78	3	4	11	5	0	0

FAPL Summary by Club

Norwich C	92/3 to 94/5		42	42	0	2	2	8	0	0
N Forest	94/5		38	38	0	2	4	1	0	0
Total			*80*	*80*	*0*	*4*	*6*	*9*	*0*	*0*

PICKERING Ally   Coventry City
Fullname: Alistair G Pickering   DOB: 23-06-71 Manchester
Debut: Liverpool v COVENTRY CITY 26/2/94 as sub
Debut Goal:

Previous Clubs Details

			Apps					Goals		
Club	Signed	Fee	Tot	Start	Sub	FA	FL	Lge	FA	FL
Rotherham Utd	Feb-90	£18,500	88	87	1	9	6	2	0	0
Coventry C	Oct-93	£80,000	35	28	7	2	3	0	0	0

FAPL Summary by Club

Coventry C	93/4 to 94/5		35	28	7	2	3	0	0	0
Total			*35*	*28*	*7*	*2*	*3*	*0*	*0*	*0*

PILKINGTON Kevin   Manchester United
Fullname: Kevin Pilkington   DOB: 09-03-78 Hitchin
Debut: MANCHESTER UTD v Crystal Palace 19/11/94 as sub
Debut Goal:

Previous Clubs Details

			Apps					Goals		
Club	Signed	Fee	Tot	Start	Sub	FA	FL	Lge	FA	FL
Manchester Utd	Jul-92	Trainee	1	1	0	0	0	0	0	0

FAPL Summary by Club

Manchester Utd	94/5		1	0	1	0	0	0	0	0
Total			*1*	*0*	*1*	*0*	*0*	*0*	*0*	*0*

PLATT David   Arsenal

Fullname: David Andrew Platt   DOB: 11-06-70 Oldham
Debut: Debut Goal:

Previous Clubs Details

Club	Signed	Fee	Apps					Goals		
			Tot	Start	Sub	FA	FL	Lge	FA	FL
Crewe Alexa	Jan-85		134	134	0	0	0	55	0	0
Aston Villa	Feb-88		121	121	0	0	0	50	0	0
Bari			29					11		
Juventus			16					3		
Sampdoria			29	29				9		
Arsenal	Jul-95	£4.75m								

POLLOCK Jamie   Middlesbrough

Fullname: DOB: 17-02-78 Stockton
Debut: MIDDLESBROUGH v Leeds United 22/8/92 as sub
Debut Goal: Sheffield Wednesday v MIDDLESBROUGH 1/5/93

Previous Clubs Details

Club	Signed	Fee	Apps					Goals		
			Tot	Start	Sub	FA	FL	Lge	FA	FL
Middlesbrough	Dec-91	Trainee	83	72	11	9	10	11	0	0

FAPL Summary by Club

Middlesbrough	92/3 to 94/5		20	15	5	0	0	1	0	0
Total			*20*	*15*	*5*	*0*	*0*	*1*	*0*	*0*

PORIC Adem   Sheffield Wednesday

Fullname: Adem Poric   DOB: 23-04-77 Australia
Debut: Everton v SHEFFIELD WEDNESDAY 26/12/94 as sub
Debut Goal:

Previous Clubs Details

Club	Signed	Fee	Apps					Goals		
			Tot	Start	Sub	FA	FL	Lge	FA	FL
St George (Australia)										
Sheffield W	Oct-93	£60,000	4	3	1	0	0	0	0	0

FAPL Summary by Club

Sheffield W	94/5		4	1	3	0	0	0	0	0
Total			*4*	*1*	*3*	*0*	*0*	*0*	*0*	*0*

POTTS Steve   West Ham United

Fullname: Steven J Potts   DOB: 08-05-71 Hartford, USA
Debut: WEST HAM UNITED v Wimbledon 14/8/93
Debut Goal:

Previous Clubs Details

Club	Signed	Fee	Apps					Goals		
			Tot	Start	Sub	FA	FL	Lge	FA	FL
West Ham Utd	Jul-83		278	268	10	31	34	1	0	0

FAPL Summary by Club

West Ham Utd	93/4 to 94/5		83	83	0	8	7	0	0	0
Total			*83*	*83*	*0*	*8*	*7*	*0*	*0*	*0*

POWELL Mark   **Bolton Wanderers**

Fullname: Mark Powell   DOB:
Debut: Debut Goal:

Previous Clubs Details			Apps					Goals		
Club	Signed	Fee	Tot	Start	Sub	FA	FL	Lge	FA	FL
Everton										
Bolton Wdrs	Nov-94	Free								

PRESSLEY Steve   **Coventry City**

Fullname: Steven Pressley   DOB: 12-10-77 Elgin
Debut: Arsenal v COVENTRY CITY 23/10/94
Debut Goal: COVENTRY CITY v Manchester United 1/5/95

Previous Clubs Details			Apps					Goals		
Club	Signed	Fee	Tot	Start	Sub	FA	FL	Lge	FA	FL
Rangers										
Coventry C	Oct-94	£600,000	19	18	1	3	0	1	0	0
FAPL Summary by Club										
Coventry C		94/5	19	18	1	3	0	1	0	0
Total			*19*	*18*	*1*	*3*	*0*	*1*	*0*	*0*

PRESSMAN Kevin   **Sheffield Wednesday**

Fullname: Kevin Paul Pressman   DOB: 07-11-71 Fareham
Debut: SHEFFIELD WEDNESDAY v Southampton 12/4/92
Debut Goal: (Goalkeeper)

Previous Clubs Details			Apps					Goals		
Club	Signed	Fee	Tot	Start	Sub	FA	FL	Lge	FA	FL
Sheffield W	Nov-85		128	128	0	7	21	0	0	0
Stoke C	Mar-92	Loan	4	4	0	0	0	0	0	0
FAPL Summary by Club										
Sheffield W	92/3 to 94/5		69	69	0	7	12	0	0	0
Total			*69*	*69*	*0*	*7*	*12*	*0*	*0*	*0*

QUIGLEY Mike   **Manchester City**

Fullname: Michael Anthony Quigley   DOB: 03-10-74 Manchester
Debut: Norwich City v MANCHESTER CITY 20/2/93 as sub
Debut Goal:

Previous Clubs Details			Apps					Goals		
Club	Signed	Fee	Tot	Start	Sub	FA	FL	Lge	FA	FL
Manchester C	Jul-89		12	3	9	0	0	0	0	0
FAPL Summary by Club										
Manchester C	92/3 to 93/4		7	3	4	0	0	0	0	0
Total			*7*	*3*	*4*	*0*	*0*	*0*	*0*	*0*

QUINN Mick　　　　　　　　　　　　　　　　**Coventry City**

Fullname:　Michael Quinn　　　　　　DOB: 03-05-66 Liverpool
Debut:　　COVENTRY CITY v Manchester City 21/11/92
Debut Goal: COVENTRY CITY v Manchester City 21/11/92

Previous Clubs Details

Club	Signed	Fee	Apps					Goals		
			Tot	Start	Sub	FA	FL	Lge	FA	FL
Derby County			0	0	0	0	0	0	0	0
Wigan Ath	Sep-79	Free	69	56	13	3	5	19	1	1
Stockport Co	Jun-82	Free	63	62	1	2	5	39	0	2
Oldham Ath	Jan-84	£50,000	80	78	2	2	4	34	1	2
Portsmouth	Mar-86	£150,000	121	115	6	7	7	54	7	6
Newcastle Utd	Aug-89	£680,000	115	110	5	7	9	59	4	0
Coventry C	Nov-92	£250,000	64	57	7	2	2	25	0	1
Plymouth Arg	Nov-94	Loan								
Portsmouth	Feb-95	Loan								
FAPL Summary by Club										
Coventry C	92/3 to 94/5		64	57	7	2	2	25	0	1
Total			*64*	*57*	*7*	*2*	*2*	*25*	*0*	*1*

QUINN Niall　　　　　　　　　　　　　　　**Manchester City**

Fullname:　Niall John Quinn　　　　　　DOB: 07-10-70 Dublin, R.Ireland
Debut:　　MANCHESTER CITY v QPR 17/8/92
Debut Goal: MANCHESTER CITY v Oldham Athletic 29/8/92

Previous Clubs Details

Club	Signed	Fee	Apps					Goals		
			Tot	Start	Sub	FA	FL	Lge	FA	FL
Arsenal	Nov-83		67	59	8	10	16	14	2	4
Manchester C	Mar-90	£800,000	171	159	12	12	19	57	2	6
FAPL Summary by Club										
Manchester C	92/3 to 94/5		89	77	12	9	12	22	1	3
Total			*89*	*77*	*12*	*9*	*12*	*22*	*1*	*3*

RADEBE Lucas　　　　　　　　　　　　　　**Leeds United**

Fullname:　Lucas Radebe　　　　　　DOB: 13-04-73 Johannesburg
Debut:　　Sheffield Wednesday v LEEDS UNITED 26/9/94 as sub
Debut Goal:

Previous Clubs Details

Club	Signed	Fee	Apps					Goals		
			Tot	Start	Sub	FA	FL	Lge	FA	FL
Kaiser Chiefs										
Leeds Utd	Aug-94	£250,000	12	9	3	2	1	0	0	0
FAPL Summary by Club										
Leeds Utd	94/5		12	9	3	2	1	0	0	0
Total			*12*	*9*	*3*	*2*	*1*	*0*	*0*	*0*

READY Karl   QPR
Fullname: Karl Ready   DOB: 15-08-76 Neath
Debut: QPR v Coventry City 20/2/93
Debut Goal: Blackburn Rovers v QPR 24/4/94

Previous Clubs Details			Apps					Goals		
Club	Signed	Fee	Tot	Start	Sub	FA	FL	Lge	FA	FL
QPR	Aug-90		39	33	6	0	2	2	0	0
FAPL Summary by Club										
QPR	92/3 to 94/5		38	32	6	0	1	2	0	0
Total			*38*	*32*	*6*	*0*	*1*	*2*	*0*	*0*

REDKNAPP Jamie   Liverpool
Fullname: Jamie Frank Redknapp   DOB: 26-06-67 Barton on Sea
Debut: Leeds United v LIVERPOOL 29/8/92
Debut Goal: LIVERPOOL v Chelsea 5/9/92

Previous Clubs Details			Apps					Goals		
Club	Signed	Fee	Tot	Start	Sub	FA	FL	Lge	FA	FL
Bournemouth	Jun-90		13	6	7	3	3	0	0	0
Liverpool	Jan-91	£350,000	110	97	13	11	18	10	0	3
FAPL Summary by Club										
Liverpool	92/3 to 94/5		104	92	12	9	18	9	0	3
Total			*104*	*92*	*12*	*9*	*18*	*9*	*0*	*3*

REEVES Alan   Wimbledon
Fullname: Alan Reeves   DOB: 20-11-71 Birkenhead
Debut: WIMBLEDON v Leicester City 10/9/94
Debut Goal: QPR v WIMBLEDON 24/9/94

Previous Clubs Details			Apps					Goals		
Club	Signed	Fee	Tot	Start	Sub	FA	FL	Lge	FA	FL
Norwich C	Sep-88									
Chester C	Aug-89	£10,000	40	31	9	3	2	2	0	0
Rochdale	Jul-91	Free	116	114	2	6	10	9	1	0
Wimbledon	Sep-94	£300,000	32	32	0	2	0	3	0	0
FAPL Summary by Club										
Wimbledon		94/5	32	32	0	2	0	3	0	0
Total			*32*	*32*	*0*	*2*	*0*	*3*	*0*	*0*

RENNIE David   Coventry City
Fullname: David Rennie   DOB: 30-08-68 Edinburgh
Debut: COVENTRY CITY v Arsenal 13/3/93
Debut Goal: Arsenal v COVENTRY CITY 14/8/93

Previous Clubs Details			Apps					Goals		
Club	Signed	Fee	Tot	Start	Sub	FA	FL	Lge	FA	FL
Leicester C	May-82		21	21	0	0	2	1	0	0
Leeds Utd	Jan-86	£50,000	101	95	6	7	7	5	1	0

			Tot		Sub	FA	FL	Lge	FA	FL
Bristol C	Jul-89	£175,000	104	101	3	9	8	8	0	0
Birmingham C	Feb-92	£120,000	35	32	3	0	1	4	0	0
Coventry C	Mar-93	£100,000	71	71	0	4	5	1	0	0
FAPL Summary by Club										
Coventry C	92/3 to 94/5		71	71	0	4	5	1	0	0
Total			*71*	*71*	*0*	*4*	*5*	*1*	*0*	*0*

RICHARDSON Kevin Coventry City

Fullname: Kevin Richardson DOB: 05-12-66 Newcastle
Debut: Ipswich Town v ASTON VILLA 15/8/92
Debut Goal: ASTON VILLA v Chelsea 2/9/92

Previous Clubs Details

			Apps					Goals		
Club	Signed	Fee	Tot	Start	Sub	FA	FL	Lge	FA	FL
Everton	Dec-80		109	95	14	13	13	16	1	3
Watford	Sep-86	£225,000	39	39	0	7	3	2	0	0
Arsenal	Aug-87	£200,000	96	88	8	9	16	5	1	2
Real Sociedad	Jun-90	£750,000	0	0	0	0	0	0	0	0
Aston Villa	Aug-91	£450,000	143	142	1	12	15	14	0	3
Coventry C	Feb-95	£300,000	14	14	0	0	0	0	0	0
FAPL Summary by Club										
Aston Villa	92/3 to 94/5		101	100	1	7	13	8	0	3
Coventry C	94/5		14	14	0	0	0	0	0	0
Total			*115*	*114*	*1*	*7*	*13*	*8*	*0*	*3*

RIDEOUT Paul Everton

Fullname: Paul D Rideout DOB: 15-08-68 Bournemouth
Debut: EVERTON v Sheffield Wednesday 15/8/92
Debut Goal: Nottingham Forest v EVERTON 7/11/92

Previous Clubs Details

			Apps					Goals		
Club	Signed	Fee	Tot	Start	Sub	FA	FL	Lge	FA	FL
Swindon T	Aug-81		95	90	5	7	3	38	1	2
Aston Villa	Jun-83	£200,000	54	50	4	2	6	19	0	3
Bari (Italy)	Jul-85	£400,000	0	0	0	0	0	0	0	0
Southampton	Jul-88	£430,000	75	68	7	7	13	19	0	2
Swindon T	Mar-91	Loan	9	9	0	0	0	1	0	0
Notts County	Sep-91	£250,000	11	9	2	1	2	3	0	0
Rangers	Jan-92	£500,000								
Everton	Aug-92	£500,000	77	63	14	7	9	23	3	6
FAPL Summary by Club										
Everton	92/3 to 94/5		77	63	14	7	9	23	3	6
Total			*77*	*63*	*14*	*7*	*9*	*23*	*3*	*6*

RIEPER Marc West Ham United

Fullname: Marc Rieper DOB:
Debut: Leeds United v WEST HAM UNITED 10/12/94
Debut Goal: WEST HAM UNITED v Blackburn Rovers 30/4/95

Club	Signed	Fee	Tot	Start	Sub	FA	FL	Lge	FA	FL
Brondby										
West Ham Utd	Dec-94	£500,000	21	17	4	0	0	1	0	0

FAPL Summary by Club

Club			Tot	Start	Sub	FA	FL	Lge	FA	FL
West Ham Utd	94/5		21	17	4	0	0	1	0	0
Total			*21*	*17*	*4*	*0*	*0*	*1*	*0*	*0*

RIGBY Malcolm   Nottingham Forest

Fullname: Malcolm Rigby   DOB: 14-03-80 Nottingham
Debut: Debut Goal:

Previous Clubs Details   *Apps*   *Goals*

Club	Signed	Fee	Tot	Start	Sub	FA	FL	Lge	FA	FL
Notts County										
N Forest	Aug-94	£50,000								

RIPLEY Stuart   Blackburn Rovers

Fullname: Stuart Edward Ripley   DOB: 21-11-71 Middlesbrough
Debut: Crystal Palace v BLACKBURN ROVERS 15/8/92
Debut Goal: Crystal Palace v BLACKBURN ROVERS 15/8/92

Previous Clubs Details   *Apps*   *Goals*

Club	Signed	Fee	Tot	Start	Sub	FA	FL	Lge	FA	FL
Middlesbrough	Nov-85		249	210	39	18	23	26	1	3
Bolton Wdrs	Feb-86	Loan	5	5	0	0	0	0	0	0
Blackburn R	Jul-92	£1.3m	117	114	3	9	15	11	2	0

FAPL Summary by Club

Club			Tot	Start	Sub	FA	FL	Lge	FA	FL
Blackburn R	92/3 to 94/5		117	114	3	9	15	11	2	0
Total			*117*	*114*	*3*	*9*	*15*	*11*	*2*	*0*

RIX Graham   Chelsea

Fullname: Graham Rix   DOB:
Debut: CHELSEA v Arsenal 14/5/95 as sub
Debut Goal:

Previous Clubs Details   *Apps*   *Goals*

Club	Signed	Fee	Tot	Start	Sub	FA	FL	Lge	FA	FL
Arsenal			351	338	13	44	47	41	7	2
Brentford		Loan	6					0		
Caen (France)										
Dundee			14					2		
Chelsea			1	0	1	0	0	0	0	0

FAPL Summary by Club

Club			Tot	Start	Sub	FA	FL	Lge	FA	FL
Chelsea	94/5		1	0	1	0	0	0	0	0
Total			*1*	*0*	*1*	*0*	*0*	*0*	*0*	*0*

ROBERTS Tony   QPR

Fullname: Anthony Mark Roberts   DOB: 05-08-73 Holyhead
Debut: QPR v Southampton 19/8/92
Debut Goal:

Previous Clubs Details			*Apps*					*Goals*		
Club	Signed	Fee	Tot	Start	Sub	FA	FL	Lge	FA	FL
QPR	Jul-87		94	94	0	7	7	0	0	0

FAPL Summary by Club
QPR	92/3 to 94/5		75	75	0	7	4	0	0	0
Total			*75*	*75*	*0*	*7*	*4*	*0*	*0*	*0*

ROBERTSON Sandy   Coventry City

Fullname: Alexander Robertson   DOB: 27-04-75 Edinburgh
Debut: COVENTRY CITY v QPR 22/1/94 as sub
Debut Goal:

Previous Clubs Details			*Apps*					*Goals*		
Club	Signed	Fee	Tot	Start	Sub	FA	FL	Lge	FA	FL
Rangers										
Coventry C	Jan-94	£250,000	4	0	4	0	0	0	0	0

FAPL Summary by Club
Coventry C	93/4 to 94/5		4	0	4	0	0	0	0	0
Total			*4*	*0*	*4*	*0*	*0*	*0*	*0*	*0*

ROBINSON Matt   Southampton

Fullname: Matthew Robinson   DOB: 24-12-78 Exeter
Debut: SOUTHAMPTON v Sheff Wed 29/4/95 as sub
Debut Goal:

Previous Clubs Details			*Apps*					*Goals*		
Club	Signed	Fee	Tot	Start	Sub	FA	FL	Lge	FA	FL
Southampton	Jul-93	Trainee	1	0	1	0	0	0	0	0

FAPL Summary by Club
Southampton	94/5		1	0	1	0	0	0	0	0
Total			*1*	*0*	*1*	*0*	*0*	*0*	*0*	*0*

ROBSON Bryan   Middlesbrough

Fullname: Bryan Robson   DOB: 12-01-61 Witton Gilbert
Debut: Middlesbrough v MANCHESTER UNITED 3/10/92
Debut Goal: Wimbledon v MANCHESTER UNITED 8/5/93

Previous Clubs Details			*Apps*					*Goals*		
Club	Signed	Fee	Tot	Start	Sub	FA	FL	Lge	FA	FL
WBA	Aug-74		198	194	4	12	18	39	2	2
Manchester Utd	Oct-81	£1.5m	345	326	19	35	51	74	10	5
Middlesbrough	May-94	Free	22	21	1	0	0	1	0	0

FAPL Summary by Club
Manchester Utd	92/3 to 93/4		29	15	14	3	6	2	0	0
Total			*29*	*15*	*14*	*3*	*6*	*2*	*0*	*0*

ROCASTLE David   Chelsea

Fullname: David Carlyle Rocastle   DOB: 03-05-71 Lewisham
Debut: Ipswich Town v LEEDS UNITED 3/10/93 as sub
Debut Goal: LEEDS UNITED v Manchester City 13/3/93

Previous Clubs Details			Apps					Goals		
Club	Signed	Fee	Tot	Start	Sub	FA	FL	Lge	FA	FL
Arsenal	Dec-84		218	204	14	20	33	24	4	6
Leeds Utd	Jul-92	£2m	25	17	8	3	3	2	0	0
Manchester C	Dec-93	Swap	21	21	0	2	0	2	0	0
Chelsea	Aug-94	£1.25m	28	26	2	1	3	1	0	1
FAPL Summary by Club										
Leeds Utd	92/3 to 93/4		25	17	8	3	3	2	0	0
Manchester C	93/4 to 93/4		21	21	0	2	0	2	0	0
Chelsea	94/5		28	26	2	1	3	1	0	1
Total			74	64	10	6	6	5	0	1

ROSARIO Robert   Nottingham Forest

Fullname: Robert Michael Rosario   DOB: 05-03-70 Hammersmith
Debut: COVENTRY CITY v Middlesbrough 15/8/92
Debut Goal: Wimbledon v COVENTRY CITY 22/8/92

Previous Clubs Details			Apps					Goals		
Club	Signed	Fee	Tot	Start	Sub	FA	FL	Lge	FA	FL
Norwich C	Dec-83		126	115	11	14	11	18	3	3
Wolves	Dec-85	Loan	2	2	0	0	0	1	0	0
Coventry C	Mar-91	£600,000	59	54	5	3	4	8	0	2
N Forest	Mar-93	£400,000	27	25	2	0	1	3	0	0
FAPL Summary by Club										
Coventry C	92/3 to 93/4		28	28	0	1	1	4	0	0
N Forest	92/3 to 94/5		11	10	1	0	0	1	0	0
Total			39	38	1	1	1	5	0	0

ROSENTHAL Ronny   Tottenham Hotspur

Fullname: Ronny Rosenthal   DOB: 05-10-67 Haifa, Israel
Debut: Nottingham Forest v LIVERPOOL 16/8/92 as sub
Debut Goal: LIVERPOOL v Aston Villa 19/9/92

Previous Clubs Details			Apps					Goals		
Club	Signed	Fee	Tot	Start	Sub	FA	FL	Lge	FA	FL
Liverpool	Mar-90	£1m	74	32	42	8	9	21	1	1
Tottenham H	Jan-94	£250,000	35	25	10	4	1	2	4	0
FAPL Summary by Club										
Liverpool	92/3 to 93/4		30	16	14	1	3	6	0	1
Tottenham H	93/4 to 94/5		35	25	10	4	1	2	4	0
Total			65	41	24	5	4	8	4	1

ROSLER Uwe　　　　　　　　　　　　**Manchester City**
Fullname:　Uwe Rosler　　　　　　DOB: 16-11-72 Attenburg
Debut:　　Arsenal v MANCHESTER CITY 20/8/94
Debut Goal: MANCHESTER CITY v West Ham United 24/8/94

Previous Clubs Details			*Apps*				*Goals*		
Club	Signed	Fee	Tot	Start	Sub	FA	FL	Lge	FA FL
D Dresden									
Manchester C	Mar-94	£750,000	31	29	2	4	4	15	5 2
FAPL Summary by Club									
Manchester C	94/5 to 93/4		31	29	2	4	4	15	5 2
Total			*31*	*29*	*2*	*4*	*4*	*15*	*5 2*

ROWLAND Keith　　　　　　　　**West Ham United**
Fullname:　Keith Rowland　　　　　DOB: 02-09-75 Portadown,
Northern Ireland
Debut:　　Norwich City v COVENTRY CITY 16/1/93 as sub
Debut Goal:

Previous Clubs Details			*Apps*				*Goals*		
Club	Signed	Fee	Tot	Start	Sub	FA	FL	Lge	FA FL
Bournemouth	Oct-89		72	65	7	8	5	2	0 0
Coventry C	Jan-93	Loan	2	0	2	0	0	0	0 0
West Ham Utd	Aug-93	£110,000	35	27	8	4	3	0	0 0
FAPL Summary by Club									
Coventry C	92/3 to 93/4		2	0	2	0	0	0	0 0
West Ham Utd	93/4 to 94/5		35	27	8	4	3	0	0 0
Total			*37*	*27*	*10*	*4*	*3*	*0*	*0 0*

ROY Bryan　　　　　　　　　　**Nottingham Forest**
Fullname:　Bryan Roy　　　　　　DOB: 13-02-74 Amsterdam
Debut:　　Ipswich Town v NOTTINGHAM FOREST 20/8/94
Debut Goal: Ipswich Town v NOTTINGHAM FOREST 20/8/94

Previous Clubs Details			*Apps*				*Goals*		
Club	Signed	Fee	Tot	Start	Sub	FA	FL	Lge	FA FL
Ajax	Jul-87		126	126	0	0	0	17	0 0
Foggia	Nov-92		20	20	0	0	0	3	0 0
N Forest	Aug-94	£2.5m	37	37	0	2	4	13	0 0
FAPL Summary by Club									
N Forest	94/5 to 93/4		37	37	0	2	4	13	0 1
Total			*37*	*37*	*0*	*2*	*4*	*13*	*0 1*

RUDDOCK Neil　　　　　　　　　　　**Liverpool**
Fullname:　Neil Ruddock　　　　　　DOB: 10-05-72 Wandsworth
Debut:　　Southampton v TOTTENHAM HOTSPUR 15/8/92
Debut Goal: TOTTENHAM HOTSPUR v Liverpool 31/10/92

Previous Clubs Details			*Apps*					*Goals*		
Club	Signed	Fee	Tot	Start	Sub	FA	FL	Lge	FA	FL
Millwall	Mar-86		0	0	0	0	0	0	0	0
Tottenham H	Apr-86	£50,000	9	7	2	2	0	0	1	0
Millwall	Jun-88	£300,000	2	0	2	0	2	1	0	3
Southampton	Feb-89	£250,000	107	100	7	10	15	9	3	1
Tottenham H	May-92	£750,000	38	38	0	5	4	3	0	0
Liverpool	Jul-93	£2.5m	76	76	0	2	13	5	0	1
FAPL Summary by Club										
Tottenham H	92/3 to 93/4		38	38	0	5	4	3	0	0
Liverpool	93/4 to 94/5		76	76	0	2	13	5	0	1
Total			*114*	*114*	*0*	*7*	*17*	*8*	*0*	*1*

RUSH Matthew   West Ham United

Fullname: Matthew J Rush   DOB: 07-08-75 Hackney
Debut: WEST HAM UNITED v Swindon Town 11/9/93
Debut Goal: WEST HAM UNITED v Ipswich Town 2/4/94

Previous Clubs Details			*Apps*					*Goals*		
Club	Signed	Fee	Tot	Start	Sub	FA	FL	Lge	FA	FL
West Ham Utd	Mar-90		48	29	19	0	4	5	0	0
Cambridge Utd	Mar-93	Loan	10	4	6	0	0	0	0	0
Swansea C	Jan-94	Loan	13	13	0	0	0	0	0	0
FAPL Summary by Club										
West Ham Utd	93/4 to 94/5		33	24	9	0	3	3	0	0
Total			*33*	*24*	*9*	*0*	*3*	*3*	*0*	*0*

RUSH Ian   *Liverpool*

Fullname: Ian James Rush   DOB: 21-10-65 St Asaph
Debut: Nottingham Forest v LIVERPOOL 16/8/92
Debut Goal: Manchester United v LIVERPOOL 18/10/92

Previous Clubs Details			*Apps*					*Goals*		
Club	Signed	Fee	Tot	Start	Sub	FA	FL	Lge	FA	FL
Chester C	Jul-79		34	33	1	5	0	14	3	0
Liverpool	Apr-80	£300,000	224	224	0	24	47	139	19	25
Juventus (Italy)	Jun-87	£3.8m	115	105	10			45		
Liverpool	Aug-88	£2.2m	225	213	12	32	29	85	17	20
FAPL Summary by Club										
Liverpool	92/3 to 94/5		110	108	2	10	16	40	2	11
Total			*110*	*108*	*2*	*10*	*16*	*40*	*2*	*11*

SAMWAYS Vinny   Everton

Fullname: Vincent Samways   DOB: 28-10-71 Bethnal Green
Debut: Southampton v TOTTENHAM HOTSPUR 15/8/92
Debut Goal: TOTTENHAM HOTSPUR v Liverpool 18/12/93

Club	Signed	Fee	Tot	Start	Sub	FA	FL	Lge	FA	FL
			Apps					*Goals*		
Tottenham H	Oct-85		193	165	28	16	30	11	2	4
Everton	Jul-94	£2m	19	14	5	0	2	1	0	1
FAPL Summary by Club										
Tottenham H	92/3 to 93/4		73	73	0	8	8	3	2	1
Everton	94/5		19	14	5	0	2	1	0	1
Total			*92*	*87*	*5*	*8*	*10*	*4*	*2*	*2*

SCALES John   Liverpool

Fullname: John Robert Scales   DOB: 05-06-70 Harrogate
Debut: Leeds United v WIMBLEDON 15/8/92
Debut Goal: WIMBLEDON v Middlesbrough 9/3/93

Club	Signed	Fee	Tot	Start	Sub	FA	FL	Lge	FA	FL
			Apps					*Goals*		
Bristol Rovers	Jul-85		72	68	4	6	3	2	0	0
Wimbledon	Jul-87	£70,000	240	235	5	21	19	11	1	0
Liverpool	Sep-94	£3m +	35	35	0	7	7	2	0	1
FAPL Summary by Club										
Wimbledon	92/3 to 94/5		72	72	0	8	7	1	1	0
Liverpool	94/5		35	35	0	7	7	2	0	1
Total			*107*	*107*	*0*	*15*	*14*	*3*	*1*	*1*

SCHMEICHEL Peter   Manchester United

Fullname: Peter Boleslaw Schmeichel   DOB: 19-11-72 Glodsone, Den.
Debut: Sheffield United v MANCHESTER UNITED 15/8/92
Debut Goal:

Club	Signed	Fee	Tot	Start	Sub	FA	FL	Lge	FA	FL
			Apps					*Goals*		
Manchester Utd	Aug-91	£550,000	154	154	0	20	16	0	0	0
FAPL Summary by Club										
Manchester Utd	92/3 to 94/5		114	114	0	17	10	0	0	0
Total			*114*	*114*	*0*	*17*	*10*	*0*	*0*	*0*

SCHOLES Paul   Manchester United

Fullname: Paul Scholes   DOB: 17-11-78 Salford
Debut: Ipswich Town v MANCHESTER UTD 24/9/94 as sub
Debut Goal: Ipswich Town v MANCHESTER UTD 24/9/94 as sub

Club	Signed	Fee	Tot	Start	Sub	FA	FL	Lge	FA	FL
			Apps					*Goals*		
Manchester Utd	Jan-93	Trainee	17	6	11	3	3	5	0	2
FAPL Summary by Club										
Manchester Utd	94/5		17	6	11	3	3	5	0	2
Total			*17*	*6*	*11*	*3*	*3*	*5*	*0*	*2*

SCOTT Kevin   Tottenham Hotspur

Fullname: Kevin W Scott   DOB: 18-12-70 Easington
Debut: NEWCASTLE UNITED v Tottenham Hotspur 14/8/93
Debut Goal: NEWCASTLE UNITED v Sheffield Wednesday 5/3/94

Previous Clubs Details			*Apps*					*Goals*		
Club	Signed	Fee	Tot	Start	Sub	FA	FL	Lge	FA	FL
Newcastle Utd	Dec-84		227	227	0	16	18	8	1	0
Tottenham H	Feb-94	£850,000	16	16	0	0	0	1	0	0
Port Vale	Jan-95	Loan								
FAPL Summary by Club										
Newcastle Utd	93/4 to 94/5		18	18	0	1	2	0	0	0
Tottenham H	94/5		16	16	0	0	0	1	0	0
Total			*34*	*34*	*0*	*1*	*2*	*1*	*0*	*0*

SEAGRAVES Mark   Bolton Wanderers

Fullname: Mark Seagraves   DOB: 23-10-70 Bootle
Debut: Debut Goal:

Previous Clubs Details			*Apps*					*Goals*		
Club	Signed	Fee	Tot	Start	Sub	FA	FL	Lge	FA	FL
Liverpool	Nov-83	Amateur	0	0	0	1	1	0	0	0
Norwich C	Nov-86	Loan	3	3	0	0	0	0	0	0
Manchester C	Sep-87	£100,000	42	36	6	3	3	0	0	0
Bolton Wdrs	Sep-90	£100,000	157	152	5	17	8	8	1	0

SEAMAN David   Arsenal

Fullname: David Andrew Seaman   DOB: 20-09-67 Rotherham
Debut: ARSENAL v Norwich City 15/8/92
Debut Goal: (Goalkeeper)

Previous Clubs Details			*Apps*					*Goals*		
Club	Signed	Fee	Tot	Start	Sub	FA	FL	Lge	FA	FL
Leeds Utd	Sep-81		0	0	0	0	0	0	0	0
Peterborough U	Aug-82	£4,000	91	91	0	5	10	0	0	0
Birmingham C	Oct-84	£100,000	75	75	0	5	4	0	0	0
QPR	Aug-86	£225,000	141	141	0	17	13	0	0	0
Arsenal	May-90	£1.3m	189	189	0	28	21	0	0	0
FAPL Summary by Club										
Arsenal	92/3 to 94/5		109	109	0	13	20	0	0	0
Total			*109*	*109*	*0*	*13*	*20*	*0*	*0*	*0*

SEGERS Hans   Wimbledon

Fullname: Johannes C A Segers   DOB: 31-10-75 Eindhoven
Debut: Leeds United v WIMBLEDON 15/8/92
Debut Goal: (Goalkeeper)

Previous Clubs Details			Apps					Goals		
Club	Signed	Fee	Tot	Start	Sub	FA	FL	Lge	FA	FL
N Forest	Aug-84	£50,000	58	58	0	5	4	0	0	0
Stoke C	Feb-87	Loan	1	1	0	0	0	0	0	0
Sheffield Utd	Nov-87	Loan	10	10	0	0	0	0	0	0
Dunfermline A	Mar-88	Loan	0	0	0	0	0	0	0	0
Wimbledon	Sep-88	£180,000	263	262	1	22	26	0	0	0
FAPL Summary by Club										
Wimbledon	92/3 to 94/5		114	113	1	12	13	0	0	0
Total			*114*	*113*	*1*	*12*	*13*	*0*	*0*	*0*

SELLARS Scott   Newcastle United
Fullname: Scott Sellars   DOB: 28-11-69 Sheffield
Debut: LEEDS UNITED v Aston Villa 13/9/92
Debut Goal: NEWCASTLE UNITED v Ipswich Town 23/3/94

Previous Clubs Details			Apps					Goals		
Club	Signed	Fee	Tot	Start	Sub	FA	FL	Lge	FA	FL
Leeds Utd	Jul-83		74	72	2	4	4	12	0	1
Blackburn R	Jul-86	£20,000	202	194	8	11	12	35	1	3
Leeds Utd	Jul-92	£800,000	7	6	1	0	2	0	0	0
Newcastle Utd	Mar-93	£700,000	55	54	1	3	5	5	0	1
FAPL Summary by Club										
Leeds Utd	92/3 to 94/5		7	6	1	0	2	0	0	0
Newcastle Utd	93/4 to 94/5		42	41	1	3	5	3	0	1
Total			*49*	*47*	*2*	*3*	*7*	*3*	*0*	*1*

SELLEY Ian   Arsenal
Fullname: Ian Selley   DOB: 15-06-78 Chertsey
Debut: ARSENAL v Blackburn Rovers 12/9/92
Debut Goal:

Previous Clubs Details			Apps					Goals		
Club	Signed	Fee	Tot	Start	Sub	FA	FL	Lge	FA	FL
Arsenal	May-92		40	35	5	3	6	0	0	0
FAPL Summary by Club										
Arsenal	92/3 to 94/5		40	35	5	3	6	0	0	0
Total			*40*	*35*	*5*	*3*	*6*	*0*	*0*	*0*

SHARP Kevin   Leeds United
Fullname: Kevin Phillip Sharp   DOB: 20-09-78 Ontario, Canada
Debut: Crystal Palace v LEEDS UNITED 17/4/93 as sub
Debut Goal:

Previous Clubs Details			Apps					Goals		
Club	Signed	Fee	Tot	Start	Sub	FA	FL	Lge	FA	FL
Auxerre (France)										
Leeds Utd	Oct-92	£60,000	16	11	5	0	0	0	0	0

Leeds Utd	92/3 to 94/5		16	11	5	0	0	0	0	0
Total			*16*	*11*	*5*	*0*	*0*	*0*	*0*	*0*

SHARPE Lee   Manchester United

Fullname: Lee Stuart Sharpe   DOB: 28-05-75 Halesowen
Debut: Aston Villa v MANCHESTER UNITED 7/11/92
Debut Goal: MANCHESTER UNITED v Coventry City 28/12/92

			Apps					Goals		
Club	Signed	Fee	Tot	Start	Sub	FA	FL	Lge	FA	FL
Torquay Utd	May-88		14	9	5	0	0	3	0	0
Manchester Utd	May-88	£185,000	162	139	23	23	21	17	1	9

FAPL Summary by Club

Manchester Utd	92/3 to 94/5		85	79	6	13	6	13	1	2
Total			*85*	*79*	*6*	*13*	*6*	*13*	*1*	*2*

SHAW Paul   Arsenal

Fullname: Paul Shaw   DOB:
Debut: Nottingham Forest v ARSENAL 3/12/94 as sub
Debut Goal:

			Apps					Goals		
Club	Signed	Fee	Tot	Start	Sub	FA	FL	Lge	FA	FL
Arsenal			1	0	1	0	0	0	0	0
Burnley	Mar-95	Loan								

FAPL Summary by Club

Arsenal	94/5		1	0	1	0	0	0	0	0
Total			*1*	*0*	*1*	*0*	*0*	*0*	*0*	*0*

SHEARER Alan   Blackburn Rovers

Fullname: Alan Shearer   DOB: 01-09-74 Newcastle
Debut: Crystal Palace v BLACKBURN ROVERS 15/8/92
Debut Goal: Crystal Palace v BLACKBURN ROVERS 15/8/92

			Apps					Goals		
Club	Signed	Fee	Tot	Start	Sub	FA	FL	Lge	FA	FL
Southampton	Apr-88		118	105	13	14	18	23	4	11
Blackburn R	Jul-92	£3.3m	103	97	6	6	12	81	2	7

FAPL Summary by Club

Blackburn Rovers	92/3 to 94/5		103	97	6	6	12	81	2	7
Total			*103*	*97*	*6*	*6*	*12*	*81*	*2*	*7*

SHERIDAN John   Sheffield Wednesday

Fullname: John Joseph Sheridan   DOB: 02-10-68 Manchester
Debut: SHEFFIELD WED v Blackburn Rovers 31/10/92
Debut Goal: SHEFFIELD WED v Manchester United 26/12/92

Previous Clubs Details			Apps					Goals		
Club	Signed	Fee	Tot	Start	Sub	FA	FL	Lge	FA	FL
Leeds Utd	Mar-82		230	225	5	12	14	47	1	3
N Forest	Jul-89	£650,000	0	0	0	1	0	0	0	0
Sheffield W	Nov-89	£500,000	178	174	4	18	24	25	3	3
FAPL Summary by Club										
Sheffield W	92/3 to 94/5		81	78	3	11	13	7	1	2
Total			*81*	*78*	*3*	*11*	*13*	*7*	*1*	*2*

SHERINGHAM Teddy   Tottenham Hotspur

Fullname: Edward Paul Sheringham   DOB: 03-04-70 Walthamstow
Debut: NOTTINGHAM FOREST v Liverpool 16/8/92
Debut Goal: NOTTINGHAM FOREST v Liverpool 16/8/92

Previous Clubs Details			Apps					Goals		
Club	Signed	Fee	Tot	Start	Sub	FA	FL	Lge	FA	FL
Millwall	Jan-84		220	205	15	12	17	93	5	8
Aldershot	Feb-85	Loan	5	4	1	0	0	0	0	0
N Forest	Jul-91	£2m	42	42	0	4	10	14	2	5
Tottenham H	Aug-92	£2.1m	99	96	3	11	8	52	8	5
FAPL Summary by Club										
N Forest	92/3 to 94/5		3	3	0	0	0	1	0	0
Tottenham H	92/3 to 94/5		99	96	3	16	12	84	12	8
Total			*102*	*99*	*3*	*16*	*12*	*85*	*12*	*8*

SHERWOOD Tim   Blackburn Rovers

Fullname: Timothy Alan Sherwood   DOB: 03-02-73 St Albans
Debut: Crystal Palace v BLACKBURN ROVERS 15/8/92
Debut Goal: BLACKBURN ROVERS v Norwich City 3/10/92

Previous Clubs Details			Apps					Goals		
Club	Signed	Fee	Tot	Start	Sub	FA	FL	Lge	FA	FL
Watford	Feb-87		30	23	7	9	5	2	0	0
Norwich C	Jul-87	£175,000	71	66	5	4	7	10	0	1
Blackburn R	Feb-92	£500,000	126	121	5	9	14	11	1	0
FAPL Summary by Club										
Blackburn Rovers 92/3 to 94/5			116	115	1	9	14	11	1	0
Total			*116*	*115*	*1*	*9*	*14*	*11*	*1*	*0*

SHIPPERLEY Neil   Southampton

Fullname: Neil Shipperley   DOB: 31-10-78 Chatham
Debut: Southampton v CHELSEA 10/4/93 as sub
Debut Goal: CHELSEA v Wimbledon 12/4/93

Previous Clubs Details			Apps					Goals		
Club	Signed	Fee	Tot	Start	Sub	FA	FL	Lge	FA	FL
Chelsea	Sep-92		37	26	11	3	6	7	1	1
Watford	Dec-94	Loan								
Southampton	Jan-95	£1.25m	19	19	0	4	0	4	2	0

SILENZI Andrea   Nottingham Forest

Fullname: Andrea Silenzi   DOB: 10-2-66, Rome
Debut: Debut Goal:

Previous Clubs Details

			Apps					Goals		
Club	Signed	Fee	Tot	Start	Sub	FA	FL	Lge	FA	FL
Lodigiani (C2)	1984		49					18		
Arezzo (B)	1987		19					0		
Reggiana (C1)	1988		67					32		
Napoli (A)	1990		39					6		
Torino (A)	1992		56	(not inc 94/5)				20		
N.Forest	Jul-95	£2.5m								

SHORT Craig   Everton

Fullname: Craig Short   DOB: 25-06-68, Bridlington
Debut: Debut Goal:

Previous Clubs Details

			Apps					Goals		
Club	Signed	Fee	Tot	Start	Sub	FA	FL	Lge	FA	FL
Scarborough	Oct-87		63	61	2			7		
Notts County	Jul-89		128	128	0			6		
Derby County	1992		81+					6+		
Everton	Jul-95	£2.5m								

SIMPSON Fitzroy   Manchester City

Fullname: Fitzroy Simpson   DOB: 27-02-74 Br'd on Avon
Debut: MANCHESTER CITY v QPR 17/8/92
Debut Goal: MAN CITY v Nottingham Forest 3/10/92

Previous Clubs Details

			Apps					Goals		
Club	Signed	Fee	Tot	Start	Sub	FA	FL	Lge	FA	FL
Swindon T	Jul-88		104	78	26	3	10	9	0	1
Manchester C	Mar-92	£500,000	71	58	13	6	6	4	0	0
Bristol C	Sep-94	Loan								

SINCLAIR Frank   Chelsea

Fullname: Frank Mohammed Sinclair   DOB: 04-12-75 Lambeth
Debut: Manchester City v CHELSEA 20/9/92
Debut Goal: Wimbledon v CHELSEA 10/4/95

Previous Clubs Details			Apps					Goals		
Club	Signed	Fee	Tot	Start	Sub	FA	FL	Lge	FA	FL
Chelsea	May-90		77	77	0	9	9	1	0	0
WBA	Dec-91	Loan	112	112	0	12	11	4	1	0
FAPL Summary by Club										
Chelsea	92/3 to 94/5		102	102	0	11	11	3	1	1
Total			*102*	*102*	*0*	*11*	*11*	*3*	*1*	*1*

SINCLAIR Trevor   QPR

Fullname: Trevor Sinclair
Debut: QPR v Liverpool 18/8/93   DOB: 03-03-77 Dulwich
Debut Goal: QPR v Sheffield Wednesday 24/8/94

Previous Clubs Details			Apps					Goals		
Club	Signed	Fee	Tot	Start	Sub	FA	FL	Lge	FA	FL
Blackpool	Aug-90	Trainee	112	84	28	7	8	15	0	0
QPR	Aug-93		65	62	3	2	6	8	0	2
FAPL Summary by Club										
QPR	93/4 to 94/5		65	62	3	2	6	4	0	1
Total			*65*	*62*	*3*	*2*	*6*	*4*	*0*	*1*

SINTON Andy   Sheffield Wednesday

Fullname: Andrew Sinton
Debut: Manchester City v QPR 17/8/92   DOB: 20-03-70 Newcastle
Debut Goal: Manchester City v QPR 17/8/92

Previous Clubs Details			Apps					Goals		
Club	Signed	Fee	Tot	Start	Sub	FA	FL	Lge	FA	FL
Cambridge Utd	Apr-83		93	90	3	3	6	13	0	1
Brentford	Dec-85	£25,000	149	149	0	11	8	28	1	3
QPR	Mar-89	£350,000	160	160	0	13	14	22	2	0
Sheffield W	Aug-93	£2.75m	50	47	3	8	6	3	0	0
FAPL Summary by Club										
QPR	92/3 to 94/5		36	36	0	2	4	7	0	0
Sheffield W	93/4 to 94/5		50	47	3	4	10	3	0	0
Total			*86*	*83*	*3*	*6*	*14*	*10*	*0*	*0*

SLATER Robbie   Blackburn Rovers

Fullname: Robert Slater
Debut: Southampton v BLACKBURN ROVERS 20/8/94   DOB: 23-11-68 Ormskirk
Debut Goal:

Previous Clubs Details			Apps					Goals		
Club	Signed	Fee	Tot	Start	Sub	FA	FL	Lge	FA	FL
Lens										
Blackburn R	Aug-94	£300,000	18	12	6	1	1	0	0	0
FAPL Summary by Club										
Blackburn Rovers	94/5		18	12	6	1	1	0	0	0
Total			*18*	*12*	*6*	*1*	*1*	*0*	*0*	*0*

SMALL Bryan Aston Villa

Fullname: Bryan Small   DOB: 16-11-75 Birmingham
Debut: ASTON VILLA v Blackburn Rovers 19/10/92
Debut Goal:

Previous Clubs Details			*Apps*					*Goals*		
Club	Signed	Fee	Tot	Start	Sub	FA	FL	Lge	FA	FL
Aston Villa	Jul-90		35	31	4	3	2	0	0	0
Birmingham C	Sep-94	Loan								
FAPL Summary by Club										
Aston Villa	92/3 to 94/5		28	23	5	0	2	0	0	0
Total			*28*	*23*	*5*	*0*	*2*	*0*	*0*	*0*

SMITH Paul Nottingham Forest

Fullname: Paul Smith   DOB:
Debut: Debut Goal:

Previous Clubs Details			*Apps*					*Goals*		
Club	Signed	Fee	Tot	Start	Sub	FA	FL	Lge	FA	FL
Hastings Town										
N Forest	Jan-95	£50,000								

SNEEKES Richard Bolton Wanderers

Fullname: Richard Sneekes   DOB:
Debut: Debut Goal:

Previous Clubs Details			*Apps*					*Goals*		
Club	Signed	Fee	Tot	Start	Sub	FA	FL	Lge	FA	FL
Fortuna Sitard										
Bolton Wdrs	Aug-94	£150,000	38	37	1	1	8	6	1	1

SOUTHALL Neville Everton

Fullname: Neville Southall   DOB: 17-09-82 Llandudno
Debut: EVERTON v Sheffield Wednesday 15/8/92
Debut Goal: (Goalkeeper)

Previous Clubs Details			*Apps*					*Goals*		
Club	Signed	Fee	Tot	Start	Sub	FA	FL	Lge	FA	FL
Bury	Jun-80	£6,000	39	39	0	5	0	0	0	0
Everton	Jul-81	£150,000	453	453	0	58	58	0	0	0
Port Vale	Jan-83	Loan	9	9	0	0	0	0	0	0
FAPL Summary by Club										
Everton	92/3 to 94/5		123	123	0	9	12	0	0	0
Total			*123*	*123*	*0*	*9*	*12*	*0*	*0*	*0*

SOUTHGATE Gareth Aston Villa

Fullname: Gareth Southgate   DOB: 04-09-74 Watford
Debut: CRYSTAL PALACE v Blackburn Rovers 15/8/92
Debut Goal: CRYSTAL PALACE v Blackburn Rovers 15/8/92

Previous Clubs Details			Apps					Goals		
Club	Signed	Fee	Tot	Start	Sub	FA	FL	Lge	FA	FL
Crystal Palace	Jan-89		110	106	4	1	17	12	0	5
Aston Villa	Jun-95	£2.5m								
FAPL Summary by Club										
Crystal Palace	92/3 to 94/5		75	75	0	8	13	4	0	4
Total			*75*	*75*	*0*	*8*	*13*	*4*	*0*	*4*

SPACKMAN Nigel   Chelsea
Fullname: Nigel J Spackman   DOB: 03-12-64 Romsey
Debut: CHELSEA v Norwich City 12/9/92
Debut Goal:

Previous Clubs Details			Apps					Goals		
Club	Signed	Fee	Tot	Start	Sub	FA	FL	Lge	FA	FL
Bournemouth	May-80		119	118	1	7	5	10	0	0
Chelsea	Jun-83	£40,000	141	139	2	8	23	12	1	0
Liverpool	Feb-87	£400,000	51	39	12	5	7	0	0	0
QPR	Feb-89	£500,000	29	27	2	0	2	1	0	1
Rangers	Nov-89	£500,000								
Chelsea	Aug-92	£485,000	51	47	4	6	4	0	0	0
FAPL Summary by Club										
Chelsea	92/3 to 94/5		51	47	4	6	4	0	0	0
Total			*51*	*47*	*4*	*6*	*4*	*0*	*0*	*0*

SPEED Gary   Leeds United
Fullname: Gary Andrew Speed   DOB: 09-09-73 Hawarden
Debut: LEEDS UNITED v Wimbledon 15/8/92
Debut Goal: Aston Villa v LEEDS UNITED 19/8/92

Previous Clubs Details			Apps					Goals		
Club	Signed	Fee	Tot	Start	Sub	FA	FL	Lge	FA	FL
Leeds Utd	Jun-88		219	202	17	14	19	37	4	8
FAPL Summary by Club										
Leeds Utd	92/3 to 94/5		114	113	1	10	7	20	4	2
Total			*114*	*113*	*1*	*10*	*7*	*20*	*4*	*2*

SPENCER John   Chelsea
Fullname: John Spencer   DOB: 12-09-74 Glasgow
Debut: Norwich City v CHELSEA 19/8/92 as sub
Debut Goal: CHELSEA v Manchester City 9/1/93

Previous Clubs Details			Apps					Goals		
Club	Signed	Fee	Tot	Start	Sub	FA	FL	Lge	FA	FL
Lisbung (HK)	(From Rangers - Trainee)									
Morton	1988		4					1		
Rangers	1989		13					1		
Chelsea	Aug-92	£450,000	71	52	19	12	5	14	1	0

Chelsea	92/3 to 94/5	71	52	19	12	5	14	3	0
Total		*71*	*52*	*19*	*12*	*5*	*14*	*3*	*0*

SPINK Nigel   Aston Villa

Fullname: Nigel Philip Spink   DOB: 09-08-62 Chelmsford
Debut: Ipswich Town v ASTON VILLA 15/8/92
Debut Goal: (Goalkeeper)

Previous Clubs Details			*Apps*				*Goals*		
Club	Signed	Fee	Tot	Start	Sub	FA	FL	Lge	FA FL
Aston Villa	Jan-77	£4,000	359	357	2	28	45	0	0 0

FAPL Summary by Club

Aston Villa	92/3 to 94/5	53	51	2	4	6	0	0	0
Total		*53*	*51*	*2*	*4*	*6*	*0*	*0*	*0*

SPOONER Nick   Bolton Wanderers

Fullname: Nicholas Spooner   DOB: 06-06-75 Manchester
Debut: Debut Goal:

Previous Clubs Details			*Apps*				*Goals*		
Club	Signed	Fee	Tot	Start	Sub	FA	FL	Lge	FA FL
Bolton Wdrs	Jul-89	Trainee	23	22	1	3	4	2	0 0

SRNICEK Pavel   Newcastle United

Fullname: Pavel Srnicek   DOB: 11-03-72 Ostrava,Czech'kia
Debut: NEWCASTLE UNITED v Tottenham Hotspur 14/8/93
Debut Goal: (Goalkeeper)

Previous Clubs Details			*Apps*				*Goals*		
Club	Signed	Fee	Tot	Start	Sub	FA	FL	Lge	FA FL
Banik Ostrava									
Newcastle Utd	Feb-91	£350,000	111	111	0	10	8	0	0 0

FAPL Summary by Club

Newcastle Utd	93/4 to 94/5	59	59	0	5	6	0	0	0
Total		*59*	*59*	*0*	*5*	*6*	*0*	*0*	*0*

STAMP Phillip   Middlesbrough

Fullname: Phillip Stamp   DOB: 13-12-79 Middlesbrough
Debut: Debut Goal:

Previous Clubs Details			*Apps*				*Goals*		
Club	Signed	Fee	Tot	Start	Sub	FA	FL	Lge	FA FL
Middlesbrough	Feb-93	Trainee	10	8	2	1	2	0	0 0

STAUNTON Steve   Aston Villa

Fullname: Stephen Staunton   DOB: 20-01-73 Drogheda
Debut: Ipswich Town v ASTON VILLA 15/8/92
Debut Goal: ASTON VILLA v Crystal Palace 5/9/92

Club	Signed	Fee	Apps					Goals			
			Tot	Start	Sub	FA	FL	Lge	FA	FL	
Liverpool	Sep-86	£20,000	65	55	10	16	8	0	1	4	
Bradford C	Nov-87	Loan	8	7	1	0	2	0	0	0	
Aston Villa	Aug-91	£1.1m	138	137	1	12	14	14	0	0	

FAPL Summary by Club

| Aston Villa | 92/3 to 94/5 | | 101 | 100 | 1 | 8 | 12 | 10 | 0 | 0 | |
| *Total* | | | *101* | *100* | *1* | *8* | *12* | *10* | *0* | *0* | |

STEIN Mark   Chelsea

Fullname: E Mark S Stein   DOB: 29-01-70 South Africa
Debut: CHELSEA v Oldham Athletic 30/10/93
Debut Goal: Southampton v CHELSEA 27/12/93

Previous Clubs Details

Club	Signed	Fee	Apps					Goals			
			Tot	Start	Sub	FA	FL	Lge	FA	FL	
Luton T	Jan-84		54	41	13	9	5	19	3	0	
Aldershot	Jan-86	Loan	2	2	0	0	0	1	0	0	
QPR	Aug-88	£300,000	33	20	13	3	4	4	1	2	
Oxford Utd	Sep-89	Swap	82	72	10	3	4	18	0	0	
Stoke C	Sep-91	£100,000	94	94	0	4	8	50	0	8	
Chelsea	Oct-93	£1.5m	42	39	3	9	0	21	2	0	

FAPL Summary by Club

| Chelsea | 93/4 to 94/5 | | 42 | 39 | 3 | 9 | 0 | 21 | 2 | 0 | |
| *Total* | | | *42* | *39* | *3* | *9* | *0* | *21* | *2* | *0* | |

STEWART Simon   Sheffield Wednesday

Fullname: Simon A Stewart   DOB: 02-11-77 Leeds
Debut: Ipswich Town v SHEFFIELD WEDNESDAY 10/3/93
Debut Goal:

Previous Clubs Details

Club	Signed	Fee	Apps					Goals			
			Tot	Start	Sub	FA	FL	Lge	FA	FL	
Sheffield W	Jun-92		6	6	0	0	1	0	0	0	

FAPL Summary by Club

| Sheffield W | 92/3 to 94/5 | | 6 | 6 | 0 | 0 | 1 | 0 | 0 | 0 | |
| *Total* | | | *6* | *6* | *0* | *0* | *1* | *0* | *0* | *0* | |

STEWART Paul   Liverpool

Fullname: Paul Andrew Stewart   DOB: 08-10-68 Manchester
Debut: Nottingham Forest v LIVERPOOL 16/8/92
Debut Goal: LIVERPOOL v Sheffield United 19/8/92

Previous Clubs Details

Club	Signed	Fee	Apps					Goals			
			Tot	Start	Sub	FA	FL	Lge	FA	FL	
Blackpool	Oct-81		191	188	3	7	11	56	2	3	
Manchester C	Mar-87	£200,000	51	51	0	4	6	27	1	2	
Tottenham H	Jun-88	£1.7m	131	126	5	9	23	28	2	7	
Liverpool	Jul-92	£2.3m	32	28	4	1	6	1	0	0	

Crystal Palace	Jan-94	Loan	18	18	0	0	0	3	0 0
Wolves	Sep-94	Loan							
Burnley	Feb-95	Loan							
FAPL Summary by Club									
Liverpool	92/3 to 93/4		32	28	4	1	6	1	0 0
Total			*32*	*28*	*4*	*1*	*6*	*1*	*0 0*

STONE Steve   Nottingham Forest

Fullname: Steven Brian Stone   DOB: 21-08-75 Gateshead
Debut: Middlesbrough v NOTTINGHAM FOREST 20/2/92
Debut Goal: Middlesbrough v NOTTINGHAM FOREST 20/2/92

Previous Clubs Details			*Apps*					*Goals*		
Club	Signed	Fee	Tot	Start	Sub	FA	FL	Lge	FA	FL
N Forest	May-89		99	97	2	4	10	11	0	0
FAPL Summary by Club										
N Forest	92/3 to 94/5		53	52	1	2	5	6	0	0
Total			*53*	*52*	*1*	*2*	*5*	*6*	*0*	*0*

STRACHAN Gordon   Coventry City

Fullname: Gordon David Strachan   DOB: 10-02-61 Edinburgh
Debut: LEEDS UNITED v Wimbledon 15/8/92
Debut Goal: QPR v LEEDS UNITED 24/10/92

Previous Clubs Details			*Apps*					*Goals*		
Club	Signed	Fee	Tot	Start	Sub	FA	FL	Lge	FA	FL
Manchester Utd	Aug-84	£500,000	160	155	5	22	13	33	2	1
Leeds Utd	Mar-89	£300,000	197	188	9	14	19	37	2	3
Coventry C	Mar-95	Free	5	5	0	0	0	0	0	0
FAPL Summary by Club										
Leeds Utd	92/3 to 94/5		70	62	8	7	6	7	1	1
Coventry C	94/5		5	5	0	0	0	0	0	0
Total			*75*	*67*	*8*	*7*	*6*	*7*	*1*	*1*

STUART Graham   Everton

Fullname: Graham Charles Stuart   DOB: 25-10-74 Tooting
Debut: CHELSEA v Oldham Athletic 15/8/92
Debut Goal: Norwich City v CHELSEA 19/8/92

Previous Clubs Details			*Apps*					*Goals*		
Club	Signed	Fee	Tot	Start	Sub	FA	FL	Lge	FA	FL
Chelsea	Jun-89		87	70	17	7	11	14	1	2
Everton	Aug-93	£850,000	58	46	12	7	4	6	2	1
FAPL Summary by Club										
Chelsea	92/3		39	31	8	1	6	9	0	1
Everton	93/4 to 94/5		58	46	12	7	4	6	2	1
Total			*97*	*77*	*20*	*8*	*10*	*15*	*2*	*2*

STUBBS Alan — Bolton Wanderers

Fullname: Alan Stubbs
Debut:

DOB: 07-10-75 Liverpool
Debut Goal:

Previous Clubs Details

Club	Signed	Fee	Apps					Goals		
			Tot	Start	Sub	FA	FL	Lge	FA	FL
Bolton Wdrs	Jul-90	Trainee	176	156	20	17	16	5	2	4

SULLIVAN Neil — Wimbledon

Fullname: Neil Sullivan
Debut: Southampton v WIMBLEDON 17/10/92
Debut Goal:

DOB: 25-02-74 Sutton

Previous Clubs Details

Club	Signed	Fee	Apps					Goals		
			Tot	Start	Sub	FA	FL	Lge	FA	FL
Wimbledon	Jul-88		16	15	1	0	0	0	0	0
Crystal Palace	May-92	Loan	1	1	0	0	0	0	0	0

FAPL Summary by Club

| Wimbledon | 92/3 to 94/5 | | 14 | 13 | 1 | 0 | 0 | 0 | 0 | 0 |
| *Total* | | | *14* | *13* | *1* | *0* | *0* | *0* | *0* | *0* |

SUMMERBEE Nicky — Manchester City

Fullname: Nicholas J Summerbee
Debut: Sheffield United v SWINDON TOWN 14/8/93
Debut Goal: SWINDON TOWN v Manchester City 1/9/93

DOB: 27-08-75 Altrincham

Previous Clubs Details

Club	Signed	Fee	Apps					Goals		
			Tot	Start	Sub	FA	FL	Lge	FA	FL
Swindon T	Jul-89		112	89	23	6	10	6	0	3
Manchester C	Jun-94	£1.5m	41	39	2	4	6	1	0	2

FAPL Summary by Club

Swindon T	93/4 to 94/5		38	36	2	2	3	3	0	2
Manchester C	94/5		41	39	2	4	6	1	0	2
Total			*79*	*75*	*4*	*6*	*9*	*4*	*0*	*4*

SUTTON Chris — Blackburn Rovers

Fullname: Christopher Roy Sutton
Debut: Arsenal v NORWICH CITY 15/8/92
Debut Goal: NORWICH CITY v QPR 17/10/92

DOB: 11-03-77 Nottingham

Previous Clubs Details

Club	Signed	Fee	Apps					Goals		
			Tot	Start	Sub	FA	FL	Lge	FA	FL
Norwich C	Jul-91		102	89	13	10	9	35	5	3
Blackburn R	Jul-94	£5m	40	40	0	2	4	15	2	0

FAPL Summary by Club

Norwich C	92/3 to 93/4		79	73	6	4	7	33	2	3
Blackburn Rovers	94/5		40	40	0	2	4	15	2	0
Total			*119*	*113*	*6*	*6*	*11*	*48*	*4*	*3*

TALBOYS Steven — Wimbledon

Fullname: Steven John Talboys   DOB: 19-09-70 Bristol
Debut: Norwich City v WIMBLEDON 5/12/92
Debut Goal: WIMBLEDON v Tottenham Hotspur 1/10/94

Previous Clubs Details			Apps					Goals		
Club	Signed	Fee	Tot	Start	Sub	FA	FL	Lge	FA	FL
Wimbledon	Sep-92	£10,000	31	26	5	1	2	1	0	0
FAPL Summary by Club										
Wimbledon	92/3 to 94/5		21	16	5	1	2	1	0	0
Total			21	16	5	1	2	1	0	0

TAYLOR Ian — Aston Villa

Fullname: Ian V Taylor   DOB: 05-06-72 Birmingham
Debut: SHEFFIELD WED v Tottenham Hotspur 20/8/94
Debut Goal: SHEFFIELD WEDNESDAY v Newcastle Utd 22/10/94

Previous Clubs Details			Apps					Goals		
Club	Signed	Fee	Tot	Start	Sub	FA	FL	Lge	FA	FL
Port Vale	Jul-92		83	83	0	6	4	28	1	2
Sheffield W	Jun-94	£1m	14	9	5	0	4	1	0	1
Aston Villa	Dec-94	£1m	22	22	0	2	0	1	0	0
FAPL Summary by Club										
Sheffield W	94/5		14	9	5	0	4	1	0	1
Aston Villa	94/5		22	22	0	2	0	1	0	0
Total			36	31	5	2	4	2	0	1

TEALE Shaun — Aston Villa

Fullname: Shaun Teale   DOB: 11-03-68 Southport
Debut: Ipswich Town v ASTON VILLA 15/8/92
Debut Goal: ASTON VILLA v Middlesbrough 17/1/93

Previous Clubs Details			Apps					Goals		
Club	Signed	Fee	Tot	Start	Sub	FA	FL	Lge	FA	FL
Bournemouth	Jan-89	£50,000	100	99	1	5	8	4	1	0
Aston Villa	Jul-91	£300,000	147	146	1	13	15	2	0	3
FAPL Summary by Club										
Aston Villa	92/3 to 94/5		105	104	1	8	13	2	0	2
Total			105	104	1	8	13	2	0	2

THOMAS Michael — Liverpool

Fullname: Michael Lauriston Thomas   DOB: 25-08-71 Lambeth
Debut: LIVERPOOL v Southampton 1/9/92
Debut Goal: LIVERPOOL v Norwich City 25/10/92

Previous Clubs Details			Apps					Goals		
Club	Signed	Fee	Tot	Start	Sub	FA	FL	Lge	FA	FL
Arsenal	Dec-84		163	149	14	17	23	24	1	5
Portsmouth	Dec-86	Loan	3	3	0	0	0	0	0	0
Liverpool	Dec-91	£1.5m	55	39	16	10	4	4	2	0

Liverpool	92/3 to 94/5	38	23	15	5	4	1	0	0
Total		*38*	*23*	*15*	*5*	*4*	*1*	*0*	*0*

THOMAS Scott   Manchester City

Fullname: Scott L Thomas   DOB: 31-10-78 Bury
Debut: Nottm Forest v MANCHESTER CITY 6/5/95 as sub
Debut Goal:

Previous Clubs Details			*Apps*					*Goals*		
Club	Signed	Fee	Tot	Start	Sub	FA	FL	Lge	FA	FL
Manchester C	Mar-92	Trainee	2	0	2	0	0	0	0	0

FAPL Summary by Club

Manchester C	94/5	2	0	2	0	0	0	0	0
Total		*2*	*0*	*2*	*0*	*0*	*0*	*0*	*0*

THOMPSON Alan   Bolton Wanderers

Fullname: Alan Thompson   DOB: 23-12-77 Newcastle
Debut: Debut Goal:

Previous Clubs Details			*Apps*					*Goals*		
Club	Signed	Fee	Tot	Start	Sub	FA	FL	Lge	FA	FL
Newcastle Utd	Mar-91		16	13	3	1	0	0	0	0
Bolton Wdrs	Jul-93	£250,000	64	53	11	4	12	13	1	2

THORN Andy   Wimbledon

Fullname: Andrew Charles Thorn   DOB: 13-11-72 Carshalton
Debut: CRYSTAL PALACE v Blackburn Rovers 15/8/92
Debut Goal: CRYSTAL PALACE v Leeds United 20/12/92

Previous Clubs Details			*Apps*					*Goals*		
Club	Signed	Fee	Tot	Start	Sub	FA	FL	Lge	FA	FL
Wimbledon	Nov-84		107	106	1	9	7	2	0	0
Newcastle Utd	Aug-88	£850,000	36	36	0	0	4	2	0	1
Crystal Palace	Dec-89	£650,000	128	128	0	10	19	3	0	4
Wimbledon	Oct-94	Free	23	22	1	3	1	1	0	0

FAPL Summary by Club

Crystal Palace	92/3 to 94/5	34	34	0	0	5	1	0	3
Wimbledon	94/5	23	22	1	3	1	1	0	0
Total		*57*	*56*	*1*	*3*	*6*	*2*	*0*	*1*

THORSTVEDT Erik   Tottenham Hotspur

Fullname: Erik Thorstvedt   DOB: 29-10-66 Stavanger, Norway
Debut: TOTTENHAM HOTSPUR v Coventry City 19/8/92
Debut Goal: (Goalkeeper)

Previous Clubs Details			*Apps*					*Goals*		
Club	Signed	Fee	Tot	Start	Sub	FA	FL	Lge	FA	FL
Eik, Viking (Norway)										
Borussia Mon.										

IFK (Sweden)

			Tot	Start	Sub	FA	FL	Lge	FA	FL
Tottenham H	Dec-88	£400,000	173	171	2	14	25		0	0	0

FAPL Summary by Club

Tottenham H	92/3 to 94/5	60	58	2	6	7		0	0	0
Total		*60*	*58*	*2*	*6*	*7*		*0*	*0*	*0*

TILER Carl   Nottingham Forest
Fullname: Carl Tiler   DOB: 12-01-74 Sheffield
Debut: Blackburn Rovers v NOTTINGHAM FOREST 5/9/93
Debut Goal:

Previous Clubs Details   *Apps*   *Goals*

Club	Signed	Fee	Tot	Start	Sub	FA	FL	Lge	FA	FL
Barnsley	Aug-88		71	67	4	5	4	3	0	0
N Forest	May-91	£1.4m	69	67	2	6	11	1	0	0
Swindon T	Nov-94	Loan								

FAPL Summary by Club

N Forest	92/3 to 94/5	40	40	0	5	5		0	0	0
Total		*40*	*40*	*0*	*5*	*5*		*0*	*0*	*0*

TINKLER Mark   Leeds United
Fullname: Mark Roland Tinkler   DOB: 25-10-78 Bishop Auckland
Debut: Sheffield United v LEEDS UNITED 6/4/93
Debut Goal:

Previous Clubs Details   *Apps*   *Goals*

Club	Signed	Fee	Tot	Start	Sub	FA	FL	Lge	FA	FL
Leeds Utd	Nov-91		13	8	5	0	0	0	0	0

FAPL Summary by Club

Leeds Utd	92/3 to 94/5	13	8	5	0	0		0	0	0
Total		*13*	*8*	*5*	*0*	*0*		*0*	*0*	*0*

TISDALE Paul   Southampton
Fullname: Paul Tisdale   DOB: 15-01-77 Malta
Debut: Sheff Wed v TOTTENHAM HOTSPUR 2/1/95 as sub
Debut Goal:

Previous Clubs Details   *Apps*   *Goals*

Club	Signed	Fee	Tot	Start	Sub	FA	FL	Lge	FA	FL
Southampton	Jun-91	Junior	6	0	6	1	1	0	0	0
Northampton T	Mar-92	Loan	5	5	0	0	0	0	0	0

FAPL Summary by Club

Southampton	94/5	6	0	6	1	1		0	0	0
Total		*6*	*0*	*6*	*1*	*1*		*0*	*0*	*0*

TOWNSEND Andy   Aston Villa
Fullname: Andrew David Townsend   DOB: 24-07-77 Maidstone
Debut: CHELSEA v Oldham Athletic 15/8/92
Debut Goal: CHELSEA v Norwich City 12/9/92

Previous Clubs Details			*Apps*					*Goals*		
Club	Signed	Fee	Tot	Start	Sub	FA	FL	Lge	FA	FL
Southampton	Jan-85	£35,000	83	77	6	5	8	5	0	0
Norwich C	Aug-88	£300,000	71	66	5	10	4	8	2	0
Chelsea	Jul-90	£1.2m	110	110	0	7	17	12	0	7
Aston Villa	Jul-93	£2.1m	64	64	0	5	10	4	0	1
FAPL Summary by Club										
Chelsea	92/3 to 93/4		41	41	0	1	6	4	0	3
Aston Villa	93/4 to 94/5		64	64	0	5	10	4	0	1
Total			*105*	*105*	*0*	*6*	*16*	*8*	*0*	*4*

TURNER Andrew   Tottenham Hotspur

Fullname: Andrew Peter Turner   DOB: 24-03-79 Woolwich
Debut: Southampton v TOTTENHAM HOTSPUR 15/8/92
Debut Goal: TOTTENHAM HOTSPUR v Everton 5/9/92

Previous Clubs Details			*Apps*					*Goals*		
Club	Signed	Fee	Tot	Start	Sub	FA	FL	Lge	FA	FL
Tottenham H	Apr-92		38	33	5	3	4	4	0	0
Wycombe Wd	Aug-94	Loan								
Doncaster Ro	Oct-94	Loan								
FAPL Summary by Club										
Tottenham H	92/3 to 94/5		20	8	12	1	2	3	0	0
Total			*20*	*8*	*12*	*1*	*2*	*3*	*0*	*0*

UNSWORTH David   Everton

Fullname: David G Unsworth   DOB: 17-10-77 Chorley
Debut: EVERTON v Liverpool 7/12/92
Debut Goal: EVERTON v Arsenal 29/10/94

Previous Clubs Details			*Apps*					*Goals*		
Club	Signed	Fee	Tot	Start	Sub	FA	FL	Lge	FA	FL
Everton	May-92		51	48	3	5	4	4	0	0
FAPL Summary by Club										
Everton	92/3 to 94/5		49	47	2	5	4	3	0	0
Total			*49*	*47*	*2*	*5*	*4*	*3*	*0*	*0*

VICKERS Steve   Middlesbrough

Fullname: DOB: 14-10-71 Bishop Auckland
Debut: Debut Goal:

Previous Clubs Details			*Apps*					*Goals*		
Club	Signed	Fee	Tot	Start	Sub	FA	FL	Lge	FA	FL
Tranmere R	Sep-85		311	310	1	19	21	11	3	5
Middlesbrough	Dec-93	£700,000	26	25	1	2	0	3	0	0

VONK Michael   Manchester City

Fullname: Michael Christian Vonk   DOB: 29-10-72 Netherlands
Debut: MANCHESTER CITY v QPR 17/8/92

Debut Goal: MANCHESTER CITY v Oldham Athletic 29/8/92

Previous Clubs Details

Club	Signed	Fee	Apps					Goals		
			Tot	Start	Sub	FA	FL	Lge	FA	FL
Manchester C	Mar-92	£500,000	91	87	4	7	5	4	0	1

FAPL Summary by Club

| Manchester C | 92/3 to 94/5 | | 82 | 79 | 3 | 7 | 5 | 4 | 0 | 2 |
| *Total* | | | *82* | *79* | *3* | *7* | *5* | *4* | *0* | *2* |

WADDLE Chris — Sheffield Wednesday

Fullname: Christopher Roland Waddle
DOB: 15-12-64 Felling
Debut: Everton v SHEFFIELD WEDNESDAY 15/8/92
Debut Goal: SHEFFIELD WEDNESDAY v Everton 6/2/93

Previous Clubs Details

Club	Signed	Fee	Apps					Goals		
			Tot	Start	Sub	FA	FL	Lge	FA	FL
Newcastle Utd	Jul-80	£1,000	170	169	1	12	8	46	4	2
Tottenham H	Jun-85	£590,000	138	137	1	14	21	33	5	4
Marseille	Jul-89	£4.25m	0	0	0	0	0	0	0	0
Sheffield W	Jun-92	£1m	77	71	6	12	16	8	3	0

FAPL Summary by Club

| Sheffield W | 92/3 to 94/5 | | 77 | 71 | 6 | 12 | 15 | 8 | 3 | 0 |
| *Total* | | | *77* | *71* | *6* | *12* | *15* | *8* | *3* | *0* |

WALKER Andrew — Bolton Wanderers

Fullname: Andrew Walker
DOB: 07-04-69 Glasgow
Debut:
Debut Goal:

Previous Clubs Details

Club	Signed	Fee	Apps					Goals		
			Tot	Start	Sub	FA	FL	Lge	FA	FL
Motherwell			77	65	12	11	6	17	2	1
Celtic		£350,000	108	86	22	11	15	40	6	8
Newcastle Utd	Sep-91	Loan	2	2	0	0	1	0	0	0
Bolton Wdrs	Jan-92	£160,000	67	61	6	12	3	44	8	1

WALKER Ian — Tottenham Hotspur

Fullname: Ian Michael Walker
DOB: 01-11-75 Watford
Debut: Southampton v TOTTENHAM HOTSPUR 15/8/92
Debut Goal:

Previous Clubs Details

Club	Signed	Fee	Apps					Goals		
			Tot	Start	Sub	FA	FL	Lge	FA	FL
Tottenham H	Dec-89		88	87	1	8	2	0	0	0
Oxford Utd	Sep-90	Loan	2	2	0	0	1	0	0	0

FAPL Summary by Club

| Tottenham H | 92/3 to 94/5 | | 69 | 68 | 1 | 8 | 5 | 0 | 0 | 0 |
| *Total* | | | *69* | *68* | *1* | *8* | *5* | *0* | *0* | *0* |

WALKER Des — Sheffield Wednesday

Fullname: Desmond Sinclair Walker   DOB: 27-11-69 Hackney
Debut: SHEFFIELD WEDNESDAY v Aston Villa 18/8/93
Debut Goal:

Previous Clubs Details			*Apps*					*Goals*		
Club	Signed	Fee	Tot	Start	Sub	FA	FL	Lge	FA	FL
N Forest	Nov-83		264	259	5	27	40	1	0	0
Sampdoria	May-92	£1.5m	0	0	0	0	0	0	0	0
Sheffield W	Aug-93	£2.75m	80	80	0	7	10	0	0	0
FAPL Summary by Club										
Sheffield W	93/4 to 94/5		80	80	0	7	10	0	0	0
Total			*80*	*80*	*0*	*7*	*10*	*0*	*0*	*0*

WALLACE Rod — Leeds United

Fullname: Rodney Seymour Wallace   DOB: 03-10-73 Greenwich
Debut: LEEDS UNITED v Wimbledon 15/8/92
Debut Goal: LEEDS UNITED v Tottenham Hotspur 25/8/92

Previous Clubs Details			*Apps*					*Goals*		
Club	Signed	Fee	Tot	Start	Sub	FA	FL	Lge	FA	FL
Southampton	Apr-88		128	111	17	10	19	44	3	6
Leeds Utd	Jun-91	£1.6m	134	129	5	9	8	39	0	3
FAPL Summary by Club										
Leeds Utd	92/3 to 94/5		101	95	6	8	5	28	0	1
Total			*101*	*95*	*6*	*8*	*5*	*28*	*0*	*1*

WALSH Gary — Manchester United

Fullname: Gary Walsh   DOB: 22-03-72 Wigan
Debut: Ipswich Town v MANCHESTER UNITED 24/9/94
Debut Goal:

Previous Clubs Details			*Apps*					*Goals*		
Club	Signed	Fee	Tot	Start	Sub	FA	FL	Lge	FA	FL
Manchester Utd	Apr-85	Junior	50	49	1	0	7	0	0	0
Airdrieonians	Aug-88	Loan								
Oldham Ath	Nov-93	Loan	6	6	0	0	0	0	0	0
FAPL Summary by Club										
Manchester Utd		94/5	10	10	0	0	3	0	0	0
Total			*10*	*10*	*0*	*0*	*3*	*0*	*0*	*0*

WALSH Paul — Manchester City

Fullname: Paul A M Walsh   DOB: 02-10-66 Plumstead
Debut: MANCHESTER CITY v Wimbledon 12/3/93
Debut Goal: Ipswich Town v MANCHESTER CITY 29/3/93

Previous Clubs Details			*Apps*					*Goals*		
Club	Signed	Fee	Tot	Start	Sub	FA	FL	Lge	FA	FL
Charlton Ath	Oct-79		87	85	2	4	9	24	1	6

Club	Signed	Fee	Tot	Start	Sub	FA	FL	Lge	FA	FL
Luton T	Jul-82	£400,000	80	80	0	4	5	24	3	1
Liverpool	May-84	£700,000	77	63	14	8	12	25	3	4
Tottenham H	Feb-88	£500,000	128	84	44	8	15	19	0	2
QPR	Sep-91	Loan	2	2	0	0	0	0	0	0
Portsmouth	Jun-92	£400,000	73	67	6	3	8	13	0	4
Manchester C	Mar-94	£750,000	51	51	0	3	6	16	1	2
FAPL Summary by Club										
Manchester C	93/4 to 94/5		51	51	0	3	6	16	1	2
Total			*51*	*51*	*0*	*3*	*6*	*16*	*1*	*2*

WALTERS Mark   Liverpool

Fullname: Mark Everton Walters   DOB: 03-06-68 Birmingham
Debut: Nottingham Forest v LIVERPOOL 16/8/92
Debut Goal: LIVERPOOL v Sheffield United 19/8/92

Previous Clubs Details

Club	Signed	Fee	Apps					Goals		
			Tot	Start	Sub	FA	FL	Lge	FA	FL
Aston Villa	May-82		181	168	13	12	21	39	1	6
Rangers	Dec-87	£500,000	0	0	0	0	0	0	0	0
Liverpool	Aug-91	£1.25m	93	58	53	8	12	14	0	4
Stoke C	Mar-94	Loan	9	9	0	0	0	2	0	0
Wolv'n Wan	Sep-94	Loan								
FAPL Summary by Club										
Liverpool	92/3 to 94/5		68	40	28	5	8	11	0	2
Total			*68*	*40*	*28*	*5*	*8*	*11*	*0*	*2*

WARHURST Paul   Blackburn Rovers

Fullname: Paul Warhurst   DOB: 27-09-73 Stockport
Debut: Everton v SHEFFIELD WEDNESDAY 15/8/92
Debut Goal: Nottingham Forest v SHEFFIELD WED 12/9/92

Previous Clubs Details

Club	Signed	Fee	Apps					Goals		
			Tot	Start	Sub	FA	FL	Lge	FA	FL
Manchester C	Jun-88		0	0	0	0	0	0	0	0
Oldham Ath	Oct-88	£10,000	67	60	7	9	8	2	0	0
Sheffield W	Jul-91	£750,000	66	60	6	8	9	6	4	5
Blackburn R	Sep-93	£2.7m	36	24	12	2	5	2	0	0
FAPL Summary by Club										
Sheffield W	92/3 to 93/4		33	29	4	7	7	6	5	3
Blackburn Rovers	93/4 to 94/5		36	24	12	9	12	2	5	3
Total			*69*	*53*	*16*	*16*	*19*	*8*	*10*	*6*

WARNER Vance   Nottingham Forest

Fullname: Vance Warner   DOB: 04-09-78 Leeds
Debut: NOTTINGHAM FOREST v Crystal Palace 2/1/95
Debut Goal:

Previous Clubs Details			Apps					Goals		
Club	Signed	Fee	Tot	Start	Sub	FA	FL	Lge	FA	FL
N Forest			2	2	0	0	1	0	0	0

FAPL Summary by Club

N Forest	94/5		1	1	0	0	0	0	0	0
Total			*1*	*1*	*0*	*0*	*0*	*0*	*0*	*0*

WATSON Steve   Newcastle United

Fullname: Stephen C Watson   DOB: 02-04-78 North Shields
Debut: NEWCASTLE UNITED v Tottenham Hotspur 14/8/93
Debut Goal: NEWCASTLE UNITED v Swindon Town 12/3/94

Previous Clubs Details			Apps					Goals		
Club	Signed	Fee	Tot	Start	Sub	FA	FL	Lge	FA	FL
Newcastle Utd	Jul-90		113	97	16	8	7	7	0	0

FAPL Summary by Club

Newcastle Utd	93/4 to 94/5		59	51	8	3	7	6	0	0
Total			*59*	*51*	*8*	*3*	*7*	*6*	*0*	*0*

WATSON Dave   Everton

Fullname: David Watson   DOB: 21-11-65 Liverpool
Debut: EVERTON v Sheffield Wednesday 15/8/92
Debut Goal: Middlesbrough v EVERTON 10/4/93

Previous Clubs Details			Apps					Goals		
Club	Signed	Fee	Tot	Start	Sub	FA	FL	Lge	FA	FL
Liverpool	May-79		0	0	0	0	0	0	0	0
Norwich C	Nov-80	£100,000	212	212	0	18	21	11	1	3
Everton	Aug-86	£900,000	306	304	2	38	34	22	5	6

FAPL Summary by Club

Everton	92/3 to 94/5		106	105	1	8	11	4	2	1
Total			*106*	*105*	*1*	*8*	*11*	*4*	*2*	*1*

WATSON Gordon   Southampton

Fullname: Gordon William George Watson   DOB: 21-03-76 Sidcup
Debut: Everton v SHEFFIELD WEDNESDAY 15/8/92 as sub
Debut Goal: Oldham Athletic v SHEFFIELD WEDNESDAY 7/4/93

Previous Clubs Details			Apps					Goals		
Club	Signed	Fee	Tot	Start	Sub	FA	FL	Lge	FA	FL
Charlton Ath	Apr-89		31	20	11	1	2	7	0	7
Sheffield W	Feb-91	£250,000	43	24	19	6	8	13	2	3
Southampton	Mar-95	£1.2m	12	12	0	0	0	3	0	0

FAPL Summary by Club

Sheffield W	92/3 to 94/5		57	24	33	6	10	15	2	3
Southampton	94/5		12	12	0	0	0	3	0	0
Total			*69*	*36*	*33*	*6*	*10*	*18*	*2*	*3*

WATSON Kevin — Tottenham Hotspur

Fullname: Kevin Edward Watson
DOB: 04-01-78 Hackney
Debut: Sheffield Wed v TOTTENHAM H 27/9/92 as sub
Debut Goal:

Previous Clubs Details

Club	Signed	Fee	Apps Tot	Start	Sub	FA	FL	Goals Lge	FA	FL
Tottenham H	May-92		5	4	1	1	2	1	0	1
Brentford	Mar-94	Loan	3	2	1	0	0	0	0	0
Barnet	Feb-95	Loan								

FAPL Summary by Club

Tottenham H	92/3 to 93/4		5	4	1	1	2	0	0	1
Total			*5*	*4*	*1*	*1*	*2*	*0*	*0*	*1*

WATTS Julian — Sheffield Wednesday

Fullname: Julian D Watts
DOB: 18-03-75 Sheffield
Debut: Liverpool v SHEFFIELD WEDNESDAY 3/3/93
Debut Goal:

Previous Clubs Details

Club	Signed	Fee	Apps Tot	Start	Sub	FA	FL	Goals Lge	FA	FL
Rotherham Utd	Jul-90		20	17	3	4	1	1	0	0
Sheffield W	Mar-92	£80,000	5	3	2	0	0	0	0	0
Shrewsbury T	Dec-92	Loan	9	9	0	0	0	0	0	0

FAPL Summary by Club

Sheffield W	92/3 to 93/4		4	3	1	0	0	0	0	0
Total			*4*	*3*	*1*	*0*	*0*	*0*	*0*	*0*

WEBSTER Simon — West Ham United

Fullname: Simon P Webster
DOB: 21-01-68 Earl Shilton
Debut: WEST HAM UTD v Blackburn Rovers 30/4/95 as sub
Debut Goal:

Previous Clubs Details

Club	Signed	Fee	Apps Tot	Start	Sub	FA	FL	Goals Lge	FA	FL
Tottenham H	Dec-81		3	2	1	0	0	0	0	0
Exeter C	Nov-83	Loan	26	26	0	0	0	0	0	0
Huddersfield T	Feb-85	£15,000	118	118	0	7	7	4	0	0
Sheffield Utd	Mar-88	£35,000	37	26	11	6	5	3	0	0
Charlton Ath	Sep-90	£50,000	127	127	0	6	7	7	0	0
West Ham Utd	Jul-93	£525,000								
Oldham Ath	Mar-95	Loan								

FAPL Summary by Club

West Ham Utd	93/4 to 94/5		5	0	5	0	0	0	0	0
Total			*5*	*0*	*5*	*0*	*0*	*0*	*0*	*0*

WEGERLE Roy — Coventry City

Fullname: Roy Connon Wegerle   DOB: 20-03-68 Johannesburg, SA
Debut: Coventry City v BLACKBURN ROVERS 29/8/92
Debut Goal: BLACKBURN ROVERS v Norwich City 3/10/92

Previous Clubs Details

Club	Signed	Fee	Tot	Start	Sub	FA	FL	Lge	FA	FL
Tampa Bay (USA)										
Chelsea	Jun-86	£100,000	23	15	8	2	0	3	1	0
Swindon T	Mar-88	Loan	7	7	0	0	0	1	0	0
Luton T	Jul-88	£75,000	45	39	6	1	10	10	0	8
QPR	Dec-89	£1m	75	71	4	11	5	29	1	1
Blackburn R	Mar-92	£1.2m	34	20	14	5	6	6	2	4
Coventry C	Mar-93	£1m	54	47	7	5	5	9	1	1

FAPL Summary by Club

Blackburn Rovers	92/3 to 93/4		22	11	11	5	6	4	2	4
Coventry C	92/3 to 94/5		54	47	7	10	11	15	3	5
Total			*76*	*58*	*18*	*15*	*17*	*19*	*5*	*9*

WETHERALL David — Leeds United

Fullname: David Wetherall   DOB: 15-03-75 Sheffield
Debut: Southampton v LEEDS UNITED 19/9/92
Debut Goal: LEEDS UNITED v Chelsea 24/3/93

Previous Clubs Details

Club	Signed	Fee	Tot	Start	Sub	FA	FL	Lge	FA	FL
Sheffield W	Jul-89	Trainee	0	0	0	0	0	0	0	0
Leeds Utd	Jul-91	£125,000	84	82	2	10	5	5	3	0

FAPL Summary by Club

Leeds Utd	92/3 to 94/5		83	82	1	10	5	5	3	0
Total			*83*	*82*	*1*	*10*	*5*	*5*	*3*	*0*

WHELAN Noel — Leeds United

Fullname: Noel Whelan   DOB: 31-12-78 Leeds
Debut: Sheffield Wednesday v LEEDS UNITED 4/5/93
Debut Goal: LEEDS UNITED v Arsenal 23/8/94 as sub

Previous Clubs Details

Club	Signed	Fee	Tot	Start	Sub	FA	FL	Lge	FA	FL
Leeds Utd	Mar-93		40	25	15	2	3	7	0	1

FAPL Summary by Club

Leeds Utd	92/3 to 94/5		40	25	15	2	3	7	0	1
Total			*40*	*25*	*15*	*2*	*3*	*7*	*0*	*1*

WHELAN Phil — Middlesbrough

Fullname: Philip James Whelan   DOB: 08-03-76 Stockport
Debut: IPSWICH TOWN v Aston Villa 15/8/92
Debut Goal:

Previous Clubs Details			Apps					Goals		
Club	Signed	Fee	Tot	Start	Sub	FA	FL	Lge	FA	FL
Ipswich T	Jul-90		69	64	5	3	7	2	0	0
Middlesbrough	Mar-95	£300,000	0	0	0	0	0	0	0	0
FAPL Summary by Club										
Ipswich T	92/3 to 93/4		61	56	5	3	7	0	0	0
Total			*61*	*56*	*5*	*3*	*7*	*0*	*0*	*0*

WHISTON Peter   Southampton

Fullname: Peter M Whiston   DOB: 05-01-72 Widnes
Debut: Newcastle United v SOUTHAMPTON 27/8/94 as sub
Debut Goal:

Previous Clubs Details			Apps					Goals		
Club	Signed	Fee	Tot	Start	Sub	FA	FL	Lge	FA	FL
Plymouth Arg	Dec-87		10	4	6	1	0		0	0
Torquay Utd	Mar-90	Free	40	39	1	1	5	1	1	0
Exeter C	Sep-91	£25,000	85	85	0	10	7	6	0	0
Southampton	Aug-94	£30,000	1	0	1	0	0	0	0	0
FAPL Summary by Club										
Southampton	94/5		1	0	1	0	0	0	0	0
Total			*1*	*0*	*1*	*0*	*0*	*0*	*0*	*0*

WHITBREAD Adrian   West Ham United

Fullname: Adrian R Whitbread   DOB: 23-10-75 Epping
Debut: Sheffield United v SWINDON TOWN 14/8/93
Debut Goal: SWINDON TOWN v Tottenham Hotspur 22/1/94

Previous Clubs Details			Apps					Goals		
Club	Signed	Fee	Tot	Start	Sub	FA	FL	Lge	FA	FL
Leyton Orient	Nov-89		125	125	0	11	11	2	1	0
Swindon T	Aug-93	£500,000	35	34	1	2	0	1	0	0
West Ham Utd	Aug-94	Swap +	8	3	5	0	3	0	0	0
FAPL Summary by Club										
Swindon T	93/4		35	34	1	2	0	1	0	0
West Ham Utd	94/5		8	3	5	0	3	0	0	0
Total			*43*	*37*	*6*	*2*	*3*	*1*	*0*	*0*

WHITE David   Leeds United

Fullname: David White   DOB: 31-10-71 Manchester
Debut: MANCHESTER CITY v QPR 17/8/92
Debut Goal: MANCHESTER CITY v QPR 17/8/92

Previous Clubs Details			Apps					Goals		
Club	Signed	Fee	Tot	Start	Sub	FA	FL	Lge	FA	FL
Manchester C	Oct-85		285	273	12	22	26	81	4	11
Leeds Utd	Dec-93	Swap	38	27	11	6	0	8	2	0

WHITTINGHAM Guy   Sheffield Wednesday

Fullname: Guy Whittingham
Debut: ASTON VILLA v Manchester United 23/8/93 as sub
DOB: 11-11-68 Evesham
Debut Goal: Everton v ASTON VILLA 31/8/93

Previous Clubs Details			*Apps*					*Goals*		
Club	Signed	Fee	Tot	Start	Sub	FA	FL	Lge	FA	FL
Portsmouth	Jun-89		160	149	11	10	9	88	10	3
Aston Villa	Jul-93	£1.2m	18	13	5	0	2	3	0	0
Wolves	Feb-94	Loan	13	13	0	1	0	8	0	0
Sheffield W	Dec-94	£700,000	21	16	5	3	0	9	0	0
FAPL Summary by Club										
Aston Villa	93/4 to 94/5		25	17	8	0	5	5	0	1
Sheffield W	94/5		21	16	5	3	0	9	0	0
Total			*46*	*33*	*13*	*3*	*5*	*14*	*0*	*1*

WHYTE Derek   Middlesbrough

Fullname: Derek Whyte
Debut: Coventry City v MIDDLESBROUGH 15/8/92
DOB: 01-09-72 Glasgow
Debut Goal:

Previous Clubs Details			*Apps*					*Goals*		
Club	Signed	Fee	Tot	Start	Sub	FA	FL	Lge	FA	FL
Celtic			216	211	5	26	19	7	0	0
Middlesbrough	Aug-92		113	112	1	2	8	2	0	0
FAPL Summary by Club										
Middlesbrough	92/3		35	34	1	3	1	0	0	0
Total			*35*	*34*	*1*	*3*	*1*	*0*	*0*	*0*

WIDDRINGTON Tommy   Southampton

Fullname: Thomas Widdrington
Debut: Crystal Palace v SOUTHAMPTON 26/9/92
DOB: 22-11-75 Newcastle
Debut Goal: SOUTHAMPTON v Chelsea 27/12/93

Previous Clubs Details			*Apps*					*Goals*		
Club	Signed	Fee	Tot	Start	Sub	FA	FL	Lge	FA	FL
Southampton	May-90		54	47	7	6	3	1	0	0
Wigan Ath	Sep-91	Loan	6	5	1	0	0	0	0	0
FAPL Summary by Club										
Southampton	92/3 to 94/5		51	45	6	7	2	1	0	0
Total			*51*	*45*	*6*	*7*	*2*	*1*	*0*	*0*

WILCOX Jason
Blackburn Rovers

Fullname: Jason Malcolm Wilcox   DOB: 16-03-75 Farnworth
Debut: BLACKBURN ROVERS v Arsenal 18/8/92
Debut Goal: Middlesbrough v BLACKBURN ROVERS 5/12/92

Previous Clubs Details

Club	Signed	Fee	Tot	Start	Sub	FA	FL	Lge	FA	FL
Blackburn R	Jun-89		160	148	12	11	14	19	1	0

FAPL Summary by Club

Blackburn R	92/3 to 94/5		93	89	4	11	12	15	1	0
Total			*93*	*89*	*4*	*11*	*12*	*15*	*1*	*0*

WILKINS Ray
QPR

Fullname: Raymond Colin Wilkins   DOB: 15-09-60 Hillingdon
Debut: Manchester City v QPR 17/8/92
Debut Goal: QPR v Tottenham Hotspur 3/10/92

Previous Clubs Details

Club	Signed	Fee	Tot	Start	Sub	FA	FL	Lge	FA	FL
Chelsea	Oct-73		179	176	3	11	7	30	2	2
Manchester Utd	Aug-79	£825,000	160	158	2	10	15	7	1	1
Milan	Jul-84	£1.5m								
Rangers	Nov-87	£250,000								
QPR	Nov-89	Free	154	153	1	13	13	7	2	0
Crystal Palace	May-94	Free	1	1	0	0	0	0	0	0
QPR	Nov-94	Free	2	1	1	0	0	2	0	0

FAPL Summary by Club

QPR	92/3 to 94/5		68	67	1	2	8	5	0	0
Crystal Palace	94/5		1	1	0	0	0	0	0	0
Total			*69*	*68*	*1*	*2*	*8*	*5*	*0*	*0*

WILKINSON Paul
Middlesbrough

Fullname: Paul Wilkinson   DOB: 31-10-68 Louth
Debut: Coventry City v MIDDLESBROUGH 15/8/92
Debut Goal: MIDDLESBROUGH v Leeds United 22/8/92

Previous Clubs Details

Club	Signed	Fee	Tot	Start	Sub	FA	FL	Lge	FA	FL
Grimsby T	Nov-82	Amateur	71	69	2	6	10	27	1	5
Everton	Mar-85	£250,000	31	19	12	3	4	6	1	7
N Forest	Mar-87	£200,000	34	32	2	5	3	5	2	1
Watford	Aug-88	£300,000	134	133	1	7	4	52	0	1
Middlesbrough	Aug-91	£550,000	162	159	3	11	16	50	5	8

FAPL Summary by Club

Middlesbrough	92/3		41	41	0			15		
Total			*41*	*41*	*0*			*15*		

WILLIAMS Paul — Coventry City

Fullname: Paul R C Williams DOB: 12-09-73 Leicester
Debut: COVENTRY CITY v Newcastle United 18/8/93 as sub
Debut Goal:

Previous Clubs Details

Club	Signed	Fee	Tot	Start	Sub	FA	FL	Lge	FA	FL
Stockport C	Jul-89		70	61	9	4	3	4	0	0
Coventry C	Aug-93	£150,000	14	8	6	3	2	0	0	0
WBA	Nov-93	Loan	5	5	0	0	0	0	0	0
Huddersfield T	Nov-94	Loan								
Huddersfield T	Mar-95	Loan								

FAPL Summary by Club

Coventry C	93/4 to 94/5		14	8	6	3	2	0	0	0
Total			*14*	*8*	*6*	*3*	*2*	*0*	*0*	*0*

WILLIAMS John — Coventry City

Fullname: John N Williams DOB: 12-05-72 Birmingham
Debut: COVENTRY CITY v Middlesbrough 15/8/92
Debut Goal: COVENTRY CITY v Middlesbrough 15/8/92

Previous Clubs Details

Club	Signed	Fee	Tot	Start	Sub	FA	FL	Lge	FA	FL
Swansea C	Aug-91	£5,000	39	36	3	3	3	11	0	0
Coventry C	Jul-92	£250,000	80	66	14	2	4	11	0	0
Notts County	Oct-94	Loan								
Swansea C	Feb-95	Loan								

FAPL Summary by Club

Coventry C	92/3 to 94/5		80	66	14	2	4	11	0	0
Total			*80*	*66*	*14*	*2*	*4*	*11*	*0*	*0*

WILLIAMS Mike — Sheffield Wednesday

Fullname: Michael Anthony Williams DOB: 22-11-73 Bradford
Debut: SHEFFIELD WEDNESDAY v Southampton 12/4/93
Debut Goal: SHEFFIELD WEDNESDAY v Ipswich Town 14/5/95

Previous Clubs Details

Club	Signed	Fee	Tot	Start	Sub	FA	FL	Lge	FA	FL
Sheffield W	Feb-91		17	14	3	0	2	1	0	0
Halifax T	Dec-92	Loan	9	9	0	0	0	1	0	0

FAPL Summary by Club

Sheffield W	92/3 to 94/5		17	14	3	0	2	1	0	0
Total			*17*	*14*	*3*	*0*	*2*	*1*	*0*	*0*

WILLIAMSON Danny — West Ham United

Fullname: Daniel Williamson DOB: 06-12-77 Newham
Debut: Arsenal v WEST HAM UNITED 30/4/94 as sub
Debut Goal: WEST HAM UNITED v Southampton 7/5/94

Previous Clubs Details			Apps					Goals		
Club	Signed	Fee	Tot	Start	Sub	FA	FL	Lge	FA	FL
West Ham Utd			7	6	1	0	0	1	0	0
FAPL Summary by Club										
West Ham Utd	93/4 to 94/5		7	6	1	0	0	1	0	0
Total			*7*	*6*	*1*	*0*	*0*	*1*	*0*	*0*

WILSON Clive   Tottenham Hotspur

Fullname: Clive A Wilson   DOB: 14-11-65 Manchester
Debut: Manchester City v QPR 17/8/92
Debut Goal: QPR v Manchester City 6/8/92

Previous Clubs Details			Apps					Goals		
Club	Signed	Fee	Tot	Start	Sub	FA	FL	Lge	FA	FL
Manchester C	Dec-79		109	107	2	2	10	9	0	2
Chester C	Sep-82	Loan	21	21	0	0	0	2	0	0
Chelsea	Mar-87	£250,000	81	68	13	4	6	5	0	0
QPR	Jul-90	£450,000	172	170	2	8	16	10	1	1
Tottenham H	Jun-95	Free								
FAPL Summary by Club										
QPR	92/3 to 94/5		119	119	0	6	10	6	1	1
Total			*119*	*119*	*0*	*6*	*10*	*6*	*1*	*1*

WINTERBURN Nigel   Arsenal

Fullname: Nigel Winterburn   DOB: 12-12-67 Nuneaton
Debut: ARSENAL v Norwich City 15/8/92
Debut Goal: ARSENAL v Oldham Athletic 26/8/92

Previous Clubs Details			Apps					Goals		
Club	Signed	Fee	Tot	Start	Sub	FA	FL	Lge	FA	FL
Wimbledon	Aug-83		165	164	1	12	13	8	0	0
Arsenal	May-87	£407,000	272	271	1	30	35	5	0	3
FAPL Summary by Club										
Arsenal	92/3 to 94/5		102	102	0	13	16	1	0	1
Total			*102*	*102*	*0*	*13*	*16*	*1*	*0*	*1*

WISE Dennis   Chelsea

Fullname: Dennis Frank Wise   DOB: 17-12-70 Kensington
Debut: CHELSEA v Blackburn Rovers 26/8/92
Debut Goal: Aston Villa v CHELSEA 2/9/92

Previous Clubs Details			Apps					Goals		
Club	Signed	Fee	Tot	Start	Sub	FA	FL	Lge	FA	FL
Wimbledon	Mar-85		135	127	8	11	14	26	3	0
Chelsea	Jul-90	£1.6m	152	150	2	11	19	33	2	6
FAPL Summary by Club										
Chelsea	92/3 to 94/5		81	80	1	6	10	13	0	3
Total			*81*	*80*	*1*	*6*	*10*	*13*	*0*	*3*

WOAN Ian   Nottingham Forest

Fullname: Ian Simon Woan   DOB: 15-12-71 Heswall
Debut: NOTTINGHAM FOREST v Liverpool 16/8/92
Debut Goal: Coventry City v NOTTINGHAM FOREST 9/1/93

Previous Clubs Details

Club	Signed	Fee	Tot	Start	Sub	FA	FL	Lge	FA	FL
N Forest	Mar-90	£80,000	122	114	8	11	11	21	1	1

FAPL Summary by Club

N Forest	92/3 to 94/5		65	62	3	5	4	8	0	0
Total			*65*	*62*	*3*	*5*	*4*	*8*	*0*	*0*

WOODS Chris   Sheffield Wednesday

Fullname: Christopher Charles Eric Woods   DOB: 15-11-63 Boston
Debut: Everton v SHEFFIELD WEDNESDAY 15/8/92
Debut Goal:

Previous Clubs Details

Club	Signed	Fee	Tot	Start	Sub	FA	FL	Lge	FA	FL
N Forest	Dec-76		0	0	0	0	7	0	0	0
QPR	Jul-79	£250,000	63	63	0	1	8	0	0	0
Norwich C	Mar-81	£225,000	216	216	0	19	26	0	0	0
Rangers	Jun-86	£600,000								
Sheffield W	Aug-91	£1.2m	99	98	1	10	13	0	0	0

FAPL Summary by Club

Sheffield W	92/3 to 94/5		58	57	1	8	9	0	0	0
Total			*58*	*57*	*1*	*8*	*9*	*0*	*0*	*0*

WORTHINGTON Nigel   Leeds United

Fullname: Nigel Worthington   DOB: 05-11-65 Ballymena, N.Ireland
Debut: Everton v SHEFFIELD WEDNESDAY 15/8/92
Debut Goal: SHEFFIELD WEDNESDAY v Norwich City 10/1/93

Previous Clubs Details

Club	Signed	Fee	Tot	Start	Sub	FA	FL	Lge	FA	FL
Notts County	Jul-81	£100,000	67	62	5	4	11	4	0	0
Sheffield W	Feb-84	£125,000	338	334	4	29	41	12	0	1
Leeds Utd		£2.225m	27	21	6	4	2	1	0	0

FAPL Summary by Club

Sheffield W	92/3 to 93/4		71	70	1	9	10	2	0	1
Leeds Utd	94/5		27	21	6	4	2	1	0	0
Total			*98*	*91*	*7*	*13*	*12*	*3*	*0*	*1*

WRIGHT Mark   Liverpool

Fullname: Mark Wright   DOB: 02-08-67 Dorchester on Thames
Debut: Nottingham Forest v LIVERPOOL 16/8/92
Debut Goal: LIVERPOOL v Southampton 1/9/92

Club	Signed	Fee	Tot	Start	Sub	FA	FL	Lge	FA	FL
Oxford Utd	Aug-80		10	8	2	1	0	0	0	0
Southampton	Mar-82	£80,000	170	170	0	17	25	7	1	2
Derby County	Aug-87	£760,000	144	144	0	5	15	10	0	0
Liverpool	Jul-91	£2.2m	91	89	2	9	10	3	0	0

FAPL Summary by Club

Liverpool	92/3 to 94/5		70	68	2	0	9	3	0	1
Total			*70*	*68*	*2*	*0*	*9*	*3*	*0*	*1*

WRIGHT Ian   Arsenal

Fullname: Ian Edward Wright   DOB: 04-11-67 Woolwich
Debut: ARSENAL v Norwich City 15/8/92
Debut Goal: Liverpool v ARSENAL 23/8/92

Previous Clubs Details

Club	Signed	Fee	Tot	Start	Sub	FA	FL	Lge	FA	FL
Crystal Palace	Aug-85		225	206	19	11	19	90	3	9
Arsenal	Sep-91	£2.5m	131	129	2	12	18	80	11	16

FAPL Summary by Club

Arsenal	92/3 to 94/5		101	99	2	12	15	56	11	14
Total			*101*	*99*	*2*	*12*	*15*	*56*	*11*	*14*

WRIGHT Alan   Aston Villa

Fullname: Alan Geoffrey Wright   DOB: 29-09-75 Ashton-under-Lyme
Debut: Crystal Palace v BLACKBURN ROVERS 15/8/92
Debut Goal:

Previous Clubs Details

Club	Signed	Fee	Tot	Start	Sub	FA	FL	Lge	FA	FL
Blackpool	Apr-89		98	91	7	8	12	0	0	0
Blackburn R	Oct-91	£400,000	69	63	6	5	8	1	0	0
Aston Villa	Mar-95	£1m	8	8	0	0	0	0	0	0

FAPL Summary by Club

Blackburn R	92/3 to 94/5		41	35	6	4	8	0	0	0
Aston Villa	94/5		8	8	0	0	0	0	0	0
Total			*49*	*43*	*6*	*4*	*8*	*0*	*0*	*0*

WRIGHT Tommy   Middlesbrough

Fullname: Thomas E Wright   DOB: 11-01-70 Dunfermline
Debut: Coventry City v MIDDLESBROUGH 15/8/92
Debut Goal: MIDDLESBROUGH v Leeds United 22/8/92

Previous Clubs Details

Club	Signed	Fee	Tot	Start	Sub	FA	FL	Lge	FA	FL
Leeds Utd	Jan-83	Amateur	91	73	8	4	5	24	3	1
Oldham Ath	Oct-86	£80,000	112	110	2	3	8	23	2	2

Leicester C	Aug-89	£350,000	129	122	7	4	8	22	0	0
Middlesbrough	Jul-92	£650,000	53					5		

FAPL Summary by Club

Middlesbrough	92/3	36	34	2			5
Total		*36*	*34*	*2*	*0*	*0*	*5*	*0*	*0*

YATES Steve   QPR

Fullname: Stephen Yates   DOB: 30-01-74 Bristol
Debut: QPR v Liverpool 18/8/94
Debut Goal: Aston Villa v QPR 14/1/95

Previous Clubs Details

Club	Signed	Fee	Apps					Goals		
			Tot	Start	Sub	FA	FL	Lge	FA	FL
Bristol R	Aug-93		197	196	1	11	9	0	0	0
QPR	Aug-93	£650,000	52	49	3	2	3	1	0	0

FAPL Summary by Club

QPR	93/4 to 94/5	52	49	3	2	3	1	0	0
Total		*52*	*49*	*3*	*2*	*3*	*1*	*0*	*0*

YEBOAH Anthony   Leeds United

Fullname: Anthony Yeboah   DOB: 07-06-70 Kumasi, Ghana
Debut: LEEDS UNITED v QPR 24/1/95 as sub
Debut Goal: LEEDS UNITED v Everton 22/2/95

Previous Clubs Details

Club	Signed	Fee	Apps					Goals		
			Tot	Start	Sub	FA	FL	Lge	FA	FL
Eintracht Frankfurt										
Leeds Utd	Jan-95	£3.4m	18	16	2	2	0	12	1	0

FAPL Summary by Club

Leeds Utd	94/5	18	16	2	2	0	12	1	0
Total		*18*	*16*	*2*	*2*	*0*	*12*	*1*	*0*

YORKE Dwight   Aston Villa

Fullname: Dwight Yorke   DOB: 04-11-75 Tobago, West Indies
Debut: ASTON VILLA v Leeds United 19/8/92
Debut Goal: ASTON VILLA v Crystal Palace 5/9/92

Previous Clubs Details

Club	Signed	Fee	Apps					Goals		
			Tot	Start	Sub	FA	FL	Lge	FA	FL
Aston Villa	Nov-89	£120,000	128	92	36	15	11	24	7	1

FAPL Summary by Club

Aston Villa	92/3 to 94/5	76	57	19	8	8	11	3	1
Total		*76*	*57*	*19*	*8*	*8*	*11*	*3*	*1*

FA PREMIER LEAGUE
EX-PLAYERS LIST

Name	Club(s)	Season(s)	Apps	Gls
ADAMS, Micky	Southampton	92/3–93/4	57	4
ADAMS, Neil	Oldham Athletic	92/3–93/4	45	9
	Norwich City	93/4–94/5	47	3
AGNEW, Steve	Leicester City	94/5	11	0
AKINBIYI, Ade	Norwich City	93/4–94/5	15	0
ALLEN, Clive	West Ham United	93/4–94/5	7	2
ALLAN, Derek	Southampton	92/3–94/5	1	0
ANDERSSON, Patrik	Blackburn Rovers	92/3–93/4	12	0
ANDREWS, Ian	Southampton	93/4–93/4	5	0
ANGELL, Brett	Everton	93/4–94/5	20	1
ANTHROBUS, Steve	Wimbledon	92/3–94/5	5	0
APPLEBY, Matthew	Newcastle United	93/4–94/5	1	0
BAKER, Clive	Ipswich Town	92/3–94/5	48	0
BANGER, Nicky	Southampton	92/3–94/5	34	8
BANNISTER, Gary	Nottingham Forest	92/3	31	8
BARLOW, Andy	Oldham Athletic	92/3–94/5	6	0
BARNES, David	Sheffield United	92/3–93/4	15	0
BARTLETT, Neal	Southampton	92/3–93/4	8	0
BECKFORD, Darren	Norwich City	92/3–93/4	8	1
	Oldham Athletic	92/3–93/4	14	6
BEESLEY, Paul	Sheffield United	92/3–93/4	64	2
BEINLICH, Stefan	Aston Villa	92/3–93/4	14	1
BERNARD, Paul	Oldham Athletic	92/3–93/4	65	9
BERRY, Greg	Wimbledon	92/3–93/4	7	1
BLAKE, Mark	Aston Villa	92/3–93/4	1	0
	Leicester City	94/5–94/5	30	3
BODEN, Chris	Aston Villa	94/5–94/5	1	0
BODIN, Paul	Swindon Town	93/4	32	7
BOOTY, Martyn	Coventry City	93/4	2	0
BOUND, Matthew	Southampton	92/3–93/4	4	0
BOWEN, Mark	Norwich City	92/3–94/5	119	8
BOWMAN, Robert	Leeds United	92/3–94/5	4	0
BOWRY, Robert	Crystal Palace	92/3–94/5	29	0
BOZINOSKI, Valdo	Ipswich Town	92/3–94/5	9	0
BRADSHAW, Carl	Sheffield United	92/3–93/4	57	2
	Norwich City	94/5–94/5	26	1
BREITKREUTZ, Matthias	Aston Villa	92/3–93/4	5	0
BRENNAN, Mark	Oldham Athletic	92/3–93/4	25	3
BROWN, Richard	Blackburn Rovers	92/3	2	0

Name	Club(s)	Season(s)	Apps	Gls
BRYSON, Ian	Sheffield United	92/3	16	3
BUTLER, Peter	West Ham United	93/4–94/5	31	1
BUTTERWORTH, Ian	Norwich City	92/3–93/4	51	1
CAREY, Brian	Leicester City	94/5–94/5	12	0
CARR, Stephen	Tottenham Hotspur	93/4–93/4	1	0
CARTER, Jimmy	Arsenal	92/3–94/5	19	2
CASCARINO, Tony	Chelsea	92/3–93/4	29	6
CHAPMAN, Lee	Leeds United	92/3–94/5	40	14
	West Ham United	93/4–94/5	40	8
	Ipswich Town	94/5–94/5	16	1
COCKERILL, Glenn	Southampton	92/3–93/4	37	0
COLEMAN, Chris	Crystal Palace	92/3–94/5	73	6
COLLETT, Andrew	Middlesbrough	92/3	2	0
CORK, Alan	Sheffield United	92/3–93/4	46	5
COTTERELL, Leo	Ipswich Town	94/5–94/5	2	0
COWAN, Tom	Sheffield United	92/3–93/4	21	0
COWANS, Gordon	Blackburn Rovers	92/3–93/4	24	1
	Aston Villa	93/4–93/4	12	0
COX, Ian	Crystal Palace	94/5–94/5	11	0
CRAMB, Colin	Southampton	93/4–93/4	1	0
CROOK, Ian	Norwich City	92/3–94/5	106	3
CROSBY, Gary	Nottingham Forest	92/3–94/5	23	1
CULVERHOUSE, Ian	Norwich City	92/3–93/4	83	1
CURETON, Jamie	Norwich City	94/5–94/5	17	4
DALEY, Tony	Aston Villa	92/3–94/5	40	3
DAVIS, Paul	Arsenal	92/3–94/5	32	1
DEARDEN, Kevin	Tottenham Hotspur	92/3–94/5	1	0
DIGBY, Fraser	Swindon Town	93/4–94/5	28	0
DIXON, Kerry	Southampton	92/3–94/5	9	2
DOBBS, Gerald	Wimbledon	92/3–93/4	29	1
DOBSON, Tony	Blackburn Rovers	92/3–93/4	19	0
DONAGHY, Mal	Chelsea	92/3–93/4	68	3
DOWIE, Iain	Southampton	92/3–94/5	92	21
	Crystal Palace	94/5–94/5	15	4
DOYLE, Maurice	QPR	92/3–93/4	6	0
DUBERRY, Michael	Chelsea	93/4–94/5	1	0
DURIE, Gordon	Tottenham Hotspur	92/3–93/4	17	3
DURRANT, Ian	Everton	94/5–94/5	5	0
DURRANT, Lee	Ipswich Town	93/4–93/4	7	0
DYER, Bruce	Crystal Palace	94/5–94/5	16	1
EADIE, Darren	Norwich City	93/4–94/5	41	5
ELLIOTT, Paul	Chelsea	92/3–94/5	7	0
ELLIS, Kevin	Ipswich Town	94/5–94/5	1	0
FALCONER, Willie	Middlesbrough	92/3	28	5
	Sheffield United	93/4–93/4	23	3

Name	Club(s)	Season(s)	Apps	Gls
FENWICK, Terry	Tottenham Hotspur	92/3	5	0
	Swindon Town	93/4–93/4	26	0
FERGUSON, Darren	Manchester United	92/3–93/4	18	3
FLEMING, Craig	Oldham Athletic	92/3–93/4	60	0
FORREST, Craig	Ipswich Town	92/3–94/5	74	0
FOSTER, Colin	West Ham United	93/4–94/5	5	0
FRANCIS, Trevor	Sheffield Wednesday	92/3-93/4	6	0
FROGGATT, Stephen	Aston Villa	92/3–93/4	26	2
GAGE, Kevin	Sheffield United	92/3–93/4	48	0
GALE, Tony	West Ham United	93/4	32	0
	Blackburn Rovers	94/5	15	0
GALLOWAY, Mike	Leicester City	94/5–94/5	5	0
GANNON, John	Sheffield United	92/3–93/4	41	1
GAYLE, John	Coventry City	93/4–93/4	3	0
GAYLE, Brian	Sheffield United	92/3–93/4	44	5
GEE, Phil	Leicester City	94/5–94/5	7	2
GERRARD, Paul	Oldham Athletic	92/3–93/4	41	0
GIBSON, Terry	Wimbledon	93/4–93/4	8	1
GILLESPIE, Gary	Coventry City	94/5–94/5	3	0
GITTENS, John	Middlesbrough	92/3	13	0
GLOVER, Lee	Nottingham Forest	92/3–93/4	14	0
GODDARD, Paul	Ipswich Town	92/3–93/4	29	3
GORDON, Dale	West Ham United	93/4–93/4	8	1
GORDON, Dean	Crystal Palace	92/3–94/5	51	2
GOSS, Jeremy	Norwich City	92/3–94/5	84	9
GRAY, Andy	Tottenham Hotspur	92/3–93/4	19	2
GRAYSON, Simon	Leicester City	94/5–94/5	34	0
GREGORY, David	Ipswich Town	92/3–94/5	4	1
GREGORY, Neil	Ipswich Town	94/5–94/5	3	0
GROENENDIJK, Alphonse	Manchester City	93/4–94/5	9	0
GROVES, Perry	Arsenal	92/3–94/5	1	0
	Southampton	93/4–94/5	15	2
GUENTCHEV, Bontcho	Ipswich Town	92/3–94/5	61	6
GUNN, Bryan	Norwich City	92/3–94/5	104	0
GUPPY, Steve	Newcastle United	94/5–94/5	0	0
HALLE, Gunnar	Oldham Athletic	92/3–93/4	63	6
HALLWORTH, Jon	Oldham Athletic	92/3–93/4	35	0
HAMMOND, Nicky	Swindon Town	93/4–93/4	13	0
HARKES, John	Sheffield Wednesday	92/3	29	2
HARPER, Alan	Everton	92/3	18	0
HARTFIELD, Charlie	Sheffield United	92/3–93/4	25	0
HENDRY, John	Tottenham Hotspur	92/3–93/4	8	0
HENRY, Nick	Oldham Athletic	92/3–93/4	55	6
HESKEY,	Leicester City	94/5–94/5	1	0

Name	Club(s)	Season(s)	Apps	Gls
HILL, Colin	Leicester City	94/5–93/4	24	0
HODDLE, Glen	Chelsea	93/4–94/5	31	1
HODGES, Glyn	Sheffield United	92/3–93/4	62	6
HODGES, Lee	Tottenham Hotspur	92/3–93/4	4	0
HOLDEN, Rick	Manchester City	92/3–93/4	50	3
HORLOCK, Kevin	Swindon Town	93/4–94/5	38	0
HORNE, Barry	Middlesbrough	92/3	4	0
HOUGHTON, Ray	Aston Villa	92/3–94/5	95	6
	Crystal Palace	94/5–94/5	10	2
HOWIE, Scott	Norwich City	93/4–94/5	2	0
HOYLAND, Jamie	Sheffield United	92/3–93/4	40	2
HUMPHREY, John	Crystal Palace	92/3–94/5	53	0
HURLOCK, Terry	Southampton	92/3–93/4	32	0
HURST, Lee	Coventry City	92/3–93/4	35	2
INCE, Paul	Manchester United	92/3–94/5	116	19
INGEBRIGTSEN, Kare	Manchester United	92/3–93/4	15	0
IRELAND, Simon	Blackburn Rovers	92/3–93/4	1	0
IRONSIDE, Ian	Middlesbrough	92/3	12	0
JEMSON, Nigel	Sheffield Wednesday	92/3–93/4	31	5
JOACHIM, Julian	Leicester City	94/5–93/4	15	3
JOBSON, Richard	Oldham Athletic	92/3–93/4	77	7
JOHNSON, Gavin	Ipswich Town	92/3–94/5	73	6
JOHNSON, Andrew	Norwich City	92/3–94/5	11	1
JOHNSTON, Mo	Everton	92/3–94/5	13	3
JONES, Cobi	Coventry City	94/5–94/5	21	2
JONES, Steve	West Ham United	93/4–94/5	10	2
KAMARA, Chris	Sheffield United	92/3–94/5	8	0
	Middlesbrough	92/3–92/3	5	0
	Sheffield United	93/4–93/4	16	0
KARL, Stefan	Manchester City	93/4–94/5	6	1
KAVANAGH, Graham	Middlesbrough	92/3	22	2
KEIZERWEERD, Orpheo	Oldham Athletic	92/3–94/5	1	0
KELLY, Alan	Sheffield United	92/3–94/5	63	0
KENNY, Billy	Everton	92/3–93/4	17	1
KILCLINE, Brian	Newcastle United	93/4	1	0
KINNER, Justin	Wimbledon	92/3–93/4	1	0
KLINSMANN, Jurgen	Tottenham Hotspur	94/5–94/5	41	22
KUBICKI, Dariusz	Aston Villa	93/4	2	0
LAKE, Paul	Manchester City	92/3	2	0
LAKE, Mike	Sheffield United	92/3	6	0
LAUNDERS, Brian	Crystal Palace	94/5–94/5	2	0
LAWS, Brian	Nottingham Forest	92/3	33	0
LAWRENCE, Jamie	Leicester City	94/5–94/5	17	1
LEWIS, Neil	Leicester City	94/5	16	0
LING, Martin	Swindon Town	93/4	33	10

Name	Club(s)	Season(s)	Apps	Gls
LINIGHAN, David	Ipswich Town	92/3–94/5	112	4
LITTLEJOHN, Adrian	Sheffield United	92/3–93/4	46	11
LIVINGSTONE, Steve	Blackburn Rovers	92/3–93/4	2	0
	Chelsea	92/3–92/3	1	0
LOWE, David	Leicester City	94/5–94/5	29	8
LYDERSON, Pal	Arsenal	92/3–93/4	8	0
McDONALD, David	Tottenham Hotspur	92/3–94/5	2	0
McDONALD, Neil	Oldham Athletic	92/3–93/4	7	0
McGEE, Paul	Wimbledon	92/3–93/4	3	0
McGRATH, Lloyd	Coventry City	92/3–93/4	36	0
McKINNON, Ray	Nottingham Forest	92/3	6	1
McLAREN, Ross	Swindon Town	93/4–93/4	12	0
McMAHON, Sam	Leicester City	94/5–94/5	1	0
McMAHON, Steve	Manchester City	92/3–94/5	69	1
MAHORN, Paul	Tottenham Hotspur	93/4	1	0
MAKEL, Lee	Blackburn Rovers	92/3–93/4	3	0
MARGETSON, Martyn	Manchester City	92/3–93/4	1	0
MARKER, Nicky	Blackburn Rovers	92/3–93/4	38	0
MARRIOT, Andy	Nottingham Forest	92/3	5	0
MARSH, Mike	Liverpool	92/3-93/4	30	2
	West Ham United	93/4-94/5	49	1
	Coventry City	94/5	15	2
MARSHALL, Andy	Norwich City	94/5–94/5	21	0
MARSHALL, Dwight	Middlesbrough	92/3	3	0
MARSHALL, Ian	Oldham Athletic	92/3–93/4	27	2
	Ipswich Town	93/4–94/5	47	13
MARSHALL, Scott	Arsenal	92/3–93/4	2	0
MARTYN, Nigel	Crystal Palace	92/3–94/5	79	0
MASON, Paul	Ipswich Town	93/4–94/5	43	6
MASSEY, Stuart	Crystal Palace	92/3–94/5	1	0
MATHIE, Alex	Newcastle United	93/4–94/5	24	4
	Ipswich Town	94/5–94/5	13	2
MATTHEW, Damian	Chelsea	92/3–94/5	4	0
	Crystal Palace	94/5–94/5	4	0
MEGSON, Gary	Norwich City	92/3–94/5	46	1
MILLER, Paul	Wimbledon	92/3–94/5	19	2
MILLIGAN, Mike	Oldham Athletic	92/3–93/4	81	3
	Norwich City	94/5–94/5	26	2
MILLS, Gary	Leicester City	94/5–94/5	1	0
MILTON, Simon	Ipswich Town	92/3–94/5	52	5
MITCHELL, Paul	West Ham United	93/4–94/5	1	0
MOHAN, Nicky	Leicester City	94/5–94/5	23	0
MOODY, Paul	Southampton	92/3–93/4	8	0
MOORE, Kevin	Southampton	92/3–93/4	32	2
MORAN, Kevin	Blackburn Rovers	92/3–93/4	55	5

Name	Club(s)	Season(s)	Apps	Gls
MORAN, Paul	Tottenham Hotspur	92/3–93/4	8	0
MORGAN, Philip	Ipswich Town	94/5–94/5	1	0
MORRIS, Chris	Middlesbrough	92/3–94/5	23	1
MORRISON, Andy	Blackburn Rovers	93/4–93/4	5	0
MORTIMER, Paul	Crystal Palace	92/3–93/4	1	0
NDAH, George	Crystal Palace	92/3–94/5	25	1
NEWHOUSE, Aiden	Wimbledon	92/3–94/5	1	1
NEWMAN, Ricky	Crystal Palace	92/3–94/5	37	3
NEWMAN, Rob	Norwich City	92/3–94/5	82	5
NEWSOME, Jon	Leeds United	92/3–94/4	66	1
	Norwich City	94/5–94/5	35	3
NICOL, Steve	Liverpool	92/3–94/5	67	1
NIJHOLT, Luc	Swindon Town	93/4–94/5	32	1
NILSSON, Roland	Sheffield Wednesday	92/3–92/3	70	1
NORFOLK, Lee	Ipswich Town	94/5–94/5	3	0
O'BRIEN, Liam	Newcastle United	93/4–92/3	6	0
O'LEARY, David	Arsenal	92/3	11	0
	Leeds United	93/4–93/4	10	0
O'NEILL, Keith	Norwich City	94/5–94/5	1	0
OLDFIELD, David	Leicester City	94/5	14	1
OLNEY, Ian	Oldham Athletic	92/3–93/4	44	25
ORGLYSSON, Thor	Nottingham Forest	92/3	20	1
ORMONDROYD, Ian	Leicester City	94/5–93/4	6	1
OSBORN, Simon	Crystal Palace	92/3–93/4	31	2
PALMER, Roger	Oldham Athletic	92/3–93/4	25	0
PALMER, Steve	Ipswich Town	92/3–94/5	55	1
PARKER, Garry	Aston Villa	92/3–94/5	70	11
	Leicester City	94/5–94/5	14	2
PARKINSON, Gary	Middlesbrough	92/3	4	0
PATTERSON, Darren	Crystal Palace	94/5–94/5	22	1
PAZ, Adrian	Ipswich Town	94/5–94/5	17	1
PEAKE, Andy	Middlesbrough	92/3	33	0
PETTERSON, Andy	Ipswich Town	92/3–94/5	1	0
PEYTON, Gerry	Chelsea	92/3–94/5	1	0
PHELAN, Mike	Manchester United	92/3–93/4	13	0
PHILLIPS, James	Middlesbrough	92/3–94/5	40	2
PHILPOTT, Lee	Leicester City	94/5–93/4	23	0
PIECHNIK, Torben	Liverpool	92/3–93/4	17	0
PITCHER, Darren	Crystal Palace	94/5–94/5	25	0
POINTON, Neil	Oldham Athletic	92/3–93/4	60	3
POLSTON, John	Norwich City	92/3–94/5	96	1
POOLE, Kevin	Leicester City	94/5–94/5	36	0
POPESCU, Gica	Tottenham Hotspur	94/5–94/5	23	3
POWELL, Lee	Southampton	92/3–93/4	3	0
POWER, Lee	Norwich City	92/3–93/4	23	6

Name	Club(s)	Season(s)	Apps	Gls
PREECE, Andy	Crystal Palace	94/5–94/5	20	4
PRIOR, Spencer	Norwich City	93/4–94/5	30	0
PROCTOR, Mark	Middlesbrough	92/3	11	0
RADOSAVIJEVIC, Pedray	Everton	92/3–93/4	46	4
RANSON, Ray	Manchester City	92/3–93/4	17	0
REDMOND, Steve	Oldham Athletic	92/3–93/4	64	1
REID, Peter	Manchester City	92/3–93/4	24	0
RITCHIE, Andy	Oldham Athletic	92/3–93/4	12	3
ROBERTS, Iwan	Leicester City	94/5–93/4	37	9
ROBINS, Mark	Norwich City	92/3–94/5	67	20
	Leicester City	94/5–94/5	17	5
ROBINSON, Stephen	Tottenham Hotspur	93/4–94/5	2	0
ROBINSON, Mark	Newcastle United	93/4–94/5	16	0
ROBSON, Mark	West Ham United	93/4–94/5	3	8
ROBSON, Stewart	Coventry City	92/3–93/4	16	0
RODGER, Simon	Crystal Palace	92/3–94/5	27	2
ROGERS, Paul	Sheffield United	92/3–93/4	52	6
ROWETT, Gary	Everton	93/4–93/4	2	0
SALAKO, John	Crystal Palace	92/3–94/5	52	4
SANCHEZ, Lawrie	Wimbledon	92/3–93/4	42	6
	Swindon Town	93/4–94/5	8	0
SANSOM, Kenny	Coventry City	92/3–93/4	21	0
	Everton	92/3–92/3	7	1
SAUNDERS, Dean	Liverpool	92/3–93/4	6	1
	Aston Villa	92/3–94/5	112	38
SCHWARZ, Stefan	Arsenal	94/5–94/5	34	2
SCOTT, Andy	Sheffield United	92/3–93/4	17	2
SEDGLEY, Steve	Tottenham Hotspur	92/3–93/4	64	8
	Ipswich Town	94/5–94/5	26	4
SHARPE, Graeme	Oldham Athletic	92/3–93/4	55	16
SHAW, Richard	Crystal Palace	92/3–94/5	74	0
SHERIDAN, Tony	Coventry City	92/3–93/4	9	0
SHERON, Mike	Manchester City	92/3–93/4	71	17
	Norwich City	94/5–94/5	21	1
SHIRTLIFF, Peter	Sheffield Wednesday	92/3–93/4	20	0
SHUTT, Carl	Leeds United	92/3–93/4	14	0
	Manchester City	93/4–93/4	7	0
SINNOTT, Lee	Crystal Palace	92/3	19	0
SLATER, Stuart	Ipswich Town	93/4–94/5	55	2
SLAVEN, Bernie	Middlesbrough	92/3	18	4
SMITH, David	Norwich City	92/3–93/4	13	0
SMITH, Richard	Leicester City	94/5–93/4	12	0
SMITH, Alan	Arsenal	92/3–94/5	75	8
SNODIN, Ian	Everton	92/3–94/5	52	1
SPEEDIE, David	Southampton	92/3–94/5	11	0

Name	Club(s)	Season(s)	Apps	Gls
STEJSKAL, Jan	QPR	92/3–93/4	41	0
STERLAND, Mel	Leeds United	92/3–93/4	3	0
STOCKWELL, Mike	Ipswich Town	92/3–94/5	96	5
STRANDLI, Frank	Leeds United	92/3–93/4	14	6
SUTCH, Daryl	Norwich City	92/3–94/5	55	3
SWAILES, Chris	Ipswich Town	94/5–94/5	4	0
TANNER, Adam	Ipswich Town	94/5–94/5	10	2
TANNER, Nicky	Liverpool	92/3–94/5	4	0
TARICCO, Mauricio	Ipswich Town	94/5–94/5	0	0
TAYLOR, Shaun	Swindon Town	93/4–94/5	42	14
THOMAS, Geoff	Crystal Palace	92/3	29	2
THOMPSON, Garry	QPR	92/3–94/5	4	0
THOMPSON, Neil	Ipswich Town	92/3–94/5	73	3
THOMPSON, Steve	Leicester City	94/5–94/5	19	0
THOMSEN, Claus	Ipswich Town	94/5–94/5	33	5
THORNLEY, Ben	Manchester United	93/4–94/5	1	0
TOLSON, Neil	Oldham Athletic	92/3–94/5	3	0
TRACEY, Simon	Sheffield United	92/3–93/4	25	0
	Manchester City	94/5–94/5	3	0
	Norwich City	94/5–94/5	1	0
TUTTLE, David	Tottenham Hotspur	92/3–93/4	5	0
	Sheffield United	93/4–93/4	31	31
ULLATHORNE, Robert	Norwich City	93/4–94/5	43	4
VAN DEN HAUWE, Pat	Tottenham Hotspur	92/3–94/5	18	0
VAUGHAN, Tony	Ipswich Town	94/5–94/5	10	0
VENISON, Barry	Newcastle United	93/4–94/5	65	1
WALLACE, Danny	Manchester United	92/3	2	0
WALLACE, Ray	Leeds United	92/3–93/4	7	0
WALSH, Steve	Leicester City	94/5–93/4	5	0
WARD, Ashley	Norwich City	94/5–94/5	25	8
WARD, Mitch	Sheffield United	92/3–93/4	48	1
WARD, Mark	Everton	92/3–93/4	46	2
WARD, Gavin	Leicester City	94/5–93/4	6	0
WARK, John	Ipswich Town	92/3–94/5	101	13
WATTS, Grant	Crystal Palace	92/3	4	0
WARZYCHA, Robert	Everton	92/3–93/4	27	1
WEBB, Neil	Manchester United	92/3–93/4	1	0
	Nottingham Forest	92/3–92/3	9	0
WHELAN, Ronnie	Liverpool	92/3–93/4	40	2
WHITE, Steve	Swindon Town	93/4–93/4	6	0
WHITE, Devon	QPR	92/3–94/5	26	9
WHITEHOUSE, Dane	Sheffield United	92/3–93/4	52	10
WHITLOW, Michael	Leicester City	94/5–94/5	28	2
WHITTON, Steve	Ipswich Town	92/3–93/4	39	4
WHYTE, Chris	Leeds United	92/3–93/4	34	1

WILLIAMS, Brett	Nottingham Forest	92/3	9	0
WILLIAMS, Geraint	IpswichTown	92/3–93/4	37	0
	Ipswich Town	93/4–94/5	72	1
WILLIAMS, Paul	Sheffield Wednesday	92/3–93/4	7	1
	Crystal Palace	92/3–94/5	22	18
WILLIS, Jimmy	Leicester City	94/5–93/4	29	2
WILMOT, Rhys	Crystal Palace	94/5–94/5	6	0
WILSON, Terry	Nottingham Forest	92/3	5	0
WIRMOLA, Jonas	Sheffield United	93/4–93/4	8	0
WITSCHGE, Richard	Blackburn Rovers	94/5–94/5	1	0
WITTER, Tony	QPR	93/4–93/4	1	0
WOOD, Steve	Southampton	92/3–93/4	31	0
WOODTHORPE, Colin	Norwich City	92/3–93/4	27	0
WRIGHT, Johnny	Norwich City	94/5–94/5	2	0
WRIGHT, Richard	Ipswich Town	94/5–94/5	3	0
WRIGHT, Tommy	Newcastle United	93/4–93/4	3	0
YALLOP, Frank	Ipswich Town	92/3–94/5	54	3
YOUDS, Eddie	Ipswich Town	92/3–94/5	49	1
YOUNG, Eric	Crystal Palace	92/3–94/5	51	6

Form 'n Encounter Guide

Our unique *Form 'n Encounter Guide* will allow you to plan your season's FA Carling Premiership schedule by providing you with a form guide which helps you to predict what are likely to be the most exciting games to attend on a day-by-day basis. Listed are the results from the previous Premiership encounters for the matches. Please do check that the game you are looking to attend is on before you set out. Match dates and ko times are all subject to change to cope with TV schedules and the like.

Dates given for the European club competitions are based on the Wednesday of the week – however, this date is normally reserved exclusively for UEFA Champions' League fixtures, UEFA Cup matches are generally played on the Tuesday and Cup-Winners' Cup ties on the Thursdays. Clubs involved in the latter may move subsequent league matches to the Sunday.

Date	Match /Event	92-93	93-94	94-95
09-Aug	*European Preliminary Round 1st Legs*			
13-Aug	*Littlewoods Pools FA Charity Shield*			
	Blackburn Rovers v Everton (Wembley)			
19-Aug	Aston Villa v Manchester United	1-0	1-2	1-2
19-Aug	Blackburn Rovers v QPR	1-0	1-1	4-0
19-Aug	Chelsea v Everton	2-1	4-2	0-1
19-Aug	Liverpool v Sheffield Wednesday	1-0	2-0	4-1
19-Aug	Manchester City v Tottenham Hotspur	0-1	0-2	5-2
19-Aug	Newcastle United v Coventry City	–	4-0	4-0
19-Aug	Southampton v Nottingham Forest	1-2	–	1-1
19-Aug	West Ham United v Leeds United	–	0-1	0-0
20-Aug	Arsenal v Middlesbrough	1-1	–	–
22-Aug	Bolton Wanderers v Newcastle United	–	–	–
22-Aug	Leeds United v Liverpool	2-2	2-0	0-2
22-Aug	Middlesbrough v Southampton	2-1	–	–
23-Aug	*European Preliminary Round 1st Legs*			
23-Aug	Coventry City v Manchester City	2-3	4-0	1-0
23-Aug	Everton v Arsenal	0-0	1-1	1-1
23-Aug	Manchester United v West Ham United	–	3-0	1-0
23-Aug	Nottingham Forest v Chelsea	3-0	–	0-1
23-Aug	QPR v Wimbledon	1-2	1-0	0-1
23-Aug	Sheffield Wednesday v Blackburn Rovers	0-0	1-2	0-1

Date	Match	92-93	93-94	94-95
23-Aug	Tottenham Hotspur v Aston Villa	0-0	1-1	3-4
26-Aug	Bolton Wanderers v Blackburn Rovers	–	–	–
26-Aug	Coventry City v Arsenal	0-2	1-0	0-1
26-Aug	Everton v Southampton	2-1	1-0	0-0
26-Aug	Leeds United v Aston Villa	1-1	2-0	1-0
26-Aug	Manchester United v Wimbledon	0-1	3-1	3-0
26-Aug	Middlesbrough v Chelsea	0-0		
26-Aug	Nottingham Forest v West Ham United	–	–	1-1
26-Aug	QPR v Manchester City	1-1	1-1	1-2
26-Aug	Sheffield Wednesday v Newcastle United	–	0-1	0-0
26-Aug	Tottenham Hotspur v Liverpool	2-0	3-3	0-0
29-Aug	Arsenal v Nottingham Forest	1-1	–	1-0
29-Aug	Blackburn Rovers v Manchester United	0-0	2-0	2-4
29-Aug	Wimbledon v Sheffield Wednesday	1-1	2-1	0-1
30-Aug	Chelsea v Coventry City	2-1	1-2	2-2
30-Aug	Liverpool v QPR	1-0	3-2	1-1
30-Aug	Manchester City v Everton	2-5	1-0	4-0
30-Aug	Southampton v Leeds United	1-1	0-2	1-3
30-Aug	West Ham United v Tottenham Hotspur	–	1-3	1-2
06-Sep	*International: England v Croatia (Wembley)*			
09-Sep	Blackburn Rovers v Aston Villa	3-0	1-0	3-1
09-Sep	Bolton Wanderers v Middlesbrough	–		
09-Sep	Coventry City v Nottingham Forest	0-1	–	0-0
09-Sep	Everton v Manchester United	0-2	0-1	1-0
09-Sep	Manchester City v Arsenal	0-1	0-0	1-2
09-Sep	QPR v Sheffield Wednesday	3-1	1-2	3-2
09-Sep	Southampton v Newcastle United		2-1	3-1
09-Sep	Tottenham Hotspur v Leeds United	4-0	1-1	1-1
09-Sep	West Ham United v Chelsea	–	1-0	1-2
09-Sep	Wimbledon v Liverpool	2-0	1-1	0-0
12-Sep	*European First Round 1st Legs*			
16-Sep	Arsenal v West Ham United		0-2	0-1
16-Sep	Aston Villa v Wimbledon	1-0	0-1	7-1
16-Sep	Chelsea v Southampton	1-1	2-0	0-2
16-Sep	Leeds United v QPR	1-1	1-1	4-0
16-Sep	Liverpool v Blackburn Rovers	2-1	0-1	–
16-Sep	Middlesbrough v Coventry City	0-2		
16-Sep	Newcastle United v Manchester City	–	2-0	0-0

Date	Match	92-93	93-94	94-95
16-Sep	Nottingham Forest v Everton	0-1	–	2-1
16-Sep	Sheffield Wednesday v Tottenham Hotspur ...	2-0	1-0	3-4
20-Sep	*Coca Cola League Cup Second Round 1st Legs*			
23-Sep	Arsenal v Southampton	4-3	1-0	1-1
23-Sep	Aston Villa v Nottingham Forest	2-1	–	0-2
23-Sep	Blackburn Rovers v Coventry City	2-5	2-1	4-0
23-Sep	Newcastle United v Chelsea	–	0-0	4-2
23-Sep	QPR v Tottenham Hotspur	4-1	1-1	2-1
23-Sep	Sheffield Wednesday v Manchester United ...	3-3	2-3	1-0
23-Sep	West Ham United v Everton	–	0-1	2-2
23-Sep	Wimbledon v Leeds United	1-0	1-0	0-0
27-Sep	*European First Round 2nd Legs*			
30-Sep	Bolton Wanderers v Queens Park Rangers ...	–	–	–
30-Sep	Chelsea v Arsenal	1-0	0-2	2-1
30-Sep	Coventry City v Aston Villa	3-0	0-1	0-1
30-Sep	Everton v Newcastle United	–	0-2	2-0
30-Sep	Leeds United v Sheffield Wednesday	3-1	2-1	0-1
30-Sep	Manchester United v Liverpool	2-2	1-0	2-0
30-Sep	Middlesbrough v Blackburn Rovers	3-2	–	–
30-Sep	Nottingham Forest v Manchester City	0-2	–	1-0
30-Sep	Southampton v West Ham United	–	0-2	1-1
30-Sep	Tottenham Hotspur v Wimbledon	1-1	1-1	1-2
04-Oct	*Coca Cola League Cup Second Round 2nd Legs*			
10-Oct	*International: Norway v England (Oslo)*			
14-Oct	Aston Villa v Chelsea	1-3	1-0	3-0
14-Oct	Blackburn Rovers v Southampton	0-0	2-0	3-2
14-Oct	Bolton Wanderers v Everton	–	–	–
14-Oct	Leeds United v Arsenal	3-0	2-1	1-0
14-Oct	Liverpool v Coventry City	4-0	1-0	2-3
14-Oct	Manchester United v Manchester City	2-1	2-0	5-0
14-Oct	QPR v Newcastle United	–	1-2	3-0
14-Oct	Tottenham Hotspur v Nottingham Forest	2-1	–	1-4
14-Oct	Wimbledon v West Ham United	–	1-2	1-0
18-Oct	*European Second Round 1st Legs*			
21-Oct	Arsenal v Aston Villa	0-1	1-2	0-0
21-Oct	Chelsea v Manchester United	1-1	1-0	2-3
21-Oct	Coventry City v Sheffield Wednesday	1-0	1-1	2-0
21-Oct	Everton v Tottenham Hotspur	1-2	0-1	0-0

Date	Match	92-93	93-94	94-95
21-Oct	Manchester City v Leeds United	4-0	1-1	0-0
21-Oct	Middlesbrough v Queens Park Rangers	0-1	–	–
21-Oct	Newcastle United v Wimbledon	–	4-0	2-1
21-Oct	Southampton v Liverpool	2-1	4-2	0-2
21-Oct	West Ham United v Blackburn Rovers	–	1-2	2-0
25-Oct	*Coca Cola League Cup Third Round*			
28-Oct	Aston Villa v Everton	2-1	0-0	0-0
28-Oct	Blackburn Rovers v Chelsea	2-0	2-0	2-1
28-Oct	Bolton Wanderers v Arsenal	–	–	–
28-Oct	Leeds United v Coventry City	2-2	1-0	3-0
28-Oct	Liverpool v Manchester City	1-1	2-1	2-0
28-Oct	QPR v Nottingham Forest	4-3	–	1-1
28-Oct	Sheffield Wednesday v West Ham United	–	5-0	1-0
28-Oct	Tottenham Hotspur v Newcastle United	–	1-2	4-2
28-Oct	Wimbledon v Southampton	1-2	1-0	0-2
01-Nov	*European Second Round 2nd Legs*			
04-Nov	Arsenal v Manchester United	0-1	0-0	0-0
04-Nov	Chelsea v Sheffield Wednesday	0-2	1-1	1-1
04-Nov	Coventry City v Tottenham Hotspur	1-0	1-0	0-4
04-Nov	Everton v Blackburn Rovers	2-1	0-3	1-2
04-Nov	Middlesbrough v Leeds United	4-1	–	–
04-Nov	Newcastle United v Liverpool	–	3-0	1-1
04-Nov	Nottingham Forest v Wimbledon	1-1	–	3-1
04-Nov	Southampton v QPR	1-2	0-1	2-1
04-Nov	West Ham United v Aston Villa	–	0-0	1-0
08-Nov	Newcastle United v Blackburn Rovers	–	1-1	1-1
15-Nov	*International: England v Switzerland (Wembley)*			
18-Nov	Aston Villa v Newcastle United	–	0-2	0-2
18-Nov	Blackburn Rovers v Nottingham Forest	4-1	–	3-0
18-Nov	Bolton Wanderers v West Ham United	–	–	–
18-Nov	Leeds United v Chelsea	1-1	4-1	2-3
18-Nov	Liverpool v Everton	1-0	2-1	0-0
18-Nov	Manchester United v Southampton	2-1	2-0	2-1
18-Nov	QPR v Coventry City	2-0	5-1	2-2
18-Nov	Sheffield Wednesday v Manchester City	0-3	1-1	1-1
18-Nov	Tottenham Hotspur v Arsenal	1-0	0-1	1-0
21-Nov	Arsenal v Sheffield Wednesday	2-1	1-0	0-0

Date	Match	92-93	93-94	94-95
21-Nov	Middlesbrough v Tottenham Hotspur	3-0	–	–
22-Nov	*European Third Round 1st Legs*			
22-Nov	Coventry City v Manchester United	0-1	0-1	2-3
22-Nov	Everton v QPR	3-5	0-3	2-2
22-Nov	Manchester City v Wimbledon	1-1	0-1	2-0
22-Nov	Nottingham Forest v Leeds United	1-1	–	3-0
22-Nov	Southampton v Aston Villa	2-0	4-1	2-1
22-Nov	West Ham United v Liverpool	–	1-2	0-0
25-Nov	Arsenal v Blackburn Rovers	0-1	1-0	0-0
25-Nov	Chelsea v Tottenham Hotspur	1-1	4-3	1-1
25-Nov	Coventry City v Wimbledon	0-2	1-2	1-1
25-Nov	Everton v Sheffield Wednesday	1-1	0-2	1-4
25-Nov	Manchester City v Aston Villa	1-1	3-0	2-2
25-Nov	Middlesbrough v Liverpool	1-2	–	–
25-Nov	Newcastle United v Leeds United	–	1-1	1-2
25-Nov	Nottingham Forest v Manchester United	0-2	–	1-1
25-Nov	West Ham United v QPR	–	0-4	0-0
25-Nov	*Coca Cola League Cup Fourth Round*			
02-Dec	Aston Villa v Arsenal	1-0	1-2	0-4
02-Dec	Blackburn Rovers v West Ham United	–	0-2	4-2
02-Dec	Bolton Wanderers v Nottingham Forest	–		
02-Dec	Leeds United v Manchester City	1-0	3-2	2-1
02-Dec	Liverpool v Southampton	1-1	4-2	3-1
02-Dec	Manchester United v Chelsea	3-0	0-1	0-0
02-Dec	Sheffield Wednesday v Coventry City	1-2	0-0	5-1
02-Dec	Tottenham Hotspur v Everton	2-1	3-2	2-1
02-Dec	Wimbledon v Newcastle United	–	4-2	3-2
06-Dec	*European Third Round 2nd Legs*			
09-Dec	Bolton Wanderers v Liverpool	–	–	–
09-Dec	Chelsea v Newcastle United	–	1-0	1-1
09-Dec	Coventry City v Blackburn Rovers	0-2	2-1	1-1
09-Dec	Everton v West Ham United	–	0-1	1-0
09-Dec	Leeds United v Wimbledon	2-1	4-0	3-1
09-Dec	Manchester United v Sheffield Wednesday	2-1	5-0	1-0
09-Dec	Middlesbrough v Manchester City	2-0	–	–
09-Dec	Nottingham Forest v Aston Villa	0-1	–	1-2
09-Dec	Southampton v Arsenal	2-0	0-4	1-0
09-Dec	Tottenham Hotspur v QPR	3-1	1-2	1-1

Date	Match	92-93	93-94	94-95
12-Dec	*World Cup 1988 – Draw for Qualifying Competition*			
13-Dec	*International Date*			
16-Dec	Arsenal v Chelsea	2-1	1-0	3-1
16-Dec	Aston Villa v Coventry City	0-0	–	0-0
16-Dec	Liverpool v Manchester United	1-2	3-3	2-0
16-Dec	Manchester City v Nottingham Forest	2-2	–	3-3
16-Dec	Newcastle United v Everton	–	1-0	2-0
16-Dec	Sheffield Wednesday v Leeds United	1-1	3-3	1-1
16-Dec	West Ham United v Southampton	–	3-3	2-0
16-Dec	Wimbledon v Tottenham Hotspur	1-1	2-1	1-2
17-Dec	*Euro 96 – Draw for Finals*			
23-Dec	Coventry City v Everton	0-1	2-1	0-0
23-Dec	Leeds United v Manchester United	0-0	0-2	2-1
23-Dec	Liverpool v Arsenal	0-2	0-0	3-0
23-Dec	Manchester City v Chelsea	0-1	2-2	1-2
23-Dec	Middlesbrough v West Ham United	–	–	–
23-Dec	Newcastle United v Nottingham Forest	–	–	2-1
23-Dec	QPR v Aston Villa	2-1	2-2	2-0
23-Dec	Sheffield Wednesday v Southampton	5-2	2-0	1-1
23-Dec	Wimbledon v Blackburn Rovers	1-1	4-1	0-3
26-Dec	Arsenal v QPR	0-0	0-0	1-3
26-Dec	Aston Villa v Liverpool	4-2	2-1	2-0
26-Dec	Blackburn Rovers v Manchester City	1-0	2-0	2-3
26-Dec	Bolton Wanderers v Leeds United	–	–	–
26-Dec	Chelsea v Wimbledon	4-2	2-0	1-1
26-Dec	Manchester United v Newcastle United	–	1-1	2-0
26-Dec	Nottingham Forest v Sheffield Wednesday	1-2	–	4-1
26-Dec	Southampton v Tottenham Hotspur	0-0	1-0	4-3
26-Dec	West Ham United v Coventry City	–	3-2	0-1
30-Dec	Arsenal v Wimbledon	0-1	1-1	0-0
30-Dec	Aston Villa v Sheffield Wednesday	2-0	2-2	1-1
30-Dec	Blackburn Rovers v Tottenham Hotspur	0-2	1-0	2-0
30-Dec	Bolton Wanderers v Coventry City	–	–	–
30-Dec	Chelsea v Liverpool	0-0	1-0	0-0
30-Dec	Everton v Leeds United	2-0	1-1	3-0
30-Dec	Manchester United v QPR	0-0	2-1	2-0
30-Dec	Southampton v Manchester City	0-1	0-1	2-2
30-Dec	West Ham United v Newcastle United	–	2-4	1-3

Date	Match	92-93	93-94	94-95
01-Jan	Coventry City v Southampton	2-0	1-1	1-3
01-Jan	Leeds United v Blackburn Rovers	5-2	3-3	1-1
01-Jan	Liverpool v Nottingham Forest	0-0	–	1-0
01-Jan	Manchester City v West Ham United	–	0-0	3-0
01-Jan	Middlesbrough v Aston Villa	2-3	–	–
01-Jan	Newcastle United v Arsenal	–	2-0	1-0
01-Jan	QPR v Chelsea	1-1	1-1	1-0
01-Jan	Tottenham Hotspur v Manchester United	1-1	0-1	0-1
01-Jan	Wimbledon v Everton	1-3	1-1	2-1

06-Jan   *FA Cup (Littlewoods Pools) Third Round*
10-Jan   *Coca Cola League Cup Fifth Round*

Date	Match	92-93	93-94	94-95
13-Jan	Bolton Wanderers v Wimbledon	–	–	–
13-Jan	Coventry City v Newcastle United	–	2-1	0-0
13-Jan	Everton v Chelsea	0-1	4-2	3-3
13-Jan	Leeds United v West Ham United	–	1-0	2-2
13-Jan	Manchester United v Aston Villa	1-1	3-1	1-0
13-Jan	Middlesbrough v Arsenal	1-0	–	–
13-Jan	Nottingham Forest v Southampton	1-2	–	3-0
13-Jan	QPR v Blackburn Rovers	0-3	1-0	0-1
13-Jan	Sheffield Wednesday v Liverpool	1-1	3-1	1-2
13-Jan	Tottenham Hotspur v Manchester City	3-1	1-0	2-1
13-Jan	West Ham United v Manchester City	–	3-1	3-0

Date	Match	92-93	93-94	94-95
20-Jan	Arsenal v Everton	2-0	2-0	1-1
20-Jan	Aston Villa v Tottenham Hotspur	0-0	1-0	1-0
20-Jan	Blackburn Rovers v Sheffield Wednesday	1-0	1-1	3-1
20-Jan	Chelsea v Nottingham Forest	0-0	–	0-2
20-Jan	Liverpool v Leeds United	2-0	2-0	0-1
20-Jan	Manchester City v Coventry City	1-0	1-1	0-0
20-Jan	Manchester United v Leeds United	2-0	0-0	0-0
20-Jan	West Ham United v Manchester United	–	2-2	1-1
20-Jan	Wimbledon v QPR	1-2	1-1	1-3

24-Jan   *International Date (not UEFA)*
27-Jan   *FA Cup (Littlewoods Pools) Fourth Round*

Date	Match	92-93	93-94	94-95
03-Feb	Arsenal v Coventry City	3-0	0-3	2-1
03-Feb	Aston Villa v Leeds United	1-1	1-0	0-0
03-Feb	Liverpool v Tottenham Hotspur	6-2	1-2	1-1
03-Feb	Manchester City v QPR	1-1	3-0	2-3
03-Feb	Newcastle United v Sheffield Wednesday	–	4-2	2-1
03-Feb	Southampton v Everton	0-0	0-2	2-0

Date	Match	92-93	93-94	94-95
03-Feb	West Ham United v Nottingham Forest	–	–	3-1
03-Feb	Wimbledon v Manchester United	1-2	1-0	0-1
07-Feb	*International Date (not UEFA)*			
10-Feb	Bolton Wanderers v Aston Villa	–		–
10-Feb	Coventry City v Chelsea	1-2	1-1	2-2
10-Feb	Everton v Manchester City	2-3	1-0	1-1
10-Feb	Leeds United v Southampton	2-1	0-0	0-0
10-Feb	Manchester United v Blackburn Rovers	3-1	1-1	1-0
10-Feb	Middlesbrough v Newcastle United	–		
10-Feb	Nottingham Forest v Arsenal	0-1		2-2
10-Feb	QPR v Liverpool	0-1	1-3	2-1
10-Feb	Sheffield Wednesday v Wimbledon	1-1	2-2	0-1
10-Feb	Tottenham Hotspur v West Ham United	–	1-4	3-1
11-Feb	*Coca Cola League Cup Semi-Final 1st Leg*			
14-Feb	*Coca Cola League Cup Semi-Final 1st Leg*			
17-Feb	*FA Cup (Littlewoods Pools) Fifth Round*			
17-Feb	Arsenal v Manchester City	1-0	0-0	3-1
17-Feb	Aston Villa v Blackburn Rovers	0-0	0-1	0-1
17-Feb	Chelsea v West Ham United	–	2-0	1-2
17-Feb	Leeds United v Tottenham Hotspur	5-0	2-0	1-1
17-Feb	Liverpool v Wimbledon	2-3	1-1	3-0
17-Feb	Manchester United v Everton	0-3	1-0	2-0
17-Feb	Middlesbrough v Bolton Wanderers	–		
17-Feb	Newcastle United v Southampton	–	1-2	5-1
17-Feb	Nottingham Forest v Coventry City	1-1	–	2-0
17-Feb	Sheffield Wednesday v QPR.....................	1-0	3-1	0-2
21-Feb	*Coca Cola League Cup Semi-Final 2nd Leg*			
24-Feb	Blackburn Rovers v Liverpool	4-1	2-0	3-2
24-Feb	Bolton Wanderers v Manchester United	–	–	–
24-Feb	Everton v Nottingham Forest	3-0	–	1-2
24-Feb	Manchester City v Newcastle United	–	2-1	0-0
24-Feb	QPR v Leeds United	2-1	0-4	3-2
24-Feb	Southampton v Chelsea..........................	1-0	3-1	0-1
24-Feb	Tottenham Hotspur v Sheffield Wednesday ...	0-2	1-3	3-1
24-Feb	West Ham United v Arsenal	–	0-0	0-2
24-Feb	Wimbledon v Aston Villa	2-3	2-2	4-3
25-Feb	*Coca Cola League Cup Semi-Final 2nd Leg*			

Date	Match	92-93	93-94	94-95
02-Mar	Coventry City v West Ham United	–	1-1	2-0
02-Mar	Liverpool v Aston Villa	1-2	2-1	3-2
02-Mar	Manchester City v Blackburn Rovers	3-2	0-2	1-3
02-Mar	Middlesbrough v Everton	1-2	–	–
02-Mar	Newcastle United v Manchester United	–	1-1	1-1
02-Mar	QPR v Arsenal	0-0	1-1	3-1
02-Mar	Sheffield Wednesday v Nottingham Forest ...	2-0	–	1-7
02-Mar	Tottenham Hotspur v Southampton	4-2	3-0	1-2
02-Mar	Wimbledon v Chelsea	0-0	1-1	1-1
06-Mar	*European Quarter Finals 1st Legs*			
09-Mar	*FA Cup (Littlewoods Pools) Sixth Round*			
09-Mar	Arsenal v Liverpool	0-1	1-0	0-1
09-Mar	Aston Villa v QPR	2-0	4-1	2-1
09-Mar	Blackburn Rovers v Wimbledon	0-0	3-0	2-1
09-Mar	Bolton Wanderers v Tottenham Hotspur	–	–	–
09-Mar	Chelsea v Manchester City	2-4	0-0	3-0
09-Mar	Everton v Coventry City	1-1	0-0	0-2
09-Mar	Nottingham Forest v Newcastle United	–	–	0-0
09-Mar	Southampton v Sheffield Wednesday	1-2	1-1	0-0
13-Mar	Liverpool v Chelsea	2-1	2-1	–
16-Mar	Leeds United v Everton...........................	2-0	3-0	1-0
16-Mar	Manchester City v Southampton	1-0	1-1	3-3
16-Mar	Middlesbrough v Nottingham Forest	1-2	–	–
16-Mar	Newcastle United v West Ham United	–	2-0	2-0
16-Mar	QPR v Manchester United	1-3	2-3	2-3
16-Mar	Sheffield Wednesday v Aston Villa	1-2	0-0	1-2
16-Mar	Tottenham Hotspur v Blackburn Rovers	1-2	0-2	3-1
16-Mar	Wimbledon v Arsenal	3-2	0-3	1-3
20-Mar	*European Quarter Finals 2nd Legs*			
23-Mar	Arsenal v Newcastle United	–	2-1	2-3
23-Mar	Blackburn Rovers v Leeds United	3-1	2-1	1-1
23-Mar	Bolton Wanderers v Sheffield Wednesday ...	–	–	–
23-Mar	Chelsea v QPR	1-0	2-0	1-0
23-Mar	Everton v Wimbledon	0-0	3-2	0-0
23-Mar	Manchester United v Tottenham Hotspur	4-1	2-1	0-0
23-Mar	Nottingham Forest v Liverpool	1-0	–	1-1
23-Mar	Southampton v Coventry City	2-2	1-0	0-0

Date	Match	92-93	93-94	94-95
24-Mar	*Coca Cola League Cup Final (Wembley)*			
27-Mar	*International Date*			
30-Mar	Aston Villa v West Ham United	–	3-1	0-2
30-Mar	Blackburn Rovers v Everton	2-3	2-0	3-0
30-Mar	Bolton Wanderers v Manchester City	–	–	–
30-Mar	Liverpool v Newcastle United	–	0-2	2-0
30-Mar	Manchester United v Arsenal	0-0	1-0	3-0
30-Mar	QPR v Southampton	3-1	2-1	2-2
30-Mar	Sheffield Wednesday v Chelsea	3-3	3-1	1-1
30-Mar	Tottenham Hotspur v Coventry City	0-2	1-2	1-3
30-Mar	Wimbledon v Nottingham Forest	1-0	–	2-2
31-Mar	*FA Cup (Littlewoods Pools) Semi Finals*			
03-Apr	*European Semi Finals 1st Legs*			
06-Apr	Arsenal v Leeds United	0-0	2-1	1-3
06-Apr	Chelsea v Aston Villa	0-1	1-1	1-0
06-Apr	Coventry City v Liverpool	5-1	1-0	1-1
06-Apr	Manchester City v Manchester United	1-1	2-3	0-3
06-Apr	Middlesbrough v Sheffield Wednesday	1-1	–	–
06-Apr	Newcastle United v QPR	–	1-2	2-1
06-Apr	Nottingham Forest v Tottenham Hotspur	2-1	–	2-2
06-Apr	Southampton v Blackburn Rovers	1-1	3-1	1-1
06-Apr	West Ham United v Wimbledon	–	0-2	3-0
08-Apr	Aston Villa v Southampton	1-1	0-2	1-1
08-Apr	Blackburn Rovers v Newcastle United	–	1-0	0-0
08-Apr	Bolton Wanderers v Chelsea	–	–	–
08-Apr	Leeds United v Nottingham Forest	1-4	–	1-0
08-Apr	Liverpool v West Ham United	–	2-0	0-0
08-Apr	Manchester United v Coventry City	5-0	0-0	2-0
08-Apr	QPR v Everton	4-2	2-1	2-3
08-Apr	Sheffield Wednesday v Arsenal	1-0	0-1	3-1
08-Apr	Wimbledon v Manchester City	0-1	1-0	2-0
13-Apr	Arsenal v Tottenham Hotspur	1-3	1-1	1-1
13-Apr	Chelsea v Leeds United	1-0	1-1	0-3
13-Apr	Coventry City v QPR	0-1	0-1	0-1
13-Apr	Everton v Liverpool	2-1	2-0	2-0
13-Apr	Manchester City v Sheffield Wednesday	1-2	1-3	3-2
13-Apr	Middlesbrough v Wimbledon	2-0	–	–
13-Apr	Newcastle United v Aston Villa	–	5-1	3-1

Date	Match	92-93	93-94	94-95
13-Apr	Nottingham Forest v Blackburn Rovers	1-3	–	0-2
13-Apr	Southampton v Manchester United	0-1	1-3	2-2
17-Apr	*European Semi Finals 2nd Legs*			
24-Apr	*International Date*			
27-Apr	Aston Villa v Manchester City	3-1	0-0	1-1
27-Apr	Blackburn Rovers v Arsenal	1-0	1-1	3-1
27-Apr	Bolton Wanderers v Southampton	–	–	–
27-Apr	Leeds United v Newcastle United	–	1-1	0-0
27-Apr	Manchester United v Nottingham Forest	2-0	–	1-2
27-Apr	QPR v West Ham United	–	0-0	2-1
27-Apr	Sheffield Wednesday v Everton	3-1	5-1	0-0
27-Apr	Tottenham Hotspur v Chelsea	1-2	1-1	0-0
27-Apr	Wimbledon v Coventry City	1-2	1-2	2-0
01-May	*UEFA Cup Final 1st Leg*			
04-May	Chelsea v Blackburn Rovers	0-0	1-2	1-2
04-May	Coventry City v Leeds United	3-3	0-2	2-1
04-May	Everton v Aston Villa	1-0	0-1	2-2
04-May	Manchester City v Liverpool	1-1	1-1	2-1
04-May	Middlesbrough v Manchester United	1-1	–	–
04-May	Newcastle United v Tottenham Hotspur	–	0-1	3-3
04-May	Nottingham Forest v QPR	1-0	–	3-2
04-May	Southampton v Wimbledon	2-2	1-0	2-3
04-May	West Ham United v Sheffield Wednesday ...	–	2-0	0-2
08-May	*Cup-Winners' Cup Final*			
11-May	*FA Cup (Littlewoods Pools) Final (Wembley)*			
15-May	*UEFA Cup Final 2nd Leg*			
18-May	*Possible England International Date*			
22-May	*Champions' Cup Final*			
08-Jun	*Euro96 Starts (Wembley)*			
	Group Matches 10,11,13,14,15,16,18,19 June			
22/3-Jun	*Quarter Finals (Anfield, Villa Park, Old Trafford, Wembley)*			
26-Jun	*Semi Finals (Old Trafford/Wembley)*			
30-Jun	*Final (Wembley)*			